The Blackwell Companion to Political Sociology

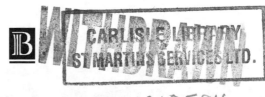

BLACKWELL COMPANIONS TO SOCIOLOGY

The *Blackwell Companions to Sociology* provide introductions to emerging topics and theoretical orientations in sociology as well as presenting the scope and quality of the discipline as it is currently configured. Essays in the Companions tackle broad themes or central puzzles within the field and are authored by key scholars who have spent considerable time in research and reflection on the questions and controversies that have activated interest in their area. This authoritative series will interest those studying sociology at advanced undergraduate or graduate level as well as scholars in the social sciences and informed readers in related disciplines.

The Blackwell Companion to Political Sociology

Edited by

Kate Nash and Alan Scott

BLACKWELL
Publishers

First published 2001

2 4 6 8 10 9 7 5 3 1

Blackwell Publishers Inc.
350 Main Street
Malden, Massachusetts 02148
USA

Blackwell Publishers Ltd
108 Cowley Road
Oxford OX4 1JF
UK

Library of Congress Cataloging-in-Publication Data

The Blackwell companion to political sociology / edited by Kate Nash and Alan Scott.
    p.   cm. — (Blackwell companions to sociology)
  Includes bibliographical references and index.
  ISBN 0–631–21050–4 (alk. paper)
    1. Political sociology.   I. Nash, Kate, 1958–   II. Scott, Alan.   III. Series.

JA76.B58   2000
306.2—dc21
                                                                    00–037830

British Library Cataloguing in Publication Data
A CIP catalogue record for this book is available from the British Library.

Typeset in 10.5/12.5pt Sabon
by Kolam Information Services Pvt Ltd, Pondicherry, India
Printed in Great Britain by
TJ International Ltd., Padstow, Cornwall

This book is printed on acid-free paper.

Contents

List of Contributors

Arnaldo Bagnasco is Professor of Sociology at the University of Turin. A leading economic sociologist, he is well known for his work on economic development and the Third Italy; his publications include La *problematica territoriale dello sviluppo Italian* (1977) and *Small Firms and Economic Development in Europe* (editor with C. F. Sabel, 1995).

Sigrid Baringhost is Professor of Politics at the University of Siegen, Germany. She is author of *Politik als Kampagne. Zur medialen Erzeugung von Solidaritaet* [politics as campaign: on the media production of solidarity] (1998) and *Fremde in der Stadt* [strangers in the city] (1991).

David Beetham is Professor of Politics at the University of Leeds and Director of the Centre for Democratic Studies. An initiator of the "democratic audit," he also acts as a consultant to The Council of Europe. Publications include *Max Weber and the Theory of Politics* (second edition, 1985), *The Legitimation of Power* (1991) and, with C. J. Lord, *Legitimacy and the European Union* (1998).

Richard Bellamy is Professor of Politics at the University of Reading. His publications include *Liberalism and Modern Society: An Historical Argument* (1992) and *Liberalism and Pluralism: Towards a Politics of Compromise* (1999). He is currently directing a research project on European Constitutionalism and Citizenship.

Robert W. Connell is Professor of Education at the University of Sydney. He is author of *Masculinities* and *Gender and Power* and a senior editor of *Theory and Society*.

Colin Crouch is a Professor in Sociology at the European University Institute, Florence and an External Scientific member of the Max-Planck-Institute for Society Research at Cologne. He is chairman of the editorial board of *The Political Quarterly* and a member of the editorial board of *Stato e Mercato*. He is currently working on a project with colleagues in France, Germany, Italy, and the UK, studying local production systems of small firms in various European countries. Recent books include *Industrial Relations and European State Traditions* (1993); *Are Skills the Answer?* (with David Finegold and Mari Sako, 1999), and *Social Change in Western Europe* (1999).

Keith Dowding is Reader in Public Choice and Public Administration at the London School of Economics and Political Science. He is the author of *Rational Choice and Political Power* (1991) and *Power* (1996) and the co-editor of the *Journal of Theoretical Politics*.

Michael Drake teaches sociology at the University of East Anglia, Norwich. His doctoral thesis is titled "Problematics of Military Power: Government, Discipline and the Subject of Violence" (publication forthcoming), and he has published articles on the relation between organized violence and political order. He is curently working on the military rationality of recent and projected armed intervention in the context of globalization.

Alan Finlayson is Lecturer in Politics at the University of Swansea, Wales. He is the author of articles on New Labour, Loyalism, and theories of nationalism and co-author of *Contemporary Social and Political Theory: An Introduction* (1999).

Joe Foweraker is Professor of Government at the University of Essex. He is the author of *Citizenship Rights and Social Movements* (1997) and *Theorizing Social Movements* (1995), as well as major monographs on Brazil, Spain, and Mexico.

Patrick Le Galès is CNRS Senior Research Fellow at CEVIPOF (Sciences Po Paris) and Associate Professor of Sociology and Politics at Sciences Po, Paris. He is the author of *Politiques urbaines et développement local: une comparaison franco-britannique* (Paris: L'Harmattan, 1993) and "State and cities in Europe" in *West European Politics*, 1998 (with A. Harding),and editor of *Regions in Europe, The Paradox of Power* (with C. Lequesne, 1998) and *Cities in Europe* (with A. Bagnasco, 2000). He is the editor of the *International Journal of Urban and Regional Research*.

Pierre Hamel is Professor of Urban Planning and Sociology at the University of Montreal. Currently, his research interests are focused on new models of urban governance and social movements. He has recently finished a research project on local democracy and public consultation. His books include *Action Collective et Démocratie Locale* (1991) and *Urban Movements in a Globalising World* (co-editor, forthcoming).

Barry Hindess is Professor of Political Science in the Research School of Social Sciences at the Australian National University. His most recent books are *Discourses of Power: from Hobbes to Foucault* (Blackwell Publishers, 1996) and *Democracy* (in press).

Bob Jessop is Professor of Sociology at Lancaster University. He is the author of *The Capitalist State* (1982), *Nicos Poulantzas* (1985), and *State Theory* (1990). He has also published numerous journal articles and short works on state theory, Marxist political economy, postwar British politics, and welfare state restructuring.

Peter John is Reader in Politics and Sociology at Birkbeck College, University of London. He is author of *Analysing Public Policy* (1998) and has published papers in such journals as *British Journal of Political Science*, *Political Studies*, *West European Politics*, *Public Administration*. He was educated at the universities of Bath and Oxford, and has worked for the Policy Studies Institute, and Keele and Southampton univerisites.

Herbert Kitschelt is Professor of Political Science at Duke University. His recent book publications are *The Transformation of European Social Democracy* (1994), *The Radical Right in Western Europe* (1995), and, co-authored with Zdenka Mansfeldova, Radoslaw Markowski, and Gabor Toka, *Post-Communist Party Systems* (Cambridge University Press, 1999).

Stefan Lange is Lecturer in Sociology at the Fernuniversität (Open University) in Hagen, Germany. Together with D. Braun he is author of *Politische Steuerung Zwiochen System und Akteur* [Political guidance between System and Actor] (Opladen 2000) and with U. Schimank "Wisscnschaft in Mittel- und Osteuropa: Die Transformation der Akademieforschung" [Science in Middle- and East Europe. The Transformation of Research inside the Academies of Science] in *Leviathan* 26, 1997.

Ruth Lister is Professor of Social Policy in the Department of Social Sciences, Loughborough University. She is author of *Citizenship: Feminist Perspectives* (1997).

Louis Maheu is Professor of Sociology at the University of Montreal. He has published extensively on the topic of social movements, including an edited collection in English, *Social Movements and Social Classes: the Future of Collective Action* (1995). He is the Chair of the ISA Research Committee on Social Movements and Social Class.

David S. Meyer is Associate Professor of Sociology at the University of California–Irvine. He is author of *A Winter of Discontent: the Nuclear Freeze and American Politics* and numerous articles on social protest movements.

Kate Nash is Lecturer in Sociology at Goldsmiths College, University of London. Her most recent publications are *Universal Difference: Feminism and the Liberalism Undecidability of Women* (1998), *Contemporary Political Sociology: Globalization, Politics and Power* and an accompanying reader (both published by Blackwell Publishers, 2000).

Aletta J. Norval is Senior Lecturer in Political Theory in the Department of Government, University of Essex and Director of the Doctoral Programme in Ideology and Discourse Analysis. She has published widely on issues in post-structuralist political theory, and theories and politics of race and ethnicity. Her recent publications include *Deconstructing Apartheid Discourse* (Verso), and two co-edited volumes entitled *South African in Transition. New Theoretical Perspectives* (Macmillan), and *Discourse Theory and Political Analysis. Identities, Hegemonies and Social Change* (forthcoming).

David Owen is Senior Lecturer in Political Theory and Assistant Director of the Centre for Post-Analytic Philosophy at the University of Southampton. He is the author of *Maturity and Modernity* (1994) and *Nietzsche, Politics and Modernity* (1995), editor of *Sociology After Postmodernism* (1998), and co-editor of *Foucault Contra Habermas* (1999).

Jan Pakulski is Professor of Sociology at the University of Tasmania, Australia. He is co-author of *Postmodernization* (1992) and *Death of Class* (1996).

Antonino Palumbo is Research Fellow in Political Philosophy at the University of Palermo (Sicily). He is author of "Processi di rifroma e codici etici della pubblica amministrazione in Gran Bretagna" [administrative and ethical reforms in the British civil service] in L. Sacconi (ed.) *Etica della pubblica amministrazione* [ethics and public administration], Milan: Guerini Editore, 1998 and "Il problema dell'authorita assoluta nei modelli neohobbesiani della scelta razionale" [the problem of absolute sovereignty in Hobbsian rational choice models], *Theoria politica*, 1997.

Max Pensky is Associate Professor of Philosophy at Binghamton University, State University of New York, USA. He has edited Jürgen Habermas's *The Past as Future* (1995) and *The Postnational Constellation* (2000) and written several articles on Habermas and the German political public sphere.

Gianfranco Poggi is currently Professor of Sociology at the European University Institute, Florence. Well known for his work on the state and on social theory, his book publications include *The State: its Nature, Development and Prospects* (1990) and *Forms of Social Power and their Relations* (forthcoming).

Donatella della Porta is Professor of Political Science at the University of Florence. Among her recent publications are *Social Movement, Political Violence and the State* (1995); *Social Movements: an Introduction* (with Mario Diani, Blackwell Publishers, 1999); *Corrupt Exchanges* (with Alberto Vannucci, 1999).

Giovanna Procacci is Professor of Sociology at the University of Milan. A leading authority on the work of Michel Foucault, her English publications include "Social economy and the government of poverty" in G. Burchell et al. (eds.) *The Foucault Effect* (1991). Recent publications include (in Italian) a book on governing poverty (1998).

Larry Ray is Professor of Sociology at the University of Kent. He is author of *Theorizing Classical Sociology* (Open University Press, 1999) and editor (with Andrew Sayer) of *Culture and Economy After the Cultural Turn* (Sage, 1999).

Roberta Sassatelli teaches Sociology at the University of East Anglia, Norwich and at the University of Bologna. She works on cultural sociology, particularly the sociology of the body and consumption. She is author of an ethnographic study, *Anatomia della Palestra* [The anatomy of the Gym] (Mulino, 1998) and "From value to consumption," *Acta Sociologica*, 2000.

Uwe Schimank is Professor of Sociology at the Fernuniversität (Open University) in Hagen, Germany. He is author of *"Theorien gesellschaftlicher Differenzierung"* [theories of societal differentiation] (Opladen, 1996), *Handeln und Strukturen. Einfuehrung in die akteurtheoretische Soziologie* [action and structures. An introduction to an actor-centered sociology] (Weinheim 1999), and, together with R. Mayntz and P. Weingart, is editor of *East-European Academies in Transition* (Dordrecht, 1997).

John Schwarzmantel is Senior Lecturer in Politics at the University of Leeds. He is author of *Socialism and the Idea of the Nation* (Harvester–Wheatsheaf, 1991); *The Age of Ideology, Political Ideologies from the American Revolution to Postmodern Times* (Macmillan, 1998).

Alan Scott is Professor of Sociology at the University of Innsbruck. Recent publications include *The Limits of Globalization* (editor) (Routledge, 1997) and "War and the Public Intellectual: Cosmopolitanism and Anti-cosmopolitanism in the Kosovo Debate in Germany," *Sociological Research Online* 4(2), 1999.

John Scott is Professor of Sociology at the University of Essex and Adjunct Professor at the University of Bergen. He is the author of *Corporate Business and Capitalist Classes* and *Stratification and Power*.

Yasemin Nuhoğlu Soysal is Senior Lecturer in Sociology at the University of Essex. She is author of *Limits of Citizenship: Migrants and Postnational Membership in Europe* (University of Chicago Press, 1994), and most recently "Citizenship and Identity: Living in Diasporas in Postwar Europe?" *Ethnic and Racial Studies*, 23(1) January 2000.

Judith Squires is a Lecturer in Political Theory at the University of Bristol. She is author of *Gender in Political Theory* (Polity Press, 1999) and co-editor of

Feminisms (Oxford University Press, 1997). She is reviews editor for the *International Feminist Journal of Politics*.

John Street is a Reader in Politics at the University of East Anglia. He is the author of *Politics and Popular Culture* (Polity Press, 1997) and is one of the editors of the journal *Popular Music*.

John B. Thompson is Reader in Sociology at the University of Cambridge and Fellow of Jesus College, Cambridge. His publications include *The Media and Modernity: A Social Theory of the Media* (Polity Press, 1995) and *Political Scandal: Power and Visibility in the Media Age* (Polity Press, 2000).

Fran Tonkiss is Lecturer in Sociology at Goldsmiths College, University of London. Her publications include *Market Society and Modern Social Thought* (with D. Slater, Polity Press) and *Trust and Civil Society* (with A. Passey, N. Fenton and L. Hems, Macmillan).

Danilo Zolo is Professor of Philosophy and Sociology of Law at the University of Florence. He is author of *Democracy and Complexity. A Realist Approach* (Polity Press, 1992) and *Cosmopolis. Prospects for World Government* (Polity Press, 1997).

Acknowledgments

A number of contributors to this volume deserve thanks not merely for their contributions, but also for making specific suggestions on possible topics or authors. Among those we would like to mention are Patrick Le Galès, David Owen, Nino Palumbo, Roberta Sassatelli and John Scott. A number of non-contributors played a similar role through additional comments and suggestions. Among these were Emilio Santori, Anna-Marie Smith, and Neil Washbourne. Thanks are also due to the anonymous reviewers of the original proposal whose constructive comments the editors have attempted to respond to in the execution of the project. John Irving and Laura Serratrice provided fine translations of chapters 21 and 38 respectively.

Introduction

KATE NASH AND ALAN SCOTT

Editors of a volume such as this are at the outset confronted with a simple choice. Either they can attempt to impose conceptual order on the area by selecting one of a number of possible paradigms and asserting, or simply tacitly assuming or pretending, that the one that they have selected is, is becoming, or should be *the* dominant or only legitimate paradigm, or they can seek to "tell it as it is" and to represent all the voices seeking attention or perspectives vying for position within the field. Either option has its advantages and limitations. The first may achieve order but at the price of partiality. The second is in danger of creating a cacophony of voices which all too often talk past, or simply seek to drown out, each other. At the same time, representative approaches are bound to be both too inclusive – leaving the boundaries of the discipline or subdiscipline open and vague – *and* not inclusive enough; something is bound to slip through the net; someone's favored topic is going to be under-represented or omitted. We have chosen the second option with all its attendant dangers. Thus, postmodernist perspectives vie with rational choice; institutionally focused approaches are to be found alongside broad theoretical position statements; opposing definitions of what counts as "political" are set alongside each other. We have in effect taken the somewhat quaint but attractive term "companion" rather literally. A companion is not a lexicon or dictionary. It does not aspire to be definitive. It is more an invitation to partake in, or at least eavesdrop on, a debate, or debates.

The problem of boundaries is particularly intense in the case of a subarea like political sociology which exists within or between the two disciplines which have formed it, and in turn partly been formed by it: political science and sociology. To put the point more sharply, is political sociology any more than a transit station through which new(ish) issues or perspectives travel before they become established within one or other of the two more institutionally secured disciplines? If the answer were unambiguously "yes" then a companion to political sociology would be a considerably slimmer volume than the one you have in your hands. By assuming that political sociology is more than just such a transit station we have risked another possible boundary problem. The list of topics included here might leave political scientists wondering what part of their discipline is *not* political sociology and may awake the suspicion that political sociology is a Trojan Horse. A similar suspicion might well be raised in the minds of sociologists when they see how much of cultural and economic sociology can be included under the rubric of political sociology.

These dangers have been intensified by developments within political science and sociology themselves which have, for example, pointed up the previously underestimated political importance of culture (e.g. in the analysis of social movements or of new forms of citizenship). At the same time, globalization is said to call into question the centrality of the basic unit of political analysis – nation-states – *and* sociological analysis – national societies. Such developments, or alleged developments, have in turn stimulated new forms of analysis, for example of cultural or identity politics. Theoretical developments beyond as well as within these disciplines – for example, feminism, postmodernism – have caused a radical rethinking of the nature and purpose, or even legitimacy, of the social sciences. One possible conclusion from such developments is that political sociology (or the social sciences generally) are caught within a framework which is itself redundant and that such matters would be better addressed through newer (and thus more innovative?) disciplines such as cultural studies. Thus new contenders emerge and turf wars intensify. An alternative interpretation is that political sociology, precisely because of its location in the gaps of the conventional boundaries drawn between the political, cultural and economic is, and always has been, in a particularly good position to absorb and transmit emerging developments, to understand the ambiguity of these – possibly arbitrary – boundaries and to recognize the intimacy of the connections between these "spheres." Assuming this more benign, or convenient, interpretation we have sought both to include newer debates and to range beyond "the political" to include aspects of "economic" or "cultural" life where these touch on the concerns of contemporary political sociologists and political scientists (e.g. social capital, or ethnicity and citizenship).

It follows that there is necessarily an element of arbitrariness in the – equally necessary – division of the book into sections. The first section includes overviews of the most prominent theoretical perspectives on power and politics represented in the following pages. The second, "state and governance," gathers articles in which relations between the state and different institutions, organizations, and groups in society are central issues. The articles in the third section, "the political and the social," are less directly concerned with action oriented towards the state. They deal with the very definitions of social space implied in different divisions between state and society; with collective action which does not necessarily take the state as its focus; and with forms of citizenship in which the distinction between social and political is particularly difficult to draw. Finally, the fourth section takes the topical theme of "political transformations" as its rationale.

Several of the chapters "speak to each other" across these divisions: disagreeing with each other, providing an example to support a case made elsewhere, or discussing the same material from a different point of view. The days when social scientific debates could be neatly characterized with reference to one or two dichotomies (Marxist vs. Weberian; structural vs. action approaches, or even modern vs. postmodern) are over. As a result of this pluralization, or perhaps fragmentation, of social scientific discourse, this volume contains a broad range of shadow debates. As editors, we have cross-referenced these points of contact and contrast where we find them most useful or interesting. Given the complexity and diversity of current debates, we have chosen to gather the chapters according to topics rather than impose an even more artificial categorization in terms of schools or perspectives. But there is also continuity across the volume in that all the contributors were asked to address the most recent developments in their area of study, as well as providing background to welcome newcomers to ongoing debates. It should, therefore, be something of a companion to current events as well as to the discipline of political sociology.

Part I

Approaches to Power and the Political

1

Developments in Marxist Theory

Bob Jessop

Marxist approaches to power are distinctive in focusing on its relation to class domination in capitalist societies. Power is linked to class relations in economics, politics, and ideology. The aim of much recent Marxist analysis has been to show how class power is dispersed throughout society, in order to avoid economic reductionism. In capitalist societies the state is considered to be particularly important in securing the conditions for economic class domination. Marxists are also interested in why dominated classes collude in their oppression and address issues of resistance and strategies to bring about radical change. In this chapter, as well as a summary of the main trends in contemporary Marxism, Jessop also offers a brief assessment of its disadvantages as a sociological analysis of power: its neglect of social domination that is not directly related to class; a tendency to overemphasize the coherence of class domination; the continuing problem of economic reductionism; and the opposite danger of a voluntaristic account of resistance to capitalism.

Marxists have analyzed power relations in many different ways. But four interrelated themes typify their overall approach. The first of these is a concern with power relations as manifestations of a specific mode or configuration of class domination rather than as purely interpersonal phenomena lacking deeper foundations in the social structure. The significance thus attached to class domination by no means implies that all forms of power are always exercised by social actors with clear class identities and class interests. It means only that Marxists are mainly interested in the causal interconnections between the exercise of social power and the reproduction or transformation of class domination. Indeed Marxists are usually well aware of other types of subject, identity, antagonism, and domination. But they consider such phenomena largely in terms of their relevance for, and their overdetermination by, class domination. Second, Marxists are concerned with the links – including discontinuities as well as continuities – between economic, political, and ideological class domination. Despite the obvious centrality of this issue, however, it prompts widespread theoretical and empirical disagreements. For different Marxist approaches locate the bases of class power primarily in the social relations of production, in control over the state, or in intellectual hegemony over hearts and minds. I will deal with these alternatives below. Third, Marxists note the limitations inherent in any exercise of power that is rooted in one or another form of class domination and try to explain this in terms of structural contradictions and antagonisms inscribed therein. Thus Marxists tend to assume that all forms of social power linked to class domination are inherently fragile, unstable, provisional, and temporary and that continuing struggles are needed to reproduce the conditions for class domination, to overcome resistance, and to naturalize or mystify class power. It follows, fourthly, that Marxists also address questions of strategy and tactics. They provide empirical analyses of actual strategies intended to reproduce, resist, or overthrow class domination in specific periods and conjunctures; and they often engage in political debates about the most appropriate identities, interests, strategies, and tactics for dominated classes and other oppressed groups to adopt in order to challenge, most effectively, their subaltern position.

POWER AS A SOCIAL RELATION

Marxists are interested in the first instance in powers as capacities rather than the exercise of power as the actualization of such capacities. They see these capacities as *socially structured* rather than as *socially amorphous* (or random). Thus Marxists focus on capacities grounded in structured social relations rather than in the properties of individual agents considered in isolation. Moreover, as these structured social relations entail enduring relations, they involve reciprocal, if often asymmetrical, capacities and vulnerabilities. A common paradigm here is Hegel's master–slave dialectic – in which the master depends on the slave and the slave on the master. Marx's equivalent case is, of course, the material interdependence of capital and labor. At stake in both instances are enduring relations of reproduced, reciprocal practices rather than one-off, unilateral impositions of will. This has the interesting implication that power is also involved in securing the continuity of social relations rather than producing radical change. Thus, as Isaac notes, "[r]ather than A getting B to do something B would not otherwise do, social relations of power typically involve both A and B doing what they *ordinarily* do" (1987: 96). The capitalist wage relation is a particularly useful example here. For, in voluntarily selling their labor-power for a wage, workers transfer its control and the right to any surplus to the capitalist. A formally free exchange thereby becomes the basis of factory despotism and economic exploitation. Nonetheless, as working class resistance in labor markets and the labor process indicate, Marxists note that the successful exercise of power is also a conjunctural phenomenon rather than being guaranteed by unequal social relations of production. They regard the actualization of capacities to exercise power and its effects, if any, as always and everywhere contingent on circumstances. Moreover, as capacities to exercise power are always tied to specific sets of social relations and depend for their actualization on specific circumstances, there can be no such thing as power in general or general power – only particular powers and the sum of particular exercises of power.

GENERAL REMARKS ON CLASS DOMINATION

Marxism differs from other analyses of power because of its primary interest in class domination. In contrast, Weberian analyses, for example, give equal *analytical* weight to other forms of domination (status, party); or, again, radical feminists prioritize changing forms of patriarchy. But Marxists' distinctive interest in class domination is not limited to *economic* class domination in the *labor process* (although this is important) nor even to the economic bases of class domination in the wider economy (such as control over the allocation of capital to alternative productive activities). For Marxists see class powers as dispersed throughout society and therefore also investigate political and ideological class domination. However, whereas some Marxists believe political and/or ideological domination derive more or less directly from economic domination, others emphasize the complexity of relations among these three sites or modes of class domination.

Even Marxists who stress the economic bases of class domination also acknowledge that politics is primary in practice. For it is only through political revolution that existing patterns of class domination will be overthrown. Other Marxists prioritize the political over the economic not just (if at all) in terms of revolutionary struggles but also in terms of the routine reproduction of class domination in normal circumstances. This makes the state central to Marxist analyses not only in regard to political power in narrow terms but also to class power more generally. For the state is seen as responsible for maintaining the overall structural integration and social cohesion of a "society divided into classes" – a structural integration and social cohesion without which capitalism's contradictions and antagonisms might cause revolutionary crises or even lead, in the telling phrase of the *Communist Manifesto* [1848], to "the mutual ruin of the contending classes."

Economic Class Domination

Marxism is premised on the existence of antagonistic modes of production. Production involves the material appropriation and transformation of nature. A mode of production comprises in turn a specific combination of the forces of production and social relations of production. The productive forces comprise raw materials, means of production, the technical division of labor corresponding to these raw materials and the given means of production, and the relations of interdependence and cooperation among the direct producers in setting the means of production to work. The social relations of production comprise social control over the allocation of resources to different productive activities and over the appropriation of any resulting surplus; the social division of labor (or the allocation of workers to different activities across different units of production); and class relations grounded in property relations, ownership of the means of production, and the form of economic exploitation. Some Marxists emphasize the primacy of the forces of production in producing social change but the majority view (and current wisdom) is that the social relations of production are primary. Thus most Marxists now regard the social relations of production rather than the productive forces as the basis for economic class domination. Indeed it is these social relations that shape the choice among available productive forces and how they get deployed in production.

Given the primacy of the relations of production in economic class domination, some Marxists emphasize the power relations rooted in organization of the labor process. This is considered the primary site of the antagonism between capitalists and workers and is the crucial site for securing the valorization of capital through direct control over labor-power. Various forms of control are identified (e.g. bureaucratic, technical, and despotic), each with its own implications for forms of class struggle and the distribution of power between capital and labor. Other Marxists study the overall organization of the production process and its articulation to other aspects of the circuit of capital. Thus emphasis is placed on the relative importance of industrial or financial capital, monopoly capital or small and medium enterprises, multinational or national firms, and firms interested in domestic growth or exports. Different modes of economic growth are associated with different patterns of power. Atlantic Fordism, for example, based on a virtuous circle of mass production and mass consumption in relatively closed economies, was compatible for a time with an institutionalized compromise between industrial capital and organized labor. This supported the Keynesian welfare national state with its distinctive forms of economic, social, and political redistribution. But increasing globalization combined with capital's attempts to increase labor market flexibility have undermined these conditions and encouraged a neo-liberal assault on the postwar compromise in several countries (see Crouch, chapter 22, and Tonkiss, chapter 23, in this volume).

Political Class Domination

Marxist accounts of political class domination begin with the state and its direct and indirect roles in securing the conditions for economic class domination (see Poggi, chapter 9, in this volume). The state is emphasized for various reasons: first, since market forces themselves cannot secure all the conditions needed for capital accumulation and are prone to market failure, there is a need for some mechanism standing outside and above the market to underwrite it and compensate for its failures; second, economic and political competition between capitals necessitates a force able to organize their collective interests; third, the state is needed to manage the many and varied repercussions of economic exploitation within the wider society. Marxists argue that only if the state can secure sufficient institutional integration and social cohesion will the extra-economic conditions for rational economic calculation and, a fortiori, capital accumulation be secured. This requires a sovereign state that is relatively autonomous from particular class interests and can articulate and promote a broader, national-popular interest. Where this project respects the decisive economic nucleus of the society, then the state helps to secure economic as well as political class domination. This is often held to be more likely in bourgeois democratic political regimes than dictatorial regimes (see Moore

1957; Gramsci 1971; Poulantzas 1978; Offe 1984; Jessop 1990; and Barrow 1993).

There are three main Marxist approaches to the state: instrumentalist, structuralist, and "strategic–relational." Instrumentalists see the state mainly as a neutral tool for exercising political power: whichever class controls this tool can use it to advance its own interests. Structuralists argue that who controls the state is irrelevant because it embodies a prior bias towards capital and against the subaltern classes. And strategic-relational theorists argue that state power is a form-determined condensation of the balance of class forces in struggle. I now illustrate these three views for the capitalist state. Different examples would be required for states associated with other modes of production.

Instrumentalists regard the contemporary state as a *state in capitalist society*. Ralph Miliband expresses this view well in writing that "the 'ruling class' of capitalist society is that class which owns and controls the means of production and which is able, by virtue of the economic power thus conferred upon it, to use the state as an instrument for the domination of society" (1969: 22). More generally, those who talk of the "state in capitalist society" stress the contingency of state-economy relations. For, despite the dominance of capitalist relations of production in such a society, the state itself has no inherently capitalist form and performs no necessarily capitalist functions. Any functions it does perform for capital occur because pro-capitalist forces *happen* to control the state and/or because securing social order also *happens* to secure key conditions for rational economic calculation. If the same state apparatus were found in another kind of system, however, it might well be controlled by other forces and perform different functions.

Structuralists regard the state as a *capitalist state* because it has an inherently capitalist form and therefore functions on behalf of capital. This view implies a correspondence between form and function such that the state is *necessarily* capitalist. But what makes a state form capitalist and what guarantees its functionality for capital? Structuralists argue that the very structure of the modern state means that it organizes capital and disorganizes the working class. Claus Offe (1972, 1984) has developed this view as follows. The state's exclusion from direct control over the means of production (which are held in private hands) means that its revenues depend on a healthy private sector; therefore it must, as a condition of its own reproduction as a state apparatus, ensure the profitability of capital. Subordinate classes can secure material concessions only within the limits of the logic of capital – if they breach these limits, such concessions must be rolled back. But capital in turn is unable to press its economic advantages too far, however, without undermining the political legitimacy of the state. For, in contrast to earlier forms of political class domination, the economically dominant class enjoys no formal monopoly of political power. Instead the typical form of bourgeois state is a constitutional state and, later, a national-popular democratic state. This requires respect for the rule of law and the views of its citizens.

The strategic-relational approach was initially proposed by a Greek Communist theorist, Nicos Poulantzas and has subsequently been elaborated by the British state theorist, Bob Jessop. Poulantzas extended Marx's insight that capital is not a thing but a social relation to propose that the state is also a social relation. Marx showed how continued reproduction of the material and institutional forms of the capital relation shaped the dynamic of capital accumulation and the economic class struggle – but the dominance of these forms could not in and of itself guarantee capital accumulation. This depended on capital's success in maintaining its domination over the working class in production, politics, and the wider society. In his later work Poulantzas applied this insight to the capitalist state. He saw the modern form of state as having certain inbuilt biases but argued these were insufficient in themselves to ensure capitalist rule. Indeed they even served to reproduce class conflict and contradictions within the state itself so that the impact of state power depended heavily on the changing balance of forces and the strategies and tactics pursued by class and non-class forces (Poulantzas 1978).

The suggestion that the state is a social relation is important theoretically and politically. Seen as an institutional ensemble or repository of political capacities and resources, the state is by no means a class-neutral instrumentarium. It is inevitably class-biased by virtue of the structural selectivity that makes state institutions, capacities, and resources more accessible to some political forces and more tractable for some purposes than others. This bias is rooted in the generic form of the capitalist state but varies with its particular institutional matrix. Likewise, since it is not a subject, the capitalist state does not and, indeed, cannot, exercise power. Instead its powers (in the plural) are activated through changing sets of politicians and state officials located in specific parts of the state apparatus in specific conjunctures. If an overall strategic line is ever discernible in the exercise of these powers, this results from a strategic coordination enabled by the selectivity of the state system and the organizational role of parallel power networks that cross-cut and thereby unify its formal structures. However, as Poulantzas notes, this is an improbable achievement. For the state system itself is necessarily shot through with contradictions and class struggles and the political agents operating within it always meet resistances from specific forces beyond the state, which are engaged in struggles to transform it, to determine its policies, or simply to influence it at a distance. It follows, if one accepts this analysis, that there is no end to political class struggle. Only through its continual renewal can a capitalist power bloc keep its relative unity in the face of rivalry and fractionalism and maintain its hegemony (or, at least, its dominance) over the popular masses. And only by disrupting the strategic selectivity of the capitalist state through mass struggle at a distance from the state, within the state, and to transform the state, could a democratic transition to democratic socialism be achieved.

Ideological Class Domination

Marx and Engels first alluded to ideological class domination when they noted in *The German Ideology* [1845–6] that "the ruling ideas of any age are the ideas of the ruling class" and related this phenomenon to the latter's control over the means of intellectual production. Their own work developed a number of perspectives on ideological class domination – ranging from the impact of commodity fetishism through the individualism generated by political forms such as citizenship to the struggles for hearts and minds in civil society. Marxist interest in the forms and modalities of ideological class domination grew even stronger with the rise of democratic government and mass politics in the late nineteenth century and the increased importance of mass media and national-popular culture in the twentieth century. Various currents in so-called "Western Marxism" have been strongly interested in ideological class domination – especially whenever a radical socialist or communist revolution has failed to occur despite severe economic crisis or, indeed, during more general periods of working-class passivity. Successive generations of the Frankfurt School have been important here but there are many other approaches that work on similar lines.

A leading figure who has inspired much work in this area is Antonio Gramsci, an Italian Communist active in the interwar period. Gramsci developed a very distinctive approach to the analysis of class power. His chief concern was to develop an autonomous Marxist science of politics in capitalist societies, to distinguish different types of state and politics, and thereby to establish the most likely conditions under which revolutionary forces might eventually replace capitalism. He was particularly concerned with the specificities of the political situation and revolutionary prospects in the "West" (western Europe, USA) as opposed to the "East" (i.e. Tsarist Russia) – believing that a Leninist vanguard party and a revolutionary coup d'état were inappropriate to the "West."

Gramsci identified the state in its narrow sense with the politico-juridical apparatus, the constitutional and institutional features of government, its formal decision-making procedures, and its general policies. But his own work focused more on the ways and means through which *political, intellectual, and moral leadership* was mediated through a complex ensemble of institutions, organizations, and forces operating within, oriented towards, or located at a distance from the state in its narrow sense. This approach is reflected in his controversial definition of the state as "political society + civil society" and his related claims that state power in western capitalist societies rests on "hegemony armored by coercion." Gramsci also defined the state as: "the entire complex of practical and theoretical activities with which the ruling class not only justifies and maintains its dominance but manages to win the active consent of those over whom it rules" (1971: 244). He argued that states were always based on variable combinations of coercion and consent (or force and hegemony). For Gramsci, *force* involves the use of a coercive apparatus to bring the mass of the people into conformity and compliance with the requirements of a specific mode of production. Conversely, *hegemony* involves the successful mobilization and reproduction of the "active consent" of dominated groups by the ruling class through the exercise of political, intellectual, and moral leadership. It should be noted here that Gramsci did not identify force exclusively with the state (e.g., he referred to private fascist terror squads) nor did he locate hegemony exclusively within civil society (since the state also has important ethico-political functions). But his overall argument was that the capitalist state should not be seen as a basically coercive apparatus but as an institutional ensemble marked by a variable mix of coercion, fraud-corruption, and active consent. Moreover, rather than treating

specific institutions and apparatuses as purely technical instruments of government, Gramsci was concerned with their social bases and stressed how their
functions and effects are shaped by their links to the economic system and civil
society.

One of Gramsci's key arguments is the need in the advanced capitalist democracies to engage in a long-term war of position in which subordinate class forces
would develop a hegemonic "collective will" that creatively synthesizes a revolutionary project based on the everyday experiences and "common sense" of
popular forces. Although some commentators interpret this stress on politico-
ideological struggle as meaning that a parliamentary road to socialism would be
possible, Gramsci typically stressed the likelihood of an eventual war of maneuvre with a military-political resolution. But this would be shorter, sharper, and
less bloody if hegemony had first been won.

The Articulation of Economic, Political, and Ideological Domination

The relations among economic, political, and ideological domination can be
considered in terms of the structurally-inscribed selectivity of particular forms of
domination and the strategies that help to consolidate (or undermine) these
selectivities. The bias inscribed on the terrain of the state as a site of strategic
action can only be understood as a bias relative to specific strategies pursued by
specific forces to advance specific interests over a given time horizon in terms of
a specific set of other forces, each advancing their own interests through specific
strategies. Particular forms of state privilege some strategies over others, privilege the access of some forces over others, some interests over others, some time
horizons over others, some coalition possibilities over others. A given type of
state, a given state form, a given form of regime, will be more accessible to some
forces than others according to the strategies they adopt to gain state power. And
it will be more suited to the pursuit of some types of economic or political
strategy than others because of the modes of intervention and resources that
characterize that system. All of this indicates the need to examine the differences
among types of state (e.g. feudal vs. capitalist), state forms (e.g. absolutist,
liberal, interventionist), modes of political representation (e.g. democratic vs.
despotic), specific political regimes (e.g. bureaucratic authoritarian, fascist, and
military or parliamentary, presidential, mass plebiscitary, etc.), particular policy
instruments (e.g. Keynesian demand management vs. neo-liberal supply-side
policies), and so on (see Jessop 1982, 1990).

Whereas Jessop, building on Poulantzas, tends to emphasize the structural
moment of "strategic selectivity," Gramsci focused on its strategic moment. In
particular, against the then prevailing view that the economic base unilaterally
determined the juridico-political superstructure and prevailing forms of social
consciousness; Gramsci argued that there was a reciprocal relationship between
the economic "base" and its politico-ideological "superstructure." He studied
this problem in terms of how "the necessary reciprocity between structure and
superstructure" is secured through specific intellectual, moral, and political

practices that translate narrow sectoral, professional, or local interests into broader "ethico-political" ones. Only thus, he wrote, does the economic structure cease to be an external, constraining force and become a source of initiative and subjective freedom (1971: 366–7). This implies that the ethico-political not only co-constitutes economic structures but also gives them their rationale and legitimacy. Where such a reciprocal relationship exists between base and superstructure, Gramsci spoke of an "*historic bloc.*" He also introduced the concepts of *power bloc* and *hegemonic bloc* to analyze respectively the alliances among dominant classes and the broader ensemble of national-popular forces that were mobilized behind a specific hegemonic project. The concept of hegemonic bloc refers to the *historical unity* not of structures (as in the case of the historical bloc) but *of social forces* (which Gramsci analyzed in terms of the ruling classes, supporting classes, mass movements, and intellectuals). An hegemonic bloc is a durable alliance of class forces organized by a class (or class fraction) which has proved itself capable of exercising political, intellectual, and moral leadership over the dominant classes and the popular masses alike. Gramsci notes a key organizational role here for "organic intellectuals," i.e., persons able to develop hegemonic projects that express the long-term interests of the dominant or subaltern classes in "national-popular" terms. Gramsci also emphasized the need for a "decisive economic nucleus" to provide the basis for long-term hegemony and criticized efforts to construct an "arbitrary, rationalistic, and willed" hegemony which ignored economic realities.

CONCLUDING REMARKS

To conclude, the Marxist approach to power and its exercise involves the following four interests: (1) power and class domination; (2) the mediations among economic, political, and ideological class domination; (3) the limitations and contradictions of power that are grounded in the nature of capitalism as a system of social relations; and (4) the role of strategy and tactics. These interests indicate both the strengths and weaknesses of the approach. First, in privileging class domination, Marxism tends to ignore other forms of social domination – patriarchal, ethnic, "racial," hegemonic masculinities, inter-state, regional or territorial, etc. At best these figure as factors that overdetermine the forms of class domination and/or get modified by changes in class relations. Second, there is a risk of overemphasizing the structural coherence of class domination at the expense of its disjunctures, contradictions, countervailing tendencies, etc. Notions of a unified ruling class belie the messiness of actual configurations of class power – the frictions within and across its economic, political, and ideological dimensions, the disjunctions between different scales of social organization, the contradictory nature and effects of strategies, tactics, and policies, the probability of state as well as market failures, and the capacity of subaltern forces to engage in resistance. Many concrete analyses reveal this messiness and complexity but these qualities often go unreflected in more abstract Marxist theorizing. Third, Marxists risk reducing the limits of economic, political, and ideological power to the effect of class contradictions. But there are other sources of failure too. Finally, whilst an emphasis on strategy and tactics is important to avoid the structuralist fallacy that capital reproduces itself quasi-automatically and without need of human action, there is a risk of voluntarism if strategy and tactics are examined without reference to specific conjunctures and broader structural contexts.

Further Reading

Detailed discussions of Marxist theories of power and of the state can be found in C. W. Barrow's *Critical Theories of the State: Marxist, neo-Marxist, post-Marxist*. Madison: University of Wisconsin Press, 1993 and B. Jessop's *State Theory: Putting Capitalist States in their Place*. Cambridge: Polity Press, 1990.

2

Developments in Pluralist and Elite Approaches

RICHARD BELLAMY

Pluralist accounts are offered as liberal or radical alternatives to Marxism. They are based on the idea that society itself is pluralist: with respect to its differentiated functions, interests and values, and – in the most recent versions of pluralism – radically different perspectives and identities. While earlier pluralists saw differences as negotiable and commensurable, ultimately assuming common ground between conflicting groups, recent philosophical pluralists see conflicts as potentially irresolvable: values are incommensurable so there is no single reasonable choice between them. As Bellamy points out, a radical democratic pluralism must find ways of negotiating or fairly resolving such conflicts. For elitists this problem does not arise since they are convinced that society is, and must be, ruled by an elite. Pluralism and elitism are combined in the work of Weber who argued that the democratic government of complex, modern societies was only possible where it consisted of competition between the elites of political parties. At the end of the chapter Bellamy asks whether this pessimistic view is really justified: are ordinary people incapable of making the difficult decisions required in pluralist societies?

Pluralist approaches to politics have been associated with functional differentiation and the division of labor, the related plurality of ideals and interests, and the plural identities stemming from such factors as multicultural-ism, ethnicity, and gender. Pluralists claim political power either is or should be distributed in ways that respect these divisions. Though these cleavages are related to class distinctions, pluralists resist attempts to assimilate the one to the other. Their analyses are offered as liberal or radical alternatives to Marxism. Elitism is both a response and a challenge to pluralism. Elite theorists argue power either resides with a ruling class or that it should do. At worst pluralism is mere appearance, offering a cover for elite rule; at best it signifies a plurality of elites.

I begin by exploring the three main varieties of political pluralism outlined above. All appear incomplete. Pluralism runs deeper than these approaches appreciate, disturbing the integrity of each of them. A proposed fourth variety avoids these difficulties. I then survey the main elite critiques of pluralism. Max

Weber's position emerges as the most philosophically profound and sociologic-ally plausible. However, his belief that pluralist politics must be elitist rather than democratic proves too pessimistic.

PLURALISM

The earliest pluralist theories focused on the functional pluralism deriving from the division of labor. A doctrine associated with the English pluralists F. W. Maitland, J. N. Figgis, Ernest Barker, G. D. H. Cole, and Harold Laski, they had been influenced by the ideas of the German jurist Otto von Gierke and the French scholars Emile Durkheim and Léon Duguit (Hirst 1989; Laborde 2000). Four related themes characterized their writings, though each thinker prioritized and interpreted them in different ways. These were:

1 The principle of functional representation.
2 The notion of corporate personality.
3 The critique of state sovereignty.
4 The organic view of society.

I shall explore each in turn.

These pluralists contended people feel a greater allegiance to functional asso-ciations than they do to territorial units. Since individuals spend more time at work than anywhere else, professional groups such as trade unions had pride of place within their scheme. However, they also acknowledged the significance people attach to membership of associations such as churches and clubs, and accepted we had interests as consumers as well as producers. From their per-spective, territory appeared triply flawed as a basis for political representation . First, they argued territorial representation assumes it is possible to represent the "general will" or "common good" of the people within a given constituency. But individual interests are complex and split between a variety of associations, with no one person likely to have the same allegiances and concerns as anyone else. Second, functions and territory do not always map onto each other. Those functions and associations that individuals have an interest in might well cross over several constituencies and even the borders of several states. Third, they believed territorial forms of representation view functional and associational life as voluntary. The power a given employer or church exerts over people is treated as the freely chosen result of taking a job or entering a given sect. There is no need to democratize these entities, therefore, to guarantee the freedom of their members. Individuals can simply join another organization that suits them better. By contrast, these pluralists contended our autonomy was intimately tied up with these associations being self-governing. The prime locus of demo-cratic participation should be the various groups to which we belong, with each electing representatives to a federal legislature to devise the rules governing relations between them.

The reasoning behind much of this argument stems from their concept of corporate personality. They thought entities such as religious and industrial bodies are more than mere means for the satisfaction of individual interests. Membership of them partly defines those individual interests by shaping someone's identity as, say, a Catholic miner. Consequently, an individual's capacity for self-development depends upon the ability to collectively develop those groups which fashion who they are. This argument both parallels and weakens the case for national self-determination. The notion of corporate personality was opposed to both methodological individualism and a holism that turned individuals into mere cyphers of the collectivity. Instead these pluralists attempted to synthesize the two perspectives. They claimed individuality presupposes the collective goods and social relations provided by associational life but that these associations have no worth or existence apart from the individuals who compose them. This view led them to oppose the treatment of corporations as legal "fictions." The favorite example of John Figgis was the Free Church of Scotland case of 1900. The Free Church had merged with the United Presbyterian Church by a majority of 643 votes to 27. The minority claimed the merger was an *ultra vires* act and took the majority to court. The House of Lords ruled in their favor by arguing their position was truer to the sect's principles and awarded the dissenters the Church's assets. Figgis saw the Lords ruling as denying the free development of groups and hence of those who belonged to them (Figgis 1913: 21–2). For it reified Church doctrine into something distinct from the view of it held by Church members.

Their pluralist critique of state sovereignty also entered here. Figgis thought the ruling illustrated how a central authority could illegitimately override the express will of citizens. These pluralists identified sovereignty with a "unitary" or "monistic" state. Like the territorial view of representative democracy, this doctrine mistakenly assumed citizens possessed a general will which could be expressed by some central sovereign power, be it a monarch or a unitary legislative body supposedly representing the people. Particular associations were distrusted as self-seeking factions that undermined a commitment to the common good. However, the value consensus and commonality of interests presupposed by this theory largely reflected the concerns of hegemonic groups, especially those possessing economic power. In reality, the interests and ideals of ordinary citizens were far more diverse. Moreover, they could only get a hearing if their associations, such as trade unions, were empowered within the political system. This proposal was seen as extending the federal principle from territory to function, though without power being organized in a hierarchical manner. Instead they favored a more confederal arrangement which gave each association a high degree of autonomy within its specific domain. Different circumstances and spheres of activity called for different regulative regimes and norms. The best way to capture this diversity was to disperse sovereign power horizontally amongst appropriate bodies rather than to devolve it down from the center.

An organic view of society prompted the belief that relations between associations would prove largely self-regulating and harmonious once their reciprocal ties were appreciated. To the extent a state was necessary it was as the locus of a confederal body capable of bringing this mutual dependence to light . Thus the demands of employee and employer organizations, and of producers and consumers, were to be reconciled via a heightened awareness of the complementary character of their respective needs. Durkheim (1957), for example, largely reconceived politics as communication, with the state the recipient and channel of this information. Laski (1921) and Figgis (1913) were a little less sanguine, and accepted that occasionally the state might need to mediate conflict.

Pluralism of this variety flourished in the period 1915–25. It was a response to the challenges to liberal democracy posed by syndicalist and Marxist socialism and, to a lesser extent, fascism. It sought a middle way between individualism and collectivism, though some thinkers – notably G. D. H. Cole and Laski – were firmly on the left of the political spectrum. Though inspired in Britain by the Hegelian idealism of T. H. Green, particularly in their view of corporate personality and organicism, they followed him in rejecting a metaphysical conception of the state. Instead, they looked to mediaeval, pre-Hobbesian notions of sovereignty, a lineage evident in references by Cole (1920) and others to guilds. It was thus quite different in character to state corporatist doctrines. The apparent triumph of communism and fascism in the 1930s made pluralism seem unrealizable and most of its proponents abandoned it.

Recently, debates about the weakening of the state by globalization and the related reorientation of the left to meet New Right critiques of statist versions of socialism have given the doctrine a new lease of life in the guise of associative theories of democracy (Hirst 1994; Cohen and Rogers 1995). These drop the organicism and see associations as voluntary. Yet this step undermines crucial aspects of the pluralist argument. As we saw, the earlier pluralists justified extending democratic politics to civil society precisely because membership of certain functional associations was as inescapable as residence in a state and, in their broader role in framing our identities, as, if not more, important to individual autonomy as the self-determination of peoples. The underlying organicism also explained why these thinkers were unconcerned by possible collective-action problems resulting from the wealthy defecting from schemes for public welfare, say, or certain functional groups exploiting their positional advantage to get extra funding from others. As shall we see, elitists believe such behavior inevitable. The new associationalists respond by advocating the equalization of resources. Even if this proposal would successfully eliminate these problems, a matter of dispute, it begs the questions of where the consensus for such a scheme might come from given pluralism, and what authority might establish it given the alleged weakness of states.

The second main variety of pluralist politics potentially faces similar difficulties, since it treats all groups as organized interests vying for power. Though its proponents claim a descent going back to James Madison, this form of pluralism originated in the 1950s from the work of contemporary North American political scientists such as David Truman (1951) and Robert Dahl (1956, 1989). The key to their thesis, and their answer to the elitists, arises from a particular analysis of power and its distribution within western democracies. Power they define as the capacity to act so as to control another's responses. That capacity rests on a variety of different kinds of resource and the relative share of them held by those involved. They make two central claims in this regard. First, they maintain that modern dynamic societies are highly differentiated and contain a plurality of different sorts of social group. As a result, people hold multiple memberships and occasionally conflicting allegiances to very diverse groups. There are also multiple centers and sources of power within the society, economy, and polity which compete with and, to some extent, balance each other. Churches, schools, and the media; different firms and distinct political institutions and parties all vie for the attention of citizens, as well as offering a variety of locations where they can seek, exercise, or be subject to power.

Second, these circumstances mean no one type of resource, such as economic and financial influence, is dominant. They accept inequalities exist, and that wealth gives the rich access to far more political resources, from education through to direct access to politicians, than the poor. However, within democracies the capacity to mobilize popular support stems from a number of factors. Some resources will be relevant in certain contexts, others in different ones. The organizational power of certain unions and their strategic position in a pivotal industry can mean their relatively poor members may sometimes take on rich individual businessmen or governments, for example. Similarly, getting the support of a given religious or ethnic group can be crucial in certain elections or votes in the legislature. Much will depend on the complexion of the electorate and the nature of the policy. Nor need numbers be the deciding factor. In certain fora and for issues involving some form of expertise, status and knowledge can give particular individuals, such as academics or clergy, influence far beyond either their financial resources or the size of their group.

These two factors lead them to contest the contrasting critiques of democracy made by the elite theorists examined in the next section, on the one hand, and liberals, on the other. Elitists argue democracy simply acts as a cover for the domination of a ruling class. Pluralists counter that no such cohesive minority exists (Dahl 1989: ch. 19). We belong to many groups with often very different agendas. It is unlikely that the same people will consistently line up with each other on every issue. Nor will the same people be similarly important across all spheres of social, economic, and political life. As we saw, these pluralists believe there are competing centers and sources of power, the influence of which waxes and wanes according to the policy. Even if each group is dominated by an elite, they will be unable to collectively form a ruling class. For much the same reasons, the liberal fear of the "tyranny of the majority" proves equally unfounded (Dahl 1989: chs. 15–18). Any majority is best characterized as a coalition of minorities. Moreover, the composition of that coalition will alter according to what is being decided and where. People's multiple membership of groups make all coalitions unstable because it will be hard to construct a package of policies all can consistently agree on. Thus, people will tend to find themselves in a majority coalition on some issues and in a minority one on others. So long as elections are regular and competitive, then a pluralist society will be what Dahl calls a "polyarchy." That is, it will possess a democratic system where different minorities rule in a plurality of different loci, thereby rendering both dictatorship and demagogic populism impossible. Power is shared and bargained between numerous groups representing diverse interests. The structures of the state offer a neutral terrain for these negotiations. As a result, a "competitive equilibrium" emerges as different groups are constrained to reach mutually beneficial compromises.

Pluralists have been criticized for having an overly optimistic view of the distribution of power (Bachrach and Baratz 1962; Lukes 1974). Critics argue their analysis proves incomplete because they only look at actual decision making. For power has already been exercised in both setting the agenda and in constructing the ways and fora where decisions get made. Social, cultural, and economic factors may systematically bias the political system so that certain policy-conflicts never get aired. Far from being neutral, the procedures and character of the state can discriminate against certain groups and favor others. It is no accident that the poor are far less likely to vote than the moderately wealthy. These pluralists tend to view voter apathy as a positive sign, reflecting trust and agreement with the government, for example, rather than alienation, lack of access, and a sense of impotence (Dahl 1956: 132–3; Almond and Verba 1963). They reply that the "non-decision-making" process can be almost impossible to identify, especially if its presence rests on counterfactual assertions of what voters would want if they were capable of expressing their "authentic" interests. Some have conceded nonetheless that they failed to acknowledge the systematic imbalance produced by the capitalist system itself. It is not just that differences of economic power create inequalities in other political resources, a matter they always acknowledged. The requirements of private accumulation systematically limit the policy options available to governments (Linblom 1977: 122–3; Dahl 1985: 55). Dahl suggests that democratizing economic enterprises through schemes for workers democracy that gives them a say in management of the enterprise offers one means for restoring the balance (Dahl 1989: chs. 22–3). Put another way, he supplements interest group pluralism with the functional pluralism of Cole and Laski.

These pluralists hold that the multiple membership of diverse groups produces cross-cutting cleavages within society. In consequence, politics becomes less zero-sum and a consensus on the procedural norms and limits of democracy develops. They believe the resulting shared civic culture explains the success of contemporary liberal democracies. However, the new social movements that emerged in the late 1960s challenged this analysis, revealing a whole series of groups who feel their interests had been excluded from official politics (see Meyer, chapter 15 and Hamel and Maheu, chapter 24, in this volume). Some of these groups reflect horizontal or segmental cleavages within society arising from ethnicity, culture, language, gender, religion, and so on. Though the members of groups organized on these lines usually differ amongst each other in other respects and hold a range of interests and ideals similar to that found in the population at large, they nonetheless feel these divisions are primary. These cleavages define their core beliefs and identities and hinder cooperation with people from different groups with whom they share other concerns.

This third variety of pluralism has profound consequences for politics. It disrupts agreement on the means, ends, and limits of democracy. Political debate in such circumstances can appear more zero-sum and less amenable to bargaining. The trading of interests is easiest when those concerned accept that they are of the same kind or translatable into some common medium of exchange, such as material resources. However, if people feel they hold different perspectives and values then they may either not be able to fix on terms of agreement or desire that these be negotiated first rather than simply accepting a set up which they believe entrenches the views of their interlocutors. As a result, they will seek protection from external interference or desire mechanisms that guarantee them a say in debates about the very structure of the political system.

Will Kymlicka (1995: 26–33) has identified three forms of group-differentiated rights resulting from such demands: self-government rights, polyethnic rights, and special representation rights. Self-government rights are commonest amongst regionally based national minorities, such as the Welsh and Scots, and can lead to demands for secession. Though Kymlicka overlooks this possibility, self-government rights can also be established on a non-territorial basis along the lines advocated by the English school of pluralists. Territorially dispersed minorities can in this way nonetheless belong to their own trade union organizations and even run their own education and health-care systems. Usually such groups seek polyethnic rights, however. These give exemptions from certain laws that disadvantage them, permitting Sikhs not to wear motor cycle helmets, for example, or Jews and Muslims to trade on Sundays. More controversially, such rights can also extend to more positive measures, such as an entitlement to deal with public authorities in a minority language and to have minority languages and religions taught in schools. Such rights aim less at self-government than reconciliation with and assimilation into the majority culture. Finally, special representation rights seek to equalize the say of minority groups within the legislative process. These measures range from creating constituencies favorable to the election of representatives from such groups or even reserving a number of seats for them in the legislature; through encouraging quotas within the established political parties or employing electoral systems, such as PR, that favor the setting up of group-based parties; to directly or, as might result from the measures already mentioned, indirectly ensuring power sharing in the executive. This last set of mechanisms has been taken up by women's, gay, lesbian, and disabled groups as well as racial, ethnic, religious, and national minorities.

These three sets of group rights are not mutually exclusive, and many political systems contain a selection from each of them. Kymlicka justifies group rights using the impeccably liberal principles of equality and autonomy. He argues that when identities and the cultures on which they draw are structurally disadvantaged, those concerned lack an equal chance to live according to their values. To the extent these disadvantages are unchosen, they are analogous to involuntary unemployment or sexual discrimination. Group rights are similar to social security schemes and affirmative action, therefore, protecting individuals from the (often unwitting) discriminatory impact of the political and economic choices of the wider society. However, liberal critics worry that unless groups have a liberal ethos, external protection may lead to infringements of the rights of dissenting individuals within them. Self-government rights in particular benefit some groups but, as Kymlicka concedes, they may merely reconfigure the problem for others, since most self-governing or newly autonomous regions will contain substantial minorities of their own. Restrictions on the use of English by the Anglophone minority in Quebec offers an example of this dilemma, as does the exemption of Amish children from compulsory education regulations in the United States.

Though Kymlicka sees such cases as exceptions rather than the rule, there is a general concern that group rights are inherently conservative, entrenching and possibly even imposing a particular identity on groups that reinforces majority prejudices and discourages their recognition by and engagement with the wider society. For example, some Asian groups have argued that designating them as "black" involved just such an imposed and prejudicial identity (Modood 1994). These faults have also been associated with the most common form of this variety of pluralist politics, consociationalism. Its chief proponent, Arend Lijphart (1968) has defined consociationalism in terms of four principles: a grand coalition or power-sharing executive; segmental autonomy involving either territorial or non-territorial forms of self-government; proportionality as a principle of political representation, civil service appointments and the allocation of public funds; and minority veto. This political system combines the first and third of Kymlicka's group rights and invariably establishes certain polyethnic rights too. Its success depends on the ability of elites within the Grand Coalition to deliver the acquiescence of their followers in return for a mutually beneficial carve-up of resources. Thus, the elites have a vested interest in preventing dissent within their ranks and of perpetuating divisions. It is a largely negative strategy, aimed at achieving a modus vivendi between groups rather than mutual recognition.

Consociationalism also assumes a particular and rather partial view of differences (Barry 1975). It favors those focused on hierarchical organizations capable of partly defining and stabilizing the beliefs of their members. Religions typically display these features, with the clergy establishing church doctrine, and so do some ideologies. However, differences based on ethnicity and those associated with new social movements rarely possess these characteristics. The historical constructs of the human capacity for reflection and interpretation, they are internally contested and open to development. They are usually more informally organized and have less clear cut programmes. They are less concerned with a fair division of the spoils so much as with the shape and nature of the polity within which such resources get defined as well as distributed. This conception of difference invites a more positive view of group rights. They serve not only as protective devices but also foster mutual recognition between minority groups and the majority by enabling them to take an equal part in defining the political culture of the polity. They belong to, and are themselves defined through, an agonistic politics where the demand for recognition of one's own differences entails a reciprocal willingness to recognize and engage with those of others, including dissidents within one's group (Young 1990; Taylor 1994; Tully 1995). The difficult task for a pluralist polity lies in achieving a balance between the negative or protective mechanisms and those positive devices that encourage dialogue.

This fourth and radical variety of pluralist politics draws on the ontological and epistemological pluralism of certain philosophers (Bellamy 1999). This philosophical doctrine refers to the nature of values and the relations between them. Philosophical pluralists claim there are many moral and non-moral values and different ways of combining, interpreting, and evaluating them. The crux comes when this plurality motivates contrary courses of action, generating conflicts between individuals, groups, societies, and cultures. Between incompatible, contested, and possibly incommensurable values and valuations, no choice appears the only reasonable one. This position challenges the three main varieties of pluralist politics. The first variety treats pluralism as the manifestation of an underlying if complex social unity, albeit one that would only emerge through the collaboration of the various parts of the body politic. Radical pluralists would agree with Luhmann (1982), however, in linking functional differentiation with a high degree of reflexivity which makes communication between different spheres difficult. The norms of work and family, church and state, friends and neighbors, can impose contrasting and incompatible claims on individuals that defy rational resolution. The second variety identifies pluralism with the strategic pursuit of sectional, subjective interests. But this assumes all values are tradable and can be ranked or weighed employing some common denominator. The third variety sees pluralism in terms of objective identities of either a primordial or doctrinaire kind, over which their possessors have little control. This position overlooks the complexity of both ways of life and the principles and values they contain. There are internal conflicts within cultures as well as external clashes between them. A radical and democratic pluralist politics must either find ways of negotiating such conflicts or propose fair procedures for resolving them. It is to the elitist denial of this possibility that we now turn.

ELITISM

Elite theory arose from similar dissatisfactions with liberal democracy to the pluralists' (Bottomore 1964; Parry 1969). Originating with the Italian political sociologists Gaetano Mosca (1939) and Vilfredo Pareto (1935) and developed further by the Germans Roberto Michels (1958) and Max Weber (1994) in much the same period as the English pluralists were writing, it gained a new lease of life in the 1940s, 1950s, and 1960s in the Marxist critiques of North American pluralists by James Burnham (1941), C. Wright Mills (1956) and others. Elitists share the pluralists' scepticism about portraying democracy in terms of the general will or majority rule. However, they believe these terms overlook not minorities but a minority – the ruling elite.

Elitists generally divide the ruling class into two groups: what Mosca called "the generals" who exercise power, and a much larger group or "officer class" from whom these rulers are drawn (1939: 50, 404). However, their explanations of the rise, fall, and desirability of elites differs widely. Thus, Pareto asserts that elites always had and would rule. Unfortunately, beyond an assumption as to the gullibility of the mass, he never says why. Instead, he focuses on how their rule is exercised. His analysis is more psychological than social. He contends humans are largely moved by "non-logical" reasoning arising from certain psychic dispositions that he terms "residues" (1935: paras. 867–70). Two are particularly important: the "instinct of combinations," by which he means a capacity for shrewdness and for inventiveness, and the "persistence of aggregates" or conservative tendency (1935: paras 888–9). Following Machiavelli, Pareto believes both qualities are necessary to govern. Rulers must possess the cunning of "foxes" to build consent whilst having the strength of "lions" needed to impose law and order. He believed the balance between the two residues went in cycles that related to those in the economy and society as a whole. Prosperity favored the first but ultimately ended in anarchy and a desire for authority associated with the second, a phase that led in its turn to stagnation and a return to a more creative and flexible ethos. He sees this pattern as a universal law and cites evidence from ancient Greece to the present (1935: paras. 2053–9, 2230–6). But his categories are so vague that almost any event can be tailored to fit them (Bellamy 1987: ch. 2).

Mosca's theory proves far more promising. He notes the qualities of the elite vary according to the needs and values of a given society, with military prowess giving way to the capacity to win friends and influence people. Elites always rule, regardless of whether power flows down, as in autocratic societies, or up, as in liberal ones. Their recruitment depends on the balance of two tendencies: the aristocratic, whereby the elite recruits from its own members, or the democratic, when the rulers draw on the ruled (1939: ch. 15). Autocratic organizations can nonetheless display democratic tendencies, as in the Catholic Church, and liberal societies aristocratic ones, as in political dynasties such as the Nehru family. Though elite rule favors the aristocratic tendency, its survival depends on some element of the democratic. If the character of the elite changes, Mosca thought the inevitable existence of an elite does not. The reason lies in the organizational superiority of a minority (1939: 53). A minority can form itself into a cohesive group more easily than the mass, and act more quickly and decisively. It is this point that Michels picks up and develops into an "iron law of oligarchy" (1958: 418). He argues that coordination problems, the need for expertise and sheer efficiency dictate that organizations of any size need leaders. Since power breeds power, the strategic advantages of leadership make those who possess them difficult to control.

These arguments challenged Marxist claims, later refined by Mills, that attributed the existence of a ruling class to the possession of economic power. Elites could never wither way, making a democratic socialism as much of a sham as any other form of democracy. Pareto characterized appeals to popular rule or the general will as mere rhetorical devices. Socialist politicians were by and large "foxes," who used state funds to buy and manipulate their supporters. Socialist beliefs were simply "derivations" of class 1 residues. Mosca took a less cynical and more sophisticated view. Mass democracy had given rise to party organizations. He claimed the real ruling class were the "Grand Electors," the party bosses who raise funds and ran the electoral machine. They choose the politicians and control the political agenda. The electorate do not select a government, they are recruited by the parties to vote for candidates and policies over which they have little say. Michels' refinement of this thesis drew on extensive research on the German Socialist Party (SPD). He showed that, notwithstanding their egalitarian and democratic ethos, the requirements of campaigning, funding, organizing speakers and so on had given rise to a professional party elite. Nevertheless, Mosca's later writings give the elite argument a pluralist and democratic twist. Allowing his own sympathies to come to the fore, he argued that representative democracies achieve a felicitous combination of autocratic and liberal principles, on the one hand, and aristocratic and democratic tendencies, on the other. As a result, the ruling class comes to incorporate the plurality of interests within society. He remained a cautious democrat, however, fearing populism and wishing the suffrage had remained the privilege of the middle class (Bachrach 1969).

The link between pluralism and elitism was not fully explored until Weber. His concern with the bureaucratization of modern societies had inspired much of Michels' work. Elites became a necessity for Weber as the only source of meaningful direction and initiative in an increasingly formalized and rule-bound society. He believed capitalist economies remained sufficiently dynamic to contain competing organizations, be they companies, parties, or states, each with a distinct group of rival elites. He took the epistemological and ontological aspects of pluralism seriously, appreciating the challenge they posed to politics. He believed pluralism made rational deliberation on the common good impossible. The only way to resolve plural conflicts between competing goods or types of moral claim was through radical, existential choices. However, ordinary people were not able to make such choices, locked as they were into the routines of everyday life. Inspired by Nietzsche, he claimed only exceptional individuals had this capacity. Democratic politics he now reconceptualized as a struggle between rival party leaders to win popular support, a process that selected politicians with suitably charismatic qualities (Bellamy 1992: ch. 4; Weber 1994: 309–69).

Though his view of democracy as a competition between plural elites has been highly influential (Schumpeter 1956), Weber's view of the masses is too pessimistic. Ordinary people are shrewder judges of the impact of policies on their lives than he allows. They daily confront political issues from the price of food to schooling, transport, employment opportunities and so on. They are also no strangers to the hard choices posed by pluralism, constantly juggling the competing commitments of friends and fellow citizens, family and work, God and Mammon, amongst others. Moreover, collective decisions can be easier than personal ones. In context, choices appear less stark with numerous subsidiary reasons guiding the selection of particular options. People's different preference schedules and their ability to collaborate to facilitate each others activities also allow trade-offs and compromises to emerge. Choosing between health and knowledge as such may be impossible, but communities can sensibly decide to invest more in swimming pools than libraries, say. They do so by referring to numerous additional factors, such as the state of health of the population or the relative ease of buying a book as opposed to building a pool, and by negotiating compromises, for example cutting a deal over subsidies for orchestras and theatres to win over the library supporters. Democracy plays a crucial role here, communicating the necessary information concerning the population's priorities and reconciling them to the decision by involving them in it. The key lies in devising a political system that allows the different views expression whilst nonetheless promoting a decision which affords all mutual respect (Bellamy 1999: chs. 5 and 6). Such a system would remain a representative rather than a direct democracy, but need not be elitist in any strong sense provided adequate methods of accountability and responsiveness to the electorate exist. As we saw, none of the models of pluralist politics examined in the last section are totally adequate to this task. Each, however, may be partially adequate, suggesting that a plurality of different kinds of politics offers the best route to meeting the pluralist and elitist challenges.

Further Reading

Bellamy, R. P. 1992: *Liberalism and Modern Society: An Historical Argument*. Cambridge: Polity Press.
Bellamy, R. P. 1999: *Liberalism and Pluralism: Towards a Politics of Compromise*. London and New York: Routledge.
Kekes, J. 1993: *The Morality of Pluralism*. Princeton, N.J.: Princeton University Press.
Mc Lennan, G. 1995: *Pluralism*. Buckingham: Open University Press.
Nichols, D. 1974: *Three Varieties of Pluralism*. London: Macmillan.
Parry, G. 1969: *Political Elites*. London: George Allen and Unwin.

3

Rational Choice Approaches to Analyzing Power

Keith Dowding

The methodology of rational choice theory is game theory. The assumption of this approach is that actors seek to maximize their utility – to get as much of whatever it is they want as they can. Although there are great, perhaps insuperable, problems in using game theory to study power in actual social settings, models developed using this approach may help us understand some of the difficulties in measuring power in society. In this chapter, Dowding explores the advantages and drawbacks of using cooperative and non-cooperative game theory to study voting in the European Union. Finally, he argues that rational choice theory may overcome the duality of structure and individual within which debates over power are invariably caught. It analyzes the relationship between actors whose preferences are "suggested," though not determined, by the position they hold in society.

Power is a central concept in political science and sociology. Both in the study of institutions, which can be seen as devices for controlling the power of and enabling actors to do things, and in the study of policy development and implementation. In this sense political science could be said to be about power. In economics, however, power as a concept is hardly used at all. Indeed *the* major modern textbook on microeconomics (Kreps 1990) does not mention "power" in the index except in the context of monopolies. However, as Kreps makes clear, game theory is now a standard tool of economics and though not acknowledged there, provides a handy means by which to examine political or social power in society.

The most obvious uses of game theory to understand power is in the context of voting games. Cooperative game theory has been used to study the power of individual voters in voting situations. Cooperative game theory examines the resources voters can bring to bear to help attain their preferred outcome, demonstrating that some voters may have more power than their voting strength initially appears to offer. This provides a good starting point for analyzing power but has limitations, and may give a misleading analysis of the overall power of actors in different institutional settings. Here non-cooperative game theory provides a more thorough analysis. I will examine these approaches with regard to the power of different institutional actors in the European Union (EU), a topic of much recent dispute. Quantifying power in the setting of voting games is relatively easy. Quantifying the power of actors in broader social settings is much harder if not impossible. However, the lessons learned by examining analytic approaches to measuring power in voting games can help us to conceptualize some of the problems of analyzing power in society. I turn to this later in the essay, where I also demonstrate that the oft-made distinction between power seen as a "structural force" and power as a capacity of actors is a chimera. Actors have power given the structures in which they find themselves.

Von Neumann and Morgenstern (1944) created game theory. The first part of their book differs conspicuously from the second and this distinction survives today in cooperative and non-cooperative game theory. Non-cooperative game theory is the more fundamental. It requires a complete description of the rules of the game so that the individual strategies available to the players can be studied in detail. The aim is to find the equilibrium strategies to discover the solution to the game. Cooperative game theory is concerned with situations where players can negotiate, before the game is played, about what to do in the game. It is assumed that these negotiations can be concluded with a binding agreement so the precise strategies available to the players do not matter. Thus, once we know the game being played the only thing which matters is the preferences of the players.

Von Neumann and Morgenstern (1944) used cooperative game theory to simplify strategic situations by summarizing each alternative facing a player in a game with a single number. Simply, their account of expected utility theory specified the conditions under which an individual's preferences over risky alternatives could model behavior as the individual maximized the expected value of her utility function. Cooperative games are ones where the opportunities available to each coalition of players can also be described by a single number. Lloyd Shapley (1953) proposed summarizing the complex possibilities facing each player in a game in a characteristic function form by a single number representing the "value" of playing the game. The value of a game with $N = \{1, \ldots, n\}$ players would be a vector of n numbers representing the value of playing the game in each of its n positions. The Shapley value (see Roth, ed., 1988 for extensive discussion) allows a calculation of the worth of each player to some winning coalition given the rules of the game. Together with Martin Shubik he proposed using the Shapley value to study a class of simple games which may straightforwardly be taken to model voting rules. The Shapley–Shubik power index attempts to measure the voting power of individual members on a committee (Shapley and Shubik 1954). They ask "when is an individual voter decisive in securing her preferred outcome?" They imagine a group of actors all willing to vote for some measure. Each person votes one after the other until a bare majority is reached, the voting ceases, and the measure is declared passed. The last person to vote for the measure is credited with being decisive, her vote having secured the bare majority. This person is called the *pivotal voter* or *pivot*. This scheme does not represent a real method of voting; rather it is a device to try to capture the voting power of individual voters. The power of each voter is then given by how often each is, or could be, the pivotal voter. The pivot can then be defined:

$$P_i = m(i)/n!$$

Here P is the power of the voter i in a set of voters $\{1, 2, ..., n\}$ and m(i) is the number of times that i is *pivotal* in securing that outcome (n! means n factorial and if $n = 4$ then $4! = 4 \times 3 \times 2 \times 1 = 24$). Being pivotal is defined: when the voting rules define q votes as a winning number:

$$(n + 1)[q][n \text{ or}] \ n/2 + 1[q][n].$$

The pivotal position is the qth position in any ordered sequence of votes, there being n! ordered sequences. Thus:

$$\sum_{i=1}^{n} P_i^n = 1$$

Under this definition a voter's power is determined by the number of times she is pivotal in relation to the number of possible ordered sequences. In other words, the power of any given voter is the probability that that individual is the final member of a minimum winning coalition. The power of all members of a committee always sums to 1.

When each person has one vote on a committee of *n* the voting power of each is $1/n$. However, with weighted voting the model demonstrates that voting power is less obvious. For example, *a*, *b*, and *c* are three parties in a legislature of 100 members. Party *a* has 49 members, party *b* 48 members, and party *c* 3 members. Despite Party *c* having far fewer members it has the same voting power as *a* and *b* since its votes are required by each of the other parties in order to secure a majority. The Shapley–Shubik index give the following power to parties in the European Parliament (EP), see table 3.1.

Other rival power indices have been created (see Felsenthal and Machover 1998). Whilst bearing similarities these indices do not all provide exactly the same numerical evaluations of players power, nor rank the players' position

Table 3.1 Party group power in the European Parliament in 1999

	Percentage of seats	S-S Power under simple majority	S-S Power under absolute majority
PES	34.2	.348	.506
EPP	28.8	.229	.315
UPE	8.9	.105	.39
IEN	8.5	.105	.39
ELDR	6.5	.057	.39
EUL	5.4	.057	.39
G	4.5	.057	.15
ERA	3.2	.043	.06
Percentage of seats to win		50.2(314)	66.8 (418)

Source: Hix 1999, p.82.

identically in more complex voting games. (To download a program for calculating different voting power indices see http://www.mzes.uni-mannheim.de/
arb2/pow.html). Since the scores produced by the indices are not identical this
causes problems in their precise interpretation, and the indices are sensitive to
particular underlying assumptions which may not be obvious. However, they
share the feature that they are constructed by assigning a score to each voter v for
all winning coalitions C in which v is pivotal such that $C-v$ is not winning. The
scores are then normalized such that the sum of the power of each voter is 1.
Recently these indices have been used to assess the power of each nation in the
EU Council of Ministers (CM). Table 3.2 shows the Shapley–Shubik scores for
the CM.

The power of each nation in the CM, or the power of coalitions of nations such
as "large nations" or the "poor nations," can then be calculated given the weighted
votes of each and the precise rules governing winning coalitions. This is of obvious
interest since, for example, it has been argued (Johnston 1995) that the largest
member states (Germany, the UK, France, and Italy) have more powerwhen the
blocking majority is 27 than when it is 23; thus John Major's negotiating
position was against British interests as Major saw them. Other writers have

Table 3.2   Voting weights and voting power in the Council under Qualified
Majority Voting

Country	Population (millions)	Votes	Citizens per vote (million)	Power (Shapley–Shubik)	Citizens relative to S-S Power
Germany	81.7	10	8.2	.117	698
UK	58.6	10	5.9	.117	500
France	58.1	10	5.8	.117	496
Italy	57.7	10	5.8	.117	493
Spain	39.1	8	4.9	.096	407
Netherlands	15.5	5	3.1	.055	282
Greece	10.5	5	2.1	.055	191
Belgium	10.2	5	2.0	.055	185
Portugal	9.9	5	2.0	.055	180
Sweden	8.9	4	2.2	.045	198
Austria	8.1	4	2.0	.045	180
Denmark	5.2	3	1.7	.035	149
Finland	5.1	3	1.7	.035	146
Ireland	2.6	3	0.9	.035	74
Luxembourg	0.4	2	0.2	.021	19
Total Votes		87			
Required to Adopt		62			
Required to Block		26			

Source: Modified from Hix 1999, p.70.

examined the actual and potential voting rules to see the relative powers of nations in terms of the GDP, population, and other factors to question the wisdom of the actual voting rules (see Steneunberg et al. 1999). Similar applications of the indices have been given to nations and political groups within the European Parliament (see Hix 1999). As far as this analysis goes, there is nothing wrong with using power indices in this manner. They can be used to demonstrate the relative voting power (or voting resources) of voters or groups of voters within voting assemblies. However, there are a number of criticisms of this approach. One, which will be examined in more detail below, is that they confuse the measuring of voting *power*, which is the difference an actor can make in getting what she wants, with the *probability* that some actor will actually achieve what she wants. In criticizing the power index approach Garrett and Tsebelis (1999) argue that the "likely influence" of each nation is related to their centrality in policy space and not the normalized power index score. More correctly we should say that the probability of a nation getting what it wants is related to its centrality in policy space. This is not the same as its power because it is ludicrous to suggest that countries can become more influential by discovering the preferences of other nations, then lining up their votes in the middle. All attempts to incorporate connectedness into power index calculations confuse the probability of coalitions forming with the normalized voting power of the constituent members of the coalitions. More importantly however, Garrett and Tsebelis argue that the cooperative game theory approach ignores institutional features of the EU which affects our assessment of the relative powers of actors within it. We need to use non-cooperative game theory.

Figure 3.1 represents the Garrett–Tsebelis argument. In order to simplify they assume the Council has 7 members and a qualified majority (QMV) is 5 from 7 (approximates 62 of 87). They represent the battles in the EU on a single dimension of "pro" versus "anti" further integration, and assume actors have ideal

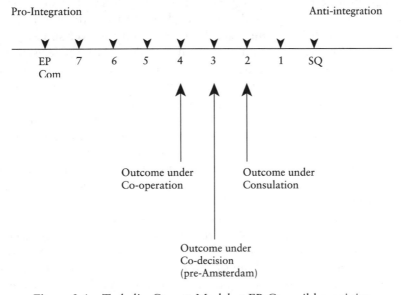

Figure 3.1   Tsebelis–Garrett Model at EP-Council bargaining

points on the dimension and Euclidean preferences; that is, they want outcomes as close as possible to their ideal points. In figure 3.1 we have member states at different ideal points along the single dimension, the Commission (Com) and European Parliament (EP) are represented as more integrationist, and the status quo (SQ) less integrationist than any state.

They then examine the likely outcomes, given these assumptions, from different institutional arrangements in the European Union. Under the "consultation procedure" the final decision is made by the Council. When the unanimity rule holds, this means that the least integrationist state will veto any proposal which is not closer to its ideal point (1) than the SQ. Thus it would not veto a proposal at point (2) which is as close to point (1) as SQ. Under the cooperation procedure the Council also makes the final decision, but it now has to decide whether to accept EP amendments by QMV or reject them, replacing them with its own proposal decided by unanimity. By analogy with the consultation procedure the latter course will end up at point (2). But the EP, which is more integrationist, only needs the support of state 3 for the Council to support its proposal under QMV. State 3 is pivotal. Under this analysis the EP should make a proposal at point (4) because state 3 is indifferent between 2 and 4.

Under the co-decision procedure, the EP has the final say. This would seem to give the EP more power. However, Tsebelis argued that the cooperation procedure made the EP the "agenda-setter" since it can forward proposals the Council is more likely to accept than reject. But under the co-decision procedure this agenda-setting power lies with the Council. In fact Garrett and Tsebelis argue that the Council may try to stop agreement (normally reached through the Conciliation procedure) in order to get its own preferred policy reached under this procedure by QMV (called the Common Position, CP). All the EP can do is to unconditionally reject the Council's preferred policy CP, but in figure 3.1 the EP is more integrationist than any member state so it will always prefer the Council's position to that of the SQ. The CP will be located at position 3 because under QMV state 3 is the pivotal actor and thus can force its own ideal point.

Garrett and Tsebelis's argument has been criticized for over-simplifying parts of the process. However, I am not concerned with details of EU decision-making here (the interested reader should start with Hix 1999), but rather to demonstrate these simple games illustrate two aspects of power. First, the precise institutional rules which exist are just as important for the final outcome as the preferences of actors. Secondly, because they suggest the counter-intuitive result that the co-decision procedure of the Maastricht Treaty reduced the power of the EP (Tsebelis 1994). This example demonstrates that without careful analysis of what different institutions mean for the strategic actions of players in a game, we may have incorrect intuitions about what we think will happen under constitutional reform.

The key in both the cooperative and non-cooperative approach is seeing the "pivotal actor" as being powerful. In the Shapley–Shubik score, decisiveness is measured in the number of times it is logically possible for each actor to be pivotal given no assumptions about the preferences of the players and no specific institutional rules governing the game. If each player has the same voting resources each will be equally powerful. In weighted voting, such as with parties in table 3.1 where the "weight" of each party group is composed of their number of MEPs, the power of each group is measured by the number of times the party group is likely to be pivotal given the respective weights and the precise voting rules governing each decision. With non-cooperative games, preferences are assumed. In the example above, the seven states, the EP, and the Council are placed on a single ideological dimension and which player turns out to be pivotal depends upon the precise decision-making rules which are adopted. Different players are pivotal under each procedure. Whatever the rules therefore, and given the spread of preferences, however the pivotal player is created it seems to be all-powerful for it is able to determine the outcome – it is able to ensure policy conforms to its ideal point. What makes a player powerful is the rules, and the spread of preferences. If someone just happens to be at the center of the spectrum they are able to get what they want. But this seems to be luck rather than power because it makes no sense to change your preferences in *order* to be pivotal and thereby get what you want. This makes a mockery of "wants." (Though note, it does make sense to pretend your preferences are something other than they really are, in order to be pivotal in one voting game in order to make deals in other voting games.) Brian Barry (1991) takes up this idea of luck, and we can see that the concept of "luck" and its extension has a powerful effect on the analysis of power in society.

Barry defines luck as the probability of getting what you want without trying. Success is how often one gets what one wants. The difference between success and luck is an individual's decisiveness. So success = luck + decisiveness. Thus the notion that Shapley–Shubik were trying to develop with the number of sequences in which some voter is pivotal divided by the number of possible sequences is, in Barry's terms, a measure of their decisiveness. And like the Shapley–Shubik power index, for any given individual each of these measures will take a value between 0 and 1, but the scores of all members do not have to sum to 1.

The decisiveness and luck of an actor vary according to the preferences of other actors, but an actor's power remains the same. It is a disposition, analyzable counteractually by taking into account all possible preference orderings. Power here is about being able to get what you want, but no single person nor any group can get anything done in every possible world: thus in an absolute sense no one has political power. From this we learn that every powerful actor is powerful because of the resources they bring to a bargain with other actors. Power always depends upon a coalition of mutual or allied interests. Dictators rely upon many other people; their army, their police, their secret police, their cabinet and so on. All these people, or some subset of them, could conspire and overthrow the dictator. Dictators survive by forming coalitions with others and stopping rival coalitions forming by sowing doubts in others' minds and turning potential partners against each other. The dictator offers positive and negative incentives to the others in order to gain their support and stop their challenge. In order to understand even the most obvious examples of power we need to understand the nature of coalition formation and the nature of bargaining. All political power is a form of reciprocal or bargaining power.

One may prefer to be lucky than decisive, for then one gets what one wants without trying. One may rather share the same interests with the powerful than be one of them. Individuals must make judgments about getting what they want by taking into account the interests they share with others, and judgments about power must be judgments about groups rather than individuals. What individuals take into account in these calculations are the resources that others could bring to bear against them in any social situation. The power of others is assessed solely in terms of their resources. These resources include both "external" resources – money, legal rights, institutional authority for example – and "internal" resources such as physical strength, determination, and persuasiveness. In order to study power we need to study the resources of different groups in society, understand their preferences and model their relationship to one another. But there is one resource that is less tangible than the others: reputation. Firms may respond to other firms encroaching upon their product markets by setting prices so low they are unprofitable. By doing so they create a reputation for aggressively protecting their market and thereby making future encroachments less likely. A player in a game of Chicken may always play the hawk strategy, no matter how great the potential losses if she meets another hawk, in order to convince potential opponents to play dove and thereby bring greater rewards to herself. A small boy may refuse to hand over his pocket money to the bully no matter how badly the bully beats him. If the beating brings costs to the bully (he scrapes his knuckles, gets blood on his shirt, and looks lesser in the eyes of others for not being able to force the boy to hand over his money), then the bully is more likely to pick on another victim in the future. Reputation is a key element in bargaining and game theory. It depends on players having incomplete and imperfect information. If players had complete and perfect information there would be no room for reputation, for there would be no room for players to pretend they were anything other than what they are. The importance of information arises from its asymmetry. It shows that we cannot simply read off actors' power from their resources – the so-called "vehicle fallacy" (Morriss 1987: 18) which equates power with its vehicle – and shows that determinate game-theoretic accounts are impossible. It also provides a means by which we can understand how playing the game can change the preferences of the player. I return to this below.

We have seen that getting what you want may be determined by luck as much as by power. But are some people inherently lucky? If we imagine that preferences are randomly distributed in simple voting game, as assumed in the Shapley–Shubik model, then luck, like decisiveness will be equally distributed. But we know that preferences are not randomly distributed. Different groups have different sets of preferences because of the sorts of people they are. As Marx argued, one's material conditions determines one's interests, but so does one's ethnicity and one's personal history. Democratic theory has struggled to come to terms with persistent minorities (Dahl 1956, 1989) and in voting games these individuals constantly lose out. Their individual power in the voting game is no less than that of members of the majority, but they are systematically unlucky (Dowding 1991, 1996: ch. 4). Why systematically unlucky? If "luck" is getting what you want without trying, systematic luck is regularly getting what you want because of who you are. Systematic luck attaches to certain locations within the social and institutional structure. Luck in this sense is closer to fortune or destiny than to simple chance. There is an important disjunction between getting what you want and outcome power, even when we expect that certain types of people get what they want without trying. Political science tends to denote people by their social locations – they are capitalists, or developers, or bureaucrats, or party activists – they are not denoted by their personal identities. Actors denoted by their social location have powers based upon their social resources, and they also have luck based upon their social location.

We can understand this with the classic example from the community power debate. In most communities the major issue over time concerns local development strategies. Time and again case studies show developers clashing with local citizen groups. The former wanting industrial development, large shopping malls, or high-price housing, the latter opposing development altogether, or wanting local amenities and low-price housing. Neither side always gets its way. Clark and Goetz (1994) reckoned about a quarter of their study of 179 cities had viable anti-development movements. The question is, do these movements get their way as often as their resources suggest they should? In the community power debate between pluralists and elitists (Bellamy, chapter 2, in this volume) one of the key issues was over evidence. Elitists claimed that powerful forces determined the political agenda which was canted towards their interests. The pluralists (notably Polsby 1980) demanded evidence, which was hard to find. On the one hand they asked for a demonstration that the elites were actively working to shape the agenda in their favor. On the other hand they demanded evidence that citizens cared as much as the "radical" critics (such as Lukes 1974) claimed. Evidence was hard to find, which led some to believe, wrongly, that somehow it was inherently impossible to empirically examine power. Rational choice analysis allows us to have our cake and eat it. We can see why some elites are advantaged through being systematically lucky, and understand under-mobilization through the collective action problem.

Developers tend to be systematically lucky. That is not to say they do not lobby for local growth strategies. Rich interests give small fortunes to different politicians, often backing both sides, in order to get politicians to help them, and also lobby for public support for schemes which they claim will boost the local economy or smarten up slum areas. But these powers are boosted by the fact their interests coincide with those of politicians. Developers promise a boost to the local economy and politicians know their re-election chances are enhanced when the local economy is doing well. We can split the growth game into two. A positive-sum game over the growth possibilities, and a zero-sum game over where and what sort of development is to occur. The first game is positive-sum because everyone may gain. (In practice some lose.) Developers and landed interests gain even more through growth than does the local community, but if local jobs are created or secured then many in the local community will gain. If developers agree to provide some low-cost housing as a result of bargaining with local politicians for building rights, then local people may gain more directly. In so far as the developers are able to gain because others gain too, they are pushing at an open door. To that extent they are lucky. What is in their interests is in others' interests too. This is an important aspect of the power structure. In a capitalist society capitalists are systematically lucky because the welfare of everyone is dependent upon the state of the economy and capitalism is the motor of the economy.

On the other side, citizen groups find it harder to overcome their collective action problems. Over thirty years of research on the collective action problem have shown that many factors affect the ability of groups to mobilize. They include how "obvious" one's interests are, the relative costs of taking part in collective action, the size and interactiveness of the group, the number of non-rival demands, whether the affected interests involve potential losses or potential gains, the shape of the production function of the collective good, the quality of personnel in a group, the possibility of an organization providing selective incentives, the possibility of joint action with other interests and so on (see Dowding 1996). For example, some interests in diffuse goods (whose benefits are widely spread around the population), such as clean air, are notoriously difficult to mobilize group action for since many people suffer but only marginally, whilst polluters face big clean-up costs. (Of course the "two" sides here may be the same people – "air breathers" and "car drivers.") Rational choice approaches have revolutionized our study of mobilization and thereby help us to understand the nature of power in society.

Generally speaking, those who have studied power either take a structuralist or individualist account. Rational choice analysis allows us to transcend this ancient debate. It is individualist in that it assumes actors act, but these actors are denoted by their structural characteristics, their social roles. A structure is the relationship between variables, and in society people are the variables. Different people may take up the same social role, and by bringing their own unique characteristics may have effects upon social outcomes. But people tend to have only marginal effects, because their power, their luck, and their preferences (or interests) are "structurally suggested" (Dowding 1991, 1996) to them by their social role. These make social structures relatively enduring and tend to systematically freeze the power and luck structure on to those social roles. Rational choice and game-theory analyze by examining the relationship between actors whose preferences are assumed to have been determined (or "suggested") by the position they hold in society, and seeing how those actors interact given their relationships as denoted by the institutional and social structures of society. It thus allows us to model why actors do not always act even when their interests appear threatened, understand why some actors seem to get what they want more often than their relative resources seem to suggest they should, and track coalitional formation and political bargaining of the strategically inclined to show why some groups win those political battles because of their pivotal position in different types of games.

Further Reading

Barry, B. 1991: *Democracy and Power.* Oxford: Oxford University Press.

Felsenthal, Dan S. and Machover, M. (1998): *The Measurement of Voting Power.* Aldershot: Edward Elgar.

Dowding, K. 1991: *Rational Choice and Political Power.* Aldershot: Edward Elgar.

Dowding, K. 1996: *Power Buckingham.* Milton Keynes: Open University Press.

4

Power, Government, Politics

BARRY HINDESS

Foucault's nominalist understanding of power cautions against reification. It also suggests there is little to say of interest about power as such and in general. Foucault studied specific, relatively stable configurations of power: domination and the government of a state. Domination is a hierarchical relationship in which the margin of liberty of the subordinated is extremely restricted. Government in this sense is understood more widely than "the supreme authority in states," as action aimed at influencing the way individuals regulate their own behavior. For Foucault the two senses are linked in that the aim of modern government of the state is to conduct the affairs of the population in the interests of the whole. This is not restricted to *the* government, but is performed also by agencies in civil society. The two senses of "government" are also linked by the use made of individual liberty in governmentality; seen in liberalism as setting limits to government action, scholars of governmentality analyze it as actually providing a means for the extension and consolidation of the state. Despite the contributions of this approach to our understanding of the uses of freedom, however, Hindess argues that two important aspects of liberal politics are neglected by analyses of governmentality. First, the politically oriented activity of partisan groups such as parties. Secondly, authoritarian aspects of liberal government. He argues that the approach needs to be extended to encompass these.

To ask the question "how do things happen?," Michel Foucault insists, is also "to suggest that power as such does not exist" (1982a: 217). The point of his comment is not to deny the reality of situations in which one individual or group exercises power over others but rather to caution against reification: that is, against the treatment of power as a capacity to impose one's will that some people (the powerful) possess in greater quantities than others. He goes on to claim that power over others should be seen as a matter of "the total structure of actions brought to bear" (1982a: 220) on their behavior. Thus, to adapt a well-known expression of the reified view of power, what happens when A gets "B to do something that B would not otherwise do" (Dahl 1957: 204) is that A brings various actions to bear on B's conduct. To say, as Robert Dahl does, that "A has power over B" is simply to claim that there is some connection between

A's actions and B's response. The reference to A's power is not an explanation of the change in B's conduct; rather it serves as a convenient kind of short-hand, an alternative to describing what interactions take place between them.

Since social interaction is always a matter of acting on the actions of others, this nominalistic view of power suggests that power relations will often be relatively unproblematic. It also suggests that power is an ubiquitous component of social life and that there is therefore little of value to be said about the nature of power as such and in general. Nevertheless, in spite of this last point, there are some relatively stable configurations of power that Foucault chooses to write about at length: domination and the government of a state. Domination is a hierarchical relationship in which the margin of liberty of the subordinated parties is severely restricted. This is "what we ordinarily call power" (1988c: 12) and, in Foucault's view, it should be resisted: the problem, he suggests, is to establish conditions in which games of power can be played "with a minimum of domination" (1988c: 18). There are passages in his discussion of government in which he proposes a closely related politics of resistance, this time directed against the state. When he insists, in the closing section of his Tanner Lectures on Human Values, that liberation "can only come from attacking...political rationality's very roots" (1981: 254) his argument is clearly directed against the political rationality that, in his view, underlies the modern government of the state.

There are striking parallels, and equally striking contrasts, between Foucault's normative critiques of domination and government and the arguments of critical theory. (The differences are discussed in Hindess 1996; Ashenden and Owen (eds.) 1999.) Critical theorists take a different view of these matters (see, for example, Fraser 1989; McCarthy 1992). Of more interest to the substantive analysis of politics, however, are his accounts of the emergence of the political rationality of government in the early modern period and the subsequent development of liberalism as a specific form of governmental reason. These accounts have inspired a substantial body of academic work, sometimes called the governmentality school, devoted to the study of government in the modern West (see Burchell et al. 1991; Barry et al. 1996; Dean and Hindess 1998 for useful samples. There are recent surveys of the field in Dean 1999; Rose 1999).

This chapter begins by outlining the Foucaultian treatment of government, and of liberalism as a specific rationality of government, and considers its implications for the study of politics. It then moves on to show how this treatment must be adapted to take account, first, of the significance for government of what Max Weber calls "politically oriented action," and, secondly, of authoritarian aspects of liberal political reason.

GOVERNMENT

In contemporary political analysis the term "government" is commonly used to denote what Aristotle calls "the supreme authority in states" (1988c, III, 1279a 27) a usage which suggests that government should be seen as emanating from a single center of control – albeit one which may sometimes be divided, for example, between executive, legislature and judiciary, or between national and sub-national levels. However, it can also denote a kind of activity, in which case the term is applied more broadly. Thus Aristotle discusses "the government of a wife and children and of a household" (ibid., 1278b 37–8), a form of rule which he distinguishes both from the government of a state and from the rule of a master over his slave. In yet another usage it refers to a rule that one exercises over oneself. Foucault insists that, while they may work on different kinds of materials, and accordingly face somewhat different problems, there is nevertheless a certain continuity between these diverse usages: they share an underlying concern to affect the conduct of the governed. Thus, rather than act directly on the actions of individuals, government aims to do so indirectly by influencing the manner in which individuals regulate their own behavior. Government, in this sense, is clearly a special case of power: while it is a matter of acting on the actions of others (or of oneself), the fact that it does so indirectly, through its influence on conduct, means that government involves an element of calculation that is not necessarily present in every exercise of power. Government differs from domination, another special case of power, in allowing the governed a certain margin of liberty in regulating their own behavior, aiming to work primarily by influencing the manner in which they do so.

However, while he emphasizes the continuity between these various forms of government, Foucault also insists on the distinctive character of the modern art of government – "the particular form of governing which can be applied to the state as a whole" (1991: 91). We can see what is involved here by turning to another aspect of Aristotle's treatment of government: the claim that each form of government has its own proper purpose or *telos*. Thus, the government of a slave is "exercised primarily with a view to the interest of the master" while the government of a household is "exercised in the first instance for the good of the governed" (1988c: 34–7, 39). In the case of the state, Aristotle maintains, the only true forms of government are those "which have a regard to the common interest," the others being "defective or perverted" (ibid., 1279a, 17–21).

The art of government, as Foucault describes it, takes up a version of this classical perspective by claiming that the state should be "governed according to rational principles which are intrinsic to it" (1991: 96–7). Foucault insists that the normative claims of this art of government should be distinguished from two alternative perspectives: justification of rule in terms of a universal order laid down by God (and therefore not intrinsic to the state) and "the problematic of the Prince," which is primarily concerned with "the prince's ability to keep his principality" (1991: 90). His point in making these distinctions is not to endorse the classical view of the purpose or *telos* of government – quite the contrary, as we have seen – but rather to present the modern government of the state as a systematic attempt to realize that purpose.

As he describes it, then, the art of government is not concerned primarily with the business of taking over the state, keeping it in one's possession or subordinating it to some external principle of legitimacy but rather with the work of conducting the affairs of the population in the interests of the whole. Government, in this sense, is not restricted to the work of *the* government and the agencies it controls. Much of it will also be performed by agencies of other kinds, by elements of what is now called civil society: churches, employers, financial institutions, legal and medical professionals, voluntary associations. The work of governing the state as a whole, then, extends far beyond the institutions of the state itself.

Perhaps the most influential aspect of Foucault's work on government has been his treatment of liberalism as a rationality of government. Liberalism is commonly regarded as a normative political theory that regards the maintenance of individual liberty as an end in itself and therefore as setting limits of principle to the objectives and means of action of government. Individual liberty is central to Foucault's account of liberalism too, but it is seen in a very different light. The crucial issue here concerns the governmental significance of the belief that members of the population to be governed are endowed with a capacity for autonomous, self-directing activity: what does that belief entail for the practical work of government? Foucault's account of liberalism focuses on the implication that government should aim to make use of this capacity, that the maintenance and promotion of suitable forms of individual liberty may be advantageous to the state itself.

A particularly significant illustration of this liberal perspective can be found in Adam Smith's *The Wealth of Nations*. Smith describes the aim of political economy as being "to enrich both the people and the sovereign" (1976: 428) and he argues that this aim is best served by promoting the free activities of economic agents. This argument turns on a view of economic activity as a system of interaction in which the conduct of participants is regulated by prices for goods and labor that are themselves established by the free decisions of the participants themselves – in effect, by numerous individual decisions to buy or to sell, or to seek a better deal elsewhere. Since these prices are established within the system itself, this view suggests that external interference in economic inter-action – by the state setting prices or minimum wages, for example – will reduce the efficiency of the system overall. Thus, when he examines the police regula-tion of economic activity or the workings of the mercantile system, Smith's aim is to show that they detract from the wealth of the nation overall.

Liberalism, as Foucault describes it, treats this image of the self-regulating market as a model for other aspects of society. Accordingly, it regards the populations of modern states as encompassing a variety of domains – the sphere of economic activity, the workings of civil society, the processes of population growth and so on – each one regulated, in large part, by the free decisions of individuals in the course of their interactions with others. This perception suggests that, once they have been securely established, these domains of free interaction will function most effectively if external interference is reduced to a minimum. Thus, rather than subject activity within these domains to detailed regulation by the state, liberal government will aim to establish and to maintain conditions under which the domains themselves will operate with beneficial effects for the well-being of the population and of the state itself. This liberal view, in turn, implies that effective government must be based on reliable know-ledge of the processes and conditions that sustain these patterns of free interac-tion. It suggests, in other words, that liberal government will depend on the abstract and theoretical knowledge of social life provided by economics and the other social sciences.

Governmentality scholars have adapted this account of liberalism to the analysis of neo-liberal attempts to govern through the decisions of autonomous individuals. They have focused, in particular, on the governmental uses of individual choice and empowerment and on the more general promotion of market or quasi-market regimes as indirect means of government (for examples, see Cruikshank 1999; Valverde 1998). To say that individual choice, personal empowerment, and markets are widely employed as instruments of government is not to say that the freedom they offer is illusory – although it may sometimes be extremely limited – but it is to insist that individual liberty cannot be seen simply as a limit to the reach of government. In fact, as the market model suggests, the use of individual liberty as a means of governing the population must rely not only on regulation by the state but also on the existence of suitable patterns of individual conduct and on the regulation of that conduct by others. Neo-liberal government, on this view, will be particularly dependent on the expertise of psychiatrists, counsellors, financial advisers and the like, all of whom assist their clients to develop appropriate ways of conducting their own affairs, and, at another level, on the efforts of economists and others to extend the model of market interaction to the analysis of all areas of human activity.

POLITICS AND GOVERNMENT

To see what this account of the government of the state contributes to our understanding of politics we have only to observe that "politics," "political," and other such terms frequently refer precisely to the work of government. Foucault adopts this usage throughout his discussions of government and its rationalities, and it is characteristic also of the governmentality literature. I have already noted, for example, that the critique of *political* reason which Foucault develops in his *Tanner Lectures* (Foucault 1981) is in fact directed against the art of government outlined above: against a political reason that concerns itself with the government of the state and with recruiting other forms of government, especially the government of oneself, to its own purposes. (This last feature of political reason is the central focus of Foucault's normative critique.) He is careful, as we have seen, to distinguish this rationality of the government of a state from understandings of government that are not *political* in this specific sense – from those whose *telos* is derived, for example, from the interests of spiritual or secular powers.

Thus, the Foucaultian analysis of government is itself a contribution to the understanding of an important kind of politics: one that aims to govern the population of a state in the interests of the whole. Similarly, the Foucaultian accounts of liberal and neo-liberal government contribute to the understanding of influential contemporary versions of this politics: versions that aim to govern as far as possible by promoting certain forms of freedom and arranging conditions so that the resulting activity furthers the common good. Perhaps the most significant contribution of this literature has been its careful exploration of the ways in which this governmental politics extends beyond state agencies to make use of practices of individual self-government and of diverse elements of civil society.

Nevertheless, there are many aspects of politics which this powerful analysis of government simply fails to address. One is the politics of resistance that Foucault invokes in his normative critiques of domination and political reason. For our purposes, however, the more important silences of the governmentality literature concern, first, the politically oriented activity that Max Weber describes in the first section of *Economy and Society* and, secondly, authoritarian aspects of liberal government.

GOVERNMENT AND PARTISAN POLITICS

Weber describes action as being politically oriented if:

> it aims at exerting influence on the government of a political organization; especially at the appropriation, redistribution or allocation of the powers of government. (Weber, 1978: 55)

Action may be "politically oriented" without participating in the work of government itself. Where the focus of Foucault's "political reason" is on the overall pursuit of the interests and the welfare of the state and the population ruled by the state, that of Weber's "politically oriented action" is on the partisan activities of parties, pressure groups and social movements and, of course, of individuals or factions within them. Politically oriented action could well be motivated by religious doctrine or the problematic of the Prince, both of which Foucault distinguishes from the *political* concerns of the art of government.

In fact, while politically oriented activity may not be directly governmental, the problem of how to deal with it has always been one of the central concerns of the art of government. Its failure to consider the governmental implications of such activity is one of the more serious limitations of the Foucaultian treatment of government. We can begin our discussion of this point by observing that the scope for a certain kind of partisanship is already inscribed in the classical view of the purpose or *telos* of government – a view which the modern art of government also adopts. Far from preventing partisanship, the identification of this *telos* with the common interest (or some equivalent) serves rather to establish the terms in which partisan dispute will be conducted. Thus, in a pattern that will be familiar to political activists of all persuasions, the common interest and more particular sectional interests are thought to be quite distinct and yet are frequently confused: invocation of the one becomes a standard means of promoting the other and an opponent's appeal to the common interest is readily seen as just another sectional maneuvre.

While the conduct of partisan dispute in such terms will be present under any form of government, we should expect it to flourish where the freedom of members of the subject population is promoted by the predominant rationality of government. David Hume notes, for example, that partisan groups are:

> plants which grow most plentifully in the richest soil; and though absolute governments be not wholly free from them, it must be confessed, that they rise more easily,

and propagate themselves faster in free governments, where they always infect the
legislature itself, which alone could be able, by the steady application of rewards
and punishments, to eradicate them. (Hume, 1987: 55–6)

The most notable feature of this passage is its view of partisan politics as a
damaging infection. This fear of what partisanship might do to government has
been a long-standing feature of governmental reason but, as Hume's comment
indicates, it is has a particular resonance for liberal and neo-liberal rationalities
of government.

This point suggests that the characterization of liberal and related rationalities
of government in terms of their emphasis on governing through the decisions of
autonomous individuals is seriously incomplete: they are also substantially concerned to defend the proper purposes of government from the impact of partisan
politics. It is partly for this reason that secrecy and deliberate misdirection are so
commonly employed by even the most liberal of governments. The neo-liberal
push of recent decades has taken this defense further by corporatizing and
privatizing various kinds of state activity, insulating central banks from political
control, and promoting the use of market or contractual relationships between
and within government agencies and between those agencies and citizens.

At one level the aim of such devices is to minimize inducements for citizens to
engage in politically oriented action by enabling them to pursue their concerns in
other ways, notably through contract and the market: the promotion of certain
kinds of individual autonomy also serves to inhibit political participation. At
another, it is to limit the partisan influence of parties, pressure groups, and
public officials by removing significant areas of public provision from the
realm of political decision, and relying instead on suitably organized forms of
market interaction. This, of course, is less a reduction in the overall scope of
government than a change in the means by which government is exercised: a
form of government that works through the administrative apparatuses of the
state is displaced in favor of one that works on individuals and organizations
through the disciplines imposed by their interactions with others in market and
quasi-market regimes. Since this limited dismantling of the administrative apparatuses of the state is itself conducted by partisan politicians and their chosen
advisers, those who are not persuaded by the neo-liberal case – and many of
those who are – will see in this procedure ample scope for the pursuit of new
forms of partisan advantage.

LIBERAL AUTHORITARIANISM

Authoritarian rule has always played a significant part in the government
of states, even where liberal political reason has been influential. Nineteenth-
century western states restricted the freedom of important sections of their own
populations and some forcibly imposed their rule on substantial populations
outside their own national borders. Even now, coercive and oppressive practices
continue to play an important part in the government of western societies: in the
criminal justice system, the policing of inner-city areas and the urban poor, the

provision of social services and, of course, the management of large public and private organizations. Elsewhere, in much of Latin America, parts of South-East Asia, central and eastern Europe, authoritarian rule has been used as an instrument of economic liberalization (see Zolo, chapter 38, in this volume).

What do these practices have to do with the liberal government of freedom? With few exceptions (notably Valverde 1996) contributors to the governmentality literature have seen the relationship between them as largely external. Thus, while Nikolas Rose (1999) observes that coercive and oppressive practices must now be justified on the liberal grounds of freedom, these practices play little part in his account of liberal government itself. Or again, Mitchell Dean (1999) insists that any attempt to govern through freedom will have to acknowledge that some people may just have to be governed in other ways. These accounts capture important aspects of liberal political reason, but the government of unfreedom is more central to its concerns than either would suggest.

We can see what is at issue here by returning to the significance for government of the belief that members of the population are naturally endowed with a capacity for autonomous, self-directing activity. One obvious implication seems to be that government should make use of this capacity, and the Foucaultian account of liberal and neo-liberal government has therefore focused on its deployment of individual liberty. In fact, the implications are rather more complex: individuals may be naturally endowed with a capacity for autonomous action but this does not mean that the capacity will always be fully realized. Modern political thought has generally taken the contrary view: that there are indeed contexts in which suitable habits of self-government have taken root, but many more in which they have not. Liberals have usually seen the realization of this capacity for autonomous action in historical and developmental terms, suggesting that it will be well established amongst numerous adults only in relatively civilized communities; that extended periods of education and training are required if individuals are to develop the necessary habits of self-regulation; and that, even under favorable conditions, there will be those who cannot be relied on to conduct their affairs in a reasonable manner. They have argued that, where this capacity is not well developed, government simply cannot afford to work through the free decisions of individuals: children must be constrained by parental authority and uncivilized adults subjected to authoritarian rule. John Stuart Mill's comments on the people of India and other colonial dependencies provides a well-known example of this liberal perspective. Since they are not, in his view, "sufficiently advanced... to be fitted for representative government," they must be governed by the dominant country or its agents:

> This mode of government is as legitimate as any other, if it is the one which in the existing state of civilization of the subject people, most facilitates their transition to a higher stage of improvement. (1977: 567)

Liberal political reason has been concerned with the subject peoples of imperial possessions as much as with the free inhabitants of western states, with minors and adults judged to be incompetent as much as with autonomous individuals. Western colonial rule has now been displaced but its developmental perspective remains influential in the programs of economic and political development promoted by independent, post-colonial states and by international agencies.

Authoritarian government in these cases has a paternalistic rationale: its aim is to move towards its own eventual abolition. A rationale of a different kind rests on the point, noted earlier, that liberalism is substantially concerned to defend the work of government from the impact of partisan politics. The corporatization and privatization of state agencies might seem to reduce the threat of certain kinds of partisanship, but there will also be cases in which more direct measures seem to be required. These range from limitations on parliamentary and intra-party debate to the direct suppression of political opposition. In societies where paternalistic attitudes toward the bulk of the population are already well-entrenched, the supposed imperatives of economic reform have often provided governments and their international supporters with powerful liberal grounds for the restriction of political freedom.

MOVING ON

The Foucaultian studies of government, and of liberal and neo-liberal government in particular, have made substantial contributions to our understanding of the significance of freedom, choice, and empowerment in the government of contemporary western populations. There are, nevertheless, important areas of politics, and indeed of government, which these studies have not addressed. This chapter has commented, all too briefly, on two of these – political partisanship and liberal authoritarianism – and suggested that they are central to the analysis of liberalism and of modern government more generally, both in the West and elsewhere. To insist on the importance of these areas, however, is not to raise an objection to the governmentality perspective. The point, rather, is to show that it has considerably more to offer our understanding of contemporary politics than it has yet been able to deliver.

Further Reading

Dean, M. 1999: *Governmentality*. London: Sage.
Dean, M. and Hindess, B. 1998: "Introduction: government, liberalism, society." In M. Dean and B. Hindess (eds.), *Governing Australia: Studies in Contemporary Rationalities of Government*. Cambridge and Melbourne: Cambridge University Press.
Rose, Nikolas 1999: *Powers of Freedom: Reframing Political Thought*. Cambridge: Cambridge University Press.

5

Society, Morality, and Law: Jürgen Habermas

MAX PENSKY

Habermas's recent work has focused on "communicative rationality," a form of power embodying Enlightenment ideals of freedom and equality which has the potential to counterbalance the administrative and strategic power of modern social structures. To this end Habermas's theory emphasizes intersubjective rationality. He sees the instrumental rationality of the isolated subject on which Enlightenment models of individual autonomy were founded as part of the problem of the "colonization of the lifeworld" by the state and economy, rather than as articulating the possibility of democratic resistance to its systemic tendencies. Pensky's chapter outlines the range of theoretical resources Habermas uses to build his sociological theory of communicative action and show how it may be philosophically grounded. Finally, he discusses how Habermas applies his theory of communicative rationality to the question of the legitimacy of modern democratic law in *Between Facts and Norms*.

Jürgen Habermas is arguably the most influential social theorist of the second half of the twentieth century. In a body of work beginning in the late 1950s, Habermas has covered an enormous range of problems and disciplines, and produced a stunning array of interlocked theoretical works: historical analyses, epistemology and philosophical anthropology, social theory, moral philosophy, legal theory, a huge amount of political analysis, even literary criticism. However, this sprawling œuvre – which shows no sign of slowing down – has remained remarkably consistent in the basic normative and theoretical commitments that form the foundation of all else that Habermas writes: the internal connection between rationality and agreement, and the attempt to delineate the normative implications of this connection in a critical theory of democratic society, morality, and law. This half-century-long project has established Habermas's social theory as the most prominent consensualist treatment of power in the twentieth century. Human rationality, Habermas argues, consists in a capacity for intersubjective coordination of action based on universal capacities for communicative competence, an ability to create a shared lifeworld through discursive practices. Hence, rationality is a "communicative power" that embodies the normative ideals of equality and freedom characteristic of the

Enlightenment conceptions of human reason. At the same time, communicative rationality constitutes a stubborn counterbalance to the forms of administrative and strategic power that characterize modern social structures.

Jürgen Habermas was born in Düsseldorf in 1929. After university study in philosophy and related fields, he received a doctorate in 1954 with a dissertation on Schelling. Until the end of the 1950s, Habermas served as Theodor W. Adorno's assistant at the Institute for Social Research in Frankfurt am Main, and in 1962 he published his first major work, *The Structural Transformation of the Public Sphere* (1989).

That early work already set the course for much of Habermas's subsequent theory. In a mixture of historical analysis and theoretical reconstruction, Habermas argued that the liberal public sphere that emerged in the early democratic societies of eighteenth-century Europe embodied a fundamental normative ideal of reason as critical discourse and intersubjective agreement. The public sphere constituted a set of institutionally unbounded discourses, distinct both from the state and civil society, understood narrowly as competing individual economic interests in which citizens could direct the actions of state and market through a process of collective will-formation guided through open, critical public discussion of matters of collective concern (see Ray, chapter 20, in this volume). Thus Habermas first posited the notion that political and legal legitimacy consisted in formal processes of mutual understanding, in which individuals enter into discursive practices not just with the goal of strategic success and utility maximization, but primarily with the goal of reaching an unforced agreement through settled procedures of argument. The anti-Weberian claim that such processes of reaching understanding and collective will-formation constituted a vital if fragile third mode of social coordination in addition to (and increasingly in conflict with) the forces of the modern administrative state and economy, would remain a central contention for Habermas's political sociology.

Habermas traces the historical genesis of the public sphere from the literary salons, voluntary societies, and other groups occupying the narrow space between state and emerging economy in the eighteenth century, showing how the gradual emergence of a self-consciously political conception of the public sphere was vital for the ideal of democratic self-governance and popular sovereignty, while simultaneously generating an inevitable tension between the universalistic conception of right and rationality on which it based itself, and the exclusionary practices in which those rights were extended only to a delimited segment of the population. In the second half of the work, Habermas traces the collapse of the Enlightenment public sphere in the late nineteenth and twentieth centuries. As state and society expand and differentiate, they gradually extend their own functional imperatives into the public sphere. The rise of large-scale social welfare states in the twentieth century marks the end of the liberal public sphere, as capitalist modernity systematically closes down the narrow space for free and open collective deliberation and control of complex sociopolitical processes. *The Structural Transformation of the Public Sphere* ended on a sombre note, offering little in the way of a positive recommendation for countering the decline of the public sphere in the contemporary world. But the book lays down a program for a critical, politically oriented sociology to which Habermas has remained remarkably true over the past four decades. Political modernity is characterized above all by a tension between two different forms of modernization: one rationalization in the form of increasing technical control, Weberian *Zweckrationalität;* the other a development of communicative reason that embeds itself institutionally in modes of democratic procedure and subjectively in a post-traditional, universalistic value orientations. While nothing internal to these two rationality problematics marks them as destined to enter into contradiction with each other, the specific history of modernization that has been the central object of study of modern sociology is in large measure the story of the gradual – and gradually worsening – tension between them. The democratic, radically egalitarian potential inherent in processes of social communication is gradually thwarted by non-communicative, ultimately strategic modes of bureaucratic and administrative control that characterize the modern social state. Virtually all of Habermas's chief works since *Structural Transformation of the Public Sphere* are attempts to render this global diagnosis into more precise and coherent theoretical language.

In his *magnum opus*, the massive, two-volume *Theory of Communicative Action* (1984, 1987), Habermas addresses the need for a theory of rationality to ground the basic distinction between communication and strategic control, a relation whose imbalance Habermas would continue to insist was at source of the social pathologies of modernity. Habermas was thus faced with the task of a theory of communicative reason.

The first premise in this massive undertaking is the inadequacy of the philosophical model of the isolated, autonomous subject, and the demand instead that any successful theory of rationality be based upon an intersubjective model of rationality and agency. And the second is the demand that an intersubjective model of reason and agency in turn be based upon a philosophy of language – understood in the performative sense as speech – rather than a philosophy of consciousness. Habermas draws on his extensive work in the areas of speech-act theory and the philosophy of argumentation from the 1970s. Focusing on the basic features of any successful intersubjective communication, Habermas develops a "universal pragmatics" that specifies the condition for the communicative competence of persons. In addition to the material content of linguistic communication (the locution), successful communication requires that speaker and hearer are able to coordinate and adjust their mutual expectations according to the illocutionary force associated with a locution. Such force is the normally implicit aspect of a speech act, in which a speaker associates a given speech act with a form of validity claim. An illocutionary force attaches to any utterance, implying that the speaker "promises" to a hearer that the utterance is valid – that is, that it makes a (usually implicit) validity claim. And validity claims, in turn, serve as promissory notes that the speaker can resolve any challenge to her utterance's validity by providing reasons.

An utterance can raise a validity claim, however, in four distinct ways. Speech-act theory distinguishes, first, the logical coherence or the formal-syntactical correctness of an utterance; second, the truth of an utterance or its claim to refer to a state of affairs in an objective world open to intersubjective disagreement; third, the rightness of an utterance or its conformity to intersubjectively grounded norms; and fourth, the truthfulness or authenticity of an utterance, or its claim to represent the authentic internal state or disposition of the speaker. Thus, the modes of illocutionary force (Habermas focuses on the last three; truth, rightness, and truthfulness) correspond to three different forms of validity claim, demarcating three different modes of justification. And these modes of justification, finally, imply three distinct kinds of argumentative demand, related to three pragmatically constituted "worlds": an objective world about which we may expect (and challenge) claims to factual truth, an intersubjective world in which we raise claims to normative rightness, and a subjective world in which we may raise claims concerning the truthfulness or authenticity of a subject's linguistic presentation of an internal state.

Habermas thus argues for an internal connection between meaning and validity: the ability to understand the meaning of an utterance is the ability to take a yes or a no position in a (real or potential) argument in which a speaker gives reasons for the validity of the utterance, in which validity can be asserted in the form of truth, rightness, or truthfulness.

Habermas's adoption of speech-act theory thus leads to a theory of communicative reason, which attempts to reconstruct the basic intuition that rationality as such is above all characterized by the capacity for the giving and taking of reasons as a mode of coordinating actions. Rather than attaching primarily to a subject, communicative rationality now is an attribute chiefly of forms of communicative interaction. And such a mode of rationality is to be seen in sharp contrast to strategic or means-ends rationality. The theory of universal pragmatics that grounds the universal character of communicative reason also endows it with a strongly idealizing element, one that, in turn, is meant to capture the essentially normative intuitions caught up with the notions of practical reason characteristic of modern deontological moral theories. Unlike teleological action, communicative action is guided by processes of communication in such a way that success can be registered only via the ideal of a rational consensus among agents as a result of a discursive process. Hence, the reconstructable idealizations that constitute such a situation – the universal pragmatic conditions for the possibility of a violence-free consensus, in which each discourse participant is capable of speaking and hearing, taking unforced and unmanipulated positions of yes or no on contested claims, and so on – serve as claims about the universality of reason. The pragmatically unavoidable elements of any successful process of argumentation over problematized claims to factual or normative validity turn out *also* to be accurate reconstructions of the basic moral thrust of the tradition of the European Enlightenment, in which intact procedures of collective will-formation define both the essentially normative character of the well-run democratic polity and the inherently social dynamic in even the most individualistic notions of the autonomous rational agent.

Much of the *Theory of Communicative Action* is taken up, perhaps not surprisingly, with the attempt to show the relevance of this highly idealizing notion of communicative reason for a modernity characterized above all by secularization and the pluralism of contemporary worldviews. In the transition from a theory of rationality to a reconstruction of the problem of reason for the basic tasks of sociology, Habermas will claim that his theory of communicative reason can settle the otherwise intractable problems of a theory of modernity, the rationality problem, and problems of sociological methodology better than the other competing models for the theorization of human action: teleological, normatively regulated, or dramaturgic action.

In the first volume of the *Theory of Communicative Action*, Habermas's chief interlocutor is Weber. Habermas accepts much of Weber's basic orientation: social and cultural modernity in the West is characterized above all by the emergence of new modes of reason, and the dynamic of rationalization is fundamentally the work of differentiating spheres of validity. As all traditional social and cultural forms of meaning are progressively devalued, occidental rationality generates increasingly distinct and self-maintaining spheres – modern lifeworlds are obliged to disintegrate into differentiated models of culture, society and economy, and personality.

The distinction between strategic and communicative reason permits Habermas to formulate a simple, powerful objection to Weber's theory of modernization as rationalization: Weber had correctly understood that western modernity was best analyzed as a process of rationalization in which traditional lifeworlds were institutionally differentiated into autonomous value-spheres, whose criteria of legitimacy and efficacy were internal to the spheres themselves. Understood as the institutionalization of rational conduct, the spheres of science and technology, law and morality, and aesthetics were united, if at all, only in their commitment to rationality understood uniquely and explicitly as *Zweckrationalität*, as a means-ends rationality that allowed for little or no rational reflection on the worthiness or value of ends themselves. No higher-order perspective, whether religious or metaphysical, was available to encompass the overall relations of these spheres to one another; no holistic account of reason could provide a critical position from which to lodge a protest against the loss of freedom and loss of meaning arising from the rationalization of life. Weber's famous "iron cage" of rationality, however, appears as a seriously one-sided mistake of emphasis on Habermasian terms. Unable to identify the fundamental differences between strategic and communicative rationality, Weber was unable to grasp the pathological aspects of the *strategic* rationalization of culture, society, and personality *as opposed to* their communicative rationalization – in other words, Weber mistook as inevitable and without alternative a rationalization process that consisted, in reality, in a historical struggle over whether the communicative-rational potential of emerging modern institutions would be realized or thwarted by strategic considerations.

The second volume of the *Theory of Communicative Action* is given over to a reconceptualization of the relation between systems theory and microsociology. In Durkheim and Mead, Habermas borrows, *mutatis mutandis*, some of the basic tools for a general reintegration of social-action theory and Parsonian functionalism. Drawing on the notions of individual ontogenesis and social integration that he had developed over the course of the 1970s, Habermas reads Mead's symbolic interactionism as a basic blueprint for a communicative theory of individuation through socialization. The internal link between individual states, attitudes, preferences, and personality structures with social structures via the institutionalized processes of intersubjective communication provides a basis for the public nature, and rational criticizability, of even the most internal aspects of personality – social integration thus emerges as a mediating link between the symbolic transmission of lifeworlds and the ongoing functioning of social institutions. The utopian perspective of a context of communication free from domination once again connects with the Enlightenment ideal of the rational autonomy of persons considered as responsible moral agents, whose actions and intentions are the proper objects of rational criticism and justification by self and others. Mead's vision of "universal discourse" thus emerges in its full Kantian implications, without Kant's monological reduction. And systems theory is meant to provide a plausible account for the various external factors missing in Mead's account of individual ontogenesis.

This underlying normative–political vision is important as a background for Habermas's integration of systems theory and action theory (cf. Lange and Schimank, chapter 6, in this volume), since it amounts to an integration of a theory of modernity (phylogenesis) and of personality (ontogenesis) via a theory of communication. This entails a reconstruction of the process of phylogenesis in which social institutions and practices are gradually transformed, generating social solidarity less and less via their sacral or ritualistic function (the reference to Durkheim here is explicit) and increasingly according to differentiated and autonomous processes of communication (here the reference to the transformed Weberian theory of modernity from the first volume comes into its own). The disenchantment of social systems, their dwindling ability to generate social solidarity and solve factual or normative disputes via a pre-established consensus of traditional interpretations, means that social functions gradually come to depend ever more on the communicative competencies of subjects who nevertheless undergo a process of ontogenesis only through those very same functions. Hence the Weberian process of social modernization as the internal differentiation of value-spheres at the institutional level, Durkheim's investigation of the tasks of manufacturing social solidarity in the consequence of the secularization of worldviews, and Mead's theory of ontogenesis as a process of symbolic interaction with a generalized other all merge into a theory of the rationalization (or linguistification) of modern lifeworlds.

Habermas's reformulation of the notion of the lifeworld as it developed from competing traditions in comparative sociology is one of the most significant, and difficult, aspects of his analysis. For Habermas, the phenomenological approaches of Husserl and Schutz were overly concerned with the problem of symbolic reproduction and the transmission of traditional stores of symbolic meaning, and too little concerned with the dynamic of personalization and socialization; Mead, by contrast, overemphasized just these factors and thus missed the role that the lifeworld plays in placing limits to processes of ontogenesis, rather than merely providing neutral reservoirs of meaning for such processes.

In a highly characteristic move, Habermas constructs a discourse between the varying candidates for a theory of the lifeworld, producing a multilevel model far more complex and nuanced than any previous approach. To summarize crudely, Habermas argues for a model of the lifeworld as *both* an unproblematic horizon or background against which any form of social action must bear meaning, *and* the reservoir of symbolically structured meanings, situation inter-pretations and explanations that provide both the sources of possible disagree-ment and problems that social actors must face, as well as the store of material for any possible solution. For Habermas, the lifeworld thus cannot be restricted to cultural interpretations, but must include, in symbolically accessible form, the level of social institutions and personality structures as well. Hence the lifeworld is in a dynamic process of self-unfolding in which all three aspects – culture, society, and personality – are in constant, mutual dialogue. Likewise, the three tasks of cultural reproduction, the manufacture of social solidarity, and social integration cannot be separated but rather must be regarded as mutually inter-twined processes of the interface between a communicative lifeworld and com-municatively competent social actors. These competencies, finally, are rooted in processes of arriving at consensus on validity claims that have become problem-atic, and that social actors must solve in order to maintain a social order. Hence the basic structure of communicative competence, in which agents can recognize the kinds of reasons and hence the forms of discourse that would satisfy a range of differing illocutionary forces, maps onto the differentiated modes in which social actors can reflectively experience their own lifeworld. Cultural reproduc-tion, socialization, and social integration are in the end isomorphic with the internal structures of illocutionary claims, discussed above, that form an objec-tive, intersubjective, and subjective world. The institutionalized differentiation of (scientific) facts, (legal–moral) values, and (aesthetic– expressive) internal states, the hallmark of western modernity, rests upon the differentiation of objective, intersubjective, and subjective worlds latently contained as universal structure of communicative competence itself.

The basic task of the second volume, the distinction between lifeworld and system, grows out of the most pressing problem of the discourse-theoretic recon-struction of the lifeworld. Under the presuppositions of a theory of modernization as rationalization, if the lifeworld is regarded as a source of problems which are to be solved by the communicative accomplishments of social actors themselves, then how does sociology explain the pathologies of modernity? As we have seen, Habermas wishes to use the theory of communicative rationality to argue that Weber's thesis on its own cannot adequately capture the underlying dynamic of social pathologies: the destructive relation between communicative rationality and instrumental rationality, arising from the manner in which system and life-world differentiate over the course of modernity itself. Making this claim plau-sible, however, entails some serious revisions in basic sociological approaches.

Habermas draws attention to the familiar problem of the inadequacy of both interpretive and functionalist approaches in sociology to provide a plausibly complete explanation of the phenomenon of social reproduction as a whole. In addition to the more familiar problems concerning causation in the explanation of social action, interpretive sociology proves incapable of theorizing the sys-temic role of social institutions, the constraining function of tasks of material reproduction, or the systemic character of social pathologies. Systems theory, by contrast, apart from the familiar criticisms of methodological individualism and the explanation of social facts as an object domain, seems unable to relate the function of social institutions to the everyday lifeworld perspectives of real social actors. Hence, Habermas proposes a reintegration of system and lifeworld perspectives by reconceiving the lifeworld itself as a "boundary-maintaining system": taken with a certain degree of methodological objectification, the interpretive accomplishments of social actors who respond to ongoing problematizations of their own lifeworld through secured processes of collective communication in effect participate in a system whose aggregate function is the task of symbolic reproduction of the lifeworld itself. It is only once we understand how the lifeworld takes on the function of systemic maintenance that we see how material reproduction (at the level of system) and symbolic reproduction (at the level of lifeworld) are tied together. Social system is, in other words, merely a self-reproducing lifeworld conceptualized under different terms. This compatibilist move helps Habermas interpret how social systems emerge from out of modern lifeworlds, differentiating themselves off from them while nevertheless remaining rooted in them both on the level of institutions and in terms of the work of social integration.

That change in terms, however, proceeds not just according to methodological choices of the social theorist but as a response to actual historical processes. Modern societies are ones in which a linguistified lifeworld increasingly places the systemic tasks of cultural reproduction, socialization, and social integration onto the shoulders of social agents, resulting in a peculiar integration of lifeworld and system on the cultural, social, and individual level. But one characteristic dynamic of modernization is the problem of increasing social complexity that generates a process of "decoupling" of system and lifeworld, as social institutions steadily unburden actors from the tasks of system maintenance through their own interpretive achievements. Once decoupled, however, social systems increasingly differentiate themselves off from the lifeworld through an internal rationalization process, as modes of functional integration steadily distance themselves from the modes of social integration rooted in the lifeworld – much as Weber described. But modern social subsystems – economy and political administration chief among them – respond to the pressures of system maintenance under the conditions of growing complexity essentially by the *elimination* of communicative rationality in favor of strategic modes. Economic and administrative subsystems, in other words, develop inherently non-communicative steering media for their own internal function, even as they remain tied institutionally to the lifeworld.

The result of this paradoxical decoupling, in which essentially non-linguistic steering media articulate themselves in social subsystems that nevertheless maintain their institutional rootedness in lifeworld structures, is Habermas's own version of what, in classical critical social theory, would have been described as the anonymous aspect of social domination. The communicative structures of a rationalized lifeworld are gradually infiltrated by strategic systemic imperatives: the anonymous steering mechanism of market forces via division of labor (money) and bureaucratic administration via hierarchically structured relationships (power) thus gain an ever-greater share in the ongoing work of the symbolic reproduction of the lifeworld, even as they disburden lifeworld participants from the need to reach substantive consensus over increasingly complex social functions. The result is that these subsystems "colonize" communicative structures, replacing the discursive aspect of a successful lifeworld – ongoing cultural reproduction, social integration, and socialization steered via the ideal of unforced consensus – with the "delinguistificd" imperatives of instrumental action. The thesis of the "inner colonization of the lifeworld" is thus meant to explain how the Weberian thesis of the anomic and pathological dimension of modernization can be better explained by a system–lifeworld model articulated via a distinction between communicative and instrumental rationality. The "juridification" of everyday life and the transformation of citizens into subjects of economic and administrative processes beyond their power, the slow creep of instrumental reason into the tiniest capillaries of lifeworld structures, the loss of collective control over the choice of reasonable social goals – these ills of modernity can now be diagnosed as a colonization of the communicative "power" of an intact modern lifeworld by systemic imperatives that have become destructive of it. The *Theory of Communicative Action* thus retains the essential claim of a critical social theory: the historically contingent factors that have produced an *imbalanced* pattern of rationalization in western societies can be effectively countered by mobilizing the power of intact communicative processes themselves.

Following the *Theory of Communicative Action*, Habermas produced a series of influential articles in the 1980s and 1990s that developed a "discourse ethics," an attempt to transfer the basic elements of Kantian moral deontology into the intersubjective, discourse-based model developed in his earlier work. The 1990s also saw the publication of Habermas's theory of morality and law. *Between Facts and Norms* (1996) undertakes the reconstruction of the internal relation between modern positive law, modern deontological moral theory, and the discursive basis of constitutional democracy.

The problem of modern law emerges sharply from Habermas's revision of Weber's thesis of modernization: in the context of rationalized lifeworlds, fragmented worldviews and the gradual encroachment of systemic imperatives onto the communicative lifeworld, modern law constitutes a set of coercive codes, above all legal rights, that together demarcate a sphere in which the strategic actions of isolated individuals can harmonize with each other, without requiring such individuals to come to a substantial consensus over their actions; at the same time, as *rights*, they make a rational claim concerning the sphere of freedoms that persons ought not to be deprived of. Modern constitutional law thus constitutes coercible limits *for others* concerning one's own self-interested actions; as such they demonstrate the familiar paradox of modern positive law, its simultaneous assertion of factual coercion over those ruled by it, and its validity, or its claim to legitimacy, to *deserve* its coercive power, on the basis of the reasonable consent by those ruled. Between the "is" of legal positivity and the "ought" of claims to rights grounded in normative insights, modern law coerces subjects whom it simultaneously defines as the subjects of self-legislation, moral-legal persons who recognize the validity of the same law that coerces them, based upon the rightness of the procedures according to which law is produced. Hence this internal contradiction traces back to the basic paradox of "right": how free subjects exercise their rational autonomy in order to bring themselves under legal restraint.

The paradoxes implicit in this demand come out most clearly in recent controversies between "liberalism" and "communitarianism": Modern natural-law theories, including Kant and Rawls, have tended to insist on the derivative character of positive law to universal morality, discounting the coercive facticity of law in favor of the law's dependence on the abstract character of individual, subjective moral rights, whose recognition and free exercise the law is intended to protect. Communitarian approaches, by contrast, emphasize the internal entwinement of law and morality on the level of particular communities and the forms of life that their legality expresses, hence on the *particular* popular sovereignties embodied in legal orders. Both liberalism and communitarianism, in other words, "solve" the tension between coercive positive law and morality by consigning the former, in one way or another, to the latter. One of the basic tasks of *Between Facts and Norms* is to argue that an intersubjective, discourse-based approach will show that positive law can neither be reduced to a dimension of morality, whether universal or particular, nor can it be *merely* positive as an arbitrary source of coercion and restraint. Rather, a philosophy of law must analyze the *common* source of moral and legal intuitions in the basic structures of discursive procedures, while simultaneously emphasizing the *differentiation* and *interrelation* of law and morality for modern democratic legal orders. In the end, this more differentiated model intends to show that the basic cognitive insights underlying the principle of popular sovereignty in democratic societies – collective self-legislation according to a principle of discourse – reveals the rational kernel of both democracy and the rule of law.

How is law legitimate? This question, at the heart of *Between Facts and Norms*, leads to the claim that there is an internal, conceptually necessary relation between the rule of law as embodied in modern constitutional legal orders and the deliberative processes of public will-formation and public processes of coming to understanding that characterize democracy in its truest sense; that is, as a process of self-governance and self-legislation, as opposed to an administrative system based on political representation via voting functions. Legal rights, providing a set of protections for individuals, guarantees their private autonomy as utility-maximizers at the same time as, ideally, it secures the public autonomy of a democratic collective that imposes laws upon itself only through reasonable processes of collective will-formation and deliberation. Hence the internal relation between the rule of law and democratic processes traces back to the more fundamental internal relation between public and private autonomy, a fact that liberalism, with its stress on private autonomy, and communitarianism, with its stress on the forms of public autonomy tied to particular popular sovereignty, have each neglected. As they ground the possibility of a democratic political order, discursive procedures grant positive law its validity only insofar as they enable (and oblige) subjects to see themselves as the addressees and the authors of law *at the same time*.

In his attempt to move beyond the liberal–communitarian divide, Habermas argues that the "discourse principle" – "Only those norms are valid to which all affected persons could agree as participants in rational discourses" – provides not just the basic intuition underlying modern moral theory, but indeed of the rational basis for the legitimate adjudication of *any* socially valid norm, whether moral or otherwise. Hence modern positive law and modern morality both trace back to the discourse principle, which ties them together as two coeval moments of the broader development of the rational basis of modern constitutional democracies. The demand that law's legitimacy rests on the basic discursive conditions for normativity as such, while law simultaneously satisfies the factual need for concrete rights for individuals' pursuit of their own private autonomy, shows the link between modern legal orders and modern universalistic morality. While linked internally, however, modern law and morality nevertheless remain distinct – law can no longer be understood as an expression or reflection of moral insights, even if it shares with them the basic structure of discursive redemption of social norms. The result of this claim is a vision of positive law as a system of basic rights, the realization of which will differ substantially from one society to the other, but which would remain formally consistent in the integrity of the discursive procedures – and the normative foundation – that ties it internally with deliberative democracy. Habermas's system of basic rights – the classic negative liberties, rights to political membership and due process, political participation, and social rights – reconstruct, *mutatis mutandis*, the standard schedule of basic, political, and social rights. But rather than seeing these rights as the standard expressions of moral claims, or seeing them just as the purely contingent outcomes of historical struggles, Habermas's approach now understands the schedule of basic legal rights in a complex relation to moral insights, mediated through the same set of discursive practices on which modern democracies as such are based.

Of course, the author of *The Theory of Communicative Action*, with its exploration of the bases of modern social pathologies, has no idealizing illusions concerning the state of modern law: what Habermas described in Weberian terms as the "juridification" of the lifeworld in his earlier work is still very much in force in *Between Facts and Norms*. And indeed, much of the book is dedicated to an exploration of the *external* tensions between the claims of public and private autonomy implicit in law and democracy, and forms of social power that counteract those claims. But in its insistence on a discursive foundation for both the relatedness and the distinction between law and morality, Habermas's philosophy of law also calls for a fundamental legal paradigm shift parallel to the one he has called for in the domains of social and moral theory: the ultimate subject of law is the intersubjective process of coming-to-understanding itself, a process from which our modern conceptions of legal persons, moral agents, and democratic modes of life ultimately stem.

Further Reading

Habermas's chief theoretical works are the two-volume *Theory of Communicative Action* (1984: 1987), and *Between Facts and Norms* (1996). A lucid overview of his work can be found in William Outhwaite, *Habermas: A Critical Introduction* (Cambridge: Polity Press, 1994).

6

A Political Sociology for Complex Societies: Niklas Luhmann

Stefan Lange and Uwe Schimank

Luhmann's systems theory is universal, intended to cover all social phenomena. He sees social systems as essential to reduce the unbearable complexity of the world. Modern society is made up of a number of self-referential subsystems organized around binary codes that structure their communications and may make them antagonistic or indifferent to other subsystems. Unlike Parsons, whose work influenced Luhmann, he does not see society as a harmonious, functioning whole, but rather as fragmented and riven with contradictions. Power for Luhmann is the medium of communication of the political subsystem. Lange and Schimank outline here Luhmann's account of the crisis of the welfare state and his recommendations for a reduced role for politics. Luhmann argues that the political subsystem is only one among others, it can not command them, and there is no common language within which it makes sense for them to allow "power" to take precedence over other codes. The authors argue that ultimately Luhmann's systems theory has much in common with liberal ideas of societal self-regulation. According to Luhmann, the interventionist welfare state stretches the political subsystem beyond its functional capacities; it should restrict itself to regulation.

At least with respect to the catchword "complexity," every student of political sociology sooner or later comes into contact with the ambitious and sophisticated work of German sociologist Niklas Luhmann (b. December 8, 1927; d. November 6, 1998). Apart from his colleague and in many respects rival Jürgen Habermas, Luhmann is surely the most internationally famous German theorist of society since Max Weber. Many of Luhmann's works were recently translated into English (see Further Reading, p. 70). In the next few years even more translations of his most important books will follow, making the Anglo-Saxon public more familiar with the many facets of his extensive lifework.

Luhmann's ambitious theoretical program covers all aspects of social life. It is truly what he himself calls a "super-theory" of the social in general (Luhmann 1984: 19). This theory of social systems covers the whole range of social phenomena, from interactions lasting only a few seconds up to societies surviving for centuries. Its origins can be traced back to the years 1960–1, when Luhmann, after having studied law and working as a higher public servant for several years, quit this career to study sociology under Talcott Parsons in Harvard. Here Luhmann made himself familiar with the state of the art sociological systems theory as well as with Parsons's theory of the functional differentiation of modern society. Since the mid-1960s, Luhmann started to work out a sociological systems theory of his own, including a highly original theory of societal differentiation. The implications of this theory of modern society for political sociology shall be spelled out in this chapter.

TWO APPROACHES TO SOCIAL SYSTEMS

Before we turn to our main topic, we have to sketch very briefly the two analytical approaches to social systems which Luhmann adopted in the two distinct phases of his work. In contrast to Parsons, from the beginning Luhmann treated social systems not just as analytical categories but as empirical facts. One of his major works opens with the bald assertion: "social systems exist" (Luhmann 1984: 30). But in agreement with Parsons, in the first phase of his work which lasted until the mid-1970s, Luhmann conceived of social systems as *open* systems existing in a complex environment. Two general functions of such systems are highlighted. One function of all social systems, also emphasized by Parsons and by political scientist David Easton, is the transformation of inputs from their environment into outputs. For example, the political system receives demands and support from other societal areas, and produces out of these "raw materials" collectively binding decisions.

But there is another even more basic function of social systems which Luhmann, in line with German philosophical anthropology (Arnold Gehlen, Helmut Plessner) emphasized. It is basically the same idea which Peter L. Berger and Thomas Luckmann took up in their theory of institutions (Berger and Luckmann 1966). Namely, without institutions, we would live in an unendurable anomie because, in contrast to animals, we have no instincts with which to categorize and "explain" the world to ourselves. For Luhmann (1967), social systems reduce the vast, meaningless complexity of the world in line with our very limited capacity to handle complexity. Within a particular social system, an actor can be quite sure that only very few of all of the things which might happen within the social world in general will actually occur. In order to *reduce complexity*, each system erects and maintains boundaries of meaning. For instance, a conversation as an interaction system has a certain topic to which all actors involved adhere so that everybody can concentrate on it and forget about all other subjects. Thus, society at large consists of numerous social systems on different levels (interactions, organizations, societal subsystems) so that actors know all the time in which particular system or systems they are situated. This in turn provides them with situational meaning. In particular they know what they are up to at any given moment. As consumers in the economic system, their goals are quite different from those they have when they are voters in the political system.

Since the mid-1970s Luhmann began to develop a new meta-theoretical approach that led to a radical "paradigm change in social theory" (Luhmann 1984: 15–23). He adopted from the new biology of cognition developed by Humberto Maturana and Francisco Varela the concept of self-referentially *closed* or autopoietic social systems. *Autopoiesis* literally means self-production. An autopoietic system produces its elements from its elements and, in this way, maintains its structural identity over time even though all of its elements change. The basic element of social systems is communication. Individual social systems reproduce themselves by producing their specific kinds of communication from earlier communications of exactly the same kind. For instance, in the social system of science assertions of truth are the specific kind of communication. These assertions, usually made in scientific publications, lead to other such assertions, and – within science – not to political declarations or declarations of love. Any scientific publication, if it provokes any reactions at all, is either affirmed and finally taken for granted or rejected by later publications. It does not matter with respect to the reproduction of science as a social system which of these two reactions occur. In either case science continues. Either new research questions are taken up on the basis of the taken-for-granted truth of the respective publication, or its research question is taken up again and critically reexamined. Both reactions result in new publications. Thus, science reproduces itself as a societal subsystem by an unending sequence of publications.

Social systems operating in this way are self-referentially closed because they basically consist of chains of communications which refer to other communications of the same kind. In this way, "provinces of meaning" – to borrow a term from Alfred Schutz – are constituted which have no "window" to the social world outside. It is obvious that this fundamental feature of social systems explains even better how they reduce the complexity of the world. However, this closure of social systems with respect to relevant frames of meaning goes along with an openness to their environment with respect to resources and functional performance. The science system, for instance, needs financial resources, among other things, and gets them from the state, or from industry, or from the military. In the other direction, science provides these and other societal subsystems with knowledge they can use for their purposes. Thus, the economy relies heavily on science for production technologies, the military for technologies of destruction, or politics for expertise and advice. Thus, the initial input–output perspective is included within the autopoiesis perspective on social systems. But the primary emphasis on closure which Luhmann insists on during the second phase of his work emphasizes a social system's fundamental *autonomy*. Neither resource dependency upon its environment nor considerations of performance for the environment intervene directly in the communicative self-production of the respective social system. Which assertions of truth are regarded as valid, and which are falsified is determined solely according to criteria of science itself.

THE FUNCTIONAL DIFFERENTIATION OF MODERN SOCIETY

Applying these general ideas about social systems to modern society, Luhmann states that modern society consists of a limited number of societal subsystems – about a dozen in all – each of which guides its communications by means of a specific binary code (Luhmann 1986). The *subsystems* are: the economy, the political system, law, religion, science, the arts, mass-media, education, health care, sports, and family and intimacy. *Binary codes* are "world-constructions with a claim to universality" (Luhmann 1986: 78). This means: every social event can potentially be understood in terms of a certain binary code. The science system's binary code is "true"/ "untrue," the legal system's "legal"/"illegal." Thus, if someone has a car accident and explains it by a sudden failure of the brakes, a scientist may investigate whether this was really the case and, if so, causally responsible for the accident whereas a judge may clarify whether the car's brakes were maintained according to legal provisions, and who was legally responsible for doing so. Each subsystem's binary code shines a highly selective searchlight onto the social world, illuminating certain corners of it and leaving the rest in darkness.

Switching on all of these searchlights, society as a whole becomes illuminated. This was the initial promise of those theorists who, like Emile Durkheim or Talcott Parsons, understood *functional differentiation* as a division of labor advantageous to all subsystems as well as to society at large. Like Weber before him, Luhmann does not share such an inherently harmonious view. The former portrayed modern society as a "polytheism" of "value-spheres." This brings about either antagonistic conflicts, or a thoughtless indifference between religion and science, science and politics, politics and arts, arts and economics, etc. (Weber 1919: 27–8). Similarly, for Luhmann each societal subsystem tends to overemphasize its own code-determined perspective on social events. For science, only itself is important, and the same holds true for all other subsystems. Accordingly, each subsystem combines a highly selective perception of societal affairs with a universal interference into them and a rather self-assured attitude. The overall result is an effective multiplication of society accompanied by many strong contradictions (Luhmann 1990: 420–1). Borrowing a term from philosopher Gotthard Günther, Luhmann calls this the *"poly-contextruality"* of modern society. No archimedean point exists from which we could have the one and only correct judgment of things happening in society. Since all societal subsystems make essential contributions to the reproduction of society at large, and none of them can substitute any other, each of them is a functional prerequisite for society. Modern society would break down without the economy, but also without mass-media or without a health-care system; and the latter could not be replaced by politics or education. In this sense, "'modern society' . . . is a society without a top and without a center" (Luhmann 1981: 22).

By now it should be evident that Luhmann challenges the three most familiar ways in which modern society interprets itself, each with a long philosophical and ideological heritage. First, modern society, in his view, is not capitalist society because the economy is not its center. It is just one subsystem among others. Secondly, in Luhmann's view, modern society is not culturally shaped by a "civil religion" consisting of moral values which overrule all subsystemic codes (Cohen and Arato 1994: 299–341). Here, Luhmann departs especially from Parsonian sociological thought. And thirdly, modern society is not ruled by the political system. Politicians do not stand on top of society governing its affairs and development. This last point will be our special concern in the rest of this chapter.

THE POLITICAL SUBSYSTEM OF MODERN SOCIETY

In a "poly-contextual" society the political system can neither represent society as a moral community, as prescribed by ancient Greek political thought, nor can politics be an organized body with unlimited sovereignty and the power to force society by command – as the early modern political thinker Thomas Hobbes put it. Under modern conditions the political system is just one of society's functional subsystems, no more important or influential than the others. Following Parsons and other theorists of modern politics, Luhmann (1968, 1981) defines the special function of the political system for society as the *production of collectively binding decisions*, anytime and anywhere such decisions are needed by other societal subsystems. To fulfil its function the political system uses *power* as its generalized medium of communication. The binary code of having or not having power ("powerful"/"powerless") guides all political operations. Gaining power, increasing one's power, or at least preventing its decrease is what politics is about.

This struggle for power takes place in a highly differentiated internal structure of modern politics. Luhmann points out that the political system is differentiated into three further subsystems – public administration, party politics, and the public – whose interplay generates a *cycle of power*.

Binding decisions are definitely produced by the *public administration* which works strictly according to formal and substantial rules, treating everybody

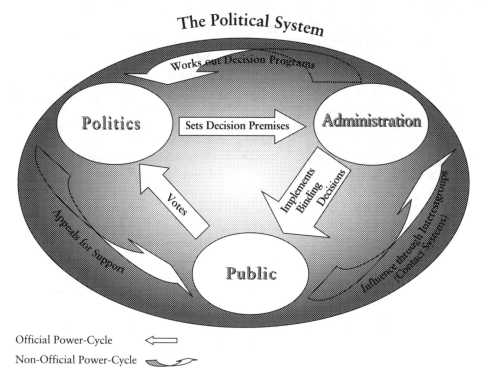

Figure 6.1   The political system

impartially and *sine ira et studio*. This gives specific administrative decisions their procedural legitimacy. However, the administration cannot itself generate the general legitimacy – or "diffuse support" – for politics. This is the contribution of *party politics*. In democracies, political parties and individual politicians as their representatives struggle with each other in elections which are a competition for limited positions in parliament and government. Those in government are powerful in the sense of being able to shape political programs into decision premises for public administration. Those in opposition are powerless but attempt to become powerful by winning the next election. Parties distinguish themselves especially by framing their substantial programs either as progressive or conservative – in traditional terms, left or right (Luhmann 1974). Thus, any societal event or problem can become a topic of political communication in one of these two versions, or even in mixtures of progressive and conservative elements. The alternatives which the parties present give the *public* as the electorate a choice. In elections the public is not able to express its manifold demands in a differentiated way; it is merely able to vote for programs and persons which are selected and presented by the political parties. Representative democracy as the specific form of modern political systems does not allow the public to shape its concrete demands and interests directly into substantial collectively binding decisions. It is precisely this which gives subsystemic autonomy to modern politics, making it an autopoietic production of power from power in which specific demands from the public are taken into account only insofar as they affect considerations of power.

According to Luhmann, this power-cycle represents the official self-description of modern political systems. But this is only half the story. The other half is an *unofficial power-cycle* which becomes necessary to the degree that the official one is "stressed with complexity" (Luhmann 1981: 47). During the last decades, political parties have been less and less able to aggregate and present political programs which reflect and satisfy the public's increasing and increasingly heterogeneous demands. Supported by lobbies, interest- and single-issue-groups, the public addresses its demands directly to the administration. Manifold "contact systems" between public and administration have developed, from corporatism to participation of citizen's groups in administrative decision-making (Luhmann 1969: 201–18). Based on such negotiations, the administration works out decisions on its own and confronts governments and parliaments with them. This puts political parties more and more into the paradoxical position that they have to appeal to the public for support for political decisions which organized parts of the public have already arranged with the administration. In this informal direct democracy, parties partly lose their function of buffering the administration from the public. But this, in turn, results in a corresponding loss of autonomy of the political system from its environment. The public, consisting of individual citizens – usually organized in corporate actors to pool their power – with all their concrete interests, tends to overload the political system with specific demands. The self-description of a political system with such a predominance of the unofficial power cycle is the interventionist welfare state.

THE STRUCTURAL CRISIS OF MODERN WELFARE STATES

Here we are already dealing with Luhmann's diagnosis of the structural crisis of contemporary politics, and his prescriptions to politicians as to what they should do about this situation. Ultimately, this crisis originates from an essential feature of functional differentiation. All functionally specialized subsystems of society tend towards an infinite perfection of their performance. With respect to individual members of society, this hypertrophy finds its main expression in the principle of *inclusion*. Inclusion implies the promise of all societal subsystems that ultimately every member of society shall benefit from their performance, and moreover that they will steadily increase the quantity and quality of these benefits. Thus, everybody shall profit from unlimited medical progress, educational opportunities, economic affluence, a wide variety of news provided by the mass media, legal chances to defend their rights, etc. An escalating interplay between subsystems and individuals is at work here. On one side, the subsystems's codes have no provisions to stop these expansions of performance. For instance, science never has enough truths. It is as insatiable in this respect as the health-care system is with regard to improvements of medical diagnosis and therapy. On the other side, individuals construct and maintain their identity in modern society – as Luhmann states – mainly by putting forward claims with regard to the performance of societal subsystems. Thus, supply push and demand pull work in tandem (Luhmann 1983).

However, many claims for inclusion are not sufficiently satisfied or even get refused by societal subsystems which lack the resources to fulfil everything which is wanted of them. This inability of other subsystems produces the overload of modern politics. *Inclusion into the welfare state* means basically that the political system is supposed to compensate for the inclusion deficits of other societal subsystems (Luhmann 1981). Especially when those political parties which represent the progressive version of political demands reinforce such an *expansionist* understanding of the role of the political system. Luhmann (1983: 108) states that nowadays every achieved level of inclusion "...is the base for a quest for 'more' of the same, even though anybody knows that this can't go on indefinitely." For a long time, materialist issues dominated the agenda of the welfare state. But since the mid-1970s even post-materialist issues like technological risks, environmental pollution, animal rights, or the rights of lifestyle communities (such as homosexuals) have entered the political scene, making things even more difficult. The political system can hardly refuse these demands because party competition leads even the conservatives to extend the welfare state. It seems almost impossible to win an election with a political program which announces the intention to lower the level of inclusion.

These welfare state policies, however, have led to a simultaneous *inflation of money, law, and political power* – the three principal instruments of political intervention into society (Luhmann 1981, 1983). The welfare state's need for money has led to chronic economic inflation and growing state debts, a juridification of all aspects of social life has gone along with declining acceptance of specific laws, and an increasing bureaucracy has stifled market forces and other forms of societal self-regulation. In this way, Luhmann describes the reality and tendencies of the German welfare state of the 1970s and 1980s as a trajectory of crisis.

What could be done to stop this unfavorable development which might ultimately ruin the political system? Luhmann gives a twofold answer which nicely captures what has happened in many European countries during the 1980s and 1990s, first formulated by conservative parties – starting with British Thatcherism – but sooner or later adopted by socialists and social-democrats as well. A *restrictive* understanding of politics replaced the former expansionist one. Initially, all governments had to proclaim practical constraints manifesting themselves mainly as empty treasuries which made it impossible to satisfy public demands for even more welfare policies. Lack of resources are the only convincing argument against the welfare state. But Luhmann went further, admonishing politicians to stick to this restrictive understanding of politics even after fiscal crises of the state had been addressed. A strict refusal of welfare state policies should be the permanent future conception of the political system's role in society. This plea is theoretically based on Luhmann's general analysis of political guidance within a "poly-contextual" society.

POLITICAL GUIDANCE AND SOCIETAL EVOLUTION

Up to the mid-1980s Luhmann treated the functional differentiation and overall complexity of modern society as a serious obstacle to successful *political guidance,* but not as rendering it an impossibility . But later he absolutely denied any possibility for rational societal goal-attainment through interventionist policies. This "radicalization" (Scharpf 1989) of Luhmann's theoretical position, which departs from all conventional political science approaches, must be understood in the context of his general shift towards the autopoiesis paradigm of social systems.

According to Luhmann (1991), analyzing political decision-makers as actors who are able to cause deliberate changes in other subsystems of society such as the economy fits with the self-understanding of modern politics but not with its reality. A truthful sociological or political science analysis should dissociate itself from this self-deception of politicians. Luhmann gives two main reasons why the successful political guidance of societal dynamics is an illusion. First of all, as already mentioned, in a "poly-contextural" society all subsystems are equal in rank. No structural hierarchy exists between them. The political system is not at the top where it could command other subsystems. Secondly, subsystems do not possess a common language as a basis for mutual understanding (Luhmann 1989). For example, as the language of the economy is that of costs and prices it cannot understand political interventions based on the language of power, nor adapt to them according to political intentions. Economic compliance with the imperatives of political power would presuppose a "blunted differentiation" (Colomy 1990: 470) of both subsystems. As we know by now from the real-life experiment of socialism, under these conditions political guidance may reach its goals. But this political success is not at all successful economically. Instead, it brings about an immense economic inefficiency which is accompanied by a ruin of society at large.

With these arguments against political guidance, Luhmann does not deny that political interventions do have effects in other societal subsystems. Since the self-referentially closed subsystems are open as well, there are effects – but only by chance would they correspond to what was intended politically. Nevertheless, Luhmann (1984: 645) reassures us: "for survival evolution is sufficient." More precisely, he counts on the *co-evolution of societal subsystems by their "structural coupling"* (Luhmann 1995, 1997: 536–7). Each autopoietic system evolves according to its own rules, but by mutual interference they adapt to each other at least as far as to ensure a minimal degree of societal integration. For example, the science system may recognize that by raising certain research topics more financial resources from the economy can be acquired than by other topics; and the economy may become aware of the fact that the implementation of certain innovative technologies leads to higher profits. Both subsystems operate strictly according to their own logic, being totally indifferent to the logic of the respective other subsystem. Still, science adapts to the needs of the economy, and vice versa. Many other examples could illustrate such dynamics of co-evolution which are functional to society at large. But of course, as Luhmann admits, there is nothing inherent to co-evolution which guarantees societal integration. Co-evolution may also bring about societal disintegration. Luhmann (1992: 138) leaves us with the laconic remark: "everything works fine as long as it works fine."

Luhmann's radical scepticism towards interventionist policy-making has provoked many criticisms. His opponents have stressed that Luhmann's argumentation misunderstands the essence of modern policy-making. They pointed out that the aim of political interventions is not to replace or suppress the self-referential codes of the economy or other functional subsystems. Such attempts which did occur and may again are evolutionary regressions from the level of functional differentiation which modern society has reached. In this respect, Middle and East European state socialism or German national socialism clearly were aberrations within modernity. In contrast, what the political system usually more modestly attempts, and can indeed achieve, though by no means easily and all of the time, is to steer organizations in other societal subsystems in order to channel their autopoiesis in certain directions (Mayntz 1988; Scharpf 1989; Schimank 1992). In addition, the political system aims for "contextual guidance" of the interplay of particular subsystems, again by explicitly respecting their autopoiesis (Teubner and Willke 1984; Willke 1992). Corporatist arrangements and policy networks may be interpreted in this way. To these critiques Luhmann (1993, 1994) has replied that without doubt there might be some chances of short-term success for policies which proceed according to principles of "incrementalism" or "piece-meal engineering" (Lindblom 1959; Popper 1961). However, he insisted on his point that the general and long-term outcome of policies is highly uncertain, contrary to what politicians and political scientists frequently tell the public and believe themselves about the role of the political system within modern society.

CONCLUSION

In the long run it is surely hard to say to what degree societal stability or change in certain respects has been brought about by political guidance or by the co-evolution of autopoietic subsystems. Luhmann states that ambitious – and costly – political interventionism according to the expansionist ideology of the welfare state predominantly does harm to modern society. Despite radical differences in general theoretical premises, we can discover a strong correspondence between Luhmann's theory of societal evolution and liberal ideas of societal self-regulation by "invisible hand mechanisms" (Ullmann-Margalit 1978), from Adam Smith to Friedrich A. Hayek and others. In Luhmann, we find core elements of the "realist" liberal understanding of modern political theory translated into the new language of systems theory supplied by recent developments in the natural sciences.

Taking Luhmann seriously, one might wonder why modern society still has a political system. Does society really need one, if political guidance is impossible? Or is the self-deception of politicians so convincing that all other societal sub-systems also take for granted that political guidance is beneficial and even essential to them? So, is this the message of Luhmann's "sociological enlight-enment" of "poly-contextural" society with respect to its political system; that the best thing that could happen to the former would be the disappearance of the latter?

Such an "anarchist" reading of Luhmann's political sociology would be going too far. First of all, his restrictive understanding of politics has a substantial core. Luhmann does insist on the societal need for collectively binding decisions produced by the political system. These binding decisions are legal norms by which the political system programs the legal subsystem of modern society. This structural coupling of political and legal system regulates societal conflicts, as it is expressed most succinctly in the German tradition of the "*Rechtsstaat.*" The important thing about a political system restricting itself to this function is that it contributes essentially to the regulation of conflicts occurring within other societal subsystems such as the economy, but has no aspirations at all to use political criteria to guide what happens elsewhere in society. Regulation, not guidance, is what politics should be about. With this message reminiscent of the nineteenth century Luhmann sends us into the twenty-first.

In addition, Luhmann would admit that even the misleading expansionist self-understanding of the welfare state unintentionally might do some good to society. The welfare state can be a quite useful instrument of symbolic politics. Thus, addressing certain issues to the welfare state might give other societal subsystems time to deliberate and implement decisions of their own in these matters. For example, making environmental pollution a political issue shifts attention away from the economy – even if this subsystem is declared to be the prime cause of this problem. Firms can get on with their work and gradually adapt to the problem under the cover of political controversies, expert hearings, negotiations, and so on. Moreover, political rhetoric may legitimize decisions – and non-decisions – of other societal subsystems about such problems. Again, the political system serves as a buffer which allows other subsystems's autopoiesis to continue. In these ways, by decoupling "action" and "talk," the fiction of the welfare state helps modern society to carry on with its "hypocrisy" (Brunsson 1989) of continually perfecting the attainment of the common good.

Further Reading

The major Works by Luhmann in English on the general theory of society and political sociology are:

Luhmann, Niklas 1982: *The Differentiation of Society. Selected Writings* Translated by Stephen Holmes and Charles Larmore, New York: Columbia University Press. .

Luhmann, Niklas 1989 [1986]: *Ecological Communication*. Trans. John Bednarz Jr. Chicago, IL.: The University of Chicago Press.

Luhmann, Niklas 1990 [1981]: *Political Theory in the Welfare State*. Trans. John Bednarz Jr. Berlin and New York: de Gruyter.

Luhmann, Niklas 1993 [1991]: *Risk: A Sociological Theory*. Trans. Rhodes Barret. Berlin and New York: de Gruyter.

Luhmann, Niklas 1995 [1984]: *Social Systems*. Trans. John Bednarz Jr. and Dirk Baecker. Stanford, CA: Stanford University Press.

Luhmann, Niklas 1998 [1992]: *Observations on Modernity*. Trans. William Whobrey. Stanford, CA: Stanford University Press.

7

"Postmodern" Political Sociology

DAVID OWEN

The central categories of modern sociology have been called into question in two different ways. For the sociology of postmodernity, transformations in social reality mean they are no longer useful and new theories need to be developed to provide an accurate account of its processes. For postmodernist sociology, following Foucault, what is at issue is the modes of acting and thinking through which "knowing subjects" and "reality" as such are constituted. From this point of view, sociology is not a science of society but an "ethics of truth." Owen discusses the example of the concept of "society" to illustrate postmodern political sociology. A condition of the emergence of modern sociology, it holds in place a way of describing and evaluating "reality" as an international order of sovereign states and the demarcation of citizens and aliens; and an understanding of political rule structured by the problematic of society and the individual. Central to postmodern political sociology is concern that ethical and political reasons are transformed into juridical and scientific problems, disenfranchising individuals and groups faced with legal and scientific experts.

In its classic "modernist" form, political sociology is concerned with the sociological analysis of political phenomena ranging from the State, to civil society, to the family, investigating topics such as citizenship, social movements, and the sources of social power. The lineage of this discipline is typically traced from such thinkers as Montesquieu, Smith, and Ferguson through the "founding fathers" of sociology – Marx, Durkheim, and Max Weber – to such contemporary theorists as Gellner, Giddens, Habermas, and Mann. Given the range and value of work which has been – and still is – produced within this trajectory of thought, it might reasonably be asked how, if at all, the development of a so-called "postmodern" political sociology contributes to our understanding of ourselves as political agents. To produce a satisfying answer to this question requires that we begin by differentiating two ways in which the central categories and theories of modern sociology have been called into question. These two routes will be presented in terms of a contrast between the sociology of postmodernity and postmodernist sociology. This clarification provides the basis from which to reflect on "postmodern" political sociology by considering some examples of this type of enquiry before sketching the salient features of the family of approaches gathered together under this title.

I

The contrast between the sociology of postmodernity and "postmodern" sociology can be elucidated in terms of the difference between an epistemic and an ethical problematization of the central categories and theories of modern sociology. The former presents the argument that certain transformations of social reality entail that the epistemic power of these categories and theories (i.e. their capacity to generate satisfying accounts of the phenomena in question) has been significantly undermined. The latter argues that the hegemonic status of the style of reasoning expressed in and through such categories and theories, and the limits that this places on our ways of thinking about ourselves as political agents, is itself an appropriate object of ethical reflection. Let's consider each in turn.

The sociology of postmodernity is an *epochal* form of sociological reflection which can be taken as conforming to Bauman's injunction that:

> rather than seeking a new form of postmodernist sociology...sociologists should be engaged in developing a sociology of postmodernity (i.e. deploying the strategy of systematic, rational discourse to the task of constructing a theoretical model of postmodern society as a system in its own right, rather than a distorted form, or an aberration from another system). (Bauman 1992: 61)

Enquiries conducted in terms of this epochal mode of reflection have produced the thesis that a related set of practices and processes are transforming our experience of space and time (Harvey 1989) and producing a distinct social formation characterized by a complex (non-mechanical) system which "appears as a space of chaos and chronic indeterminacy, a territory subjected to rival and contradictory meaning-bestowing claims and hence perpetually ambivalent" (Bauman 1992, 1993). This shift is given expression, it is claimed, in processes of "postmodernization" (Crook, Pakulski, and Waters 1992; see also Pakulski, chapter 35, in this volume) which can be discerned in relation to social stratification (Pakulski and Waters 1996), culture (Foster 1983; Featherstone 1990), modes of economic organization (Lash and Urry 1987, 1993), the production and circulation of knowledge (Stehr 1994), the role of mass media and information technologies (Baudrillard 1983), and the impact of globalization on the nation-state (Robertson 1992).

An exemplary instance of the problematization of the central categories and theories of modern sociology which characterizes the sociology of post-modernity is given by Pakulski's and Waters' (1996) argument that our societies are increasingly organized in status-conventional terms which denude the category of "class" of its explanatory power with respect to the analysis of access to economic resources, political power, and prestige. Waters also provides a clear expression of the intellectual spirit of this approach when he remarks:

the key task that remains is the development of a macro-theoretical paradigm that can match the brilliant capacity of Marx and Weber to theorize a new principle of social stratification. They managed to avoid the dangers of retrospection, to avoid theorizing classes as "new estates" and we too must seek likewise to avoid theorizing emergent status-conventional arrangements as "new classes." (1997: 38)

For the purposes of this discussion, the crucial point to note, as the citations from Bauman and Waters both illustrate, is that this type of endeavor does not significantly depart from the classic ambitions of sociological thought, namely, to provide an accurate account of the nature of our social reality in terms of theoretical models which map its inner processes. In other words, the standard features of sociological theory in its orthodox modernist form can be discerned in this more recent set of theories:

Such theories are in agreement that immediate empirical evidence is quite insufficient to provide an adequate explanation of social phenomena. Further, mainstream sociology requires that explanation of the phenomena or happenings must be adduced to a mechanism that gives rise to such surface phenomena. Precisely what these mechanisms are and how they are linked to the observational data is a matter of dispute. But that such mechanisms are linked, and connected causally to empirical features of the world, is not at issue. (Velody 1989: 127)

In this respect at least, contemporary debates between the advocates of "postmodernization" and of "reflexive modernization" (e.g. Beck, Giddens) have an epistemologically localized character.

By contrast, "postmodern" or, more precisely, postmodernist sociology does not attempt to provide theoretical articulations of the (hidden) inner processes of social reality; on the contrary, its concern is with the artefactual character of the practices – understood simultaneously as modes of acting and of thinking – "through which one can grasp the lineaments both of what was constituted as real for those who were attempting to conceptualize and govern it, and of the way in which those same people constituted themselves as subjects capable of knowing, analyzing, and ultimately modifying the real" (cf. Dean 1994; Foucault 1994: 318). This mode of enquiry can be seen as asking three questions (Tully 1999). First, how have we come to think and act with respect to x in the ways that we do? Second, what are the effects and costs of this way of thinking and acting? Third, how might we think and act otherwise than we do? Perhaps the best way to conceptualize this kind of enquiry, as Tom Osborne has argued brilliantly in *Aspects of Enlightenment* (1998), is as "an ethics of truth" which acts in the service of our powers of freedom, as a form of ethical work in which the enquirer seeks to tell the truth about, and thus to reevaluate, the value of specific ways of reflecting on ourselves and the world. The relevant point has been neatly put by Mitchell Dean:

If sociology ceases to be viewed as a science of society, as an analytic of truth concerning what can be said about a distinctive interconnected unity, then we can begin to grasp it as a different thing altogether. If we place it on the side of a critical ontology, it becomes an investigation into the conditions of existence of what we take to be our present and how we have come to think and act on ourselves and others. Given this, the notion of society need not be definitive of sociology...I want to suggest that sociology is less a mode of production of truth than a kind of truth-telling, a contemporary form of what the ancient world called parrhesia... Sociology is hence a "diagnostic" that investigates the limits and possibilities of how we have come to think about who we are and what we do, of how we act on ourselves and others, and the present in which we find, and indeed discover, ourselves. (Dean 1997: 206)

We can clarify what is involved in this "postmodern" approach by offering a description of it.

Quentin Skinner has recently reminded us, that "it is remarkably difficult to avoid falling under the spell of our own intellectual heritage":

As we analyze and reflect on our normative concepts, it is easy to become bewitched into believing that the ways of thinking about them bequeathed to us by the mainstream of our intellectual traditions must be the ways of thinking about them. (1998: 116)

He goes on to suggest that:

[t]he history of philosophy, and perhaps especially of moral, social and political philosophy, is there to prevent us from becoming too readily bewitched. The intellectual historian can help us to appreciate how far the values embodied in our present way of life, and our present ways of thinking about those values, reflect a series of choices made at different times between different possible worlds. This awareness can help to liberate us from the grip of any one hegemonal account of those values and how they should be interpreted and understood. Equipped with a broader sense of possibility, we can stand back from the intellectual commitments that we have inherited and ask ourselves in a new spirit of enquiry what we should think of them. (1998: 116–17)

The contrast between the intellectual historian and the postmodernist sociologist in this context is simply that whereas the former focuses on demonstrating the historically contingent character of our ways of reflecting on x by tracing the emergence and development of these ways of reflecting on x, the latter seeks to offer an account of how the emergence and development of our ways of reflecting on x are interwoven with the emergence and development of particular forms of conduct and practical identities – and, thus, of how our ways of reflecting on x have become hegemonic, of how this hegemony is sustained, and of the effects of domination that taking these ways of reflecting on x as the ways of reflecting on x engenders.

There are two central methodological features of this approach. First, it dispenses with "the constituent subject" in order "to arrive at an analysis which can account for the constitution of the subject within a historical framework" (Foucault 1984b: 59). Second, it advances the claim that "there is no power relation without the correlative constitution of a field of knowledge, nor any knowledge that does not presuppose and constitute at the same time power relations" (Foucault 1977: 27). This latter claim has been much misunderstood. It does not, for example, mean that power and knowledge are identical or, even more bizarrely, that knowledge is simply a product and instrument of domination. Rather this thesis is simply that advanced by Wittgenstein which argues that our ways of reflecting on the world are inextricably interwoven with, and sustained by, our ways of acting in the world. These two features of postmodernist approaches to sociology are combined to generate a practice which seeks to account for the emergence and development of particular forms of subjectivity by attending to the formation of particular practices (i.e. ways of thinking and acting) and tracing the effects of these practices.

We can specify this kind of enquiry in relation to "political sociology" in terms of an investigation of "political rationalities" or "rationalities of rule" (Rose 1996). This phrase refers to (1) the aspects of our thought and action that have been brought under (or excluded from) the concept of the political (*le politique*) and the domains of our thought and action that have been marked out by the concept of politics (*la politique*) – and (2) the ways in which those aspects of our practical identities and forms of our practical conduct that are demarcated by the concepts of the political and politics respectively have been problematized within an assemblage of practical systems. So, for example, an investigation of contemporary political rationalities with respect to those aspects of our practical identities marked out by the concepts of class, race, gender, or culture would attend to the ways in which these aspects have become politicized (i.e. constituted as objects of political reflection and action) or de-politicized, the specific forms of this politicization or de-politicization (i.e. the particular styles of political reasoning and practical systems within which reflection on these aspects of our practical identities is situated) and the practical effects of this way of fabricating our political experience of ourselves and others.

We can, then, distinguish postmodernist sociology from the sociology of postmodernity in terms of a distinction between an ethical and an epistemic criticism of the central categories and theories of modern sociology. However, the abstract character of the discussion may not be unduly helpful; consequently, let us turn to an illustration of "postmodern" political sociology in terms of an example.

II

To situate the example which will be provided in this section, we can begin by noting that from this postmodernist perspective, modern political sociology is an appropriate object of investigation precisely because it acts to hold in place a way of describing and evaluating "the real" as a social reality constituted by, for example, an international order of sovereign states, global markets, the demarcation of citizens and aliens, etc. Consequently, I shall offer an example of this approach which illustrates the ethical problematization of modern political sociology. This example concerns the concept of society which secures the modernist project of political sociology.

As Mitchell Dean points out in the remarks cited above, the concept of society need not be definitive for sociology, yet it is arguably the case that the emergence of the concept of society is a necessary condition for the formation of sociology as a distinct form of knowledge, and as a discipline. This is just to say that the concept of society as "a distinct, substantial and enduring entity" (Hindess 1998: 65) comprising "the sum of bonds and relations between individuals and events – economic, moral, political – within a more or less bounded territory governed by its own laws" (Rose 1996: 1) makes possible the formation of a new plane of knowledge, that is, a new way of describing and problematizing human relations in terms of, for example, the relationship between society and the individual – and, relatedly, from the nineteenth century on, a new plane of governance, that is, a way of governing organized in terms of the problematic of society and the individual which seeks to govern from "the social point of view." As Nikolas Rose points out, the "political rationalities that have played so great a part in our own century – socialism, social democracy, social liberalism – may have differed on many things, but on this they agreed – one must pose the question of how to govern from 'the social point of view'" (1996: 3).

So, for example, Dean refers to the formation from the mid-nineteenth century of policy assemblages such as "the Social Question," "Social Promotion," "Social Defense," "Social Security," and "Social Insurance" which involve institutions such as "schools, juvenile courts, government departments, police stations, unemployment exchanges, wage-fixing tribunals, borstals, baby health and family planning clinics, and so on" and qualified personnel such as "the general practitioner, the social worker, the professional police officer, the child psychologist, the career public servant, and so on" (1997: 211–12). In other words, as Rose remarks:

> "The social" was certainly a hybrid domain, emerging out of a whole lot of little lines of mutation that occurred in most European nations and in North America over the course of the nineteenth century and the first half of the twentieth. But it formed as the plane upon which all these little lines came to intersect, a way of problematizing all manner of ills, speaking about them, analyzing them and intervening upon them. (1996: 3)

As Rose points out, "the social" is a plane on which "human intellectual, political and moral authorities, within a limited geographical territory, thought about and acted upon their collective experience for about a century" (1996: 3). In this respect, the social sciences and, in particular, sociology can be grasped as the forms of knowledge which develop on (and develop) the plane of "the social," and the institutionalization and professionalization of these forms of knowledge as disciplines can be understood in terms of the development of the hegemony of "the social" as a way of thinking about, and acting on, our collective experience which is elaborated through categories such as "social relations" (Marx), "social facts" (Durkheim), and "social action" (Weber). This hegemony is given its most direct expression in the sixth of Marx's "Theses on Feuerbach": "Feuerbach resolves the religious essence into the human essence. But the human essence is no abstraction inherent in each individual.

In its reality it is the ensemble of the social relations" (1975: 423). In this respect, it is not the least of the functions of sociology that it acts to hold in place the modern concept of society which is presupposed by, and given expression in, debates concerning "the social point of view."

The pertinence of this sketch for reflecting on modern political sociology becomes clear when we note that while recent work on, for example, nationalism has been concerned to explore the artefactual character of the category "nation," such reflections have not been extended to the concept of society deployed in such analyses. As Hindess points out:

> Perhaps the most surprising feature of this literature is that many of those who insist on the invented or artefactual character of nations continue to treat societies as if they were altogether more substantial entities. Ernest Gellner, for example, presents nations and nationalism as if they were characteristic phenomena of certain kinds of society, appearing only in those endowed with a modern state. He also observes that: "Not all societies are endowed with states. It immediately follows that the problem of nationalism does not arise for stateless societies..." Thus, while nations are regarded as fabrications, the societies in which they appear or fail to appear are seen as having a more enduring status. Similarly, Eric Hobsbawm's analyses of the invention of tradition, in which the nation and national tradition are seen as being of central importance, presents such inventions as occurring "more frequently when a rapid transformation of society weakens or destroys the social patterns for which 'old' traditions had been designed..." (1998: 64)

Yet, as Hindess notes, one of the ironies of this unreflective appeal to the concept of society is that "the particular concept of society employed" in these discussions of nations and nationalism "is a more recent historical innovation than that of the nation itself" (1998: 65; cf. Wolf 1988). Far from being simply given, the modern concept of society is an artefact of the European process of state-building – later exported to the rest of the world – which, from the Treaty of Westphalia onward, facilitated "the ability of a number of states to each impose a substantial degree of exclusive control over a territory and the population within it" (1998: 65; cf. Hirst 1997). The significance of this point is twofold.

First, the unreflective adoption of this concept of society as a basic category of reflection acts to hold in place an understanding of human beings, of the human population, as naturally divided into a series of sub-populations or "societies." This "natural fact," in turn, acts as a basis on which to differentiate our relations to others in terms of whether or not they are members of our society in ways which facilitate certain forms of acknowledgment and interaction – and obstruct others. Not the least of these differentiations concerns our political relations to others since it is part of this picture that, ideally, each society has its own sovereign state (a point demonstrated by the way in which stateless societies are conceptualized as a political problem) – and, concomitantly, our relations to others are divided into our relations to fellow-citizens or nationals, on the one hand, and our relations to aliens, on the other (Hindess 1998).

Two examples of how this picture is held in place are provided by David Campbell's *Writing Security* (1998) and Nevzat Soguk's *States and Strangers*

(1999). Campbell demonstrates, with respect to the United States, how *foreign* policy acts "as a political practice central to the constitution, production and maintenance of American political identity" (1998: 8). More specifically, he shows both how the production of the foreign is integral to the reproduction of the orthodox picture of state sovereignty, citizenship, and nationhood, *and* how the history of the constitution of "the American foreign" is central to an adequate understanding of the history of American political identity. Relatedly, Soguk elucidates the constitutive role of the international refugee regime in maintaining a picture of the world as naturally divided into sovereign states composed of, and responsible for, their citizen-members. Tracking the history of European and, later, global state-building, Soguk demonstrates the central place of the figure of the refugee in the statist imaginary as the "exceptional" other whose presence (real or imagined) is a necessary condition of producing and maintaining the "normality" of the international order of sovereign states – and, concomitantly, the identification of citizenship with membership of a territorially bounded society. In both cases, these authors show how these practices of statecraft, and the picture that they hold in place, entail the denial of a political voice to the stranger (the foreigner, the refugee), while, simultaneously, obstructing the acknowledgment of this denial of political voice as a form of domination.

Second, the unreflective adoption of this concept of society as a basic category of reflection also acts to hold in place an understanding of political rule which is structured in terms of the problematic of society and the individual. This "natural fact" acts to shape and orient the space of political reason (i.e. the political imaginary) in terms of the limit-cases of an ideal of fully individualized society, on the one hand, and an ideal of fully socialized individuals, on the other hand. One might think of libertarianism and communism as examples of political rationalities which approximate to these limit-ideals – and precisely to that extent remain simultaneously utopian and dystopian forms of rule. The attempt to offer a dialectically nuanced resolution of the aporetic relationship of these two limit-ideals – a task undertaken speculatively by Hegel in the *Philosophy of Right* – has issued in the simultaneous assertion and reassertion of individual rights, on the one hand, and of social norms, on the other, which takes the practical shape of the normalization of rights and the juridification of norms. These phrases can be clarified by considering some examples.

The normalization of rights refers to the ways in which the human sciences have become integral to judicial judgment. Thus, for example, in *Discipline and Punish*, Foucault traces the ways in which criminal law becomes interwoven with psychiatric knowledge in the nineteenth century such that "crime":

> the object with which penal practice is concerned, has profoundly altered...Under-cover of the relative stability of the law, a mass of subtle and rapid changes has occurred. Certainly the "crimes" and "offences" on which judgment is passed are also juridical objects defined by the code, but judgment is also passed on the passions, instincts, anomalies, infirmities, maladjustments, effects of environment or heredity; acts of aggression are punished, so also, through them is aggressivity; rape, but at the same time perversions; murders, but also drives and desires. But, it will be objected, judgment is not actually being passed on them; if they are referred

to at all it is to explain the actions in question, and to determine to what extent the subject's will was involved in the crime. This is no answer. For it *is* these shadows lurking behind the case itself that are judged and punished. They are judged indirectly as "attenuating circumstances" that introduce into the verdict not only "circumstantial" evidence, but something quite different, which is not juridically codifiable: the knowledge of the criminal, one's estimation of him, what is known about the relations between him, his past and his crime, and what might be expected of him in the future. (1977: 17–18)

This transformation of "crime" corresponds to the emergence of "criminality" as an object of knowledge. Concomitantly, "a quite different discourse of truth is inscribed in the course of the penal judgment":

The question is no longer simply: "Has the act been established and is it punishable?" But also: "What *is* this act, what *is* this act of violence or this murder? To what level or to what field of reality does it belong? Is it a fantasy, a psychotic reaction, a delusional episode, a perverse action?" It is no longer simply: "Who committed it?" But: "How can we assign the causal process that produced it? Where did it originate in the author himself? Instinct, unconscious, environment, heredity? It is no longer simply: "What law punishes this offence?" But: "What would be the most appropriate measures to take? How do we see the future development of the offender? What would be the best way of rehabilitating him?" A whole set of assessing, diagnostic, prognostic, normative judgements concerning the criminal have become lodged in the framework of penal judgement. (1977: 19)

Another example is provided by the shift in international refugee law from the various arrangements, conventions, and institutions which, in the first half of the twentieth century, introduce the refugee as a juridical figure defined in terms of "categories (i.e., persons of a certain origin not enjoying the protection of their country)" (UNHCR Handbook s.37, cf. 1951 Convention Article 1 A(1) for these earlier instruments) to the contemporary construction of the refugee, in the 1951 Geneva Convention Relating to the Status of Refugees and the 1967 New York Protocol to the Convention Relating to the Status of Refugees, as one who:

owing to a well-founded fear of being persecuted for reasons of race, religion, nationality [as belonging to a "people"], membership of a social group or political opinion is outside the country of his nationality [as membership of a state] and is unable or, owing to such fear, is unwilling to avail himself of the protection of that country; or who, not having a nationality and being outside the country of his habitual residence . . . is unable, or, owing to such fear, is unwilling to return to it. (1951 Convention Article 1 A (2); 1967 Protocol Article 1 (2). The insertions are mine.)

The judgment that an applicant is or is not a refugee is now not simply a judgment whose truth is specifiable in terms of knowing what the origin of the applicant is, knowing whether the laws of their country protect persons of that origin and knowing refugee law – rather it involves a whole series of knowledges (psychological, sociological, linguistic, geopolitical, etc.) and techniques

(medical and psychiatric evaluation, disclosure interviews, detention, etc.) designed to elicit the truth of the applicant's state of mind (is it fear?) and the level of
reality or fantasy to which this state of mind belongs (is it well-founded?).

By contrast, the juridification of norms refers to the ways in which various social
norms become subject to legal codification such that certain forms of behavior are
not simply designated as "abnormal" by reference to a given norm, but become
subject to legal sanctions. A prominent recent example is the development of
"speech codes" governing the kinds of utterances with respect, say, to gender and
ethnicity which can be legitimately spoken. Other related examples include the
development of sexual harassment laws and laws on parental responsibility and
liability for the actions of their children. The significance of this process is that it
facilitates the extension and generalization of norms across multiple domains of
government because the juridification of a given norm (such as equal treatment)
with respect to some particular domain (such as gender) constructs a logic such
that the extension of this norm, via law, to other domains (such as race) is impelled
by the principles of legal reasoning (for example, consistency).

Perhaps the central concern of postmodern political sociologists with respect to
both of these developments is the way in which they transform the space of ethical
and political reasons into a juridico-scientific space that is centered around the
figure of the expert-judge. Or, to put it plainly, the way in which these developments disenfranchise the voice of individuals and groups by limiting the entitlement to speak to the relevant legal and scientific experts (Ashenden 1996). Given
the emphasis on power relations taken by this approach, this reference to the
disenfranchisement of the voice of individuals and groups may sound slightly
strange – but if so, this is misleading. After all, to say that power relations are
omnipresent is not to say (incoherently) that they are omniscient. On the contrary,
on this account, power relations presuppose the possibility of resistance because
power can only be exercised over free subjects insofar as they are free (this is the
sense in which power is distinct from force). In this respect, the existence of power
relations *per se* is not a problem, rather it is the existence of highly asymmetrical
power relations – relations of domination – which poses a problem for human
freedom insofar as such relations of domination block the exercise of *effective*
resistance. Of course, one of the ways in which such relations of domination
emerge and are held in place is through forms of knowledge which describe a given
way of thinking and acting as natural, necessary, or obligatory. In this context, we
can see that the concern of the postmodernist political sociologist is the ethical
task of describing the contingent process by which we develop this understanding
of ourselves in order to free ourselves from the "natural," or "necessary," or
"obligatory" appearance of this picture so that we can grasp the effects of
domination that this understanding engenders as effects of domination – and
begin the experiment of thinking and acting differently (Tully 1999).

CONCLUSION

On the basis of these reflections, we can see how apposite it is to describe
postmodern political sociology as an ethics of truth in the service of our powers

of freedom. Whereas both the sociologies of modernity and of postmodernity seek to conceptualize the real as accurately as possible, postmodern political sociology questions the value of our ways of conceptualizing the real. Whereas sociologies of modernity and of postmodernity seek to demarcate and specify the epochal character of human history, postmodern modern political sociology questions the value of such epochal claims. By cultivating an engaged scepticism toward the limits of current ways of thinking, postmodern political sociology seeks to cultivate an ethos of critical freedom in which, as Deleuze puts it: "Thought thinks its own history (the past), but in order to free itself from what it thinks (the present) and be able finally to 'think otherwise' (the future)" (1988: 119).

Further Reading

Dean, M. 1994: *Critical and Effective Histories*. London: Routledge.
Osborne, T. 1998: *Aspects of Enlightenment*. London: UCL Press.
Owen, D. (ed.) 1998: *Sociology After Postmodernism*. London, Sage.

8

Studying Power

JOHN SCOTT

There are three dominant methodological traditions through which power is studied in empirical political sociology. The reputational approach looks at those who are believed to have power. Increasingly, however, it is thought that this is evidence only of images of power on the part of those asked. Structural approaches focus on strategic positions in the central organizations and institutions of a society. Decision-making approaches are based on the claim that the reputational and positional approaches ignore what actually happens when decisions are made. Scott favors the structural approach, arguing that it can, and should, incorporate the insights of the others: decision-making can only be studied where there is understanding of the important structures within which decisions are taken; and perceptions of power can best be understood where there is independent knowledge of the positions people believe to be powerful.

The principal approaches to the study of power have generally be seen as bitter rivals and as offering mutually exclusive paradigms of research. They have each come to be associated with quite distinctive methods of research and analysis. Indeed, it has even been claimed that the theoretical starting point determines not only the choice of research methods but also the substantive conclusions that can be drawn from the research (Walton 1966). These suggested links are far too strong. There are, indeed, affinities between theoretical approaches and research methods, resulting in the formation of distinct research traditions, but these are not tight and rigid connections. The merits and demerits of the various research methods can be considered independently of the particular theoretical approach that is adopted. Although I concentrate on the virtues of one tradition, I take it as axiomatic that the theoretical approaches that are associated with these traditions must be seen as complementary perspectives rather than as all-or-nothing rivals (Moyser and Wagstaffe 1987b).

It is possible to identify three dominant research traditions. These are the reputational approach, the structural approach, and the agency or decision-making approach (Crewe 1974). Each of these traditions is associated with a study that exemplifies its research methods and techniques and that has provided a model for later researchers. Figure 8.1 presents a simplified summary of

Table 8.1 Research traditions and research methods

Research tradition	Paradigmatic study	Preferred research methods		Object of analysis
		Data collection	Data analysis	
Reputational	Hunter (1953)	Expert judgment, interviews	Voting, ranking, and rating scores	Images of power
Structural	Mills (1956)	Documents	Frequency distributions, social network analysis	Positions of power
Decision-making	Dahl (1961)	Observation, interviews	Policy outcomes	Agencies of power

the links between the research traditions and their preferred methods of research.

The reputational approach to power has as its main concern those who are *reputed* to be powerful. While it has often been assumed that this method can give direct evidence on actual power relations, it has increasingly come to be realized that, in fact, it evidences only *images* of power. Structural approaches to power focus directly on the attributes of strategic positions in the central organizations and institutions of a society. These positions are held to be central to the control of the resources that are the basis of power, and the occupants of these positions are the central actors in the exercise of power. Decision-making approaches have been based on the claim that reputational and positional approaches have been overly formalistic. They have looked at formal, official definitions of power and have ignored what really happens when decisions are made. Not all of those who occupy positions of formal authority will be equally involved in all the various stages of decision making, and the only proper way to investigate power, it is held, is to do so directly at its point of exercise.

My own position is that the structural approach has the most to offer to researchers on power and that it provides a basis for incorporating the insights of the rival approaches. It is possible to study decision making only if we have an understanding of the structure within which these decisions are made, and perceptions of power can best be studied if we have some independent knowledge of what it is that the participants are trying to perceive. The starting point for any study of power, then, must be a structural analysis.

Each tradition relies on particular techniques of data collection and data analysis. Many of these techniques are used very widely in the social sciences, and I will not attempt to give a comprehensive coverage of such techniques as survey methods, interview methods, and the use of documents. Instead, I will concentrate on those features of these research methods that are most particular to the study of power and that raise particular issues in power research. As the focus of this discussion is on studying power, I have not discussed the research methods used in elite studies more generally, where the focus is not on power but on elite attitudes, values, and behavior (Putnam 1973; see also Moyser and Wagstaffe 1987a).

Power can be studied at a number of levels of analysis, and these will figure in this discussion. Some research has focused its attention on the national level, investigating power relations in and around the nation-state. An important tradition of research, however, has been concerned with power at the community level, in towns and cities within nation-states. There are, of course, important theoretical and substantive issues that surround the choice of an appropriate level of analysis, as well as about the extent to which global power relations should be considered alongside the national and the local. However, the research issues that arise in each of these areas are, in general, similar, and there is little need to make explicit reference to the level of analysis here.

IMAGES AND DECISIONS

The paradigmatic study for the reputational approach is that of Floyd Hunter (1953), for whom the central concern in a study of power was to identify those people who, according to general opinion in their community, exercise the greatest amount of power. It is perceptions or images of social positions and their occupants that are of interest to Hunter. In this respect, Hunter's work is similar to studies of images of class (Warner 1949; Lockwood 1966; Bulmer 1974) and of images of society more generally. In his work, however, he tends to gloss the distinction between images of power and the actual exercise of power. Hunter's "positional" approach to power saw it as "the acts of men [*sic*] going about the business of moving other men to act in relation to themselves or in relation to organic or inorganic things" (Hunter 1953: 2–3, emphasis removed). (Note that all the writers considered in detail here followed the sexist practice of referring to "men" instead of "people," and there is little or no discussion of the practices through which women have been excluded from power. In the direct quotations used in the rest of this chapter, I have left the argument in the words actually used by the researcher.) The resources that made such power possible were seen as being tied to social positions, and so the focus of any investigation must be on those who occupy prominent positions in various types of groups or associations. This starting point is the same as that of the structural approach, but Hunter wanted to move from structures to reputations.

In his study of community power in the financial, commercial, and industrial center of Atlanta, Georgia (called "Regional City" in the original report), Hunter aimed to identify powerful individuals in four arenas of power – business, government, civic affairs, and "society leaders and leaders of wealth" (Hunter 1953: 169). He sought key informants in the leading organizations and associations in each of these arenas, asking them to name the Chairmen and other leaders in the principal organizations in each of the four arenas of power. Many such office holders could, of course, have been identified from published documentary sources, as has been the case in more explicitly structural research, but Hunter was keen to tap into the knowledge and opinions of his key informants from the beginning.

The lists produced by the key informants were given to a panel of "judges," whose job it was to use their knowledge to reduce them to a more manageable "top ten of influence" in each arena. The panel of judges was supposed to be representative of the community in terms of religion, sex, age, and ethnicity, and they were also supposed to be representative of business and the professions (though no attempt was made to ensure that they were representative of other occupational groups). The community influentials – seen as the holders of power – were defined as the 40 people who received the largest number of votes from the panel of judges. (Note, however, that while the panel of judges was supposed to be representative of middle-class opinion, there is evidence that they were far less representative even than this. Hunter found that no African Americans appeared on the list. This reflects, of course, the lack of power – real or reputed – held by African Americans in the southern states of America in the 1950s, but it also seemed, to Hunter, to reflect the unwillingness or inability of his key informants to recognize those African Americans who did achieve positions of power. To overcome this, Hunter made an *ad hoc* extension to his research by carrying out a parallel sub-study within the black community, arguing that there was a divided structure of black–white power. This argument is analogous to Warner's claims about black–white class relations in the Deep South (Warner 1936; see also Davis 1941).

This was, of course, an arbitrary limitation, and Hunter's claim that these people were typical of a larger group of powerful persons (Hunter 1953: 61) highlights a problem that occurs in all projects where only a sub-set of the powerful are studied. This is the problem of sampling. When a researcher does not cover the whole of the target population, whether by accident or design, it is important that the nature and representativeness of the resulting sample is examined. In general, it would be preferable to use explicit sampling criteria in the first place, though this may not be possible when the size and compositions of the target population is unknown or unspecified.

While it purports to investigate the actual holders of power, the reputational approach, at best, provides evidence on *images of power*. The images disclosed are those of the expert judges, or the larger social groups of which they are representative. As such, it is important for a reputational study to identify clearly its target group: is the aim of the research to identify those that a whole society rates as the most powerful, or those that one class, sex, or ethnic group within it rates as the most powerful? Such questions can be answered only on the basis of some knowledge about the actual structures of power and the wider social structure.

The paradigmatic study for the decision-making approach to power is that of Robert Dahl (1961), one of the earliest critics of Hunter and structural approaches. Structural, or positional, approaches, he argued, presupposed that an elite exists, and a methodology that concentrates on top positions will inevitably conclude that an elite does, in fact, exist. The whole process, he argued, is circular. For Dahl, the existence of an elite had to be demonstrated through the direct investigation of decision making. He holds that "A has power over B to the extent that he can get B to do something that B would not otherwise do" (Dahl 1957: 202–3), and this is studied by measuring the actual participation of position holders in specific key decisions (see Lukes 1974 and the "Introduction" and the reprints of key contributions by Dahl, Lukes, and others in Scott 1994. Also Bellamy, chapter 2 and Hindess, chapter 4, in this volume).

Paradoxically, Dahl also began his research with the identification of structural positions. His study of New Haven, Connecticut, in the 1950s identified a large number of positions that he thought had the potential for power and influence in the community. These included office holders in the city administration (elected and appointed), local businessmen, and various "social and economic notables." The latter were large property holders and directors, and those active in "Society" activities. While this starting point looks little different from that of Hunter, Dahl was not using it to delineate a group of actual power holders. Rather, he wanted simply to identify a large population of *potential* holders of power, so that he could then go on and identify which of them were involved in the active exercise of power. This was the question that was to be investigated through an examination of their participation in the making of key decisions in the community.

Dahl's study of politics and his decision-making methodology have been emulated by many other political scientists and sociologists, though few have undertaken the kind of detailed and careful investigation of processes and policy outcomes that Dahl himself undertook. At the level of community power are the studies of Vidich and Bensman (1968), Birch (1959), and Wildavsky (1964), while at the national level there have been Rose (1967) in the United States and Hewitt (1974).

Dahl concentrated on a number of "issue-areas" – urban redevelopment, local schooling, and nominations for political office – and within each he looked at specific decisions such as the formation of a Citizen's Action Commission, the redevelopment of particular streets and squares, the introduction of eye tests in schools, changes to educational budgets, policies for dealing with delinquency at school, nominations for election as mayor, and proposals for a new city charter. Dahl and his researchers sought to use interviews, observations, and documents to identify who proposed particular alternatives, who spoke in discussions, when and how proposals were modified or rejected, and who voted for each proposal when a final decision was arrived at. He concluded that a great many people were involved in initiating or vetoing proposals, and that they tended to be actively involved only in those areas where they had particular professional or occupational interests. Only the democratically-elected politicians were centrally involved in more than one proposal (Dahl 1961: 181–3). The positional resources of the economic and social notables gave them only the *potential* for power, but very few of them either tried or succeeded in converting their potential into actual influence in decision-making processes. He further argued that political decisions were shaped by the lobbying and pressuring activities of a variety of groups. The outcome of decision-making processes did not uniformly express the interests or advantages of any one group. Power in New Haven was "pluralistic" rather than elitist (see also Polsby 1980).

The problems with the decision-making approach are, of course, that there is no certainty that researchers will either get access to those who really make decisions or be able to uncover the key participants. To the extent that decisions are made behind closed doors, away from the glare of public scrutiny, then political scientists and sociologists are unlikely to be able to observe these decisions or to interview those involved (Bachrach and Baratz 1963, 1975). This critique points to the need to investigate the "non-decision-making" processes that occur behind the scenes and that serve to keep some issues out of the overt decision-making process. From this standpoint, the "potential" power inherent in structural positions has a far greater significance than Dahl allowed.

The necessity for a structural framework is also apparent in the need for an objective criterion for identifying which decisions are the most important or strategic in a community. Which decisions are important, and which are not, is a matter that can be decided only in relation to the overall structure of the society and the distribution of advantages and disadvantages within it. Without such information, the researcher may end up looking only at the marginal and unimportant decisions that the real rulers could safely leave to others. The implication of this kind of criticism, then, is that the very structural concerns that Dahl sought to eliminate must, indeed, find their place in a comprehensive investigation of power.

STRUCTURES OF POWER

If structures of power are to form the centerpiece of power research – and both Hunter and Dahl began with the identification of structural positions – how is this to be carried out? The paradigmatic study for this approach is that of Mills (1956), who used the positional method to study national level power in the United States. Where Hunter and Dahl identified positions of power simply as their starting points, Mills saw this as central to the whole project. Power, he held, resides with all those "who are able to realize their will, even if others resist it" (Mills 1956: 9). While the identity of the particular individuals is recognized to be important, it is the attributes of the positions that they occupy that are seen as more fundamental to power relations. Someone exercises power as an occupant of a particular position, subject to the constraint exercised by the occupants of other positions. Without their positions, individuals have no significant power.

Power has its location in the top positions in the institutional hierarchies that define the social structure of a society, and the distribution of power varies with the shape taken by this structure. As the institutional hierarchies of a society become more centralized, so the distribution of power becomes more concentrated: "As the means of information and of power are centralized, some men come to occupy positions in American society from which they can look down upon, so to speak, and by their decisions mightily affect, the everyday worlds of ordinary men and women" (Mills 1956: 3). Mills's central concept of the power elite follows from this view of power. The institutional hierarchies form a structure of power, and it is the overlapping and interlocking of their top positions that forms a power elite. A power elite, then, comprises the "men whose positions enable them to transcend the ordinary environments of ordinary men and women; they are in positions that allow them to make decisions that have major consequences" (Mills 1956: 3–4).

Mills saw three institutional hierarchies at the heart of the power elite in the United States of the 1950s. These were the economic, the political, and the military hierarchies. As the identification of positions of power was to be the heart of his study, Mills sought to be as comprehensive and as systematic as he could in his use of evidence. Instead of relying on the knowledge of key informants, he went directly to the documentary sources that provided a full coverage of these positions. Although his precise selection criteria varied from case to case, Mills did make great attempts to be systematic and rigorous in his data collection. In most cases, he collected data for the full set of positions over three generations.

Within the economic arena, Mills noted the twentieth-century growth of the corporate sector at the expense of personal, privately-owned enterprises. He therefore focused his attention on those positions that formed what he called the "corporate rich." This category included holders of substantial wealth (termed the "very rich") and holders of corporate office (the "corporate executives"). The very rich were operationally defined as those men and women with assets of $30 million or more, and lists of names were compiled from a variety of official, corporate, and secondary sources (on the use of documentary sources in power and other studies see Scott 1990b). He defined "corporate executives" rather loosely as the "top two or three command posts in each of those hundred or so corporations which . . . are the largest" (Mills 1956: 126), and similar data on them were collected by his Ph.D. student, Suzanne Keller.

This definition of corporate executives highlights a general problem in positional studies of power. This is the problem of defining and bounding the positions that are to be studied, sometimes referred to as the problem of system boundaries. While any such decisions are likely to be arbitrary, it is important that the criteria are both clear and consistently applied. For example, we must know whether the category of "top" corporations includes the largest 50, 100, 200, or 500 corporations, and we also need to know by what criterion "size" is measured. Similarly, we must know which actual positions are to count as the "top" positions within them. Do we include just the President (Chief Executive), all the office holders, or all the directors? There is no simple answer to such questions, as the boundary criteria that needs to be used will vary from one situation to another.

In the political and military arenas, Mills focused his attention on what he called "the political directorate" and "the warlords." The political directorate is a category that includes all the leading positions of state: President, Vice President, Speaker, Cabinet members, and Supreme Court Justices. His list also included a number of positions that had grown in importance in executive decision-making over the course of the century. These were the Under Secretaries, Directors of Departments, Members of the Executive Office of the President, and White House Staff. The warlords were all Generals and Admirals, including – most importantly – those holding office in the Pentagon. Like the political directorate, these office holders were identified from official documents that listed the positions and their occupants. As with the corporate rich, the boundaries of the "top" positions in the political and military hierarchies were, inevitably, drawn arbitrarily, as a decision must always be made about which positions are important enough to include. An attempt to set out a framework for such matters in relation to identifying a political elite can be found in Giddens (1973).

Mills's power elite comprised the overlapping groups of the corporate rich, the political directorate, and the warlords. This emphasis on the analysis of overlapping memberships has been a central characteristic of structural studies of power. These studies have investigated the overlap among positions of power by the more or less systematic use of methods of social network analysis. Hunter had used these same techniques rather more systematically. He used rudimentary methods of social network analysis to construct sociograms of interaction among the reputedly powerful, concluding that there was evidence for the existence of various "crowds" or "cliques" within the leadership group (Hunter 1953: 77–8).

The systematic use of social network analysis has gradually become more central to structural research on power, as the advanced techniques developed since the 1960s have allowed more rigorous investigations into the formation of cliques and other sub-groupings. In social network analysis, individual positions are represented as points in a diagram or as rows in a matrix, while the social relations that connect these positions are represented as lines connecting the points or as the individual cells of the matrix. Mathematical techniques are now available to chart the size and structure of social networks through such measures as density, centralization, and fragmentation (Scott 1991b; Wasserman and Faust 1994). Density measures the coherence or integration of a network – how closely connected its members are. Centrality, on the other hand, concerns the relative prominence of members in the network. At an overall level, centralization measures examine the extent to which a network is organized around focal units. Particularly important measures in structural analysis are those that identify cliques, clusters, and other sub-groupings that cross-cut the formal boundaries of institutions (Knoke 1994).

The most systematic and theoretically-sophisticated examples of the use of the structural approach come from the work of Domhoff (1967; 1971; 1979; 1998) and those influenced by him. In these studies, structures of powerful positions are investigated in relation to the social background and policy preferences of those who occupy them. Domhoff has explored the consolidation of capitalist class power through the formal and informal networks involved in the special-interest process, the policy-formation process, the candidate-selection process, and the ideology process. In Britain, a similar approach has been used in works by Guttsman (1963), Miliband (1969), and Scott (1991c). Scott has shown that the "old boy" networks of British politics can be explored through the structural analysis of power blocs and the structure of intercorporate relations in business. Such work has recently been enlarged in the growing number of studies into policy networks (see Marsh 1998; see John, chapter 13, in this volume).

The approach has been especially important in analyses of economic power in large corporations (see Mizruchi 1982; Scott and Griff 1984; Mintz and Schwartz 1985; Stokman et al. 1985; see also Scott 1991a. Some of the key studies of political and economic elites using these methods can be found in Scott 1990a). Such work has examined interlocking directorships and inter-corporate shareholdings, showing the organization of economic power around structured relations between industrial and financial interests (Scott 1997). Central to many such studies has been a critical examination of the managerialist ideas of writers such as Burnham (1941) and Berle and Means (1932), who share many of the assumptions of the pluralist writers. Rejecting this point of view, the works of Mintz and Schwartz in the United States and Scott in Britain have documented the existence of structures of bank centrality through which finance capitalists are able to coordinate the affairs of the numerous corporate boards on which they sit. Through their interlocking directorships, these multiple directors become the most important force in the corporate power structure.

Conclusion

Each of the traditions that I have reviewed has produced important work, showing the potential and the value of the particular methods used to study power. However, each also has its limitations, and I have tried to sketch these out. The trite conclusion is undoubtedly that no one tradition has a monopoly of the truth, and they must, ideally, be combined in a single research design (Dowding 1996: 58ff and see also 1995 where he down-plays the significance of structural concerns in an otherwise useful survey. This seems to be based on his appraisal of the limited results appearing in the relatively new area of policy network research). This is not to say that they carry equal weight. I have argued that the structural approach provides the best basis for integrating the results of research on participation in decision making and the images of power that motivate participants. It provides powerful techniques for mapping and measuring power relations, and it provides the essential framework for understanding processes of decision-making power.

Further Reading

Scott, J. (ed.) 1990: *The Sociology of Elites*, 3 vols., Cheltenham: Edward Elgar.
Scott, J. (ed.) 1994: *Power*, 3 vols., London: Routledge.
Wartenberg, T. E. (ed.) 1992: *Rethinking Power*. Albany: State University of New York Press.

Part II

The State and Governance

9

Formation and Form
Theories of State Formation

GIANFRANCO POGGI

The state is not universal. It emerged in its modern form between the twelfth and eighteenth centuries in western Europe. Poggi focuses on three principal accounts of its formation. The managerial perspective, which emphasizes the top-down aspect of the process: the establishment of increasingly effective political administration over larger and larger territories. The military perspective which, following Weber, emphasizes the state's monopoly of legitimate violence, with particular reference to war. And the economic perspective which, following Marx, sees the state as an outcome of class struggle between producers and exploiters in a capitalist mode of production. Poggi sees each of these perspectives as making important contributions to our understanding of state formation, and, indeed, to our understanding of all aspects of political sociology.

This essay gives a summary and highly selective account of the most significant sociological perspectives on the early and intermediate phases of what one may call statualization – a set of processes taking place in western Europe between the twelfth and the eighteenth century, in the course of which the practice of rule, as concerned a diminishing number of generally larger and more clearly delimited territories, became to a growing extent:

- depersonalized. That is, rule is (in principle) vested in offices rather than in physical individuals as such;
- formalized. The practice of rule increasingly refers to norms which expressly authorize it, mandate it, and control it;
- integrated. Rule increasingly takes into account other aspects of the social process, recognizes their significance and makes some contribution to their persistence, while being at the same time
- differentiated from them. Rule, that is, addresses distinctive concerns and employs special resources (material and symbolic). Finally, it is
- organized. This expression suggests two related and at the same time contrasting phenomena: on the one hand, rule is exercised by and through a plurality of subjects (individual and collective), on the other these subjects constitute together a single unit, which overrides their plurality.

WHY DEAL WITH THESE MATTERS?

As recently as thirty years ago, a work such as this one would probably not have contained an essay devoted to our present topic. At the time, political sociology largely left political institutions to political science. The latter, in turn, showed little concern with "the state" as such, much less with the question of how it had developed. Subsequently, it fell largely to sociologists (though some of these were active both in sociology and in political science) to "bring the state back in" (Evans, Rueschemeyer, and Skocpol (eds.) 1985). Some of them expressly thematized where, when, how, and why the state had come into being and become the key political institution of modernity.

The state was put on the agenda, from the 1960s on, by diverse developments. Some of these were of a pragmatic nature: for instance, the feeling that in the West the "long boom" and the prevalence of social peace owed much to various forms of public intervention in, and regulation of economic and social processes, which shifted and sometimes seemed to erase the state/society divide. On the radical side, some authors emphasized the role played by the welfare state in moderating social conflicts, while others wondered about how long it could continue to play that role.

There were also more specifically intellectual reasons for thematizing the state and its developments. In particular, for reasons not to be discussed here, the nature of modernity and the peculiarity of the West began to exercise the minds of some sociologists, and both these overlapping topics necessarily led to an increased awareness of how distinctive and significant western political arrangements had been, from the Middle Ages on.

Much of the resultant work was inspired by a new appreciation of the theoretical legacy of Max Weber, emphasizing his own concern with juridical and political developments. Oddly enough, however, scholars who appealed chiefly, instead, to Marx's legacy, also moved toward the same themes, in spite of the fact that previously the Marxist tradition had de-emphasized them. In the intellectual climate of the social sciences in the 1970s, marked by a hegemony of Marxism, in some form or other, much of what went under the name of "state theory" was in fact a more or less sophisticated exercise in advanced Marxology, bent upon the peculiar task, say, of "deriving the category of the state" from the concept of capital, or of commodity (Holloway and Picciotto (eds.) 1978; Jessop 1982). But some Marx-inspired authors engaged in a less venturesome, more substantial inquiry into the phases and modalities of the development of the modern state. Even today, some of the more significant contributions to these topics come from authors who appeal to some extent, more or less expressly, to the Marxist tradition (Block 1987).

More recent impulses have come, on the one hand, from the growing significance of such concepts/phenomena as nationalism, citizenship, or the public sphere; on the other, from the increasingly problematical nature of the relationship between "state (or politics) and markets." The accounts of state development, chosen for attention below, emphasize in turn what one may call the managerial, the military, and the economic aspects of "the state's story."

THE MANAGERIAL PERSPECTIVE

My chief witness concerning this view is a short work which has been largely ignored in the current discussion about that story: *On the Medieval Origins of the Modern State*, by the American historian Joseph Strayer. One reason for putting it first is its explicit focus on the early phases of that story, coupled however with a suggestion that "the modern state, wherever we find it today, is based on the pattern which emerged in Europe in the period 1100 to 1600" (Strayer 1970: 12). Over this time:

> [w]e are looking for the appearance of political units persisting in time and fixed in space, the development of permanent, impersonal institutions, agreement on the need for an authority which can give final judgements, and acceptance of the idea that this authority should receive the basic loyalty of its subjects. (Strayer 1970: 10)

The book's relevance in our context rests on its focus on the top-down aspect of the process, that is, on the developing practices and assumptions concerning the political administration of larger territories. Strayer emphasizes both the traits common to most western European experiences (for instance, the practices of consultation between rulers and other powerful individuals or bodies or the importance of law) and some of the contrasts relating to these matters between countries, especially England and France.

The key process, in Strayer's view, consists in the establishment of increasingly effective modes of management of larger and larger territories, put into place on behalf of rulers by growing bodies of professional administrators. He thus concerns himself to a large extent with the evolving practices relating to the recruitment, training, and employment of those administrators, and with the distinctive practices which they develop (often quite self-consciously) and which later become to an extent traditional.

How distinctive and pointed this argument is, in spite of the low-key way in which Strayer advances it, shows what is missing from it – in particular, any bloody-minded, Schmittian sense of the heroic distinctiveness of the political enterprise, of the centrality of the confrontation with "the Other," of the momentousness and drama of political decision, of "the demoniac face of power" (Ritter 1979).

As Strayer depicts it, the development of the modern state is chiefly an ongoing, low-profile process of inventing and adopting/adapting marginally (though sometimes markedly) more effective ways of collecting and husbanding resources, of controlling their employment, of providing services (especially judicial and "police" services) to local communities. As he remarks pointedly, "the first permanent institutions in western Europe dealt with internal not external affairs. High courts of justice and Treasury Departments existed long before Foreign Offices and Departments of Defense" (Strayer 1970: 26).

The individuals active in these primordial offices play the key role in getting a population, in spite of its intense localism, to accept and value the existence of a centrally controlled framework of rule to which it increasingly refers in defining its interests and obligations, and to develop a sense of trans-local commonality (this, Strayer argues, happened first in England). Thus, political units in the process of becoming states are not seen in the first place as conquering entities, but as the growing estates of dominant dynasties, assisted chiefly by managers intent, day-in day-out, upon tending and increasing the dynasty's possessions.

Strayer refers occasionally to the role played in the above process by ecclesiastical personnel, who contributed to it on the one hand a distinctive concern with establishing and maintaining peace, on the other some critical resources, such as literacy and the use of Latin as a trans-local language; and a sense of what it means for a local collectivity (a parish, an abbey) to belong to a higher one (a diocese, the Church at large, a religious order as a whole).

Some years after the publication of Strayer's book, a distinguished legal scholar, Harold Berman, made at length in an impressive book, *Law and Revolution*, a much stronger version of that argument. He does not simply point to the contribution made by ecclesiastics and their distinctive ways of thinking and acting to the construction of states, but holds that "the first state in the West was that which was established in the church by the papacy in the late eleventh and the twelfth century" (Berman 1983: 276). This is chiefly because the Gregorian reformation made express and sustained use of sophisticated, text-based, secular, "rational," institutionally differentiated legal discourse in order to institute, activate, and coordinate ecclesiastical organs – and such discourse was later much used, in properly political bodies, to orient and control binding decisions, including those involving the threat of or the recourse to violence.

Although Strayer had already acknowledged the uses of law in the performance of managerial tasks, Berman follows and complements an earlier tradition of legal and constitutional history in emphasizing the wider significance of law in state-building. Why is law important, and particularly enacted, non-customary law? For one thing, it permits two contrasting requirements to be fulfilled: on the one hand it reduces the contingency in the conduct of public bodies and in the determination of the obligations of subjects/citizens toward them, by tying them to expressly promulgated commands valid in principle "wherever and whenever"; on the other hand, each such law is itself contingent, for, by following certain procedural rules (themselves juridical in nature), it can be set aside by another one. Thus, administrative and judicial bodies can be programed to act in predictable ways, but that programing is itself variable. Also, the validity of existent bodies of law can be extended to new territories, facilitating their incorporation in a given polity.

Furthermore, in the West, on various grounds, law long enjoyed high moral and cultural prestige. It is a sophisticated, highly literate intellectual product, which can be systematized, taught, and examined, and can thus assist rulers and their top administrators in the process of selecting and training the specialized personnel which, through the first centuries of the modern state, is increasingly called upon to replace the feudal and the clerical elements in manning the political establishment. To this extent, Berman's sustained concern with the legal dimension in the development of papal institutions usefully complements Strayer's primary emphasis on other aspects of the management of royal territories.

THE MILITARY PERSPECTIVE

The state is the central political institution; *qua* political, it has an intrinsic connection with violence, emphasized in a famous definition of the state by Weber which Randall Collins has elaborated as follows:

> By "state" we mean a way in which violence is organized. The state consists of individuals in possession of firearms and other weaponry and willing to put them to use: in the version of political organization found in the modern world, these individuals claim the monopoly of such use . . . The state is, in the first instance, the army and the police. (Collins 1975: 181)

Although the distinction itself between army and police is a historical product, and can be institutionalized to a different extent, this statement suggests two different ways in which this theme can be elaborated: one which emphasizes primarily what we may call the "internal" uses of organized violence – law enforcement, the repression and suppression of threats to the public order by the police and the judicial system – and one which emphasizes its "external" uses – war and the military establishment. But in the literature on state development the first mode of elaboration is much less significant, although moves in this direction could be derived, in particular, from Foucault's writings on punishment and surveillance (Foucault 1977; see also Hindess, chapter 4, in this volume). The second, on the other hand, has been much elaborated on in the past, and recently has enjoyed something of a revival. It is, furthermore, more likely to inspire reflections about other significant themes of political theorizing, such as the moral significance of violence in general and war in particular, or on such concepts as sovereignty, territory, the states system, political obligation.

In the context of a discussion about state development, the argument for the significance of war is straightforward. From the beginning, the modern state was shaped by the fact of being essentially intended for war-making, and primarily concerned with establishing and maintaining its military might. In turn, the fortunes of war played the decisive role in shaping the map of Europe and thus the original context of the states system, which found in war the irreplaceable instrument for periodically revising its equilibrium.

Early in the twentieth century Otto Hintze claimed most succinctly that according to all comparative studies, "all state constitution is originally war constitution, military constitution" (Hintze 1970: 53). Later elaborations of this thesis emphasize not so much a direct link, say, between the distribution of military capacities within a population and the structure of the polity, but rather an indirect one: each state derives its institutional arrangements chiefly from the ways in which it goes about providing itself with "the sinews of war" – the material resources necessary to equip itself militarily. Bertrand de Jouvenel's statement of the argument exemplifies this emphasis:

> The intimate tie between war and power is a constant feature of European history . . . If a feudal monarchy succeeded in getting financial aid from the vassals at more

and more frequent intervals and could thus increase the number of mercenaries in its employ, the others had to copy it. If in the end these aids were consolidated into a permanent tax for maintaining a standing army, the movement had to be followed. For, as Adam Smith remarked, "Once the system of having a standing army had been adopted by one civilized nation, all its neighbors had to introduce it; security reasons made it inevitable, for the old militias were quite incapable of resisting an army of this kind." (de Jouvenel 1962: 142)

A recent, very strong restatement of this point, by Tilly (1992), suggests that state structures in general be understood as secondary products of the rulers' efforts to provide themselves with military resources. On the face of it, this might seem to apply only to the core administrative and fiscal structures, those established in the early and middle phases of state development; but one might argue that even arrangements typical of its late phases, and apparently remote from military concerns, sometimes have a military rationale. For instance, some of the early welfare state provisions introduced by the British state were a response to the realization, in the course of the Boer war, that many of the young males brought up in the industrial conurbations were in inadequate physical condition, and thus barely fit for fighting.

A significant component of this kind of argument has always been the connection between the challenge of war on the one hand, and a tendency to tighten the hold of the center on the political organs of the periphery of the state on the other hand. In other words, the proximity, the awareness, and the urgency of that challenge have generated and sustained the "centralization trend" typical of maturing states. Note that this connection is not a prerogative of European states; it can be found in United States, operating in a very different environment, and originally fashioned with the express intent of transcending the European experience. For instance, a recent book by R. F. Bensel (1990) emphasizes the role played by the American Civil War in fostering the progress of central political institutions both in the US and in the Confederacy.

Two significant aspects of the military perspective on state development may be noted. In the first place, its frequent emphasis on fiscal arrangements creates a kind of thematic overlap with what I have called the managerial perspective. In the second place, by the same token it also connects the study of political arrangements with the arrangements dominant in two other spheres of social experience: on the one hand the economy, on the other technology – particularly, of course, the technology of warfare.

This last connection, in particular, is extensively explored in some of the more sophisticated studies developing the military perspective. Warfare technology, itself, is a complex matter: one aspect of it is strictly material, and has to do with the power, precision, and other operational features of the military hardware; the other is largely social, and is constituted chiefly by the ways in which military manpower is raised, trained, deployed, organized, monitored, motivated, etc.

Recent studies have made much of the relationship between the early-modern "military revolution," characterized largely in material terms, and changes in the political, fiscal, administrative arrangements of European states. The title and subtitle of Brian Downing's, *Military Revolution and Political Change: Origins of Democracy and Autocracy in Early Modern Europe*, neatly convey the message (Downing 1992).

In fact, title and subtitle suggest two different emphases, in this book as well as in others adopting the same perspective: a (let us call it) "narrative" emphasis, stressing continuities and discontinuities – of military practice in this case – and the relative adaptations; and a comparative emphasis, stressing instead the variations in those adaptations. In the latter perspective what matters are the different, indeed divergent ways in which rulers respond to developments in the technology (material and social) of warfare.

The broadest generalization suggested by writings advancing this perspective, is that the military revolution makes it necessary for states, if they want to remain in business, to commandeer more resources than the arrangements inherited from the late-medieval past can put at their disposal. Those arrangements (which can be subsumed under one variant or the other of the so-called *Ständestaat*, or "polity of estates") must be either suppressed or complemented by others which increase the discretion of rulers and/or capitalize on the parallel process of economic modernization.

In most cases, the ancient pattern of decentralized military capacity and of *ad hoc* financial levies is replaced by one of three arrangements, all of which substantially increase the extraction of resources to be put to military uses. The main contrast lies perhaps between Prussia and England: the first develops a pattern of "authoritarian" extraction, associated chiefly with a new, centrally imposed and run system of taxation; the latter, a pattern of "negotiated" extraction, which involves first the court, later Parliament as the representative organ of society, and which taps the new resource base constituted by an increasingly commercialized economy via both taxation and (increasingly) a flexible, responsible public debt system. But one must add at least the French pattern, whereby the monarch puts the state in hock by means of a ruinous process of indebtment with which taxation can never catch up.

One reason why much attention has been recently devoted to how such matters were settled in the seventeenth and early eighteenth century is the sense that each of the patterns (and their variants) makes a huge difference to the nature of the state at large, including whether, to what extent, and at what point, it opens itself to constitutionalism, representative government, liberalism. (A book by Thomas Ertman 1997, is particularly significant in this context.) But of course, the perspective also includes later developments in the relation between war and state-making; in particular, it is often claimed that there is a significant connection between, at one end, the advent of mass armies in the late eighteenth century and early nineteenth century, and continuing since then; at the other end, "the entry of masses into politics" characteristic of the later part of the nineteenth and of the twentieth century. In other terms, the military perspective on state development lends itself to extensive and sophisticated elaboration.

THE ECONOMIC PERSPECTIVE

In the interpretation just discussed, the development of the modern state finds its basic rationale in a phenomenon – war – which is a (perhaps *the*) most signific-ant aspect of the political sphere. The next interpretation, however, shifts the focus to a different sphere, the economic one, where the processes of production and distribution of material wealth take place, and views as aspects and com-ponents of those processes, and of the resulting conflicts, political phenomena in general, and the formation and development of the state in particular. This line of thinking has as its main proponents Karl Marx and various thinkers chiefly inspired by him; thus my exposition of it must seek to convey, in however elementary a fashion, the main contentions of Marx's views on politics and the state (see also Jessop, chapter 1, in this volume).

Human life can only be sustained through labor. Beyond a minimal threshold of effectiveness, labor, in its interaction with nature, can yield a greater product than is strictly necessary to reconstitute the individual's capacity to labor, in the form both of product which is surplus to the consumption needs of producers and of embodied products of past labor to be used as instruments of further labor. But both surpluses, being objectivized, can be taken away from those producing them, and put to the service, and placed under the control, of individuals not themselves responsible for producing them.

Typically, the privilege of consuming more than one contributes to the social production process is enjoyed by a minority who make the majority work to own advantage; thus it is intrinsically invidious and contentious, and exposed to the risk of being challenged by the majority. On this account, the minority/majority relationship is always potentially unstable, and must be stabilized by processes external to those of material production: chiefly, the production of symbolic and ideological resources which moderate or divert the majority's resentment of and opposition to their condition, and an asymmetric allocation also of the capacity to exercise coercion.

This capacity (grounded on control over the means of violence, including organization) may play either a direct role in the production/exploitation process (as in slavery or serfdom) or only (or chiefly) an indirect role. In particular, the "feudal mode of production" required the overt submission of the producers to the political superiority of the exploiters, and to the threat of open coercion, because some means of production were under the producers' immediate con-trol. This situation was compatible with (and indeed conducive to) the decen-tralization of authority, and of coercive resources characteristic of feudalism in its political aspects.

However, in the capitalist mode of production, according to Marx, exploita-tion is achieved in a covert manner, not by expressly subjecting the producers to the exploiters, but by means of voluntarily entered, contractual relations between formally free individuals, once these have been dispossessed of any autonomous control over the means of production. This pattern required that rearrangement of political relations and of juridical arrangements which is the core of state development, at any rate in its domestic aspects. In particular:

- Capitalism entails production for the market, centered on exchange values, not on use. As such it requires orderly, purposefully organized cooperation within units and secure exchange between units. An intrinsic aspect of state formation and of the unification of jurisdictions it involves is the widening territorial reach of power centers, which standardize and secure relations between many individuals across wide spaces, making production and exchange easier and more calculable, and more open to continuing rationalization.

- The development of the modern state is associated, particularly on the Continent, with two fundamental developments in the field of private law: the return to the absolute Roman conception of property (*dominium*), and the establishment of contract as the key device for the creation and transmission of rights. Both are indispensable to the mobilization of wealth and to the creation of contingent, open-ended, cash-oriented relations between exchange partners.

- In particular, the contractualization of employer/employee relations allows capitalists to dismiss any responsibility for the workers' livelihood, to treat labor (power) as commodity, buying it to the extent and for the duration required for production and in the light of present or expected market demand and on terms set in turn by the market. According to Marx, this construction of employer/employee relations is critical because it hides the intrinsically exploitative character of the employment relation, wherein the systematic inferiority of all employees (*qua* members of a class) toward all employers (*qua* members of a class) allows the latter to extract unpaid labor from the former, without seeming to.

- The secular movement from "status" to "contract" characteristic of modern law also leads to the emergence of a new kind of collective actor – *class*: a unit of a non-corporate nature, based purely on the convergence of the factual interests of its components, rather than on publicly recognized privileges. To this socio-economic development corresponds, in political terms, a long-run movement toward the formal equality of all citizens which is characteristic of the state.

The absolutization of property allows the abolition of property forms of a communal nature, and thus the expropriation of resources which previously allowed the members of subaltern groups to subsist autonomously, if only on a collective basis, forcing them into the new dependency characteristic of salaried labor. "Absolute" property also entitles those who own it to a privileged claim on the deployment of that coercive power which the state has progressively monopolized and vested in the police and the judiciary. Furthermore, within the new places of production, and signally within the factory, it grounds a despotic control by the capitalist over the expenditure of labor power by workers and over their product, to the end of maximizing profit.

These aspects of the "statualization" of political relations deliver significant, indeed essential requisites of the formation and advance of the capitalist mode of production. Like other, premodern forms of political order, the state is thus critically implicated in upholding the central form of inequality, that constituted by the control, or the exclusion from control, over the means of production characteristic of a given situation: ruling practices secure the exploitation process and the advantages of the dominant minority. For the same reason, all significant changes in the socioeconomic order presuppose a substantial development in the means and the relations of production, but must also have a political dimension, resulting in the changed nature of the ruling class. Thus, for all the differences it may reveal in its phases and in its locales, the modern state also entails the ascent of the bourgeoisie to a dominant political role. In a famous sentence of the Manifesto, "the government is but the executive committee of the bourgeoisie."

For this very reason Marx, Engels, and many Marxist authors display a certain interest in political developments, assuming that certain developments in the formation of public policies, and particularly those centering on the emergence of parties, would in turn play a role in the political dimension of the socialist revolution. However Marx himself, at any rate from the mid-1840s on, paid little sustained attention to major changes in the institutional forms of the state. One might suspect that a more or less explicit economistic bias, while it allows Marx and others to develop (what strikes me as) an insightful view of the process of state development as a whole, seriously limits their capacity for appreciating some significant aspects of it.

At any rate, in the early twentieth century, following Hobson, Lenin interprets imperialism as the "supreme phase" of capitalism, allowing the ruling classes of the West to delay its inevitable fate, and placing the class struggle on what we would call today a global footing. By and large, Marx-inspired writers treat war as the extreme limit case of the conflict between "national fractions" of capital over opportunities for accumulation and/or as ways of diverting the working masses from pursuing their class interest. They interpret fascism chiefly as a different, but not hugely different way of organizing and conducting the business-as-usual of the state in countries where financial capital has prevailed over other forms, and where the bourgeoisie feels particularly threatened by the class war.

Valuable as some of these interpretations may be, they mostly revolve on the question, What kind of political order is necessary for what kind of economic order? Since the latter is conceptualized in a rather simple way, as a succession of only four modes of production (ancient, feudal, Asiatic, capitalist) this mode of analysis becomes essentially unilinear, and pays little attention to the historical variants of the respective political orders – a lack of attention which in the twentieth century was to have unfortunate practical consequences, such as the early refusal of the communist parties outside the Soviet Union, but controlled by the Comintern, to take on board the gravity of the appearance of fascism, and to make a resolute stand for the defense of democratic institutions in the West.

But the interpretation outlined above is only a partial rendering of the Marxist perspective on state development, reflecting only its "objectivist," systemic/functionalist side. Marx's own thinking has another side which emphasizes the class struggle, and acknowledges to some extent the plurality of its protagonists, the variety of the respective interests, and the strategic component in their relations (which class allies itself with which, against which, with what success or lack of it). In this context, it can attribute some significance, among other things, to the various political arrangements associated with those strategies and with their outcomes.

Within the Marxist camp (broadly understood) the best work in this manner, as concerns our topic, is probably that done by Perry Anderson (Anderson 1974a, 1974b). However, an even more impressive, imaginative framework of analysis focused on classes and their strategies, and expressly concerned with varieties of political development and (among other things) of state construction, is embodied in a masterpiece by Barrington Moore, jr. (1969) *Social Origins of Dictatorship and Democracy*. I wind up this chapter by briefly considering this book because, while reflecting upon the early modern era, it is concerned chiefly with a later development, the commercialization of the countryside, and seeks to account for even later ones, such as the nazism and fascism, and the communist-led revolutions of the twentieth century. It also has an expressly comparative focus, as its title itself makes clear.

Moore's relationship to Marx and Marxism is complex. He shares that tradition's tough-minded emphasis on revolution and on revolutionary violence, the attribution to classes and class interest of the key role in historical develop-ment, the assumption that the key relationship between dominant and subaltern groups is one of exploitation, however masked by pretences to the "functional" contribution of the former to the welfare of the latter, the systematic discounting of the significance of "values" and other cultural factors. However, as indicated above, he considers the countryside as the central stage of modernization pro-cesses, and landowners and peasants as its protagonists; he adds to these the ruler and its apparatus, and the town-based burgher and then bourgeois groups – but the working class is nearly nowhere, even in considering twentieth-century events.

Even Moore's construction of, at any rate some moments in the development of, the bourgeoisie is at variance from the standard Marxist construction. He somewhat half-heartedly concedes, in particular, that the French revolution may be labelled "bourgeois," but points out that the bourgeoisie in question had little to do with capitalism proper, and even less with industrial capitalism.

Furthermore, Moore problematizes the Marxist assumption that exploited and oppressed groups will revolt; he also has an acute sense of the contingent nature of major social developments and of the attendant ironies – see for example one of his chapter headings: "England and the contribution of violence to gradualism"! It is again ironic that those revolutions in which peasants have played the most significant role (in the twentieth century, the Russian and the Chinese) are also those which in the end imposed on them the greatest costs and defeats. Even more significant, in our context, is Moore's sense that political institutions matter, and so do differences between them; particularly valuable are those that impose constraints on arbitrary rule, allow the development of just and rational rules, and give the populace some voice in their making.

Finally, as I have already suggested, Moore attaches great weight to the strategic components in the operation of major social groupings, and partic-ularly to their positive or negative alignments and the resultant arrangements in the political sphere. The argument to this effect is, alas, too complex to be reviewed here. But when all is said and done, as I see the matter, *Social Origins*, in an original and sophisticated manner, interprets many critical aspects of political modernization, including some relating to the timing, nature, and shape of statualization, chiefly in the light of the interests of groups constituted around questions of control or exclusion from economic resources. On these grounds, it develops a significant, though of course controversial, interpretation of such events as the great revolutions of the twentieth century, and the rise of fascism and of collectivist states.

CONCLUSION

We have come a long way from a ruler's attempt to increase his dynastic patrimony and optimize its management at the very beginnings of the modern state, to mention an attempt to analyze the fateful contrasts in the nature of the state enterprise in its twentieth-century phase. In this manner, the proposed, simple tripartition between "perspectives" adopted by major students of state development appears relevant not just to the topic of this essay but to others pursued in the volume.

  One may ask oneself which of these perspectives appears more relevant and reliable. The answer would have to be, predictably, that each has something to contribute, and that one should attempt, if anything, to achieve a synthesis between them rather than compel a choice. Some recent works already mentioned expressly aim at such a synthesis: for instance, Tilly's utilizes insights proper to the military and the economic perspectives; and Ertman does the same thing within a framework which, by emphasizing the significance of administrative arrangements, may remind the reader also of the managerial perspective. And one may already see the elements of a masterful synthesis in some of Max Weber's many contributions to the topic, culminating perhaps in the wonderfully compressed version offered in "The Profession and Vocation of Politics" (Weber 1994).

Further Reading

Evans, P. B., Rueschemeyer, D., and Skocpol, T. (eds.) 1985: *Bringing the State Back In*. Cambridge: Cambridge University Press.
Moore, B. jr. 1969: *Social Origins of Dictatorship and Democracy: Lord and Peasant in the Making of the Modern World*. Harmondsworth: Penguin.
Poggi, G. 1990: *The State: its Nature, Development and Prospects*. Cambridge: Polity Press.
Strayer, J. R. 1970: *On the Medieval Origins of the Modern State*. Princeton: Princeton University Press.

10

Political Legitimacy

David Beetham

Claims to political legitimacy try to ground the occupation of positions of political power, to show why they are rightful and why those subject to them should obey. Political sociology is concerned with their effectiveness; the conditions under which legitimacy is realized or eroded and what happens when it fails. The most important writer for the study of political legitimacy is Weber who set the basic questions that must be addressed. Who is the audience for legitimacy claims: the general public or the administration? What is the relation between principles of legitimacy and the organization of systems of power? Weber's own typology of power systems is, however, inadequate to the variety of types that have existed in the twentieth century. Beetham refines it to account for differences between liberal democracy, Marxist–Leninism, theocracy, and fascism. He then discusses why it is that the liberal–democratic mode of legitimacy has become globally prevalent at the start of the twenty-first century.

Since the dawn of human history, those occupying positions of power, and especially political power, have sought to ground their authority in a principle of legitimacy, which shows why their access to, and exercise of, power is rightful, and why those subject to it have a corresponding duty to obey. Mostly such claims to legitimacy have been taken for granted by those involved in power relations. However, where the possession or exercise of power has been substantially contested, whether because it breaches some important interest or established principle of legitimacy, or the principles themselves have proved inadequate to new social circumstances and political forces, then serious reflection and argument about what makes power rightful has taken place. It has usually been the task of philosophers to elaborate such reflection into a considered theory or theories, and to test legitimacy claims against accepted standards of normative validity and discursive argument. From at least the time of the ancient Greeks onwards the study of legitimacy has been central to the practice of political philosophy, through its analysis of normative principles of the right and the good.

The study of legitimacy as a subject for political sociology, by contrast, is comparatively recent, beginning only with the twentieth century. As befits a social science, political sociology's focus is much more empirical than the normative tradition of philosophy. Its concern is less with the abstract validity of legitimacy claims than with their acknowledgment by the relevant social agents, and with the consequences that follow from that acknowledgment for the stability of a system of rule and for the manner in which it is organized. Political sociology is concerned with questions such as: what difference does legitimacy make to the exercise of power? Who constitutes the audience for legitimacy claims? What happens when legitimacy is eroded, or is lacking altogether? What difference do the historically and socially varying bases or principles of legitimacy make to the manner in which political power is organized? Underlying all these questions is a more basic one: what exactly is "legitimacy" as a subject for political sociology?

It was Max Weber in his *Economy and Society* (1978 [1922]) who made legitimacy a key subject in the systematic study of power relations and typologies of power, and hence a central concern for political sociology. Anyone who studies the subject has therefore to come to terms with what Weber wrote about it. In my view, two features of Weber's analysis are important and valuable, while others have proved misleading. The best way of introducing the subject, and debates about it, is to consider these features in turn.

First is what Weber had to say about the significance of legitimacy for power relations, and the instability of systems of authority where legitimacy is lacking. "Custom, personal advantage, purely affectual or ideal motives of solidarity," he wrote, "do not form a sufficiently reliable basis for a given domination. In addition, there is normally a further element, the belief in *legitimacy*" (Weber 1978: 213). In other words, where there is general recognition of the legitimacy of authority, its commands will be followed without the widespread use of coercion, or the constant fear of disobedience or subversion. In this Weber was echoing an earlier observation by the political theorist Rousseau, who wrote that "the strongest is never strong enough to be master, unless he transforms strength into right and obedience into duty" (Rousseau 1963 [1762]: 6).

However, a number of other social theorists have since challenged the assumption that a general recognition of the legitimacy of authority is necessary either to its reliability or to its durability. For most of human history, they would argue, systems of power have been maintained by the effective organization of the means of coercion. What has kept those subordinate in line has been their lack of any means of resistance, and, above all, their belief in their own impotence. This position has been put most forcefully by James C. Scott (1990: ch. 4). The point of the symbolic and ideological elaborations of authority, he argues, is not so much to convince the subordinate of the rightfulness of their subordination – claims which they are perfectly capable of seeing through – as to create an impression of impregnable power, which it is pointless to resist. It is this aura of impregnability, he argues, rather than of moral superiority, that is essential to the stability and durability of power. In so far as legitimacy claims matter, it is to the powerful themselves. It is they who need to be convinced of the rightfulness of their rule if they are to have the self-confidence to maintain it; they constitute the chief audience for their own legitimacy claims (see also Abercrombie and Turner 1978).

Now it should be said that Weber himself was aware of different levels of audience for legitimacy claims. In particular, he was insistent that it was primarily those who were involved in the administration and enforcement of a system of power who had to be convinced of its legitimacy, if the supreme power holders were not to be vulnerable to a "palace coup," or, as in the late Roman Empire, to any usurper who could offer the imperial guards more pay and booty. Moreover, he acknowledged that broader strata of subordinates might submit simply out of helplessness, because there was no alternative. "A system of domination may be so completely protected," he wrote, "on the one hand by the obvious community of interests between the chief and his administrative staff as opposed to the subjects, on the other hand by the helplessness of the latter, that it can afford to drop even the pretence of legitimacy" (Weber 1978: 214).

Yet Weber regarded such a condition as the exception rather than the norm. The norm is for a system of power "to establish and cultivate the belief in its legitimacy." The reason is not far to seek. The more that a power structure is dependent on those subordinate to it for the achievement of its purposes, and especially where the quality of their performance matters, the more essential is it that the relationship is constructed according to an acknowledgment of reciprocal rights and duties such as only a principle of legitimacy can provide. This is particularly true of the modern state, which requires those subject to its authority not only to obey its laws, but to pay their taxes, cooperate with its policies, and even to fight in its defense.

Take, for example, the payment of taxes. By definition, no one likes paying taxes. But it makes an enormous difference to a system of tax collection if people acknowledge the right of the state to tax them and accept the system as broadly fair. Then the vast majority will pay up without demur. Naturally, the administrative arrangements will have to be efficient, and there will have to be compulsion at the margin to deal with backsliders, and to convince the rest that there are no "free riders." But a state where people acknowledge no duty to pay taxes will have to engage in enormously expensive systems of enforcement, which will substantially reduce the overall take, and may even, as in contemporary Russia, compromise its capacity to raise taxes altogether. This means that the effectiveness and the legitimacy of a system of power are not distinct and separable elements, as many sociologists have assumed (see Lipset 1983: ch. 3). This is because the capacity of political authorities is also dependent upon their moral authority or standing among those whose cooperation is required for them to achieve their purposes. So the first main significance of legitimacy lies in the contribution it makes, alongside the organization of the means of administration and coercion, to the reliability, effectiveness, and durability of a system of power.

The second important point Weber had to make about the significance of legitimacy concerned the relationship between the different ideas or principles of legitimacy and the way systems of power were organized in practice. "According to the kind of legitimacy which is claimed," he wrote, "the type of obedience, the kind of administrative staff developed to guarantee it, and the mode of exercising authority, will all differ fundamentally...Hence it is useful to classify the types of domination according to the kind of claim to legitimacy typically made by each." (Weber 1978: 213). Weber is highlighting two things here. All institutional arrangements for the organization of power embody legitimating ideas or principles, which determine how power is attained and by whom, how it is exercised, and within what limits. Understanding institutions is therefore not just a question of giving an empirical description of how they operate, but of exploring the regulative ideas which help explain why they are organized as they are. And it follows, secondly, that we can most usefully construct a typology of different historical and contemporary power systems according to their different legitimating principles or ideas. It was on just such a basis that Weber organized his own political sociology in *Economy and Society*.

This is an important insight, which has significant implications for socio- logical practice, and relates to the broader Weberian method of "interpretative sociology" (Weber 1978: 4–22). The limitation of it lies not in the method itself, but in the particular typology of power systems that Weber constructed from his threefold legitimating principles: traditional, rational-legal, and charismatic, respectively (Weber 1978: 215–16). There is not space to explain fully here what is inadequate with this typology, but it can be summarized as follows: although the three legitimating ideas may help to define what is distinctive about modern, in contrast to pre-modern systems of law and administration, they provide a wholly inadequate basis for characterizing the different political regime types that have existed in the course of the twentieth century. Compar- ative political scientists who have tried to use the Weberian typology for this purpose have usually produced more obfuscation than light. It is not particularly helpful to be told that both liberal democracy and fascism are different variants of charismatic authority, one more rule governed than the other; or that com- munist systems comprised a unique combination of the traditional, rational- legal, and charismatic types (Heller 1982).

To construct a more adequate typology we need to address a basic question: what exactly is it that makes political authorities legitimate, and acknowledged as such by those subordinate to them? The answer lies in an interpretative analysis of the grounds for that acknowledgment, which reveals that legitimacy is multidimensional, not monodimensional: it is constructed from rules, justifi- cations grounded in societal beliefs, and actions expressive of recognition or consent (Beetham 1991: ch. 1). Political authority is legitimate, we can say, to the extent that:

1 it is acquired and exercised according to established rules (legality);
2 the rules are justifiable according to socially accepted beliefs about (i) the rightful source of authority, and (ii) the proper ends and standards of government (normative justifiability);
3 positions of authority are confirmed by express consent or affirmation of appropriate subordinates, and by recognition from other legitimate author- ities (legitimation).

The three levels are not alternatives, since all contribute to legitimacy; together they provide the subordinate with moral grounds for compliance or cooperation with authority. The fact that all are required is shown by the different negative words used to express the different ways in which power may lack legitimacy. If there is a breach of the rules, we use the term "illegitimacy"; if the rules are only weakly supported by societal beliefs, or are deeply contested, we can talk of a "legitimacy deficit"; if consent or recognition is publicly withdrawn or withheld, we speak of "delegitimation."

The most extreme example of *illegitimacy* is usurpation or *coup d'etat* – power attained in violation of the rules. Examples of *legitimacy deficit* are enormously varied: from situations where changing societal beliefs leave existing institutional arrangements unsupported, or those where people have widely diverging beliefs, say, about which state they should belong to; to situations where government is chronically unable to meet the basic purposes, such as welfare or security, which people believe it should. Legitimacy deficits usually only become critical when some performance failure of government exposes a fundamental doubt about its rightful source of authority. Examples of *delegitimation* include acts of widespread public opposition to a regime, of which revolutionary mobilization is the most extreme example. Revolutions follow a typical course from chronic legitimacy deficit of the regime (doubtful or disputed source of authority compounded by performance failure), through its delegitimation by mass oppositional mobilization which splits the governing apparatus, to an illegitimate seizure of power which heralds its reconstruction under a new set of legitimating principles.

The different dimensions of legitimacy outlined above constitute only the most general or abstract framework, the specific content of which has to be "filled in" for each historical society or political system. They provide a heuristic tool to guide analysis. Is political authority valid according to the rules? The relevant rules have to be specified, their conventional or legal form established, the mode of adjudication appropriate to them determined for the given context, and so on. Are the rules justifiable in terms of the beliefs and norms of the particular society, and are these norms relatively uncontested? We need to examine the specific beliefs current in the society about the rightful source of authority, on the one hand, and the proper ends and standards of government, on the other. Are there, finally, actions expressive of consent to authority on the part of those qualified to give it, as well as recognition by other authorities? Who counts as qualified, and what actions count as appropriate, will be determined by the conventions of the given society or system of power, as also what other kinds of authority there are whose recognition has legitimating force.

This overall framework can be used to construct a typology of twentieth-century political systems or regime types according to the different dimensions of legitimacy outlined: their characteristic form of law or legality; their distinctive source of authority; their publicly defined ends or purposes of government; and their typical mode of consent. The results of this typology are to be found in the accompanying table, in which the different systems are portrayed in their most typical form ("ideal-typical" to use the Weberian term).

Military dictatorship has been included here as a limiting case of a non-legitimate political order, born of illegitimacy, and lacking both a rightful source of authority and any mode of expressed consent. Such legitimacy as military regimes have is based entirely on their purpose or mission – to save society from chaos – and is typically defined as transitional, to promote the restoration of a

Table 10.1 Typology of twentieth-century regimes

Regime type	Form of law	Source of authority	Ends of government	Mode of consent
traditional	custom/precedent	hereditary/the past	well-being within traditional order	assembly of social elite
fascist	sovereign will	leadership principle	national purity/ expansion	mass mobilization
communist	sovereign will	party monopoly of Marxist–Leninist truth	building communist future	mass mobilization
theocratic	sacred texts	divine will interpreted by the hierarchy	purifying moral order	various
liberal-democratic	constitutional rule of law	the people through competitive election	individual rights and protection	competitive election
military dictatorship	decree	none	restore order and national unity	none

normal legitimate order. Like all regimes whose legitimacy is limited to the dimension of performance, they are vulnerable once performance falters and their failure exposes their lack of any valid source of authority. Legitimate political orders, in contrast, which are secure in their source of authority, are able to withstand shocks and performance failures, and to effect routine changes of administration which do not threaten the legitimacy of the system itself.

Use of the regime typology can help us to identify what is distinctive about the liberal – democratic mode of legitimacy, in comparison with others, and also help explain why it has come to prevail over the course of the twentieth century. It will be useful to start with its source of authority and mode of consent, since these are the most characteristic democratic features, and bring us to the heart of the difference with the other political systems. First, in liberal democracy the source of political authority lies with the people, and the right to rule derives from electoral choice, rather than from heredity and the past (traditional system), from the party's monopoly of the truth (Marxist–Leninism), from religious authorization (theocracy), or from the exceptional qualities of the leader (fascism). Ever since the principle of popular sovereignty was announced in the eighteenth century, who has counted as "the people" has been a matter of contestation, as progressively those who have been excluded from the political nation – the propertyless, women, racial and other minorities – have demanded inclusion. At the same time, where the boundaries of the nation-state should be drawn has become problematized in a way it never was when the state was regarded simply as the property of the ruling family, and its borders could be altered at will, according to dynastic convenience or military conquest.

Many have argued that nationalism is the major legitimating idea of modern politics, and certainly it has been central in determining the spatial dimensions of the state, and which state people should belong to. It has also been widely used to bolster the legitimacy of rulers, especially non-democratic ones, and to delegitimize those who could be accused of selling out to foreign powers. Yet nationalism does not of itself provide any legitimating basis for appointment to political office, or for a particular kind of political system, and in this key respect it does not constitute an alternative, say, to communism. Moreover, since its legitimating force derives from the same principle as that of democracy – that political authority stems from the people – its articulation always invites the challenge that the people should express the "nation's will" for themselves, through an electoral process, rather than have it merely proclaimed by higher authorities on their behalf.

This brings us to the second key feature of liberal – democratic legitimacy, which is the distinctive method through which consent is expressed to political authority. It is often argued that "consent" as such is distinctive of liberal democracy, but this is mistaken. All political authorities throughout history have sought to bind in key subordinates through actions which express consent to, and confer public recognition on, their authority, and in so doing contribute to its legitimacy. Where systems differ is in who among their subordinates is qualified to give consent or confer recognition, and through what kinds of action. In a traditional system it is key notables who do so through swearing an oath of allegiance, kissing hands, or some other public symbolic act. In posttraditional systems those who are qualified include the population at large. In fascist and communist regimes, however, consent is expressed through acts of mass acclamation and mass mobilization in the regime's cause, which have their counterpart in the secret suppression of all dissent. What is distinctive about liberal democracy is that the process through which consent is conferred – popular election – is the same as that through which political authority is appointed in the first place, whereas in all other systems the expression of consent *follows* the process of appointment to office, which is determined by other means (heredity, priestly selection, inner-party choice, self-appointment, etc.). So it would be more accurate to say that it is the popular *authorization* of government, rather than popular *consent* to it, that is the distinctive feature of liberal–democratic legitimation.

The two other dimensions of liberal–democratic legitimacy exemplify more the characteristically liberal than the democratic components of the portman-teau construct "liberal democracy." Its distinctive purpose of government lies in the protection of individual rights, initially the liberty rights of the eighteenth-century bourgeois revolutions, then increasingly also during the twentieth century the welfare rights of the social–democratic tradition. This emphasis on individual rights contrasts with a variety of collective purposes characteristic of other regime types. And its distinctive mode of legality lies in the constitutional rule of law, in contrast to the customary law of traditional systems, the sacred law of theocratic ones, or law as the expression of sovereign will, whether of the leader or the revolutionary party, as in fascist or communist ones.

Why is it that the liberal–democratic mode of legitimacy, and form of political system, has become globally prevalent by the start of the twenty-first century? This is partly for negative reasons, that other forms of legitimate political order have proved ill-adapted to some key aspect of contemporary economic and social conditions, and have lost their internal legitimacy. The hereditary monopoly of political authority characteristic of traditional systems has proved vulnerable to the modern requirement of a career open to talent, and to popular demands for inclusion in the political process. The Marxist–Leninist goal of a communist society came up against the inherent limits of its system of economic planning, and the party's claim to exclusive knowledge of the workers' interests proved increasingly out of step with their own perceptions of them. The fascist pursuit of radical national goals has typically led to self-destructive wars; or, where these have been avoided, an authority vested in the person of an individual leader has proved unable to survive his death. Theocracies have proved vulnerable to fundamentalisms that have quickly forfeited popularity, or else they have provoked adherents of other faiths to open disaffection or civil war. Each system has had its own internal crisis tendencies, inherent in its legitimating principles or procedures, which have eventually proved terminal (Beetham1991: ch. 6).

Liberal democracy has become prevalent, in contrast, because it has proved the only sustainable legitimate order compatible with the conditions of market capitalism, on the one side, especially in its most advanced form, and with the requirements of multicultural societies on the other. Market capitalism's anti-paternalist principles – individuals are the best judge of their own interests, are responsible for their own fate, and are sovereign in the consumer market – have over time led to the demand for people to be sovereign in the political sphere also, and have undermined all paternalist forms of legitimacy, especially as education has become widespread. At the same time, the increasingly global dimensions of communication have made closed political systems, claiming a monopoly of information and ideology, unsustainable. Finally, the potential antagonisms between different communities cohabiting the same state, which are normal for most contemporary states, can only be peacefully resolved through the methods of dialogue and respect for equal rights, such as are intrinsic to liberal–democratic procedures.

The long-term superiority and survivability of liberal democracy's legitimating principles and procedures do not mean that they are themselves unproblematic. Indeed, they contain their own inherent crisis tendencies. One stems from the inescapable tension between the economic and social inequalities that are as intrinsic to capitalism as to pre-capitalist economic systems, and the equality of citizenship and political voice that democracy promises. This tension requires carefully crafted institutional compromises within the party and political system if it is not to prove unmanageable. The main alternatives are either a pseudo-democracy in which the mass of the people is effectively excluded from power and influence despite the formal exercise of the vote; or else a reversion to dictatorship, when the demands of the masses prove too threatening to the interests of economic and social elites. The second recurrent problem lies in the majoritarian procedure of democracy, which encourages political mobilization along ethnic lines in divided societies, and threatens the permanent exclusion of minorities from power and influence, with the prospect of consequent degeneration into civil war. Again, this requires carefully crafted institutional procedures, such as a form of consociational democracy, to resolve (Lijphart 1977).

It is important to stress, however, that liberal democracy's crisis tendencies, where they have not been institutionally resolved, have never proved terminal, in the sense that they have marked a transition to a different legitimate political order. At most they have led to the suspension of legitimacy, in military dictatorship or other forms of exceptional regime, whose rationale is precisely that they are temporary. These have usually ended in turn with attempts to restore the liberal–democratic form of legitimacy once more. In this sense the twentieth century, though not history itself, has ended with liberal democracy triumphant.

This dominant position has been reinforced at the international level also. For most of the past few centuries, recognition by the international state system has been an important contributor to the domestic legitimacy of states, particularly for newly established regimes. However, this recognition has simply required that regimes demonstrate a *de facto* capacity to exercise power within their territory, and especially within the capital city, and has been quite neutral as to the form of regime, which has been regarded as entirely a domestic matter. Increasingly, however, states are now being required to meet externally monitored legitimacy requirements if they are to achieve full international recognition. At first this has been a human rights requirement, according to the standards of the International Covenant on Civil and Political Rights, as it has increasingly become accepted that how a state treats its own citizens is no longer just an internal matter for the state concerned (Rosas 1995). Since 1989, however, the requirement that a state also meet liberal–democratic principles and procedures in its mode of political organization has started to become generalized as an internationally accepted norm. This norm provides strong external legitimation to domestic political forces engaged in democratization, and is also given practical effect through positive measures of democracy support and through negative pressure where aid, trade, and debt interdependencies are involved.

The liberal–democratic principle of legitimacy has become most fully developed as an international norm within the European political space, as applications from the former communist countries to join the economic club of the European Union have been made dependent on prior membership of the Council of Europe, with its democracy and human rights conditions (Storey 1995). These norms have also been used to legitimate external military intervention in a sovereign European state, as in the Nato war against Yugoslavia over its treatment of the Albanian population in Kosovo. This war serves to mark the decisive shift in international norms away from the principle of unconstrained sovereignty on the part of states over their own internal affairs, regardless of how they treat their populations. It also underlines the deeply problematic character of external intervention, while states still retain a monopoly of physical force over their own territories. There is a serious disjunction, in other words, between the developing normative framework at the international level, and the means available to enforce it.

The development of a democracy and human rights "mission" on the part of the European Union has served to focus attention on the legitimacy of its own political arrangements, which is both contested politically and a source of disagreement among analysts. On the one hand are those who model the EU's authority on that of international institutions, whose legitimacy is derived from recognition by member states, and whose audience for legitimacy claims are the states' own bureaucracies. On the other hand are those who argue that the supranational dimension of the EU's institutions, and the impact its policy and legislation has on the lives of citizens, requires a direct rather than merely indirect form of legitimation; and that this can only be constructed on liberal–democratic principles (see Beetham and Lord 1998: ch.1). At all events, it is clear that political legitimacy in the European political space now involves an inter-active, two-level relationship, between the European levels and that of individual states. In this, the EU is simply the most developed example of what can be seen as a more general feature of political legitimacy in the contemporary world: it is no longer determined simply at the domestic level of the individual state, as it has been for the past few centuries, but is increasingly dependent also on the state's conformity to norms defined at the international level.

Further Reading

Beetham, D. 1991: *The Legitimation of Power.* Basingstoke: Macmillan.
Beetham, D. and Lord, C. J. 1998: *Legitimacy and the European Union.* Harlow: Addison-Wesley-Longman.

11

Gender and the State

R. W. CONNELL

Feminists agree that the state is a gendered institution. How this should be theorized is, however, disputed. The initial feminist critique of gender-ignorant theories of the state resulted in the concept of the patriarchal state, but this is too monolithic. Poststructuralist and postmodern feminist thought tends to abandon the concept of "the state" altogether. What is needed is a theory that is sensitive to diversity, especially in relation to imperialism, postcolonialism, and the international state. Gendered power in relation to the state is complex in contemporary societies, with the impact of globalization, the establishment of "private states" in gated communities, and the disintegration of nation-states following the rise of ethnicity as a principle of political organization. Furthermore, although men are culturally dominant and the state is masculinized, there are groups of men who do not share the power accorded by hegemonic masculinity. Nor do all women share the same relationship to the state. It is important to look at how inequalities and exclusions are produced and at possible strategies for change.

THE GENDER-STATE

Every day we switch on the television to watch the news, and every day men in suits look back at us, speaking seriously into the cameras. Some of those men own the cameras, of course, but many of them simply run the government.

The fact that the institutions of government are run by *men* specifically, not women, is so familiar that most citizens simply take it for granted as a fact of life. It is of course a tradition: men have dominated the public realm in the past (Hearn 1992). But it is a tradition that persists, in a world self-consciously modern or postmodern, with surprising force. The predominance of men over women in positions of power is, statistically, one of the most striking inequalities of contemporary life. Men generally make up about 90 percent of national legislatures, and a higher percentage of top office-holders – cabinet members, senior judges, generals, and elite civil servants.

Not long ago, this fact of life was also a fact of law. Modern feminism began with a struggle for the right to vote, that is, for women's entry into the institutions of the liberal state. Except in a few theocratic states, this struggle has been won; women now have the formal right to be everything from an astronaut to secretary-general of the United Nations. Yet apart from some isolated women (e.g. the current US Secretary of State), and a few countries (e.g. Norway) where women have arrived in parliaments in force, men still run the show. Why?

In everyday discussion, gender (or "sex") is taken to be the attribute of an individual. In social science too, reference to "masculinity" or "femininity" is usually taken as reference to differences in personal traits, temperament, or desire, produced by interpersonal interaction along the lines of "sex roles." With such a conception of gender, there can only be an incidental connection with the state.

It has gradually come to be recognized that this view of gender is inadequate. Gender is also an aspect of institutions and large-scale cultural processes (Connell 1987). Gender is embedded in organizational divisions of labor, in organizational cultures, in symbolic systems, and in patterns of emotional attachment and hostility. Seeing gender this way makes it possible to analyze the state as inherently a gendered institution, inherently a site of gender politics.

During the 1980s such a view spread among thinkers influenced by socialist and radical feminism, resulting in a series of attempts to define a feminist theory of the state. The best known is the work of MacKinnon (1989) in the United States, though other scholars in North America and Europe contributed. Gender issues have been brought into discussions of bureaucracy (Grant and Tancred 1992), international relations (Peterson 1992), and other familiar debates about states. A few years ago I tried to summarize this emerging perspective (Connell 1990) in six theses:

(1)   The state is the central institutionalization of the power relations of gender (power relations being one of the major substructures of gender relations). Conversely the state is, at a fundamental level, constituted by gender relations. The state appears "masculine" because it is a condensation of men's gender power over women. Traditional state theory cannot see gender where only men are present. But where only men are present, we are dealing with a powerful gender effect.

(2)   The state is a gendered institution, marked by its internal gender regime. The social relations within the state are ordered through: (i) a gender division of labor among state personnel, (ii) gendered power relations, for instance in the social definition of legitimate authority, (iii) a structure of emotional relations, including the social construction of sexuality. It is typical of modern state structures that the centers of state power, such as the centers of military and economic decision-making, are heavily masculinized. Though women are not categorically excluded from the state, their interests tend to be represented in more peripheral state agencies, as Grant and Tancred (1992) point out.

(3)   Through its position in gender relations, and its internal gender regime, the state has capacity to regulate gender – and also has incentives to do this. The state develops agencies and policies concerned with gender issues, and acts to

regulate gender relations in the society as a whole. This is not a marginal aspect of state operations. It involves a whole range of policy areas, from housing through education to criminal justice and the military (Franzway et al. 1989).

(4) State activity not only regulates existing gender relations. It also helps to constitute gender relations and the social categories they define. The best-analyzed example is the role of repressive laws and state-backed medicine in constituting the category of "the homosexual" in the late nineteenth century (Greenberg 1988). "The prostitute" was a category constituted by similar processes; "the pedophile" is a category, once medical, now being constituted by law and electoral politics. In somewhat less dramatic form, the categories of "husband" and "wife" are also constituted by state actions ranging from the legal definition of marriage to the design of tax policy and income security systems (Shaver 1989).

(5) Because of these activities and capacities, the state is the key stake in gender politics. It is the focus of most political mobilization on gender issues. Indeed, the rise of the liberal state, with its characteristic legitimation through citizenship, was the focus of a historic change in the form of gender politics. Gender politics, formerly almost entirely local, became mass politics for the first time through the woman suffrage movement.

(6) Since gender relations are historically dynamic, marked by crisis tendencies and structural change, the state as a gendered institution is liable to crisis and transformation. The complex gender politics of the shift from the postwar welfare state to the "downsized" neo-liberal state is an important example.

These points are drawn from the first wave of feminist theorizing on the state. Broadly speaking, that research took as its model the Marxist analysis of the state as a condensation of class relations. This gave the analysis of the gender-state a certain solidity and realism.

But that approach also had limitations, and has come under criticism. Watson (1990) questions whether feminism needs a theory of the state at all; this is a category of patriarchal social theory, and feminism may be better suited by a more fluid understanding of power. Broadly, poststructuralist feminism has de-emphasized issues about institutions in order to focus on culture, identity, and discourse; while postmodern feminism has questioned the universalized claims of "rights" through which feminism has long attempted to influence the liberal state.

At the same time, the sociology of gender has increasingly recognized the internal complexity and multiple forms of gender (Lorber 1994). The attempts to construct a theory of the state have almost all been conducted in rich metropolitan countries; in developing countries, both gender issues and state structures may take very different shapes.

The initial feminist critique of gender-ignorant social theory was entirely justified – and as the examples given at the start of this paper show, constantly needs restating. But the concept of the patriarchal state outlined above was too monolithic, and needs rethinking.

What should replace it is, however, still in dispute. Poststructuralist and postmodern thought tends to abandon the concept of "the state" as such, replacing it with discursive conceptions of "governmentality" or with discussions of local and specific powers. I consider this approach is inadequate. It gives limited understanding of a society of which large-scale organizations are a central feature. It gives little grip on issues of violence, especially the large-scale violence which is so important a feature of twentieth-century history. It gives little understanding of economic issues, and material inequalities ranging from the distribution of wealth to inequalities of health. (The importance of these material issues is not a matter of Marxist dogma, but of the everyday experience of the majority of the population.) And therefore it gives little grip on the *practical* problems of feminist politics, of how one actually contests and changes gender inequality (Eisenstein 1991).

Finally, postmodernism, though rhetorically emphasizing postcolonial diversity, gives little understanding of the actual history of colonialism, anti-colonial struggle, and the creation of the contemporary world order. To this issue I will now turn.

Imperialism, Gender, and the Multiplicity of States

Much writing about politics (including this book) uses the singular universal, "the state." But states are not all the same, did not all arise from the same historical processes, and do not all work the same way. To think that "the state" is always the same is a highly Eurocentric – perhaps more exactly, North-Atlanto-centric – view of the world. Most states in the contemporary world took their modern form because of western imperialism. Imperialism was a gendered process from the start; so the gender patterning of states is linked to the gender dynamics of imperialism.

Colonial States

Colonial conquest often involved a direct assault on gender arrangements. The Portuguese conquerors of Brazil forced indigenous "Indians" into slavery on plantations, or into village settlements rigidly controlled by the church, in which their pagan ways (and languages) would be lost; and imported literally millions of African slaves to provide a labor force for the sugar and coffee industries, disrupting the gender order of indigenous society on both sides of the Atlantic. The Spanish conquerors of Mexico and neighboring Central and North America did similar things, including a violent attack on "sodomy," nearly obliterating the intermediate gender category (the so-called "berdache") that was traditional in many indigenous communities (Williams 1986).

Economic exploitation under settler colonialism in Africa impacted just as strongly. A major disruption of gender relations was required to produce labor forces for plantations and mines. The resulting pattern of poverty, labor migration, and male labor forces living in barracks, produced distinctive gender arrangements – which themselves were subject to disruption and change as the economics of mining changed (Moodie and Ndatshe 1994).

In constructing a social order after conquest, the colonizers produced racialized gender orders. Initial conquest often meant widespread interracial sex (rape, concubinage, and sometimes marriage). But by the high tide of colonialism in the late nineteenth century, all the major empires were operating color bars connected to a gender division of labor. The colonial states were controlled by men, for whom wives were imported from the metropole. The social relations of colonial society revolved around "white women" who directed labor forces of domestic servants but were forbidden political expression (e.g. in Papua New Guinea, Bulbeck 1992).

Postcolonial States

The process of decolonization necessarily challenged the imperial gender order. Some anti-colonial movements mobilized women's support and contested traditional forms of patriarchy, the Chinese communist movement being the best known case (Stacey 1983).

It is familiar, however, that the establishment of a postcolonial or postrevolutionary regime has often meant the reinstallation of patriarchy. Mies' (1986) sardonic observations on the cults of Marxist Founding Fathers are all too apt. The intimidation of women by Islamic-revival movements in Iran, Afghanistan, and some Arab countries is a current example, where feminist attitudes among women are seen as evidence of the western corruption of religion and culture (Tohidi 1991).

Yet the current is not all one way. Women have achieved a considerable level of influence within the Islamic republic of Iran. The postcolonial state in India has provided a political environment in which a feminist movement could develop, known internationally through the journal *Manushi* (Kishwar and Vanita 1984). Of the five successor states to the British Indian Empire, three have had women Prime Ministers and a fourth nearly did.

Metropolitan States

Imperialism impacts on society in the metropole as well as in the colonies. The tremendous scale of the social surplus concentrated in the imperial centers, and now in the financial centers of the global economy, changes the conditions of gender politics. It supports, for instance, the rising expectation of life and the drastic drop in birthrate that has transformed the experience of married women. The politics of reproduction take a different shape in such circumstances. This became a point of tension between third-world and first-world feminisms in the 1980s.

Women's political citizenship developed first on the frontier of European settler colonialism (in North America and Australasia); next in the metropole. Citizenship, however, has been progressively emptied of political content and replaced by the status of consumer, as the commercialization of everyday life and culture intensifies. This has produced an extensive commodification of sexuality, constituting heterosexual men as collective consumers of women's sexual services (e.g. through advertising and pornography).

Thus women's increased presence in the public realm has been counterbalanced by a decline of the public realm itself, and a relocation of power into market mechanisms dominated by men. The old form of state patriarchy, with masculine authority embedded in bureaucratic hierarchies, was vulnerable to challenge through equal rights campaigns.

New forms of management which commodify state services (privatization, corporatization, program budgeting), and neo-liberal administrative reform agendas (Yeatman 1990), have reconstituted state power in forms less open to feminist challenge. It is no accident that these organizational reforms coincided with a "taxpayers' revolt" and tax concessions to business, budgetary attacks on social services (which tend to benefit women), and higher military expenditure in major powers (benefiting mostly men).

The International State

A striking feature of twentieth-century political history is the attempt to overcome the anarchy of the system of sovereign states through permanent international institutions. Some of these agencies link territorial states without themselves having a territorial base. The International Labor Organization is one of the oldest, followed by the League of Nations, the United Nations and its various agencies, the World Bank and International Monetary Fund. Other agencies follow the more traditional pattern of regional customs unions or trading blocs, gradually developing into federal states. The most important of these at present is the European Union.

These agencies too are gendered, and have gender effects. For the most part their gender regimes replicate those of the territorial states that gave rise to them. The international agencies have, however, a specific importance in gender politics as means for the globalization of gender relations. As Stromquist (1995) notes, gender policies at the international level may be more progressive than their local realizations.

This dynamic surfaced in the most explicit address to gender politics by the international state, the United Nations Decade for Women. The international conferences marking the Decade became an arena for conflict over the global significance of western feminism – whether this was a new form of cultural imperialism, or a vital support for indigenous women's movements challenging the patriarchal power of postcolonial states. The fact that the American delegation to the 1985 Nairobi conference was led by the daughter of the most reactionary president in recent US history, with the evident intention of preventing any feminist outcomes, lent an element of black humor to this story. At the follow-up 1995 conference in Beijing, despite vigorous resistance by a coalition of conservative religions and states, and continuing divisions over sexual politics, documents supporting the empowerment of women in a range of fields were produced (Bulbeck 1998).

In other respects international agencies have reinforced rather than challenged local patriarchy. The "male bias" in most development aid is familiar – so scandalous, eventually, that aid agencies such as the World Bank were persuaded to set up special programs for women. But the general economic policies pursued by international agencies since the debt crisis of the 1980s have disadvantaged women. The austerity programs forced on debtor governments have squeezed the welfare sector, on which women are generally more dependent than men, and has favored market mechanisms, which are mostly controlled by men.

We must also acknowledge the scale of intergovernmental links in the realm of violence and espionage. Military aid is the largest single component of international aid. The resources transferred go overwhelmingly into the hands of men. In many cases the armed forces supported by these links became the main political power. These cases include Indonesia, the largest Islamic country in the world; Brazil and Argentina, the largest countries in South America. Military dictatorships are, without exception, patriarchal dictatorships.

GENDER AND THE COMPLEXITIES OF POWER

Mainstream theories of the state tend to erase other powers. For instance, the famous Weberian definition of the state as the holder of the monopoly of legitimate force in a given territory ignores the force used by husbands toward wives. This is a widespread social pattern, whose legitimacy is only now being widely contested, as terms like "domestic violence" come into use (Dobash and Dobash 1992).

Can we regard husbands as a power group? To do so flies in the face of conventional political analysis. But in the context of gender relations, husbands may well be a group with definable interests and the capacity to enforce them. Where family structure is patriarchal, husbands' interests in their wives' sexual and domestic services are institutionalized on a society-wide basis. As shown by Hollway's (1994) study of employment practice in the Tanzanian civil service, state agencies may accommodate to this power to the extent of disrupting explicit equal-opportunity policies.

Gender-ignorant political theory has recognized limits to state power mainly in economic institutions – in corporations and markets, especially multinational corporations and international markets. There has been, without doubt, an erosion of state power over the economy in the last two decades, in the face of capital flight, global sourcing (in manufacturing), and currency deregulation. Discussions of these issues almost never register the fact that global capital is gendered.

International corporations are overwhelmingly controlled by men. They are institutionally gendered in the same ways as the state, and depend on gender divisions of labor in their workforce, for instance in "offshore" manufacturing plants with female workers and male supervisors (Enloe 1990). World capitalism involves a gendered accumulation process, whose dimensions have been shown with great clarity by Mies (1986).

Within the metropolitan countries, the global "North," another power is emerging which might be called private states. There are said to be more private "security" employees in the United States than there are police. Corporations run surveillance programs to control their own employees, commonly using computer technology. Increasing numbers of the ruling class live in "gated communities," housing complexes with fences patrolled by security employees and designed to keep out the poor, the black, and the dispossessed. These private states are gendered: controlled by men, mostly employing men, and in the case of the gated communities, en-gating women. Because their legitimacy depends on property not citizenship, private states escape the political pressure of women which the public state encounters as demands for equal opportunity and affirmative action.

The gender-state, then, is operating in a more complex field of powers than feminist theory has usually registered. This helps explain the phenomenon so forcibly brought to our attention in the 1990s, the disintegration of state structures – even apparently well developed ones such as the USSR.

Seeing the interplay of states with other gendered powers also gives some grip on what has surprised many people, the emergence of ethnicity as a basis of successor states. Given the importance of patriarchy in state legitimation, it is relatively easy to ground a new state on patriarchal local powers. Ethnicity is constituted in large measure through gender relations. The notion of extended "kinship" is central to the rhetoric of ethnicity – "our kith and kin," in the old language of British racism. As Vickers (1994) notes, ethnic politics lays heavy emphasis on women's reproductive powers. Gender relations thus provide a vehicle for new claims to authority (all the leaders of the conflicting states in the former Yugoslavia and the former USSR are men), and define boundaries of the group to which loyalty is demanded.

If we thus develop a more complicated picture of power, we must also recognize more complexity in the picture of gender. "Gender" in academic usage is often a code-word for "women." But "gender" always refers to a structure involving men as well as women. And the participants in gender relations are not two undifferentiated categories, but a complex set of groupings and relationships between groups.

Thus it has become common, in research on men and gender, to speak of "masculinities" rather than "masculinity" (Messerschmidt 1993). In most situations there is a culturally dominant gender pattern for men; but this is a dominant pattern, not a universal one. Only a minority of men may actually live an exemplary masculinity, as defined, say, by Brahmin codes in India, or Hollywood action-hero codes in the United States. Therefore we speak of "hegemonic masculinity," which means precisely that there are also subordinated masculinities (such as found among gay men), marginalized masculinities (e.g. in marginalized ethnic groups), and complicit masculinities, supporting the hegemonic code but not living rigorously by it (Connell 1995).

In the overall structure of gender relations, men are on top; but many men are not on top in terms of sexuality and gender, let alone class and race. This introduces important complexities into gender relations within and around the state. The men of oppressed ethnic groups may develop aggressive versions of hegemonic masculinity, which are criminalized when state elites perceive a problem of order. A striking example is the very high rates of violence and imprisonment among African-American men in the United States. They may also be tapped for the purposes of the state: the same group has a high level of recruitment to the US Army.

The masculinization of the state identified in feminist theory is principally a relationship between state institutions and hegemonic masculinity. This relationship is a two-way street. While hegemonic masculinity is a resource in the struggle for state power, state power is a resource in the struggle for hegemony in gender (a fact clearly apparent to both Christian and Islamic fundamentalists in current struggles).

As with masculinities, it is necessary to acknowledge the diversity of femininities within the gender order, and the complexity of women's relationships with the state. State policy has often constructed femininity as motherhood, but in class-specific or race-specific forms. For instance, welfare policy in the United States discourages young minority women from having babies, or pathologizes them when they do. Labor market policies have often attempted to constitute a docile labor force for domestic service or industrial production, while educational policies pursued the professionalization of middle-class women.

State agencies often discriminate against lesbians (e.g. in employment, in custody of children, in school curricula), and sometimes laws are passed forbidding state agencies to "promote homosexuality" – thus helping sustain women's sexual availability to men by promoting heterosexuality. But at the same time the state may provide pensions for women with dependent children under conditions that deny their sexual availability to men (e.g. through "cohabitation rules").

With increasing integration of world markets and mass communications, local gender orders are increasingly under pressure from a global culture centered in the North Atlantic countries. To some extent this makes for a standardization of gender categories. For instance, research on sexuality has shown, in countries as far apart as Brazil and Indonesia, diverse forms of same-gender sexual relationship among men being replaced by a "gay identity" patterned on the urban culture of the United States. Yet globalization is not flat-out homogenization. As Altman (1996) observes, the emerging homosexual identities of Asia are not all of one pattern; indeed the interplay between local and imported patterns creates a very complex array of sexualities and definitions of gender.

Clearly, not all gender phenomena follow a masculine vs. feminine polarity. There is also a colorful variety of inter-gender and cross-gender identities and practices (Epstein and Straub 1991). These can pose difficulties for the state. If the police arrest someone of mixed or intermediate gender, where is she/he to be imprisoned: in the men's gaol or the women's gaol? Lawsuits have already been fought over this issue. Wherever the state attempts gender segregation, in fact, difficulties arise about policing the boundaries.

CONCLUSION

Gender-ignorant theories of the state are intellectually obsolete. Politically, they can only be regarded as part of the defense of patriarchy, helping to conceal the gender effects of the institutions they purport to analyze.

Gender is important to the analysis of states, both historically and at present. Formal gender equality (e.g. equal right to vote) has not eliminated gender effects or gendered power, though it has changed the circumstances in which patriarchy operates.

Conversely, states are important in the analysis of gender. Once it is acknowledged that gender involves a large-scale structure of social relations, states must be seen as major elements of this structure.

States are not objects, internally homogeneous or fixed in character. Rather, they are configurations of relationships, nodes in wider fields of human practice. Hence they take different forms historically and exist in diverse forms now.

Gender effects are not mechanisms, fixed in their character by essential traits of men and women. No such traits exist. Gender effects are produced by social practice. Large-scale gender effects generally embody some more or less articulate political project; for instance the current shift to market mechanisms in the restructuring of states.

States cannot be understood outside the context of the global history that has produced the modern state system. Nor can their gender effects, as gender is increasingly involved in a global dynamic of change. States must be seen as a key means of the globalization of gender relationships.

At the same time, gender necessarily involves bodies, life histories, and human relationships. The largest-scale dynamics have their consequences in personal lives and face-to-face situations; theory should never lose touch with these consequences.

Some recent gender theories emphasize multiplicity, but not the relationships which produce multiplicity and limit its significance. Relational analysis is required for theories of gender and states to serve democratic purposes. If we are to end inequalities and exclusions we must know how they are produced and sustained, and what are the possible dynamics of change.

Acknowledgment

This chapter draws from a paper presented to the Symposium "Feminist Challenges to Social Theory" at the XIII World Congress of Sociology, Bielefeld, July 1994. I am grateful to all participants in this session, and to colleagues with whom I have discussed these issues in subsequent years.

Further Reading

Kreisky, Eva and Sauer, Birgit (eds.) 2000: *The Gender of Globalization*. Frankfurt am Main: Campus Verlag.
Radtke, H. Lorraine and Stam, Henderikus J. (eds.) 1994: *Power/Gender: Social Relations in Theory and Practice*. London: Sage.

12

Political Processes
Administration, Civil Service, and Bureaucracy

Antonino Palumbo

The New Right attempt to "roll back the frontiers of the state" is underpinned by an analysis derived from neoclassic economics and rational choice theory: New Political Economy (NPE). As an analysis of the state, it is inadequate: it is too simplistic when applied to agents operating in structured, complex institutions; it is unsuitable for application outside the context of the competitive market; and, ideologically driven, it supposes a stark opposition between market and state that actually produces accounts at odds with its individualistic premises. In practice, public policies based on NPE have resulted in greater inefficiencies that, ironically, provide fresh empirical evidence of the government failures they are supposed to correct.

The coming to power of Margaret Thatcher and Ronald Reagan was the starting point of one of the most ambitious social and political experiments carried out in the western world this century. The ultimate goal of this experiment was to "roll back the frontiers of the state"; that is, to reduce the power of the state in society by reforming the welfare state and, above all, the public sector and public administration. Promoting this social experiment was a blend of philosophical, political, and economic theories supplied by a composite movement identified as the New Right. First, there was the idea that the principles underpinning the welfare state were incompatible with individual liberty (Hayek 1960). Second, there was the idea that welfare policies were actually ineffective and inefficient and would, in the end, make everyone worse off (Buchanan and Tullock 1962). These criticisms point out the limits of collective action in solving problems of suboptimality and the tendency of governments and public bureaucracies to distort social incentives for their own sake. In other words, they claim that far from maximizing the common good, politics and government are a means to maximize the wealth and power of unaccountable and parasitic bureaucratic elites (Niskanen 1973; Tullock 1976).

Underpinning the New Right analyses of democracy, government, and bureaucracy there is a highly sophisticated explanatory framework derived from neoclassic economics and rational choice theory (see Dowding, chapter 3, in this volume). Following Inman (1987), I shall call it the New Political Economy

(NPE). At the center of this framework there is the fiction of the *homo oecono-micus* with its crude motivations and predictable actions and the equivalence of politics with *exchange* and democracy with *market* (see Crouch, chapter 22 and Tonkiss, chapter 23, in this volume). The application of this framework to the analysis of collective action and public choice is meant as a departure from the fragmented and inconclusive analyses proposed by sociology and political science (Mitchell and Simmons 1994). According to the New Right iconography, NPE supplies a rigorous, realistic, and value-free analysis of democracy, government activity, and the public sector. In addition, the proposed equivalence between economic and political markets allows NPE to compare the relative efficacy and efficiency of these two productive systems and indicates a direction to pursue to reform political institutions and solve social inefficiencies. I maintain that the economic framework supplied by NPE fails to fulfil those promises. First, the behavioral and methodological assumptions underpinning rational choice make those explanations too simplis-tic when applied to agents operating within highly structured institutions and unable to account for the strategic interaction of collective agencies. Second, the competitive market context within which rational choice models operate makes those explanations unsuitable and misleading when applied to domains which are of a different logical nature. Finally, the stark opposition between market and state and the superficial attention given to market failures make those analyses ideologically-laden and often inconsistent with their own premises:

> Notwithstanding these theoretical faults, NPE has been influential in modifying the way that modern man views government and political process. The romance is gone, perhaps never to be regained. The socialist paradise is lost. Politicians and bureaucrats are seen as ordinary persons much like the rest of us, and "politics" is viewed as a set of arrangements, a game if you will, in which many players with quite disparate objectives interact so as to generate a set of outcomes that may not be either internally consistent or efficient by any standards. (Buchanan 1984: 20

Moreover, as William Niskanen proudly acknowledges, "the policy implications of this literature have encouraged many 'practical experiments' in privatizing the supply of government services, primarily by American state and local govern-ments and by the British government under Prime Minister Margaret Thatcher" (1993: 269). In concluding this essay, I shall consider the policy implications of public choice theory and assess the results of the New Right's attempt to employ those policies for reforming public institutions. First, I note that public choice combines an alleged "realistic" account of the political process as the inefficient interaction of self-seeking agents with the "celebrative" proposition of the market logic and selfish behavior. Second, I maintain that far from resolving the social inefficiencies caused by government growth, the *laissez faire* policies advocated by public choice have generated new and even more complex patterns of inefficiency, thus, unwittingly supplying fresh empirical evidence for the theory of government failures.

THEORIES OF BUREAUCRACY

Following David Beetham (1996), we can single out three main theoretical perspectives from which bureaucracy has been studied. These theoretical perspectives have arrived at alternative and, sometimes, irreconcilable (i) definitions of their object of inquiry, (ii) explanatory accounts of its nature, and (iii) methods for assessing its working.

The first theoretical perspective is that of sociology and its earliest and more exhaustive synthesis is to be found in the work of Max Weber (1922). Weber sees bureaucracy as a form of organization dialectically related to the rise of the national state and modernity. According to him, the building of the national state was largely possible because of the work of the powerful bureaucratic apparatus. The latter supplied political authorities with the resources and personnel needed to break localized and traditional forms of social identity, and build national communities with centralized powers. In addition, Weber describes bureaucracy as a model of organization typical of modern capitalist society dominated by large firms with their instrumental, means-ends, rational approaches. In Weber's model, bureaucratic organizations are described as hierarchical structures operating through a rational and routinized division of work, functions, and roles. Weber puts private and public forms of organization on the same level. For him, the distinctive feature of the bureaucratic ideal-type is not the structure of ownership or the field of activity in which it operates, but the internal articulation and functional relation between offices and roles. As for its assumptions, it relies on a model of man as *role-taking*. Individuals are thought capable of identifying themselves with the values and aims of the social roles which they occupy. As a result, the analysis and assessment of diverse bureaucratic forms of organization are carried out by (i) looking at the dialectic process that caused the emergence of a particular ideal-type and (ii) studying the relation between ideal-types and historical-types.

The second theoretical framework, political science, sees bureaucracy not as a form of organization characterizing modernity, but as a more restricted set of institutions which function to implement political decisions. Bureaucracy thus identified is synonymous with government and public administration. The peculiar character of this form of organization is due to its relation with political power, and its public aims and burdens. Bureaucratic activities are distinguished from other activities for: (i) having a compulsory nature, (ii) being established by law, (iii) aiming at the common good, and (iv) operating under the constraints set by public accountability. Political science as a discipline lacks a distinct methodological approach. Its main distinctive feature resides in the claim that the political domain is not a residual category to the social or the economic. Rather, it sees the political as an autonomous sphere wherein all those activities that are of relevance to the community as a whole take place – the forum. Opposing the economic approach, political science rejects the claim that the common good can be the *by-product* of the interaction of self-concerned individual agents, or that the role of government is that of *aggregating* individual preferences (D. Miller 1993). On the contrary, it maintains that the common good can only be achieved by *intentional* collective actions emerging from a process of *deliberation*. As a result, the analysis and assessment of bureaucratic forms are carried out by (i) looking at the way in which public institutions fit within a constitutional system and (ii) comparing those institutions and that constitutional system with other equivalent institutions and with alternative constitutional systems.

Finally, NPE sees bureaucracy as both an alternative and a complement to the market. Accordingly, bureaucracy is depicted either as an institutional form of production in competition with the market, or as a *sui generis* economic entity dealing with goods that cannot be produced by the market. In the first case, NPE puts forward a sharp distinction between institutions operating within and without a competitive market framework. The term bureaucracy is employed to indicate those hierarchies and relations of authority that are alternative to the decentralized system of interactions of the market, or other than the profit-seeking institutions depicted by neoclassic economics. In the second case, the study of bureaucracy takes the form of a theory of supply for government goods and services. Such a theory attempts to offer a universalistic, and rather abstract, explanatory model of the institutional interaction that goes on within the political sector, rather than an account of the actual working of specific political systems. The economic approach to bureaucracy represents a radical conceptual alternative to the analyses carried out in sociology and political science. Underpinning this approach there is a model of man as *role shaping*. Individuals are depicted as endowed with (sets of) fixed desires and preferences which are both subjective and self-originating. In addition, social roles and functions are thought of as *equilibria* generated by the strategic interaction of self-seeking and unrelated individuals. As a result, the analysis and assessment of bureaucratic forms are carried out by (i) looking at the way in which schemes of incentive and sanctions are structured within hierarchies and (ii) comparing those schemes with the ones available in the marketplace.

Of these three theories of bureaucracy, the economic approach has acquired preeminence at both academic and governmental levels. While NPE has become a main academic subject taught across disciplinary boundaries (thus displacing more traditional approaches), public choice models have been the basis for most of the institutional reforms carried out in the 1980s and 1990s. Three main reasons have been put forward to explain the academic success of NPE *vis-à-vis* sociology and political science: its value-free inquiry, its more realistic assumptions and, finally, its rigorous analysis. These reasons do not stand critical analysis. Despite its claims, NPE has supplied an oversimplified and highly disputable analytical framework which lacks any historical knowledge of the dynamics which are at the roots of our political systems and bureaucratic institutions. In practice, the outcome of the reliance on public choice's remedies has been an array of *laissez-faire* policies with a distinct nineteenth-century flavor; reinforcing the idea that "history itself, far from being unilinear, [is] really cyclical after all" (Beetham 1993: 187).

MARKET FAILURES TO GOVERNMENT FAILURES

The attempt to develop an economic theory of politics and public administration follows the axiomatization of neoclassic equilibrium analysis, the development of welfare economics, and Keynesian macroeconomics. Equilibrium analysis and its axiomatization in the 1940s made clear that markets are prone to failure and require government intervention. As Inman puts it,

> There is a common problem which underlies all market failures, and that [...] common problem is uniquely handled by an institution which can enforce co-operative – that is, collective – behavior in a world where non-cooperative behavior is the preferred individual strategy. Government is one such institution. (1987: 650)

Such an analysis parallels and complements Keynesian macroeconomics and the idea that state intervention is a necessary condition for achieving Pareto-optimality; that is, efficient allocations of social resources. The justification of the economic role of the state as a hierarchical form of production alternative to the market has been questioned repeatedly ever since it was first stated. Three main areas have been the objects of critical attention: (i) the ability of democratic institutions to arrive at efficient social choices (Arrow 1951; Olson 1965), (ii) the neutrality of public institutions in devising and setting public policy (Buchanan and Tullock 1962; Niskanen 1971), and (iii) the effectiveness of Keynesian political economy (von Mises 1944; Hayek 1960). Largely, what goes under the name of NPE is the sum of three bodies of literature dealing with those areas of inquiry.

NPE has imported the analysis of market failures within the public domain and shown that, as for markets, state action is liable to reproduce failure. Welfare economics optimism and reliance on government have then been proven to be misplaced. A related underlying aim of these three critiques is also that of restating traditional liberal criticisms of democracy by clarifying the perverse and self-generating nature of government growth which has occurred since the development of the welfare state (Rowley 1993). In other words, NPE aspires to show that, far from filling the gaps left open by market failures, government growth has caused the emergence of a vicious circle where political attempts to solve social inefficiencies result in serving the rent-seeking attitude of politicians and bureaucrats. The most systematic attempt in this direction has been carried out by public choice theory to which I shall now turn.

PUBLIC CHOICE: METHODS AND AIMS

Public choice has its roots in the works of Anthony Downs (1957), James Buchanan and Gordon Tullock (1962), Mancur Olson (1965), and William Niskanen (1971). Following Dowding (1995b), we can single out two main aspects of public choice theory: its behavioral and methodological foundations and its equilibrium analysis. In line with NPE, public choice regards each institution operating in the public sphere as a strategic player with a well-defined utility function and a simple goal: the maximization of its expected utility. Niskanen describes this approach as:

> The "compositive" method of economics, which develops hypotheses about social behavior from models of purposive behavior by individuals, [which] contrasts with the "collectivist" method of sociology, [and] which develops hypotheses about social behavior from models of role behavior by aggregative ideal types. The [...] bureaucrat is the central figure [...] he is a "chooser" and a "maximizer" [...] not just a "role player" [...] The larger environment influences the behavior of the individual by constraining his set of possible actions, by changing the relations between actions and outcomes, and, to some extent, by influencing his personal preferences. (1971: 5)

In turn, the schemes of incentives and sanctions that characterize the institutional framework wherein interaction takes place are explained as the result of the strategic equilibrium arrived at by the players. Thus, public choice supplies an analytical device aspiring to explanatory and predictive power. This analytical device is then used to explain the self-generating growth of government, the nature of government failures and the relative inefficiency of the public sector.

Although the several authors and schools contributing to public choice share the same epistemic framework, equilibrium analysis is carried out by focusing on the strategic behavior of diverse institutional agents: electorate, politicians, government, and public bureaucracies. Accordingly, there arise three separate equilibrium analyses each of which single out a bargaining game:

- the *democracy game* between citizens and politicians for the production of public goods and redistribution of social resources;
- the *government game* between legislative and government officials for the definition of the objectives singled out in the previous game;
- the *bureaucracy game* between politicians and bureaucrats for the implementation of political decisions and the delivery of cost-effective services. (McLean 1987; Mueller 1989)

Three problems arise from the public choice framework. First, the definition of the various bargaining games underpinning equilibrium analysis is carried out *as if* they unfold in an institutional vacuum. As a result, public choice blurs the distinction between the non-cooperative interaction taking place in state-of-nature-like contexts and the equilibrium stability of alternative institutional solutions. Moreover, it underrates the force of the constitutional setting in influencing the strategic behavior of the players and the fact that the relation between players is often a relation of authority. Second, each game singled out describes the interaction between two institutional agents. To them is attributed a coherent utility function and an unambiguous motivational structure. This "black-boxing" of complex institutions like state, government, and bureaucracy assumes away the strategic relations taking place within each institution and is, therefore, inconsistent with the tenets of the "compositive" method advocated. As a result, public choice commits the selfsame "collectivist" error attributed to sociology. Lastly, the clear-cut results of the equilibrium analysis for each game are often due to the arbitrary way in which strategic power is attributed to some agents rather than others. Typically, each bargaining game takes the form of an asymmetric interaction between a weak and fragmented institutional agent ("open box") and a monolithic counterpart ("black box"). As a result, public choice inconsistently assumes that while one agent has greater difficulty in imposing its authority across the hierarchical line, the other has no difficulty whatsoever in controlling its subordinates. In short, public choice puts forward very rudimentary and questionable analyses of the overall working of the institutions composing our political systems. This is exemplified by Niskanen's "Budget-maximizing model" which I shall now discuss.

THE BUDGET-MAXIMIZING MODEL

The public choice theory of bureaucracy starts with the works of Tullock (1965), Downs (1967), and Niskanen (1971). Of these three, only the last has had a major and enduring influence on the study of bureaucracy and on the New Right political project. Niskanen defines bureaucracy in strict, and very abstract, economic terms: "bureaus are nonprofit organizations which are financed, at least in part, by a periodic appropriation or grant" (1971: 15). Bureaus are also depicted as productive units specialized "in providing those goods and services that some people prefer be supplied in larger amounts than would be supplied by their sale at a per-unit rate" (1971: 18). At the top of the bureau a senior civil servant defines the bureau's policy in line with his own self-interest. The bureaucrat's maximand (his personal goal) is "a positive monotonic function of the total *budget* of the bureau during the bureaucrat's tenure in office" (1971: 38). On the demand side, the bureau's budget is "financed by a single or dominant collective organization which, in turn, is financed by tax revenues or by more or less compulsory contributions" (1971: 24). In a bipartisan system the amount of goods thus financed is defined by the "median-voter theorem" (the sponsor's maximand). Finally, Niskanen describes the relationship between the bureau and its sponsor as a two-person bargaining game. What is the result of this bureaucracy game? Niskanen's thesis is twofold. He maintains that if the sponsor's demand level is low, the bureau will supply double the amount of the goods required. Alternatively, if the sponsor's demand level is high, the bureau will supply the exact quantity of goods required but at a much higher per-unit cost. In the first case, the bureau creates an inefficient allocation of social resources, while in the second case it is productively inefficient.

Niskanen's results depend heavily on many *ad hoc* simplifications. First, the relation between bureau and sponsor is described as characterized by asymmetric information in favor of the bureau. Whilst the bureau has full information of the sponsor's demand level, the latter is held as having defective knowledge of the production process and scarce power of control. Second, there is also an imbalance in bargaining power in favor of the bureau. Whilst the sponsor faces an "all-or-nothing" offer that it cannot reject, the bureau can use its private information of the sponsor's demand level strategically to embarrass the sponsor publicly, or even to bypass it by appealing directly to the electorate. As for the players, Niskanen portrays the sponsor as mainly passive, unable to affirm its authority over the hierarchically subordinate bureaus while incapable of evading the supervision of the electorate. On the contrary, the bureau is pictured as a compact, secretive, and clever player with a single goal and a clear strategy. Now, these assumptions are highly questionable. In fact, not only are they empirically unwarranted, but rely on an arbitrary and partial "black-boxing" of the players and on a too rudimentary definition of the bargaining game.

As for the asymmetric information between sponsor and bureau, Moe (1997) points out that Niskanen confuses two separate issues: information control and agenda setting. This confusion is at the roots of the twofold conclusion reached by Niskanen. In fact, whereas the bureau's agenda setting power is responsible for the allocative inefficiency, the bureau's productive inefficiency is due to its information control. A strong bureau's agenda control seems, however, not just unrealistic, but at odds with public choice analysis of the *democratic game* and *government game*. These two other games also rely on the maximizing behavior of variously identified collective agents (i.e. interest groups, political parties, politicians, ministers, the state). Now, if we allow those agents to have some degree of agenda setting power, their relation with the bureau will be that of a zero-sum game. Therefore, Niskanen needs to clarify how it is possible for the bureaucrat to have such a vast agenda setting power. The public choice story cannot have too many, all too powerful villains, otherwise they will compete against each other and neutralize the power they hold over the electorate. Furthermore, to attribute to the bureau too much information control power underrates the real ability of the politicians to supervise their officials. Parliamentary subcommittees, independent auditors, public service users and bureaucrats' whistle-blowers represent many organizations and sources of information that can complement and reinforce the direct control operated by the sponsor.

In Niskanen's model a crucial source of power is the "all-or-nothing" threat used by the bureau. This power is overstated and unwarranted. Several critics have pointed out that the bargaining power of the bureau cannot be positively related to the whole production, but only to the "reversion level"; that is, the production level prior to the budget review. In turn, this connects with the maximand of the bureaucrat. Niskanen assumes that the latter is positively related to the bureau's budget. Such an assumption, however, does not follow from utility maximization. For, by definition, the bureaucrat cannot appropriate the budget surplus, as the management in the profit-seeking firm does. At most, what is available for appropriation is the bureaucrat's "discretionary budget," that is, "the difference between his total budget and the minimum cost of producing the expected outcome" (Niskanen 1975: 245). Niskanen (1975) is an attempt to meet those objections by revising the basic budget-maximizing model in two directions. First, he redefines the bureaucrat's maximand by relating it to both the "reversion level" and the "discretionary budget." Second, he tries to integrate his equilibrium analysis by using a better account of the supervising power of the politicians. The upshot is a U-turn concerning the agenda setting power of the bureaucrats and their role in distorting the allocation of social resources. Bureaus are still left with a degree of information control which explains why they are productively less efficient than profit-seeking firms. However, this information power is the result of a further simplification. In discussing political control, Niskanen claims that its effectiveness is reduced by (i) the costs involved in carrying such an activity out properly, and (ii) the free-riding problem arising between the legislative and executive who are supposed to do the job. By so doing, however, Niskanen is making the one-sided action of opening the box labelled as "sponsor," while keeping the lid on the "bureau" box.

Dunleavy (1991) gives us an example of what the "bureau" box will look like when this lid is also removed. First, he shows that Niskanen's bureau is nothing more than a collection of departments and agencies composing each department: delivery agency, regulatory agency, transfer agency, contract agency, control agency. Second, Dunleavy also shows that the bureau's budget is very often the sum of a number of different types of budget: (i) a *core budget*, which includes salaries, personnel, and administrative costs; (ii) a *bureau budget*, which includes debt interests and variable contract costs with private firms; (iii) a *program budget*, which includes funds for which the agency is the sponsor of other bureaus; (iv) a *super-program budget*, which includes all the previous budgets and the funds raised by the other agencies. The resulting possibility is of intra- and inter-departmental competition, and the chance of coalitions between the sponsor and subsets of the bureau which render Niskanen's budget-maximizing model far too rudimentary. In fact, not only is the bureaucrat's self-seeking attitude now often shown as unrelated to the bureau's budget but, even when it is so related, it still needs to be specified (i) *which* budget and (ii) *what* the bureaucrat's real power of maximizing that budget is. Clearly, once we open the black-boxes of "sponsor" and "bureau" alike, the result of the bargaining game between the two becomes indeterminate and extremely sensitive to the constitutional setting within which it unfolds. Lacking a clear-cut information power over the sponsor, it is not clear whether there is any *a priori* reason for claiming that bureaus are productively more inefficient than their profit-seeking counterparts.

This conclusion seems shared even by Niskanen himself, who now claims that:

> Bureaus are inefficient suppliers of government services as measured by the interests of the general population, though not in terms of the interests of the members of the legislature. In that sense [...] most of the problems often attributed to bureaus are more fundamentally caused by the structure and decision rules of the legislature, for which bureaus are merely their preferred agents. (1993: 278)

Thus, he admits that the bureaucrat is, perhaps, not the villain of the story and that the *bureaucratic game* is, perhaps, not the relevant game that could explain the self-generating nature of government growth. However, similar arguments used to question Niskanen's model can be replicated concerning the *democratic game* and the *government game* and come up with the same results. In short, I maintain that public choice has failed to fulfil its promise to put political science on solid foundations. Instead, it has ended with a too simplified and ambiguous definition and analysis of the agents, relations and processes taking place in the public arena, and with an *a priori* assertion of the inefficiency of public bureaucracies that is theoretically ungrounded.

The Social Experiment: Rolling Back the Frontiers of the State

NPE has had a massive influence on the New Right critique of big government and public bureaucracies and inspired the 1980s and 1990s reform movement led by the conservative governments of Margaret Thatcher, Ronald Reagan, and their successors. In some instances this sounds ironical for, although public choice presents itself as a research project into government failures, its main criticisms have always been accompanied by clear policy indications. Two major concerns are at the center of NPE's critique: the role of the state and the efficiency of the public sector. While the growth of the modern state is seen as a vicious process causing inefficient allocation of social resources, the public sector is blamed for creating and holding an artificial monopoly power that explains its productive inefficiency. According to this diagnosis, the best solution is that of returning bits of the public sector to the private sector, changing the sources of supply of public services by using market alternatives, and introducing forms of competition within the public administration (Niskanen 1973). The several waves of reform that have repeatedly hit the British Civil Service since early 1980s clearly follow public choice *laissez-faire* solutions and its quest for allocative and productive efficiency and show the limits of such an approach.

Two phases characterize the Conservatives' attempt to reform the British institutions of government. In the first phase (1979/1987), the aim of the government was just that of reducing the relevance of the public sector and improving the productive efficiency of the Civil Service. Means to these ends were the tightening of financial constraints on public spending, the privatization of public assets and the revision of the attitudes of public management toward production and delivery of goods and services. Since 1988, however, the government has engaged in deep structural and organizational reforms which have set in motion controversial and, sometimes, inconsistent processes of change. First, the Civil Service has undergone a process of decentralization designed to make the whole organization more flexible and manageable. Second, the government has established "internal virtual markets" within which the newly created administrative agencies are supposed to vie. Lastly, a blend of privatization, performance related pay, and citizens' charters has been employed to make the public sector more entrepreneurial and the bureaucrats more responsive to consumers' needs (Palumbo 1996). The two phases seem to pursue diverse and not fully compatible goals. Whereas in the first phase the objective of the government is to enhance the productive efficiency of the Civil Service by a better involvement of middle and lower rank managers, the second phase aims at dismantling the Weberian-type of bureaucracy that characterizes the old Civil Service and substituting it with market networks. In turn, these two phases rely on alternative philosophical perspectives. Whereas the first appeals to a philosophy that recognizes the validity of the theory of market failures and is concerned with the efficiency of a "core" of state's activities that has to be retained, the second perspective appeals to the self-regenerating powers of the market and sees public bureaucracies as irredeemable.

What is the result of this array of institutional reforms? A global evaluation of these reforms is not an easy task, for some of the processes are still in progress. It is clear, however, that far from reducing the role of the state in society and increasing the efficiency of society at large, the whole process is creating paradigmatic cases of market failures and affecting the Civil Service's overall effectiveness. In fact, while the process of decentralization has further increased the internal complexity of the Civil Service and, consequently, the risk of coordination failures, the development of internal markets has augmented the strategic interaction between and within agencies. The upshot is the emergence of new asymmetric relations and schemes of incentives which justify a narrow self-seeking behavior. Meanwhile, the privatization process has produced a host of new monopolitistic agencies which are clearly beyond the direct control of the departments, and the growth of a new managerial class whose top salaries are tenfold those of the old mandarins. Last but not least, the various attempts to distinguish and separate administration and policy-making have caused the redefinition of roles and responsibilities between bureaucrats and politicians, thus further blurring the lines of accountability and undermining the work ethics of the Civil Service. In short, what arises is the impression that the overall reform process lacks a clear economic and social cost-benefit analysis, and that the way in which some reforms have been carried out simply represents a tribute to the simplistic suggestions of public choice and the free-market rhetoric of the New Right.

CONCLUSION

NPE's challenge to traditional theories of bureaucracy has had the effect of establishing the economic approach as the dominant paradigm within the social sciences and inspiring large-scale reforms of welfare institutions. At the center of this new paradigm there is a well-defined explanatory model derived from rational choice and neoclassic economics. Its application to the analysis of political institutions and public bureaucracies has led to an allegedly value-free and rigorous account of the institutional interaction that goes on within the political sector. Moreover, by comparing the relative efficiency of the public sector and the market, NPE has supplied clear-cut policy indications as to how to harness the self-seeking attitudes of politicians and bureaucrats alike, and improve the efficiency of society at large. I have cast doubts on both the theoretical and practical achievements of NPE. I have argued that the behavioral and methodological assumptions underpinning rational choice make the explanations supplied by NPE too simplistic when dealing with the strategic interaction of individual agents within highly structured institutions. Also, I have stressed that the "black-boxing" technique imported from neoclassic economics makes public choice accounts of the interaction between political and bureaucratic institutions far too rudimentary and inconsistent with the chosen individualistic platform. Finally, I have claimed that in comparing bureaucratic and market supply, and in proposing the latter as a solution to government failures, public choice fails to draw any lesson from the theory of market failures, to note that actual markets are crowded with hierarchical systems of production that mirror public bureaucracies, and to acknowledge that each institutional form of production can be a historical solution to market breakdowns.

Those theoretical weaknesses have led to simplistic policy indications and self-defeating institutional reforms. First, public choice's call for privatization relies on an ambiguous account of the nature of the monopoly position of the public sector. In fact, if bureau supply concerns the production of "those goods and services that some people prefer be supplied in larger amounts than would be supplied by their sale at a per-unit rate" (Niskanen 1971: 18), it is not clear whether a return to the market will be feasible at all. In other words, if this monopoly position is a solution to a market failure, then privatization will simply create a private monopoly, free from any relation of authority and, therefore, even more difficult to control. A further source of ambiguity surrounds the call for institutional reforms designed to introduce competition and a "new managerial culture" within the public sector. Paradoxically, those suggestions imply the creation of internal markets that revoke the arguments in favor of market socialism and welfare provision fiercely criticized by NPE. Moreover, they pay little attention to the "transaction costs" that those solutions involve and show scarce understanding of the reasons (both theoretical and historical) behind the raising of hierarchical forms of organization. Finally, they rely on analyses à la Niskanen which miss the simple fact that "the bureau may be a monopoly, but the bureau *head* is not a monopolist" (Wintrobe 1997: 446). In short, I maintain that NPE has failed to separate market failures arguments from Keynesian arguments and has put forward solutions that have no bearing on allocative efficiency and show no clear benefits for the consumers.

Further Reading

Beetham, D. 1996: *Bureaucracy*, second edition. Buckingham: Open University Press.
Dunleavy, P. 1991: *Democracy, Bureaucracy and Public Choice*. Hemel Hempstead: Harvester Wheatsheaf.
Green, D. and Shapiro, I. 1994: *Pathologies of Rational Choice: A Critique of Applications in Political Science*. New Haven, CT: Yale University Press.
Niskanen, W. A. 1994: *Bureaucracy and Public Economics*. Cheltenham: Edward Elgar.

13

Policy Networks

PETER JOHN

The study of policy networks offers more insight into how policy is made than the traditional study of political institutions. Decisions are shared between networks of interrelated public and private sector decision-makers who share common expectations and interests. This opens up a central problem of political sociology: the tension between public accountability and the inaccessibility of the policy-making process. The study of policy networks tends to be carried out using case studies because of their context-dependent character. They have focused principally on policy networks at the nation-state level (despite the central assumption of the approach that networks permeate all levels of government). Somewhat different traditions have emerged in different national contexts. Here John briefly describes those of North America, Britain, and Europe. He also discusses the research on subnational policy networks and comparative studies. Finally, he gives some indications of future directions the approach may take towards offering a more explanatory framework, given criticisms of the over-descriptive nature of current studies of policy networks: rational choice theory; formal network analysis; and more detailed case studies.

The image of the network has captured the imagination of public policy scholars. Because public decision-making is so complex, researchers and commentators find that the network metaphor summarizes many of the underlying features of the contemporary policy process. The network idea neatly suggests the manner in which powerful individuals, located in the maze of public and private organizations that govern a policy domain, such as health or public education, connect with each other. Bureaucrats, politicians, experts, and interest group representatives usually discuss public problems and devise the means for their solution. They have common interests that lead them to cooperate and to share ideas. Over time these interactions and exchanges form networks of interrelationships and sets of common expectations. The argument is that these networks are generally bounded in some way and in part are separate from others. To an extent they are obscured from the public glare. Researchers generally ascribe to each network a set of relatively stable characteristics, such as types of exchanges and sets of values that differ according to the sector in question, such as whether it is health, education, or agriculture policy.

As well as offering some simplicity, the study of policy networks promises more insight into how policy is made than the traditional study of political institutions. While the prominence of constitutions and law-making bodies imply that power rests with formal office holders, who are supposed to be accountable to the public, common sense and detailed studies of public decision-making suggest that the sharing of decisions between many public and private sector decision-makers is a much more realistic account of what actually happens. Institutions are important in setting the context of policy, but network studies stress the way in which each domain of public regulation and the nature of public problems and their solution generate certain kinds of relationships and particular patterns of shared interests.

The policy network literature illuminates some of the central concerns of political sociology. By stressing the relationships between different types of power holders, the approach highlights the close connections between the apparatus of the state and institutions of civil society. Public bureaucracies, legislatures, and other public bodies have close links to associations and market organizations. Writers on policy networks stress the blurred boundary between the state and society, and it is networks that fuse the public and private. By studying these partially institutionalized relationships, researchers may study topics like the power of economic elites in policy and the socialization of professional groups. The nature of the network concept ensures researchers discuss the distribution of political power and the exclusion of weak groups from arenas of public decision-making. The power of these largely hidden networks of actors highlights one of the central problems of liberal democracy: the tension between the public aim of accountability and the inaccessibility of the policy-making process. While these concerns appear in mainstream political sociology, the policy network school suggests there are different relationships and implications depending on the public problem. The literature thus adds many nuances to the study of the state. Although policy network analysis simplifies public decision-making, at the same time it acknowledges the variation across and within political institutions.

The network is a portable concept that can be applied to any public arena. Where there is politics there is bound to be networks because the organizations and people involved usually form relationships with each other. The ubiquity of networks partly explains the ease with which the idea has been applied across, within, below, and above nation-states, in what amounts to a massive expansion of the research topic since the 1970s. Whilst researchers can rely on the broad notion of the network to communicate to other scholars, they can adapt the concept to the topic under study.

The context dependent character of network studies predisposes scholars to examine particular examples. Network researchers typically study one domain or sector of public activity, usually at the nation-state level. The investigator sets up semi-structured interviews with the main participants to pose questions about relationships between the decision-makers and to explore examples of policy change and stability. Researchers prize "thick" description, such as detailed case studies, and the approach neatly lends itself to edited book collections and journal special issues (e.g. Schubert and Jordan 1992; Marsh and Rhodes 1992; Marsh 1998) where the editor compares the insights that come from the cases and categorizes what the contributors have found.

THE VARIETY OF APPROACHES

While policy network studies share many similarities, there are two main differences in the way in which researchers approach the topic (leaving aside formal network analysis for the moment). The first is over who are the participants to the network. Are they organizations or individuals? Most researchers investigate connections between the bureaus, agencies, and groups in a policy domain; others examine the individual bureaucrats, politicians, lobbyists, experts, and consultants. The argument for the former unit of analysis is that it tends to sum up most of what is going on – individuals usually act in an organizational capacity where, for example, one bureaucrat can substitute for another. Limiting the possible networks makes the research process manageable. The argument for taking the people as the focus is that organizations are always fragmented and individuals form the building blocks of networks. There is no necessary conflict between these approaches if an organizational approach recognizes the role of individuals and *vice versa*, but the former shows its limitations when researchers seek to measure networks precisely. All that results from organizational analysis is the truism that all public organizations are connected together, a finding which is unlikely to surprise the academic and practitioner communities.

The second difference is between scholars who assume that resources and bargaining characterize networks and others who regard them as a means to transmit ideas. The former sort of researcher draws on Benson's account of the interdependence of organizations (1975), which was applied and popularized by Rhodes (1986, 1988) in his "power-dependence" model. Rhodes argues that organizations seek to deploy different sorts of resources, such as finance and legal sanctions, to obtain what they want from other organizations. The resulting interdependence creates the policy network. The importance of bargaining is implicit in most studies, but recently writers of a rational choice persuasion have taken forward the approach (see below).

Alternatively networks are seen to be constituted by and bound together by ideas. Thus there are epistemic communities of actors who debate common sets of ideas, such as on the international politics of the environment (Haas 1992). In another formulation, policy advocacy coalitions of actors within the same policy domain engage in policy orientated learning (Jenkins-Smith, St. Clair, and Woods 1991; Sabatier and Jenkins-Smith 1993). Within the environmental policy sector, for example, there may be competing coalitions, one for and one against economic development, each with a different set of ideas about how the world works and views about the most appropriate solution. The participants shift positions in their coalitions when they are subject to external changes, such as an economic crisis. In a further refinement, using again the rather too familiar case study of environmental policy, some analysts refer to discourse coalitions where language and debate characterize the relationships between the participants in public decision-making (Hajer 1993, 1997). But the multiplication of labels disguises a similar description that can be summarized as "decision-making = policy networks + ideas."

INSTITUTIONAL CONTEXTS

In keeping with the generally descriptive and reflective character of the policy network approach, most studies cluster in national groups and observe the particularities of and variations within their political institutions. Not only what they describe is different, they approach the topic in a particular way.

North America

The pioneers of the policy network approach were the scholars who studied subgovernment in the US. Here the network idea emerged gradually. What researchers noted first were the close relationships between the types of decision-makers: the executive agencies, Congressional Committees, and interest groups. The participants cooperated in patterns of closed exchanges – hence the use of the term subgovernment. Bentley (1908) set out the field, but it is really Griffith (1939) and Freeman (1955) who led the way with the use of metaphors like the "iron triangle" and "whirlpool" to describe relations between the groups and organizations. The network idea also linked the study of the pork barrel with studies of the close relationships between members of Congress and the particular industries and groups in a district (Maas 1951; Ferejohn 1974). The closed politics of legislative subcommittees allowed them to distort the distribution of public resources to favor districts where there was a powerful member of Congress.

With the emergence of policy studies as part of the discipline of political science in the late 1960s and 1970s, the network idea started to take off (see Jordan 1990 for a review). By stressing the predominance of pressure groups, many studies acknowledged the power of private interests that permeate the weak US state. The fairly autonomous "private governments" can evade scrutiny by democratic institutions and critical publics. Indeed, the subgovernment thesis contributed to the critique of pluralism during the late 1960s with accounts of how private interests captured the public realm (Cater 1964; McConnell 1970). The results of this research reflected the fragmentation of US political institutions and the strength of producer groups.

Heclo's (1978) frequently cited essay popularized the term "issue network" to capture the more fluid and changeable form of political relationships that had emerged in the US after the dramatic events of the late 1960s and early 1970s. Heclo argued that the emergence of more participatory forms of politics, the interest group explosion, and the fragmentation of power in Congress had shattered the cosy world of subgovernments. Instead there were shifting coalitions, made up of the old actors alongside many new ones from the expanded

Congressional staffs, new interest groups, and the lawyers and consultants that congregate in Washington. After Heclo, many studies adapted the network idea to capture the complexity of the relationships between old and new political actors, either across the political system as a whole (e.g. Gais, Peterson, and Walker 1984) or in specific areas such as health care reform (e.g. Peterson 1993). Probably the most thorough attempt to apply the network idea is Browne's study of agricultural policy, which examines the pressure on networks from constituents and state level actors (Browne 1995). Another excellent and nuanced study is Stein and Bickers' (1995) refinement of the pork barrel politics model through a quantitative analysis of the transactions within policy networks. However, there is no US policy network school in the European sense. Researchers have tended to use the idea to investigate other topics, such as the diffusion of innovations (Mintrom and Vergari 1998), the pork barrel, and government aid to industry (Verdier 1995).

In the US network research has also taken on a specialized and methodologically self-conscious character. One strand is the burgeoning sociometric literature. For example, one piece of research example uses network techniques to study the strategies of lobbyists (Carpenter, Esterling, and Lazer 1998). The authors deploy Granovetter's (1973) insight that individuals gain more information through their "weak" ties to other networks than through their "strong" ones to people they know well. Through some impressive data analysis, they show that information in Washington passes through these weak ties and that lobbyists' access depends on these contacts. Another example is the quantitative literature that tests hypotheses from the policy advocacy coalition framework (Sabatier and Jenkins-Smith 1993). Through coding the joint representations of agencies and interest groups to Congressional committees in successive years, they draw a picture of how coalitions change over time thereby meeting a frequent criticism that network studies are largely static in theory and method.

Britain

Network concepts dominated British policy studies for much of the 1980s and 1990s. The field grew out of one of the classic studies of British pressure groups: Richardson and Jordan's *Governing Under Pressure* (1979). Richardson and Jordan's book was path breaking because it utilized network ideas to refine and elaborate understandings of British politics. The work marked a move away from the preoccupation with parties and parliament toward a realization of the importance of the hidden world of policy communities. Notable too was Heclo's and Wildavsky's (1974) detailed accounts of personal networks within the Treasury and across Whitehall. The focus of both studies was the closed and elite character of Britain's governing culture. The former observed close relationships in policy communities of civil servants and producer groups; the latter examined the exclusive group of civil servants, centered in the Treasury, whose personal contacts spanned "village" Whitehall. While these two studies laid the ground, it was Rhodes' (1986, 1988) account of British intergovernmental relations and Marsh and Rhodes' (1992) edited book collection on policy networks in Britain that created the interest. Other studies focused on policy sectors, such as agriculture (Smith 1990, 1991; Jordan, Maloney, and McLaughin 1994), education (Raab 1992), subnational government (Gray 1994), water (Richardson, Maloney, and Rudig 1992), and community care (Hunter and Wistow 1987), and government-industry relations (Wilks and Wright 1987). There were also theoretical contributions (Rhodes 1990; Jordan 1990; Rhodes and Marsh 1992; van Warden 1992). The policy network idea influenced three UK Economic and Social Research Council research programs: the intergovernmental relations initiative, the relations between government and industry initiative, and much of the local governance program.

Commentators note the ambition of some of these studies (Dowding 1995; Thatcher 1998). Writers in the British policy network school have not been content to use the idea as a metaphor or as a descriptive device, but they have set out typologies and have imputed causal power to networks. Rhodes and Marsh made a great play of the distinction between different types of policy network, particularly between the loose and open "issue network" of the Heclo variety and the closed and exclusive policy community. The former occur in some policy sectors, such as consumer affairs, but communities are more the norm in European states. The key idea is that "The existence of a policy network, or more particularly a policy community, constrains the policy agenda and shapes the policy outcomes" (Rhodes and Marsh 1992: 197). The critics have highlighted the lack of clarity in this account. Dowding (1995) writes that the attempts to build a theory "fail because the driving force of explanation, the independent variables, are not network characteristics per se but rather characteristics of components within networks. These components both explain the nature of the network *and* the nature of the policy process." Fortunately, in keeping with English empiricist academic culture, much of the theory is only a brief introduction to descriptive accounts of policy-making in various policy sectors. The network framework becomes a way of organizing the empirical material rather than a model that generates a test. The reader is free to ignore the theoretical claims. As Marsh and Rhodes admit, the policy network is more a research tool than a theory (Marsh 1998; Rhodes and Marsh 1994).

European Country Studies

A different kind of ambition has affected the Europeans. They too have created a massive literature. Some of the leading writers have advocated policy networks as a new form of governance (e.g. Kenis and Schneider 1991; Kooiman 1993), many of whom form part of what has been called the Max-Planck School (see Borzel 1998; pp. 258–65 for a review). These writers stress policy networks are a form of social organization in response to political problems of coordination. Networks facilitate coordination by creating trust and reducing transaction costs. While this idea is fairly straightforward and has useful applications (see Hindmoor 1998 discussed below), these writers make a linguistic meal of it by adding layers of jargon. Just as with the corporatist debate of the 1970s and 1980s, which again was also influenced by German political science, the literature is heavy with conceptualizations of the problem, but has produced few models and testable hypotheses.

The love of theory has affected the French version of policy networks. French writing on public policy has taken a long time to develop as administrative studies have either been dominated by lawyers or organizational theorists, the latter in the school led Michel Crozier. Partly influenced by cross-national debates, a French version of a policy network account has now emerged, marked by the appearance of an edited book (Le Galès and Thatcher 1995). The main exponent and investigator is Pierre Muller who has espoused policy networks as a form of social mediation, making the explanation rather similar to the German account (Jobert and Muller 1987), though some of the empirical findings confirm a more familiar reality of differences between policy sectors and relatively stable closed policy communities. The main unique finding of the French literature is the importance of the professional *corps* at the heart of policy networks.

TERRITORIAL NETWORKS

It is ironic that most research on policy networks has been at the central state level when one of the assumptions of the approach is that networks permeate and link levels of government. Recently, studies of subnational policy networks have appeared (e.g. Bennett and Krebs 1993; Gray 1994; Melbeck 1998; John and Cole 2000). Above the nation-state, some researchers have examined networks at the EU level (e.g. Peterson 1989; Peterson 1995; Bomberg 1998) where the approach has facilitated descriptions of the plethora of bureaus and organizations on the Brussels scene, and has complemented the institutionalized writing on EU decision-making. Just as at the national level, the critics are in hot pursuit with the same set of criticisms – with the added one that the EU is very different from the policy communities surrounding national bureaucracies (Kassim 1994). More innovative than the replications of national studies is the recent explosion of writing on multi-level governance, which has at its core an account of networks between and across the subnational, national, and the supranational levels (e.g. Jeffery 1997). The idea is that policy-making is characterized by interdependence and exchange at all levels of governance.

COMPARATIVE STUDIES

The final example of policy network studies attracts less criticism. There is a small but growing literature comparing policy networks (e.g. Atkinson and Coleman 1989; Marsh 1998). Here the descriptive character of policy network studies can be used to great effect. Rather than seeking to explain policy outputs and outcomes from networks, the researcher can use the comparative method to explain changes to the network. The network becomes what it should usually be: a dependent variable. In this manner, other theories can take the weight of explanation and the researcher can make inferences from the differences and similarities of the networks under study.

FUTURE DIRECTIONS

As indicated by the comparative studies, the policy network approach has the potential to contribute to political science, but at present the descriptive nature of the idea means that it offers useful accounts of policy-making, rather than forming a major part of an explanation. Indeed, the critics are highly pessimistic about attempts to create more intellectual rigor, and prefer modest studies (Dowding 1995; Thatcher 1998). Perhaps it would be best to leave the concept in its current open-ended definition so it is always ready to be interpreted by the researcher who uses it? But there are three possible ways forward.

Rational Choice

The first way forward is to use rational choice theory. Dowding (1995: 145) argues that "the bargaining model and game theory can be fruitfully applied to understand the nature of policy networks." As networks result from bargaining and strategic interaction, researchers may investigate the institutions that create the payoffs to the participants and also examine the effect of the games on the choices of the actors. The recommendation is more easily written than researched as it is very hard to measure the preferences of players in policy games as these change rapidly and are largely hidden from view. The games are likely to be very complex indeed and cannot be represented as a two person or even n-person prisoners' dilemma. The most likely result of a rational choice policy study is that the language of games can be applied as a metaphor to understand the interactions within the domains. But this may end up as similar to policy network analysis as it would be useful and illuminating, but not hard social science. Such an approach would not test a model, but would appeal to intuitions to understand what has happened.

There are, however, some studies in the pipeline which may correct this pessimistic view (e.g. Dowding et al. 1999). The best published one so far is by Hindmoor (1998) who uses transaction cost analysis to give analytical bite to the study of policy networks. He argues that policy communities emerge to reduce transaction costs and to facilitate cooperation and trust. He takes the case study of the formation of the British National Health Service to show that this happened. His conclusion is a surprising defense of Rhodes and Marsh's argument that networks matter. The empirical work is not an impregnable test of a model, as he does not test for other explanations for the emergence of the policy community, but the paper is highly persuasive.

Network Analysis

The second route is to seek improvements to formal network analysis. Network analysis measures the occurrence or frequency of relationships between the members of a network. It draws on a branch of mathematics called graph theory to analyze the properties and structure of networks. The implication of the research is that network structure – whether determined within or from without the networks – counts as it affects the information flows and thus the distribution of power across social organizations. So far the approach and technique have been mainly applied to social relationships (Wasserman and Galaskiewicz 1994; Wasserman and Faust 1994), with specific research on the spread of diseases, searches for employment, kinship relationships, and other social situations. The application to politics has been late. It emerged mainly in the study of elite local and central networks in the 1970s. Formal policy network studies appeared in the late 1980s led by a group of US sociologists. The classic study is by Laumann and Knoke (1987) who examine the differences in policy networks by multidimensionally scaling the distances between actors in US energy and health sectors. In contrast, Heinz and his colleagues find the absence of a core to a network in their study of Washington elites (Heinz, Laumann, Nelson, and Salisbury 1993). Another group of researchers explore the similarities and differences in labor policy networks between the US, Germany, and Japan (Knoke, Pappi, Broadbent, and Tsujinaka 1996). The research discovers that different state traditions and histories of government intervention in the economy are important sources of variation in network structure.

Both policy network researchers and the critics are unhappy with formal analysis. Rhodes argues that "definitional and theoretical proliferation prevail and social network analysis tends to be preoccupied with description and the measurement of linkages" (1990: 295). Keith Dowding writes that "network analysis has proved inadequate in providing fully determined causal analysis of particular networks in structural terms" (1995: 158). He reviews studies, including some of those cited above, to show their meagre or trite results. Thatcher (1998) raises methodological concerns about the selection of the members of the network, the reliability of the responses and bias in the application of techniques, though he only gives one example of these deficiencies.

The critics are right to highlight the limitations of the research tool and its application. One could add further criticisms. It is not clear what the network measures. By counting contacts it is not possible to know whether the research has picked up symbolic, ceremonial, operational, implementation matters as well as policy choices. It is possible that networks merely reflect the ephemera of politics rather than show important relationships and illuminate political power. Second, the boundaries of networks are unclear (Laumann, Marsden, and Prensky 1992), especially policy networks. It would seem that the precise measures used in network analysis impose an arbitrary simplicity onto a complex world. The third criticism is that network analysis is usually cross-sectional and only provides a snapshot of very fluid sets of relationships. If networks change rapidly, it is hard to generalize precisely about what relationships the network measures capture.

These criticisms, however, are largely unfair. They apply a measuring rod that few scientists, let alone social scientists use. The real world is messy and research tools are crude. Social researchers usually recognize these limitations by sensitively applying research methods and techniques rather than blindly running computer packages or throwing up their hands in despair. The problems of network analysis are the familiar ones in quantitative research. Researchers must take care in identifying the network and its boundaries, be aware about changes over time and use their knowledge about the research context to make sensible judgments. Most of all, the critics should realize that even getting modest research results requires a massive effort and that a research subarea usually builds up in knowledge slowly over time. Moreover, while some of the early policy network studies did not yield staggering results, the field has started to move ahead. There is now a literature that, for example, tests changes over time (e.g. Konig 1997), explores visual representations of networks (Brandes et al. 1998) and performs computer simulations of the effect of power and policy preferences on network structures and policy outputs (Stokman and Zeggelink 1996). A recent collection of papers have been brought together in the *Journal of Theoretical Politics* called "Modelling Policy Networks," which includes essays on the formation of policy networks (Konig and Brauninger 1998), the lobbying work by Carpenter et al. (1998) discussed above, and the application of power and policy maximization measures to decision-making in Amsterdam (Stokman and Berveling 1998). The diversity of studies and their interesting results do not suggest the field is an intellectual dead end.

Improved Case Studies

Given the discussion of the benefits of formal modelling, the third and final route to better studies of policy networks may sound surprising. There is a need for more detailed description. What is missing from some of the accounts of policy networks is the feel of the policy process, the complexity of personal and professional connections and the multilayered character of relationships between individuals. So many studies skim the surface with just an account of the decision-making context, an identification of the main participants, and a discussion of the change in policy, when in reality the intensity and perversity of contemporary decision-making needs an approach which can examine the complexity of the links and show how personal contracts can affect policy outcomes and the transfer of policy ideas from place to place. In short, researchers need to push the theory along with rational choice, to model with network analysis but to understand the context with much more thorough descriptions. The tendency toward simplification through modelling and hypothesis testing needs to be complemented by qualitative insights.

Further Reading

Heclo, H. and Wildavsky, A. 1974: *The Private Government of Public Money*. London: Macmillan.

Rhodes, R. A. W. 1990: "Policy networks: A British perspective." *Journal of Theoretical Politics* 2: 293–317.

Richardson, J. J. and Jordan, G. 1979: *Governing Under Pressure: The Policy Process in a Post-Parliamentary Democracy*. Oxford: Martin Robertson.

Stein, R. M. and Bickers, K. 1995: *Perpetuating the Pork Barrel*. Cambridge: Cambridge University Press.

Dowding, K. 1995: "Model or metaphor? A critical review of the policy network approach." *Political Studies* 43: 136–58.

14

Parties and Political Intermediation

HERBERT KITSCHELT

There are two main ways of distinguishing parties from other techniques
for pursuing political objectives: institutional definitions emphasize the
arena in which collective political action takes place; functional definitions
see parties as political alliances for solving problems of collective action
and social choice. Kitschelt here combines the two approaches, asking,
What are the institutional conditions under which the functional criteria
for constituting a political party are met? Different institutional conditions
result in different types of political parties: those with a program that offer
credible policy initiatives and clientalist parties that offer a direct exchange
of goods for votes. In Europe, programmatic parties prevail and political
sociologists have focused on their relation to social divides and cleavages.
Another – oddly unrelated – field of investigation is that of party competition, primarily studied from a rational choice theory perspective. The study
of party organization is rather under-developed – there has been a tendency
to treat parties as unitary actors; the existing literature in political sociology is largely inspired by Michels's early work on party oligarchy. However, new controversies have been generated by debates over the precise
form parties now take in postindustrial democracies. In the final section
Kitschelt outlines two main alternative developments for political parties:
the technocratic–monological model in which existing parties maintain
their dominance aided by professional advice; and the postmodern pluralist
interpretation which sees the potential for a proliferation of new parties
appealing to an increasingly sophisticated and differentiated electorate.

Interest groups, social movements, and political parties are specific techniques
individuals choose to pursue political objectives by pooling resources. People's
goals are *political* when they seek authoritative decisions that are ultimately
backed up by coercion in order to (re)distribute material or non-material life
chances, rights, and privileges. Whether political pursuits take the form of a
political party hinges upon *institutional* or *functional* attributes that distinguish
parties from other modes of collective mobilization.

Institutional definitions of political parties emphasize the arena in which
individuals become collective political actors. Politically motivated individuals
form parties when they combine resources to compete for electoral office. The

institutional definition of parties presupposes the existence of competitive, representative oligarchies or democracies. These polities confer civil and political rights on some or all competent adult members. These include the rights to vote and run as candidates for legislative and executive political office, as well as the rights to articulate political demands, to assemble and to organize collectively.

Functional definitions conceptualize parties as political alliances that articulate and aggregate political demands, or, in a more current vocabulary, that solve problems of collective action and social choice in the pursuit of political goals (Aldrich 1995). When the fruits of political action are shared by an entire community (non-excludability), then no individual member may have an incentive to contribute to the production of that good whenever her costs of fighting for that good exceed her personal benefits of enjoying the good (Olson 1965). Parties represent a technique for solving this problem by making individuals contribute to collective interest articulation and by preventing them from free-riding on the labor of others. Parties also aggregate interests and solve the social choice problem if they employ political organization to identify and to pursue a common preference ordering among political goods that all members support and that overrides their individual preference rankings. The emergence of a social choice function, something we may call a "shared political program" in the context of party politics, helps a democratic community based on majority rule to overcome the potential chaos of perpetually cycling majorities that may result from the individual members' heterogeneous political preference rankings (cf. Riker 1982).

The functional definition of political parties is both wider and narrower than the institutional definition. On the one hand, it qualifies collective political mobilization as parties even *outside* the context of competitive oligarchies or democracies, provided such joint undertakings solve problems of collective action and social choice in the pursuit of political goals (e.g. the Bolsheviks in Tsarist Russia). On the other, it characterizes only a *subset* of politicians' electoral vehicles as political parties within competitive democracies, namely those that articulate *and* aggregate political interests. The empirical discrepancy between the entities institutional or functional definitions identify as parties generates an interesting research question: What are the institutional conditions under which bands of office-seeking politicians will meet the functional criteria for constituting a political party? In a nominalist epistemology, conceptual definitions are a matter of taste, practicality, and theoretical intuition. Once entities have been conceptually defined, however, understanding the way they relate to each other in the empirical world is a matter of developing theoretical propositions and testing them with empirical evidence.

I will first discuss conditions under which entities that qualify as parties by institutional criteria are also parties in the functional sense, i.e. are primarily based on joint programmatic appeals (section 1). I then examine what sort of programmatic political demands structure party alternatives (section 2). This leads me to consider theories of party competition (section 3) and party organization (section 4), followed by final thoughts on the current development of parties in postindustrial democracies (section 5).

Before addressing these issues, let me note two other analytical schemes that may guide the study of parties. They will appear implicitly and explicitly in my discussion, but do not organize the flow of the exposition. First, we may investigate individual parties as self-contained units or as elements of a party system. Analysis of individual parties must often refer back to the systemic configuration of parties in the institutional settings of the polity and vice versa. Second, focusing on individual parties, we may examine them in three respects: (i) as collective undertakings in the electorate that assemble coalitions of supporters; (ii) as strategic units in representative bodies, such as legislatures, or executives (e.g. party coalitions), and (iii) as organizational structures with internal processes of membership recruitment and strategic decision-making.

In the 1950s and 1960s, students of party politics embraced a "bottom-up" theoretical perspective, yielding a *sociology of politics* that treats parties primarily as the result of extra-political economic and cultural processes. Since the 1970s, social scientists have shifted toward a "top-down" *political sociology* which views parties as governed by ambitious elites who bring together social coalitions for strategic purposes under imperatives of electoral competition within the party system. Party goals are not so much an emanation from society as a strategic choice governed by imperatives of competition. Instead of opting for one of the two perspectives on party politics, I find it more useful to examine the interaction between bottom-up and top-down forces shaping the dynamics of party systems.

1 PROGRAMMATIC OR NON-PROGRAMMATIC PARTIES

Politically ambitious citizens solve their collective action problem of running for office by investing in an administrative–technical infrastructure (clerical staff, communication technology, headquarters, public relations materials, etc.) that enables them to harness economies of scale in advertising their candidates, to simplify the voters' choices by offering them recognizable labels on the ballot and even to monitor or physically ensure their supporters' voting turnout by delivering them to the polling stations. Parties solve their social choice problem by working out comprehensive programs through a democratic process of deliberation, the monocratic *fiat* of a leader, or some intermediate oligarchical option. These programs detail policies the parties wishes to pursue if elected to legislative or executive office and relates them to the parties' past policy record. Often allegiance to basic commitments of the program serves as the criterion to admit citizens to party membership.

If politicians address neither the collective action nor the social choice problem, they have no party. We then encounter a situation of *individual representation* where personalities advance their political objectives based on personal public name recognition. Where a multiple of politicians solve the social choice problem of rallying around a program, but not the collective action problem of building an infrastructure to turn out the vote, they approximate the situation of *caucus or framework parties* (Duverger 1954) before the advent of universal suffrage; for example, in the British parliament of the mid-nineteenth century.

Here, politicians coordinated around policy positions, but did not avail themselves of a political machine to advertise their legislative conduct and promote
their reelection.

In twentieth-century mass democracies with universal suffrage, politicians
almost always have to solve the collective action problems through organization
building in the pursuit of political office and power. But they do not necessarily
solve the social choice problem as well. Political parties around the world often
run without a programmatic platform that details credible policy initiatives. A
credible program proposes to compensate electoral supporters *indirectly* for
their vote through policy changes that will affect citizens regardless of whether
they did or did not support the party that won office. By contrast, parties
without credible programs may still attract voters by proposing to them a *direct
exchange* in which citizens surrender votes and financial support for parties,
while the parties, through their public office holders, compensate these supporters through personal monetary payments, gifts in kind, public sector jobs,
housing, favorable regulatory decisions, or government procurement contracts.
In direct exchange, only those voters receive rewards who actually supported the
ruling party or parties. Direct exchange creates *clientelist parties* without party
programs with or programs that lack credibility.

At least three theories, in combination, identify the conditions under which
clientelist or programmatic parties prevail. First, *modernization theories* argue
that poor citizens and, at the systemic level, polities in poor countries support
clientelist parties. Poor citizens want immediate gratification through direct
political exchange, discount the future, and often rely on localized, face-to-face
relations between patrons and clients that facilitate the emergence of clientelist
parties. Conversely, with rising affluence and education and citizens' increasing
spatial social mobility, particularly inside a growing middle class, the better-off
citizens defect from clientelism because they develop a longer time horizon, put
less value on direct clientelist pay-offs (such as unskilled public sector jobs or
public housing), and realize the collective economic costs of a clientelist allocation of public resources.

Second, *statist theories* of clientelism and programmatic party competition
focus on the strategic choices of politicians in the process of democratization
(Shefter 1978). Where the extension of suffrage precedes the rise of a professional state bureaucracy, at least those politicians who initially have access to the
state apparatus can avail themselves of a non-professional bureaucracy and build
clientelist parties. Where this process precedes industrialization, like in the
United States, they might as well preempt the formation of class-based, policy-
oriented working-class parties by offering direct material inducements to the
poverty-stricken expanding working class. More generally, the early rise of
clientelist parties in non-professional state machineries disorganizes programmatic parties. Even in contemporary new Latin American, Southeast Asian, and
Eastern European democracies, the trajectory of professional state building may
affect the nature of exchanges parties seek with electoral constituencies
(Kitschelt et al. 1999). But the existence of large state-owned or state-subsidized
sectors of the economy open to patronage may also explain the existence of
clientelist practices in advanced industrial democracies (Austria, Italy, Japan).

These arrangements come under duress through a growing urban professional middle class unaffiliated with the clientelist party pillars of politics, exacerbated by the economic crisis of state-subsidized industries in the 1980s and 1990s.

Third, *institutionalist theories* argue that the programmatic cohesiveness of parties depends on electoral laws and executive–legislative relations. Where electoral laws personalize relations between voters and individual representatives, such as in first-past-the-post single-member district systems or in multi-member district systems with citizens casting votes for individual candidates, particularly if these votes accrue not to the party list as a whole (non-pooling), clientelist direct exchange between constituencies and politicians is more likely (cf. Katz 1980; Ames 1995; Carey and Shugart 1995). Regardless of electoral district size, a lack of the party central organization's control over the candidate nomination process, such as in systems with primaries, promotes clientelist linkages.

Executive–legislative relations also affect the programmatic cohesiveness of parties. Polities with directly elected presidencies, enjoying strong decree powers, legislative veto powers, powers to appoint and dismiss cabinets, and a host of other prerogatives to influence executive decisions, promote clientelist parties and undercut programmatic competition (Harmel and Janda 1982; Linz and Valenzuela 1994). The personalization of the highest office in the state facilitates direct exchange relations in which presidents award personal favors to individual legislators and constituency members for past and present support. Moreover, presidents employ clientelist incentives and compensation to individual deputies in order to make legislatures compliant to their wishes, thus undermining the programmatic cohesiveness of political parties.

Neither sociological modernization theories nor political science statist and institutional theories, each on their own, can fully explain the distribution of clientelist and programmatic parties and party systems. Descending from party systems to individual parties, *political ideology* may also play an important role in the nature of citizen-party linkages through direct or indirect exchange. Parties with universalist ideologies, like market liberalism or Marxian socialism, are more geared toward programmatic appeals than parties with particularist ideologies based on ethno-national, linguistic, or religious friend–foe identifications that justify the unequal treatment of citizens within the same polity.

In a nutshell, widespread poverty, a non-professional state apparatus (often together with a large state-regulated and subsidized business sector), personalistic electoral laws and governance arrangements, and particularist ideologies favor clientelist parties that do not resolve social choice problems. Conversely, programmatic parties become more likely with rising and widely distributed economic affluence in a polity, a professional state apparatus, impersonal electoral laws, and a collegial cabinet executive dependent on parliamentary majority support.

2 THE NATURE OF PROGRAMMATIC DIVISIONS

Inspired by the experience of European democracies in the twentieth century, most party theorists essentially take the prevalence of programmatic party identities and programmatic competition on "cleavage dimensions" for granted and primarily ask what sorts of dimensions are likely to dominate the democratic political struggle. Cleavages signal a divide between groups in society. But this notion is very colorful and involves a great deal of conceptual ambiguity that requires clarification (cf. Lipset and Rokkan 1967; Rae and Taylor 1970; Lijphart 1977, 1984; Bartolini and Mair 1990). As a linguistic definitional convention, let me distinguish between "divides," "cleavages," and "competitive dimensions" relevant for parties' programmatic appeals. Divide is the generic term for group differences based on citizens' personal traits (e.g. location in the social structure), organizational affiliations or attitudes, and preferences. Cleavages are those divides that are durable, usually because they "entrap" individuals in certain social locations, such as class, or networks. *Social cleavages* are group divides developing in the social organization and public opinion outside party politics. *Political cleavages* are group divides mapped onto party alternatives. Not every social or political divide is a cleavage as well. For example, the question of left or right side driving in Sweden in the 1950s was a temporary divide that never crystallized to become a political cleavage. Furthermore, not every social cleavage also translates into a political cleavage. For example, urban–rural divides have given rise to party alternatives only in a minority of West European democracies.

Competitive dimensions, finally, are only those political cleavages on which party politicians find it worthwhile taking positions with the expectation of attracting new voters. Competitive dimensions thus presuppose voter elasticity, contingent upon politicians' programmatic appeals. Where voters are inelastic in their support profiles, political cleavages constitute *dimensions of identification* (cf. Sani and Sartori 1983). For example, church attendance predicts voting behavior in just about all western and Latin American democracies, yet at the turn of the millennium only in a limited subset of these countries would politicians consider religious–moral issues to be a competitive dimension in electoral politics.

The number of competitive dimensions in a democratic polity is typically much smaller than the number of social and political cleavages. First of all, some social cleavages never make it onto the map of political cleavages because the start-up costs of party formation are too high, the salience of the divide is too low, or existing parties have already partially incorporated the alternatives. Second, many political cleavages constitute dimensions of identification. Third, politicians will do their best to combine salient political divides in mutually reinforcing programmatic packages. If we know a party's position on one salient political cleavage, the chances are we can also predict its position on another divide. From the bottom up, the reason is that voters have limited cognitive capacities to process complex political information. It helps them to conceptualize political alternative in packages situated on a single dimension that often can be conveniently converted into spatial left–right metaphors. From the top down, party politicians may be eager to reduce the dimensionality of political spaces in order to maintain the integrity of their own parties and prevent internal splits, prompted by cross-cutting cleavages.

Sophisticated political sociologists always knew that neither a purely sociological bottom-up nor a purely political-elite driven top-down theory could account for political cleavages and competitive dimensions (Lipset and Rokkan 1967). Lipset and Rokkan's famous four cleavage dimensions in European politics represent only *social cleavages*. The first two, the center/periphery and the religious denominational or religious/secular divides, are associated with the national revolution of state formation in fifteenth-through twentieth-century Europe. The second set of urban–rural and social class cleavages relate to the social dislocations and conflicts brought about by the industrial revolution. Whether or not these social cleavages translate into political cleavages, let alone competitive dimensions, according to Lipset and Rokkan hinges on a host of institutional and strategic conditions.

Much of the literature since Lipset and Rokkan's seminal article has focused on reconsidering the list of social cleavage dimensions they proposed and on the conditions under which they convert into political cleavages and competitive dimensions. From the vantage point of the new millennium, the original list of cleavages appears dated and historically as well as geographically contingent. Outside western Europe, ethno-cultural cleavages that are not fully captured by Lipset and Rokkan's center/periphery divide have certainly played an increasing role (cf. Lijphart 1977; Horowitz 1985). Conversely, some of their key cleavages have faded and are now better redescribed as special cases of a broader analytical scheme. The literature on social and political cleavage divides outside western Europe is now growing, covering regions such as Latin America (Dix 1989; Collier and Collier 1991) or Eastern Europe (Kitschelt 1992; Evans and Whitefield 1993; Fish 1995; Kitschelt et al. 2000).

One approach to the study of cleavages is inductive, based on survey research (cf. Knutsen and Scarbrough 1995). While valuable, it tends to inflate the number of cleavage dimensions, focus on social divides and underappreciate the *reductive effect* of political elites on competitive dimensions. Analytical approaches tend to focus more on salient political divides and competitive dimensions. My own favorite classification relies on three categories (cf. Kitschelt 1992). First, distributive cleavages concern citizens' market positions and material benefits. These social cleavages are sufficiently intense to convert into political cleavages in almost all programmatically–based party systems, even though they tend to be suppressed in clientelist systems. Class and urban–rural divides are special cases of the distributive cleavage dimension, just as are divides between sectors and occupational groups. The divide concerns economic policy preferences running from support for spontaneous market exchange as the preferred mode of allocating scarce resources to a preference for a state-governed distributive policy. Second, sociocultural cleavages divide individualist and universalist libertarians who also embrace participatory collective decision-making and a broad scope of personal freedom of lifestyles from collectivist, particularist authoritarians who endorse top-down binding commands and individual compliance with group rules. Third, ethno-cultural cleavages define friend–foe relations based on ascriptive and often immutable group membership and concern the very political definition of citizenship.

Social and political cleavages that fall under these three headings may be analytically distinct, but they often reinforce each other in empirical reality, though in different configurations. For example, where ethnic minorities are both politically and economically disadvantaged, they may opt for a state-led distribution of scarce resources rather than market allocation. Conversely, ethnic minorities with economic advantages may favor spontaneous market allocation of economic assets. Much future research must account for contrasting alignments of political cleavages and their contribution to competitive dimensions in party systems particularly in the more recently founded democracies.

Social scientists have advanced explanations of social cleavages in a top-down or a bottom-up mode. For extreme proponents of the elite-centered view, citizens are like pieces of clay in the hands of politicians as master-potters who mold the cognitive and normative orientations of their subjects and rally them around parties. Thus, whether citizens believe in social class as the leading political divide depends on the effort politicians make to frame political conflict in terms of class (Przeworski 1985). Conversely, sociologists have argued that it is preexisting social conditions, such as religious pluralism, ethnic heterogeneity, and class inequality that structure the rise of political alternatives. Neither of these alternatives may be entirely convincing. Accounting for the number and ideological configuration of parties in a party system or the rise of new parties is likely to involve both reference to the sociocultural conditions of a society as well as the institutional and strategic opportunities political elites are facing. Thus, electoral laws stipulating high thresholds of representation and imposing high entry costs on the entrepreneurs of new parties, may restrain the number of political cleavage lines in a system, but they cannot fully explain the party system format and the substantive programmatic alternatives incorporated in the party system (cf. Cox 1997: ch. 11). In the same spirit, the rise of new left-libertarian or right-authoritarian parties in western Europe depends not only on electoral laws and other entry thresholds, but critically both on the underlying socio-economic conditions of different societies and their existing strategic alignments that provide more or fewer incentives for politicians to build new independent parties (Kitschelt 1989, 1995).

A, by now, old debate, going back to the early 1960s, concerns the disappearance of social and political cleavages in favor of a "dealigned" electorate, ready to switch sides based on temporary issue appeals, and willing to follow broad "catch-all" parties that have lost their grounding in specific electoral constituencies (cf. Kirchheimer 1965; Dalton, Flanagan, and Beck 1984). While the demise of Marxian socialism, the change of the class structure of advanced capitalist democracies, and the rise of mixed economies with comprehensive welfare states have certainly dismantled the programmatic alternatives on distributive politics that prevailed in West European democracies in the first half of the twentieth century (cf. Inglehart 1990: chs. 5, 8), it is questionable whether the party affiliations of electorates have become more unstructured and whether economic policy conflicts play a lesser role for contemporary political competition. What observers in the 1960s and 1970s initially described as "dealignment" has often turned out to be the beginning of a "realignment" of political forces where distributive conflicts are cast in a new way and where they associate with new sociocultural divides. An upward shift in the parties' net volatility of electoral support from one election to a subsequent one would be a plausible signal of the decreasing stability of partisan alignments. After an upward blip in the 1970s, these volatility rates settled back to a historically familiar pattern and show little sign of a permanent upward shift (cf. Bartolini and Mair 1990).

Compared to advanced industrial democracies, it is much harder to determine whether political cleavage alignments congeal in most of the new Latin American, Southeast Asian, and East European party systems. The newness of democratic competition, as well as incentives to build clientelist exchange relations between voters and politicians may jointly inhibit the consolidation of cleavage dimensions. In such polities, initially hordes of political entrepreneurs with independent proto-parties crowd the electoral arena and it may take several elections before the institutional rules of democratic competition, together with the new patterns of socioeconomic and cultural governance in these countries, cause a shake-out among these contenders and reduce the number of parties to manageable complexity. Until then, the parties' and party systems' volatility rates in these democracies tend to be extremely high. Sometimes, however, these bald indicators are not sufficiently detailed to determine the quality of electoral volatility. Stability is certainly greater, first, if volatility derives from the circulation of voters among existing parties rather than between them and new parties and when, second, voters circulate only among parties with similar issue appeals rather than across the boundaries between blocs and sectors of programmatically similar parties.

3 PARTY COMPETITION

The literature on political party alignments should have a natural affinity to the study of party competition, but these two fields have often remained divorced from each other. Whereas the former tends to attract political sociologists and comparative political scientists, the latter draws on economists and rational choice theorists broadly conceived. Whereas the former is more inductive, *ad hoc* historical and empirical, the latter is more formal, general, and deductive, but often void of empirical analysis (for an overview, see Ordeshook 1997 and Schofield 1997). More work needs to be done at the interstices of these two fields.

The most influential theory of party competition originates in Anthony Downs' (1957) spatial theory of competition and information processing. The model assumes politicians and parties seeking executive political office, rather than votes or policies for their own sake. Voters are information misers who recognize only the barest outlines of politicians' announced policy positions, base the estimation of politicians' credibility on their perceived past performance, and vote for the party that is closest to their own ideal policy preference. As a consequence, parties frame their appeals to be in the proximity of as many voters as they need to maximize their chances for winning executive office, contingent upon the constraints imposed on them by the strategies of their competitors. To convert this general underlying model of party position taking and voter choice into empirically operational propositions is a difficult undertaking, as legions of formal theorists have discovered (see Enelow and Hinich 1984, 1990). Downs' main medium-voter theorem, that parties in a two-party contest will make appeals close to the ideal preferences of the median voter, applies only under highly idealized conditions (for example, no entry threats by new parties or abstention by voters; unidimensionality of party competition; voter preferences focused on the next election only). Under conditions of multi-party competition, by contrast, it is more likely that parties have incentives to spread their appeals over the entire range of the competitive policy dimensions, contingent upon institutional restrictions imposed on the entry of new competitors.

Several factors complicate the formal analysis of party competition and usually make it difficult to rigorously derive empirically relevant equilibrium strategies for political parties from formal analysis: the multi-dimensionality of party competition, the multiplicity of competitors and virtual competitors (entry threat), sophisticated voting for "second best" alternatives, long-term party strategies (sacrificing votes now to win them later), or short-term heterogeneity of party objectives (office-seeking, vote-seeking, policy-seeking: see Strom 1990a). Nevertheless, the spatial party competition literature has also had tremendous influence on the literature discussing inter-party coalition formation (for recent works, see Laver and Schofield 1990; Strom 1990b; Schofield 1993; Laver and Shepsle 1996). The literature on both party competition and coalition formation can branch out in two directions at this time. On the one hand, it can seek to refine the formal models to derive more realistic and testable equilibrium strategies. On the other, it can seek to impose *behavioral restrictions* on voters' and politicians' rationality and thus make it easier to derive equilibrium conditions. An early example of this strategy is Sartori's (1976) analysis of moderate and polarized multi-party pluralism. I, for one, find the latter strategy more feasible, interesting, and relevant for political sociology (cf. Kitschelt 1994). Even formal theorists begin to have second thoughts about the marginal payoffs of further progress through more sophisticated formal models (Ordeshook 1997: 268–70). Recent work on the constraints for party competition imposed by electoral laws begins to consider these behavioral limitations as well (cf. Cox 1997).

Two behaviorally inspired theories have challenged the spatial models of party competition and called for amendments, if not fundamental revisions of the model. First, Budge and Farlie (1983) developed a salience theory of competition based on the assumption that most issues are valence issues such that voters agree on the desirable outcome (e.g. low unemployment), but ascribe different competence to political competitors in realizing such objectives. The competitive skill of politicians then consists in their ability to advance the salience of those issues for which their party "owns" the credibility and competence attribution of the electorate and de-emphasize the issues owned by competitors. The problem of this theory is that issues usually can be mapped onto competitive dimensions (Hinich and Munger 1996) and thus can be understood in the spatial–positional model. Empirically, the investigations inspired by the valence/salience theory of competition employed measurement instruments that led them back to spatial models (for a critique: Kitschelt 1994: 201–3).

The other interesting, behaviorally inspired model of competition is the *directional theory* advanced by Rabinowitz and MacDonald (1989) and giving rise to a voluminous controversy (e.g. Iversen 1994; Westholm 1997). Parties must express clearly articulated, though not extreme, positions to catch the voters' attention. Voters support the parties that have such stark positions on the side of the issue they are leaning toward, even if another party is spatially closer to the voters' position, but on the other side of the issue. This theory would explain why parties attract votes from moderates even if they pursue non-centrist strategies. The directional theory is imaginative, but the current state of the debate shows that it ultimately provides few, if any, improvements on the empirical predictions of spatial theories of party competition.

All of the models of party competition I have introduced so far essentially take the distribution of voter preferences on salient issues as given, but not as induced by party competition itself. Although there have always been claims that politicians shape social and political divides (e.g. Przeworski 1985), there is little systematic evidence of this being the case. For example, socialist class appeals could not rally the overwhelming share of the emerging working class in precisely those European democracies where the Catholic church had begun to organize the poor and eventually the industrial workers. The reverse does not apply: lower-class mobilization based on religious appeals was not prompted by the failure of socialist politicians to articulate a clear message. Nevertheless, as Lipset and Rokkan's (1967) work, and that of later writers, suggest, in the longer run, elite strategies at time $t1$, such as the introduction of confessional schools or the construction of particular welfare state institutions, may have an impact on the nature and distribution of citizens' preference schedules many years later at time $t2$. For all practical purposes, party politicians with relatively short time horizons of one or two electoral terms simply cannot hitch their electoral success to the hope to shift the opinion of large electoral constituencies profoundly on issues they find salient, or to create entirely new issues citizens have not found salient in the past. Thus, while *ex post* politicians' strategies leave their imprint on voter preferences, *ex ante* it is very difficult for politicians to choose competitive strategies with that purpose in mind. In the short and medium run, parties take the menu of policy issues as given, even though they may experiment with modifications they introduce at the margins.

4 PARTY ORGANIZATION

Theories of political alignments and party competition tend to treat parties as unitary actors inside which the resolution of social choice problems leads to a single shared internal collective preference schedule. This idealization is useful for some purposes, but often unrealistic when studying parties' strategic choices in the electoral and the legislative arena. A theoretically guided literature on studying parties as internal polities with conflicts, competition, and coalition formation is still underdeveloped, but would nevertheless require a separate article. Both a more inductive, historical-comparative and a more formal, deductive literature take their clues from Michels's (1962 [1911]) seminal book on party oligarchy. According to Michels, democracies require mass member-ship party machines. These, in turn, involve division of labor and delegation of decision making to leaders. For the sake of preserving their political office, the latter ultimately develop different interests than their rank-and-file followers and erect an oligarchy that supports the societal and political status quo, even if their constituencies and party activists demand radical social change.

Taking off from Michels and Weber (1958 [1919]), the historical–comparative literature has developed numerous typologies of political party organizations (cf. Duverger 1954; Kirchheimer 1965; Janda and King 1985; Panebianco 1988). What underlies all these models, however, is the belief that in the late nineteenth and twentieth century, with the diffusion of universal suffrage as catalyst, the competitive struggle of parties necessitated the emergence of mass membership parties capable of turning out the vote and "encapsulating" electoral support, often in complex organizational webs which included economic interest groups and sociocultural associations. With the advent of the modern mass media and the dissolution of tightly-knit social subcultures, however, large party member-ship organizations have lost some, although not all, of their political missions. Rather than physically turning out the vote, they provide the cadres of candid-ates, for the large number of local and regional electoral offices parties must fill and serve as recruitment mechanisms for political leadership positions, among other tasks. Moreover, the decline of mass membership parties varies contingent upon institutional rules of party competition, party ideology, and electoral constituency (for an overview, see Katz and Mair 1992; Mair 1997). What is controversial, however, is the extent to which postindustrial democracies gen-erate electoral-professional parties, governed by politicians and hired campaign technicians (Panebianco 1988) or even "cartel parties," in which politicians, by virtue of public campaign financing and assistance within the administrative structure of the state, can detach themselves from their rank-and-file (Katz and Mair 1994, 1996; Mair 1997). These party structures may be supplemented, if not displaced, by postindustrial framework parties in which leaders, on one side, enjoy increasing degrees of freedom in the choice of policy objectives *vis-à-vis* their members, but in which comparatively small groups of rank-and-file acti-vists, on the other, can selectively mobilize, team up with, or supplant members of the leadership, and affect party strategy in dramatic ways (cf. Kitschelt 1989, 1994, 1999).

In the spirit of Michels's theory, the more formal literature on party organi-zation has typically started with a principle-agent model in which party activists, whose incentive to participate is political ideology rather than office holding, are pitted against party leaders who are willing to sacrifice ideology for winning office (Schlesinger 1984; Panebianco 1988; Strom 1990a). These approaches postulate a curvilinear distribution of political preferences, with a party's electoral constituencies being comparatively moderate, the party's rank-and-file activists tending to be radical ideologues, and the party leadership intent on overriding the activists in order to maintain and broaden the voters' allegiance (May 1973). Empirically, it appears, however, that party leaders are often as radical or more radical than party activists (Iversen 1994). Even theoretically, within the logic of spatial competition, the disparity between leaders and activists may be expected only in a two-party system with little chance for new party entry and few incentives for political leaders to spread their appeals over the salient competitive dimension(s), and even there only under particular circumstances. Moreover, a model that relies on a simple vertical preference split between principals and agents does not capture the horizontal divisions between segments of leaders and their followers that result in political organizations that permit internal competition, as do many parties.

As in the case of party competition, what is needed is a combination of insights flowing from the inductive, historical–comparative and the deductive formal literature to advance the analysis of party organization. The formal literature forces theorists to clarify their basic premises about the preferences and calculations of actors and the contingencies that affect their choices. The behavioral approach can explain how actors choose from alternatives under conditions of bounded rationality, based on beliefs, precedents, and experiences, and thus do not take all the alternatives into account which a fully rational calculation of their best strategy of office-seeking would require. The behavioral models, however, have to identify how and why they restrain the feasibility set of the actors' consideration of alternatives against the backdrop of the underlying rational formal models.

5 CONTROVERSIES ABOUT PARTIES IN POSTINDUSTRIAL DEMOCRACY

Very few analytical subjects in the study of parties and party systems, and certainly none of those covered in this brief overview, are non-controversial. In a similar vein, these controversies extend over all possible geographic areas where party conduct can be studied, whether it is the formation of party systems and party organization in Latin America, postcommunist eastern Europe, and Southeast Asia, or the transformation of parties in advanced western postindustrial polities. Without doubt, hitherto controversies about the dynamics of advanced capitalist democracies have yielded the richest literature, but also for this set of polities, there is considerable uncertainty about the interpretation of current developments.

Few voices, however, expect the utter displacement of parties by other vehicles of interest articulation and association, even though anti-party sentiments well-up in many democracies. While democracy does not exhaust itself in elections and legislative maneuvring where parties have their prime fields of activity, a democracy without formal rules of representation in legislatures, based on universal suffrage and the equal weight of each citizen's vote in the election of territorially-based districts, is all but inconceivable. Corporatist governance of interest groups and direct democratic action by social movements may supplement the democratic process, but they cannot take over the task structure of parties in elections or legislatures.

Let me conclude with two alternative scenarios that mark opposite end-points of a range of developments political sociologists conceive as possible within the realm of party competition in contemporary established western democracies after the decline of socialist class politics and of other traditional cleavages (e.g. religion). Let me label these alternatives the technocratic–monological and the postmodern pluralist interpretations (for inspiration, see Mair 1997; Kitschelt 1999). According to the technocratic view, the existing parties are able to maintain their dominance with the aid of professional advice. They can incorporate new societal demands, aided by the waning of strong ideological convictions in an increasingly fluid electorate, aroused only by sudden bursts of interest in localized topics. In this vision, parties continue to gravitate toward the "catch-all" model of converging programmatic appeals and dealigned voters who switch party affiliation contingent upon minor differences between the contenders. The technocratic scenario expects the prevalence of small nodes of electoral professionals, surrounded by a mantle of career-oriented, ambitious party activists, and large and unorganized electoral constituencies whose sentiments parties sound out through opinion polls. By virtue of state financing and entrenchment in the state apparatus (in legislatures and bureau-cracies) these dominant parties can avert the entry of new competitors or co-opt them.

In the alternative pluralist postmodern vision, there is potential for a proliferation of new parties and a displacement of old parties, as societies develop increasingly sophisticated and differentiated electoral constituencies, making it difficult for established "omnibus" parties to resolve the electoral trade-offs they face by trying to incorporate new issue dimensions into the existing organizational and political alignments they represent. While the old Marxian class or religion-based voter divisions lose their importance for the voter's affiliation with parties, they give way to new, more differentiated social divisions based on occupational market position, job autonomy, types of social interaction, partners in the employment setting, and based on patterns of lifestyle and consumption outside work. Parties cultivate different lifestyle niches with fairly specific signals. As a consequence, they tailor their programs to their target constituencies rather than confine themselves to vacuous generalities. Internally, the parties will be minimally efficient, fluid associations where the boundaries between leaders and activists are not always clear and where agents at different levels bargain over the party's message and strategies. These parties enjoy no monopoly powers over an increasingly lethargic electorate, but are always vulnerable to moderately sophisticated, vigilant constituencies whose voters or activists always consider defection to their party's old and new competitors. As a consequence, niche parties have to display considerable responsiveness to their constituencies in order to remain electorally viable.

Neither of these alternatives is likely to reflect the current developments in western party systems fully. But it is important to imagine extreme scenarios in order to identify interesting research controversies. The international prolifera-tion of democratic party competition since the mid-1970s will stimulate more scenario building that may prompt theoretical and empirical research.

Further Reading

Kitschelt, H., Mansfeldova, Z., Markowski, R. and Toka, G. 1999: *Post-Communist Party Systems. Competition, Representation, and Inter-Party Cooperation*. Cambridge: Cambridge University Press.
Mair, P. (ed.) 1990: *West European Party Systems*. Oxford: Oxford University Press.
Ware, A. 1996: *Political Parties and Party Systems*. Oxford: Oxford University Press.

15

Protest and Political Process

David S. Meyer

To understand social protest movements, it is necessary to look at how
politics and the influence of the state permeate areas of life not usually
considered political. Social movements are characterized in the following
ways: they address the state to adjudicate disputes and make binding
decisions; they challenge cultural codes and transform participants' everyday lives; as well as conventional, they also use non-conventional political
means; they are not unitary actors but are composed of a multiplicity of
organizations, groups, and individuals. Social movements are also related
to the political process in that they rise and decline according to conditions
created by the state. They take different forms according to whether the
state is repressive or liberal–democratic. Critical to their emergence is the
construction of political opportunities on the part of state elites. Meyer
concludes with an analysis of the effects of social movements in three
distinct but interdependent areas: public policy, culture, and the lives of
participants.

A woman seeking an abortion at a Planned Parenthood clinic anywhere in the
United States these days is likely to walk past "street counsellors" who will plead
with her not to "murder her unborn child." Brandishing graphic pictures of
aborted fetuses, they will scream and threaten her, with damnation if not
violence. These protesters want not only to stop each woman they encounter
from having an abortion, but also to encourage government to make it more
difficult for women to get legal abortions. Their allies often choose alternate
tactics, ranging from lobbying legislators to shooting doctors. Government
regulates not only access to abortion, but the distance from the clinic entrance
that protesters must stay. The politics of protest outside mainstream political
institutions is thus tightly tied to politics and policy inside political institutions.
We can understand the politics of protest only by analyzing its relationship to the
more routine politics within mainstream politics.

Although social movements like the anti-abortion movement continue to
challenge day-to-day routine politics, they have in themselves become somewhat
routine. Much of the activity falls into conventional categories, but a great deal
of protest politics slips beneath the radar of social science (for reviews, see Meyer

2000; Meyer and Tarrow 1998). Fuller understanding of the sources and impacts of social protest movements requires considering factors frequently missing from conventional political analysis. We need to recognize broader sources and arenas of politics, different and additional sources of political power, and a wider range of significant actors. Politics and the influence of the state permeate areas of social life not generally considered political. The sources of political power are not simply those recognized in constitutions, laws, or academic studies of voting or public opinion. And influence is to be found not only in policies and laws, but also in the ways people live their lives.

I begin by describing the social movement, distinguishing it from other social and political phenomena. Protest politics, I argue, are the product of people trying to come to terms with circumstances they view as unacceptable by employing ostensibly non-political means to political ends. I then consider the circumstances under which social movements emerge and the general dynamics of their development. Next, I examine the multiple impacts of social movements on state and society. I conclude with a discussion of the impact that understanding social movements and protest politics generally can have on contemporary political analysis.

PROTEST POLITICS AND SOCIAL MOVEMENTS

Like military planners and political pundits, social movement analysts are generally fighting and defining the last war, leading to distorted views of the contemporary phenomena. A very brief and schematic review of the development of scholarship can lead us to a more comprehensive evaluation of movements. Analysts of social movements considering protest politics in the 1950s, with the memory of Nazism painfully fresh, wrote with fascism in mind, and thus defined movements as dysfunctional, irrational, and exceptionally dangerous (e.g. Kornhauser 1959). They contrasted movements with less disruptive and more routine interest group politics, which they saw as representatives of citizen concerns in healthier and more pluralist polities. The implication was that social movements were an alternative to "real" politics, and potentially very dangerous. Effective political institutions would allow citizens to exercise influence in more moderate ways; unruly protest would be unnecessary.

If political openness and the wide distribution of resources were to quell or preempt protest, the movements of the 1960s in exactly the most open and democratic polities provided a shock to social science. Empirical studies of student activists found that they were more likely than their less active colleagues to be politically oriented, socially engaged, and psychologically well-adapted (Kenniston 1968). Policy-oriented analysts recognized that social unrest led to concessions from government (Piven and Cloward 1971), and reconceptualized protest strategies as rational efforts by those poorly positioned to make claims on government through conventional means. For those left outside of the pluralist arena, protest was a "political resource" (Lipsky 1968; McCarthy and Zald 1977); protest augmented rather than supplanted conventional strategies of influence.

But protest is also more than this. Protest serves as a vehicle not only for expressing political claims, but also for building communities, forging connections among people, and constructing a sense of self. Social movements develop, in embryo, the world in which they want to live, creating in microcosm the larger political structures they envision (or "prefigurative politics," see Breines 1982). Protest movements include both efforts to transform society and the politics of transforming one's more immediate community and one's self. The world outside the social movement involves political claims, representation, and institutional politics; the world inside involves the production of identity and meaning. These are complementary rather than conflicting aspects of the reality of social protest. Let me suggest four consistent elements that distinguish social movements from other social and political phenomena.

First, *social movements make claims on the state* or some other authority seen to have the capacity to redress activist concerns. The development of the nation-state itself, Tarrow has pointed out, made possible the development of the modern social movement (Tilly 1978; Tarrow 1998). The state has the capacity to process claims, adjudicate disputes, and make decisions binding on losers. Movements may also seek to enlist or provoke other social or political institutions, both below and above the level of the nation-state, to augment their influence on the state. Nonetheless, the state remains the focal point of social movement claims and activities. In the case of the Greensboro sit-in movement, for example, protesters engaged local business directly, but also sought to mobilize portions of the federal government on their behalf. Anti-abortion protesters target local landlords who rent to women's health clinics, but also seek to mobilize support from more risk-adverse allies.

Second, *social movements challenge cultural codes and transform the lives of their participants*. Protest is about more than the claims expressed on placards. Women who march though parks *en masse* at midnight, for example, are not simply urging local governments to improve police protection, but asserting power and confidence for themselves, "taking back the night." Such a march can succeed even if political leaders do not respond with policy reforms. The permeability of the state to dissident claims affects how directly activists target it.

For this reason, Vaclav Havel (1985), facing circumstances that made direct challenge to the Communist state of Czechoslovakia exceedingly difficult, implored his allies to "live in truth," to carve out a sphere of human activity autonomous from state-sponsored social institutions, seeking some transcendent vision of justice and humanity, as an end in itself, and as a means of exercising leverage on the state. Havel offered that this could entail, initially, refusing to mouth the slogans of workers' rule that decorated daily life. Havel's notion was that by such living, often through almost silent protest, dissidents could carve out a public space autonomous from the state, in which they could build civil society.

Third, *social movements use means additional to those offered and accepted by mainstream politics*. Movements may engage in conventional political activities, such as lobbying, running electoral campaigns, and conducting public education campaigns. They will also, however, employ non-conventional means of proffering their claims in visible challenges. Such activities can include demonstrations, boycotts, pickets, civil disobedience, and political violence. Although conventional political analyses treat these tactics as epiphenomena, apart from the more important (and more conventional) political expressions, contemporary protest politics mandate that we look at a broader definition of what comprises politics, beginning with choices individuals make in their personal lives and human interactions.

Of course, individual states draw the boundaries of what comprises acceptable political conduct differently. Peace and democracy activists in the former East Germany expressed their concerns by wearing patches depicting a statue of a workman banging swords into ploughshares. Employing the symbol of a statue given to East Germany by the Soviet Union represented a politics of irony more than confrontation; nonetheless, the government banned the symbol. Activists then identified themselves and provoked opposition by sporting blank patches (Tismaneanu 1989; Meyer and Marullo 1992). The important point here about movements is that challengers pick tactics that place them at the edges of political legitimacy. They are defined by their dynamic interaction with mainstream politics.

Fourth, *movements are comprised of a diverse field of organizations and actors working in pursuit of the same general goals* rather than unitary actors. The boundaries marking a social movement from society in general are fluid; formal organizations, subtle tendencies, and critical dissidents rise and fall rapidly. Allied groups cooperate (generally) in pursuit of political goals and compete (frequently) for support from other citizens and for recognition as legitimate representatives of the movement.

Competitive tension between organizations can make movements more effective. The Greensboro students who started a national civil rights sit-in campaign were not affiliated with the major civil rights organizations of the day, although they were certainly were influenced by established organizations, particularly the National Association for the Advancement of Colored People (NAACP) and the Southern Christian Leadership Council (SCLC). Ella Baker, who had been instrumental in creating the SCLC after the successful bus boycott in Montgomery, persuaded the SCLC to sponsor a national conference to create a new student-based organization, SNCC (Sitkoff 1981). Baker, who was frustrated by the dominance of SCLC by a small group of ministers, shepherded SNCC's creation, and its initial vision of itself as a movement organization committed to grassroots activity.

Forming a new organization is a way to engage a neglected constituency, give voice to new claims and emphases, and support different tactics. In this case, SNCC was explicitly targeted toward youth generally, and students in particular; it emphasized voting rights and engaged in community campaigns and direct action. SNCC gave the older civil rights organizations a radical edge that made the movement as a whole more volatile and less predictable, establishing a greater presence in American political life in the 1960s.

Similarly, Randall Terry, an American vehemently opposed to abortion, founded Operation Rescue when he grew frustrated with what he saw as the relative invisibility and passivity of the anti-abortion movement. Operation Rescue's non-violent and confrontational politics at abortion clinics invigorated less confrontational organizations, and also mobilized an abortion rights opposition. At the same, for a time, its efforts reduced the amount of anti-abortion violence (Meyer and Staggenborg 1996).

Movements are transient and volatile political phenomena that are about more than the expressed claims they explicitly express. Social movements attempt to change public policy, political coalitions, and how people live their lives. Sometimes they succeed – to some degree. But movements are inherently unstable; they give way to more routinized and institutionalized political forms that incorporate, ignore, or normalize social movement claims (Meyer and Tarrow 1998). The processes by which this takes place reflect the peculiar political location of movements, at the edges of mainstream legitimacy.

The Trajectory of Social Protest

If movements are indeed transient phenomena, then it is important to look at the circumstances under which they arise, how they develop in interaction with mainstream politics, the ways they fade, and the residue or impact they leave. Why do people *sometimes* choose to challenge long-standing policies, such as segregation in the United States, or social injustices such as discrimination, or conditions such as Soviet domination of eastern Europe? Four freshmen who sat up late one January night in Greensboro decided the time had come to do something, but why did the time arrive in 1960, not 10 years earlier or later?

The range of contestable issues and available tactics at any time is shaped by the experiences of the constituencies mobilized and audiences targeted, and particularly by the degree of tolerance the state offers. In repressive regimes that restrict political participation severely, the decision to engage in activism often involves embracing an identity of "dissident" laden with real risks. In the Czechoslovakia of 1968–89, circulating *samizdat* literature, attending house meetings, refusing to join the communist party, or signing a charter of human rights, were all high-risk political strategies. The repressive state made activities taken for granted in liberal polities both political and risky.

In contrast, choosing to participate in liberal polities necessitates decisions about how to participate and with whom. When the state offers readily accessible, relatively low cost and essentially no-risk means of participation – such as voting or political campaigning – to choose protest movement activity is not obviously "natural." People resorting to non-conventional or movement activities should occur only when they believe that more conventional routes to influence are either not available or not effective. People choose to participate in a social movement not only for instrumental political influence but also to cultivate and fulfil some sense of their own identity.

Finally, there is the critical issue of choosing which claims to make and issues to engage. Paradoxically, this may be somewhat simpler in more repressive or closed polities: when conventional means of political access are restricted, virtually all demands for political change first necessitate pressing for political openness. Again, during the cold war, dissidents across the former Eastern

Europe, despite their divisions on fundamental issues, united behind the basic principles of democratic participation.

In contrast, in open polities it is possible to engage on a broad spectrum of political issues. Organizers press their special claims, trying to link them to potential activists' concerns. Issue activists try to launch new campaigns, but only periodically do their entreaties reach responsive audiences in the political mainstream and threaten to alter the normal conduct of politics. Although it is easiest analytically to focus on their efforts, attributing success or failure to the tactics or rhetoric of appeals for mobilization, this is fundamentally mistaken. External political realities alter the risks or costs that citizens are willing to bear in making decisions about whether to engage in political activism and what issues are viable for substantial challenges. It makes sense to be more concerned about nuclear war, for example, when the president of the United States suggests that it may be inevitable and survivable, and increases spending on nuclear weapons; it also makes sense to distrust the more conventional styles of politics that produced such a president (Meyer 1990). Similarly, it seems more reasonable to organize for women's rights when the state establishes a commission on women, formally prohibits discrimination, and suggests that it may play a role in combating it (Costain 1992). Activists are not ineluctably linked to one set of issues. An American activist concerned with social justice may protest against nuclear testing in 1962, for voting rights in 1964, against the war in Vietnam in 1967, and for an Equal Rights Amendment in 1972 without dramatically altering his perception of self or justice. Rather, he will be responding to the most urgent, or the most promising, issues that appear before him. In this way, the issues that activists mobilize around are those the state sets out as challenges and opportunities.

The important point is that movements arise within a particular constellation of social and political factors. Movements do not decline because they run out of gas, recognize their failures, or because adherents get bored and move on to something else (contrary to, e.g. Downs 1972). Rather, protest movements decline when the state effects some kind of new arrangement with at least some activists or sponsors. Such arrangements can include repression, incorporating new claims or constituencies in mainstream institutions, and policy reform. Protest campaigns dissipate when activists no longer believe that a movement strategy is possible, necessary, or potentially effective. Repression inhibits the perception of possibility. In contrast, when established political institutions such as parties and interest groups, take up some of the claims of challenging social movements, the perception that extra-institutional activity is necessary erodes.

CONSTRUCTING POLITICAL OPPORTUNITY

Regardless of the objective conditions of political alignments, potential participation, or public policy, movements don't emerge unless substantial numbers of people are invested with feelings of both urgency and efficacy. The job of the organizer is to persuade significant numbers of people that the issues they care about are indeed *urgent*, that alternatives are *possible*, and that the constituencies they seek to mobilize can in fact be invested with *agency* (Gamson and Meyer 1996).

But organizers do not construct these interpretations in a vacuum, nor do potential activists interpret each new appeal solely on its own terms. Both operate in a larger political environment, a crucible in which their values are honed. Critical to the successful emergence of protest movements is a positive feedback loop through which well-positioned elites reinforce both an alternate position on issues, and the choice of protest as a strategy. In the case of civil rights in the United States, for example, the Supreme Court's 1954 decision, *Brown v. Board of Education*, legitimated criticism of segregation and offered the promise of federal government intervention as a powerful ally against southern state and local governments. The decision suggested new possibilities for social organization.

Organizers recognize then that in order first to promote, and then to sustain activism, they need to build and reinforce not only a shared understanding of a social problem but also a sense of community. The sources of community and the struggles for change differ from context to context and movement to movement. Successful labor organizers in Poland built unions around the shared experiences of their members, both at the workplace and at home, addressing the range of concerns in both spheres. East German dissidents organized in the Protestant Church, while the intellectuals in Czechoslovakia who spearheaded the revolution of 1989 found political space in the now-famous Magic Lantern theatre. The first step in launching any effective political campaign is searching out and filling available free spaces, nurturing in embryo the social values activists want to see expressed in the larger society. Even in a repressive state with an under-developed civil society, social movement mobilization is the activity of the organized, *en bloc*, rather than a mystical melding of atomized individuals.

THE EFFECTS OF SOCIAL PROTEST MOVEMENTS

Social movements challenge current public policies, and sometimes they also alter governing alliances and public policy. This is not, however, the end of their influence. Movement activists aspire to change not only specific policies but also broad cultural and institutional structures; they therefore can affect far more than their explicitly articulated targets. Movements change the lives of those who participate in them in ways that can radically reconstruct subsequent politics, including subsequent social protest movements. Movements build communities of struggle – communities that can sustain themselves and also change in unanticipated ways. We can see the influence of protest movements in three distinct but interdependent areas: public policy, culture, and participants (Meyer and Whittier 1994). Each of these is important not just for its impact on the larger society, but also for its direct and indirect effects on other social movements.

- *Policy*: Movements generally organize and mobilize around specific policy demands ranging from passing a civil rights ordinance to ending a war.

Activists also seek to represent their concerns and their claimed constituencies within mainstream political institutions, to speak for those
who protest. Public policy includes symbolic and substantive components,
and policy makers can make symbolic concessions to try to avoid grant-
ing the aggrieved group's substantive demands or giving it new power.
In domestic policy, elected officials can offer combinations of rhetorical concessions or attacks, in conjunction with symbolic policy
changes, to respond to or preempt political challenges (Edelman 1971).
Visible appointments to high-level positions, rhetorical flourishes, and
symbolic policy changes may quiet, at least momentarily, a challenging
movement demanding substantive reforms. Both symbolic and substantive
concessions in response to pressure from one social movement change the
context in which other challengers operate. They open or close avenues of
influence, augment or diminish the pressure a movement can bring to bear,
or raise or lower the costs of mobilization. Thus, movements can
alter the structure of political opportunities they and others face in the
future.

- *Culture*: Social movements struggle on a broad cultural plane where state
policy is only one parameter (Fantasia 1988; Whittier 1995). Movements
must draw from mainstream public discourse and symbols to recruit new
activists and advance their claims, yet they must also transform those
symbols in order to create the environment they seek. Symbols, meanings,
and practices forged in the cauldron of social protest often outlive the
movements that created them. The familiar peace symbol, for example,
designed to support the British Campaign for Nuclear Disarmament in the
1950s, migrated to the United States during its antiwar movement, back to
Europe in the 1980s, and to Asia as a rallying point for pro-democracy
movements in the 1990s.

  Indeed, in the absence of concrete policy successes, movements are likely
to find culture a more accessible venue in which to work, building support
for subsequent challenges on matters of policy. In the late 1970s and 1980s,
eastern European dissidents chose explicitly "antipolitical" strategies of
participation, in a deliberate attempt to create a "civil society," that is, a
set of social networks and relationships independent of the state. Publication of *samizdat* literature, production of underground theatre, and appropriating western rock music to indigenous political purposes, were all
important political work for democratic dissidents. This battle, in the
least promising of circumstances, proved to be critical in precipitating
and shaping the end of the cold war.

- *Participants*: Finally, social movements influence the people who participate in them. As the Greensboro veterans noted, taking responsibility for
changing the segregated South changed their lives forever. People who
participate in movements step into history as actors, not simply as victims,
and this transformation is not easily reversible. Movement activists forge
new identities in struggle, identities that carry on beyond the scope of a
particular campaign or movement. Someone who has forged an identity in
the struggle of collective action and exercised political power through

membership in a community of struggle will not readily submit to being acted upon by distant authorities in the future.

Activists come to see themselves as members of a group that is differentiated from outsiders. They interpret their experiences in political terms, and politicize their actions in both movement contexts and everyday life. Collective identities constructed during periods of peak mobilization endure even after protest dies down. One-time movement participants continue to see themselves as progressive activists even as organized collective action decreases, and they make personal and political decisions in light of this identity. Veterans of Freedom Summer, for example, became leading organizers in the peace and student movements of the 1960s, the feminist and anti-nuclear movements of the 1980s, and beyond (McAdam 1988). By changing the way individuals live, movements affect longer term changes in the society.

In summary, movements can influence not only the terrain upon which subsequent challengers struggle, but also the resources available to challengers and the general atmosphere surrounding the struggle. In changing policy and the policymaking process, movements can alter the structure of political opportunity new challengers face. By producing changes in culture, movements can change the values and symbols used by both mainstream and dissident actors. They can expand the tactical repertoire available to new movements. By changing participants' lives, movements alter the personnel available for subsequent challenges.

Further Reading

McAdam, Doug. 1982: *Political Process and the Development of Black Insurgency*. Chicago: University of Chicago Press.

McAdam, D., McCarthy, J. D., and Zald, M. N. (eds.) 1996: *Comparative Perspectives on Social Movements: Political Opportunities, Mobilizing Structures, and Cultural Framings*. Cambridge: Cambridge University Press.

Meyer, D. S. and Tarrow, S. (eds.) 1998: *The Social Movement Society*. Lanham, MD: Rowman & Littlefield.

Piven, F. F. and Cloward, R. A. 1979: *Poor People's Movements*. New York: Vintage.

Tarrow, S. 1998: *Power in Movement*, second edition. Cambridge: Cambridge University Press.

Tilly, C. 1978: *From Mobilization to Revolution*. Reading, MA: Addison-Wesley-Longman.

16

The Media and Politics

John B. Thompson

All forms of mediated communication involve the transmission of information or symbolic content through time and space. They create forms of interaction in which participants are unlikely to confront each other directly "face-to-face." This is not new, but the mass media introduce new dimensions to the exchanges enabled by them: their institutions are commercial; their products are oriented toward a plurality of potential recipients; recipients have relatively little influence over the process of this production. Empirical studies of the effects of the mass media on the political process have tended to focus on their impact on attitudes and behavior, especially voting behavior in elections. Also important is their effect on the electoral practices of candidates and political parties. A wider question is that of how the rise of the mass media has altered the very relationship between rulers and ruled. Developing Habermas's idea of the public sphere, Thompson argues that the development of communication media has created new forms of publicness which are no longer linked to sharing a common locale. While this means that politicians have become increasingly sophisticated at manipulating their public images, it also makes politics more open and accessible than ever before.

The Nature and Development of the Media

The term "media" is commonly associated with particular forms of communication which have become pervasive features of contemporary societies, such as newspapers, magazines, radio, cinema, and television. But these particular forms of communication represent only some of the many ways in which information and symbolic content can be fixed in technical media of various kinds and transmitted to others, or stored for subsequent use. In the most fundamental sense, the term "media" refers to these various kinds of material substrata and the institutional forms by means of which information and symbolic content can be fixed and transmitted to others. Hence the use of paper for writing, the use of the telephone for communicating with others, and the use of computer technologies for storing and exchanging information all involve the use of media in this sense.

One characteristic which is common to all forms of mediated communication is that they involve the transmission of information or symbolic content through time and space. The use of communication media enables individuals to transmit information and symbolic content to others who are situated in distant contexts. Hence, the use of communication media involves the creation of forms of interaction which are rather different from the forms of interaction which take place in the shared locales of everyday life. Much everyday interaction is "face-to-face interaction," in the sense that it takes place in a localized setting in which individuals share a common spatial-temporal framework and confront one another directly. But mediated interaction is "stretched" across space and perhaps also time; the participants may be situated in distant and diverse contexts, and they are unlikely to share a common spatial–temporal framework.

Understood in this broad way, communication media have been part of social and political life for several millennia. The development of systems of writing in Mesopotamia and Ancient Egypt, and the use of clay, stone, papyrus and paper for recording and transmitting information and symbolic content, involved the use of communication media in this sense (Innis 1950). But the invention of the printing press in the fifteenth century, and the subsequent rise of the printing and publishing industries, marked the beginning of something new. Thanks to the techniques of printing, it was now possible to reproduce multiple copies of texts relatively cheaply, and hence to make them available to a plurality of recipients in a commercially profitable way. The techniques of printing spread rapidly throughout Europe in the late fifteenth century, and by the sixteenth century there was a flourishing trade in books, pamphlets and other printed materials. In the early seventeenth century, regular journals of news began to appear in various European cities: these "corantos," as they were called at the time, were the precursors of the modern newspaper. By the early eighteenth century, a variety of daily and weekly newspapers were well established in most major European cities.

The rise of media institutions concerned with the production and diffusion of books, newspapers, and other symbolic material represented an important development. The gathering and circulation of information and symbolic content was increasingly linked to a range of institutionalized activities which were oriented toward the production of symbolic goods and their exchange in the marketplace. When we speak of "the media" today, we are often referring to these institutions and their products. (They are also commonly described today as "the mass media" or "mass communication," although the term "mass" can be misleading.) These institutions and their products have several important features. In the first place, these institutions are, for the most part, commercial organizations which are oriented towards financial gain. They use technical media of various kinds to produce symbolic goods which can be sold or otherwise distributed to individuals in a way which generates some kind of financial return. A second feature of media institutions is that their products are generally oriented towards a plurality of potential recipients. These goods are produced in multiple copies or transmitted to a multiplicity of receivers in such a way that they are available in principle to anyone who has the means, skills and resources to acquire them. Moreover, the flow of media products is a structured flow, in the sense that they are often produced by organizations which are largely responsible for shaping the product and its content, and then sold or transmitted to individuals who are primarily recipients. Of course, recipients can influence the production process in various ways, but this capacity is generally quite limited.

While the origins of media institutions can be traced back to the rise of the printing and publishing industries in late medieval and early modern Europe, the media have changed in many ways since the early nineteenth century. Three changes have been particularly significant. First, media institutions have become increasingly commercialized, and some have been transformed into large-scale commercial concerns. This transformation was due partly to a series of technical innovations in the printing industry, and partly to a gradual shift in the financial basis of the media industries and their methods of generating revenue. Through processes of growth and consolidation, large-scale communication conglomerates have emerged. These conglomerates – such as Time Warner, Disney, and Rupert Murdoch's News Corporation – have today become key transnational players in the production and circulation of information and communication (Herman and McChesney 1997; Bagdikian 2000).

A second and closely-related development was the globalization of communication and the emergence of global communication networks. In earlier centuries, printed materials were commonly transported over large distances and across the boundaries of kingdoms and states. But in the course of the nineteenth century the international flow of information and communication assumed a much more extensive and organized form. The development of international news agencies based in the major commercial cities of Europe, together with the expansion of communication networks linking the peripheral regions of empires with their European centers, established the beginnings of a global system of communication and information processing which, in the course of the twentieth century, became increasingly ramified and complex.

The third development was the emergence of electronically mediated forms of communication. Telegraph and telephone systems were introduced in the nineteenth century, and by the 1920s viable systems of radio broadcasting had been developed. Television broadcasting began after the Second World War and expanded rapidly in the 1950s. More recently, many media systems have been transformed by the development of new forms of information processing based on digital systems of codification – the so-called "information revolution." Digitization has led to the growing convergence of information and communication technologies on a common digital system of transmission, processing, and storage. Information and symbolic content can now be converted rapidly and relatively easily into different media forms. This development has already blurred the traditional boundaries between different sectors of the media industries and it is likely that it will continue to do so.

THE MEDIA AND THE POLITICAL PROCESS

It has long been recognized that the development of the media has important implications for the nature of politics and the political process. Early liberal thinkers, such as James Mill and John Stuart Mill, regarded an independent press as a crucial component of a liberal–democratic society. They saw the free expression of opinion through the organs of an independent press as a vital means by which a diversity of viewpoints could be expressed and the abuses of state power by corrupt or tyrannical governments could be checked. A free and independent press would play the role of a critical watchdog, scrutinizing and criticizing the activities of those who rule (J. Mill 1967; J. S. Mill 1972).

Other social and political thinkers have taken a less sanguine view. Among the early critics of the media were Max Horkheimer and Theodor Adorno, two authors associated with the Frankfurt School of critical social theory. Writing in the 1930s and 1940s, Horkheimer and Adorno feared that the development of the media – or what they called "the culture industry" – would lead to an increasingly oppressive social and political order. They used the term "culture industry" to refer to the commodification of cultural forms brought about by the rise of the entertainment industries in Europe and the United States in the late nineteenth and early twentieth centuries. The cultural goods produced by these industries are standardized and rationalized commodities which are shaped primarily by the logic of capital accumulation. These goods would not stimulate critical thinking in audiences or readers but would, Horkheimer and Adorno feared, render individuals less capable of autonomous judgment and more dependent on social processes over which they have little control. Individuals would be increasingly assimilated to the social order by their very desire for the objects produced by it (Horkheimer and Adorno 1972; Adorno 1991).

The gloomy prognosis of critics like Horkheimer and Adorno presumed that the media were capable of having a quite powerful impact on the attitudes and behavior of ordinary individuals. Whether this was true, however, and the precise nature of the impact that the media might have, were primarily empirical questions which required careful investigation. A good deal of empirical research has been done in an attempt to answer questions of this kind. Among other things, researchers have tried to determine whether the media have a discernible impact on the outcome of elections, and whether election campaigns conducted in the media have a significant impact on the decisions of voters. Studies of this kind have yielded relatively few clear-cut and generalizable conclusions. Given the complexity of electoral processes and the wide range of factors which are likely to affect outcomes, it is perhaps not surprising that researchers have found it difficult to isolate the effects of media coverage and campaigns. But the early studies did tend to suggest that the impact of the media on electoral outcomes was less significant and less direct than many commentators had supposed.

One of the first major studies of the media and elections was carried out in the United States by Paul Lazarsfeld and his associates in the 1940s and 1950s (Lazarsfeld, Berelson, and Gaudet 1948; Katz and Lazarsfeld 1955). Lazarsfeld and his associates were particularly interested in why people changed their voting intentions during election campaigns. Initially they studied the 1940 presidential election and found that exposure to media campaigns produced little alteration in people's voting intentions. Instead, the key factor influencing changes seemed to be other people. They also found that some people were particularly influential in this regard, and that these "opinion leaders" were more likely to be influenced by the media. So Lazarsfeld and his associates put forward a model of what they called "the two-step flow of communication": ideas flow from the media to opinion leaders, and from these opinion leaders they flow to other sections of the population. This model suggested that the impact of the media on most ordinary individuals was largely indirect: it was mediated by the social groups to which they belong and by significant individuals with whom they interact in their day-to-day lives.

The work of Lazarsfeld and others in the 1940s and 1950s seemed to show that the power of the media to change people's views was relatively limited. Media messages, it seemed, were much more likely to confirm and reinforce preexisting attitudes and beliefs than to change them; minor alterations might occur, but conversion to fundamentally different points of view was rare. "Persuasive mass communications functions far more frequently as an agent of reinforcement than as an agent of change," concluded Joseph Klapper in a text which became a standard reference work in the field (Klapper 1960: 15). But the thesis of minimal consequences, together with the research on which it was based, has been criticized on various grounds (see, for example, Gitlin 1978). The emphasis on short-term changes of attitude might well obscure a range of more subtle influences, and the circumstances in which elections take place today might differ in significant ways from the social and political contexts in which Lazarsfeld and others carried out their research. More recent studies have highlighted a number of important ways in which the media can shape political processes.

One important line of research, initiated in the 1970s by Maxwell McCombs, Donald Shaw and others, has focused on the phenomenon of "agenda setting" (McCombs and Shaw 1972; Dearing and Rogers 1996). Like Lazarsfeld and his associates, McCombs and Shaw were interested in the impact of the media on people's attitudes during election campaigns. They knew there was little evidence to suggest that the media directly changed people's attitudes on a significant scale, but McCombs and Shaw hypothesized that the media would set the agenda for political campaigns, influencing the salience of particular issues. In other words, while the media may not be very successful at telling people *what* to think, they may be quite successful at telling them what to think *about*. In their study of a sample of voters during the 1968 US presidential campaign, McCombs and Shaw found a high correlation between the issues emphasized by the media and the issues which voters regarded as important, a finding which they viewed as consistent with the agenda-setting hypothesis. Subsequent studies have explored the relations between news stories in the media and public attitudes on drugs, crime, race, environmental issues, and so on. These studies show that, in some cases, particular events can act as "triggers" which play a key role in putting the issue on the media agenda, and thereby turning them into public issues.

Another factor which has been explored by recent research, and which is relevant to the impact of the media, is the changing social composition of the electorate. In the period immediately after the Second World War, there was a relatively strong sense of party identification among voters in Britain, the United States, and elsewhere. This strong sense of party identification, cultivated in family contexts and local communities from an early age, might well have limited the capacity of electoral campaigns in the media to produce significant effects. But from the 1960s on, this strong sense of party identification has been eroded to some degree. The traditional working class has declined, and traditional links between social classes and political parties have weakened. At the same time, there has been an increase in the proportion of "floating voters" who are not firmly committed to a particular party. There is some evidence to suggest that the electoral choices of floating voters are more likely to be influenced by the media coverage of an election than the choices of committed voters (Harrop 1986; Miller 1991). In the run-up to the 1987 British General Election, for example, the swing to the Conservatives was much stronger among uncommitted voters than among the committed, and uncommitted voters who read the *Sun* or *Star* – two tabloid newspapers which supported the Conservatives – were more likely to swing in this direction than other uncommitted voters (Miller 1991: 194–5). Of course, evidence of this kind must be treated with caution, since it is extremely difficult to isolate the effects of any single factor. But the evidence lends some support to the view that, in a political environment characterized by a weakening of traditional party loyalties and the declining significance of social class, the potential for using the media to influence electoral outcomes at the margins – especially among floating voters – may be growing.

Whatever the precise impact of the media on the electoral choices of voters, it is clear that the existence of the media has altered the electoral practices of candidates and political parties. Elections are increasingly fought on the terrain of the media, as candidates and parties rely increasingly on media coverage and campaigns in order to present themselves and their policies to the electorate. Elections have become media events. The rise of television has accentuated this trend and has, in turn, altered its character. With the growing significance of television, politicians and parties have come to rely increasingly on techniques borrowed from advertising in order to "sell" themselves to voters. This practice became increasingly common among US presidential candidates from the 1950s on. Candidates began to employ media advisors who were trained in advertising, and spot ads on television became an increasingly central feature of election campaigns (McGinnis 1970; Jamieson 1984). Television advertising now consumes a very large and growing share of campaign budgets in both presidential and congressional elections. In Britain and many other countries, there are much stricter controls on the ability of candidates and parties to advertise on television. But some provision is usually made for candidates and parties to present themselves and their policies to the electorate via televised broadcasts.

The use of advertising techniques has also contributed to the rise of what has been called "political marketing" (O'Shaugnessy 1990; Maarek 1993). Political marketing involves more than just the use of television ads (or party political broadcasts) to promote the images and policies of candidates (or to attack their opponents). It also involves the use of techniques drawn from the world of commercial marketing to tailor the product to the needs and tastes of consumers. The use of political marketing techniques has become a common feature of American election campaigns, but marketing techniques have also become increasingly prevalent in Britain and elsewhere. The British Conservative Party under Margaret Thatcher relied heavily on the marketing expertise of Saatchi and Saatchi, the London-based advertising agency, to develop its campaign strategy for the General Election of 1979 and subsequent elections (Scammell 1995). And the reorientation of the Labor Party under Tony Blair, aimed at restoring Labor's electoral credibility after four successive General Election defeats, was based on the extensive use of methods of market research.

THE MEDIA AND THE TRANSFORMATION OF PUBLIC LIFE

While the role of the media in elections and election campaigns has been a major focus of attention for scholars interested in political communication, it is also clear that the significance of the media for politics extends well beyond the relatively limited sphere of elections. The rise of communication media has altered the very nature of politics and the ways in which political leaders relate to those over whom they rule. These changes are part of a broader transformation in the nature of public life. The distinction between "public" and "private" has a long history in western social and political thought, and these terms have acquired various senses (see Bobbio 1989; Habermas 1989a; Thompson 1995). In one sense of the term, "public" means "open" or "available." What is public, in this sense, is what is visible or observable, what is performed in front of spectators, what is open for all or many to see or hear about. What is private, by contrast, is what is hidden from view, what is said or done in secrecy or behind closed doors. In this sense, the public–private distinction has to do with publicness versus privacy, with openness versus secrecy, with visibility versus invisibility.

The development of communication media has altered the publicness or visibility of actions or events in a fundamental way. (For a more detailed discussion of this point and of the consequences which follow from it, see Thompson 1995.) Prior to the development of the media, the publicness of actions or events was linked to the sharing of a common locale: an event became a public event by being staged before a plurality of individuals who were physically present at the time and place of its occurrence. This "traditional publicness of copresence" was tied to the characteristics of face-to-face interaction. But the development of communication media – beginning with print, but including the more recent electronic media – created new forms of publicness which were no longer linked to the sharing of a common locale. An action or event could be made visible and observable by being recorded and transmitted to others who were not physically present. These new forms of "mediated publicness" did not entirely displace the role of the traditional publicness of copresence. But as new media of communication became more pervasive, the new forms of mediated publicness began to supplement, and gradually to extend and transform, the traditional form of publicness.

The changing nature of publicness has altered the conditions under which political power is exercised. Political rulers and leaders have always sought to construct self-images and manage the ways in which they appear before others, but the development of communication media has changed the nature and scope of this activity. Prior to the development of print and other media, political rulers could generally restrict the activity of managing visibility to the relatively closed circles of the assembly or court. There were occasions, such as coronations, victory marches, or royal progresses, when rulers appeared before wider audiences. But for most individuals in ancient or medieval societies, the most powerful rulers were rarely if ever seen. With the development of new means of communication, however, political rulers had to concern themselves increasingly with their self-presentation before audiences which were not physically present. Monarchs in early modern Europe, such as Louis XIV of France or Philip IV of Spain, were well versed in the arts of image-making; their images were fabricated and celebrated not only in traditional media, such as paint, bronze, and stone, but also in the newer media of print (Elliott 1985; Burke 1992). The subsequent development of electronic media (radio and especially television) created powerful new means for political rulers and leaders to construct their images, to communicate with distant others, and to appear before them in ways that were simply not possible in the past.

These new media of communication required new modes and styles of self-presentation. The traditional forms of political speech-making – the fiery rhetoric of the speech delivered to an assembled crowd, for example – were not necessarily suitable for the new kinds of communicative situations created by electronic media. The radio allowed for a more conversational style in which political leaders could address others in a more direct and personal way; the fiery rhetoric of the impassioned speech was exchanged for the conversational intimacy of the fireside chat (Jamieson 1988). Television accentuated this trend and added the symbolic richness and immediacy of the visual image. Hence, political leaders could now address distant others with the kind of directness and intimacy characteristic of face-to-face interaction, but in a way that was freed from the constraints and reciprocity of conversation in a shared locale. The impersonal aloofness of most political leaders in the past was increasingly replaced by a new kind of mediated intimacy through which political figures could present themselves not only as leaders but also as human beings, as ordinary individuals who could address their subjects as fellow citizens, selectively disclosing aspects of their lives and their character in a conversational or even confessional mode. And given the capacity of television to convey close-up images, viewers could now scrutinize their leaders' actions, utterances, and appearances with the kind of close attention once reserved for those with whom one interacted intimately in the course of one's daily life.

Under these radically altered conditions of public life, the management of visibility and self-presentation through the media has become an integral and increasingly professionalized feature of government. The conduct of government requires a continuous process of decision-making concerning what is to be made public, to whom and how, and the task of making and executing these decisions is increasingly handed over to a team of specialized personnel who are responsible for managing the relation between the government and the media. Since the early 1970s, US presidents have relied heavily on the White House Office of Communications to perform this task. Established by Nixon in 1969, the Office of Communications employs a permanent staff which is concerned with coordinating the flow of information from the White House to the media, planning interviews and television appearances by Administration officials and developing a long-term media strategy (Maltese 1994). Part of the task of the Office (and similar organizations elsewhere) is not only to control what Administration officials say and how they appear in public, but also to try, so far as possible, to influence what the media say about them (to "spin" the story), so that the Administration will appear in a favorable light.

However, despite the efforts of governments and political leaders to manage their visibility in the mediated arena of modern politics, this is an arena which is strewn with dangers and risks. Political leaders must constantly be on their guard and employ a high degree of reflexivity to monitor their actions and utterances, since an indiscreet act or an ill-judged remark can have disastrous consequences. The mediated arena of modern politics is open and accessible in a way that traditional assemblies and courts were not. Moreover, given the development of new technologies and the sheer proliferation of media organizations and sources, it is simply not possible to control completely the flows of information and the ways in which political leaders become visible to others.

Leaks, gaffes, scandals: these and other occurrences exemplify how difficult it is to manage information and self-presentation in the age of mediated visibility. The example of scandal is particularly interesting, both because the phenomenon has become so widespread today and because its consequences can be so disastrous for the individuals concerned. Scandal is not a new phenomenon; the concept can be traced back to ancient Greek, and the word became increasingly common in European languages from the sixteenth century on. But the rise of the modern phenomenon of mediated scandal dates from the late eighteenth and early nineteenth centuries (Thompson 1997, 2000). A mediated scandal is a distinctive type of event which involves the disclosure through the media of an activity that transgresses certain norms, an activity which had previously been hidden (or known only to a small circle of people) and which, on being made public in this way, may give rise to public criticism and condemnation that can have damaging consequences for the individuals concerned. Disclosure through the media endows these hitherto private activities with the status of public events: they are now visible, observable and knowable by thousands or even millions of others who become spectators of activities which they did not and could not have witnessed directly. There is a continuous line of development from the scandals of the late nineteenth century – such as the scandal that destroyed the political career of Charles Parnell, the charismatic leader of the Irish parliamentary party at Westminster – to the scandals which have become such prominent features of political life today. The events surrounding Profumo, Watergate, the Iran–Contra affair, and the Clinton–Lewinsky scandal, to name but a few, exemplify very well how difficult it is to control the flow of information and to maintain a veil of secrecy around the private activities and conversations of political leaders and others in an age which is characterized by the proliferation of mediated forms of communication.

Further Reading

Ansolabehere, S., Behr, R., and Iyengar, S. 1993: *The Media Game: American Politics in the Age of Television*. New York: Macmillan.

Jamieson, K. H. 1988: *Eloquence in an Electronic Age: The Transformation of Political Speechmaking*. New York: Oxford University Press.

Negrine, R. 1996: *The Communication of Politics*. London: Sage.

Scammell, M. 1995: *Designer Politics: How Elections are Won*. Basingstoke: Macmillan.

Thompson, J. B. 1995: *The Media and Modernity: A Social Theory of the Media*. Cambridge: Polity Press.

17

Violence and the State
The Political Sociology of War

ALAN SCOTT

> Violence has always been the *ultima ratio* in political action and power has always been the visible expression of rule and government.
>
> (*Hannah Arendt 1951: 137*)

Sociology has been criticized for failing to recognize the importance of war and violence. Those analysts who sought to redress this situation from the 1970 and 1980s onwards, for example Michael Mann, Anthony Giddens, and Charles Tilly, were concerned to develop analyses which neither reduced war to the logic of capitalism or industrialism nor explained social development exclusively with reference to a military model of society. Their focus was on the relationship of war to the formation of the modern nation-state and on the complexities of the interaction between war making/preparation and the development of (capitalist) industrialization. More recently, attention has focused on the "demilitarization" of some societies on the one hand (Martin Shaw) and new forms of genocidal nationalism on the other. The latter raises the issue of the state's possible loss of some degree of control over the means of coercion and these "new wars" (Mary Kaldor) have been interpreted as destructive responses to the pressures placed on the nation-state by globalizing forces.

As war and violence reemerged as topics of sociological analysis in the late 1970s and 1980s, it was frequently noted that war was not so much "under-theorized" by sociologists as simply ignored (see Mann 1988: 147; Joas 1991: 48). While the army as a form of association had attracted the attention of sociologists of the professions (notably, Janowitz 1960), the social significance of war itself – its impact on economic, cultural and political life – was a matter largely left to military or social historians (e.g. Marwick 1977). While there had been exceptions to this rule (e.g. C. Wright Mills 1956; Andreski 1971), the complaint was largely justified. As late as 1999, Martin Shaw, who has himself made a major contribution to the effort of rectifying this situation, felt able to note that

> At the end of the "century of total war," social theory still has a lamentable record
> of neglect of war. Wars are regular, structural features of modernity, yet they are
> still treated as abnormal intrusions into the regularities of social life. (Shaw 1999:
> par. 1.2)

This relative neglect of war and violence is paradoxical not only because of the
frequency, violence, and destructiveness of wars during the twentieth century,
but also because of the centrality they once had in sociological thought. Marx
identified colonial adventure and violent primitive accumulation as preconditions for the emergence of capitalism as a mode of production, while Weber's
famous definition of the state had the monopoly of legitimate *violence* as one of
only two of its constitutive components (territorial boundedness being the
other).

All the more remarkable then that despite this breach between older and more
recent sociological analyses of war there has nevertheless been a degree of
continuity. Weber's work illustrates this. In the midst of an account of legitimacy
he breaks off to discuss the roots of modern rational discipline (1922, Part 3,
chapter V). These he ultimately traces to ancient military training and drill. The
specific quality of rational discipline – i.e. of the "planned, trained and precise
execution of an order in which all personal critique has been suspended" (642) –
is the uniformity of obedience across a population. Discipline is the "communal
action of a mass formation" (642) and as such can only be the product of
sustained exposure to developing techniques of military drill in which even
emotional, incalculable, and irrational feelings (e.g. hatred of the enemy) are
rationally manipulated and channelled.

But Weber goes beyond this analysis to make two further points. The first is
that the technological and social formation of the military affects the constitution of both the state and society. Like monasteries, barracks are single-gender
(i.e. male) establishments which displace men from family life and private
economic interest into a world of "cloister communism." This in turn impacts
upon the society from which these men – whose economic and sexual requirements have still to be met – have been removed. Furthermore, he hints that
specific forms of military discipline are compatible with specific forms of state
(e.g. the perfected infantry drill of Sparta with aristocracy, cities based upon
naval discipline with democracy). Secondly, Weber asserts that the rational
discipline of the army is a condition for the emergence of the rational discipline
of the modern capitalist firm: "Army discipline is the mother's knee of discipline generally. The second great teacher of discipline is the large economic
concern" (647). The exposure to military discipline, just like the exposure to
factory or office discipline, intensifies in proportion to the extent to which
the means of production (in this case the means of warfare) are removed from
the worker/soldier. Military discipline then makes a major contribution to the
emergence and dissemination of instrumental rationality in the spheres of economics and politics. Some three-quarters of a century later, one of the most
influential theorists of the relationship between war and state formation could
be found making essentially the same point: "our culture is permeated by the
desirability of team discipline, of mathematically precise logistical planning, of

split second timing: all qualities which are most closely paralleled in our society by the requirements of warfare" (Mann 1988: 133–4).

Thus, despite the fact that Weber "failed to develop any sociological analysis of the emergence and impact of war" (Joas 1991: 55) his assertions foreshadow two central areas of concern among subsequent sociologists of war: (i) the origins and implication of external discipline and self control; (ii) the interdependency of war, the formation of the modern nation-state and capitalism. In sociology, then, the main concern was, and largely remains, with the role of the military, war, and violence in the formation of modernity.

THE ORIGINS OF EXTERNAL DISCIPLINE AND SELF-CONTROL

The concern with the nature of external and internal discipline and its possible military origins reappears in the work of Norbert Elias. The interesting question for Elias is not why people fight but rather "how is it possible that so many people can normally live together without fear of being struck or killed by stronger parties" (1988: 178). The answer lies in the wider implications of the state's monopoly of legitimate violence. In modern societies individuals physically fight on their own behalf so infrequently because populations have been "pacified"; their direct access to the means of warfare has gradually been removed and the legitimate use of personal violence has declined to a point where individuals' use of violence has to be warranted in terms of self-defense and proportionality of the response to the danger of the attack. Pacification of the population is merely the other side of the concentration of violence in the state: "we live within an organization whose rulers have at their disposal groups of specialists authorized to use physical violence if necessary to prevent all other citizens from using violence" (179).

The increasing concentration of the means of violence also has a cultural and psychological dimension: "taboos against violence, which are so deeply impressed upon adolescents in developed state-regulated societies, are closely linked with the growing effectiveness of the state monopoly of violence" (180). This personal/psychological pacification, which developed over many centuries, is manifested in the development of modern manners, child-rearing practices, gender relations, and so on. The story of the emergence of modernity that Elias relates in the *Civilizing Process* (1994 [1939]) is one in which knightly societies based upon a code of personal honor and individual reputation gave way to courtly societies in which the courtiers, unlike their knightly predecessors, had no recourse to the direct use of arms. Pacified courtly manners then become generally disseminated throughout society and external control is gradually replaced by self-control exercised, above all, via the monitoring of bodily needs and capacities – including aggression (cf. Sassatelli, chapter 29, in this volume). As an account of internal pacification generally, this emphasis upon the court may be too narrowly focused and may underestimate the diversity of the process. As the American historical sociologist Charles Tilly notes, "disarmament of the civilian population took place in many small steps: general seizures or weapons at the end of rebellions, prohibitions of duels, control over the production of weapons, introduction of licensing for private arms, restriction on public displays of armed force" (1992: 69).

Elias recognizes a paradox and a danger in this process of the taming of violence: "in domestic relations violence among people is taboo and, whenever possible, punished. In international relations a different standard prevails. Every large state continuously prepares for acts of violence against other states" (1988: 181). As individuals become more pacified, so the capacity of states to violently disrupt their lives increases. No fully developed higher authority exists (as yet) to regulate the violence concentrated in modern nation-state. Modern societies are (generally) internally safer, but at the same time more vulnerable to occasions of largely unregulated violence between states. Furthermore, a pacified population is also the potentially defenseless victim of its own state, as for example in cases of internal repression or genocide. Thus, individual and social pacification on the one hand and modern industrialized total war and even genocide on the other appear here as two sides of the same coin. I shall return to some of the implication of this later.

The Interdependency of War, The Formation of the Modern Nation-State, and Capitalism

Behind the "rediscovery" of war and violence as topics of sociological analysis by theorists like Michael Mann and Anthony Giddens lay a broadly neo-Weberian motivation, namely resisting forms of reductionism. Thus Giddens' influential *The Nation-State and Violence* forms part of his broader critique of historical materialism. Both authors sought to demonstrate the independent role of war making and war preparation in the formation of the modern state. In this spirit, Giddens argues that "surveillance (in its various forms and aspects) must be regarded as an independent source of power, maximized in the modern state, which has to be as much of a concern in social critique as questions of material inequality or the nature of polyarchy" (1985: 310). The state's monopoly of legitimate violence, its role in internal pacification and surveillance, and the ever increasing differentiation of military, political, and economic power (see Crouch, chapter 22, in this volume) were all taken to be indications of the autonomy of the modern state. Given this autonomy, the state was necessarily much more than a tool of class rule. The relationship between political and economic power (between the nation-state and capitalism) had to be rethought. Furthermore, war making and state making were taken to be intimately linked. In Mann's words: "though states have other purposes too, they have been *principally* concerned throughout history with warfare" (1988: 130).

The influence of war preparation and making is felt far beyond state formation: in architecture (see Virilio 1994), in the European motorway system (started by Nazi Germany in the 1930s, continental motorways retain their NATO signposts and numbering), in innovative forms of manufacture from early mass production to the Internet (American Defense Department 1960s/70s). The emergence of modern forms of citizenship is also frequently linked to the mass nature of industrial warfare. The extension of the franchise in Britain to some categories of women over the age of 30 in 1918 has been interpreted as a "reward" for their role in the war effort in the First World War, while social citizenship, in the form of welfare, often accompanied or immediately followed war (e.g. the implementation of the Beveridge Report after 1945). As Giddens notes "if the sovereign state is inherently a polyarchic order, in which citizenship rights are the 'price paid' by the dominant class for the means of exercising its power, citizenship in turn implies acceptance of the obligations of military service" (1985: 233) (but see Lister, chapter 30, in this volume).

Despite this emphasis on the autonomy and influence of war, neither of these authors was content to return to a strictly military interpretation of the emergence of modern social and state forms. Reductionism had to be resisted whether it took an economic or militarist form. Michael Mann's 1984 essay "Capitalism and militarism" (reprinted in Mann 1988) offers one of the clearest expressions of this anti-reductionist and anti-functionalist view. Mann's starting point is the assertion that while militarism is a central element of modern societies it "derives from geo-political aspects of our social structure which are far older than capitalism" (128). From this he seeks to demonstrate (a) the centrality of militarism in the formation of the modern state and (b) that there is a vital but contingent relationship between militarism and capitalism. The impact of capitalism on the military and war is essentially the same as its impact in other areas, e.g. communication, technology, production. Capitalism massively increases the technical base of warfare: "when capitalism pioneered industrialism, it proved capable of generating repeating rifles, heavy bore field guns, high explosives, tanks, ironclad battleships, fighters and bomber aircraft, submarines, rockets and nuclear weapons" (133). The range of diplomacy, of clientele relations, etc., is increased as surely as, and in step with, the range of communication and weaponry. The culture of military life is rationalized and even growing sections of the population are drawn into militarism (just as they are into factory production). But precisely because the relationship between militarism and capitalism is contingent, modern militarism "though pioneered by capitalism, became the common property of industrialism" (143). Ironically, as Mann himself later notes (1988: xi), the effort to avoid the reduction of militarism to capitalism (or indeed industrialism) brings him close to another potentially reductionist explanation, namely realism: "the enemies [of those who desire peace] are . . . the common geo-political pretensions of the super-powers, the same pretensions as Greece and Persia, Rome and Carthage, possessed, now rendered more technically alarming to the world" (144).

A parallel development was emerging among Marxist analysts. E. P. Thompson's "exterminism thesis" – i.e. the view that militarism had an inherent exterminist logic (Thompson 1982) – ascribes a similar degree of autonomy to militarism. Thus ironically, Marxists like Thompson were moving away from economistic explanations and towards the kind of position represented by Mann and Giddens – i.e. one in which the logic of militarism might be said to match or compete with the "logic of capital." The cold war and peace movement context is clearly relevant here. With the Star Wars project, dual-track strategies, "mutually assured destruction," the stationing of Pershing and cruise missiles in Western Europe and massive oppositional citizens' movements as the background, it is not surprising to see a high degree of autonomy and considerable causal power being ascribed to military and war imperatives.

Although working within the same broad paradigm – the attempt to link war, state formation, and capitalism – Charles Tilly provides a perhaps more differentiated account; one which emphasizes the diversity of paths and conditions for these interactions and interdependencies. Like Giddens and Mann, he links the emergence of the institutions of the modern nation-state to the requirements of war preparation and war making:

> If war drove states, it did not exhaust their activity. On the contrary: as a by-product of preparations for war, rulers willy-nilly started activities and organizations that eventually took on a life of their own: courts, treasuries, systems of taxation, regional administration, public assemblies, and much more. (Tilly 1992: 75)

Similarly, the emergence of capitalism is said to be closely but contingently linked to military requirements: "capitalists serve states, when they are willing to do so, as lenders, as mobilizers of loans, and as managers or even collectors of revenues to repay loans" (85–6). As warfare became more complex and resource intensive, so too it came to require a more highly monetized economy and greater availability of credit. This interdependence creates conditions under which a mutual benefit can be gained by rulers and capitalists, and in which more monetized economics will facilitate more successful war machines. Tilly characterized the relationship as set out in figure 17.1.

But Tilly's distinctive contribution lies in his emphasis upon the historical diversity possible within these broad interdependencies. Specifically, he identifies two distinctive developmental paths: the "coercion-intensive" and the "capital-intensive." Where cities were sparse – and therefore trade links weak – state formation took the form of the creation of high-level coercive structures: "states commonly formed without either the collaboration or the effective opposition of local capitalists" (132). Where cities were linked into networks, and thus trade links strong, weaker state structures tended to emerge "in close collaboration with the local capitalists" (132). Russia and the states of Eastern Europe followed the coercive path, while Tilly offers Flanders, the Rhineland, and the Po Valley as examples of the second. Between these lay a mixed form of development – exemplified by Britain – in which there was an approximate

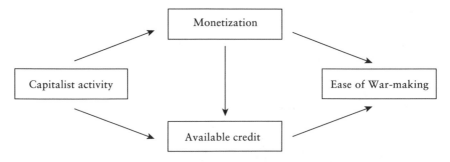

Figure 17.1   "How the presence of capital facilitates war making"

From Tilly 1992 : 86.

balance between coercion and capital (the "capitalized coercion path"). This broad ideal type enables Tilly to do two things: first, to show the complexities of the relationship between military, state, and capitalism; secondly, to argue that convergence around a standard nation-state form is a relatively recent, and indeed not yet completed, development.

So the sociological analysis of war, state formation, and (capitalist) industrialization can be characterized as an evermore sophisticated and complex narrative of the emergence of modernity via an account of the interactions between modern forms of war making, administration, monetized economies, and citizenship. It is an account which attempts to avoid reductionism while also increasingly seeking to give due weight to the variety of these interactions.

CHANGING NATURE OF WAR AND VIOLENCE

Thus far we have been concerned with the relationship between warfare, violence and the emergence of modern forms of state, economy, and citizenship. More recently, however, debates have been taken up with a possible discontinuity in or even partial reversal of the processes discussed so far. The new "multicentric world of postinternational politics" (Rosenau 1990: 40) is one in which we may be witnessing the nation-state's potential decomposition in the face of globalization, the gradual withdrawal of the masses from direct involvement with war making, war's *post*industrialization, the pacification of public (and military) in the West on the one hand and the emergence of new forms of "genocidal nationalism" (Ray 1999) on the other. Just as much of the debate in the 1980s has to be understood in the context of a particularly hot phase of the cold war, these more recent developments can be interpreted as attempts to come to terms with the very different circumstances obtaining since the collapse of the Soviet model of communism; a context characterized by new ethnic conflicts, by the disintegration of some states and the – sometimes violent – emergence of others (see Schwarzmantel, chapter 36, in this volume). The new paradigm of war is no longer the precarious stand-off between super-powers plus small proxy wars, but rather bloody ethnic conflicts such as Rwanda, Bosnia, and Kosovo or isolated acts of aggression – e.g. Iraq's invasion of Kuwait. These developments have found their intellectual echo in a new synthesis, or rather syntheses, of the elements discussed above. Debate is shifting from the formation of the nation-state to its possible *de*formation.

Changes in the Relationship between the Military and Society

An early attempt to come to terms with these changing circumstances was Martin Shaw's *Post-Military Society* (1991). The question Shaw addressed was whether the processes of "pacification" entailed by the state's monopoly over violence and militarization might not eventually lead us out of military society. Among the forces undermining military society is the changing nature of warfare itself: "the 'mode of warfare' has evolved beyond classical total war" (67). Specifically, technological innovations in war making – nuclear weapons, inter-

ballistic missiles, smart bombs, etc. – mean that war, while still involving massive potential civilian losses, no longer entails mass mobilization on the model of industrial warfare: "the nuclear age sees a re-privatization of war by the elites" (76). Under such conditions it is no longer necessary to form society around military needs. This is, paradoxically, especially true of the most militarily powerful country in history, the USA: "America is predominantly a consumer, commodity-based, society in which 'armaments culture' is inserted as an important 'element but not the core'" (84). Furthermore, Shaw suggests that "instead of the militarization of society, they [mass mobilization and conscription] posited a civilianization of the military" (73). He has in mind here new freedoms to unionize within European continental armies (e.g. in Holland), the loosening of regulations governing conscious objection (e.g. in Germany and Austria), etc. Conscription is both on the decline and a likely source of the civilianization of the military; an importer of "civilian values into the military context" (86) – e.g. the number of conscientious objectors in (the then) West Germany rose from 4,000 in 1964 to 77,000 in 1988. This may explain why the demilitarization of society may be stronger in countries with conscription than in those with professional armies only (though Switzerland may be something of an exception here).

Outside the military "the nation, in the West, is mobilized 'not as players but as *spectators*'" (78). The general demilitarization of society at large then makes it increasingly difficult to demand real sacrifice; "popular support [for war] is shallow and volatile" (79), and thus war has to be presented almost as a game like the Olympics or like a video game (e.g. Reagan's Star Wars program) in which no one really dies or suffers. Shaw uses the Gulf War as the major example of this tendency. Shaw is not implying here that this presentation of the Gulf War corresponded to the reality "on the ground," but he would want to argue that this public attitude was a constraint on the conduct of the war. He may not wish go as far as the French sociologist Jean Baudrillard did with his (in)famous quip that the "Gulf War did not take place" (see Baudrillard 1995), but Shaw does suggest that war must be virtualized at least in its presentation to western publics. Subsequent developments, such as NATO's unprecedented exclusive use of aerial bombardment during its intervention in Kosovo, would seem to confirm Shaw's analysis.

Two contrasting forms of weakening or loss of the state's monopoly of violence seem to be emerging: on the one hand we have many of the history's most militaristic nations now bound into political and military alliances (e.g. the EU and NATO respectively) which constrain their ability to act alone plus an increasingly demilitarized public, on the other hand we are witnessing the emergence of new forms of violence and conflict in weaker and less stable states which – in a quite different way – undermine those states' monopoly of the means of coercion. These two aspects come together in the case of ethnic wars and genocide and in debates surrounding western intervention in such cases.

Genocide and Terror, Then and Now

Attempts to understand genocide and terror have gained a renewed relevance and urgency in the light of the conflicts which have emerged in the wake of changes in the world order since 1989. Sociologists' neglect of genocide was broken by Zygmunt Bauman's *Modernity and the Holocaust* (1989). Yet the pattern which we have observed above – the continuity between earlier and contemporary analysts and the overriding concern with the relationship between violence and modernity – can be seen just as clearly in the sociological discussion of genocide. In Bauman's case the direct link is provided by the work of the political theorist Hannah Arendt whose *The Origin of Totalitarianism* of 1951 proposed what might be called the "continuity thesis," namely the view that totalitarianism is not an aberration within modernity, but an ever present danger requiring only a specific combination of some of modern society's core characteristics.

For Bauman too, the holocaust was not premodern and irrational, but was the product of organized modernity; it was planned, organized, and instrumentally rational. Thus, he argues that modern racism is quite distinct from premodern prejudices or fear of strangers: "*Racism is a policy first, ideology second. Like all politics, it needs organization, managers and experts*" (74). The preconditions for modern genocide were precisely those through which Weber and Marx defined modernity: instrumental rationality, bureaucratic domination; the centralization of the means of coercion and machinofacture. Bauman comes close to the Critical Theorists' argument of the 1940s and 1950s by suggesting that instrumental rationality within a bureaucratic hierarchy replaces substantive and ethical reflection with mere technical performative criteria: "*the irrelevance of moral standards for the technical success of the bureaucratic operation*" (101). The monolithic nature of modern hierarchies anaesthetizes moral sentiments and responsibility becomes "free-floating." Again like the Critical Theorists, he argues that technical operations hide and dehumanize (reify) the subjects of their operations and, like Elias, notes that internal pacification renders populations defenseless. The centralization of the means of violence and administration forces those in subordinate positions to behave rationally while freeing those at the top from any such necessity: "in the rational world of modern bureaucracy, the irrational adventurer is the dictator" (138). Bauman sets out to do two things. First, to show that the holocaust is not a German problem alone, but a problem for European modernity; it "*brings together some ordinary factors of modernity which normally are kept apart*" (94). Secondly, he calls on individual defiance for rational rules and regulations as a means of preventing the reoccurrence of such planned ("gardened") acts of inhumanity: "terror remains effective as long as the balloon of rationality has not been pricked" (203).

But an interpretation which emphasizes the degree of continuity between "normal" modernizing and rationalizing forces and the holocaust can also be challenged on the basis of sociological analysis. One example here is Wolfgang Sofsky's close analysis of the nature of Nazi rule in *Ordnung des Terrors* (1993). Sofsky does not dissent from Bauman's general thesis that the holocaust was uniquely modern – that is to say it presupposed the apparatus of bureaucracy, concentration of violence, industrialization, etc. Nevertheless, there are two crucial differences: (i) whereas Bauman's starting point is a general diagnosis of modernity from which he deduces aspects of the holocaust, Sofsky's point of departure is the social structure of the concentration camp itself from which he then works upwards towards generalizations about the nature of Nazi rule (and terror in general); (ii) this procedure leads to a difference of interpretation, or at least emphasis: whereas Bauman stresses not just the modernity of the holocaust but also its "normality" – i.e. the high degree of continuity between Nazism and the normal institutions of organized modernity – Sofsky argues that the concentration camp regime was unique – i.e. that there is a degree of discontinuity between the social structure of the camp and that of the factory or office.

Perhaps the best illustration of this point lies in the difference between the terms "deterrent" (*Abschreckung*) and "terror" (*Schrecken*). Social control within the modern factory or bureaucracy is achieved through deterrent: actors are encouraged to behave in certain kinds of ways through a variety of deterrents and rewards. They know that if they do what is required from them punishment will be avoided. There is a high degree of both predictability of outcome (for both sub- and super-ordinates) and economy; deterrent is instrumentally rational and efficient. In contrast, terror is deployed arbitrarily in such a way that the actors cannot know how to avoid punishment through modifying their behavior. Terror is neither instrumentally rational in any transparent sense, nor is it a means of social control capable of directing behavior in a predictable fashion. Terror is not a means towards an end but an end in itself. Such non-instrumentalist power, Sofsky dubs "absolute power"; its aim is not *control* over subjects' actions but total *domination* over the subjects themselves; a domination which he argues can only find its full expression in their extermination. Again in contrast to Bauman, Sofsky also argues that "the bureaucracy of the concentration camp was anything but monolithic" (127). The principles of the SS for example were grounded more in camaraderie than in rational discipline. Not, as in a bureaucracy, absolute obedience, but absolute loyalty was its basic principle. This allowed a high degree of autonomy and discretion resulting in a degree of chaos and lack of coordination untypical of modern bureaucracies.

Such issues have again been raised in the light of what Mary Kaldor (1999) has called "new wars"; wars in which ethnic groups seek to gain state power through the pursuit of a brutal identity politics of ethnic cleansing and genocide; wars which violate the most basic human rights. Shaw draws the distinction between new wars and industrialized total war as follows:

> What is new about "new wars" is that the classically genocidal policy of murderous ethnic expulsion has been transformed from a sub-theme in classical total war, into the main thrust of wars conducted by authoritarian states like Serbia and Croatia, together with their ethnic-nationalist parties and statelets in Bosnia. This can be seen as a degeneration of classic total war. (Shaw 1999: par 2.9)

While the contemporary conditions are different in key respects from those analyses by Bauman and Sofsky – e.g. they were not conditions of state break-up – issues of the instrumentality and mechanisms of terror have again been raised. Kaldor and Shaw interpret new genocidal wars as particularly destructive responses to globalizing forces which are said to weaken nation-states. They are attempts to reconsolidate state structures around exclusive ethnic identities. One aspect of the normal process of state making, namely the creation of a single legitimate culture within a given territory (see Gellner 1983), takes a particularly bloody turn.

One sociological response to this "new" situation has been to develop a more anthropologically-sensitive analysis which moves beyond questions of state formation, power, and rivalry to focus downwards, as Sofsky did, on the actual application and mechanisms of terror. This is evident in the following observation in which Larry Ray, referring to the conflict in Kosovo, links violence with cultural formation and shows how ethnicity and gender become salient in "new wars":

> A special case of public commemoration are what Durkheim ... called "sad celebrations," that is, piacular (expiatory, atoning) rites which fuse mourning and melancholy with sacrifice and violence. Their effect is to generate anger and the need to avenge the dead and discharge collective pain, manifesting in real or ritual violence. Victims are sought outside the group, especially among resident minorities "not protected by sentiments of sympathy" and women serve more frequently than men as objects of cruellest rites of mourning and as scapegoats. (Ray 1999: para. 2.5)

Similarly, Ronit Lentin argues than in order to understand wartime rape an analysis is necessary in which the complexities of the relationships between gender, ethnicity, and nation are fully acknowledged: "we are beginning to understand, wartime rape is not only about sex, nor only about power, but about the social construction of gender and, in times of war, about the gendered constructions of ethnicity and nation" (Lentin 1999: para. 3.9).

The focus on the micro level and on the anthropology of war can, but need not, lead us to underestimate the degree of political and instrumental manipulation of ethnic antagonisms. In a newspaper article on war in Kosovo, Sofsky, in line with his interpretations of the holocaust, emphasized the autonomy of the "gangs" who perpetrated much of the violence during NATO's air campaign (Sofsky 1999), but in retrospect it appears that this "spontaneous" violence was more under control and planned than may have been evident at the time. We may not be so far away after all from Weber's characterization of discipline as the instrumentally rational manipulation of the irrational.

But "new wars" have opened-up new divisions at a more macro and overtly political level too. This can be seen particularly clearly in the debates occasioned by NATO's intervention in Kosovo which saw a sharp difference emerging between the "cosmopolitan" supporters of the intervention and their critics (see Scott 1999). Mary Kaldor's analysis is representative of the cosmopolitan perspective. Like other cosmopolitans, for example Jürgen Habermas, Kaldor defends both NATO's intervention and the universalism of human rights discourse against the cultural particularism of the "warlords." An appeal to the universal rights of the world citizen and to Kant's ideal of perpetual peace is set against relativism and cultural particularism. Here "globalization" plays a double role. Globalization in the sense of the weakening of states is said to contribute to the emergence of new forms of reactionary particularism, while globalization in the sense of increased cultural pluralism plus the lifting of the rights of state citizens to the new global level of the "world citizen" (Habermas 1999) is viewed by cosmopolitans as a potential source of resolution of such conflict; as a means to protect citizens even against their own governments.

Critics of this view point to inconsistencies in the West's responses (e.g., while Kosovo raised questions of human rights, Chechenya seemed largely to be a matter of Russian internal affairs), to unintended consequences and side-effects of intervention (Zolo 1997) or to the ways in which the stated humanitarian ends are systematically at odds with the logic of the military means (Drake 1999); or else have argued that violence is immanent within the universalizing project itself (Caygill 1993).

The sociology of war and violence reflects current events precisely because it was and is a reflection *on* those events. What we have seen, and continue to see, are responses to contemporary developments and concerns informed by arguments inherited from a variety of sociological traditions. In this process core notions such as rationalization, modernity, bureaucratization, and so on are themselves transformed and renewed.

Further Reading

Charles Tilly (1992) offers a sophisticated analysis of the relationship between state formation, capitalism, and war making drawing on both Weberian and Marxist analysis. The nature of recent conflicts is discussed by Mary Kaldor (1999). A critique of the cosmopolitan position to which Kaldor adheres can be found in Danilio Zolo (1997). The works by Bauman (1989) and Sofsky (1993) provide powerful but contrasting sociological accounts of the nature of genocide. In this chapter I have not discussed an alternative approach to the analysis of war and violence which draws upon Foucault and upon postmodernist thought, for which see Michael Drake, *Problematics of Military Power* (Frank Cass: 2001).

18

Revolution

Michael Drake

Studies of revolution have tried to define a general phenomenon. This positivist approach is of limited empirical use because the definition is made in abstraction from particular cases so that there are many instances that do not fit and which must then be denied the status of "revolution." The Iranian revolution of 1979 and the Eastern European revolution of 1989 exploded the grand theoretical analyses of the political sociology of revolution and attempts to incorporate them into a revived (late-) modernization theory reveal analyses as tautological rather than explanatory. More recently, there have been attempts at "multifactorial" accounts, acknowledging the importance of culture and ideology. These are preferable to the explanations based on universal instrumental rationality to which they are opposed, but – like other contemporary theories – they fail to question the assumption that revolutions involve the seizure of sovereign political power. Charles Tilly's recent work on political process is considered, but Drake argues that ultimately his approach collapses the sociology of revolution into the study of the variable contexts of an invariant object, rather than achieving the radical rethinking of methodology he proposes. Drake also considers a third approach to studies of revolution, that focusing on historical tradition and the meaning of revolutions. He concludes with a discussion of Foucault's conception of power in which the political figures as the domain of the possible, rather than as sovereign power.

This essay is concerned not so much with the dynamics or mechanisms of revolution itself, as with the way in which sociologists have tried to define a general phenomenon of revolution in order to compare instances and develop explanations. This approach, I argue, ultimately and inevitably reduces processes to a category and is unable to think revolution beyond a normative concept of order which revolutionary actions, and sometimes ideologies, have aimed to transcend. There is thus always a misfit between the category of analysis and the concept in practice.

The definitions which analytically differentiate revolution from "normal" politics, and which isolate it as a distinct, irruptive phenomena in the flow of historical time, ultimately construct their sociological category as a closed event within the normative order of unitary sovereignty. They are thus unable to comprehend revolution as the opening of political possibility, with the paradoxical effect that the analytical category of revolution is ultimately forced back into the premodern meaning of revolution as a cyclical turn of the wheel of human history within a given order of the world. For the Renaissance, that order was still the order of God; for sociology, it is the order of the social necessity of sovereign power. To paraphrase Foucault, we have not yet cut off the king's head in the sociological analysis of revolution.

This chapter begins from but does not follow the conventions of overviews of subdisciplinary fields in sociology, for reasons which should be quickly apparent. Rather than using conventional schemas to present the range of theories of revolution that inform empirical study, I have chosen to concentrate on more recent debates and the issues these raise, using the contributions to undertake a critical investigation into the enterprise of theorizing revolution.

PERSPECTIVES IN THE SOCIOLOGY OF REVOLUTION

It is conventional for overviews of the sociology of revolution to begin by classifying a huge and diverse range of scholarship into distinctive theoretical perspectives (Kimmel 1990; Sztompka 1993; Goodwin 1994), enabling comparisons between very different theoretical approaches to identify strengths and weaknesses toward the construction of theoretical synthesis that will avoid the problems of existing theory. Drawing up the tasks and problematics for a *general* theory of revolution thus tends to treat divergent theories as a division of labor within a unifiable program of enquiry orienting upon a given object.

Michael Kimmel's overview, for example, identifies three major approaches, mapping distinct perspectives within each and outlining specific theories within them. His concluding synopsis is worth quoting at length as an exemplary map of the field:

> Non-structural theories present significant problems; aggregate psychological models emphasize individual motivations, but lose sight of social structural preconditions of revolution; and structural functionalist reliance on value consensus in a stable social system incorporates cultural analysis into a discussion of mobilization, but underplays the critical causal role of social classes, the world market, or the state as a repressive institution . . . [W]orld systems models downplay the causal role of class relations and the autonomous roles of culture and politics . . . A more traditional Marxist focus on these class relations devalues the autonomous role of the state and may . . . decontextualize the revolutionary society from a larger international frame. The state-centered theories of revolution are as structurally sound as the states they analyze are unsound, locating the revolutionary moment as a moment of state collapse and reconstruction in the aftermath of class-based struggles from below. But . . . [they] tend to overlook the significance of conscious human activity in the process of revolution . . . Tilly's synthesis comes closest to addressing all the major issues and allowing for a multidimensional model of revolution. But even he undervalues class struggle as well as world-economic variables . . . [I]n generating a model of political contention that places the state at

the analytic center and observes the way in which groups mobilize themselves and their resources to struggle with the state, Tilly undervalues economic variables altogether... (Kimmel 1990: 217–18)

Contending theories are usually informed by wider debates in social theory, applying partisan approaches to the phenomenon of revolution, but syntheses situate themselves within their self-delineated field of the sociology of revolution and address themselves to tasks which they identify for a *general theory* of revolution, functional requirements that provide performative criteria by which any theory can be evaluated. Synthesizing overviews thus tend to return the sociology of revolution to a positivist model of knowledge that constitutes the sociologist as a discursive entrepreneur, legislating the tasks for sociological practice in an ironic replication of the absolutist exercise of legislative power that classically triggers revolution itself.

The Sociology of Revolutions

Such approaches thus define their criteria of validity in abstraction from empirical events and particular factors, opening an epistemological gap between theory and political realities: when the results are applied, they tend to deny the revolutionary character of events that do not fit the criteria by which a general theory of revolution is validated. Pursuit of a general theory of revolution through theoretical critique not only requires the project to legislate the tasks of theory, but to define the object itself, since the validity of theory becomes the gauge by which to evaluate whether a revolution has objectively taken place. Such approaches initially acknowledge the problematic conceptualization of revolution itself (Kimmel 1990; Calvert 1996), but set it aside in favor of an *a priori* working definition. Whatever their theoretical intentions, they thus remain trapped within the positivist tendency for hypothesis to become hypostasis, when the theoretical function displaces the object that is to be explained by the concept. This procedure produces an inherent tautological tendency, as definitive *a priori* conceptualization ensures that the sociology of revolution is never confronted with the possibility of empirical refutation of that conceptualization, since non-corroborative evidence can simply be dismissed as outside the defined object. To put it more simply, cases that do not fit a particular model are not "really" revolutions. Kimmel (1990) points out that even strict application of the criteria of success would limit the number of revolutions to about 20, excluding many fruitful examples.

Once a category of revolution is established and the problematic of conceptualization and non-corroborative data thereby dismissed, the usual procedure is to rush headlong to engage the category with key concerns of sociology; not with means and ends, but with structure and agency. This concern is an effect of the shift in sociology from accounts of one-sided socioeconomic determination of social structure and the consciousness of actors, to approaches that privilege either structure *or* agency as causal (e.g. Skocpol 1979; Taylor 1988). More recently, attempts to theorize some kind of mediation between structure and agency have produced a further shift of focus, from causes to the interaction of multifactorial component elements.

Deeply embedded in ideological normativity, postwar sociology tended to view revolution in terms of a pathology manifesting itself in either social systemic dysfunction or the psychology of elite leadership. The main challenge to this hegemony in mainstream sociology came in the form of Barrington Moore's recognition of the primarily peasant basis of revolutionary forces under the leadership of intellectual elites (1967), providing a perspective radicalized further by Theda Skocpol's structuralist focus upon the role of the state as a quasi-independent factor (1979). Like Moore's earlier revisionary focus, her theorization was embedded in the context of the cold war bipolar division of global hegemony, in which revolutions appeared successfully only in the hegemonically under-determined spaces on the periphery of the great divide where prospectively marginalized rural peasant classes were threatened by economic and political modernization, rather than in the hegemonic core where states were comparatively securely established in relation to subordinate industrial classes. As Max Weber argued in his methodological writings, the historical context of social science tends to provide a selective focus for theorization and analysis (Weber 1949). For Skocpol, the context of bipolar hegemony focused theoretical attention on the periphery, while the basis of security of the contextual global order in mutual recognition of sovereignty in stabilized core states highlighted the role of structurally differentiated political factors (especially the state) for her analysis of the internal mechanisms of revolution.

The other general strand of grand-theoretical analysis was developed in Eisenstadt's historicization of systems analysis, by setting the pathological concept of revolution in the context of a world modernization process, in which the form of political and social systems of both East and West corresponded to a global phase of social and economic development. In this perspective, revolution figured as a specific, dissonant and catastrophic effect of local adaptations to the developing global environment that disequilibriated a given social system.

Both these approaches were fundamentally undermined by the Iranian revolution of 1979 and the eastern European revolutions of 1989. The Iranian revolution was undertaken against the modernizing regime of the Shah and saw the successful ascendancy of forces that appeared archaic to progressivist perspectives, in the form of the Shi'ite mullahs and their social basis in the bazaar economy, which effectively displaced modern forces such as the intelligentsia, the industrial bourgeoisie and the working class from center stage of the revolution. The contextual frame of modernization-based theories of revolution was thus exploded, particularly with the proliferation of Islamicist revolutionary movements across the Middle East and Northern Africa. Against Skocpol's schema, the primacy of urban forces and cultural forms in the Iranian revolution provided an empirical counter-factual of historical significance to the state-centered analytical focus which neglected the role of precisely these factors.

The eastern European revolutions were similarly urban and aimed at more than a simple substitution of sovereign authority. These revolutions occurred in the core, and their inevitable object, the destruction of the monolithic regime of bipolar hegemonic dominance, imploded the contextual frame of peripheralist theories of revolution in the tradition of Moore and Skocpol. Attempts to incorporate them into a revived (late-) modernization theory in which they figure as economically and historically determined expressions of a shift in the world-process, as the overthrow of social and political systems corresponding to an outmoded stage of modernization, simply reveals such analysis as tautological, rather than explanatory (Kumar 1996).

Causal/Component Accounts

While the Iranian Revolution of 1979 dispelled the association between modern political revolution and Enlightenment narratives of the progress of Reason, the eastern European revolutions of 1989 invoked crisis for the self-definitively predictive function of the sociology of revolution, particularly in the USA. Jeff Goodwin's review article in the journal *Theory and Society* provided an over-view of recent contributions and a focus for responses from different perspect-ives. Goodwin celebrates the turn in the sociology of revolution away from "Enlightenment 'metanarratives' around the inexorable expansion of individual freedom or the forces of production," but returns it to precisely the same condition of knowledge in which those metanarratives were grounded by evalu-ating the shift as "progressive and liberating" (Goodwin 1994: 731–2).

Studies in the structural perspective have made this shift away from progress-ivist or evolutionary frameworks and totalizing accounts in attempts to expand the dimensions of structural determinism beyond the socioeconomic by devel-oping "multifactorial" causal accounts. However, these attempts "to explore the complex interconnections among state power, civil society, and cultural systems" result in "reifying these analytic concepts into concrete 'spheres' or 'levels' of social life" (Goodwin 1994: 758). Goodwin thus praises the increasing "em-phasis on the potential autonomy of states . . . as well as of culture," but fails to see in the autonomy accorded to these categories the source of the tendency to structural reification (Goodwin 1994: 732).

Goodwin argues for greater emphasis on ideological and cultural dimensions in the multifactorial picture, categories which enable critique of the pretensions of rational-choice theories that impute a universal instrumental rationality to all social actors as if the cognition of agents could always be rendered transparent to the theorist by simple application of the "rationality principle" of goal-oriented calculation of variable means and ends; as if this calculative reason was un-mediated by culture and ideology. Aya defends the "situational logic" of imput-ing rational calculation to actors by ascertaining goals and constraints to model their situation and then proceeding to infer the intentional action implied by this model (Aya 1994: 773), but his universalized concept of rational social action originates from Max Weber's studies of the culturally and historically specific constitution of modern subjectivity and its particular and even unique "ration-ality" (Sayer 1991). Taylor (1988) has offered another defense of rational choice theory by restricting its scope to the explanation of actions of "ordinary" participants in revolution (in contrast to ideologically motivated revolution-aries), but it is difficult to see how the rational calculus of interests can be abstracted from cultural and ideological context, even for the political innocence presupposed in "ordinary" people. Taylor's categorical division of actors dispels precisely what has to be explained, that is, the *political participation* of "the masses." Furthermore, it still requires a social context for "ordinary" participants – a prior, traditional *community* as the source of their values and categories of perception. His "weak" rational choice theory thus itself invokes a reified concept of culture.

On the other hand, Goodwin's call for recognition of the role of culture in structuralist accounts fails to follow through the implications of cultural mediation to question the concept of revolution itself. His proposal to expand the scope of the theory of revolution still universalizes a culturally and historically specific object (the Jacobin aim of revolution as the conspiratorial elite seizure of sovereign political power). The argument that revolutions will always tend toward the seizure of sovereign power because the international context of the states-system determines this object (Giddens 1985; Calvert 1996), simply elevates the essentialization of political sovereignty to another level, and fails to comprehend cultural and ideological dimensions that traverse the boundaries upon which the nation-state system depends.

Goodwin's appeal for structural accounts to include culture and ideology exposes the limit of a universal concept of revolution by introducing a subjective dimension. If actors' cognition is structured by culture and ideology, then their object of revolution may not correspond to the concept of revolution that theory sets itself the task of explaining. For instance, it can be argued convincingly that while it did not attain sovereign power, the multi-movement revolt generally formulated under one of its manifestations, May 1968, has nonetheless revolutionized global society, politicizing whole areas of everyday life that were hitherto considered to be "natural," functional, necessary, and simply unquestionable (Foucault 1980a; Habermas 1987). This revolution of modernity has proceeded through cultural and ideological struggles of plural movements, circumventing sovereign power without projecting a totalistic social transformation. In this sense, the project of the sociology of revolution to integrate structurally divided categories in a "multifactorial" account of revolution that ultimately refers the object back to the conceptual criteria of sovereign power, has been outflanked by the strategies of revolutionaries and the genealogy of revolution itself.

Their struggles are not oriented by an instrumental relation between means and ends, as in the sociological model. Rather, the dissolution of that instrumental division was an integral aspect of the revolution in revolutionary strategy that enabled its subversion of the given order. And after all, the ultimate object of all modern revolutionaries has not been to merely establish a new order in the given political domain, but to open new domains of struggle by extending the frontiers of what is thinkable and what is possible. It is this aim to inaugurate new conditions of social life which distinguishes modern revolution from the Renaissance concept. In this sense, the object of revolution posited by the definitional strategies of the sociology of revolution thus represents a bogus modernity.

Charles Tilly's response to Goodwin's diagnosis of current problems obstructing the progressive advance of the sociology of revolution accepts that "we need better analyses of culture in revolution," but rather than extending the theoretical compass, much less reviewing the operational concept, he proposes that we can (and should) focus the concept of culture by conceiving it primarily in terms of "rival and shared understandings," concerning on the one hand formal constitutional relations ("rights and obligations of chief actors...[and]...the previous history of citizen-state relations" in a given polity), and on the other, elements of calculative rationality ("likely outcomes of different available forms of collective action...[and]...the relative desirability of those outcomes") (Tilly 1994: 802). Culture is thus reduced to the ideology of constitutional rights and relations (a sovereign object) on the one hand, and on the other to a form of *verstehen* that posits a (sovereign) subject of calculative rationality.

Narrowing down culture in this way, it is possible to retain a universal sociological concept of revolution against the subjective particularism introduced by cultural variables. However, if "culture in revolution" is no more than ideology in its *narrow* sense of popular understandings of the formal political constitution, plus a universalizable principle of rational calculus, then we really do not need it in order to grasp how "culture, state and revolutionary action interact incessantly," since culture is already subsumed in the latter two categories and its "rival and shared understandings" of these does little more than mediate between them.

Farideh Farhi's response to Goodwin offers more productive suggestions. She calls for greater attention to "the evolving relationship between culture and ideology" (Farhi 1994: 786), pointing out how in the Iranian case, the "ideologization" of Islam constituted the contested (that is, political) terrain of the revolution itself, while culture was itself reconstructed in the ideological entrepreneurship of the clerics' use of culture as ideology to establish their political dominance in the revolutionary Iranian state. However, Farhi's theorization of the interrelation of culture, politics, and ideology implicitly undercuts her own conception of revolution as "a political break," raising the question of where the political is located by problematizing the boundaries between the proper spheres of politics and culture upon which her structural sociology of revolution depends for its units of analysis.

Charles Tilly's Conditional Revolution

More recently, Tilly has shifted his position in relation to the mainstream sociology of revolution. Tilly (1995) argues that merely definitional accounts and tautological "predictions" are an effect of the methodological approach that constructs invariant models of a social condition or process. He does not deny the importance of "transhistorical regularities," but argues that they do not constitute "recurrent structures and processes" in the form posited by invariant models. This begs the question of how we can have non-recurrent transhistorical regularities, but Tilly's answer is simply that, "time, place and sequence strongly influence how the relevant processes unfold" (Tilly 1995: 1601), that is, the study of variable *contexts* should be substituted for *a priori* modelling in which concept and context are defined as essentially integral. In this contribution of

Tilly's, it becomes clear that his approach collapses the sociology of revolution back into the study of the variable contexts of an invariantly conceptualized object, though this does not appear to be his intention.

Tilly polemicizes against the "monadic thinking" that posits "coherent durable monads rather than contingent transitory connections among socially constructed identities," since such models do not represent political realities but "assume a political world in which whole structures and sequences repeat themselves time after time in essentially the same form." Invariant models are utilized across a range of perspectives and theories of revolution, conceptualizing their object in terms of essential characteristics that can include "causal, sequential or transactional links among the elements," but for any such approach the object is validated only by these "essential universals," and thus appears as invariant (Tilly 1995: 1595–7). (As I shall show, however, Tilly's own approach has to follow the same path and is thus inherently prone to precisely the same tendency.) The mainstream sociology of revolution is characterized by this method, and the resulting gap between theory and political realities invokes a theoretical preoccupation with "improving the model" by expanding the scope of invariant definition (Goodwin's call to include culture and ideology in the theory of revolution would provide an example of this tendency). However, Tilly's own claims to escape this orbit seem to be delusory, deriving from an elision of terms within his own schema which hides its complicity with the very approaches he sets out to debunk.

Tilly prefers the metaphor for revolution of a traffic jam to that of an earthquake, but seems to neglect its historically specific conditions and its implicit reference to a transitional condition. Tilly's metaphor figuratively predisposes the analysis of revolution to an aggregate model deriving from the aggregate social theory ultimately underpinning his enterprise (Tilly 1978). Like Talcott Parsons' analogy between social order and traffic regularities, Tilly's use of the traffic jam metaphor conceals implicit essentialist norms which prefigure substantive analysis, but which can be revealed by deconstructing an elision between two uses of the term "state power" in his schema.

Tilly argues that his own enterprise does not take "revolution" as a singular phenomenon, but distinguishes between "revolutionary situations (moments of deep fragmentation in state power) and revolutionary outcomes (rapid, forcible, durable transfers of state power)" (Tilly 1995: 1604). However, in designating "as a full-fledged revolution any combination of the two," he simply splits the singularity into two moments extending over time and thus warranting designation as "stages" of a necessary singular process that can only be described tautologically. Moreover, these two moments both orient his concept of revolution toward a singular object, here designated as "state power." In *European Revolutions* (1993), "state power" refers to the single category of *sovereignty*. Tilly's recourse to the concept of sovereignty is dictated by the need of "sociological theory" to differentiate revolutionary situations from a norm of routinized domination, and in a definition of the duality of the revolutionary process drawn from Trotsky, the first moment (a revolutionary situation) is categorically differentiated as "divided sovereignty" from the second (a revolutionary outcome) as "successful transfers of sovereign power." Sovereignty thus provides

Tilly with his own latent invariant, reducing the possibilities of power and the scope of the political to this historically and culturally specific and theoretically problematic construction (Bartelson 1995).

The study of "regionally and temporally variable forms" which Tilly (1995) urges upon the sociology of revolution, thus turns out to be no more than the study of the variable contexts of the contestation of sovereignty (a contest that is never more than transitional between unitary forms of sovereign power). This latent invariance is obscured by Tilly's secondary use of the term "state power" as one of the variables that "shape" (or influence) revolution, eliding a distinction between its use to indicate the *invariant*, sovereignty, and its use in the list of variable *contextual forms* for sovereignty, where it indicates forms of legitimacy, such as royal patrilineage or political constitutions. It is only by virtue of the former sense in which the term is used, to designate an immanently essential sovereignty as the singular object of the dual process of revolution, that "revolution turns out to be a coherent phenomenon" across the variable contexts which constitute particular causes, sequences, and outcomes.

This categorization of revolution replicates the problem of "invariant models," and Tilly's application of his theory to the eastern European events of 1989 thus attempts to adjudicate whether "full-fledged" revolutions had in fact occurred in particular national contexts, unequivocally validating political reality only for Czechoslovakia, East Germany, the Soviet Union, and Yugoslavia (Tilly 1993). Unfortunately, the outcome of revolution in precisely those cases was not the reunification and transfer of sovereign power, but the disappearance of the very sovereignties that provide Tilly with his unit of analysis. The problem here lies in a theoretical concept of revolution that takes the prior existence of a singular sovereignty as the preconditional unit of analysis, and which thus posits the division and reunification of sovereignty as the criteria for a revolutionary situation and a revolutionary outcome respectively. At the end of this book, Tilly speculated the end of the nation-state as a singular frame of analysis, but in his 1994 contribution this was only conceived in terms of "cultural particularism" as an additional factor in the scenario, i.e. as an "improvement of the model," rather than a critique of the pursuit of a general theory and conceptualization of revolution. As I have shown, despite shifting his position in more recent debates, he is unable to abandon the essentialist category in which his own ultimately normative and invariant model is grounded.

Tilly's approach appears to promise an escape from the aporias of the mainstream sociology of revolution in that his theorization of political *processes* does not depend upon the normative category of sovereignty, enabling us to see sovereignty and the state as epiphenomena of the stabilization of immediate domination-by-violence and thus to grasp the historical contingency of the emergence of categories of analysis like state formations, civil societies, polities, and communities as processes and balances, rather than reifying them as ontological, accomplished "facts" that can be defined by their essential functions. Potentially, then, Tilly's model of political processes would provide a tool with which to theorize the cases that he finds "marginal" or "uncertain" revolutions, and even instances where the revolutionary process destabilizes the condition of sovereignty itself, as in Albania and Bosnia-Herzegovina. Such analysis would need to dispense with the norms of conventional sociological approaches. Without fundamental reconceptualization, however, we will continue to produce theories that fail both in their own terms and in their relation to the phenomena that they seek to explain, because our conceptions of both the project of revolution and its theorization are dependent upon *a prioris* that entrap sociology within the very normative discourse of modernity which revolution itself may transgress.

THE MEANING OF REVOLUTION

The problems ensuing on the categorically definitive model and nation-state framework for the analysis of revolution orient us toward a third convention in the sociology of revolution, the distinction between "great" (world-historical) and "minor" (usually national) revolutions. The turn toward multifactorial accounts that seek to encompass particular, case-specific factors in sociological explanation eschews the concept of "great revolutions" as bound up with totalizing theories of mono-causal determination and grand narratives of History, but still seek to retain, in Tilly's terms, a singular transhistorical concept of revolution. Their rejection of the concept of "great" revolutions thus assumes that the distinction between "great" and "small" revolutions differentiates between cases of a singular phenomenon. However, Tilly's evaluation of the events of 1989 as "minor" revolutions suggests that such a conflation invokes acute problems in relation to political realities. In national terms, some of the events may indeed not warrant the designation of "revolution," but in wider terms it is undeniable that as an integral process the events of 1989 constituted a revolution.

The matter is not simply one of geographical scale or units of analysis, so that we could say the events of 1989 constituted a revolution at the level of the world-system but not at the scale of particular nation-states, since it is not possible to isolate national revolutions from their global and historical context. Rather than attempting to extend a singular concept across different units or scales of analysis, we might do better to recognize that the distinction between great and minor revolutions designates entirely distinct phenomena. The significance of revolution in the "great" sense, as *transnational* phenomena linked across time, not through conditional forms but by the concept itself and the meanings and ideals it bears, has exercised another set of theorists, primarily concerned with the meaning, rather than the causes or conditions of revolution. Krishan Kumar (1971) anticipated Tilly's objections to "invariant models" by using Bulmer's critique of the *a priori* method of conceptualization in social science in the simple recognition that definition is integral to the social construction of reality, so that the conceptual definition of revolution, the object, must be studied as part of the process itself, and cannot be imposed as a precondition of such study. This approach led Kumar to identify "traditions" of revolution, in which the concept is transformed in the process of social action for which it provides the object.

Kumar (1996) argues that to understand the events of 1989 we need to look to continuities with the "great tradition" which links the seventeenth-century revolutions with those of the transatlantic eighteenth century, the national revolutions of the nineteenth, and those of the Third International and the movements for national liberation in the twentieth, through the common theme of democracy (which motivated, even if it did not characterize, the Bolshevik revolution of 1917). However, unlike their more recent precedents, the revolutions of 1989 represented a break in continuity by rejecting the legacy of 1917 along with the old regimes which were ideologically associated to it, and did not look forward to a new order, but backwards, to political forms of the interwar years and ethnic, prepolitical identities. Habermas (1991) thus designated them "revolutions of recuperation." Such projects of recovery, however, can still be linked to the revolutions of 1640, 1688, and 1776, which also claimed to restore lost liberties and originated the orientation toward civil society that characterized the intellectual sources of 1989.

More forward-looking interpretations of 1989 have been advanced by evolutionary social theory, in the modernization schema which derives the collapse of the old regimes from their incapacity to adapt to the novel formations and processes of postindustrialism or late modernity. But this thesis is merely tautological, a self-affirming description that is quite unable to explain how or why, with no account of "the dynamics of mobilization and political transformation" necessary for explanation. In the same vein, postmodern views of the 1989 events characterize them by the absence of rationalizing utopian schemes which had hitherto motivated the great tradition, thus signifying the end of the Enlightenment project of reason and revolution itself. Kumar (1996) adopts a more positive interpretation, in which the links of the revolutions of 1989 to the great tradition of democracy re-open the prospect of democratic civil society in the West as well as the East, but this projection imbues his conclusion with its own utopian schema, as much belied by political realities as is the invariance of the models and concepts of the sociology of revolution that rejects such metanarrative frameworks in the name of objective validity.

More recently, Noel Parker (1999) has attempted to develop an innovative synthesis of theories of revolution of ambitious scope, contextualizing state-breakdown analyses in historical world-systems, and further attempting to unite the structure/agency dichotomy that dogged earlier attempts to develop theories capable of more specific analyses. He first establishes the "temporo-spatial dimension" of modernity as the structural context of revolutions from a synthesis of Skocpol's focus on state breakdown and Giovanni Arrighi's development of world-systems theory, which identifies an historical series of "centers" generating waves of modernization through successive global economic hegemonies (Arrighi 1994). Parker develops his ambitious thesis through the painstaking analytical qualification of previous theorizations, to construct an overarching model of such scope that it invokes an extensive review of almost all the theoretical issues of contemporary social theory, extending even to the nature of time and consciousness. This is not the place to enter into a critical review of Parker's enterprise, but this scope does require him to confront (as in Kumar's critique of structuralist approaches) the *meaning* of revolution for social action. Parker, however, conceptualizes this in terms of a "narrative" of revolution, drawing on Ricouer to provide a phenomenological equivalent to Kumar's notion of revolutionary tradition, that enables him to link this to the historical structural conditions he has drawn from his synthesis of Arrighi and Skocpol.

We are thus left with empirical and hermeneutic models of revolution (roughly corresponding to objective and subjective dimensions, and to the roles of structure and agency), which are brought together and applied to the prospect of revolution for the future. Parker draws out the significance of the Nicaraguan Sandinistas' revolutionary pluralism and the Mexican Zapatistas' use of global communications technology as examples of the way that revolution has a new role in a de-centered, globalized world-historical context, as "... the language in which the claims of forces for change in one part of the globe can be understood, and potentially sympathized with, in another," (Parker 1999: 174). Revolution, Parker seems to suggest, could thus provide the vehicle for the radical–democratic universalist project that has recently been revived in discussions of "international civil society" and "cosmopolitan democracy."

However, Parker's speculations seem foreclosed to the association of critical thought with the Enlightenment and the Kantian tradition, which locates the conditions for cosmopolitan democracy in the criteria of sovereign legitimacy and the institutions of international society which are predicated upon the states-system (Archibugi and Held 1995). Even qualified by universalist concepts of human rights, this conditional cosmopolitanism forecloses the prospect of revolution, effectively in favor of the interventionary force of an international community on behalf of the oppressed, who must themselves remain inactive victims in order to qualify (Kaldor 1999).

CONCLUSION

The morally preclusive idealism of the cosmopolitan democratic project contrasts starkly with the amoral conclusive pragmatism of postmodernism. The postmodern interpretation of 1989 as an ending or a closure derives from precisely the same source as sociology's tautological invariant models, defining the political only in terms of preexistent, given categories. Where postmodernists see only the residue of the private in the aftermath of the great tradition, the sociology of revolution sees only a cycle of sovereign power in that tradition itself. However, this delimitation of the political, and hence of the meaning and conceptualization of revolution, can be challenged.

Michel Foucault's writings on revolt can be read as ultimately nihilistic in implication (Simons 1995), as in his reference to the hopeless Attica prison revolt as an exemplar of resistance to disciplinary society (1977), or in his apparent celebration of Iranian revolutionaries "willingness to sacrifice themselves as the ultimate necessity of transgression of life itself as a condition of revolt" (1988d). However, Foucault (1984a, 1988e) also wrote of revolution in relation to Enlightenment, arguing from a text of Immanuel Kant that if we consider these as processes rather than as given objects, the task then becomes that of extending the parameters of the possible, transgressing the limits of the given, rather than tracing the conditions of limit. In this argument, Foucault is not rejecting but associating himself with a tradition of revolution and Enlightenment which has always aimed to open new fields of struggle and extend the possible. This alternative conception of the political opens onto a tradition richer than the modernity of legitimatory foreclosure, through which we might yet pursue a theory of revolution that does not substitute its analytical conditions for the object of intellectual enquiry. To do so, however, we need to abandon the conception of the political as sovereign power and embrace this other tradition in which the political figures as the domain of the possible, with revolution as its extension.

Further Reading

Bauman, Z. 1994: "A revolution in the theory of revolutions." *International Political Science Review* 15 (1): 15–24.
Tismaneanu, V. (ed.) 1999: *The Revolutions of 1989*. London: Routledge.
Touraine, A. 1990: "The idea of revolution." In M. Featherstone (ed.) *Global Culture: Nationalism, Globalization and Modernity*. Sage: London.
Vaneigem, R. 1994: *The Revolution of Everyday Life*. London: Rebel Press/Left Bank Books.

19

Terror Against the State

Donatella della Porta

It is difficult to clearly distinguish terrorism from other forms of political violence, but one distinguishing feature is that what is normally called "terrorism" is carried out by small secret groups. There have been two main approaches to its study: "terrorism studies," which tends to treat it as pathological; and the sociology of social movements which situates it on a continuum of non-conventional political protest. Della Porta outlines three analytic levels of research on terrorism. The micro-sociological perspective focuses on the characteristics of individual members of terrorist organizations. The meso-sociological perspective is used to analyze the dynamics of terrorist organizations. The macro-sociological approach deals with the types of political systems in which terrorism develops. However, analyses have dealt mainly with terrorism that emerged in western liberal-democracies in the 1960s and 1970s. New forms of terrorism that have emerged in the 1990s may raise new theoretical questions for its study.

POLITICAL VIOLENCE AND TERRORISM: A DEFINITION

Like many words imported into scientific idiom from everyday life, "terrorism" is ideologically laden. Its empirical referent varies according to social groups, political organizations, geographical area, and historic period. Heterogeneous phenomena have thus often been conflated; subsumed under the same concept and thus deprived of heuristic capacity as well as descriptive utility.

A first problem in the delimitation of the phenomenon relates to the very definition of political violence, of which terrorism would be an extreme form. In normal usage, the term *"violence"* refers to the illegitimate use of physical force against goods or persons (Graham and Gurr 1969: xvii; Tilly 1978: 176). *Political* violence is the use of physical force in order to damage a political adversary. In general, political violence consists of those repertoires of collective action which involve great physical force and cause damage to an adversary in order to attain political aims (della Porta and Tarrow 1987: 614). This definition is not, however, straightforward because the comprehension of terms like "great" or "damage" is also subjective. A certain degree of physical force is involved in many forms of protest that are usually not considered as violent *per se*. Moreover, all forms of protest seek to damage an adversary (della Porta 1995: 3).

In addition, there is the problem of discriminating between political violence in general, and its bloodier form: terrorism. While a certain degree of ritualized violence has come to be considered "normal" in a political conflict, terrorism has always been stigmatized as pathology. It was, in fact, used to indicate a point beyond which violence can be considered as terrorism. The determination of this threshold, however, presents serious difficulty. The results are no better with those definitions that, starting from the etymology of the term, consider as terrorist all those forms of political violence whose aim is to "terrorize." This conceptualization presents, first of all, the difficulty of measuring the psychological states of some individuals or groups. Moreover, focusing on fear as the expected emotional effect among their victims, this definition underestimates some important aspects of the phenomenon. Not only is the message of terrorist organizations quite diverse with respect to different groups of the population, but also the aim of many actions is that of gaining consent, rather than merely terrorizing.

A more promising way of distinguishing between different forms of violence is to start from the nature of the organizations which systematically use great physical force to damage political adversaries. Leaving aside the use of terror by the state, an important characteristic of the forms of violence that are normally counted as "terrorism" is that small, clandestine groups carry them out. The choice of going underground has in fact such important consequences for the dynamics of these organizations that adopting it changes the quality of their actions. Terrorism can be defined, then, as the activity of those small, clandestine organizations, which through a continuous and almost exclusive use of violent repertoires aim at achieving political changes or resisting such changes.

Despite this delimitation of the concept of terrorism, however, its area of application remains very wide. Not only is it the case that the size of the clandestine organizations, the forms of violence they use, and the logic of action can, in fact, change from case to case, but, above all, terrorism has been used by groups with very different ideological backgrounds and political aims. On the bases of these different aims, various typologies have been built, distinguishing ideological *versus* ethnic, right-wing *versus* left-wing, domestic *versus* international or transnational forms of terrorism (for some examples of these different forms of terrorism, see Crenshaw 1995).

Between "Extremist Groups" and Degeneration of Social Movements: a Review of the Approaches to Political Violence and Terrorism

In the social sciences different forms of violence have been studied within two broad traditions that have interacted with each other: the studies of terrorism (terrorism studies in the United States, *Extremismusforschung* in Germany) and the studies of social movements. Strangely enough, while the first approach, initially developed in the research on international terrorism, extended its attention to varied forms of national violence and also to legal organizations, the sociology of social movements narrowed its focus more and more to peaceful protest (for a review, see della Porta and Diani 1999). Concentrating on the most radical forms of political violence, terrorism studies tend to isolate their object of interest from the larger political system, explaining terrorism as a consequence of either structural strains or individual pathologies. In contrast, in social movement studies unconventional forms of protest are taken to be the result of political conflicts, mobilized by movement entrepreneurs through the use of material and symbolic incentives. The new approaches to social movements, which have flourished since the seventies to become a major field in the social sciences, developed from a critique of the assumptions shared by terrorist studies: the definition of social movements as unconscious reaction to temporary strains; the discontinuities between "normal," conventional actors and abnormal, unconventional ones; and personal frustration as the basis for individual commitment to protest. In social movement studies, protest is considered to be the product of conflicts structurally inherent in society. In order to produce collective action, however, collective actors must emerge, create collective identities and founding organizations; that is, resources and political entrepreneurs have to be available. Although more promising for understanding terrorism as an effect of a radicalization of political conflicts, the new approaches to social movements paid little attention to political violence. As was observed in a recent review of the literature, "the relationships among levels of violence and conflict, type of grievances, and the key variables of resource mobilization (resources, organization, and opportunities) remain underdeveloped" (McClurg Mueller 1992: 18).

This may explain why an influential scholar in the field described the "state of the art" in the study on political violence and terrorism as characterized by "a disturbing lack of good empirically grounded research" (Gurr 1988: 115). However, in the last decade a growing scientific literature has offered not only detailed historic accounts of some cases of terrorism, but also some first reflections on a comparative perspective. In general, the empirical research and the theoretical reflections have addressed three analytical levels: the individual, the group, and the system. In the first case, from a micro-sociological perspective, explanations refer to the personal characteristics of the militants of terrorist organizations. In the second, within a meso-sociological perspective, attention focused on the dynamics of the clandestine organizations. In the third, the principal questions of macro-sociological studies referred to the types of political systems in which terrorism has developed.

Micro-Dynamics: The Characteristics of the Militants

Many studies of the characteristics of the individual members of clandestine organizations use a psycho-sociological approach. A recurrent theme concerns the subjective motivations of adhesion to a movement. According to those who follow the hypothesis of relative deprivation (Davies 1969; Gurr 1970), the militants of the clandestine organizations come from social groups which feel frustrated because of the gap between their expectations and reality. Drawing on so called mass society theory, other studies assume that individuals who resort to forms of political violence are socially excluded (Kornhauser 1959). According to the psychology of the crowd (LeBon 1896) or to the notion of the true believer (Hoffer 1951), radical personalities are defined as frustrated individuals, blindly obedient to a leader, content to lose their "unwanted selves." The more the form of collective action has appeared as deviant with respect to established norms, the more the investigation has focused on assumed psychopathologies (Zwerman 1992).

A first criticism of this stream of studies concerns their empirical validity. Most recent investigations of terrorists' personalities converged in stating that "the more relevant characteristic of terrorists is their normality" (Crenshaw 1981: 390). Research based on the biographies of members and leaders of underground organizations failed to discover any specific personality traits or socialization deficits (della Porta 1992; Waldmann 1993). Even leaving aside the much debated theme of their empirical validity, the relative deprivation and mass society approaches fail to address a central theme: how can isolated and marginalized individuals translate strains into collective action?

The micro-sociological approach is, however, indispensable for understanding terrorism. In the first place, research points out that the decision to adhere to clandestine organizations is not an "individual" one: it develops inside dense networks of friends who share a political commitment. The groups of friends/comrades enhance the role of politics in the definition of the militants' identity and, at the same time, gradually socialize them into the use of violence. In this way, the affective and cognitive dynamics of groups' solidarity smooth the entrance into the "armed struggle," reducing the perception of individual choice and personal responsibility. In the ethnically-based terrorist groups, traditional meeting places and associations such as gastronomic societies or alpine groups in the Basque case (Wieviorka 1988) provide a reservoir for recruitment into the underground. In a similar way, recruitment has been eased by organizational networks surviving from a previous phase of military conflict – such as the Irish Republican Army (IRA) in Northern Ireland (White 1993) – as well as by family bonds with a previous generation of militants. In ideological terrorism, networks of friendship are constituted in small radical groups, active inside usually pacific social movements: the Red Brigades and Front Line in Italy (della Porta 1990, 1995) or the Red Army Fraction and the Revolutionary Cells in the Federal Republic of Germany (Neidhardt 1981; della Porta 1995) emerged from splits inside radical groups active during long protest cycles. The decision to form underground groups was taken by small networks of people with such dense ties with each other that they often refer to their own group as a "family."

In all these cases, the maintenance of commitment to the clandestine group was favored by a series of non-return mechanisms that reduced the capabilities of abandoning the group. The reduction of contacts with the external world interacted with a growing identification with the community of armed struggle. A sense of "responsibility" pushed those who were still fugitive to keep their loyalty to the terrorist organization in order to support their comrades who were in prison or had died; and those who were in prison felt "responsible" towards those who were fighting for them outside. The internalization of the ideology of the underground organization acted as a filter, distorting external reality and removing the perception of political defeat. Precisely because of their isolation from their environment, the underground organizations eventually became the sole point of reference for their members. All the aspects of the life of the militants came to depend on the underground formations as their only means of material survival as well as for retaining a form of self-respect. While the strongly-felt solidarity with other comrades in the underground made quitting the underground organizations a painful process of betraying one's own best friends, logistic needs (money, quarters, false documents, etc.) enhanced the dependence on the terrorist group (della Porta 1995).

MESO-DYNAMICS: THE CLANDESTINE ORGANIZATIONS AS VIOLENT ENTREPRENEURS

A second type of explanation of terrorism refers to the level of the group. A considerable number of analyses have used variables that refer to the ideology of underground organizations. Terrorism in democratic societies has been understood as a reaction by small groups outside the political system. In liberal society in which the channels of access to the formal decisions are open, those who aim at subverting the legitimate order employ terrorism. Isolated in a polity that supports the peaceful resolution of conflict, these ideological sects understand that they cannot persuade citizens through legal propaganda, and therefore use terrorism as a conscious strategy, consistent with the objective of the physical destruction of the enemy. In line with this analysis, the emergence of terrorism has been reduced to the action of "ideological sects," whose purpose is the abolition of individual liberty (for example, Wilkinson 1979, 1986).

From a different perspective, violent forms of conflict have been connected to the characteristics of mobilized interests. The use of radical repertoires derives from some peculiarities of the social groups involved. Political violence spreads when new challengers emerge and old polity members refuse to renounce their privileges (Tilly 1978: 52–5, 172–88). In a variation on this hypothesis, characteristics of technocratic societies are seen as thwarting the development of protest action in advanced capitalist societies: The terrorist groups then represent the only possible opposition to a pacified society (Targ 1979; Wellmer 1981).

It is not always the case, however, that the use of the terrorism may be considered as a rational choice by groups motivated by explicit ideological aims or class bases. The logic of action of clandestine formations can actually be understood only by distinguishing the explicit aims of the group from its internal ones. Like any other organization, terrorist ones must mobilize resources and allocate them to fulfil various organizational needs. Originating in the radicalization of repertoires during long protest cycles, underground groups claim to be part of wider social movements. Inside these movements they do indeed aim at recruiting activists, making propaganda for the necessity to use more violent types of actions and clandestine forms of organization. In this sense, terrorist groups act often as entrepreneurs of violence. The adoption of clandestine structures limits the range of strategic options, however, reducing further the capacity of terrorist groups to influence the desired direction of their external environment.

Research on clandestine groups active in different regions of the world has pointed out that they indeed attempt, as far as they can, to adapt their organizational structures, action strategies, and ideological discourses to their environment. The implicit, not anticipated, consequences of the choice of clandestine forms limits, however, their ability to effectively react to the external world, thus contributing to their isolation. In general, the lifecycle of these organizations may be described as a process of "encapsulation," during which they gradually give up their explicit aims of producing social and political change in order to focus instead on their own survival. In the course of this evolution, their goals become more and more radical and participation more and more totalizing as militants are forced to reduce their contacts with the external surroundings. Clandestine formations then become similar to sects, with the conservation in life of the organization as their ultimate goal. An intensification of internal solidarity and a radicalization of the forms of action follows. In the beginning, the Red Brigades, for instance, used forms of action such as setting a car on fire or symbolic kidnapping lasting only a few minutes that did not differ much from the forms of action that were accepted and used by other social movement organizations active in Italy at that time (see della Porta 1990). After a few years, however, when these forms of action failed to attract the attention of the mass media and the state started to break into the organization's headquarters and arrest its members, the first people died in shoot outs with the police or in failed kidnappings. With the passing of time, more and more brutal actions became increasingly difficult to justify to the activists of the social movements whom the Red Brigades wanted to get on their side. The indiscriminate assassinations of policemen and judges as well as "traitors" from inside their own ranks lost the terrorist organization even residual sympathy in the most radical wing of the protest movement. The residual resources came to be allocated in a kind of private war against the state, up to the point of unavoidable military defeat. In similar way, in other historic contexts, the choice of a clandestine strategy led to progressive isolation: groups as different as the Montoneros (Moyano 1995) and the Red Japanese Army (Steinhoff 1991) were assimilated by a pattern of evolution that led them to turn increasingly inward, progressively losing touch with other political actors. They increasingly used a military frame to define themselves and attack their adversaries. Bloody internal purges, including the assassinations of their own military accused of betrayal or "deviations" from the "right line," often ensued from a definition of the "inside" as an heroic elite and the "outside" as an absolute enemy. This process of encapsulation can be explained as an unanticipated consequence of the very choice of the underground: in a vicious circle, each decision reduces the possible choices in the future, transforming political organizations into closed sects.

Macro-Dynamics: Society, Politics, and Terrorism

The social science literature on political violence is rich in analyses of those environmental conditions that could contribute to its emergence and its growth.

Economic, social, political, or cultural variables have been evoked as possible causes of violent behaviors. Structural explanations, frequently based on macro-comparisons of aggregate data on violence in a large number of countries, have focused on the level of development of a society, the presence of ethnic cleavages, the degree of social differences, and the political culture. Based on individual case studies, other contributions have related the most radical forms of political violence to disturbances in the process of modernization, ineffectiveness of the coercive powers of the state, or too rapid metamorphoses in the value system. The search for the dysfunction that could cause terrorism has above all addressed the characteristics of political institutions. Elements that could act as precipitators for terrorism have been singled out, in a somewhat contradictory fashion, in governmental instability or in the lack of alternation in government; in an excess of repression or in the weakness of the state repressive apparatus; in uncompleted reform or in too radical changes (for a review, see Eckstein 1980; della Porta 1995, ch. 1).

While stimulating in their attempt to single out some causes for the emergence of violence, these structural hypotheses do not, however, seem to succeed in accounting for the complex activation of terrorist organizations, the degenera-tion of some political actors toward violence, or the evolution of political groups in the underground. In interpreting terrorism as a sign of systemic dysfunction, some of these interpretations may overlook the complex interactions between political actors that constitute the necessary link between structure and action.

In order to try to overcome these limits, more recent research on terrorism has looked at the environment as a source of opportunities and constraints for the radicalization of political conflicts. The emergence of armed formations requires, in fact, some kind of facilitation by various institutions: the police may effectively repress violence or escalate the conflict; political parties may tolerate terrorist groups or contribute to isolate them; the media may help spread the message of the armed insurgency or stigmatize clandestine formations. But, even more important for explaining the emergence of terrorist organizations are the interactions between social movements and the state. Terrorist organizations in western societies emerged inside social movements that had radicalized in the face of an inopportune and ineffective response on the part of institutional actors. Different environmental conditions help explain not only structural and ideological differences among underground groups that have emerged in differ-ent periods and countries, but also changes in the same groups over time.

Many armed groups have formed in the course of socially acute conflicts. From movements involved in long-lasting battles for political independence from, respectively, Great Britain and Spain, the IRA and the Basque ETA emerged; in the course of dramatic cycles of protest the Red Brigades were formed in Italy and the Red Army Fraction in Germany; from inside political groups mobilized for social justice and freedom rose the Montoneros in Argen-tina and the Shining Path in Peru. In all these cases social and political conflicts escalated at different speeds when social movements met with state repression and counter-movement violence. Vivid memories of brutal intervention by the police and the army against citizens who demonstrated in the street pushed many activists towards violent protest which they perceived as "legitimate defense" against state violence. The style of protest policing comes then to represent the most reliable indicator of the institutional attitudes toward democracy (della Porta and Reiter 1998).

In different situations, precipitating events reduced, at least in the eyes of the social movement activists, the legitimacy of the state institutions. The massacre of Piazza Fontana in Italy (della Porta 1995), the trial of Burgos in Spain (Jauregui Bereciartu 1981; Ibarra 1989), Bloody Sunday in Ireland (White 1993) all represented for many militants within social movements a point of no-return symbolizing the treason of democratic rules by state institutions themselves and justifying the need to seize arms against an unjust and brutal system. The lifecycle and the dimensions of clandestine organizations depend then on the degree to which social and political conflicts escalate. In democratic regimes, for example, left-wing terrorist groups have never counted for more than a few hundred members. On the other hand, armed struggle has attracted more followers where democracy appeared weaker and incapable of addressing existing social problems: in Peru, the Shining Path, appealing to the discontent of the poor farmers of the Andes, ended up controlling entire regions of the country (Palmer 1995); and in Argentina, the Montoneros contributed to the collapse of the populist regime (Gillespie 1982; Moyano 1995).

If some environmental preconditions are necessary for their emergence, terrorist organizations, however, maintain a certain decisional autonomy. Very few of the political organizations active in the above-mentioned countries chose the "armed struggle" and went underground. Terrorist organizations emerged, in fact, in the competition among various organizations belonging to the same social movement sector as a choice made by some groups to emphasize their difference from others and to stress a radical identity. The emergence of clandestine formations is the outcome of a process of polarization and fission among different factions inside social movements. This was the case, for instance, with ETA, which played an important role in the breakdown of the authoritarian regime in Spain, and continued to use violent repertoires of protest during the transition to democracy. As is clear from this example, terrorism is not necessarily a response to the hardening of repression. Once the dynamics of the underground are set in motion, clandestine organizations can even escalate their use of terrorist strategies in order to oppose a pacific solution that would reduce their space of survival.

CONCLUDING REMARKS

The development of political violence and terrorism involves complex dynamics at the macro-, meso-, and micro-level. Violence reflects an escalation of conflicts that institutions are not able to channel into peaceful decision-making process. Radicalization is a long-lasting process during which organizational resources are created for groups more prone to adopt violent repertoires and fundamentalist ideologies. In particular, underground formations provide symbolic incentives that help the development of militant identities. The choice of using terrorist strategies emerges during sustained interactions between the challengers and the representatives of the polity (della Porta 1995). Understanding these dynamics requires going beyond causal explanations. If environmental preconditions – in particular the characteristics of state repression and social movements – facilitate the emergence of violence, militant organizations tend then to act as entrepreneurs of violence reproducing the conditions for their survival.

Most of the examples of political violence and terrorism referred to up to now – that is, most of the examples social scientists have looked at – belong to a similar type, sharing a similar historical background. They developed in particular in the sixties and the seventies during periods of political turmoil when social movements asked for profound changes in society as well as in the very understanding of democracy. Very often, the institutional actors first tried to resist what they perceived as a dangerous challenge to the tranquillity and prosperity built after the Second World War. Although most of these social movements adopted non-violent forms of action, some groupings became more and more militant, in particular during street battles with the police or antagonist groups. In most cases, however, in the long run, democratic states not only defeated the terrorist groups, but also gained a new consensus, while the protestors at least succeeded in developing a new conception of democracy, with a wider legitimation of various forms of citizens' participation.

If the conflicts that have degenerated into terrorism a few decades ago seem to have found peaceful solutions, in the nineties new and even more savage forms of violence developed. If the most advanced democracies are shaken by brutal racist attacks, once again militant nationalists and religious fundamentalists spread terror, in the "Third World" as well as in the heart of "civilized" Europe. In these cases, violence is also fuelled where political opportunities are closed (or have been closed for a long time), where political entrepreneurs use terrorism to increase their power and where individuals are gradually socialized to a military image of politics. These new forms of terrorism, however, present many peculiarities compared with those we have analyzed until now. An urgent task for social scientists is to study the specific dynamics of terrorism at the turn of the millennium and thus to help find a way to avert the escalation of social and political conflicts without endangering democracy.

Further Reading

Crenshaw, Martha (ed.) 1995: *Terrorism in Context*. Philadelphia: Penn State University.
della Porta, D. (ed.) 1992: *Social Movement and Violence: Participation in Underground Organizations*. Greenwich, CT: Jai Press.
della Porta, D. 1995: *Social Movements, Political Violence and the State*. New York: Cambridge University Press.

Part III
The Political and the Social

20

State and Civil Society
Civil Society and the Public Sphere

LARRY RAY

Although these concepts have different origins and connotations, they are closely related in contemporary theory, especially in the work of those drawing on Habermas's writings. "Civil society" refers to processes of social differentiation in modern European societies in which political power was separated from other activities, so that the state became a distinct area of society among others. In seventeenth-century political philosophy, "civil society" came to be understood as essential to good government. In the critical tradition inaugurated by Hegel it is seen more problematically as an area of conflict as well as of ethics. For Marx it was equivalent to bourgeois society, an arena of class oppression and illusory emancipation. In Eurocommunism and the anti-Communist movements of Eastern Europe in which it was recently revived, it is again seen in a positive light: as the social space between the state and the economy within which voluntary associations can discuss and act to link public and private concerns. This assumes that civil society necessarily creates an active public sphere. Ray distinguishes two models, "Civil Society I" and "Civil Society II." According to the first, a democratic polity is secured by a dense network of civil associations that generate "social capital." This claim may not be justified, especially given the complexity and fragmentation of contemporary societies. According to the second, more explicitly normative model, what is needed is the generation of an alternative public sphere of autonomous self-organizing groups that will limit state power. This model may be quite particular to the situation in Eastern Europe from which it emerged. Ray outlines a number of important difficulties for the concept of civil society: the feminist critique of its gendered nature; the way in which the public sphere has failed to develop in postcommunist societies; the over-simplification of the binary opposition of civil society and state and the homogeneity of community it assumes. It is further problematized by processes of globalization that undermine the liberal–democratic state on which the existence of civil society has historically depended.

Both the concepts of civil society and the public sphere are fluid, problematic, and open to various, sometimes-conflicting interpretations. Although the concepts are closely related in contemporary debates, especially among writers drawing on Habermas, they have different origins and connotations (Seligman

1995). The notion of an active public sphere in which citizens engage in reasoned argument over affairs of state and morality derives from (idealized) notions of the ancient Greek polis in a political tradition running through Machievelli, Rousseau to twentieth-century theorists such as Arendt and Habermas. Central concepts are *virtue*, the moral requirement to be a good citizen, and rational debate. Ideas of public disputation, activity and ideally (if not necessarily) face-to-face contact imply a small-scale relatively homogeneous society. This was the kind of city-state republic, participatory rather than procedural, envisaged by Rousseau (Patomáki and Pursianen 1999). Civil society by contrast, refers to more complex, organic and differentiated orders. Certainly, "civil society" like "public sphere" originates in Greek and Roman political philosophy (Aristotle's *politike koimonia* and Cicero's *ius civile*) but is more closely identified with eighteenth-century political philosophy. The emphasis here was on the importance of a realm of privacy, economic exchange and association, and consequently the limitation of the state. The importance of contract and economic relations to many (though not all) theories of civil society invites association with the growth of the political power of the bourgeoisie in Europe. Despite these different emphases though, many theorists understand civil society as a public realm of voluntary association essential for the stability of democracy.

CIVIL SOCIETY AND SOCIAL DIFFERENTIATION

The concept of "civil society" refers to the processes of social differentiation associated with the emergence of modern European societies. With the depersonalization of political power, separated from the familial rights of monarchs, barons and landlords, the idea of the state as the personal property of the sovereign and benefice of officials slowly gave way to the idea of impersonal rule bound by rules. In the process, sovereignty was transferred from the figure of the monarch to the state, which also underwent a process of differentiation, into administrative, judicial, representative, functions. Further, the development of trade, commerce, and markets increased the complexity of economic organization whilst establishing the dual notion of social activity, divided into political and civil roles. "Civil society" described the new commercial social order, the rise of public opinion, representative government, civic freedoms, plurality and "civility." Thus civil society depicted a realm of contractual and voluntary relationships independent of the state, which thereby became merely one area of social activity among others. At the same time, political economy and philosophy began to address the question of the social context for the existence of the state (political society) the nature of which was no longer taken for granted. In particular Enlightenment social theory (e.g. Montesquieu 1949; Rousseau 1968; Condorcet 1976) regarded the despotic state as an enemy of human progress and well-being and began to examine the social conditions for democratic or constitutional forms of government.

The origins of contemporary usage can be found in seventeenth-century political philosophy. Thomas Hobbes's theory of the sovereign state (Leviathan) was premised on the existence of two branches of society – political and civil –

tied by a "social contract" between subjects and the state. Hobbes constructed a hypothetical "state of nature" in which essential human tendencies posed an ever-present threat to social peace, where "the life of man was solitary, poore, nasty, brutish and short" (Hobbes 1994: 71). However, rationality and mutual self-interest persuaded people to combine in agreement, to surrender sovereignty to a Common Power, the state, established by covenant to constrain those who would otherwise violate the social peace. With the social contract comes a separation between political and civil society – two systems in which "men [are] joyned in one Interest" as parts of the body (1994: 131). The political system is constituted by the Sovereign Power and civil society by subjects "among themselves." Although the political system was the dominant part, this expressed the idea of differentiated civil and political life as mutually sustaining systems, in which the realm of private activity, while governed by sovereign laws, was otherwise bound only by conscience (*in foro interno*) and the rules of civic association.

Disputing Hobbes's negative views of human nature, John Locke's concept of the social contact further enhanced the status of civil society, as a space of association, contract, and property regulated by the law. "Those who are united into one body, and have a common established law and judicature to appeal to, with authority to decide controversies between them and punish offenders, are in civil society one with another; but those who have no such common appeal . . . are still in the state of Nature" (Locke 1980: para. 87). Leaving the state of nature for Locke involved entering a commonwealth of men of property who contract authority to the state for their self-protection, but they do not do so unconditionally. Law is derived from God-ordained natural rights, which inhere in civil society, to which the state is ultimately answerable. Unlike Hobbes's Leviathan, which was the *product* of a covenant but not a *party* to it (and hence not bound by it), Locke's constitutional state was constrained by the law, violation of which rendered it non-legitimate.

In Hobbes and Locke though, despite differences between them, civil society was an aspect of government (Locke used political and civil society interchangeably) while in subsequent theorists, such as Adam Ferguson, it became an autonomous sphere separate from the state. The development of civil society for Ferguson reflected the progress of humanity from a simple, clan-based militaristic to complex commercial society. However, this process of social differentiation and loss of community threatened increased conflict and weakened the social fabric. Civil society, with a strong connotation of "civility," has the potential to establish a new order requiring dispersal of power and office, the rule of law, and liberal (i.e. tolerant) sentiments, which secure people and property without requiring obligation to friends and cabals (Ferguson 1966: 223). Again, civil society is inseparable from good government, but more than this, the reference to "friends and cabals" indicates an important point that is sometimes missed in subsequent debates. Civil society does not refer to just *any* kind of informal or private social relations, which exist in all societies, but to morally guided, rule following relations that make possible anonymous social exchanges. It thereby facilitates social integration in impersonal and potentially conflictual situations.

The implicit tension here between the new conflicts of commercial society and the moral demands of social peace appeared explicitly in Hegel, for whom civil society was divided between ethical life (*Sittlichkeit*) and egotistical self-interest. Civil society appears here as a process rather than in Hobbes's frozen architecture. Objective Spirit achieves self-knowledge through differentiation into discrete spheres, which nonetheless form a totality. In the family, socialization toward moral autonomy transformed biological and psychological needs into individual desires. But in complex societies, private life is transcended through association in civil society, the sphere of production, distribution, and consumption, which meets a system of needs that are modified and multiplied in the process. It has its own regulatory institutions (Justice, Public Authority, Corporations) guided by morality, although they remain instruments for achieving personal, egotistical ends. To some extent, Hegel's view of civil society anticipated Marx's critique of class polarization and dehumanization, as "the conflict between vast wealth and vast poverty steps forth, a poverty unable to improve its condition . . . [which] turns into the utmost dismemberment of will, inner rebellion and hatred" (Hegel 1967: 149–51). However, this will be overcome if the constitutional-legal state (*Rechtsstaat*) synthesizes ethical life with the public domain of civil society whilst transcending them. Differences of class, rank, and religion dissolve in universal law and formal rights.

By regarding civil society simply as the equivalent of bourgeois society, an arena of conflict, class oppression, and illusory emancipation, Marx only partially echoed Hegel's view and disregarded the latter's concept of civil society as *Sittlichkeit*. His critique of civil society was in part a critique of the limitations of Hegel's *Rechsstaat*, in which formal legal equality is merely an illusory dissolution of differences of class, rank, and religion, which masks their perpetuation within civil society. In part too though, it involved a fundamental rejection of the very process of social differentiation into institutional orders (such as private life, the economy, and civil and political association) that Hegel and most eighteenth-century theory had taken for granted. For Marx, the proletarian victory would substitute for the old civil society a classless association in which there would be neither political power nor the antagonisms of civil society (Marx 1978: 169). Marx's vision of communism was radically de-differentiated, in which boundaries between the civil and political, like those of class, nation, and religious difference, wither away. It drew on Rousseauian and radical Jacobin concepts of a public sphere of equals, along with anti-modernist nostalgia for a lost unity of humanity (Gellner 1994), rather than an organic concept of socially differentiated networks.

For much of the twentieth century the concept of civil society passed into disuse. There is some irony in that despite Marx's pejorative treatment of the term, its revival in the later twentieth century was a result first of the attempts by Eurocommunist parties to devise new strategies in the 1970s and second of its popularity among the anti-Communist movements in Eastern Europe. Eurocommunists (especially the Italian Communist Party), theoretically informed by writers like Gramsci, Bobbio, Althusser, and Poulantzas, sought to avoid more traditional Marxist economistic reductionism and simplistic polarization of social and political conflicts. Gramsci had conceived of civil society as the sphere

of non-corporeal forms of class rule, a cultural space between state and economy. Here the proletarian party could wage a cultural and ideological war to
undermine the hegemony of the ruling class, creating a counter-hegemony of
workers' clubs, social and educational organizations, assisted by the activity of
"organic intellectuals." This restated the centrality of processes of social differentiation and situated civil society within a cultural and institutional realm
rather than the economy. Despite the effectiveness of this strategy in bringing
various social movements and parties into loose coalition and debate, it already
pointed towards a post-Marxist politics in its abandonment both of materialism
and centrality of proletarian class struggle.

The second revival of civil society theory was encouraged by the collapse
of communism and its use by writers such as Vajda (1988), Konrad (1984),
Fehér and Heller (1986), and Havel (1988) to capture the essence of dissident
politics. Theorists such as Rödel, Frankenberg, and Dubiel (1989), Arato (1981)
and Cohen and Arato (1992) excavated the concept of civil society during
the disintegration of state socialism, combining ideas of radical civic republicanism with Habermas's procedural discourse ethics. The central idea of these
theories was to identify a social space for public discussion, of voluntary citizens'
associations that was neither narrowly merged with the market, nor an
adjunct to the state. Again with Eastern Europe in mind, Sztompka (1993: 73)
argued that civil society was the key to closing the chasm between public
and private realms, involving pluralism of voluntary associations, interest
groups, political organizations, and local communities markets and representative democracy as institutional arrangements linking public and personal
choices active and informed citizens. But this kind of analysis assumes that
civil society necessarily creates an active public sphere when the assumptions
underlying the two ideas may differ significantly. So, when does "civil" become
"political'?

CIVIL SOCIETY AND PUBLIC SPHERE

Clearly, for many writers, the concept of "civil society" lies at the center of
concerns with self-government, activism and privacy, separation from the state,
human rights, free economic initiatives, and the definitions of the social itself
(Keane 1988: 20). But there are various ways of connecting all these, which
imply different understandings of social organization, sometimes called "Civil
Society I" and "Civil Society II" (e.g. Foley and Edwards 1996). There is further
the question of whether models advanced are theorizations of existing social
processes or normative visions of a possible future?

One argument ("Civil Society I") runs from the Scottish moralists (such as
Ferguson) through de Tocqueville (1946) and Durkheim (1969) to contemporary
writers such as Robert Putnam (see Begnasco, chapter 21, in this volume).
According to "Civil Society I" a democratic polity is secured by being embedded
in dense networks of civil associations, such as clubs, trade associations, voluntary societies, churches, parent–teacher associations, sports clubs and the like,
that generate "social capital." The denser the networks the more secure are the

bridges between civic life and political associations along with institutions of the state. Active, voluntary, and informal groups and networks make for more stable democracy and protect against incursion by the state. The bridges envisaged here are based on institutional links along with shared moral and civic values of reciprocity (e.g. Bryant 1995). Civil society in this sense has a recursive property; it protects against state incursion yet strengthens the (liberal–democratic) state. Conversely, the absence of civil society is both an explanation and reinforcement of authoritarian yet ineffective government.

This view is consistent with the notion of organic, complex societies with high levels of social differentiation. Gellner (1994: 99–100) writes of the modern "man" as "modular," that is, having the capacity to combine associations and institutions without these being total and underwritten by ritual. Civil society creates a social "structure...not atomized, helpless and supine, and yet the structure is readily adjustable and responds to rational criteria of improvement" (Gellner 1995: 42). Civil society as a network of institutional and moral links is not monolithic but accommodates a plurality of "groups within groups, their sense of identity...always multi-layered" with many possible "we-images" along with corresponding images of the other (Mennell 1995). "Civil Society I" is less a definable social space so much as a complex web of processes and connections. In this vein, Habermas separates the social into two parts – social integration through normative communication within the lifeworld, and system integration through money and power. The lifeworld (within which Cohen and Arato situate civil society) is further differentiated into implicitly known traditions (culture), the medium of communication (society) and social identities (personality), each of which undergoes yet further internal differentiation. The potential for the expansion of public spheres exists as social movements form at contested boundaries between system and the lifeworld. An example would be environmental protests over, say, nuclear reprocessing, that force open debates about the rationality and morality of projects previously driven by technological and financial criteria.

However, the question remains as to the extent to which a public sphere of active citizens in the Arendtian or Habermasian sense is consistent with development of complex and multi layered societies? For example Habermas's (1989a) well-known critique of the erosion of the public sphere in late capitalism claims the commercialization of mass media replaced rational and unconstrained debate by public opinion research, through which political parties "extract" loyalty from publics in instrumental fashion. At the same time, increasing state intervention and the growing interdependence of research and technology resulted in a process of "technicization" whereby questions of moral value and political controversy were converted into managerial technical or planning processes (see Ray 1993: 51–3). But, especially since Habermas regards social steering by both the market and state as unavoidable (1987: 339), it is not entirely clear whether he is describing a pathological and reversible process or essentially depicting the condition of modernity. If it is the latter, then ideas of a reconstructed public sphere of active citizens may be utopian and nostalgic.

Moreover, there is the danger, as a number of commentators have noted (e.g. Mennell 1995; Foley and Edwards 1996) that a strong civil society may lead to the fragmentation of civic groups into warring factions that actually increases the risk of public violence. Ethnic and religious solidarities that undermine multinational and secular states are often cited in this context (e.g. Kaldor 1993 and Sivan 1989, respectively). However, civil society theorists would generally counter this by stressing what Cohen and Arato (1992: 421) regard as essential to civil society, namely reflection on the core of collective identities and their articulation within democratic politics. In particular, following Habermas, the crucial factor here is that we inhabit a world of morally mature post-traditional ethics, in which public debate is constrained by procedural rules. Social integration requires not that we agree over substantive matters of identity and opinion but on the rules through which public debate and conflict will be conducted. Indeed, according to Misztal (1996: 197) it is the *disengagement* of political and juridical institutions from the lived bonds of solidarity, that is a failure of "Civil Society I," that promotes new exclusive communities of trust, such as ethnic nationalism.

A second approach to the relationship between state and civil society ("Civil Society II") is associated particularly with the anticommunist movements in the 1970s and 80s, where the role of civil society is explicitly normative. Rather than embedding political processes in supportive but constraining civic networks, this conception regarded civil society as a harbinger of a new type of society – anti-political, authentic, and based on informal social solidarity. The spaces of civil society and public sphere here were often fused in that the private realm of autonomous self-organizing groups was to become an authentic public sphere alternative to the state. For Arato (1981) the seeds of new civil society germinated in *samizdat*, self-defense movements (such as the Polish KOR), the idea of self-managing democracy and permanent rights theory (Fehér and Heller 1986). Thus social movements such as Solidarity aimed to limit the state, or by-pass it altogether through alternative networks, but not to seize it as an instrument of coercion, and in this sense they were quite different from earlier and more traditional revolutionary movements (Pelczynski 1988). The early Solidarity program of *podmiotowosc* (self-management) was a radical alternative to western democracy as well as to Soviet-type socialism. The democratization of the economy was understood as part of a decentralized social order of autonomous subsystems, managed along the lines of professional self-government (Glasman 1994). These notions of self-government transcend the liberal dichotomy of public/private by bringing rational democratic procedures into everyday life, through extrapolating the networks and practices of intellectuals in the parallel polity. Cohen and Arato (1992) argue that the new public spheres in Eastern Europe could provide a model for a more general idea of civil society that is appropriate in the West too. However, they also warn against an overly polarized view of "civil society vs. the state" that was derived from a particular historical context. In contrast to the highly differentiated view outlined above, the "eastern European" model over-unifies civil society in a false solidarity and risks blocking the emergence of societal and political pluralism (1992: 67).

CRITIQUES OF CIVIL SOCIETY

It should be clear from the foregoing that civil society is an ambiguous if seductive concept and this has attracted considerable critique. Two types of critique are particularly important. First, there is the accusation that its utopian promise is flawed, in some ways echoing Marx. Second, there is the charge of ambiguity – that the complexity of the social is better appropriated through other frameworks.

The "Marxist" critique is echoed in various ways. Feminist critics have argued that the gender-neutral language of civil society and public sphere conceal how the role of citizen has been linked to the capacity to bear arms, which has been predominantly a masculine role (Fraser 1989). This fusion of citizenship, militarism, and masculinity reinforces the male occupation of the public sphere that is inscribed into the public/private dichotomy, resulting in a civil contract amongst brothers combined with the feminization of the private sphere (Pateman 1988; Okin 1991). Habermasian distinctions between public and private roles treat the family as a black box in which patriarchal power remains invisible. The male citizen-speaker role links the state and the public sphere to the family and the official economy whilst the worker-breadwinner role integrates the family with the economy and the state, confirming women's dependent status in each. It is not clear, though, whether these criticisms negate the very ideas of civil society and the public sphere or whether inclusive non-gendered institutional forms might be possible.

Another line of critique addresses the rediscovery of civil society in anti-Communist social movements. After the fall of communism some of the enthusiasm for civil society dissipated in the wake of the political demobilization and the emergence of new elites. For Tamás (1994) the revolutions of 1989 were made by the private sphere against the public with its "rational utopia" communism. However, the language of civil society was a myth, invoking a "tale of a non-coercive political order of mutual non-hierarchical contract." Indeed, for Lomax (1997) the early popular enthusiasm was betrayed by the postcommunist intellectual elite, who appropriated the term "civil society" but demobilized society and failed to develop civil initiatives and popular participation. Again, Hann (1995) argues that the model of civil society vs. the state is derived from the preindustrial history of the west and is too simplistic to examine the complex interpenetration of state and society in the communist period. A similar point is addressed in Ray (1996: 200–28). Hann sees no evidence to support the notion that an effective civil society "in the sense of public sphere" has been able to develop in Hungary in recent years. Rather, like Lomax he suggests that the term was appropriated by urban intellectuals to bemoan the fact that (especially rural) people were less willing than previously to display deference to cultural elites. However, Bernard (1996) more optimistically suggests that the initial phase of postcommunist depoliticization is temporary and public life will be reinvigorated around new interest cleavages.

Secondly, it is claimed that civil society (II especially) assumes a homogeneous community and takes too little account of functional differentiation and the interpenetration of state and society in complex societies (Seligman 1993).

Citizens confront different authorities via a series of roles – taxpayers, proponents of resolutions, voters, writers of letters to editors, supporters of interest groups etc. – that are divided according to the requirements of the political system (Luhmann 1982: 153). The binary opposition of civil society and the state could be described in terms of what Luhmann calls a political code, which simplifies and steers otherwise highly complex communications. As such it operates as a rhetorical counter to the sovereignty of the state, which invokes the myth of the collective sovereign "people." But any attempt to make this a reality, such as the unconstrained communication (supposedly) envisaged by Habermas, or the permanently open democracy of civil societarians, would be chaos (Luhmann 1982: 287–8). Again, the breadth of the meaning of "civil society" is a source of ambiguity, giving it a nebulous and undifferentiated character (Ely 1992). This may be particularly so with Habermasian accounts, (e.g. Cohen and Arato 1992) that insert the concept of the public sphere into the domain of potential communicative ethics, thus merging civil society with the routine linguistic practices. Others regard the concept as meaningless since the very existence of civil society presupposes the state, that is a state bound by legality that will not trample over civil rights (e.g. Kumar 1993).

GLOBAL CIVIL SOCIETY?

The concept of civil society discussed so far exists within the boundaries of the nation-state, which many argue has been undermined by the process of globalization. The extent to which this is occurring is a matter of controversy and should not be exaggerated. However, there may be a general trend towards "de-statization of the political system" reflected in the shift from govern*ment* to govern*ance* (Jessop 1999) where the state's role is increasingly one of coordinating multiple agencies, institutions, and systems coupled through reciprocal interdependence. According to this account, the state becomes one agent among others operating in subnational, national, and international domains. If this is the case then the notion of a "state-civil society" polarity is clearly not complex enough to grasp current intersections between the governmental and non-governmental. In this context some writers nonetheless suggest that a transnational or global civil society may be emerging. There are several possibilities here:

- Statist concepts projected and reproduced on the world stage along with shared norms, international social networks, multilevel democratic systems, and an equalization of human rights (e.g. Walker 1994; Held 1995). A post-state global civil society develops based on recognition of inalienable human rights no longer tied to specific states or national membership (e.g. Frost 1998).
- Novel forms of civic sociality are facilitated by communication technologies along with decentralized, lateral organizational forms (Ahrne 1996).
- Global social movements establish new networks, resources, and social capital, providing the infrastructure for global democratization (Walker 1994; Smith 1998).

However, an alternative scenario is an implosion of civil society, as the relation between the state and civil society envisaged by the theory is inverted. The realm of the state, that was formerly "exterior" to civil society, is becoming localized and hence "interior" to the realm of private interests (civil society) which becomes global, through transnational capital. Thus the local state may lose its cohesion and become a set of "disaggregated agencies" rather than the center of distributional politics (Miller 1993: 222). At the same time, identity and lifestyle politics, community orientations and movements supersede instrumental class and welfare politics. One consequence of this is that the nation-state cannot sustain social welfare, and peoples' vulnerability to effects of the market is increased. Meanwhile, capital gains maximum mobility across national boundaries, taking command of *space* in a way that voluntary organizations rooted more in locality and *place* cannot do (Harvey 1994: 238).

EVALUATION

Where do these observations leave the idea of civil society? I tried to indicate earlier that some accounts of civil society allow for, indeed are premised on, an organic differentiated society. To some extent, critics of the concept are reacting to utopian versions ("Civil Society II") that detach the concept from the state. On the other hand the complex intersections of global and local processes and the increasing functional differentiation of societies make problematic polarities (civil society/state) drawn from an earlier stage of social development. Civil society and public spheres are best viewed as multiple processes rather than as "sites," and as anonymously interlocked subjects and flows of communication, rather than homogeneous communities (Habermas 1992). A central theme in civil society theory, and indeed in sociology as a whole, has been the importance of embedding processes of money and power in supportive but constraining cultural and normative systems. Where civil society is positioned between the economy and polity, rather than being absorbed into either, it is possible to explore the mediating processes that connect institutional spheres to limit the extension of one into the other. Where (as is common in postcommunist societies) the boundary of the state and private activity is unclear, with few mediating institutions, the result is low trust, weak legitimacy, high crime and corruption. As a counter to these, social organizations and NGOs often strive to generate a culture of civic regulation and public accountability, such as the umbrella of anti-corruption organizations in Bulgaria, Coalition 2000. This is not to propose civil society as a panacea, but an important factor in structuring social outcomes.

If civil society is viewed as mediating other institutional orders, then one should be sceptical of ideas of a post-state or global civil society. The pursuit of interests arising from the system of needs takes place within a framework of procedural rights that allow the articulation of substantive differences of interests, roles, values, and membership of voluntary associations. Without juridical processes against which alleged violations can be protested, the "civil rights" enjoyed are very weak. So the existence of civil society does not just require the existence of non-state organizations (which would apply to Lebanon in the

1980s or to internet chat rooms) but an acceptance of rules of behavior by both government authorities and citizens that self-limit their mutual claims (White, Gill, and Slider 1993: 226–9). Further, the self-limitation of power does not arise spontaneously from the process of functional differentiation (as Luhmann suggests, 1982: 214) but implies a procedural threshold sustained by the diffusion of power through the social system. This can only occur, as Offe and Preuss (1991: 161) argue, when power is embedded (*Vegesellschaftet*) in social norms and networks, local and diverse public spheres. Despite the diffuse meanings to which the concept of civil society is open, it captures crucial features of contemporary societies in which social integration is dependent on the fixing of public institutions in cultural and moral systems of regulation. These in turn presuppose the presence of social networks and active public citizens.

Further Reading

Keane, J. ed. (1988): *Civil Society: New European Perspectives*. London: Verso. Contains a comprehensive range of contributions with a slant towards the impending changes in Eastern Europe.

Cohen, J. and Arato, A. (1992). *Civil Society and Political Theory*. Cambridge, MA: MIT Press. This is one of the most systematic recent attempts to develop a theory of civil society.

21

Trust and Social Capital

Arnaldo Bagnasco

Translated by John Irving

"Social capital" describes a resource that facilitates action which is neither individual, nor physical, but inherent in social relations. In Coleman's influential account, he used it to criticize the individualist bias of classical and neoclassical economics while preserving the rational actor paradigm. For him "social capital" is generated by authority relations, relations of trust, and unilateral transfers of control over resources; and, since it depends on networks, stable relations, ideology and other factors, it may be created, maintained, and/or destroyed. From his research on the comparative institutional performance of regional governments in Italy, Putnam concludes that social culture was a crucial variable in explaining differences between them. He sees higher levels of "civicness" – solidarity, mutual trust, and tolerance promoted by values, norms, institutions, and associations – as enhancing governments' capacities to implement political choices. Fukuyama has explored how economic efficiency depends on social capital – the capability of people to work together to achieve shared goals. The form and extent this takes varies according to national culture, religion, and family values. Bagnasco argues that the concept of social capital is a useful tool for political sociology in that it enables the exploration of the relation between state and civil society. However, Putnam's and Fukuyama's accounts under-estimate the role of politics in creating and sustaining it. Coleman's idea of social capital, based on action theory, is much more useful in this respect.

The term "social capital" is a relatively recent addition to the language of sociology and political science. It was probably used for the first time by Jane Jacobs (1961: 138). In her studies on the crisis of American cities, Jacobs stressed society's loss of self-organizational capability in neighborhoods built without a care for the perverse effects of economic action. The subsequent literature continued to place the onus on informal aspects – seen as latent components and crucial resources for the functioning of society, hence as social capital – of relational structures in highly organized societies. The subject of trust as a resource for action has also been widely developed in recent social research. Here I speak of trust only in so far as it is used to formulate the notion of social capital.

In the first section, I define the concept and examine the theoretical perspective that derives from it, with special reference to the studies of J. Coleman, the scholar most committed to the theoretical foundation of that perspective. I then present two of the most important applications of the concept to political sociology, showing how the new idea casts new light on the relationship between civic culture and the performance of political institutions, and how it can be applied to comparative analysis of capitalism in a period of difficulty for traditional political economy. In conclusion, I add a few critical observations on the future of the perspective.

A NEW TERM IN SOCIAL THEORY

The economic concept of capital refers to a stock of resources that can be used to produce goods and services for the market. It is usual to distinguish between financial capital and physical capital. Speaking of the quality of labor, Becker (1964) and other authors introduced the concept of human capital to explain wage differentials depending on investment in worker training. The idea of social capital is a further extension of the original concept of capital; it is not necessarily applied to economics, but seen more generally as a resource that facilitates action.

James Coleman introduces the concept by speaking precisely of a specific resource that facilitates action, one which is "lodged neither in individuals nor in physical implements of production," but "inheres in the structure of relations between persons and among persons" (Coleman 1994: 302).

To reason in terms of social capital is to see society from the point of view of the action potential which individuals draw from relational structures. Observed in this way, social capital seems not so much a specific object as a vantage point on society as a whole or, at any rate, on a vast, hard-to-define set of social phenomena.

Coleman claims he borrowed the concept from Loury (1977; 1987), who uses it to describe the relational resources, useful for the development of children, which families find in specific communities. He also explains that, among the first authors to use the concept explicitly, were Bourdieu (1980), Flap and De Graaf (1986), Schiff (1992) and Putnam (1993), but also that a great deal of research by anthropologists and sociologists moves in the same direction without using the term. For example, the notion of the embeddedness of economic transactions in stable social relations, which Granovetter (1985) borrows from Polanyi, can be traced to the more general notion of social capital.

Coleman first used the concept to address the problem of the formation of human capital (Coleman 1988), but he only defines it comprehensively in *Foundations of Social Theory* (1990; see also 1994). Here his general aim is clearly to construct a complex social theory criticizing the individualist bias of classical and neo classical economics, while preserving the rational actor paradigm. The rational choice perspective of sociologists differs today from that of economists in so far as it sees organizations and social institutions as contexts which affect choices and produce systemic effects (1994: 166). As we shall see, the concept of social capital is a keystone in this perspective.

Coleman begins to build his theory by imagining actors with resources over which they have control and in which they have interests. Since actors have interests in events that are under the control of others, they engage in exchanges and unilateral transfers of control which lead to the formation of permanent social relations. According to this logical sequence, authority relations, relations of trust, and the consensual allocation of rights which establish norms thus arise as the components of the social structure. These elements, however, may be seen both as components of the social structure or system and as resources for individuals pursuing their own ends. The term "social capital" describes these resources, which vary from person to person.

For individuals, social capital is an appropriable social structure. Authority relations, relations of trust and norms are forms or generators of social capital. For actors, social capital materializes in the network of relations of which they are a part, and through which they activate resources for their own strategies. Structures thus contain forms of social capital that can be activated by actors.

- *Credit-slips*, that is to say credit based on obligations to pay back. One example is the rotating loan association described by anthropologists, in which groups of friends and neighbors contribute a sum of money every month and take turns in using the central fund. Such a credit association requires a high level of trustworthiness and the extent of credit slips on which individuals can draw at any time varies greatly. A patriarch, for example, held a large concentration of social capital. As Weber has shown, the destruction of this social capital was decisive in allowing individualist strategies to contribute to the development of capitalism.
- *Information channels*, which can be established to cut the cost of information, using networks of relations that exist for other purposes.
- *Norms and effective sanctions*, as in special norms and relative forms of social control whereby self-interest should be adapted to the interests of the collectivity. It must be remembered, however, that just as norms constrain deviant actions, so they may also constrain innovativeness.
- *Authority relations*, which transfer rights of control. Even vesting authority in a charismatic leader is a way of creating social capital.
- *Appropriable social organization*, an expression used to define the possibility of appropriating an entire fabric of relations for other purposes than the ones for which it was initiated. In many cases, this possibility is connected to what anthropologists refer to as the multiplexity of relations among people bound together in more than one context (i.e. family, work, religion, and so on).

If the social capital presented so far may appear to be a sort of by-product of social structures, other forms exist which derive from specific investment in the setting up of structures to generate them. This is the case of specifically created *intentional organizations* – associations and organizations in the narrow sense. I shall return to this point later, since Coleman's critical perspective reflects the tension which exists between intentional organizations and other forms of social capital.

Social capital has the properties of a public good: namely, it is inalienable and it is not the private property of the persons who benefit from it; it is useful for certain purposes but not for others and, as circumstances change, it may lose its effectiveness. More generally, it can be created, maintained, and destroyed. We can list some of the factors which trigger these processes:

- *The closure of social networks*, due to which all or most actors are bound together. Closed structures increase possibilities for reciprocal monitoring, generating expectations and mutual norms and improving the trustworthiness of the environment. Networks are an important variable and deserve further exploration.
- The *stability of relations* in the course of time. The mobility of individuals tends to destroy social capital. The only exception is formal organizations in which positions remain, even though their incumbents change;
- *Ideology*: the Protestant doctrine of the individual's separate relation to God, for example, is a cultural factor which inhibits the creation of social capital.
- Additional factors which reduce *mutual dependence* among people include affluence and government aid. The ruling principle is that "the more extensively persons call on one another for aid, the greater will be the quantity of social capital generated" (1990: 321).

I have dwelt on Coleman's theory not only because of its quality, but also because it is continually referred to in the subsequent literature. Deviations have, however, appeared whose scope has not always been appreciated. The references which follow must, therefore, be taken as examples of important and paradigmatic applications of the theory social capital to political sociology, but also as variations on it.

CIVIC CULTURE AS SOCIAL CAPITAL

Robert Putnam conducted a major research program on the comparative institutional performance of regional government in Italy (Putnam 1993). By "institutional performance," he means the capacity of regional governments to implement political choices. Putnam sets out from the idea that, despite the fact that regions have the same institutional set-up, differences in context mean that institutions work in different ways. Following Almond and Verba (1963), he explores the hypothesis that political culture may be the decisive variable in explaining differences in performance. In their study of five countries, Almond and Verba introduced a typology of political cultures which breaks down into "participants" (rational and informed) and "subjects" (who display trust in authority and deference). A combination of the two defines the civic culture typical of well-established democracies, such as the United States and Great Britain. The lack of both dimensions defines a "parochial" type which, according to the authors, is characteristic of Italy.

Putnam reveals sharp differences in performance from one region to another, and seeks to explain them according to higher or lower levels of "civicness," by which he means the fabric of values, norms, institutions, and associations which permit and support civic commitment, the distinctive features of which are widespread solidarity, mutual trust, and tolerance. Civicness is also the opposite of Banfield's "amoral familism," based on the principle of "maximizing the short-term material advantages of the family nucleus, seeing as everyone else does" (Banfield 1958: 85). In the survey he conducted in a poor southern Italian village in the postwar years, Banfield attributed the community's failure to mobilize to address problems to this cultural complex. Civicness, on the other hand, is Tocqueville's "personal interest seen in the proper sense" or interest evaluated in the context of a wider public interest.

Putnam establishes the relationship between civicness and institutional performance through a set of statistical correlations between indicators, while seeking to control other variables. He thus identifies four macro-areas in which the quality of institutional performance corresponds to the level of civicness present. He then goes back eight centuries in search of the roots of these differences. In the twelfth century, Italy was divided into two consolidated political systems: the Norman monarchy in the South and the free communes in the center-North. The first was hierarchical and autocratic, the second republican and egalitarian, the product of free bargaining. Two different systems subsequently evolved, each according to its own logic, the first accumulating experience of "vertical" cultures and institutions, the second of "horizontal" ones. As early as the fourteenth century, it was possible to observe the four macro-areas which stand out today for their different levels of civicness, and which, with the odd adjustment, substantially reiterated primordial differences.

Putnam brings his study to an end by returning to the theory of social capital, referring in particular to Coleman. Different levels of institutional performance (but also, according to the author, of economic development) depend, in the final analysis, on different endowments of social capital. One conclusion is that both states and markets operate more effectively if the context has a rich civic tradition, that is to say an important legacy of social capital. This means that social capital contributes as much as, and perhaps more than, economic and human capital to modernization and development. In conclusion, the building of the necessary social capital is the key which opens the door of democracy.

Putnam's research has since become a benchmark for the development of the theory of social capital. It has also had a major impact on the political debate. It is almost as if the author suggests we observe America from Italy, an approach which has fuelled a lively discussion on the progressive loss of social capital in his own country (Putnam 1995, 1996).

Making Democracy Work has been praised (cf. Laitin 1995), but also criticized (e.g. Goldberg 1996; Tarrow 1996). No one questions the importance of civic culture (or social capital) in political processes, but what is in doubt is the role to attribute to civic culture in the processes analyzed and the relationship between this dimension and other aspects of social structure. One is perplexed by Putnam's final explanation of a cultural *longue durée* that is reproduced in processes of socialization and social control. True, the history of cultural characteristics moves slowly, but the persistence and variation of such characteristics needs to be explained. Hence the need to observe the combination of social interplay and the concrete choices of actors in successive moments. Political action tends to be underestimated, but ought to be re-valued, as should the true extent of economic processes. Putnam "explains too much" with social capital, reconstructing history to fit the concept itself.

SOCIAL CAPITAL AND THE POLITICAL ECONOMY OF CAPITALISM

In recent decades, the comparative analysis of the institutional set-ups of different national capitalisms has established itself in social research. Shonfield's essay on modern capitalism (1965) may be regarded as the point of departure for a vast literature, developed with a variety of theoretical tools (for a summing-up, see Trigilia 1998). *Trust* by Frances Fukuyama (1995) is the first attempt to apply the social capital perspective.

Fukuyama begins by observing that national political and economic institutions are converging, with economies increasingly oriented toward the market and integration in the global capitalistic division of labor. Social engineering has failed and the state is withdrawing from the economy. The idea that healthy political and economic institutions depend on a healthy, dynamic civil society is enjoying a revival. Civil society – firms, associations, schools, clubs, trade unions, and so on – is founded, in turn, on the family, the center of any society's cultural socialization, values, and moral precepts.

The economic and political convergence of the different countries brings to light the awareness and importance of cultural differences, which are firmly rooted in religion. Economic efficiency can be obtained inside groups in which persons work well together on the basis of common values; it depends, that is, on their endowment of social capital or, in other words, the capability of people to work together in groups and organizations in pursuit of common goals. This capability corresponds to mutual trust, the expectation of correct and cooperative behavior by others, which ultimately depends on the sharing of norms and values and on the ability to subordinate self to group interest. The accumulation of social capital is a lengthy, complex, and essentially spontaneous process. Politics is capable of destroying it unheedingly or, at best, struggles to preserve it. Culture, seen as an inherited ethical habit, thus plays a decisive role.

Different societies enjoy different endowments of social capital, and an abundance or paucity of trust is a function of different ethical codes which may be traced to different family cultures. The family may provide the basis for successful forms of small-scale enterprise, as in the industrial districts of central and Northeastern Italy, where a kind of familism is at work which extends to the local community, albeit hindering more complex economic organizations. Large corporations find fertile cultural ground in countries such as Japan, Germany, and the United States, where the family has never been a cultural impediment to extended forms of association, which are fostered by other cultural factors (by Protestant sects in the United States, for instance). Southern Italy and Russia, areas without strong families or more extended networks of trust, are examples of narrow familialism, hence their backwardness and the presence of a criminal economy within them. It is worth noting that China, France, Southern Italy, and other societies in which trust is low had experiences of strong political centralization which exhausted the social capital available there. This is not the case of Japan, the United States, and Germany.

Each national capitalism thus has a place of its own in the international division of labor. The specific culture of each selects a specific industrial structure option from those defined by markets and technologies, and the industrial structure, in turn, determines the sector of the global economy in which the country in question can achieve success.

Comparative political economy has developed different models of regulation and allocation to address problems of system integration (for example, a specific combination of aggregate economic variables which allows growth and stable employment) and social integration (for example, cultural and political acceptance of the redistributive combination obtained). This analytical school has accompanied the political experience of European forms of Keynesian capitalism. European models of economic regulation have accumulated inefficiencies and rigidities, and are ultimately jeopardized by the process of globalization which, other problems apart, has reduced the regulatory scope of national states. The most liberalist economies are the ones that are performing best at the moment.

Fukuyama's response to the new challenge is to use the idea of social capital for comparative analysis, thus liquidating the European model and allowing the "virtuous" American model to return to center-stage. In this ambitious program, he produces a large-scale synthetic framework joining past and future and backed by references to a vast literature. His book has also enjoyed great success outside academic circles, and thus deserves careful critical attention.

A TOOL TO BE HANDLED WITH CARE

The conceptual pairing of state and civil society has taken on a variety of meanings. One way of using it today is to identify the limits of politics. If politics organizes a society as a whole, civil society expresses capability and spaces for social self-organization. The concept of social capital has allowed us to explore these spaces. The collapse of communist systems and the problems encountered by Keynesian capitalism provide food for thought about the role of the state and politics in social organization. But exactly what role politics has to play remains an open question. Oddly enough, the first two comprehensive applications of the concept of social capital to political issues underestimate this problem.

Putnam assesses the performance of institutions, but fails to consider how the process of the building of the modern state has influenced the formation or the preservation of certain cultural traits (Tarrow 1996). Fukuyama defines the space of politics in a negative sense. He is not clear about what he wants politics to do; all he says is that it has to intervene as little as possible and avoid causing damage, because political action constantly risks destroying social capital. The welfare state, he argues, has often consumed social capital; by distributing subsidies it has destroyed fabrics of community self-help. It is, admittedly, important to call attention to the possible perverse effects of political action and society's loss of self-organizational capability (cf. also Ostrom 1994), but to do so is not to define the tasks of politics. Indeed, such an attitude is *de facto* negative and prejudicial.

Both authors shift their focus from politics to culture so that, for them, the question of social capital boils down to culture's functions for social integration. Albeit addressing different themes, both ultimately trace social capital to a shared culture. For Putnam, civic culture explains not only institutional performance, but also economic development. In the final analysis, Fukuyama's model explains the state and functioning of the economy in terms of market mechanisms; the reasons for adjustment to the market, he concludes, reside in culture, seen as an inherited ethical habit. This habit is the source of trust, and hence constitutes basic social capital. Both authors are attracted by the long-term duration of original cultures, and argue that historical events may have influenced the evolution of the original model, but we get the impression that everything – or almost everything – was destined to develop the way it has anyway.

To stress the limits of these applications and grasp the potential of social capital for political analysis, let us return to Coleman. Earlier I spoke of the tension which Coleman establishes between intentional organizations and other forms of social capital. In reality, he centers his attention on social capital as a by-product of social structures and the informal aspects thereof. Why?

The answer lies in the "replacement of primordial social capital" (1990: 652): namely, the social capital that used to be typical of small-scale traditional societies and now thrown into crisis by modernization. Here Coleman proves to be an heir to the classical sociologists who built the categories of modernity by difference from those of traditional society, for which they show a certain nostalgia (Nisbet 1966). The *Gemeinschaft–Gesellschaft* pairing (Tönnies 1974 [1887]) is paradigmatic in this sense, although Coleman chooses to recall Weber and his idea of modernity as rationalization-bureaucratization (Weber 1978 [1922]). The lingering problem, however, is that something needs to be replaced. Modernity fails to produce the resources it needs for integration, yet wastes others. This idea recurs today in several authors. For Habermas, capitalism lives off cultural resources which it finds in previous forms of society and consumes but fails to reproduce (Habermas 1976). On closer scrutiny, Coleman is not unduly concerned with the survival of traditional elements, although he regards them as important. He turns his attention instead to the small-scale spontaneous society of *today* in the rationalized, large-scale society of *today*. He is one of those sociologists who have rediscovered the world of direct, face-to-face interaction and how it helps us understand a society made up largely of remote, indirect interaction managed in large-scale, formalized systems of interaction (e.g. Giddens 1984; Luhmann 1984). How to fit interaction and society, micro and macro, into the analysis is an open question which every generation of sociologists posits in different ways. The perspective of Coleman's general theoretical construction moves from micro to macro. But he is also interested in the consequences of macro for micro – the destruction of small-scale social capital in formalization processes – and micro for macro – the utility for social integration of the social capital produced in direct interaction.

The difference between Coleman's idea of social capital and those of the applications described thus becomes clear. It is a basic difference of methodology and has far-reaching analytical consequences. Coleman adopts a paradigm of action, Putnam and Fukuyama a deterministic, causal paradigm (Boudon 1982). Putnam and Fukuyama develop their explanations exclusively in relation to previous situations and conditions: a certain family structure and culture, for example, foretells company size. Their analysis defines differences and explains them with correlations of this type, but the actors tend to leave the stage. Both authors know full well that the historical process intervenes to redirect lines of development at particular moments, but their references exclude individual or collective subjects oriented toward strategies that they attempt, with varying degrees of coherence and awareness, to implement in a concrete situation which at once limits them and opens alternative possibilities. This way of reconstructing historical connections and, above all, this type of attention to the present, which enhances analysis and introduces the actor to situations that are not necessarily closed, do not seem to interest them. The general limit of their deterministic approach is that, at best, it describes a correlation between phenomena but without explaining it and, sometimes, struggles to define which variable in the correlation is independent and which dependent. So is it civic culture which explains the efficiency of democratic institutions or vice versa (Barry 1970)? The fact is that the presumption that explanations are possible without real actors, their definition of the situation and intentional strategies, typically lapses into hyperfunctionalism and hyperculturalism. The actors that emerge are hyper-socialized, passive agents of economic and cultural structures.

It is possible to discuss the utility of the two paradigms at length, but it is more important now to show the differences and comparative advantages of the case in point. In an age of uncertainty and differentiation, Coleman comes out on top. In his perspective, social capital is essentially a stock of relations which an actor has for his own purposes, and which are effective since they are based on a specific culture, but also on the form of the network or other factors still. It is no coincidence that Coleman only cites examples of possible different forms of social capital. His focus on networks of relations as opposed to culture is an attempt to leave room for strategic actors, closed as little as possible in stereotyped role behavior, and protagonists of a fabric of relations in autonomous, combinatory forms. Coleman's perspective seeks to grasp progressive adjustments, combinations of different resources and "code games" rather than repetitions of crystallized cultural patterns. Developed coherently, this perspective is concerned more with the production of culture than its reproduction.

The first attempts to apply the theory of social capital to political sociology have brought to light often neglected aspects of social processes and helped to revive the political debate. Alas, their anti-political prejudice undermines the utility of the discussion. No one today questions the need to reappraise civil society's self-organizational resources, to redesign the methods and bounds of politics and to reassess the utility of the market. The theory of social capital offers the analytical resources to support these convictions. It is odd, however, that its applications have been so keen to show that politics consumes social capital, yet say so little about how it might help create it. Are we positive that welfare systems have not helped to preserve or create social capital in Europe? Are we so sure that politics in America has destroyed more social capital than the market? Towards the end of his book, Fukuyama briefly acknowledges that, albeit compatible with many institutional set-ups, capitalism consumes social capital. But is it possible to find compatible set-ups of economic growth and social integration without reappraising the regulatory role of politics?

The idea of social capital has made headway in research and has been applied in fields as diverse as the labor market, the school careers of children, the misconduct of professionals, the economic behavior of immigrants, social mobility, and so on. Simultaneously, a theoretical formulation of a "paradigm" for social capital is being developed (see Portes 1998; Sandefur and Laumann 1998) which is sure to direct research on the old and new issues of political sociology. In substance, the concept of social capital appears useful for analysis of political phenomena, but it needs to be perfected. Far from being overburdened with duties, it has to be handled with care.

Further Reading

For an informative overview, see A. Portes "Social Capital: its origins and applications in modern sociology," *Annual Review of Sociology* 24: 1–24, 1998. The best-known study of social capital is Robert Putnam's *Making Democracy Work: Civic Traditions in Modern Italy*, 1993.

22

Markets and States

Colin Crouch

The state and the market can be distinguished from other social institutions by the clarity and abstract nature of what actors within them are trying to maximize: power and material wealth respectively. Political science and economics have therefore become very distinct disciplines; unlike sociology, which is the residual social science. Historically, the development of capitalism depended on a separation of state and market in which the state guaranteed the rules and freedoms necessary for the market. This separation was compromised in the nineteenth century insofar as working-class mobilization involved the attempt to use the state to gain protection from the market, which was to be suppressed in communism, or more closely regulated in social democracy. In the late twentieth century there were two major changes: the growth of neo-liberalism with its demands for a strict separation of state and market; and increased freedom for the world market which undermined the power of organized groups in the economy and ended their involvement in economic governance. However, the way in which the rise of neo-liberalism has taken place paradoxically intensifies state-market entanglement insofar as it recommends the extension of market principles of exchange to the state itself. The neo-liberal state is far from the anonymous guardian of the level playing field advocated by both classical and neo-liberal theory.

The state and the market can be distinguished from other social institutions by the clarity and abstract character of what actors within them are trying to maximize: in the former, power; in the latter, material wealth.

While those within the state, or struggling to have access to the state, have a diversity of substantive goals, they can function effectively only if they can gain control over the capacity to give orders on the assumption that they will be obeyed. Following Max Weber's (1922: Part I, ch. 1, sec. 17) famous formulation, it is the distinctive feature of the state that in the last resort it commands a monopoly of the legitimate use of violence to support its authority. Politics, the name of the activity that focuses on access to the state, is therefore always action focused on the maximization of outcomes through command, through the attainment of power. Similarly, while actors within the market seek diversity of substantive goods and services, they can do this effectively only if they possess the means of exchange.

Economic behavior, as market action is termed, is therefore always focused on the maximization of the means of exchange – in modern economies, wealth.

Power and wealth are distinctive as goals of human activity in that they give their possessors a generalized capacity. While one is holding either power or wealth one can potentially use them for a number of different substantive ends. Once they become focused on the pursuit of a substantive objective in this way, they become limited. The pursuits of pure power and pure wealth therefore have a singular rationality, one which is compromised every time that they are converted into something specific.

The state is the primary locus for political, power-seeking behavior, and the market the primary locus for economic, wealth-seeking behavior. However, both the political and the economic can be extended by analogy to other spheres. Wherever there is power-seeking behavior we can speak of a political situation. There is for example a politics of the family: the situation where one or other family members are maneuvring against or manipulating others in order to attain their goals. Wherever there is exchange we can speak of an economic relationship. There is therefore an economics of the family, where the relations among family members are seen as a series of markets (see particularly the work of Gary Becker 1981).

It is difficult to find fundamental goals of similar abstract type in other social institutions. (The only exception is possibly religion, where action is focused on the overwhelming general need to appease powerful figures in a world beyond this one – achieving a state of grace with God in Christian terms.) It is this characteristic which early on enabled study of the state and the market to become distinct disciplines – political science and economics respectively (theology too if it is a social science) – rather than remain part of a general science of society, or sociology, and to develop their bodies of theory more strongly than that discipline.

This pattern within the structure of the social sciences is also found in many actual social representations. In formally structured societies the *virtuosi* of state and market, and those of religion, are picked out as privileged social classes: in European history these were the orders of, respectively, aristocrats, bourgeoisie, and priests; a similar pattern existed in the core caste order of Mogul India, though with the priestly caste accorded pride of place. Stratification in the rest of the population was far less systematic and clear; they were just a residuum, even though a vast majority. Similarly, the classic Greek and Roman city embodied a seat of government, a market, and a temple as the most important buildings, normally located formally in relationship to each other in the most prominent part of the city. The medieval European city followed the same pattern, with town hall, market place, and church similarly located. Other parts were less distinct and prominent; society in general was literally the poorly differentiated residuum which simply filled up the rest of available space.

Today sociology remains the residual social science. Attempts, such as that by Talcott Parsons (especially in Parsons and Smelser 1956), to claim that it was the most general, and therefore central, social science, of which political science and economics were subdisciplines, have never succeeded. One reason for this, as Carlo Trigilia (1998) has argued, is that, in conceding them their autonomy, Parsons did not go on to show how they could be reintegrated within a general social science. Another reason is this lack of a core motivational principle of action and consequent lack of institutional clarity within the residuum.

There remains the question whether either power or wealth, command or exchange, can be absorbed by the other. Can economics be reduced to political science, or *vice versa*? In practice it works only one way round. It is frequently, and today increasingly, claimed by economics that all exercises of power, as well as all other social actions, can be reduced to instances of exchange, of markets (see Dowding, chapter 3, in this volume). To obey the law, for example, can be seen as a decision to accept the constraint on behavior of obedience in exchange for the avoidance of punishment. To take a very specific example: should one see a fine for parking a car on a double yellow line as just a form of car-parking fee – distinguished from normal ones only by the fact that it is less reliably levied though particularly heavy if it is levied? Or is it an expression of the coercive power of the state to make our behavior conform to certain norms?

This approach can be extremely illuminating in requiring very precise consideration of the logic of action of groups and individuals, challenging implicit and unquestioned assumptions behind theories. In the forms of public choice and rational choice theories it has in recent years made a distinctive contribution to the study of politics and more general social action too (Russell 1979; Lewin and Vedung 1980; Elster 1986; Lane 1987; McLean 1987; Rowley 1987, 1997; Coleman and Fararo 1992; Friedman, J. 1996; Downs 1998). The main problem with this economic reductionism is that redefining all exercises of power and authority as exchanges sometimes requires either an over-elaborate re-description and analysis of what is taking place in a power relation, or a stripping out from the analysis of any elements which cannot be reduced to exchange.

There is no space here to analyse these claims of economic theory in detail (for useful critiques, see Dunleavy 1991; Dowding and King 1995; Udehn 1996). We should, however, take note of the attempt, since it is very relevant to changes taking place in the relations between states and markets, with which we shall be occupied. Arguments that economic theory can provide an adequate account of political behavior have developed alongside beliefs that the state should behave as though it were a market actor. Even within the economy itself there has been a tendency for firms to deconstruct themselves as institutions embodying authority relations between employers and employees, rejecting the insights of the Coasian theory of the firm (Coase 1937) and returning to a more purely exchanged model of the work relationship. This involves firms giving many of their employees the status of self-employed contractors and therefore declaring that their relationship with them is one of exchange, not command.

Within the political world itself, established relations between state and market have been challenged by a number of developments: moves to contractualize relations within and between government departments, making officials relate to each other as though they were in a market for each other's services; in many cases functions previously seen as part of the state have been contracted out to firms, market actors. Activities of public services are increasingly subject to the imposition of quantitative targets, which seek to reduce their activities to a number of numerical symbols – resembling a price and therefore becoming a market item. States increasingly turn to actors from the market sector to show them how to run governments as though they were businesses (see Palumbo, chapter 12, in this volume). The ideology of neo-liberalism, which has stimulated these changes, starts from the assumption that market and state should be strictly separated. That it has led to a new form of their mutual entanglement is paradoxical. To understand what has been happening it is necessary to step back and consider very briefly the historical development of relations between state and market.

AN HISTORICAL PERSPECTIVE

In medieval Europe, control over armed force gradually transformed into control over legal processes, and the set of organizations that came to be called the state became the property of relatively closed networks of families. These assigned privileges to themselves and excluded most other social groups from participation in state work. They became the European aristocracies; the most successful became monarchical dynasties. Although struggle among them was frequent and often murderous, they united in the need to restrict access to control over the emerging state to their number. Among the great majority of the population excluded from these ranks, some became able to accumulate property through buying and selling activities which grew in scope as technology advanced, increasing the range of goods and services that could be bought and sold. While the aristocracy presided over the large acres of the countryside, merchants were essentially urban people, and established their bases in the growing towns, often winning special rights and privileges for these. In this way the bourgeoisie became a separate social order, its world of exchange rivalling that of aristocratic command.

These worlds could not be kept apart. Bourgeois property and markets needed favorable law if they were to be protected from robbery and develop the complex rules and enforcements required for commerce to grow. The courts of kings and nobles were the only sources of such law. Meanwhile, these latter needed money to fight their wars and sustain their courts. While they could often get this by taking or taxing it, they also needed the cooperation of those who were able to make wealth grow – often the urban bourgeoisie. In this way the two great classes, one with its position rooted in the state, the other in the market, developed their uneasy symbiosis. They needed each other, though the power base of each threatened the other. The essential emerging demand of the bourgeoisie was that if the new capitalist economy they were developing was to thrive, it needed a very specific role from the polity: the state had to guarantee the freedoms and rules necessary for the conduct of the market, but beyond that it should not interfere (North 1990). The state should be sufficiently favorable to market interests to be willing to erect the highly elaborate institutions required: laws of property ownership and transfer, which make owners of capital responsible for their activities (otherwise they would waste resources and let down their creditors), but not so responsible that they are afraid to take initiatives. It requires a concept of bankruptcy, otherwise badly performing firms simply stay around, hoarding resources which they use inefficiently and never paying their debts; but not a bankruptcy law so severe that fear of it inhibits risk taking.

It wants capacities to share risk, so that entrepreneurship thrives; but not so extensive that agents can act irresponsibly. It wants employment contracts which make labor free and mobile; but which leave firms with scope to tie employees down with loyalty incentives.

The progress of the market certainly did not require a suppression of the state. What was essential was separation of state and market: partly and most obviously to avoid state interference in market processes. But *pari passu* it was also necessary to protect the state from special pleading by particular groups of capitalists. Ideally it ceased to be the private possession of a class, and instead became the public guarantor of the market as a level playing field. However, while this might be the interests of the market as a whole, it was not necessarily that of any one capitalist, who might seek advantages for his enterprise through political favors. Even if the maximizing principles of state and market are different, they can be converted into each other. Political power can be used to lay hands on resources that can then be used in the market, while wealth acquired in exchange can be used to buy influence in the state.

The ideal capitalist state is not a dictatorship – which will be unlikely to permit so much autonomy to the market – but a liberal polity in which political power is limited to a broad class of property owners (North 1990). Ideally none of these should be sufficiently powerful to be able to impose individual pressure on the state. Conditions approximating to this existed in a number of countries, but particularly England and the Netherlands, in the 200 years or so prior to the advance of democracy, though in neither country was the condition of an absence of privileged individual capitalists fully met.

In practice this simplified story had many vicissitudes, as it played itself out in different ways and at different speeds across Europe and, eventually, the Americas and elsewhere from the sixteenth century onwards. Here there is space to mention only one of these. In some places, by the late nineteenth century the growth of industrialization had made possible the social and political organization of some of the other groups in the largely undifferentiated, non-citizen masses, particularly skilled manual workers in industry. Many of these came to perceive that, because their numbers were so great, if they could attain political rights, they might be able to wield or at least influence state power so that state resources might offset the weaknesses they experienced in the market because of their generally low incomes. In some versions of the strategy which emerged from working-class mobilization the market was to be suppressed altogether; this became the hallmark of communist movements. In other versions it would survive, but regulated and controlled in the interests of those lacking market power; the political philosophy of social democracy. In general, the struggle between state and market changed from being that between aristocracy and bourgeoisie to that between capitalism and socialism. Briefly, was the state to limit its actions to guarantee property rights, or should it intervene to protect various classes from the operation of those markets?: the core political question of the twentieth century.

Resolution of these tensions was not easy. Sometimes (as during the fascist or Nazi periods in several countries) those thriving in the market became so afraid of the hostility of socialist forces toward it that they supported authoritarian control of the state, even though dictatorship would bring transgression of the separation of state and market so important to market capitalism. In Russia and other parts of Eastern Europe, movements acting in the name of socialism came close to destroying market processes altogether.

Generalizing very broadly, by the middle of the twentieth century the rise of the working class and its relations with established socioeconomic interests resulted in a complex web of compromises, stand-offs and mutual advantages. Outside the Soviet bloc, states in the industrial world continued to guarantee the market order, but intervened in the economy at a number of points. Some of these followed a socialist logic of protecting the working class from the market; others responded to the demand of capitalist interests themselves for protection from the instabilities of the market process. The state became a highly extended institution, carrying out a mass of economic activities as well as purely political ones, while representatives of various market interests, mainly in the form of trade unions and employers' organizations, were in turn deeply embedded in the polity.

A series of inflationary shocks in the 1970s initially produced even more complexity. Levels of taxation and of state intervention in the economy grew as governments sought restabilization, while they also tried to engage organizations of market actors in sharing the state function of economic governance with them. This compromised even further than in the preceding period the relative autonomies of state and market.

However, an underlying shift in social interests was at hand. Economic change weakened the organized manual workers who had led the challenge to the bourgeois state. The task of advocating the activist state passed increasingly to public service employees who carried out its extended functions, and whose position as creatures of that state was vulnerable. Economic globalization was about to have its impact in giving capital choices to move away from state forms that it did not like. Finally, a growth in the importance of financial as opposed to industrial capital was taking place. Financial capital possesses far greater geographical mobility, far fewer sunk costs, and can therefore escape the state, which is territory-bound. The autonomy of the market from the state was being strengthened just at the point where it had seemed to be fatally compromised. At the same time, the attempt at a total triumph of state over market in the Soviet-controlled part of Europe was collapsing. The neo-liberal ideas which had been developing in economic and political theory began to match changes in the relationships of social forces.

STATES AND MARKETS AT THE END OF THE TWENTIETH CENTURY

Subsequent developments can be examined at two levels. First, there was a straightforward neo-liberal call for the market to be left alone from state interference. In practical terms this meant reduced taxation, less public spending, and less pressure of the state on the economy in general. At the same time, increased freedom for the market would reduce the role of organized groups in the economy, leading to an end to their involvement in economic governance. The growing claims of economic theory to be able to provide better analyses of public policy than political science became very relevant at this point. It was primarily a claim in favor of clarity in objectives, in exchanges, and in means-end relationships.

As already noted, the capitalist economy is never truly free from the state, and ideally needs a particular liberal regime of property owners. Reintroducing conditions like these in the 1980s, about half a century after the spread of democracy throughout much of the advanced capitalist world and the consequent need for states to respond to the interests of the non-propertied, was a difficult task requiring political management. Parts of the population had to be persuaded that they did not want state protection from the market, while those who still did had to be politically out-maneuvred. At the same time two centuries of freedom for property-owners themselves to organize politically had produced a mass of lobbies and privileged interest groups on the side of capitalism itself. Reasserting a true separation of market and state would require a very strong and autonomous state, and indeed one almost impossible to achieve. If the state was both strong and autonomous, it would be unlikely to accept the full autonomy of the market; if it was not truly autonomous but mainly responsive to pro-market interests, it might, given the oligopolistic character of late twentieth-century capitalism, be also likely to privilege particular corporations rather than provide the true level playing field.

In fact, the most perfect reassertion of the free market came, not from one of the democracies, but from a brutal dictatorship: the military regime of General Auguste Pinochetin Chile (Drago 1998). That such a government should repress anti-capitalist, labor, and pro-welfare interests was to be expected. What was surprising was that the regime was also independent of the propertied lobbies which had long been powerful in Chilean politics. General Pinochet and his supporters were closely associated with economists from the University of Chicago, who had been the intellectual backbone of the whole neo-liberal movement (most notably, Milton Friedman – see Friedman 1962 for a political rather than technical statement). Chicago policies were implemented rigorously in Chile so that, contrary to the usual logic of state-market relations, it was a military dictatorship which clarified the market from state involvement more thoroughly than anywhere else.

The UK and the USA became the prime democratic sites for similar experiments, particularly during the governments of Margaret Thatcher and Ronald Reagan respectively – Thatcher becoming a close friend of Pinochet. The thriving condition of democracy in these two countries forced compromises with the reforms – though for the distinctive combination of a "free economy and a strong state," see Gamble 1994. Nevertheless, following the neo-liberal program of first these governments and later those of Western Europe (especially following the institution of a neo-liberal monetary regime as part of the introduction of a single European currency in most countries in the European Unions), the balance between the market and the state now corresponds more closely to the preferences of actors in the former than at any time since the Second World War – in some countries more than ever (see Tonkiss, chapter 23, in this volume).

But there were more paradoxes. As noted, the general class of property owners has an interest in sustaining a market regime as a level playing field; not in special privileges being won by individuals of its number. In economic and political theory alike this condition is fulfilled by the anonymity criterion. This requires not only that actors act anonymously in the market, but that they do so in the political process too. They have votes, and they may dispute in the law courts; and that is all.

This is however an unrealistic model. The notion of anonymity within the market itself is a fiction. Individual firms must always be trying to overcome the state of anonymity, which for them is a problem. They want customers and suppliers to know them by reputation, and they want to use that reputation as a form of power, for example, in purchaser–supplier relationships.

Economic theory has found ways of coping with this, of showing how oligopolistic competition may have wider benefits, and how it does not necessarily exclude often quite fierce competition over price or quality. However, the political problem raised does not disappear so easily. If some firms stand out by their giant size, become well-known institutions within their society, and accumulate large wealth, what is to prevent them using these advantages as political leverage? At least they will be able to lobby government for policies favorable to their market interests. At most they may engage complex and implicit exchanges of funds to political parties and either favorable state action for their interests or even the award of government contracts. In some countries and in some circumstances such exchanges may be illegal, but this is usually the case only when an exchange is very specific. One form of the relationship between states and markets is therefore a set of special relationships between politicians and state officials on one side, and firms and entrepreneurs on the other.

All politico-economic systems are vulnerable to this. Neo-liberal theorists would argue that, by disengaging state and market from the entanglements brought about by the postwar compromise between capitalism and socialism, their reforms should reduce the possibilities. However, the manner in which the rise of neo-liberalism has taken place paradoxically intensifies this particular form of state-market entanglement. The neo-liberal state defers to business interests; it believes that its own internal processes have been discredited by the years of social democratic compromise, and wishes to clean itself out by borrowing as many practices and procedures as possible from private firms. This was less true during the original, nineteenth-century capitalist period, when the state still carried something of monarchical (or in France, early republican) aura about it, and the public official was seen as a special kind of functionary, following a different professional ethic from that appropriate to the private firm. During the course of the latter twentieth century this concept of the distinctive character of public service was partially transmuted into the special role of the welfare state.

Neo-liberal theory challenges this. The ranks of state employment having swollen to include, not just a hierarchy of high-status officials, but a mass of public employees, many of whom are organized into special interest lobbies of their own, the concept of the specificity of public service is rejected. If it is "special" it is merely because it does not follow rules of profit maximization, and is therefore inefficient. Whereas, according to the neo-classical economic theory on which neo-liberalism draws, successful market actors perfectly and rationally anticipate all consequences of their actions, the state, not being a market actor, is unable to do this. Its interventions in the market are therefore virtually certain to reduce the level of rationality. This should partly be remedied by keeping the state out of the market; but for its important remaining residual functions, it must improve its rational capacity by becoming more like a firm, a market actor (Osboorne and Gaebler 1992; Fay 1997).

Ideally, state agencies should be relocated in the market; that is, privatized. Either the state privatizes the activity entirely, leaving the industry alone with its customers; or it contracts out its functions to private firms, like a large customer firm. Finally, parts of the public service which at least temporarily remain within the state must learn to act as though they were in the market – units are made either to compete with each other or to trade with each other on a purchaser–provider basis.

This logical conclusion of neo-liberal thinking breaks with the fundamental liberal principle with which it started: mutual recognition of the separate spheres of state and market, their different logics and their respective goals. Not only is the state seen as having no goals or *modi operandi* different from those of market actors, but it is seen to gain by subordinating its activities as much as possible to those of market actors.

Elements of state sovereignty are preserved through the practice of regulation, though even here there are paradoxes. Although much neo-liberal rhetoric is about deregulation of the economy, the growth of regulation and considerable innovation in its forms have been hallmarks of the period. This is because most former publicly-owned industries were in sectors in which it is difficult to have anything resembling perfect markets, mainly because the large scale of investment required to operate the primarily infrastructural industries concerned acts as an entry barrier to new firms.

Privatized industries therefore usually need to be regulated, where regulation results from recognition that markets cannot be shaped perfectly to assert the needs of customers, employees or public interests. In addition to monopoly characteristics, this might occur because of externalities – where economic action has either negative or positive consequences for third parties which cannot easily take a market form (pollution is the main example of a negative externality). It might be because it is considered that certain moral or other standards have to be maintained even if the free market would not guarantee this (as in regulation of the display of sex and violence on television). Alternatively there might be a strong belief in public policy that people should have access to certain goods even if they cannot afford or (more contentiously) would not choose to buy them (education, health services, retirement pensions). In many instances strict neo-liberals try either to deny that such problems matter (for example, adopting a libertarian position on television viewing) or to find market means of solving them (for example tackling pollution by fiscal means of making the polluter pay). However, very often the political salience of some of these issues is such that a state-governed regulatory system is established even if the service concerned is removed from direct public provision. Here, regulation continues to follow a logic of state engagement with markets typical of the postwar period.

There is however a second, more purely neo-liberal case for regulation. This is the need for a regulatory regime to ensure market actors that competition will remain fair and free and not vulnerable to arbitrary interference by the state

(Majone 1994, 1997). The regulator is there to protect the competitive order against the state as much as against abuse from within the market. Although this residually recognizes the public interest role of the state as the body most likely to install such an institution, since the state is a suspect actor from the point of view of neo-liberalism, it is unlikely to be trusted with the regulatory role itself. This logic leads to the interesting phenomenon of the private regulation of public actors. The ultimate example is the financial markets; whereas during the post-war period governments and central banks regulated the conduct of the financial markets, under conditions of deregulation and globalization it is the other way round (Boyer 2000). The markets, through their buying and selling of different currencies, pass continuous judgments on the conduct of governments, who have to obey their indications or see their currencies collapse. In the case of the European Central Bank, which has been founded by a treaty between states and therefore requires particular explicitness in its constitution, sensitivity to the priorities of the markets has been built in as the only criterion to which the Bank should respond. More formally, two particular US financial corporations, Moodys and Standard and Poor, provide rankings of the creditworthiness of governments throughout the world; effectively therefore a duopoly private enterprise is regulating a fundamental characteristic of states.

Within individual countries the privatization or contracting out of regulation as part of the general process of neo-liberal public-service reform can have similar consequences. For example, in the United Kingdom the inspection of local government departments and schools is contracted out to private firms, who are empowered to make judgments that will be supported by public authority. In some cases the enterprises providing these inspection services are also competing with local government departments to take over their functions as part of a privatization process. Here government remains the ultimate arbiter of the process, but it is a state which seeks tutelage from market actors.

These actions by the state of privatization, contracting out, sharing regulation with firms, deferring to firms on how to conduct its own business, continuously erode even further the boundaries between the state and the market, the rei forcement of which had been one of the starting points of the whole paradoxical neo-liberal exercise. This in turn increases the scope for increased transactions and contracts between politicians and individual business people – a role of the state very remote from the autonomous guardian of the level playing field of an anonymous market that was the starting point of both classical liberal and neo-liberal theory. Separation of state and market therefore appears to be a *chimera* in complex modern societies.

Further Reading

Gamble, A. 1994: *The Free Economy and the Strong State: The Politics of Thatcherism*, second edition. London: Macmillan.

Osborne, D. and Gaebler, T. 1992: *Reinventing Government: How the Entrepreneurial Spirit is Transforming the Public Sector*. Reading, MA: Addison-Wesley-Longman.

Udehn, L. 1996: *The Limits of Public Choice: A Sociological Critique of the Economic Theory of Politics*. London: Routledge.

23

Markets against States: Neo-liberalism

Fran Tonkiss

A neo-liberal consensus is the most obvious feature of the rapprochement between "left" and "right" in established liberal democracies; and neo-liberal government has spread too in Latin America and former communist countries. Emerging in the 1970s to challenge postwar corporatism, it involves a commitment to free market principles and the strict separation of economy and state. For neo-Marxists, the political and economic restructuring initiated in its name mark a shift from a Fordist regime of capital accumulation that was in crisis as a result of rigidities of production and consumption. For the neo-liberal right, the problems of the 1970s were the result of an over-extended state. From this point of view, the primary task of government is to promote economic growth in a global economy by deregulating markets, making them more "flexible." In actual fact, however, measures introduced by neo-liberals promoted a pronounced economic role for government that was in contradiction with their rhetoric of non-intervention, while attempts to "marketize" the state have produced complicated forms of re-regulation. Neo-liberalism has also promoted a restructuring of welfare and a new ideological conception of the relation between government and citizen. If the politics of a "third way" are explicitly posited against neo-liberalism, they nevertheless take up key elements of its project.

The politics of neo-liberalism is most closely associated with the radical agenda of right-wing governments in capitalist democracies during the 1980s – and signally, with the administrations of Thatcher in Britain (1979–90) and Reagan in the United States (1980–8). Over the intervening period, neo-liberal politics has lost both its novelty and its distinctly conservative credentials. The forms of economic rationalism pursued since the early 1980s by a range of social democratic and Labor governments in Europe, North America, Australia, and New Zealand suggest that neo-liberal principles have been accommodated to the politics of the mainstream left at least as easily as to those of the radical right. Indeed, the emergence of a broad neo-liberal consensus is one of the more obvious features of an alleged rapprochement between the politics of "left" and "right" (see Giddens 1994). At the same time, the spread of neo-liberal government in Latin America, and the neo-liberal shock therapy that passed for post-Communist transition in a number of ex-Soviet states, indicate that these politics are not peculiar to already liberal societies (see Przeworski 1991; Crawford 1995).

The political and economic strategies that broadly can be grouped as varieties of "neo-liberalism" reduce to a few common factors. Primary amongst these is a commitment to free market principles as the basis for economic organization. The crucial point for a political sociology of neo-liberalism is that such an attitude to the market goes with a particular conception of the state. The latter's role as an economic actor is circumscribed in ways that break with forms of welfarism and managed capitalism in liberal-democratic contexts, and with the more statist forms of corporatism or centralized planning that had typified the Latin American and Eastern European cases. In its approach to the relationship between market and state, neo-liberalism re-invents classical liberal precepts regarding the proper separation of economy from government. Moreover, neo-liberal perspectives position the market as not only the crucible for economic success, but the basis for a larger social good: the economics of the market opens onto an *ethics* of the market wherein market choices are linked to wider personal and political freedoms. The conflation of market relations with individual well-being in certain post-Communist contexts is only the most striking example of this market ethos, and has its corollary in neo-liberal reforms that have sought to correct a "culture of dependency" in a number of advanced welfare states. In these different senses, neo-liberalism stands not simply as a critique of "big government" or a retreat from the "over-burdened" state in the interests of economic efficiency, but as a *positive* state project that seeks to steer governmental forms, social institutions, and individual behavior in line with a particular vision of the free market and free society.

1 STATES AND MARKETS: THE EMERGENCE OF NEO-LIBERALISM

Neo-liberal perspectives emerged in the 1970s as a critical challenge to the postwar political and economic settlement that had underpinned liberal capitalist government since the 1950s. The established form of "managed" or "organized" capitalism was based on corporatist bargaining arrangements between national governments and the peak associations of labor and capital, twinned with national systems of welfare provision (see Crouch, chapter 22, in this volume). From the late 1960s, however, the ability of governments to steer domestic economies in concert with large corporate actors came under threat from a number of sides. These included changing patterns of international investment and trade caused by the emergence of new capitalist competitors (particularly West Germany, Japan, and newly-industrializing economies in South-East Asia and Latin America); low economic growth in increasingly stagnant large-scale production systems; the reappearance of unemployment as a serious social and economic problem; and the expanding share of national product taken by the costs of welfare bureaucracy. Entrenched unemployment existed in tandem with high inflation, in defiance of the Keynesian economic policies that predicted a trade-off between these two factors, and which in an extended way provided the basis for a broad postwar consensus in capitalist economic management.

Theorists working within a regulationist or neo-Marxist framework have viewed this constellation of factors as a "crisis" in the system of Atlantic Fordism around which postwar North American and western European economies were organized (see Aglietta 1979; Lipietz 1987; Harvey 1989; Boyer and Durand 1997). As such, it represents a crisis both of a particular mode of capitalist accumulation, and of related systems of national economic management. These economic and political arrangements were based on a complex of institutional structures, including corporatist agreements between governments, capital and labor; an Atlantic state system; production directed at domestic markets; and extended welfare systems. In contrast, an emergent set of "post-Fordist" conditions saw the weakening of corporatist consensus; the "hollowing-out" of the functions of the nation-state; internationalization of corporate ownership, production and distribution; and the retrenchment of welfare provision. On these terms, "Fordism" and "post-Fordism" do not simply represent alternative systems of production, but can be seen as extended regimes of political and economic regulation through which different forms of capital accumulation are secured. Such broad regulatory schemes should be treated with caution; a number of theorists have been sceptical about the adequacy and coherence of the post-Fordist thesis in particular (see Jessop, et al. 1988, 1990; Harvey 1989). It is certainly the case, for example, that Fordist productive systems proved compatible with a range of state and societal forms. However, the forms of market-led economic restructuring that attended the economic crisis of the 1970s (which are not, other than in a very simple sense, obviously "post-Fordist") invariably have been wedded to neo-liberal political forms.

From a political economy perspective, the economic crisis of the 1970s can be read as a problem of over-accumulation and rigidity in the Fordist system of mass production in Western Europe and North America (see Harvey 1989: 141–7). Increased technical efficiency meant that by the early 1970s fewer workers were required while output continued to expand. These problems of over-supply, given growing unemployment and falling consumer demand, posed serious problems for economic government. One response – more immediate than the tasks of wholesale economic restructuring – was for governments to release more money into their domestic economies, aiming to stimulate consumer demand and boost wider economic activity. The result, however, was a destabilizing inflationary crisis in the early 1970s which did little to reverse economic stagnation. The entrenched interests of the corporatist partners – "big labor, big capital, and big government" (Harvey 1989: 142) – compounded the sclerotic nature of large-scale production systems and inflexible labor markets. Even as the widespread experience of "stagflation" – the stubborn combination of high unemployment and high inflation – appeared to discredit Keynesian approaches to activist demand-management, welfare obligations exerted ever greater political and financial claims upon governments. On all these counts, corporatist state forms appeared exhausted – over-burdened by welfare commitments; over-extended by economic strategies that at best were ineffective, at worst positively damaging.

While presented in a thumbnail manner here, these are not simple arguments. From a different perspective – that of an emergent neo-liberal right – the situation is rather clearer. The crisis of corporatist economic management becomes readable as one of botched policy interventions, creating rapid inflation and a growing welfare bill in the face of international and internal pressures. Government activity, in this view, was a large part of the economic problem, rather than the key to its solution. The monetarist ideas originally developed by the Chicago economist Milton Friedman in the early 1950s gained increasing credence at this time, particularly in Britain and the United States. Friedman's work disrupted a Keynesian consensus in arguing that economic crises could be traced not to blips in demand, but to changes in money supply. What is more, he argued, the time-lag that existed between policy interventions and their actual economic effects served to heighten market instabilities, rather than to correct them. On both fronts the better stance for government was one of non-intervention: money supply simply should grow in line with the rate of growth in the economy; while state measures to massage demand (say, through welfare transfers or public employment programs) created market distortions at the same time as they stifled individual initiative and national competitiveness.

A distinctly neo-liberal take on the economic and political problems of the 1970s identified an over-extended state as both a chief factor behind the downturn, and the primary obstacle to recovery. The crisis of corporatist management, then, provided the stage for a radical revision of the economic role of the state; one which not only looked to the critics of Keynesianism (notably Hayek, as well as Friedman – see Hayek 1948, 1978) but found antecedents in the laissez-faire principles of classical liberal thought. Adam Smith's political economy has been ill-used as a philosophical justification for Thatcherism and Reaganism; his antipathy to the joint stock company and his sympathy for proportional taxes on wealth, amongst other things, selectively were ignored. However, Smith's directives for minimal government intervention in the conduct of trade are clear – politicians, to put it simply, cannot second-guess the superior intelligence of markets. David Ricardo, similarly, saw the meddlings of the state (along with droughts, storms, and revolutionary upheavals) as a chief cause of economic crisis. Friedman and his contemporaries followed in a lengthy and not always reputable train of liberal economists – from Thomas Malthus to Herbert Spencer – who argued for the wisdom of non-intervention as the other side of a belief in the self-regulating capacities of markets. The revival of these earlier (and sometimes only sketchily recalled) economic ideas informed a neo-liberal intellectual project that defined itself over the 1970s, providing the conceptual foundations for the accession of neo-liberal governments.

2   REFORMING THE STATE: DILEMMAS OF INTERVENTION

Neo-liberal commitments to a free market economy and a minimal state were given added impetus by the conviction that global market processes increasingly escaped the regulatory reach of nation-states. The growing propensity for "foot-loose" capital to seek offshore markets confounded governments' attempts to tie organized capital into corporatist bargains at a national level, at the same time weakening their political will to pursue uncompetitive domestic labor-market policies. From a neo-liberal standpoint, the primary economic tasks of the state were to secure the conditions for free market operations. Governments best could promote economic growth by fostering productivity in industry and efficiency in markets, notably labor markets. Such "supply-side" strategies became increasingly prevalent from the 1980s, and were geared to making markets in labor, goods, and capital more "flexible" through broad programs of deregulation. The latter included such measures as the abolition of currency controls; the deregulation of financial services and private enterprise; privatization of publicly-owned industries; the curbing of trade union powers; and abolition of wages policies and employment protection measures. While the policy mix shifted in different national contexts, neo-liberal programs tended to address a common set of economic conditions (the crisis of Fordism, industrial stagnation, globalization); developed fairly common strategies of government (based on deregulation, privatization, welfare retrenchment); and understood these changes in terms of a common and rather limited rhetoric (that of enterprise, competition, flexibility).

It is important, in this connection, to separate the rhetoric of neo-liberal government from its more substantive practices. The example of monetarism is instructive here. This little lamented economic doctrine was central to Thatcher and Reagan's prototype neo-liberalism, signalling their decisive break with Keynesian approaches to economic management – in particular the emphasis on fiscal (tax and spending) policy which assumes a pronounced economic role for government. However, if Friedman's larger message had been one of non-intervention, tight government control over money supply provided a punishing economic instrument during the 1980s. Monetarist measures were put to dramatic use in producing rapid deflation in the United States early in the decade – in this sense "Reaganomics," if it spoke the language of laissez-faire, practised a form (at times drastic) of active economic intervention. In both the US and Britain, monetarist policy early in the 1980s contributed to severe economic recessions. While the strong form of monetarism was shelved after these experiments, all the same it had succeeded in displacing Keynesian demand-management as the chief means of stabilizing a market economy. Since this period, a more conventional use of monetary policy to manage inflation (especially through controls over interest rates) has remained the favored basis for macro-economic policy.

Similarly, neo-liberal distaste for government spending did not extend, under Thatcher or Reagan, to all spheres of public investment – the most notable exemption being in defense expenditure, where the allure of lean government gave way to the perceived necessity for a "strong state" (see Gamble 1994). In a different way, neo-liberal attachments to the free market were confounded by the tendency of markets to *require* regulation. To take a key example: Britain's agreement to the Single European Act of 1985 (which provided for the creation of a single European market in 1992) was based on the premise that this would secure a free market order in Europe. As it turned out, the single "market" was instituted only via a complex of regulatory forms; "competition" mediated by a

Byzantine system of quotas, wealth transfers, employment regulations, and protection of product markets. In defiance of the deregulating thrust of neo-liberalism, the constitution of a single European market exemplifies (admittedly, in rather high relief) the manner in which markets positively *depend* on the legal and regulatory forms that shape them.

Its rather schizoid approach to questions of regulation is revealing of a basic paradox within neo-liberal politics. The dilemmas of intervention in part may be traced to the uneasy marriage of laissez-faire neo-liberalism with an authoritarian breed of social conservatism. British commentators in particular have noted the tension that existed on the Thatcherite New Right between the anti-state impulses of neo-liberalism, and paternalist forms of neo-conservatism (see Gamble 1994; Hay 1996). However, while identifiably neo-liberal economic strategies emerged in the 1980s under the auspices of right-wing governments in Britain and the US, the relationship between neo-liberalism and conservatism is not given. In an Australian context, for instance, what is generally referred to as "economic rationalism" developed, particularly during the early to mid-1990s, under Labor governments of a socially progressive nature. Similar arguments might be made regarding the neo-liberal orthodoxies of European social democratic government since the 1990s, or of neo-liberal restructuring in Latin America. Rather than deriving simply from its early coupling with conservatism, problems of intervention reside in the logic of neo-liberalism itself – as a state project that at the same time is profoundly suspicious of the overweening state. If neo-liberalism developed as an attack on "big government," it did so as a *statist* response to a very common problematic of government in capitalist societies. Welfare provision or welfare "reform," nationalization or privatization, red tape or deregulation, are all strategies concerned with the "right" relationship between state and market, public and private. They settle in different ways the question of what gets included in "the market" (health care? Air travel?), and how this entails certain demands or limits upon government. A broad strategy for the "rolling back" of the state's role in economic life might obtain across a range of policies; including the sale of public assets and enterprises, deregulation of private enterprise, "flexible" labor-market strategies, contracting out of public services to private providers, welfare reforms – the potential list is lengthy and various. The point is that specific government sell-offs (that of British Telecom, say, or the rather different and later case of France Telecom) or welfare reforms (different schemes of Workfare across the United States, or the Working Nation program in Australia) represent moments within a larger political rationality concerned to recast the relation between market and state as sites of accumulation and authority.

3   "MARKETIZING" THE STATE

While the "rolling back" of the state or the rejection of "big government" have been crucial to the rhetoric of neo-liberalism, these notions play upon a simple opposition between free market and regulatory state that belies rather more complex issues of economic regulation. For one thing, privatization and deregulation under neo-liberal governments has tended not simply to "free" incipient markets, but positively to create them in such spheres as energy, public transport, education, or health. The market forms that result, what is more, tend to be limited or managed in a number of ways – for instance via industry watchdogs, user charters, or statutory controls on consumer charges. In these contexts "market" structures are determined in large part via the actions of the state. Neo-liberal programs of deregulation are given to produce complicated kinds of *re-regulation* in the form of quangos and other semi-official bodies, public contracts, ombudsmen, detailed audit processes and the like. Such actors and instruments configure an ill-defined mode of "semi-public" governance, an awkward mediation between the increasingly notional spheres of "state" and "market."

Neither is neo-liberalism's orientation to the market confined to a (more or less) "free" realm of economic accumulation. Neo-liberal government is associated not only with the privatization of public assets and services, or the deregulation of activities in the private sector, but with moves towards a "marketized" public sector. Market-style reforms include the introduction of contract and competition between public agencies, the creation of public–private funding "partnerships," an emphasis on quantitative measures in evaluating public service outputs, and new corporate-style models of public management (see Osborne and Gaebler 1992). Such measures seek to import market logics and market structures into the design and operation of public agencies. In this conception, market forms are not antithetical to the state, but provide a model for its reorganization.

The resemblance of these "marketizing" measures to any formal definition of a competitive market is rather slight. However, it is precisely the variable nature of the organizational models that renders them so portable across different policy domains. This points to the flexible ways in which conceptions of the market function within a politics of neo-liberalism. On a primary level, neo-liberal strategies are directed toward the market as an autonomous sphere of economic exchange. On a further level, market logics shape governmental institutions and practices. And in an extended manner, a language and ethos of the market informs a general approach to the problems of government. A version of "the market," that is, does not merely mark the limits of government intervention, but becomes a model for the organization of government and a framework for policy making. As free market orthodoxies shape economic policy on inflation, unemployment, or industry, so market rationalities also are applied to more conventionally "social" domains, such as health or education. Individual citizens, it follows, may be positioned as "customers" or "consumers" in a "market" for public goods and services.

4   WELFARE, ENTERPRISE AND MARKET FREEDOMS

In these forms of "marketization," neo-liberalism as an approach to economic management opens onto a larger interest in institutions and individuals. Such a concern is especially pronounced in the welfare state reforms that are a keynote of programs of neo-liberal government. As noted earlier, expanding welfare

bureaucracies and inflated welfare bills formed part of the economic and political malaise out of which neo-liberal politics emerged in the 1970s. Against
this backdrop, the retrenchment of welfare provision was not designed simply to
reduce government spending, but rested on certain convictions regarding the
tasks of government and the duties of citizens. The litany is familiar: welfare
structures create a "culture of dependency" within which individuals come to
rely on a nanny state in ways that stifle initiative, independence, and choice (see
Mead 1986; Friedman and Friedman 1990). Neo-liberal restructuring of the
postwar system of welfare, then, goes beyond a set of technical reforms concerned with an over-extended state, to articulate a larger ideological conception
of the relation between government and citizen. On an instrumental level,
welfare cuts, "marketization," and contracting-out reduce the scale of welfare
provision. On an ethical level, they promote particular social values and varieties
of individual conduct. In a striking inversion, the structures of welfare that
originally were conceived as helping people to realize their rights as *independent*
citizens (as, for example, in the work of Marshall 1950), from a neo-liberal
perspective become tied to discourses of "dependence."

This conception of welfare is a very enduring legacy of radical neo-liberalism.
Even where the rejection of a "something-for-nothing culture" has been translated into apparently more benign discourses of "mutual obligation," the connection between welfare and an almost willful form of dependence remains a
powerful one. In this context, questions of welfare provision – and in a more
general sense, questions concerning the relation between state and citizen – have
come to be couched in a hackneyed language of "rights" and "responsibilities"
(see Mead 1986, 1997). This is especially evident in Britain, North America,
Australia, and New Zealand, where such ideas have informed family policy,
workfare programs, and the reform of welfare services for such groups as lone
parents, indigenous minorities, people with disabilities, and young people. At
the center of these policy trends is the notion that the "rights" of citizenship (in
fact, access to welfare benefits) are tied to certain obligations (most usually,
the requirement actively to look for work) – in defiance of a supposed welfare
culture of "entitlement" (see Mead 1986). This narrow discourse of
rights deflects questions of welfare away from systematic market inequalities,
toward an ethos of individual agency and duty promoted by governmental
rhetoric, but secured in an instrumental manner by increased surveillance,
means-testing, tougher eligibility criteria, and cuts in certain forms of welfare
provision.

This opens onto a further perspective on neo-liberal forms of regulation that
goes beyond a conventional model of an interventionist state. Theorists of
governmentality have examined the manner in which individual subjects come
to be implicated within neo-liberal discourses and programs – not as mute
objects of state control, but as self-conscious and self-governing individuals
(Miller and Rose 1990; Barry, Osborne, and Rose 1996). Neo-liberal techniques
of government in this sense run from the light-handed steering of a market
economy to the "self-regulating capacities" of free individuals who are enjoined
to think of themselves and others in certain economic ways (Miller and Rose
1990: 24). Regulatory effects do not simply follow from legal or political

measures, but obtain within a larger "culture" of enterprise that valorizes market freedoms and individual choice. The point is not simply that a neo-liberal notion of enterprise, for example, shapes people's behavior as economic actors, but that it extends across the boundaries of narrowly economic behavior to shape other domains of social action. Whether as consumers, as workers, or as "jobseekers," individuals might be understood as the "entrepreneurs of themselves" (Miller and Rose 1990: 25) – self-reliant, self-realizing; pursuing efficiency and productivity from the supermarket to the gym, from the sales desk or office to the classroom or unemployment center.

The conflation of market forms with individual freedoms reached its apogee in discourses surrounding the post-Communist transition in eastern Europe after 1989. The collapse of the Communist project in Europe – together with the defeat of socialist governments in Latin America, and market-style reforms in China and Cuba – was widely held to signal the failure of state planning as an alternative to free market economics, and in at least one influential view marked the almost global "triumph" of liberal capitalism as a political and economic system (see Fukuyama 1992). Compounding the inefficiencies of state planning, Soviet Communism had proved incompatible with principles of democracy and civic freedom – as evinced by the failure of reform communist movements in Hungary or Czechoslovakia, and more generally by the systematic intolerance of dissent. In the wake of 1989, the prevailing view of the liberal right was echoed in more muted ways by critics on the left who viewed the collapse of Communism against liberal capitalism's unrivalled, though uneven capacity to realize democratic freedoms together with relative material well-being (see the essays collected in Blackburn 1991).

This identification of political with economic freedoms was a powerful element of post-Communist transition. Indeed, it is arguable that conceptions of "the market" functioned as a proxy for forms of civic freedom, providing legitimacy for neo-liberal economic measures prosecuted in large part via international financial institutions and promoted by foreign governments. Notions of a "free market" commonly were defined in opposition to state control – that is, without positive characteristics in itself – and in practice represented "markets" controlled by political capitalists and their private sector cronies (see Crawford 1995). The economics of transition in several former Communist states – and particularly in Russia – rested on a mix of fierce speculation and asset-stripping by foreign and local investors, and a powerful capitalist ideology that represented the challenges facing transitional economies as a crude choice between untrammeled markets and reversion to Communism. The problems of balancing capital accumulation with state legitimation, however, proved particularly acute in contexts (like Russia or Poland) where neo-liberal restructuring occurred in the absence of existing liberal traditions or institutions. A number of theorists have identified the informal associations of civil society as a key factor in the economics of transition – the absence or suppression of such networks inhibiting development of the kinds of "social capital" that underpin and secure exchange relations (see Bagnasco, chapter 21 in this volume). The argument here is that robust social relations and institutions are not only necessary in terms of state legitimation, but are crucial for market efficiency.

5 CONCLUSION: THE "NEW POLITICS" OF NEO-LIBERALISM

An account of neo-liberalism represents an exercise in the recent history of present arrangements. One interesting sideline to debates regarding neo-liberal government in Britain in the 1980s was the question of "Thatcherism after Thatcher" – of whether Thatcherism would continue to exist as a coherent political program when Thatcher herself had exited the political scene (see Jessop et al. 1990). There were two ways of thinking about this question. On one level, the radical neo-liberal agenda pursued by the British government during the 1980s had changed institutional structures and degraded industrial structures to what appeared (and proved) an irreversible extent. On another level, sat the question of Thatcherism's ideological success. Here debate was waged over how far Thatcherite neo-liberalism had been wedded to a hegemonic project securing the "hearts and minds" of the British public; and consequently, how the left opposition might offer an effective counter-politics (see Hall 1988b; 1988c; Jessop et al. 1990). As it turned out, if the Thatcherite project did not exactly win the hearts and minds of the British electorate, it certainly turned the heads of key strategists within the British Labor Party.

If a neo-liberal right shaped liberal democracy in the latter decades of the twentieth century, its closing years saw a regrouping on the center-left, notably within the European Union and in the United States. Over the same period, severe political and economic instability in Russia, the dissipation of the Big Bang in other ex-Communist states, fears over South American economic security, and what was viewed from without as a unitary "crisis in Asia," marked in different ways the miscarriage of that raw version of neo-liberalism that so recently had stood for the "triumph" of liberal capitalist democracy. These shifts did not indicate, however, a retreat from neo-liberalism to the older certainties of statism. Rather, they saw the emergence in Europe and the United States of a declaratively "new politics" beyond both forms of social democracy oriented to the state, and a neo-liberal politics of the market (see Giddens 1998).

If the politics of a Third Way, "radical center" or a *neue Mitte* explicitly were positioned against neo-liberalism, they nonetheless took up key elements of the neo-liberal project. The emphasis within this new politics on an "enabling" state, on the "harnessing" of markets, on forms of "partnership" in social and economic government and mixed economies in health, education, or welfare reproduces the technical logic of neo-liberalism as surely as its banal language (see Blair 1998). It is arguable in this context that what have been styled as political innovations in fact represent the settled terms of a neo-liberal consensus. If neo-liberalism emerged as a radical response to forms of accumulation and legitimation crisis – of Atlantic Fordism, of Soviet-style Communism, in the economics of transition – more recently it has come to enjoy its period of consolidation and orthodoxy.

Further Reading

Harvey (1989), chapters 9–10, provides an excellent analysis of the processes of economic restructuring that underpinned neo-liberal political strategies in the 1970s and 1980s. Hay (1996), chapters 7–8, gives a clear and thorough account of the British case. Galbraith (1992) offers an economic and normative critique of neo-liberalism in the United States. Przeworski (1991) examines economic and political restructuring in Latin America and Eastern Europe.

24

The Politics of Collective Identity and Action

Beyond New Social Movements: Social Conflicts and Institutions

Pierre Hamel and Louis Maheu

Recent forms of social movements should be distinguished from the new social movements of the 1960s and 1970s. New social movements responded to new political opportunity structures created by the growth of consumption, changes in political regulation, and new forms of antagonisms produced by economic reorganization. In contrast to the labor movement, they developed in confrontation with institutional opponents (especially the state), were concerned with "life politics," and took the form of networks. Recent forms of collective action give more importance to identity, are more globally oriented and involve resistance to new forms of domination and exclusion produced by social restructuring. They also have a different relationship to institutions. Balancing non-negotiable principles with attempts to achieve concrete results, they embody the ambivalence of collective action in late modernity. Processes of domination increasingly require actors' consent so that they also offer the possibility of the construction of political public space. Social movements continually challenge the institutions of late modernity that they are also helping to define.

With the advent of late modernity, and even more so with the recent changes linked to market globalization and the growing role of information and new technologies in management of the social sphere, reflexivity has become a strategic component of action. This has led to greater uncertainty regarding the path collective action will take, prompting a number of questions that neither the actors nor researchers can side step. What can we learn from these new, recent forms of collective action or these "new" contemporary social movements, which are different from the new social movements of the 1960s and 1970s – even though they are pursuing the social and cultural criticism undertaken by the latter – in distancing themselves still further from the labor movement? What essentially characterizes them? Are they more able than the new social movements to integrate objectives of democratization in keeping with the pluralism typical of late modernity?

From the outset, it is important to underscore the double contextual change in regard to collective action that has occurred in recent years. First, we can say that the discourse and representations emphasized by the new social movements of the 1960s and 1970s no longer entirely coincide with the new demands of social integration. Whether in terms of cultural values or the democratization of public management, the ideology of these movements sometimes seems out of place for the challenges of the 1990s, which stem primarily from increasing globalization and growing social exclusion.

The other important aspect with regard to contextual change is the institutionalization of collective action. Never before in history have the resources available to social actors enabled them to reach such a level of organization (Friedman and McAdam 1992), indeed institutionalization of collective action (della Porta and Diani 1999). This is why some researchers do not hesitate to speak of "movement industries" (Zald 1992) and a "movement society" (Tarrow 1994). These categories and the analyses to which they refer apply here equally well to the environmental movement, the women's movement, and other social movements such as urban movements. At the same time, the relations that movements and their actors maintain with institutions are different. This is inducing us to re-examine the traditional view of institutions as a field of action and intervention and, in fact, the accepted definition of institutions. Finally, it should be noted that along with the density of collective actors involved in action – collective action as an intervention model has spread to all activity sectors, resulting in a veritable democratization of its tactics and strategies – we have also seen the institutionalization of the area of social movements as a research field. Over the past fifteen years, the sociology of social movements has gained a growing influence within sociology and all the social sciences. In this regard, the concerns shared by actors and researchers are producing cumulative effects in terms of the social, cultural, cognitive, and political recognition of this area of study, which is primarily an area of social and political interest.

These contextual changes are spawning fundamental questions on at least three different levels. On a first level, we see tensions emerging between, on the one hand, the material forms of collective action and, on the other hand, the conceptual categories that enable us to understand them. The primary reason for these tensions is that social movements are first and foremost theoretical constructs (Melucci 1989). Their impact lies in the societal significance that it is possible to attribute to them, which depends on our ability to identify the parameters essential to the construction of this specific type of collective action within a given social or historical context. At the same time, however, social movements can only exist through the concrete social actors that drive them. Beyond interpretative schemas and analytical categories, the materiality of collective action is grounded in conflicts, in relations of domination experienced in everyday life by social actors who mobilize and choose to engage in concrete struggles (Maheu 1995).

On a second level is the problem of relations between, on the one hand, action or forms of action and, on the other hand, the systems of constraints – and/or opportunities – with which actors interact. Given the important role that actors play in contemporary social movements, these movements must be understood from the starting point of action (Melucci 1989). However, in starting from the viewpoint of actors, their involvement, their beliefs, the networks or coalitions that they form – which are proving to be key dimensions of action – we risk overestimating the impact of mobilizations. Hence the importance of also taking into account the systems of constraints and the context within which mobilizations occur (Pickvance 1985). Moreover, due to the very nature of contemporary social movements, especially their characteristic ambivalence, and their both opportunistic and conflictual relations with institutions, we must consider their structural conditions of existence (Maheu 1995). The actors remain deeply dependent on social relations which they help to construct and define.

Finally, on a third level is the confrontation between, on the one hand, a sectorial sociology that targets the specific problems of collective action and, on the other hand, an approach that regards societal issues from the perspective of social movements. The contribution of the first viewpoint is to provide concrete knowledge on movements, their cycles, their strategies, their organizational forms. But it risks overvaluing the importance of movements in relation to social change. The second viewpoint is less concerned with concretely analyzing the processes inherent in collective action and more with understanding the phenomena of social de-structuring and restructuring. And here we have the opposite risk. The danger is a loss of knowledge on the specific nature of social movements.

Our hypothesis is that it is essential to maintain these tensions in order to grasp, beyond their complexity, the social, cultural, and political impact and significance of the recent forms of collective action. These tensions to a large extent reflect the ambivalence of contemporary social movements. At the same time, they represent a challenge for the sociology of social movements which must find a balance between, on the one hand, actors, action and a sectorial sociology and, on the other hand, concepts, social systems, and a more global sociology.

The following text is divided into three parts. First, we introduce the new forms of collective action in reference to their context. Secondly, we discuss their specific nature. Finally, we place the consequences of the recent changes in perspective, which leads us to question the political interpretations of collective action.

NEW SOCIAL MOVEMENTS

Just as the labor movement of the nineteenth century and early twentieth century highlighted the evils and impasses of industrial capitalism, in challenging the specific forms of domination inherent in class relations, so the new social movements of the 1960s and 1970s took note of the changes that had occurred on the level of consumption and in political regulation. Thus, the emergence of new forms of mobilization in the 1960s, in both Europe and North America, around issues related to lifestyles or living conditions and social integrity and milieus of belonging – whether defined in ethnic, sexual, cultural, or geographic terms – corresponded to new political opportunity structures while simultaneously reflecting the new antagonisms sparked by the growth of the productive forces of the second industrial revolution (Eder 1993).

Although the new social movements of the 1960s and 1970s were similar to the labor movement in placing at the heart of social concerns a moral protestation (Touraine 1997) defined in terms of either justice or democracy, they were nonetheless different in many ways. First, unlike the labor movement, which was a class-based movement, the new social movements called upon a collective identity which varied according to the diverse interests and experiences of the actors. These actors also helped to create a collective unit that could only develop through confrontation with institutional opponents, especially the state, and with a system of domination reinforced by liberal cultural values.

Next, the action of the new social movements coincided with a life politics which fostered a self-actualization embedded in the experience of authenticity and the exercise of freedom in a world where reflexivity is playing a growing role (Giddens 1990). This is in contrast to "emancipatory politics" which was the distinctive feature of the labor movement and which primarily sought to shatter the contradictions of capitalism.

Finally, on the organizational level and at the level of action, the new social movements did not hesitate to re-examine or move away from rigid hierarchical organizational models inherited from the more traditional forms of collective action (Tarrow 1994). This is why they more readily assumed networked forms which are fragmented and submerged in everyday life, playing the role of veritable cultural laboratories (Melucci 1989: 60).

According to some observers (Cohen and Arato 1992), the new social movements essentially sought to politicize civil society in trying to escape from representative political institutions and their bureaucratic control, which had grown as the State's economic and social role expanded. Thus, in resorting to unconventional political action (Kuechler and Dalton 1990), the actors in these movements politicized new issues – related to the body, sexual differences, cultural choices, ethnic particularities, and so on – which helped to broaden the traditional definition of politics. In emphasizing non-negotiable principles of action, because they were confronted with irreducible conflicts, involving subjectivity especially, they were nonetheless part of a modern critique of modernization. Hence the need for them to participate, with other social actors, in forging sociopolitical compromises. In contrast to those who claim that social movements are incapable of negotiating because they have nothing to offer in exchange for the concessions that might be made to them (Offe 1997: 105), it seems to us that in reiterating their beliefs regarding irreducible conflicts, these actors are renewing their capacity for intervention and are succeeding in introducing changes, as recent research has shown (Masson 1998; Séguin 1998).

New Forms of Collective Action

Even though the newness of the new social movements has never been unanimously acknowledged, most researchers have recognized that these movements differed from the labor movement in a number of ways, whether in their organization, their means of action, or their representation of social change. Whereas the labor movement was a pivotal movement in the industrial age, able to bring together a homogeneous political representation and unified action strategies, the new social movements were more diverse, more heterogeneous, more able to adapt to various contexts, and primarily focused on direct democracy and a conception of politics defined in terms of alternatives or self-management.

The more recent forms of collective action – those that have emerged since at least the early 1990s in most developed countries, and many developing nations – would come to amplify these characteristics and differences in relation to the labor movement. However, in some respects, in their discourse, representations, or action models, these new forms of collective action are unlike the new social movements. This does not mean that they do not continue to resort to the repertoire of collective action developed by the new social movements and even, we might add, to a certain extent by the labor movement. Most of the time, however, when these new forms of collective action return to these repertoires, they introduce different contents, values, and demands for action.

Recent forms of collective action are more complex, more diverse, more fragmented than new social movements. Unlike the labor movement, they are not trying to create a new vision of society, just as, unlike many of the new social movements, they are not attempting to bring together forms of organization and action based on self-actualization. They more strongly integrate the ambivalence that is inherent in collective action in the context of late modernity. The importance given to identity and of taking identity into account in action has proven to be more acutely influenced by the context within which social relations are mediated, however they are defined: resistance in the face of new forms of domination or exclusion, including social struggles against new forms of poverty; involvement in various processes of social restructuring and social recognition, which first of all means taking ethnic and cultural differences into account; participation in defining a cosmopolitan citizenship. A good example of this concern is the World March of Women in the Year 2000 that reflected a new planetary consciousness. The project was initiated by the "Fédération des Femmes du Québec," a non-partisan pressure group encouraging political education and the improvement of living conditions for women. In 1995 in Québec, this coalition organized the Women's March Against Poverty, which was very successful. Three contingents of 850 women marched during ten days to obtain specific social demands related to economic justice. The presence of women coming from countries of the South during that event brought in the idea of enlarging solidarity to other women on a global basis.

The World March of Women in the Year 2000 involved three different levels of action. The first level is action expressing solidarity by signing support cards. The second level involved the mobilization of women's movements in each country in which demonstrations are taking place connected to their local reality, even though everywhere the issue of poverty against women should be raised. The third level took the form of world rallies or demonstrations. All these actions started on March 8 of the year 2000 and ended in October of the same year with the world events. This overall mobilization pursues several goals:

promoting equality between men and women, improving women's quality of life, demonstrating women's ongoing determination to change the world, contributing in a concrete way to the elaboration of a cosmopolitan citizenship.

The recent forms of collective action are thus attempting not so much to develop solidarity as to express resistance or explore various forms of social recognition, which better satisfy the individual or subjective expectations of the actors (Ion 1994). They seek not so much to assert a principle as to achieve concrete results. Fighting for a long-term cause is subordinated to achieving short-term or medium-term results. In this spirit, actors do not hesitate to counterbalance non-negotiable principles in the context of agreements negotiated with opponents who readily become partners (Hamel 1993). In this regard, the example of recent urban movements is worth mentioning. In many European as well as North American cities, since the beginning of the 1990s, these movements have experienced new types of confrontation with the political elite and the state as cities are undergoing structural adjustments to the new world economic order while facing the erosion of welfare policies. On the one hand, grassroots organizations do not hesitate to use resources coming from governmental workfare programs in order to help recent immigrants, unemployed youth, women, or simply members of poor community neighborhoods integrate into the labor market while, on the other hand, they challenge this type of institutional solution by indicating its limitation in terms of resolving issues of social inequalities and by provoking, in many cases, its redefinition to improve sociopolitical solutions to the needs of local communities. In order to better understand recent changes in the forms of collective action, it is helpful to consider both the contextual and structural aspects in relation to which they are defined and the specific dimensions of their field of action.

Foremost among the structural changes to which recent forms of collective action have had to adapt are the sociotechnological and sociopolitical changes triggered by the processes of globalization. As a central feature of late modernity, the processes of globalization, which can be associated with the rise of the information society and the growth of new information technologies (Castells 1996), are sparking a profound reassessment of the regulatory mechanisms previously developed and controlled by the State (Giddens 1990) (see Le Galès, chapter 37, in this volume). This is prompting, in particular, the emergence of a "new political culture," in the words of Ulrich Beck (1992), which is forcing the political elite to discard the illusion of a central authority able to run society. Spiralling changes on an economic and informational level are resulting in an unravelling of the old political–institutional arrangements or compromises. State regulatory bodies are losing their effectiveness and their legitimacy, both from above, in favor of supranational authorities, and from below, in favor of local government organizations. This is why they must rethink the traditional views of control and the restrictive regulatory approaches that went along with them. Hence the increasing need to come to terms with all social forces.

In the context of a late modernity open to the pluralism of interests and identities, the general interest can no longer be unilaterally decreed by the political center. If, on an external level, the political sphere is still organized in a hierarchical way, on an internal level, it is increasingly being subjected to various processes of democratization that are changing relations of power and altering the rules of the game. In other words, the processes of political decision-making less and less often stem from a pre-established representation or a pre-existing model that would need to be implemented to counter social resistance, but rather from a process of collective action that is also a learning process, in the course of which compromises are forged.

The existence of this new political culture, which is setting up tension between a model of centralized governance and participatory management, is an issue that concerns not only policymakers but also leaders and militants in social movements. The latter in fact find themselves involved on a daily basis – whether in running community services, denouncing new forms of poverty or environmental degradation, or promoting a new conception of citizenship – in a series of transactions, exchanges, or experiments that are helping to create an open political public space. They are thus participating in approaches or practices that are redefining the status of their action.

As globalization generates profound changes in regulatory models and the political sphere, it is also affecting work as a central value in our societies, resulting in a growing social exclusion that is in turn unleashing a spiral of destabilization and uncertainty. In this context, the strategic role of information is fostering increasing reflexivity. But actors do not all have the necessary resources for their social recognition and integration. And this can be better understood by considering the main dimensions of the field of action.

Given that social actors' recognition in and through the social sphere coincides with increased individualization (Taylor 1994) – the authenticity of which can indeed only be assumed through greater subjectivity and greater individual and social responsibility – but for which access to the necessary resources has become more and more restricted or unpredictable, how can these actors mobilize? If the new social movements made it possible for individual and collective identities to converge while at the same time encouraging the recognition of personal competencies, what can we say in this regard about the new forms of collective action? Are they capable of responding to the increasing uncertainties of late modernity? To what extent can they overcome the growing non-correspondence between institutional systems and systems of action, given that institutions are less and less able to provide a stable framework for learning, normalization, and integration?

First, it is the very great diversity of social mobilizations and collective action approaches, and indeed their democratization, that is surprising. Over the past ten years, as never before, social actors have mobilized. These mobilizations are often local and limited. They sometimes bring together actors belonging to ethnic or cultural communities. In a few cases, they involve mass demonstrations against unpopular social policies. In many cases, they represent corporatist struggles or movements to protect special interests, for example, in the case of environmental issues when they seek to stop projects that threaten the quality of life of local communities. In the case of struggles involving the "excluded," whether represented by the unemployed, the homeless, or political refugees seeking asylum, actors find it difficult to form united movements due to their position and their relative lack of resources (Hérault and Lapeyronnie 1998).

The ethical and political impact of these struggles is nonetheless significant. Such struggles, however, require us to refer to the content and very definition of a social movement.

Like the labor movement and the new social movements, recent forms of collective action herald a space of social stratification of a different nature than that which characterized the configuration of social relations during the second industrial revolution or the age of expansion of the welfare state (Maheu 1995). In recent years, social actors have been confronted with processes and forms of domination that are more insidious than in the past. Like never before, these involve mechanisms of individualization (Beck 1994) and require the actors' consent. They are more of the nature of "governmentality" to use the expression of Foucault (1986), than of social control (see Hindess, chapter 4, in this volume).

This being said, approaches that call upon collective action, even when they have broken away from traditional means of political action, are not all in the nature of a social movement. We consider that social movements bring together groups of actors who challenge or contest entrenched social practices, the usual forms of decision-making, authorities, and established policies, which are simultaneously an expression of and a means of maintaining relations of inequality, domination, or exclusion. Social movements put forward demands concerning several aspects of our ways of living in society. Through organizational forms and specific action strategies, they engage in behaviors that illustrate social conflicts and contest areas of change and social stratification characteristic of our societies. This conception of social movement can help us to assess various forms of collective action and evaluate their contribution to processes of social restructuring, in taking into account their inherent tensions and ambivalences.

SOCIAL MOVEMENTS AND MODERNITY: A NEW OUTLOOK

What aspects should we emphasize to increase our understanding of collective action and social movements? The trend toward institutionalization characterizing recent forms of collective action (Scott 1990) has also meant an intensification of the ambivalent relationship that actors in movements maintain with institutions.

The question of the specific political nature of forms of collective action undoubtedly remains one of the most controversial. Within the sociology of social movements one finds viewpoints that differ not only regarding the ability of actors in movements to bring their demands onto the political stage but also regarding their rejection of established politics.

Although the legitimacy of social movements and their ability to intervene on the public and political stage alongside parties and pressure groups is universally recognized, there is no consensus as to their status. Whereas for some observers the unconventional political action of movements helps in the long term, and in an unexpected way, to stabilize the political order (Kuechler and Dalton 1990), others feel that their action retains a disruptive quality.

Another problem is the relative inability of social movements to change relations of power. This has led some researchers to underscore their fragmentation or organizational weakness and their localism (Fainstein and Hirst 1995). Others note that social movements are increasingly channeled by political-administrative mechanisms that affect the content and forms of action.

However, although these contextual elements may induce movements to emphasize self-limiting representations of politics, they do not explain the significance of radical cultural demands in relation to ethical issues involving the autonomy and social recognition of actors. This requires us to more closely examine the ambiguities and ambivalences of collective action.

In this respect, we must again stress the heterogeneity of movements. Some movements choose to make more radical demands than others. But when collective action helps to define social structures and social relations, it also involves conflictual normative choices. In other words, actors in social movements constantly challenge the institutions that they are also helping to redefine (Maheu 1996).

In these approaches, the position of the actors fluctuates between a resistance identity that seeks to combat exclusion and a proactive approach emphasizing an identity centered in specific projects (Castells 1997). In the first case, the approach is primarily defensive, whereas the second more strongly calls upon the creativity of individuals as subjects. While they use the resources available to them, new forms of collective action also distance themselves from institutional choices developed by elites, in continually reiterating the moral bases of their action.

Consequently, it is no longer only the political impact of social movements that is at issue but also the limits of politics as a system of action and of representation and regulation. In developing within a "new political culture" new forms of collective action are entering into increasingly complex systems of interaction that combine solidarity and individualization in the face of growing tensions between the globalized economy and the cultural refuge of community (Touraine 1997). At the same time, movements are questioning the effectiveness of traditional forms of state regulation.

However, in several ways, institutional forms of politics are still present in representations of action. In large part, they continue to structure communities and political networks. From this perspective, if analyses of collective action from the standpoint of contentious politics (McAdam, Tarrow, and Tilly 1996) still help us to understand the most visible aspects of the relations between social movements and political institutions, they do not enable us to comprehend what underlies them. In particular, they fail to examine the many processes, both contradictory and complementary – more broadly social than specifically political – that actors develop in their relations with institutions. This is brought to light by analyzing relations with institutions from the standpoint of the ambivalence of collective action and its main components (Hamel, Lustiger-Thaler, and Maheu 1999).

In intervening in contested areas of change, the new forms of collective action exhibit first and foremost a social stratification characteristic of our societies. They highlight the central issues in relation to which social compromises are being redefined, contributing to the definition of public-political social spaces.

In the context of late modernity, social divisions are being reinforced by the fragmentation of identities and cultures. The resulting conflicts are triggering confrontations that cannot always be linked to social movements. This is the case in corporatist struggles or defensive struggles revolving around identity or environmental issues, as in the example of the "NIMBY" movements.

Beyond their heterogeneity, fragmentation or scattered nature, and to the extent that they can be associated with new forms of collective action that are similar to social movements, these confrontations are at the heart of today's ongoing social and political restructuring. The practices that are emerging in this respect are helping to transform representations of the public-political social space as a place of transaction and mediation, while defining this space from the perspective of an issue upon which sociopolitical compromises can be based.

In recent years, collective action has engaged in various approaches of resistance and expression, all of which involve, to a greater or lesser degree, new relations with institutions and institutionalization. In this regard, we must go beyond a conception that primarily understands social movements from the perspective of a specific type of institution of civil society based solely on a public-interest orientation.

In conclusion, one can say that the future of collective action is more and more deeply rooted in new conflictual relations with institutions. From this point of view, the institutionalization of collective action is in no way a homogeneous, alternative, or transitory process. It instead corresponds to the construction of a space of confrontation, communication, and experimentation.

For actors involved in mobilizations against various forms of social exclusion, collective action is defined in relation to three major institutional dimensions, namely, the possibility: (1) of making choices; (2) of negotiating their milieus of belonging and expressing individual preferences; and (3) of satisfying their need to be recognized for what they are. On each of these levels, social exclusion involves both the context – structural dimensions – and the field of action, especially the subjectivity of the actors. For collective action, this results in tensions that can only be overcome through choices that enable actors both to express a fundamental identity and to forge compromises.

Further Reading

Bash, H. H. 1995: *Social Problems and Social Movements. An Exploration into the Sociological Construction of Alternative Realities*. New Jersey: Humanities Press.
Bauman, Z. 1998: *Globalization. The Human Consequences*. Cambridge: Polity Press.
Castells, M. 1983: *The City and the Grassroots*. Berkeley and Los Angeles: University of California Press.
Graham, K. and S. Phillips (eds.) 1998: *Citizen Engagement. Lessons In Participation In Local Government*. Toronto: Institute of Public Administration of Canada.
Melucci, A. 1996: *The Playing Self. Person and Meaning in the Planetary Society*. Cambridge: Cambridge University Press.

25

The Politics of Ethnicity and Identity

Aletta J. Norval

The theorization of ethnicity is bound up with political concerns and normative judgments so that it requires a genealogical approach. Traditional views range from primordialism to instrumentalism. Primordialists see contemporary forms of ethnic expression as a reactivation of older, sometimes biological, relations. Instrumentalists see ethnicity as a resource for different interest groups. Primordialism is essentialist: it ignores the complexity of the historical conditions under which ethnicity becomes significant and over-states the internal homogeneity of ethnic identities. Instrumentalism is nominalist: it suggests that ethnic identification is important only insofar as it is based on more material phenomena. The third main position on ethnicity is constructivism, emphasizing the historical and political processes by which it is formed and situating it in relation to other identities: racial, sexual, national, or gendered. There is a range of constructivist positions: Norval argues for a materialist poststructuralist theory against linguistic monism. She suggests that "the body" is important, but that markers of race and ethnicity are historical, social, and political rather than natural. Finally she discusses hybridity and postcolonial theories of identity concerned with diaspora, displacement, and the politics of cultural difference. Pluralism must be radicalized in order to democratize potentially exclusionary identities.

ETHNICITIES OLD AND NEW

We are suggesting that a new word reflects a new reality... The new word is "ethnicity," and the new usage is the steady expansion of the term "ethnic group" from minority and marginal subgroups ... to major elements of a society.
(Glazer and Moynihan 1975: 1)
The new politics of representation ... also sets in motion an ideological contestation around the term, "ethnicity". But in order to pursue that movement further, we will have to retheorize the concept of *difference*.
(Hall 1992a: 256)

It is interesting to return at the end of the 1990s to the literatures that first alerted us to the presence of ethnicity as a novel form of identification. Such a return should be approached, not in order to rediscover its purported origins, but to remind ourselves that the theorization of ethnicity, multiculturalism, and the emphasis on a politics of identity/difference so acutely present in our contemporary world, all have long and difficult trajectories. A few remarks on these trajectories are necessary so as to situate current theorization in a proper context. In particular, it is important to note that the history of the theorization of ethnicity is not a progressive and cumulative one. Rather, it is intimately bound up with political concerns and normative judgments. Consequently, any attempt to reconstruct its trajectory should take a genealogical form. That is, it has of necessity to start from where we are, from our current concerns and our present commitments, making visible the conditions under which particular theoretical accounts of ethnicity emerged and became disseminated. It is not possible to achieve anything approaching a full account of the complex genealogy of the uses and abuses of the term "ethnicity." To do so would require an investigation of the structural, historical, and academic contexts of emergence and surfaces on which it has been inscribed, as well as a full critical assessment of the achievements and failures of the politics and theories of ethnicity. In its stead it may be useful simply to remind ourselves of some of the main outlines and features of this trajectory. In this chapter I will trace out the movement from primordialist and instrumentalist approaches to ethnicity, to a more general engagement with questions of difference. I will give particular attention to the contribution of accounts of difference, drawing on poststructuralist and postcolonialist theorizations, that treat ethnicity as one amongst many possible forms of identification. In so doing, I aim to supplement these approaches with a consideration of the politics of difference, and its implications for the treatment of ethnicity.

Traditional debates on ethnic identity can be situated on a continuum of views ranging from primordialism to instrumentalism. That is, from views that ethnic identity stems from the givens of social existence – blood, speech, custom – which have an ineffable coerciveness in and of themselves (Geertz 1973: 259), to a view that ethnic identity is nothing but a mask deployed strategically to advance group interests that are often economic in character. The *primordialist* thesis, first discussed by Shils (1957) and elaborated upon by Geertz in the early 1960s, was and remains quite influential in discussions of ethnicity. One of the most prolific commentators on nationalism and ethnicity during the 1980s and 1990s, Anthony D. Smith (Hutchinson and Smith 1996: 6), treats contemporary forms of ethnic identification as nothing but a resurgence of more primordial identifications associated with "ethnies." Despite the emphasis in his work on the symbolic dimensions of identity, such as myths of common origin and shared historical memories, Smith retains the emphasis on the enduring, and even premodern, character of ethnicity. That is, modern forms of ethnic expression are ultimately a reactivation of older, more primordial forms. Diverging from this more culturalist turn, the 1980s also witnessed a recasting of primordialism in a sociobiological form. Van den Berghe (1986), for instance, argues that ethnicity has to be understood on the basis of kinship relations. Ethnicity for him is a manifestation of nepotism between kin that has a genetic basis. Consequently, ethnogenesis and transmission depends on "successful reproduction": ethnicity "always involves the cultural *and* genetic boundaries of a *breeding population*" (1986: 256). Primordialist approaches have been criticized, in particular, for failing to account for change, for working with overly static conceptions of ethnicity, and for naturalizing ethnic groups (Jenkins 1997: 44). More specifically, while sociobiological approaches are questioned for their biological reductionism, ethnosymbolic primordialists have been taken to task for an overemphasis on symbolic phenomena at the expense of material factors in the constitution of ethnicity. By contrast, an emphasis on the role of material interests stands at the heart of instrumentalist approaches.

Instrumentalist approaches treat ethnicity as a resource for different interest groups. Analytical emphasis, in this case, falls on analyzing and uncovering the processes through which elites mobilize groups so as to further their own self-interest. Instrumentalism, drawing its initial inspiration from the work of Barth (1969), treats ethnicity as essentially malleable and thus open to elite manipulation. Like primordialism, instrumentalism is not a homogeneous category. It encompasses both neo-Marxist and rational choice approaches. In the case of the former, ethnicity is viewed as an instrument to allow mobilization around interests that are, ultimately, grounded in social class (Wolpe 1988). Hence, ethnicity is reduced to and explicated in class terms. Something similar occurs in rational choice approaches where ethnicity is analyzed from the perspective of rational actors who choose to join groups to secure specific individual ends (cf. Hechter 1986). Both of these types of analysis signally fail to treat ethnic identification as worthy of analysis in and of itself. As a consequence, identity and identification are reduced to a level of analysis which is deemed to be somehow more fundamental and politically more significant than ethnic identity itself.

This somewhat stale debate between primordialists and instrumentalists may be recast in order to throw more light on what is at stake in the discussion, and to bring us closer to contemporary theoretical debates on identity in general, and ethnic identities in particular. In order to do so, it is useful to concentrate on the question of the "reality" of ethnicity. From this vantage point, it is possible to discern at least three diverging positions on ethnicity. In the first case, ethnicity is treated as natural, as a given and as a nodal point around which identity is organized. This nodal point has an ahistorical value: it is the core of identity, regardless of historical context; it acts as an indicator of a homogeneous group identity; it is politically, socially, and culturally salient regardless of the specific context under analysis. This *essentialism* is particularly evident in primordialist approaches to ethnicity. The main problems with treating ethnicity in an essentialist fashion consist in denying the complexity of both the specific historical circumstances under which ethnicity comes to be a significant phenomenon, and the lack of internal homogeneity of ethnic identities. In the second, ethnicity is not accorded any reality of its own. Ethnicity is merely a marker for deeper, more significant social divisions. Since it is something purely epiphenomenal, this marker is manipulable. Elites are held to be in a position to mold popular feelings through the use of ethnic symbols to achieve ends unrelated to those symbols. This *nominalism* about ethnicity is characteristic particularly of instrumentalist approaches. It suffers from a reductionism that naively suggests that the force of ethnic forms of identification arise entirely from external inducement. The obverse side of this assumption suggests that were we to understand this process properly there would be nothing of significance left to engage with: ethnicity will simply dissolve.

Since the mid-1980s there has been, primarily as a result of an increasing engagement with poststructuralist theories, a significant shift away from both axes of this debate. Both the primordialist/essentialist and the instrumentalist/ nominalist positions have come under fire from a third position, namely, *constructivism*. Whilst there are many different forms of constructivism or contextualism, commonly held tenets include *inter alia*, arguments for a context sensitive theory which is attentive to the complexities of processes of identity formation, and to the hybridity of identities, while not ignoring the political significance of ethnic forms of identification. In other words, there is, first, a shift away from the assumption of the ahistorical and given nature of ethnic identity, toward an emphasis on the analysis of the historical and political processes and practices through which it comes into being. Second, there is a break with the assumption that ethnicity is in and of itself, always, the core organizing feature of identity. This pluralization has shifted attention toward other forms of identification, be they racial, sexual, national or gendered, in short, to a preoccupation with question of *difference*. Simultaneously, it has facilitated a more politically sensitive and nuanced approach to the question of ethnicity. Whilst not assuming that it always would be politically significant, there has been a break with the instrumentalism of the nominalist position. That is, the emphasis on the constructed character of ethnic identities has also led to an acknowledgment that whether or not such identities will be politically salient is an entirely contextual matter.

FROM IDENTITY TO IDENTIFICATION

> *Every social community reproduced by the functioning of institutions is imaginary*... it is based on the projection of individual existence into the weft of a collective narrative, on the recognition of a common name... But this comes down to accepting that... *only* imaginary communities are real.
>
> *(Balibar 1991: 93)*

Despite these advances, much of the current theorization of the phenomenon of ethnicity have remained trapped in the strictures of a distinction, widely deployed in the social and human sciences, between the objective and the subjective. Separating the subjective and the objective on the grounds of the assumption that the former is "purely personal" and the latter is a "given," simply reintroduces the problematic features of the primordialism/instrumentalism divide through the back door. What is needed is a rethinking of the relation between the subjective and the objective, so as to facilitate an engagement with the social and political processes shaping ethnic forms of identification.

Recasting this distinction has been made possible by a theorization of the imaginary constitution of society (cf. Anderson 1991; Castoriadis 1987; see Finlayson, chapter 26, in this volume), a view that contains the possibility of a break with the topographical conception of the social underlying the traditional subjective/objective distinction. On this reading, far from simply "given," objectivity is nothing but that which is socially constituted, and which has become *sedimented* over time. The feature of "objectivity," thus, may be attributed to any sedimented social practice or identity. Positing objectivity in this manner has the further consequence of opening the space for the thought of *desedimentation*: any sedimented practice may be put into question by political contestation, and once its historically constituted character is revealed, it loses its naturalized status as "objectively given."

The consequences of this shift for the analysis of the phenomenon of ethnicity are far-reaching. Once the givenness and objectivity of identity is put into question, and a purely subjectivist account of ethnic identity is problematized, the way is open to develop a theoretical account of ethnic *identification*. As Ahmed (1997: 157) argues, when we can no longer assume that the subject simply "has" an identity in the form of a properly demarcated place of belonging, what is required is an analysis of the processes and structures of identification whereby identities *come to be seen* as such places of belonging. This recognition of the importance of identification should not, however, overshadow differences of approach amongst constructivist theorists.

DIFFERENT FORMS OF CONSTRUCTIVISM: FROM LINGUISTIC MONISM TO POSTSTRUCTURALISM

Constructivist positions take many forms, ranging from linguistic monism where linguistic construction is taken to be generative and deterministic through instrumentalist accounts such as those discussed earlier, to fully-fledged poststructuralist approaches. The difficulties arising from linguistic monism are many. First, if the act of construction is understood as a purely verbal act, it is unclear how such an act would be linked to the materiality of the real, since ethnic markers place certain limitations on what could "constructed" verbally. Second, as with instrumentalist accounts, construction is still understood as a unilateral process initiated from above, thus reinforcing a top-down view of the production of ethnic identity which leaves little, if any, space for human agency and resistance. Third, both of these positions fail to account for the force of ethnic identification by treating it either as a matter of individual choice, or as a matter of elite manipulation.

In order to outline an alternative, poststructuralist account of constructivism, it is necessary to specify clearly what main features such a position would have to contain. As argued earlier, it has to break with the view of ethnic identity as either imposed or merely subjective. It must, therefore, provide us with an account of the subject and of identification which takes cognisance of wider power relations while not treating such identification as if it were imposed on passive subjects. It must, in addition, be able to address the complexity and hybridity of identities, whilst avoiding linguistic determinism. It must, therefore, contain a plausible account of materiality and its role in the production of images for identification. The latter is especially important if one is to accommodate the force of radicalized identities without giving way to the spuriousness of a sociobiological approach.

RADICALIZED IDENTITIES: THE QUESTION OF MATERIALITY

Theorists such as Wallman (1978) and Eriksen (1993) have argued that physical appearance should be considered as only one possible marker of ethnic boundaries amongst many, and that ideas of race may or may not be an important factor in ethnic politics. These insights resonate with those developed from within poststructuralist theorization of identity/difference more generally. Once one moves toward a constructivist analytic proper, neither race nor ethnicity can be treated as natural givens. Indeed, both result from complicated processes of production and identification. Whether such identification takes a radicalized or an ethnicized form or both, is a matter largely if not solely of historico-political circumstances (Mason 1999: 21). Omi and Winant (1986), for instance, concentrate on the radicalization of identities in the United States, while Hall (1996) treats the movement towards hybrid ethnic forms of identification in the United Kingdom, and Norval (1996) investigates the complex interpenetration of radicalized and ethnicized forms of identification in apartheid South Africa.

Two areas in particular have to be addressed if a constructivist analytic is to be deepened in a poststructuralist direction which emphasizes the need to avoid a pure contextualism. The first concerns the theorization of the presumed materiality of the body, and of any other "physical" markers. The second is related to the first. It concerns the theorization of the politics of ethnicity. In terms of the former, Alcoff's work on racial embodiment and Butler's on the body are particularly significant. The need to deal with "the body" arises, *inter alia*, from objections against early constructivists that seemingly ignore the material visibility of color and of cultural practices and tend to absorb them into accounts of the linguistic meaning conferred upon such phenomena. In *Bodies that Matter*, Butler (1993: 30) argues that, in order to counter such linguistic determinism, one needs to the recognize that the theoretical options "are not exhausted by presuming materiality, on the one hand, and negating materiality, on the other." Rather, matter must be understood as always *posited or signified* as *prior*. The body signified as prior to signification, is then always already an effect of signification. In this manner, she puts into question the brute givenness of matter, and by implication of the body, and of color. In arguing that signifying acts delimit and contour matter she does not also suggest that the body, color, matter, does not matter. From this quite abstract starting point, it is necessary to move toward a more phenomenological approach to the body, an approach that would allow us to come to grips with the effects and the production of effects arising from embodiment.

It is here that Alcoff's work is significant, for it begins to develop an account that is both less abstract and politically more sensitive to the issues at stake

(Alcoff 1999a; 1999b). She suggests that a phenomenological approach may render our tacit knowledge about racial embodiment explicit (1999b). It may, for instance, uncover the ways in which we, without being explicitly conscious of it, read and interpret bodily markers as significant. These markers are not in any sense natural or given. She concentrates on the visual registry of embodiment, a registry which, she argues, is historically evolving, culturally variegated but which, nevertheless, has a powerful structuring influence on individual experience. The account offered by Alcoff has the further advantage of being genealogical and thus critical in character. The phenomenological descriptions, far from naturalizing and consolidating racism, reactivate the contingency of the visual registry and have, at least, the potential to disrupt the naturalization of racialization.

Thus, to point to the formation of racial or ethnic identities in this sense, and to the fact that attention needs to be given to the materialization of categories such as the body, color and other ethnic markers as a result of political practices is not also to assert that they are unimportant or irrelevant. Similarly, to emphasize the contingency of socially inscribed identities does not mean that they are fungible, that they may be picked and chosen as if from a supermarket shelf. To the contrary, it directs attention to the historical, social, and political processes through which images for identification are constructed and sustained, contested and negotiated. One consequence of this shift toward identification is that the focus of analysis of ethnic identities is laterally displaced. It is no longer adequate simply to ask "in whose interest are ethnic identities constituted?" Rather, we need to inquire into the processes through which ethnicity becomes a significant site of identification that may or may not entail a construction of the "interests" of a particular group, and that may or may not become a site of political contestation. This is perhaps the most significant element of the politics of ethnic identification today. Claims and demands made in the name of ethnic groups cannot be understood without giving attention to the dimension of identification. And identification, while it may be closely associated with felt discrimination and the unequal distribution of resources in society, cannot be reduced to the latter.

HYBRID ETHNICITIES: RETHINKING PLURALISM

The problem of reductionism occurs, not only where ethnicity is reduced to other modes of identification based, for instance, upon class but also where there is an over-concentration on the presumed homogeneity of ethnic identities. Such an emphasis on homogeneity, purity, and authenticity always occurs at the expense of the recognition of difference and diversity and it has its roots in the manner in which "plurality" was thought in early accounts of ethnicity. Jenkins (1997: 25) points out that the conceptual replacement of the "tribe" by "ethnicity" was accompanied by the development of the idea of a "plural society." Both of these changes were related to the changing postwar world and the loss of empire. In particular, it addressed the need to conceptualize, within the colonial administrative and institutional frameworks, the convergence of separate institutions for "Europeans" and urbanized local groups on the one hand, and "tribespeople" on the other. Thus, while the term "ethnicity" was an analytical category within urban anthropology, with which to make sense of these new social and cultural formations (Eade 1996: 58), the term "plural society" (taken over from Furnivall's analysis of colonial policy in South-East Asia in the 1940s) had to capture the institutional incorporation of different ethnic groups into a single state (Jenkins 1997: 26). The idea of a plural society was created in opposition to the European ideal of homogeneous nation-states. However, this recognition of plurality at the level of state institutions was based upon a homogenizing account of identity, both of the ethnicities of the colonized and of the nationhood of the colonizers. More recent developments in postcolonial theory have sought to overcome the problems associated with the assumptions underlying this model. In particular, new theorization's have problematized the idea that only "minorities" or "Third world" peoples have ethnicity, as well as the assumption that European nations were indeed internally homogeneous.

Contemporary postcolonial theories of identity are explicitly situated within the context of contemporary concerns with diaspora, displacement, and the politics of cultural difference. So, for instance, one finds an emphasis on displacement as the starting-point for rethinking questions of identity in the work of Hall, Spivak, and Bhabha. Hall utilizes this perspective to extricate the concept of ethnicity from its anti-racist paradigm, "where it connotes the immutable difference of minority experience." It then becomes a term which takes into account the historical positions, cultural conditions, and political conjunctures through which all identity is constructed. It becomes a concept connoting the "recognition that we all speak from a particular place, out of a particular history, out of a particular experience . . . We are all, in a sense, *ethnically* located and our ethnic identities are crucial to our subjective sense of who we are" (Hall 1988a: 5). For Hall, as for Juteau (1996: 55), what is important is to show the extent to which ethnicity is not the exclusive characteristic of the other. It marks every identity as such.

Bhabha, by contrast, continues to focus on the consequences of displacement for the *minority* subject. His development of the concept "hybridity" serves to act as a signifier of the irreducibility of cultural difference (1994b: 37). Before exploring this any further, it is worthwhile noting that as with other terms in this debate, that of hybridity has a longer history. As Papastergiadis shows, hybridity has shadowed every organic theory of identity, and was deeply inscribed in nineteenth-century discourses of scientific racism where it served as a metaphor for the negative consequences of racial encounters (1997: 257–79). However, for Bhabha, hybridity is precisely *not* to be understood as a mixture of pre-given identities or essences. Rather, it signifies the attempt to capture the non-purity of identity, the non-coincidence of the self with itself, and the unhomeliness of existence which arises as an effect of colonial power. The production of hybridization, moreover, "turns the discursive conditions of dominance into the grounds of intervention." (Bhabha 1994b: 171) It is from here that the concepts of homogeneous cultures and national communities, the very logic of identity conceived as pure, intact and self-sufficient, is being challenged and subverted. Bhabha thus moves almost seamlessly from a conception of hybrid identities –

exemplified in the experience of displacement – to a politics of resistance, based on transgressive discourses which aim to unsettle liberal multiculturalist and assimilative political strategies. Bhabha has frequently been criticized for his easy celebration of the condition of displacement, unhomeliness and hybridity, and for the naivete of the politics that follows from it (Ahmed 1997: 153–67; Papastergiadis 1997: 267; Norval 1999). Suffice it to mention here that the disruption of old certainties and traditional identities, by no means, lead inexorably to an acceptance of greater diversity.

The idea of hybrid identities does, nevertheless, have important consequences for our understanding of ethnicity. As Bhabha (1994a: 269) notes, it forms a response to the initial pluralism that marked the questioning of homogeneous identities. The shift away from "class" and "gender" as primary conceptual categories has resulted in an awareness of the multiple subject positions – generational, gendered, racial, locational – that inhabit any claim to identity. Thinking about identity in terms of hybridity moves beyond this pluralism of identities to focus attention on the "interstitial moments or processes that are produced in the articulation of 'differences'." (1994a: 269) As a result, the analytical questions that we seek to answer now are related to the formation of subjects that become possible in the overlapping and displacement of domains of *difference*. Difference here is not a reflection of pre-given ethnic traits set in sedimented traditions. Rather, it is to be conceived of as a complex process of negotiation, the outcome of struggles and antagonisms with dominant traditions that open up spaces through which dominant designations of difference may be resisted and recast. However, while Bhabha offers a theoretically sophisticated account of the inherently fissured nature of identity, he lacks the tools to address the complexities and ambiguities of the political struggles that emerge from these spaces. To be able to address these questions the study of ethnicity and identity must relinquish its isolation from political theory and engage with the wider theoretical concerns and conditions under which it may become politically salient.

CONCLUSION: RELOCATING THE POLITICS OF ETHNICITY

The politics of ethnicity, all too often, is associated with a study of "conflict" and its regulation in "deeply divided societies" (cf. Lijphart 1977; Horowitz 1985; McGarry and O'Leary 1993). It presupposes ethnicity and sets out to develop mechanisms to "accommodate" it. The assumptions on which this paradigm rest have been problematized along with the conception of subjectivity which informs it (Norval 1993). Based upon a conception of homogeneous, given identities, treated as if they were of necessity incommensurable, this approach perpetuates rather than accounts for the myths which have fed conflictual relations. As Taylor (1999: 123) remarks, we need to break free of the belief that "race" and "ethnicity" are simply forces that we "encounter" in politics. Instead, we need to engage with the difficult issue of learning to distinguish between a politics that arises from the legitimacy of difference and a politics resting on coercive unity. This, in turn, necessitates an engagement with the question of democracy since a politics of legitimate difference can only avoid the problem of coercive unity in so far as it is inserted into a *democratic* context, a context in which identity is open to challenge, negotiation, and renewal. While accepting that an understanding of the hybridity and ambiguity of identity in no way leads inexorably to a democratic politics, a democratic context – more than any other – facilitates accentuating "exposure to contingency and increases the likelihood that the affirmation of difference in identity will find expression in public life" (Connolly 1991: 193) .

This is where accounts of the need to move away from more traditional accounts of pluralism become pertinent (Norval 1993; Bhabha 1994a). The radicalization of traditional pluralism is akin to what Connolly (1995: xiv–xv) has called a process of active *pluralization* that seeks to turn an appreciation of established diversity into an active cultivation of difference. Pluralization, in this sense, would refer to subjecting static conceptions of "cultural diversity" based on categories such as gender, race, class, and ethnicity as givens, to the disruptive effects of a conception of difference as irreducible, and to actively cultivating the visibility of the deeply split nature of identity politically. Such an active cultivation of difference is necessary, first and foremost, because there is always the danger that ethnic forms of identification may become exclusionary and self-enclosed. This possibility arises from the very context in which ethnic forms of identification often emerge: in response to exclusionary and homogenizing nationalistic projects. There is, moreover, the danger that ethnic identifications *already* contain exclusions within them. That is why it is not enough to focus analytic attention on the articulation of ethnic demands against assimilative or homogenizing state projects. The democratic logic must go all the way down. All forms of identification must not only be open to critical interrogation, but if they are to be democratic, should foster and encourage it.

Further Reading

Alcoff, L. M. 1999a: "Philosophy and racial identity." In M. Bulmer and J. Solomos (eds.) *Ethnic and Racial Studies Today.* London: Routledge, 29–44.

Connolly, W. E. 1995: *The Ethos of Pluralization.* Minneapolis: University of Minnesota Press.

Hall, S. 1996: "Politics of identity." In T. Ranger, Y. Samad, and O. Stuart (eds.) *Culture, Identity and Politics. Ethnic Minorities in Britain.* Aldershot: Avebury, 129–35.

Jenkins, R. 1997: *Rethinking Ethnicity. Arguments and Explorations.* London: Sage.

26

Imagined Communities

Alan Finlayson

A community is a group of people who draw on the same set of symbolic resources when articulating their sense of identity. Tönnies's classic account of the shift from community to association in modern society is echoed throughout modern social theory, from Weber's sociology to Etzioni's communitarianism; though Durkheim's opposition between mechanical and organic solidarity is rather different. Nationalism is the predominant form of contemporary imagined community. It is primarily cultural and always highly specific, an aspect well-captured by Anderson's influential analysis, but somewhat neglected by Gellner's modernization theory of nationalism and Smith's emphasis on premodern forms of ethnic identification. Cultural theory has shown how shared ethnic culture and tradition are, to some extent, invented. Studies of nationalism as ideology have also contributed to our understanding of the construction of imagined communities where they become the horizon of a politics that claims to speak in the "national interest." Increasingly, political communities are being formed which are divorced from geographical territories and claims to historical authenticity.

The difficulty about theorizing or analyzing "community" is that it is itself a kind of social theory: a way of comprehending our social relationships; of imagining how we are connected to each other; of shaping our understanding of the social world, of parcelling it up and giving it meaning. As Stuart Hall argues, *apropos* national community: "we only know what it is to be English because of the way 'Englishness' has come to be represented, as a set of meanings, by English national culture...a nation is not only a political entity but something which produces meanings – a system of cultural representation... people participate in the idea of the nation as represented in its national culture. A nation is a symbolic community" (Hall 1992b: 292). A community, then, is a group of people who draw on the same set of symbolic resources when articulating their sense of identity. It is not simply one form of identity rivalling others but a sharing of the means by which identity itself is shaped (Cohen 1985). The experience of community is that of finding we interpret or explain the social world in a way congruent with, if not identical to, the understanding of others.

Community tends to be imagined as natural and "given" and hence as the basis for political organization, ethical prescriptions, and ideological claims. This is to imagine community in particular and limited ways; within boundaries or in contexts that can determine quite specific forms of action. Analyzing community therefore involves consideration of the contours of this imagining, as well as the conditions which govern its formation, with the intention of rendering more visible the processes and rules governing its creation. We will explore this firstly by examining how some classical sociological theories have conceptualized community. Then we will examine debates about the primary form of contemporary imagined community, the nation. This in turn raises questions about the ideology of community. In conclusion we will look at possible future developments in the formation of imagined communities.

COMMUNITY AND SOCIAL THOUGHT

At the end of the nineteenth century Tönnies (1974 [1887]) defined community by making a contrast with "association." The former was organic and moral, the latter contractual and amoral. The forms of association encouraged by modern life and embodied in the state were "estranged" from community life. The force of convention prevailed over consensual ethical harmony. This diagnosis of the decline of community is reflected throughout modern social thought and criticism, from Weber's theories of rationalization and disenchantment to the injunction to revive "community spirit" characteristic of recent North American communitarianism (e.g. Etzioni 1995). Indeed, it is now something of a cliché to oppose community, as something traditional and spiritual, to soulless and anomic modern life.

Durkheim, however, did not operate within this kind of framework. Employing the more subtle opposition of mechanical to organic solidarity, he found the very force of dislocation in industrial society to be the basis of social solidarity. The function of the division of labor was "to create in two or more persons a feeling of solidarity... to cause coherence among friends and to stamp them with its seal" (1933: 56). Hence, "it must have a moral character, for the need of order, harmony, and social solidarity is generally considered moral" (1933: 63). The "collective consciousness" of "traditional" community is not destroyed but made abstract. Becoming transcendental and universal, it is embodied in "the cult of individualism" and normatively expressed in liberal civil law. Thus anomie can be overcome by a new moral order intrinsic to modernity itself.

But Durkheim recognized that the *conscience collective* of traditional communities was a force for social regulation manifesting itself in a community's collective representations. While he considered the form of social solidarity found in industrial societies to be rational rather than mythic, he also recognized that "there can be no society which does not feel the need of upholding and reaffirming at regular intervals the collective sentiments and the collective ideas which make its unity and personality" (1987: 233). This might lead us to inquire into the nature of contemporary collective representations. Liberal individualism emerged as part of the transition from monarchical states to sovereign nations. Indeed, the self-determination of nations and of individuals is part of the same process: one cannot have the status of free citizen without a nation to confer it. Durkheim's "cult of individualism" exists within the confines of a national allegiance and is shaped by the collective representations of national community. Binding and normative political communities are not something from which liberalism departs.

NATIONALISM

The predominant form of contemporary imagined community is the nation. According to Anderson, nationalism takes over the imaginings of religion "transforming fatality into continuity, contingency into meaning." It is born of a modern conception of time that finds unconnected people across differentiated space occupying the same time; living in a simultaneous "meanwhile." This development, Anderson argues, was closely linked to the spread of print capitalism. In order to create viable markets it assembled varied dialects into more homogeneous languages, creating a bridge between elite clerical Latin and diverse popular vernaculars. It was this convergence between capitalism and the technology of printing that made it possible to begin imagining the national community.

Before returning to theories of the importance of communication systems for the formation of "imagined communities" we need to consider this question of the modernity of nations. For Anderson, nationalism emerges out of a set of cultural changes, themselves part of economic and political developments, that transform and reoccupy the old dynastic, absolutist states. Versions of this "modernization" thesis of nationalism are widespread and influential though not universally accepted.

The most influential "modernization" theory of nationalism is Gellner's (1983). According to Gellner, agrarian society was localized and hierarchical. The ruling class was rigidly separated from the peasantry and a clerical elite monopolized literate culture. But industrialization transformed this, making culture the key mechanism of social integration. Where agrarian society was static, industrial society is fluid. It is characterized by a division of labor, "which is complex and persistently, cumulatively changing" (Gellner 1983: 24). This variability requires facilitation from a set of generic codes, a basic training in a high culture of literacy and numeracy that is applicable across occupational fields, a commonality that transcends the particularity of artisanal labor. Thus: "in industrial society, notwithstanding its larger number of specialisms, the distance between specialists is far less great. Their mysteries are far closer to mutual intelligibility, their manuals have idioms that overlap to a much greater extent, and re-training, though sometimes difficult, is not generally an awesome task" (Gellner 1983: 26–7).

The state, holding "the monopoly of legitimate education," is the only institution capable of creating this universal high culture. Culture and politics become combined and any culture that wishes to persist must build its own "political roof." Nationalism is about this imperative that state and culture be linked. It is a response to the disruptions and transformations of industrialization that throw rigid social positioning into question and make culture, not structure, the fixing agent of social order. The apparent archaism of nationalism is a by-product of modernization itself.

Gellner has many critics. Marxists might claim that capitalist society entails a permanent dislocation in the form of the class structure on which it is built. If so, then nationalism may be an ideological phenomenon that compensates for or disguises this dislocation and not merely a functional social fact. Others might charge both Marxism and Gellner with such functionalism for in neither theory is it always clear if nationalism is to be understood as a by-product of modernization or as part of its initial propagation. Historical research suggests that claims could be made either way in different cases. Indeed, nationalism has often emerged as a force opposed to modernization and, as Breuilly remarks, it "cannot originate as a deliberate project of modernization unless one attributed phenomenal clairvoyance as well as power to nationalists" (Breuilly 1996: 156).

Anthony Smith is one of the most persistent critics of modernization theories (e.g. 1988, 1991, 1995). He emphasizes the significance of premodern social forms for understanding nationalism and argues that scholars confuse modern state formation with the building of national communities. Where some focus on the instrumental aspect of nations, their usefulness in advancing certain elite claims, Smith shows how this is too insensitive to the nature of mass support for nationalism and to the fact that it is not merely concerned with satisfying "rational" aims. He argues that a premodern core of ethnic identification (an *ethnie*) forms the basis for the deeply-held sentiments out of which nationalism develops and that such communities have been present throughout human history. Indeed, for Smith, ethnicity is a key mode of social organization. Careful to reject the argument that nationalism is simply primordial or perennial, he suggests that "*ethnies* are constituted not by lines of physical descent but by the sense of continuity, shared memory, and collective destiny." These are shared experiences, such as warfare, that generate a strong sense of belonging and the myths and rituals to reproduce it. Where these become embedded in centralized administrative systems (such as those based on religion) they foster homogeneity and give to social organization an ethnic core. These can be very durable, competing with other potential bases of identity. Smith advances a moderate defense of nationalism and nationality, arguing that it is politically and socially necessary as well as historically embedded. It helps to ground principles of national sovereignty and so protect groups while promoting interdependence (Smith 1995).

Smith's approach is a useful corrective to the more cavalier arguments that regard nationalism as merely a modern invention or a purely spurious piece of ideology. For example, although there is some truth in saying that the persistence of ethno-religious identification and conflict in Northern Ireland is related to the instrumental manipulation of elites seeking to legitimate their domination, it is also obvious that history has bequeathed the raw materials for making such identities and that they have been based on perceptions of threat that, if exaggerated, are not entirely inaccurate (see Whyte 1990).

But Gellner and Smith, in the quest for generalizable theses, deflect attention from the particular ways in which community is imagined. For Weber (Gerth and Mills 1948) the concept of nation belonged "in the sphere of values." As Walker Connor argues the nation is a "psychological bond" defining a people, differentiating it from others and cohering in "the subconscious conviction of its members" (Connor 1978; see also 1994). So we need to examine the shaping of these convictions and the generation of such values. Bearing in mind Anderson's claim that nationalism is more like kinship or religion than ideologies such as liberalism or fascism, we can see that we are dealing with a cultural phenomenon and must fashion appropriate analytical tools. When Renan (1990) famously asked "What is a Nation?" he answered that it was a "spiritual principle" and "a daily plebiscite." While this sounds overly voluntaristic we should understand it as a metaphor suggesting the process of maintaining an imaginary community, the constant making and remaking of its meanings. And in all plebiscites not everyone has an equal chance to influence the vote.

CULTURAL THEORY AND NATIONALISM

Renan also famously commented "Being a nation means getting one's history wrong." Shared ethnic culture and tradition are to some extent "invented" or at least reworked by contemporary elites (Hobsbawm and Ranger 1983). One of the crucial roles of nationalist ideologues is to gather and codify the traditions and rituals of an assumed national people, be it the revival of Gaelic sports and literature or Czech language in the nineteenth century (see Hutchinson 1987).

Nationalism is "a cultural artefact of a particular kind"; one that is "capable of being transplanted with varying degrees of self-consciousness to a great variety of social terrains, to merge and be merged with a correspondingly wide variety of political and ideological constellations" (Anderson 1992: 4). Hence we find nationalism to be a hyphenated phenomenon. There is socialist-nationalism, liberal-nationalism, pan-Arab-nationalism, and so forth.

Better then to conceive of nationalism as a mode of imagining community, within which there is further variegation, or rather which is predicated precisely on its variegation into singular forms. To study it thus requires a broad focus. Research in literary and cultural studies shows how forms of cultural production are shaped by assumptions about the nature of the national ethnic communities from which they emerge and also contribute to such social meanings of belonging. Analysts have examined cultural texts to see how such visions are codified, or disrupted within them. Such readings may be carried out on novels, dramas, films, television, popular music, or a range of popular cultural forms from past and present (e.g. Cairns and Richards 1988; Bhaba 1990; Helgerson 1992; Carter et al. 1993; Higson 1995).

Such research requires integration within larger theories of how culture is transmitted and received and how it is institutionalized within, for example, state structures or indeed political projects. Hall (1978; CCCS 1982) demonstrates how discourses around crime and deviance in seventies Britain were shaped by concepts of nationhood and race. Such discourses, Gilroy argues, involve "a distinct theory of culture and identity which can be described as ethnic absolutism" that "views nations as culturally homogeneous 'communities of sentiment' in which a sense of patriotic belonging can and should grow to become an important source of moral and political ideas" (1987: 59–60). Thatcherite "authoritarian populism" drew on a rhetoric of nation and reshaped it as part of the legitimation of a state political project.

Once opened up, the realm of culture and cultural production is very productive for understanding nationalism. The "national" heritage in the form of architecture or "natural" woodland can be seen as the embodiment of the national spirit and its preservation proof of the national loyalties of the representatives of the state (Wright 1985). Within the state, school curricula (especially literature and history) are often a battleground for shaping and defining the nation (Clark 1990; Crowley 1991) and education, as Gellner saw, is a key site for the production of the imagined community.

The institutionalization of communications is of particular importance for understanding nationally imagined communities. In many nineteenth-century European nationalisms, promotion or protection of the national language was central. Irish nationalists revived Gaelic language and culture as part of their political project. In present-day Northern Ireland Gaelic is still just such a political issue, while the Northern Protestants have emulated their rivals by reviving Ulster-Scots. In Germany Fichte demanded the purification of the language of all "alien" French words. The codification of French nationality after the Revolution involved the standardization of the language through the replacement of regional dialects with Parisian French – a task sometimes carried out at the end of a bayonet.

But as Deutsch shows, communication not only entails language but also "systems of writing, painting, calculating etc. . . . information stored in the living memories, associations, habits, and preferences . . . material facilities for the storage of information such as libraries, statues, signposts and the like" (1966: 96). The predominantly national basis to media institutions has made them of tremendous importance in the maintenance of national community. Television has been understood by its own practitioners and professionals as a means of integrating millions of domestic, family units into the rhythms and experiences of a national imaginary (Ang 1996: 5). The media, far from simply reflecting national experiences, create them by their presence as recorders of events. Be it the coronation of a monarch, the swearing in of a President or the creation of a "national" tragedy (such as the sudden death of a princess in a car crash or a football team in a penalty shoot-out), media events "integrate societies in a collective heartbeat and evoke a renewal of loyalty to the society and its legitimate authority" (Dayan and Katz 1992: 9).

We may note here the extent to which national cultural policy is shaped by concerns to protect the imagined community. National governments demonstrate anxiety over the dilution of national cultures by foreign, particularly American, media. In France quotas are imposed on radio stations to guarantee air-time for French language pop and rock music and free trade in films has been a major stumbling block for GATT. To understand imagined communities we need to examine the interrelationship between governments, cultural institutions, and the symbolic contents of nationness, perhaps focusing on the everyday aspects that reinforce a sense of national belonging. This is what Billig (1995) calls "banal nationalism." This routine reinforcement, and the institutions through which it often flows, draws us on to questions of ideology.

THE IDEOLOGY OF COMMUNITY

John Breuilly (1982: 393) argues that nationalism fulfils an important intellectual and ideological role. It helps to explain the relationship of the modern state to society, establishing its legitimacy in the nation, making government appear as a natural historical development rooted in the authenticity of the community. As such it is a belief that can influence the social actions of key persons such as missionaries, traders, and bureaucrats. Acting on the basis of assumptions about the authentic community, such functionaries can render the claims of nationalism self-evidently true: "nationalist ideology actually brings into being an imitation of its own ideas".

This opens up wider questions about the ideological nature of nationalism and the imagination of community in general. The conditions for spontaneous community certainly no longer exist (if they ever did) but the concept of community, understood as a spontaneous and self-regulating order, persists and has become the horizon of a politics that claims to speak in the "national interest." In small-scale social units it is possible that social interaction can spontaneously give rise to a communal imaginary (though it is too easy to underestimate the complexity of such societies). In communities over a certain size, face-to-face interaction with all other members is not possible and a sense of commonality inevitably requires projection into an imaginary.

Where integration is forged through similarity in lifestyle, the primary zone for a communal imaginary is the disruptive gap between people and unpredictable nature. This takes the symbolic form of the totem and social relations understood via nature. The community is built around beliefs that mediate the group's relationship to the natural environment. When the scale of social organization increases, the crucial zone for the communal imaginary becomes the relations between people. We must ground our relationship to the world but also our relationship to potentially unpredictable others by creating an imaginary community mediated through the dimensions of time and space. It is in this sense that community may be understood as ideological. As Balibar (1995) argues, adapting Marx, ideology entails the representation of particulars as universals. The modern state is "a manufacturer of abstractions precisely by virtue of the unitary fiction (or consensus) which it has to impose on society." This entails an abstracted and fictive community that "compensates for the real lack of community between individuals" (1995: 48). In Lefort's terms there is a "projection of an imaginary community under the cover of which 'real' distinctions are determined as 'natural,' their particularity is disguised under the features of the universal . . . the imaginary community rules over individuals or separate groups and imposes behavioral norms upon them" (Lefort 1986: 191). Ideology then may be nothing other than the imagining of community. Modern societies are forced continually to reimagine the grounds of their legitimacy in the form of visions of community. These imaginings obscure the real basis of community which lies in division and conflict. At the same time these imaginings specify the roles the subjects of community must aspire to.

It is not just capitalist states that have such an ideology. Many political movements are premised on a claim about community. Some versions of feminism have founded themselves on an imagined community of all women, while movements based around sexual orientation have also found it necessary to propose the existence of, as one slogan has it, a "queer nation." The implication is that the group in question forms some kind of unified collective. Rights, needs, and feelings can then be attached to it.

Psychoanalytic philosophers such as Slavoj Žižek would see such phenomena as instances of "ideological fantasy." This is not something that merely mystifies or masks the truth. It is "an illusion which structures our effective, real social relations" (1989: 47). Hence the ideology of imagined community might be what makes such social relations possible. But for Žižek this would be an imagined unity that compensates for the lack that is the absent core of all social identity.

Whether or not we agree with Balibar, or Žižek, we can see that the idea of community forms the horizon of modern ideology and politics. Where it was once possible to believe that nature or essence engendered the community, and to regard politics as the sphere of its virtuous self-expression, it is now the case that politics is often understood as the means for defending or furthering the imagined community. But we must examine closely the particularity of such claims. The community is not simply imagined as a generalized form of existence but as a particular sort of community, embodying and producing particular sorts of values. Indeed, it could be argued that what defines a particular community is the kind of subject it aims to produce. Claims about national communities also advance claims about the particular people, culture, or society they intend to represent. It is not just the rights of, say, Irish or Indian people that are proclaimed but the rights of these people as specific people with specific characteristics. Any nationalist movement has to have a people to which it refers and will always define them by constituting them as unique and different to others. As Cohen (1985) argues, communities function by defining boundaries and policing them; boundaries shaped by the dual axes of similarity and difference.

This makes it possible to analyze the intersection of concepts of community with other ideological configurations asking who is and is not included. For example, we may ask if a particular idea of community specifies gender or sexual roles (see Parker et al. 1992; Yuval-Davis 1997). Early nationalism in Ireland built itself on the projection of the nation as a suffering woman and mother to be defended by her noble Gaelic sons and eventually such a notion was codified in the 1937 constitution where the roles and rights of women were clearly specified (Finlayson 1998a). Salecl (1993) shows how gender was important to the nationalism of the new states of the former Yugoslavia. Here it intersected with claims about religion and sexual morality. The intersection of sexuality and national community can also be observed in British politics (see A-M. Smith 1995).

Political ideologies can thus be seen to legitimate their claims through an identification with the intrinsic spirit of the nation. By secreting themselves within the projected essence of the community ideologies render themselves natural (Finlayson 1998b). This is not merely a "super-structural" phenomenon, for through social institutions (of education, media, and government) ideologies can produce the very conditions of their putative naturalization.

Cohen claims that "the reality of community in people's experience inheres in their attachment or commitment to a common body of symbols" (1985: 16). But the sharing of symbols is not the same as sharing meaning. Symbols provide the means to make meaning not the meanings themselves. Community does not therefore entail a consensus about symbols. Rather symbols form the material of interpretation and understanding of community. It is a form, not a content. We might say then that community is a kind of matrix of communication and that it exists when there is a shared framework of communication between a given people. To study imagined communities is to study this matrix, searching for the principles of its symbolic ordering while remaining attentive to the specific contexts within which it is shaped and which it simultaneously reshapes. Community speaks in a mythic register, rendering its components the result of something innate. But at the same time the myth of community is invoked by the symbolic referents of which it is composed (this is why the rhetoric of community is so often solipsistic). A political sociology of community must be, in some measure, the study of these myths. This would include those pertaining to origin and descent but also the historically variable forms taken by the general myth of community. In the case of nationalism analysis needs to examine the form and function of the myth of nation, placing it in historical and institutional context while centering on its intersection with other ideologies.

CONCLUSION

As we have seen, political movements other than nationalism are premised on a claim about community. Perhaps such movements are reoccupying the conceptual forms occupied by the liberal democratic nation-state and reworking it into something new. What is most noticeable about such attempts to imagine community is that they do so in a way divorced from the geographical territories and claims to historical authenticity that are usually associated with national communities. Part of what makes this possible is that new modes of communication cut across history and territory. The mass media, which, as we have seen, play a crucial part in the imagination of community, may increasingly be the locus of different forms and scales of communion. Subcultures can form around media products and fan groups generating kinds of community that give members a sense of identity and connection, proffering what Grossberg calls "affective community" based on the intensity of shared feelings. For Baudrillard such communities of cultural consumption entail "an act of allegiance of a mythological order" where the consumer engages in "an unreal, mass relation-ship, which is quite precisely the *mass communication effect*" (1998: 107).

If communication is now a commodity then community might also become commodified. One buys into a community by sharing a product and participating in its use. Products can even be made to connote community. Television increasingly simulates a de-contextualized sense of community, inviting audiences to share in the experience of a fictive participatory "we." With the internet, the physical space and presence of community is dissolved into an allegedly "pure" communication where it is yet again reimagined. Indeed, the language of community greatly shapes discourses on new information technologies. Political movements seek to regenerate themselves as virtual communities and town halls; the computer industry invites us to enter the "global community" through our ISDN line. Here is a dream of community freed from the tiresome shackles of actual meeting, a vision of cavorting in an Athenian *agora* of the mind.

This much is fantasy but, as we have seen, the community itself is a phantas-matic mode in some degree but one increasingly faced with a global reality that impinges upon the clarity of fantasy. Visions of global community cut across and intensify feelings of belonging to particular communities, be they based on geography or some specific characteristic. While part of the logic of community is to swallow up and obliterate differences, communities are also always parti-cular. Globalization is but the attempted universalization of one such fantastic vision. Against it other visions will undoubtedly find maneuvring space to think things differently and to reimagine community. Which is to say no more than that politics and ideology are not at an end and that the struggle to imagine community still requires further investigation.

Further Reading

Anderson, B. 1993: *Imagined Communities*, second edition. London: Verso.
Billig, M. 1995: *Banal Nationalism*. London: Sage
Gellner, E. 1983: *Nations and Nationalism*. Oxford: Blackwell.
Smith, A. D. 1995: *Nations and Nationalism in a Global Era*. Cambridge: Polity Press.

27

Political Rituals

SIGRID BARINGHORST

For Durkheim, rituals were the symbolic glue that held an increasingly abstract society together. Against his view that ritual would decline in industrial society, neo-Durkheimians have identified many secular ceremonies performing the functions of constituting and expressing collective identity. In particular, rituals communicated by the mass media are seen as maintaining commitments to common values where members of society are unable to interact directly. However, contemporary processes of individualization, fragmentation, and pluralization require new understandings of how political rituals work. They are seen as generating and strengthening communities, but also as expressing conflicts, contesting national identities, and even mobilizing collectivities to challenge existing power relationships. Increasingly, it is their emotional rather than their cognitive or normative dimensions that are important. Baringhorst argues that the use of symbols to provide a language of immediate and direct evidence rather than rational argument makes ritual performances potentially dangerous and tends to erode less spectacular political participation.

PUBLIC RITUALS AS EXPRESSIVE REPRESENTATIONS OF SOCIAL UNITY

The sociologist Emile Durkheim was one of the earliest social scientists to emphasize the crucial role of rituals for social integration. Based on the general division of all things into two classes or opposed groups – the profane and the sacred – he associated rituals closely with the realm of the sacred. Certain aspects of religion, which he characterizes as "elementary," are considered indispensable for the functioning and social integration of all societies. On his assumptions religions represent social reality in two ways: on the one hand they provide individual members of societies with the necessary cognitive means to interpret social reality. On the other hand religious practices such as rituals form important social standardized and repetitive means to express and dramatize social realities. Above all they express the interdependency of the members of societies in a particular symbolic idiom. In this respect religion is seen as "a system of ideas with which the individuals represent to themselves the society of which they are members, and the obscure but intimate relations which they have with it" (Durkheim 1915: 225). "The sacred principle is nothing more or less than society hypostazised and transfigured" (Durkheim 1915: 347).

Sacred symbols and ritual assemblies appear only on the surface to be solely part of the sacred. Looked at more closely the worship of a god or other sacred being is nothing but a symbolic means of collective self-adoration of a society and of the mutual dependency of its members: "the totem is the flag of the clan," its "rallying sign," a symbolic means by which the members of the community "mutually show one another that they are all members of the same moral community and they become conscious of the kinship uniting them" (Durkheim 1915: 220, 358). Religious rituals provide the individual with a feeling of belonging and serve at the same time to maintain the indispensable conditions of social life in general. Their function is to "strengthen the bonds attaching the individual to the society of which he is a member" (Durkheim 1915: 226).

In modern societies, he argues, the cognitive function that religions fulfilled in premodern segmentary societies has been taken over by other institutions. Science has succeeded religion as the main cognitive enterprise. However, even in modern societies social integration still largely depends on "the cult and the faith." Thus its the expressive role of religion that he regards as timeless and indispensable for all societies. Public ceremonies are the symbolic glue that holds an increasingly abstract society together, that lays the foundation for public solidarity formation and the reinforcement of collectively shared values and norms.

Durkheim deplored the lack of public rituals in the society of his time as an indication of a social pathology. This state of uncertainty and confusion, however, was seen as being only transitory and finally overcome by new religious ideas and practices. Contrary to Durkheim's assumption of a far-reaching absence of rituals in twentieth-century industrial societies, many social scientists have highlighted the ubiquity of ritual behavior in the realm of the profane: not only regarding everyday social life practices, but also the crucial function of rituals in modern liberal democracies.

In 1953 Shils and Young, for instance, interpreted the British coronation ceremony as a public ritual in a clear Durkheimian sense. They interpreted it as a ritual where the sacred character of community life and communal institutions are represented symbolically and the feeling of mutual dependence of the members of the national community as well as the collective relation to the Queen and to the collective norms represented by the Queen are reinforced (Shils and Young 1953: 74). The secular ceremony is seen as a crucial act for the constitution and expression of national identity, "a great act of national communion," that shares many characteristics of a religious ritual where "the whole society is felt to be one large family" (Shils and Young 1953: 78, 80).

Blumer and others have similarly interpreted the ceremonies of investiture of the Prince of Wales (Blumer et al. 1971) as expressions and reinforcement practices of British national identity. The cultural anthropologist Lloyd Warner (1959, 1962) followed the Durkheimian assumptions in his interpretations of ceremonies of collective remembrance such as Armistice and Veteran's Day in the US-American context. The public ceremonies are regarded as political-religious rituals, as:

rituals of a sacred symbol system which functions periodically to unify the whole community, with its conflicting symbols and its opposing, autonomous churches and associations. [...] the feeling of triumph over death by collective action in the Memorial Day parade is made possible by recreating the feeling of well-being and the sense of group strength and individual strength in the group power, which is felt so intensely during the wars [...] when the feeling so necessary for the Memorial Day's symbol system is originally experienced. (Warner 1962: 8)

In *Civil Religion in America* Robert Bellah applies the Durkheimian notion that every community has a religious dimension to the American society in general (Bellah 1968). According to Bellah, the religious dimension has played a crucial role for the development of all American institutions including the political sphere. The inauguration of a president is in this respect regarded as one of the most important ceremonial events that expresses the set of shared beliefs, symbols and rituals that Bellah calls the American civil religion. "It reaffirms," as Bellah states, "among other things, the religious legitimization of the highest political authority" (Bellah 1968: 5–6).

Durkheim's theses that religious symbols serve a crucial expressive function of social representation and inclusion is explicitly taken up by Sidney Verba. Analyzing the assassination of J. F. Kennedy he attaches to political symbols – in the context of US society he refers explicitly to the president – a similar quasi-religious function of social inclusion. In this context he stresses the central role of modern mass media, particularly of television, as an agency of social integration through the broadcasting of political events. Television enables the potential participation of all members of huge territorial states and potentially reinforces the sense of national unity of all citizens:

The fact that it [the assassination crisis] involved almost total participation is important. The figures on the universality of information and involvement are overwhelming as evidence of the ability of the mass media – television in particular – to link a large nation together. Furthermore, the media communicated not only information but shared emotion. [...] It was in many cases shared by families gathered around television sets, it was shared in church services and other community ceremonials, but it was intensely and widely shared through media themselves. Not only were the emotions of individual Americans involved, but they were made clearly aware of the emotions of their fellow Americans. (Verba 1965: 355)

The crucial aspect of mass media communication for the formation of collective identity and solidarity has also been pointed out by Daniel Dayan and Elihu Katz. Drawing on Durkheim, Van Gennep, and Victor Turner, they analyze three different types of media events: contests, conquests, and coronations and illustrate them with examples like Middle East peace accords, British Royal weddings, American Presidential inaugurations, and the Olympics. In modern societies where members are not able to gather together in a direct way, mediated rituals provide an important common cultural framework and serve at the same time a significant political legitimization function for modern democracies. Key aspects of contest-oriented media events are social and political reconciliation, reunification, and reintegration:

> The message is one of reconciliation, in which participants and audiences are invited to unite in the overcoming of conflict...Almost all of these events have heroic figures around whose initiatives the reintegration of society is proposed. Even when these programs address conflict – as they do – they celebrate not conflict but reconciliation. (Dayan and Katz 1992: 12, 8)

This analysis has more recently been applied to televising of ritualized quasi-judicial hearings such as the Iran-contra hearings or the Watergate hearings (see Carey 1998).

According to the functionalist logic of all these neo-Durkheimian analyses public rituals are believed to help maintain and stabilize a cohesive social order by enforcing and expressing commitments to a common set of values (Cheal 1988: 270). However, processes of individualization and fragmentation of life-styles and the growing toleration for cultural diversity render the underlying assumptions about the necessity and existence of national consensus no longer compelling and tenable. The consensual model of society cannot explain the orderliness of the present cultural plurality and fragmentation. What is needed, therefore, is an interpretation of public rituals that takes into account the growing diversity of values and worldviews and the increasing inappropriateness of the modern ideal of a unified nation-state.

The Presence of "Others" in Modern Political Rituals

Neo-Durkheimian ritual analysis contains several implicit contentions about the relationship between ritual and value consensus: (1) political rituals are considered to be expressions of an already existing normative consensus. (2) they are interpreted as symbolic expressions of a presupposed social integration; (3) they are seen as mechanisms that generate such a normative integration and (4) rituals are interpreted as constituents of such an integration. According to the underlying normative functionalism, value integration is regarded as fundamental for social integration. It is understood to be a guarantor for balancing the whole social system (Lukes 1975: 296–8).

This rather one-dimensional interpretation of political rituals as expressions of and at the same time mechanisms for generating value consensus does not take into account the increasing "dissolution of the social." Modern liberal democracies are characterized less by value consensus than by value pluralism, a constant process of social, economic, political, and cultural change, and related internal conflicts. Their degree of value integration is much lower than presupposed by neo-Durkheimian ritual analysis. Deeply felt social cleavages are translated into diverse and volatile political identities and publicly expressed in the support for protest movements and forms of collective direct action. Thus political rituals, like rituals in all other social spheres, involve less and less generalized symbolism "because there are few central symbols, if any, that are capable of eliciting a general allegiance" (Cheal 1988: 277).

Rituals are community-generating events but they are also, particularly in modern liberal democracies, symbolic expressions of conflict and a desire for cultural and social change. Thus, their performance is not only inwardly directed creating a sense of social unity among participants; as expressions of conflicts rather than celebrations of an overarching imagined or community constituted through ritualized action, rituals are at the same time directed towards an audience of outsiders who are actually and visibly present or absent and invisible categorical referents (Baumann 1992).

Political rituals are as much about "us" as about "them." As the ritual agenda is most often the "representation of claims, both to credit and to access, of one's own group as opposed to 'others,' however contextually defined" (Baumann 1992: 102) this implication of others in ritual action can be shown regarding the heterogeneity of the ritual community, its fragmentation through cleavages of gender, age, or ethnicity, and with regard to the different modes of active participation in the same rituals and the different readings and interpretations of the same symbolic action by different participants. Handelman gives an illustrative example of the role of group difference in the ritualistic construction of community when describing the structure of the annual Palio festival of Siena. It is interpreted as a model that transforms the community by first taking it apart in the ritualistic competition and then putting it back together and thus regenerating the commune as a holistic urban entity (Handelman 1990: 116).

Political rituals such as more-or-less formalized and standardized public festivals have played a significant role in nation-formation processes (Hobsbawm and Ranger 1983) and state actors still encourage annual remembrance days, military parades, state funerals, independence days, or other rituals of national unity in order to strengthen a collective sense of national belonging. However, public rituals are very often not confirmations but contestations of essential national identities. Heterogeneity and otherness represents a constitutive aspect of public rituals in modern democracies. They are often symbolic constructions of subnational communities that are directed towards the participating "we" groups as much as directed to excluded others.

In his ethnographic analysis of the Notting Hill Carnival, Abner Cohen has shown how spectacular public rituals encompass competing performances and identities or even mobilize a collectivity to challenge existing power relationships (Cohen 1993). While political rituals initiated by official state actors are strategically employed to reinforce national identities and to legitimate existing political order and power relations, non-state actors often use ritualistic performances to renegotiate identities and to realign group boundaries (Hall and Jefferson 1993). Whether expressed as more playful ritual-like multicultural street carnivals or in more structured ways like the highly contested parades of the Orange Orders in Northern Ireland, protest rituals are staged to define a "we" group vis-à-vis a dominant or rival "they" group.

Such ritual protest is often highly controversial and sparks off conflicts about the monopoly of meaning and interpretation. Different social groups try to occupy the ritual field with their own particular ideology, symbols, and ceremonies and to define which elements of the collective memory of a community should be canonized (Dörner 1996: 26). At times protest actors successfully undermine the cohesive and legitimating function of state rituals by transforming them into rituals of contestation and opposition. Zdaislaw Mach has given an illustrative account of the transformation of Polish May Day celebrations from rituals of power confirmation to rituals of contestation of political power relations. He shows the extent to which those in power can manipulate public ritual for political ends and how public rituals can become arenas in which political rivals fight with rituals as symbolic weapons (Mach 1992). In the 1970s, state rituals like the May Day Celebrations in Poland became routinized collective actions. People's participation was a kind of recreation and leisure activity, a more unconscious than deliberate legitimization of the communist regime. The imposition of martial law in 1981 led to a deroutinization of state May Day demonstrations. The annual ritual was increasingly politicized as people became more aware of their political and ideological meaning. Abstention was a conscious political act. As a sign of political opposition the Catholic church promoted the feast of Saint Joseph the Worker as a counter-ritual and thereby provided dissidents with an opportunity to express opposition publicly, ritualistically, legitimately, as well as actively. Since the end of the Communist regime and the democratization of the Polish society both rituals lost their *raison d'être* and declined.

Collective symbolic actions of self-definition in the form of ritual takes place to strengthen social and political identities and groups solidarities, particularly in times when group boundaries are threatened, undermined, or blurred (Cohen 1985: 50). Many researchers have noted a "revival of celebrations" (Manning 1983: 4; Boissevain: 1991: 11) in western liberal democracies particularly since the 1980s. This florescence of celebrations reversed a decline of public celebratory activities and festivals that began in the years immediately after the Second World War and persisted till the 1970s. The reversal of this declining trend is largely due to an increasing awareness of collective identity and group boundaries and a growing interest in tradition and authenticity. As can be seen particularly regarding the invention or reinvention of regional and local identities, public rituals are promoted as manipulations of traditions for political ends, very often in order to claim minority group rights on the basis of ethnic, cultural, or regional differences. Public celebrations are used to threaten others and to create distinct political interest groups (Boissevain 1992: 11). As Charlett Aull Davies showed with respect to the Welsh National Eiteddfod the performative focus of public performances of regional difference shifted over the years. It started in the nineteenth century as a projection of a Welshness that would find "favor among the English," a romantic vision of a Celtic past that appealed to English imaginations. It was transformed since the 1950s through the enactment of the Welsh Rule to a public spectacle that was increasingly directed to a Welsh audience, although the provision of simultaneous translation indicated that it still remained to be also staged for an English audience (Davies 1998: 152).

POLITICAL RITUALS AS SYMBOLIC ACTIONS

While in premodern societies public rituals served the vital function of expressing and reinforcing shared values and orientations in increasingly individualized and culturally fragmented pluralist societies, their main function can be more adequately described as creating a sense of solidarity and collective identity without presupposing conformity with the goals and manifestos of political institutions, organizations, and movements. As David Kertzer has pointed out in *Ritual, Politics and Power* (1988) they are indispensable for liberal and pluralist societies because they enable the construction of group identities despite an increasing plurality of social norms and an "absence of any commonality of beliefs." In situations of conflict they produce solidarity without producing value consensus (Kertzer 1988: 66). Thus it is less their cognitive and normative than their emotional dimension that renders political rituals so vital for modern liberal societies. "...what is important in ritual is our common participation and emotional involvement, not the specific rationalizations by which we account for the rites. [...] rituals can promote social solidarity without implying that people share the same values, or even the same interpretation of the ritual" (Kertzer 1988: 67, 69).

Caroline Humphrey and James Laidlaw (1994) have defined the particular property of "ritualized action" by its non-intentionality with regard to the participants. Not that participants wouldn't have any intentions of their own, but their private and individual intentions do not matter. The identity of a ritualized act, they argue, does not depend on the agent's intention in acting (Humphrey and Laidlaw 1994: 88):

> A set of constitutive rules is accepted as determining the kinds of acts which he or she will perform. In adopting the ritual stance one accepts ... that in a very important sense, one will not be the author of one's acts... One need have no knowledge or information about the act except that it is. (Humphrey and Laidlaw 1994: 98, 102)

Thus, whether we are personally convinced of the rationality of a political cause or demand is a matter of private belief. What is of social and political relevance is only our public statement, whether we support a political claim visibly and publicly by taking part in a rally, by signing a petition, by wearing a particular emblem of group identification, or attending a public meeting.

But why is it that political rituals are so ideally suited to create political solidarity despite private differences of political opinions? The main answer is, because of their predominantly formal and dramatic quality. Rituals are highly structured, repetitive, standardized, and symbolically loaded sequences of action. It is particularly the symbolic character of rituals that distinguishes them from other repetitive forms of social action like customs or habits.

Taking part in public rituals invokes physiological stimuli and powerful emotional responses among the participants. The person who participates in a ritual "lives a life of emotion, not of thoughts" (Cassirer 1955: 24). What is important is our common participation and emotional involvement, the psychological satisfaction we derive from the ritual event. The cognitive rationalizations of these actions are of less, or no, significance. Thoughts are less relevant because the content of rituals is predominantly expressed in symbols.

Three properties of symbols enable ritual processes to create solidarity even in the absence of a uniformity of belief among participants: condensation, multivocality, and ambiguity (Kertzer 1988: 11). The verbal or iconic symbols represent and unify a variety of different meanings that interact with each other and that are particularly powerful because they reach the subconscious where they are synthesized into a new associated meaning (condensation). Symbols combine not only diverse meanings; the same symbol may also be understood by different individuals in different ways (multivocality). Symbols are thus highly ambiguous: their meaning is complex and uncertain and much less precise than a simple verbal political declaration. This ambiguity of meaning is the fundamental presupposition for the creation of feelings of collective belonging without (creating) value consensus.

While everyday life experiences are structured by social hierarchies, rituals provide experiences of social transgression. They offer individual feelings of belonging to a more generalized social entity, feelings of "communities" or even communion among participants (Turner 1969: 96; Gurvitch 1941). According to Hans-Georg Soeffner, this creation of a higher community encompasses three transgressions of everyday life: (1) the transgression of individual experiences through the *evidence* of a collectively represented intersubjectivity; (2) the transgression of individual space by dissolving the individual into a community body and community soul; (3) the transgression of time and vanity through the illusion of stopping the progression of time in the ritual, to secure a permanent presence of the higher community (Soeffner 1992: 118).

It is their particular reference to the sacred and divine and to time that renders public rituals so important for political life in modern democracies. Ideally modern processes of secularization and rationalization should have led to a clear separation between the profane and the sacred, politics and religion. According to enlightenment thinking the establishment of principles of popular sovereignty and democratic government should have reduced the use of public rituals in favor of less strategic and more discursive forms of consensus formation. Based on the notion of the citizen as an emancipated, autonomous subject, liberal democracies can theoretically be expected to be more sceptical toward the use of public rituals as means of collective identity formation and political legitimization than premodern political communities or totalitarian political systems that explicitly stress social bonds and feelings of collectivity over individual independence. Comparative political ritual analyses have given some evidence for the implied logical connection between the affinity of a society to rituals and its political ethos (Behrenbeck 1988). However, the above mentioned trend of an increase of public rituals in western European societies illustrates a growing tendency of social dedifferentiation between politics and religion. In a rapidly changing social and political environment public rituals seem to be ideally suited to provide individuals as well as collectivities with a sense of stability and continuity.

From the perspective of the individual, enduring patterns of ritual processes help to make sense of an increasingly complex and modernizing world by linking the present to the past as well as to the future. In that respect, Durkheim's interpretation of the social function of commemorative rites can also be applied to modern ceremonies of national remembrance: they serve to "revivify the most essential elements of the collective consciousness," so that "the group periodically renews the sentiment which it has of itself and of its unity." The commemorative or "representative" rites have the function of " representing or imprinting (the past) more deeply in the mind," they are ceremonies "whose sole aim is to awaken certain ideas and sentiments, to attach the present to the past or the individual to the collectivity" (Durkheim 1915: 358).

POLITICAL RITUALS IN LIBERAL DEMOCRACIES: TRANSLATING POLITICAL DISSONANCE INTO AESTHETIC CONSONANCE

Modern liberal democracies are characterized by internal frictions, a multitude of equally valid belief systems and contradicting political interests. Symbolic actions like public rituals represent extra-communicative answers to these paradoxes or contradictions. They are, as the German sociologist Hans-Georg Soeffner put it, able to translate social and political dissonances into aesthetic consonances:

> Where the symbol postulates its own reality, it aims to deny legitimacy to conceptual terms and arguments. Overdetermined and ambivalent, it represents one aspect of the human construction of reality that does not founder on its own contradictory character, but lives off it, expresses it and suggests the unity of these contradictions. (Soeffner 1991: 74)

While discursive communication aims at rational argument, the mediation of knowledge through reason, symbols provide a language of immediate and direct evidence for what is not discursively communicable. This property of direct persuasion is an enormous source of strength but also a constant potential danger of symbolic action and communication: "Symbols are able to be pursued against all reason. But this also means that they are able to construct their own worlds unaccompanied by reason; worlds which defy reason's control and monitoring, and which therefore can also create and sustain delusions" (Soeffner 1991: 75).

This is not only true with respect to the extensive use of manipulative ritual performance in totalitarian regimes like the Third Reich. Murray Edelman has given ample evidence for the strategic use of political rituals in western democracies as part of symbolic management by political elites (Edelman 1985, 1988). Political rituals are often employed as efficient and subtle means of avoiding or sometimes even suppressing public discourse and rational critique on particular political decisions or the political order in general. In his interpretation of public inauguration ceremonies, Pierre Bourdieu has emphasized the inherent danger of the symbolic power that political leaders gain through public rituals. The ceremonial confirmation of a democratically elected president creates divisions and hierarchies in the political community between the leader and the rest of the community. It expresses and gives form to a power relation, makes it visible and at the same time recognized. Like all rituals of nomination the inauguration ceremony is based on a relation of representation: "the one who is presented with symbolic power, with a new title and insignia of the political office, is the carrier of legitimacy" (Bourdieu 1982: 101). There is no legitimacy outside the act of delegation by which a political community conveys a mandate to its chosen representative. The people convey power to the representative and according to the nature of a relation of delegation the representative is, in response to that, expected to fulfil the tasks with which they were entrusted. It is only through the act of representation that the isolated subjects become a unified body. There is no political representative without a legitimating political community and there is no political community without embodiment in the representative. Inherent in the very act of delegation lays, as Bourdieu critically comments, already the possibility of usurpation. The representative gains symbolic power through the act of inauguration. From then on he speaks on behalf of the group, thus to question his words would mean to question the unity of the political community (Bourdieu 1982, 1984).

Political rituals serve the important function of providing individuals with political orientation and feelings of belonging to a wider community. These individual needs, however, can – as the world of politics widely shows – relatively easily be exploited and abused. Thus the political implications and potential effect of political rituals are highly ambivalent. On the one hand they can be interpreted as useful symbolic means of securing a democratic political order by reinforcing national bonds and traditions (rituals of national remembrance), by legitimating democratically elected elites (rituals of inauguration) or by mobilizing subnational political identities and expressing dissenting political claims (rituals of protest). The reenchanting of the political process through emotionally moving and aesthetically appealing forms of collective public performance might generally enhance political engagement and thus despite its non-rational nature contribute to the stability of liberal democracy.

Ernest Gellner has rightly stressed the integrative weakness of an understanding of politics that is solely based on enlightenment thinking and the postulate of a victory of the better argument:

> Enlightenment rationalism has a number of weaknesses, from the viewpoint of its use as a practical faith, as the foundation either for individual life or for a social order. It is too thin and ethereal to sustain an individual in crisis, and it is too abstract to be intelligible to any but intellectuals with a penchant for this kind of theorizing. Intellectually it is all but inaccessible, and unable to offer real succour in a crisis. (Gellner 1992: 86)

Even if enlightenment rationalism is not questionable as a superior cognitive strategy, truth derived from public discourse still lacks the moral validity and authority of traditional religious beliefs (Gellner 1992: 86). However, the potential dangers of a shift from discursive decision making to a generation of public consent through politics of public rituals and spectacles should not be diminished. The development of modern mass media has, as mentioned above, given political actors a powerful and attractive arena for the staging of public dramas and events (Dayan and Katz 1992; Chaney 1993) that tend to erode the chances of less spectacular and emotionally moving forms of political participation and public opinion formation.

Further Reading

Boissevain, Jeremy (ed.) 1996: *Revitalizing European Rituals*. London and New York: Berghahn Books.
Turner, Victor 1969: *The Ritual Process. Structure and Anti-structure*. London: Routledge.

28

The Politics of Popular Culture

John Street

The very definition of popular culture is political, sanctioning some forms of culture and marginalizing others. The most conventional meaning of the politics of popular culture involves the use of that culture to express political views. However, it is also important to look at the role of the state in the politics of popular culture. Censorship is an important case, whether or not it is a question of overtly political statements, since it involves the power of legitimated agencies and may be effective in constituting political identities. But even without censorship, the power of the state is significant in structuring the production and distribution of popular culture. Increasingly this is seen as an issue in relation to globalization. There is also a politics of the consumption of popular culture, tied to fears of mass culture and Americanization, and, more recently, to theories of resistance and dissent in the approach of the Birmingham school to cultural studies. Currently questions turn on the ways in which popular culture (especially music) becomes effective: how it animates feelings and thoughts through pleasure. In this respect, the study of the politics of popular culture takes us beyond conventional forms of politics to questions about the politics of identity.

During the Gulf War of 1991, it was reported that the BBC had issued an injunction, declaring certain records as unsuitable for public broadcasting (Cloonan 1998). Among the banned items were Lulu's "Boom bang-a-bang," ABBA's "Waterloo," and Kate Bush's "Army Dreamers." It was never altogether clear whether, in fact, the BBC was just issuing a set of voluntary guidelines, or whether the Corporation wanted to censor these and other records. Either way, the rumor prompted an outburst of disbelief and ridicule – surely no one was going to be offended by the sound of a Eurovision Song Contest winner? However ludicrous the BBC's behavior might seem, it was clearly inspired by the view that pop songs mattered, that playing them might be harmful.

The opposing view, the one behind the ridicule, holds by contrast that it is entirely misconceived to ban pop, indeed to bother with it at all. How can three minutes of childish rhymes and banal melodies, mass-produced by a cynically successful industry, have any significance at all? But such a question can, in turn, prompt its own angry rebuttal. If pop music is so trite and trivial, why is it that the might of the Soviet state was used to crush and control it? (Starr 1983). Why did the Communist leadership in Czechoslovakia imprison members of the rock band the Plastic People of the Universe? And why today, years after the collapse of the Soviet bloc, are musicians still persecuted in countries throughout the world? (*Index on Censorship* 1998). These competing views, about the importance or the irrelevance of popular music, frame the debate about the politics of popular culture. This debate, though, is not confined to the ways in which cumbersome and confused states lumber around suppressing music, although this is relevant, but it extends into the suggestion that popular culture itself can be seen as "dangerous" or "subversive" (and hence needs to be suppressed). More than this: the politics of popular culture, I want to suggest, cannot be limited to the way it is treated and viewed (by both its critics and defenders), but must also encompass the *pleasures* which it produces. The politics of popular culture are also the politics of fun. To sustain such claims, however, it is first necessary to look at the different ways and different places in which popular culture has appeared to be (or to become) "political."

THE POLITICS OF THE POPULAR

Popular culture becomes political in the very act of defining it. To talk about *popular* culture is to imply another kind of culture, an elite, a serious, a high culture. This distinction cannot rest simply upon sales figures or (mass) production methods. There are, after all, many examples of "high" culture which outsell so-called popular culture (the Three Tenors, for example). High culture is just as much a product of mass production as popular culture; or to put it another way: some "popular" culture emerges from small independent production companies and achieves minuscule sales. Equally, it is not clear that any neat aesthetic divide can be drawn between popular and serious culture. The values of complexity and difficulty can apply to both (Frith 1996). And yet the distinction persists.

The difference between "popular" and other forms of culture is preserved in part by the institutions which create or reinforce the distinction. The definition is a product of politics. One way this happens is through the academy which, by identifying some forms of culture as worthy of study, sanctions those cultural forms and marginalizes others. The politics of this distinction was made very apparent in the "political correctness" debate, when writers like Roger Kimball (1990) and Allan Bloom (1987) bemoaned the teaching of "popular culture" – so-called "Madonna studies," in particular – in American universities. Apart from the academy, state policies on broadcasting and cultural policies generally often serve to reinforce the distinction by allocating resources to, say, opera rather than musicals. The politics of the definition of popular culture are not confined to the actions of the state and the right. The left too stakes a claim, seeing in popular culture a counter-hegemonic force, a demonstration of popular resistance and opposition (Hall 1981; J.C. Scott 1990). To draw attention to the politics of the definition is not, however, to argue for an abandonment of the term "popular culture." Rather, it is to focus upon the ways in which popular culture is constructed by certain political processes. In adopting this focus we need to remain aware of the contingent nature of the "popular" and its politics.

It is worth adding that in exploring the politics of popular culture we are also raising questions about what "politics" refers to. Treating popular culture as "political" is to challenge many of the conventional forms of that concept, to push beyond a concern with the activity of states and parties. It is best, none-theless, to begin with seeing how very traditional definitions of the political can be applied to the most familiar of popular cultural forms.

THE POLITICS OF PROTEST

Conventionally, the politics of popular culture refers to the use of that culture to express political views. We are familiar with the ways in which film-makers, musicians, and others use their art to make a point, to support a cause. Folk music and rap include many overtly political songs. We are also now familiar with artists taking a direct part in conventional politics. Pop musicians lead campaigns to counter poverty or to end Third World debt; comedians raise money for refugees; playwrights protest at political im-prisonment. In the light of such developments, the politics of popular culture would seem to include not only the use of music, comedy, and drama to promote political ideas and values, but also the role of performers in political action. Equally familiar is the way in which popular culture is "read" politically. Douglas Kellner (1995), for instance, has shown how films like *Top Gun* encode a right-wing political ideology, one that sustained or promoted the Reaganite consensus.

But in adopting this approach to the politics of popular culture, we have to bear in mind two further thoughts, which serve to complicate this apparently simple story. The first is that the "meaning" of a song or film is not confined to the intentions and ideology of its maker. Meaning, as John Corner (1995) has pointed out, is contingent; it depends upon the context and conditions in which culture is consumed. Besides, even if meaning were contained in the text, where exactly is it to be found? Where is the meaning, say, in a song – in the words, the voice, the rhythm, the arrangement? Whatever the answer, there is unlikely to be a single, unambiguous meaning, a clear political line. Secondly, we need to be aware of the conditions that make it possible for artists to become politically salient figures. The ability to speak politically is partly a matter of genre – of what the conventions allow you to say, of what the audience expects. One of the fascinating stories within the politics of popular culture is the ways in which celebrity status has, over time, also been imbued with an element of political credibility. The rise of Bob Geldof is a prime example: from postpunk musician and jobbing pop journalist to global statesman and media entrepreneur. Just as meaning is contingent, so are the politics of popular culture; they are not intrinsic facts about a piece of cultural expression. One crucial contingency is the actions of the state.

THE POLITICS OF CENSORSHIP

Popular culture becomes political by the simple fact that the state intervenes in its production and distribution. Typically this takes the form of censorship, as the example of the BBC's reaction to the Gulf War showed. States across the world are responsible for the banning or altering of popular culture. This may be done explicitly, through officially sanctioned agencies, or it may be done more secretively. Such censorship is often assumed to be the province of totalitarian or authoritarian regimes, but liberal democratic states also engage in censorship. Almost all such societies operate a system of film classification, which regulates who is entitled to watch particular films (Matthews 1994). And in the process of classification, some films are banned (in Britain, for example, the video version of *The Exorcist* was not available until 1999) and many others are cut. The reasons for these cuts and bans – in the West, at least – are typically due to concern about portrayals of violence and sex. But there are occasions when explicitly political content is the cause of the censorship. During the 1970s and 1980s, a large number of British television programs, and several pop songs, dealing with Northern Ireland, were cut or banned.

Whether or not the reason for censorship is an explicit political message contained in a work of popular culture, the very fact of censoring is "political." It is political in the obvious sense that it relates to the operation of political power, which is used to allow or deny access to forms of entertainment or information. So even where, as in the USA, performances by the rappers 2 Live Crew were banned because of their sexual, not political, content, this becomes a political decision because of the legitimated power granted to certain agencies to act in this way. Censorship of sex may be political in another sense. It may involve denials (or marginalization) of certain sexual identities, which are themselves important to the constitution of political identities. This is a corollary of the argument of some feminists, such as Andrea Dworkin and Catherine MacKinnon, that censorship of pornography is justified because pornographic representations harm women, denying them their identity and their freedom. In short, censorship can be political, not just because of who takes the decision to censor, nor just because of the explicitly political content of the censored object, but also because of the implications for freedom and identity of censorship (or its absence).

But while it is important to think of deliberative acts of censorship as a key aspect of the politics of popular culture, there is a danger that this will obscure a more pervasive, and perhaps more important, dimension of the politics of popular culture. Too often a false dichotomy is established between "freedom of expression" and "censorship." To think of all popular culture that is not censored as free expression would be to assume that this culture emerges unhampered from some unfettered creator.

THE POLITICS OF CULTURAL PRODUCTION

Creativity has to be organized and resourced; its results have to be disseminated and consumed. These processes are as "political" (in various senses) as is censorship. The education system of a country is intimately tied to the making and consuming of popular culture. Decisions taken by central and regional authorities about what is to be taught in schools, decisions about the funding of film, music, or art colleges, these have a profound impact upon the skills – skills of creating and appreciating popular culture – which people possess. In the same way, decisions about the funding of libraries, theatres, and concert halls have an impact on what can be seen and heard. These conventional political decisions are most obviously encountered in the structuring of systems of broadcasting. The allocation of frequencies in the radiowave spectrum entails decisions about who can have access to these public goods and what they can be used for (Street 1997).

The politics of cultural production, at least as they involve the state, are most starkly focused by the impact of globalization on popular culture. For some states, a globalized popular culture represents an "Americanized" popular culture, one in which all nations dance to the same pop beat and thrill to the same Hollywood blockbuster. Such a scenario is characterized, by those fearful of it, as "cultural imperialism." The suggestion is that a nation's sense of itself, of its differences from other states, is intimately bound to its culture. Insofar as this is the case, states are in a position to acquiesce in the process of globalization or to resist it through the use of quotas and subsidies. Quotas can be used to limit the allocation of space to foreign culture. The Canadian government, for example, restricts the amount of non-Canadian music played on the radio (Straw 1993). In the same way, states subsidize local cultural production, to counteract the spread of other cultures (Rutten 1991). A similar logic applied to the French government's commitment of resources to its film industry.

Cultural production is, however, not just the province of the state. There is also a corporate politics of popular culture. Put simply, this involves the ways in which corporations responsible for the manufacturing of popular culture decide which artists or cultural forms to favor. Here, we are dealing with the micro-politics of corporate practice. Recent studies of the record industry have revealed the kind of politics involved. Keith Negus (1998) recounts how the corporate strategy of record companies has consequences for the music that is produced, and that this has a strongly political dimension. Corporations operate through a set of divisions which both reflect and create generic distinctions within music. These corporate divisions encourage the production of some musics and the marginalization of other musics. Acts that do not fit the divisional divide are not signed; and changing the corporate divisions can adversely effect those in the company. Negus shows how both salsa and African-American music suffered from these corporate practices.

Another variant on this corporate politics is provided by David Hesmond-halgh (1997). He asks whether it is possible for the production of popular culture to be run democratically. This question is prompted and explored by an examination of the independent record sector (as opposed to the "majors" and their subsidiaries). The importance of Hesmondhalgh's study is that it draws attention to the political values that organize cultural production, to the way that rights are assigned and authority allocated. The contract which performers sign with their record companies, or authors with their publishers, establish relationships of power and control. Different contracts establish different relationships. What Hesmondalgh shows is that it is at least possible to run cultural production in other ways, and in doing so he highlights the political values that constitute the norm.

Responsibility for cultural production is not confined to the state and the cultural industries. Most obviously, the media and the academy also play a part. These institutions are important to the distribution of cultural capital, the status and value that attaches to certain forms of cultural activity. It is notable, for instance, that while there are now many courses on creative writing in Universities, there are few on, say, pop song composition. Students are taught to write poems but not lyrics; they learn about John Keats not Bob Dylan; they can choose between many degree courses on film, but they have little choice if they want to study popular music; and if they take courses on film, they will spend more time watching *Citizen Kane* or *The Seven Samurai* than *Titanic* or *The Texas Chainsaw Massacre*. This divide is echoed in the way critical commentary, which serves to validate certain forms of creativity, is distributed (Shrum 1996). The allocation of space in broadsheet newspapers favors opera and classical music, not pop; and the style of writing compounds the divide: critical comment on opera is technical and serious, on pop it is emotive and flip.

To observe these features of the cultural landscape is to see the operation of a set of judgments which serve to validate or legitimate forms of cultural activity. This is clearly political, but it is not obvious what kind of politics is involved. Or to put it another way: different political positions will treat these observations differently. Some (on the left and the right) will see the fact that popular culture remains outside the mainstream, ignored by the political and cultural establishment, as a sign of its untainted populist character, with the left and right disagreeing only about the nature of the "people" which popular culture addresses. Others (also on the left and right) will see it as a sign of elitism, with the left and the right disagreeing about the justification for that elitism.

Many assumptions underlie these competing interpretations, but a central one is concerned with the relationship between production and consumption, with the degree to which the interests invested in the production of popular culture are reproduced in the experience of consuming it.

THE POLITICS OF CULTURAL CONSUMPTION

A founding document in the debate about the politics of cultural consumption was an essay written in the 1940s by Theodor Adorno and Max Horkheimer (1972). In "The Culture Industry: Enlightenment as Mass Deception," Adorno and Horkheimer wrote about the manipulative power of mass-produced culture. These were two Marxist writers who had escaped from Nazi Germany, and

Hitler's insidious mass propaganda, and found another kind of propaganda at work in their new home. Looking at the growing popularity and sophistication of the Hollywood film industry, at the use of radio as a vehicle of popular entertainment, they argued that mass culture was being deployed to reconcile the masses to their daily oppression. Mass culture stood in stark contrast to true culture which allowed people to imagine other possible worlds, to think beyond the everyday. Mass produced culture reconciled people to the everyday, while tempting them with the idea of individual freedom. In fact, the individualism of mass culture was a myth. Hollywood films, in fact, promoted obedience to the system and warned of the dangers of defiance. The way Adorno and Horkheimer coupled the production of popular culture to its message, and then to its effect, was to become a central theme in arguments about the politics of cultural consumption.

In the UK, this fear of popular culture echoed in postwar panics about the "Americanization" of British culture. But accompanying this concern was a powerful historical tradition, born of the New Left, which sought to establish the legacy of working-class culture in resisting capitalist authority. Writers like Raymond Williams, Richard Hoggart, and E. P. Thompson, while not necessarily sympathetic to mass popular culture, stood for the idea that culture could be politically progressive, rather than a form of social control. It was an idea that was to find institutional form in the Center for Contemporary Cultural Studies at Birmingham University. Under the leadership of Stuart Hall and Richard Johnson, the CCCS came in the 1970s to articulate the claim that, just as working-class culture served to voice criticism before and after the industrial revolution, so mass-produced popular culture did the same in late capitalism.

The CCCS fashioned a theoretical amalgam of Gramsci, Althusser, Barthes, and Saussure, among others, which they applied to a number of different subcultures: the punks, rastas, skinheads, and hippies. The cultural practices of these groups, the CCCS suggested, were to be understood as part of a process of resistance and subversion. Central to the argument was the thought that cultural artefacts – records, clothes, etc. – could be used by the subcultures to establish a group identity. The meanings attached to culture were not inscribed in the product, but were created by the users.

The Birmingham School's work was immensely influential. Books like Dick Hebdige's *Subculture: the meaning of style* (1979) became a manifesto for several generations of popular artists. But within the academy, criticisms of the CCCS approach were soon to be heard. Feminist critics pointed to the way in which the so-called resistant subcultures reproduced the sex divisions of the wider society (McRobbie 1991). Other critics complained at the way in which "mainstream" culture, and its followers, were implicitly condemned to a life of subservient complacency. More recently, Sarah Thornton (1995) has initiated a radical rethinking of the subcultural approach, arguing that all forms of culture – whether subcultural or mainstream – are mediated by journalists and other cultural entrepreneurs. And more importantly, she argues that the politics of these cultural groupings are not intrinsic to the groups membership or to their use of specific cultural artefacts, but that they are a product of the way in which the state and its agencies contribute to the meaning given to cultural activity. Put simply, moral panics do not describe just the reaction of outsiders, but are incorporated into the self-understanding of insiders.

Despite the criticisms and revisions, the Birmingham analysis has remained extraordinarily resilient. Its approach can still be detected in current debates about dance and rave culture, where the rhetoric of resistance still flourishes (McKay 1996). Indeed the Birmingham approach can be seen as founding the entire discipline of Cultural Studies, although as several critics have pointed out, in this transition it has been the CCCS's politics of resistance and dissent that have been lost or submerged (Gitlin 1997; Frith 1996). The argument is that Cultural Studies, while sharing the Birmingham focus on cultural consumption and the making of meaning (rather than on cultural production), has adopted a "populism" in which *all* forms of cultural consumption have been seen as "empowering," irrespective of the content and character of that culture. This indiscriminate celebration of popular culture has led Todd Gitlin (1997) to call for the abandonment of popular culture as the site of politics. Others have not been willing to resort to such drastic solutions, but have counselled a more discriminating approach to the politics involved: "pleasure" was not automatically empowering; it could also be a source of oppression.

POPULAR CULTURE AND POLITICAL ACTION

Political and social scientists have begun to examine more closely the ways in which popular culture functions within political action. Much of the attention has been upon music and, in particular, upon its role in nationalist or independence struggles (e.g. Slobin 1996). Mark Mattern (1998), for example, has written about music's contribution to collective action through the way it provides a form of communication which allows groups to establish collective meanings and interests: "By expressing common experiences, music helps create and solidify a fund of shared memories and a sense of 'who we are'" (Mattern 1998: 19). According to Mattern, the political use of music comes in three forms: the confrontational, the deliberative, and the pragmatic. The first conforms to the idea of protest music, where one side pits itself against another; the music frames the opposition. Deliberative use of music involves debates within a community about their identity – rap, Mattern suggests, contains competing visions of the African-American community. Finally, pragmatic use of music occurs when a common identity and interest already exist, and music is deployed to advance these aims. But while Mattern provides insights into how music may function within, say, Chilean politics, he says little about *how* a set of chords and notes actually fulfil these functions.

An answer of a kind is provided by Ron Eyerman and Andrew Jamison (1998), who come to their study of music's political significance from social movement theory. "Social movements," they write, "are not merely political activities"; they are also cultural forms (Eyerman and Jamison 1998: 1). Movements are to be seen as providing space – a kind of public sphere – for "cultural growth and experimentation" which entails the making and remaking of cultural traditions that are themselves generative of further political activity.

Culture shapes the way the world is viewed. Music is "both knowledge and action, part of the frameworks of interpretation and representation produced within social movements" (Eyerman and Jamison 1998: 23–4). They argue that musicians and music have a truth-bearing function. Music allows for the recounting of the experiences and the structuring of the feelings that animate political action. Eyerman and Jamison claim, for instance, that there was a powerful symbiosis between American political culture in general (and the labor movement in particular) and the radical populism within folk music. In the same way, the civil rights movement imbued soul music with "a special intensity and responsibility," and in turn, the music was able to articulate "forms of social solidarity" that become a form of "exemplary social action" (Eyerman and Jamison 1998: 77).

The weakness of this approach to popular music's political role is that the culture itself is treated with comparative glibness. Few questions are asked about how music achieves its effects, and why some music is more politically potent than others. Such questions need to be asked if we are going to understand the politics of popular culture. We need to ask why some culture is more politically effective than others. I want to suggest that a piece of music is chosen not because it "fits" the political agenda, not because it takes the "correct" line, but because it also works *as music*. Put simply, we have to understand the pleasure and the fun if we want to understand the politics.

POPULAR CULTURE AND THE POLITICS OF IDENTITY

This is not an original claim. It is made very powerfully by Robin Kelley (1998) in a critique of traditional treatments of popular culture in studies of African-American urban life. Kelley claims that much urban political sociology tends to be highly selective in its account of popular culture in ghetto life. First, it uses that culture merely to underscore stories of deprivation and misery. Secondly, it treats that culture as a political commentary on daily life. In doing this, the complex history of African-American culture is lost. The Afro hairstyle, for example, is misrepresented as simply a symbol of Black Power, when in fact it belongs equally to women's struggle for equality. Also missing from such stories is the pleasure that makes sense of cultural consumption.

The politics of popular culture – the reasons for its censorship or for its compliance in political action – can only be understood in conjunction with some account of how it animates feelings and thoughts. One way to think about this is to consider how popular culture becomes part of an identity (whether individual or collective). After all, identity is the key factor in culture's politics: the identity being denied by censorship, being appealed to by nationalism, being denied by corporate power, being reconstituted by subcultural activity. But how is identity constituted by cultural consumption, and crucially, how is it connected to pleasure? It is clearly not sufficient to note continuities between cultural forms and identities; to observe and analyze the composition of audiences is only a first stage. The main issue is what the cultural experience *gives* to those people.

If identity is seen to be an essential feature of individuals, then culture becomes merely "expressive" of those identities. Such a position limits the role of culture; rather than creating identities, it mirrors or reproduces them. To claim a cultural form for a people or group necessarily entails some element of essentialism (Lipsitz 1990). If we adopt an anti-essentialist account, then identity is constituted in the process of experiencing culture: we *feel* the identity in the pleasure we get. Simon Frith (1996) connects this anti-essentialist identity to the thought that our aesthetic response is itself also an ethical response. This is not the time to delve further into the aesthetics of popular culture, but it is important, I want to suggest, that any account of the politics of popular culture must address the way that culture works on those who hear or see it.

CONCLUSION

To adopt this position is not just to say something about how popular culture is to be analyzed but about its politics too. This chapter began by looking at the actions of that traditional political actor, the state. Censorship of popular culture is clearly important, especially to those who suffer directly from it. The point is, however, that why such censorship matters, why being denied access to popular culture is important, depends on what the culture means to people. And here the politics moves from the conventional forms – the state – to the politics of identity, and from there into the politics of pleasure, where traditional notions of politics have been radically reconstituted.

Further Reading

Adorno, T. and Horkheimer, M. (1972 [1944]): "The culture industry: Enlightenment as mass deception." In *Dialectic of Enlightenment*. London: Verso.
Kelley, R. (1998): *Yo' Mama's Disfunktional! Fighting the Culture Wars in Urban America*. Boston: Beacon Press.
Street, J. (1997) *Politics and Popular Culture*. Cambridge: Polity Press.

29

Body Politics

ROBERTA SASSATELLI

Sociology has questioned the epistemological status of the scientific study of the body, so opening up the space for exploring the political implications of bodily representations and practices. Although the body-power relation was marginal until the work of Foucault and feminist theorists, classical social theory also contributed to its emergence as a problem. In Marx's writings on labor as a corporeal process and those of Weber on discipline, the body is seen as transformed into an instrument. In other social theory, however, such as Elias's work on body rationalization, Goffman's understanding of the symbolic functions of bodily comportment, and Bourdieu's theory of embodiment and mimesis, the body is also the paramount symbol of the subject's self-possession and degree of civilization. Much of Foucault's work is concerned with modern operations of power in which body and knowledge are central, including discipline, surveillance, medicalization, and confession. Under the influence of the poststructuralist turn influenced by Foucault, feminism has confronted the body more directly than it did previously. For poststructuralist feminists, gender is not the cultural representation of biological sex, but rather the process that produces the possibility of two distinct sexes. The postmodern "plasticity" of sex, crucially articulated in the work of Judith Butler, is also taken up in studies of technology, notably that of Donna Haraway in her discussion of "cyborgs." In general there has been a trend away from considering the body as a by-product of domination, toward seeing it as the focal point of conflicts over power.

A host of contemporary phenomena, ranging from AIDS to women's rights and assisted reproduction, from gay and lesbian movements to the Human Genome Project, have foregrounded the body–power relation. Rather than formulating encompassing body typologies (Turner 1984; O'Neill 1985), sociological theory has questioned the epistemological assumptions involved in the production of natural facts, decentering the physical body of the bio-medical sciences and exploring the political implications of body representations and practices. Social constructivism has spread its wings across the wide variety of bodily experience. Bodies have acquired a history (Feher et al. 1989; Porter 1991). They have become political not only because they are shaped by productive requirements or constrained by moral rules, but also because their "naturality" is traced back to claims to truth reflecting power differences. Together with bodily matters occupying pivotal positions in political struggles, criticism of binaries such as culture/nature, body/mind, gender/sex, male/female, other/self has flourished (Rorty 1980; Butler 1990; Laqueur 1990). Corporeality itself, the way we perceive and define what it is to have and to be a body, has been problematized (Crossley 1996). Its links with different dimensions of power – be it discursive, social, or strictly political – are being explored in an effort to specify how the present social order is reproduced and to what extent it can be challenged.

Mapping body politics is an exercise in complexity reduction. The territory is, above all, unstable not least for its recent consolidation as something to be mapped. The body politics coordinates have been explicitly charted as a result of two major theoretical earthquakes – the work of Michel Foucault and the development of feminist approaches. Still, although the body–power relation has long been ancillary to other social scientific frames (Shilling 1993), much of classical sociological thought has contributed to its emergence as a problem in its own right.

DISCIPLINE, CIVILIZATION, AND TASTE

The concern with the relationship between the changing needs of an emerging industrial society and its disciplinary techniques stems from the rise of sociological reflections. The standing that Karl Marx assigned to labor as a corporeal process goes well beyond the creation of economic value. Through labor human beings can either realize themselves in harmony with nature or be alienated from themselves and their bodies, as in the capitalist mode of production. With the development of manufacture, the laborer "performs one and the same operation" all his life, becomes "detail laborer" and converts "his whole body into the automatic, specialized implement of that operation" (Marx 1977 [1887]: 321). The modern machinery-based factory is even more oppressive, reducing to a minimum the resistance the "naturally elastic" barrier of the human body. Factory discipline "exhausts the nervous system to the uttermost, it does away with the many-sided play of the muscles, and confiscates every atom of freedom, both in bodily and intellectual activity" (1977 [1887]: 398). Capitalism thus steals corporeality its meaning: the worker "only feels himself freely active in his animal function – eating, drinking, procreating, or at most in his dwelling and dressing-up, etc.; in his human functions he no longer feels himself to be anything but an animal" (Marx 1981 [1844]: 66). Marx proposes the idea that the boundaries between animality and humanity are socially constructed. This construction is however the result of domination and exploitation, something to be criticized on the basis of a truly human and natural way of being in one's own body and deploying one's own labor.

Rather like Marx, Weber considers the modern factory as an example of the rational conditioning of work performances. However, as a "uniform," "exact," "consistently rationalized" and "methodically trained" conduct, discipline is both present in every society whenever masses are to be governed steadily and acquires a special character in modern times (Weber 1978 [1922]). Modern bureaucratic discipline is both rationalized and relies on people's aspirations, working through the subjects rather than simply upon them. Weber's analysis is rich in power effects: ascetic discipline worked for certain groups as a means of social mobility, crystallized into refined means of bureaucratic domination and promoted reformist attitudes legitimizing social change in the name of ever greater rationalization. Due to "sober and rational Puritan discipline" Cromwell's "men of conscience" were, for example, technically superior to their opponents the "Cavaliers," undisciplined "men of honor." Furthermore, like Bell's (1985) medieval "holy anoretics" who managed to transcend their female disadvantage demonstrating spiritual superiority via methodical self-starvation, the bourgeoisie ascetic regime legitimized their social advancement. If the "denaturalization" of the body realized through extraordinary conducts works as to set the "chosen" apart, protestant "wordly asceticism" tempers the repressive elements of religious asceticism contrasting with the deployment of one's own professional vocation and demands that every one be a *virtuoso* (Weber 1976 [1905]). Weber thus begins to show the extent to which certain forms of body government may work as techniques of both power and empowerment even in the age of secularization.

Body government is explicitly linked to the political by Norbert Elias. Elias traces body rationalization back to the advent of the modern nation-state while retaining a dynamic framework implicating embodiment in the struggles amongst individuals and groups. Historicizing the idea that our civilization is built upon the repression of instincts (Freud 1976 [1930]; Elias 1991 [1939]) shows that changes in the shape of political control brought about by the monopolization of physical violence gave way to pacified social spaces enforcing cooperation less charged with emotions and resulting in a change of personality structure: constraints through others are converted into self-constraints. The transformation of the ruling nobility from a class of knights into a class of self-restrained, calculating courtiers is conceptualized as both an example and a catalyst for such civilizing process. The courtization of the nobility takes place together with an increased upward thrust by bourgeois strata with the necessity on the part of the former to distinguish themselves from the latter. An unconsciously operating "repulsion of the vulgar" an "increasing sensibility to anything corresponding to a lesser sensibility of lower-ranking classes" permeates the conduct of life of the courtly upper class, and this "good taste" also represents a prestige value for such circles (1994 [1939]: 499). Through an imitation-emancipation dynamic, the "code of conduct," which the leading bourgeois groups develop when they finally take over the function of the upper class, is the product of an "amalgamation" of "refinement" and "virtue."

Elias' theory of civilization suggests that in the historical development of the West a particular "civilized" bodily conduct has become widespread. In contemporary society the "pattern of self-control" has become "all-embracing," having to be deployed toward every person. Above all, it has become "more complex" and "highly differentiated" to accommodate to increased functional differentiation and the emergence of a public/private divide. Spaces for the "controlled de-control of emotions" like sport and a variety of "pleasurable" and "exciting leisure pursuits," substituting for what is "lacking" in everyday life become more important (Elias and Dunning 1986). Such a picture contrasts with Freudian visions of repression, as well as Marcusian utopias of liberation (Marcuse 1969). Indeed we may consider that while individualization, affect control, formality, and a higher shame threshold have become mankind's "second nature," the de-naturalization of the body may take the shape of practices inspired by an idealized tribal communion, informality or even excess and the grotesque (Bataille 1985; Wouters 1986). Similar practices appear, on different occasions, as forms of resistance and subversion attempting to re-define society's power structure, or as functional to its reproduction. Many commentators have associated the former with community circuits and the latter with commercialization (Lasch 1979; O'Neill 1985). Still, while research on subcultural forms shows that pleasures mediated by consumer goods are by no means merely oppressive, ostensibly counter-cultural bodily conducts or drastic body modification have been indicated as politically ambivalent. Working as a desire-producing machine allowing for the experience of dionysian communality and a desubjectified state of ecstasy, the rave scene appears to be based on a politics of difference which is indifferent to all political values other than the new (Jordan 1995). Scarification or extreme piercing on the verge of "neo-primitivism" makes clear that the body is a potential site of resistance to standardization and yet may be depoliticized as private symptom of disquiet or incorporated into the mainstream as exotic (Favazza 1996).

The trajectory indicated by the classics is twofold. On the one hand, the body is transformed into an instrument for work and labor, a utility, a function. On the other, however, the body continues to operate as the paramount symbol for the subject to demonstrate his or her being self-possessed, civilized, or otherwise valuable. The symbolic function of bodily demeanor has become prey for microsociological approaches to identity, notably in the work of Erving Goffman. As individuals' vulnerability in face-to-face interaction becomes ceremonial and locally specific, a finer body language develops. Ever more sophisticated bodily markers indicate both "diffuse social statuses" and individual "character," i.e. the actor's "conception of himself," his or her "normality" or "abnormality" (Goffman 1963a). Modern selfhood is itself only understandable in relation to the ceremonial distance that individuals keep during interaction. The "air bubble" around the body helps projecting a "sacred," "elusive," "deep" self (Goffman 1967, 1963b), something which may well constitute the taken-for-granted basis for human rights to hold still in western affectivity (Schneider 1996). Body language, however, can only to a degree be spoken strategically. As a language it talks of the subject beyond his or her intentions, and as a body it is never silent: "(a)lthough an individual can stop talking he cannot stop communicating through body idiom, he must say either the right thing or the wrong thing. He cannot say nothing" (Goffman 1963b: 35).

Like Elias, Goffman implies that with modernity there has been a shift in the attitudes towards natural functions which is by no means power-free. We could say with Georg Simmel (1997 [1908]: 118) that the modern general "aspiration to hygiene" is accompanied by embodied social distinctions to the point that "the social question is not only an ethical one, but also a question of smell." The perceptions of dirt and cleanliness have been exposed as varying between cultures and across time, being implicated in power structures (Douglas 1966; Vigarello 1988). Mary Douglas, in particular, has shown that as "a system of natural symbols" the individual body is a metaphor for the vulnerabilities and the anxieties of the political body making. If what is inside and outside the body provides a language for discussing what is inside and outside the social, it would be a mistake to think that the contemporary confinement of purity into the scientific domain of the "hygienic" marks a break with previous moralism. Indeed, the morality of bodily codes is powerfully illustrated by the potency of AIDS as a metaphor of decadence and deviance (Sontag 1988).

For all its force the metaphorical approach may risk figuring practical activity and the body merely as representation. Re-elaborating on the notion of "techniques of the body" as mimetic *habitus* assembled for the individual "by all his education, by the whole society to which he belongs, in the place he occupies it" (Mauss 1973 [1936]: 76), Pierre Bourdieu (1977a) has composed his theory of practice with a concern that human experience is not to be understood in terms of cognitive and linguistic models, but in terms of embodiment and mimesis. These are, in turn, implicated in a set of classificatory systems which "are not so much means of knowledge as means of power, harnessed to social functions and overtly or covertly aimed at satisfying the interests of a group" (Bourdieu 1984a: 477). Although accused of ignoring dissent and social transformation, Bourdieu has helped conceptualize taste as embodied disposition which works as symbolic power naturalizing the existing system of power differences. For Bourdieu, the state of the body is itself the realization of a "political mythology": lifestyle regimes reflect the cultural genesis of tastes from the specific point within the social space from which individuals originate – they are incorporated through the most elementary everyday movements inculcating the equivalence between physical and social space. Even "in its most natural appearance...volume, size, weight, etc." the body is a social product: "the unequal distribution among social classes of corporeal properties" is both realized concretely through "working conditions" and "consumption habits," and perceived through "categories and classification systems which are not independent of such distribution" (Bourdieu 1977b: 51).

BIO-POWER, SURVEILLANCE AND MEDICALIZATION

Much of Foucault's work strives to illustrate modern operations of power in which body and knowledge are central. Despite a number of criticisms – for attributing primacy to the discursive over the non-discursive realm; for overstretching the notion of power; for reducing the subject to the body and the body to a passive text; or for bestowing a somewhat essentialist quality of resistance to subjugated forms of embodiment – Foucault's work has been pivotal in recognizing that the body is directly implicated in a political field. Power relations do not simply "repress" it, they rather produce it, having "an immediate hold on it; they invest it, train it, torture it, force it to carry out tasks, to perform ceremonies and to emit signs" (Foucault 1977: 25). Power, in turn, operates as a "microphysics," as strategies and tactics working at an intermediate level between body and institutions, through everyday practices. Foucault has thus helped place emphasis on local and intimate operations of power, widening the scope of the political, something which has influenced, if not satisfied, a number of critical approaches.

In *Discipline and Punish* Foucault (1977) continues the classical preoccupation with the modern transformation of the body into a useful and docile instrument. Organizations such as schools, hospitals, armies, factories, and prisons are described as disciplinary institutions consolidating routinary systems of power working through the embodiment of self-surveillance. The mechanized organization and routinized training intimated by Marx and Weber is thoroughly analyzed by Foucault's description of discipline as coordinating people's movements and functions through time and space. Foucault however considers the body, rather than the subject, as the direct object of control. All disciplinary institutions may indeed be understood as laboratories where a new form of political rationality developed. The modern notion of sovereignty is coterminous with a shift from the right of death to the power over life, a "bio-politics" consisting of an investment in the human body (conceived as an object to be manipulated) and of an interest for the human kind (with scientific categories such as population and species replacing juridical ones as objects of political attention).

The idea that the modern nation-state consolidates itself by stimulating life to grow into prescribed forms has been widely influential. Foucault himself addressed welfare provision and the whole idea of tutelary public authority as related to an open-ended expansion of the conduct of government (Foucault 1988a; see also Hewitt 1991). Rather than an "étaticization" of society, however, Foucault suggests the inclusion of the state in a particular style of political reasoning defined as "governmentality" or the presumption that life conducts can, should, and must be administered by authority (Foucault 1991; see also Hindess, chapter 4, in this volume). Indeed, through a multifarious network of governance, regulatory interventions are increasingly important in the management of human bodies. This includes practices as diverse as insurance technologies (Defert 1991; Castel and Ewald 1991); diffuse, localized, and internalized techniques governing consumption of allegedly dangerous products such as alcohol (Valverde 1998); medical regulation concerning the boundaries of life – euthanasia and abortion on the one hand, assisted reproduction on the other (Bordo 1993; Hendin 1997); and the consolidation of a national and international jurisprudence concerning the boundaries within life – i.e. addressing citizenship rights or human rights in terms of sex change (Haslam 1986).

Whatever the definition of the political, nothing can illustrate better the insidious duplicity of bio-politics than the analogies between the eugenic measures developed in many western countries and those developed by the Nazi dictatorship (Burleigh and Wipperman 1991). Initially fuelled by hopes to eradicate defective genes, a huge number of persons were sterilized without their consent from the beginning of the century up to the early sixties in the US, mostly belonging to social groups considered racially inferior like African-Americans and Native Americans (Reilly 1991). Attention to the link between population control and racial issues has recently been renewed by the development in Europe of an intense debate about immigration. In this context, Foucauldian approaches may provide an historically-based perspective on racialized social relations starting from the establishment of a colonial order where the European individual and political bodies are set against a savage "other" (Stoler 1995).

Together with the objectifying qualities of modern political rationality, Foucault envisaged subjectifying ones: a shift in the notion of sovereignty is echoed by a shift in the notion of subjectivity, from subjects with ascribed identities to free citizens who are asked to produce themselves. Foucault's later work does not do without the body, though. It rather shifts to the modern preoccupation with uncovering one's "true" self predicated on body–mind dualism. In *The History of Sexuality* he addresses the practices by which individuals were led to acknowledge themselves as "subjects of desire," where desire located in the body contains "the truth of their being, be it natural or fallen" (Foucault 1985: 5). The development of psychoanalysis epitomizes the fact that the "truth" of individuals is no longer linked to their position in the universal order of things, but is constructed around a normalizing notion of inner responsibility requiring an endless hermeneutics of the self. While psychoanalysis is part of the "confessional" machinery that it ostensibly redresses, repression is not accounted for as an historical fact. On the contrary, power takes on a productive character as testified by the "multiplication of discourses concerning sex" in the fields of exercise of power which "exploit it as the secret" (Foucault 1978: 17, 35).

Even Foucault's earlier works on the medicalization of insanity and the birth of medical discourse may be included in this picture if we consider that modern political rationality not only makes organic life enter the art of the possible, but also does so by employing and negotiating with a number of expert discourses. In particular, a concern with medical truths implicated in a network of power relations is developed in the *Birth of the Clinic* (Foucault 1976). Examining medical treatises, Foucault analyzes the metamorphosis which leads to the establishment of pathological anatomy: disease becomes a "collection of symptoms" necessarily expressed in the human body and integral to the disease itself rather than an abstract pathological "essence." This is accompanied by a medical "gaze that dominates" the body by rendering its depth a visible object, with the anatomy lesson becoming itself a powerful representation of political power as in Rembrandt's famous painting. When the notion of a pathological essence infiltrating the body is replaced by the idea of the body itself becoming ill, death is transformed into disease and degeneration, a dispersed and uneven failure of the body. This opens the space for the medicalization of death, for its treatment as dirt, and for the institutionalization of the dying (Aries 1978; Elias 1994 [1939]). Similarly, while in the greco-roman tradition sexual intercourse was part of a regime of life governed through a measure/excess dialectic, with modernity it was inscribed in a therapeutic model working on the basis of the normal/pathological distinction (Foucault 1978; 1985). The web of scientific practices operating on the body produced a *"scientia sexualis"* constructing sexuality as an empirical and natural object of enquiry and as the secret essence of the individual. Once again truth is revealed as a historically specific category:

the body has no inherent truth; rather, truths on the body are constructed through various categorizing strategies.

FEMINISM(S), TECHNOLOGIES, AND DISCOURSES

Since its emergence feminist thought has conceived the body as a site of female oppression. However, while early socialist-feminists were striving to counter-balance the gender-blindness of much classical sociology by conceptualizing the interdependence of capitalism and patriarchy, recent works confront the body more directly. First, feminist research has considered the minute and mundane practices that associate women with the body confining them to a life centered on its maintenance (Wolf 1991; Bordo 1993; Weitz 1998). These feminist concerns can now be usefully matched by research addressing masculine embodiment in its own right. If the ways men inhabit their bodies have emerged as correlated to patriarchy, studies addressing traditional symbols of masculinity such as muscles, and less obvious areas of male involvement such as fashion, show that old visions of masculinity are negotiated in the face of the changing power balances between the sexes (Wacquant 1995; Nixon 1996).

Secondly, contemporary feminism has developed a criticism of the earlier gender/sex division which inscribed sex in a dehistoricized biological difference. Despite scepticism about Foucault's inattention to the condition of women, the poststructuralist turn within feminism has changed the framing of gender while retaining it as its key organizing category. Together with a politics stressing the diversity amongst women (hooks 1982), gender has become understood not as a cultural representation of a biological given, but as the process that produces in the body the possibility of two distinct sexes. The biological foundation is exposed as only apparently clear: gendered bodies are unstable cultural constructions, whose purpose is to delimit and contain the "threatening absence of boundaries between human bodies" (Epstein and Straub 1991). This has given way to rethinking gender/sex as a semiotics of corporeality constituting identities and self-representations.

The author most associated with such a poststructuralist turn is Judith Butler. In *Gender Trouble* Butler (1990) proposes to deconstruct the system of signs through which feminine identity has been linked to the heterosexual matrix. Considering gender as a performative, something which "is always a doing, although not a doing by a subject that comes before the deed," Butler insists that as a "continuous discursive practice," gender "remains open to intervention and re-signification" (1990: 25, 33). Having dismissed expressive notions of femininity, she believes that the realization of a feminist politics of the body is to be built upon the same technologies and everyday practices inscribing gender/sexuality onto the body. Subversive performances such as cross-dressing are thus contemplated as revealing the "imitative nature" of gender. Despite the lack of sociological analysis, Butler's agenda implies an emphasis on how different social contexts offer local rules consolidating gender through ritualistic repetitions. Drawing on Bourdieu's *habitus*, in her later work Butler stresses that this consolidation takes the shape of a social "materialization of corporeality whereby "the 'force' of the performative is never fully separable from bodily force" (Butler 1993: 9, 1997: 141). As Bourdieu (1998) himself writes, using amongst others Nancy Henley's work on body politics and non-verbal communication (Henley 1977), gender cannot be reduced to a voluntaristic act, being consolidated both in matter – posture, demeanor, size, etc. – and in symbols – classifications and categories – which speak of the subject. Butler's subversion is thereby revealed as fragile, always in danger of surreptitiously reproducing dualism. Still, her theoretical move clearly signals the aspiration to recuperate corporeality in a postdualistic fashion. To this end the body/power relation is openly constructed in such a way that the body is the weaker, plastic term of the equation, with the result that some feminists have accused her of endorsing a postmodern paradigm of plasticity which obliterates "real" differences.

Butler has been crucial in consolidating the study of the politics of sex and sexuality. The normative convergence of the male/female dichotomy and heterosexuality was already implicit in Foucault's (1980b) presentation of the memories of Herculine Barbin and, above all, it was clearly related to performativity in Harold Garfinkel's (1967) well-known essay on Agnes. Here Garfinkel analyzes how Agnes, an "intersexed" person, tries to "secure her rights to live in the elected sex status," learning to be a woman while presenting herself as a "natural" one. Agnes' struggle for a sex-change operation which would satisfy her male boyfriend too, shows the potency of the male/female duality and discloses the performative, imitative nature of femininity without assimilating all attributes or performances. Above all, the different chances available to Agnes and to the nineteenth-century hermaphrodite Herculine show that the plasticity of the truth of the body has penetrated materiality, consolidating paths for unprecedented physical transformation.

An approach to plasticity is clearly articulated in Donna Haraway's work on "cyborgs," Haraway (1991) argues for a feminist agenda addressing the cultural politics of an info-technic society that has modified the "nature" of the organic. The "cyborg," as a "hybrid of machine and organism," is at the same time a "creature of reality" – witness, for example, the increasing acceptance of cosmetic surgery (Davis 1995) – and a "creature of fiction," an "imaginative resource." As such it works as a political platform to rethink the boundaries between animality and humanity, the artificial and the organic, the physical and non-physical. In particular, the "cyborg" is set as a creature of a postgender world providing an "argument for pleasure in the confusion of boundaries and for responsibility in their construction" and a new "ontology" for an "oppositional" and "utopian" politics (Haraway 1991: 150–1). Despite its proclaimed utopian tone, Haraway's work has offered a new perspective on how technology, traditionally identified as oppressive for women and alien to them, may become a major source of female resistance. Feminists have reappraised the potential of assisted reproduction. Approaches stressing that pre-natal medicine and assisted reproduction are forms of patriachical domination undermining women's rights, displaying dangerous continuities with eugenics, producing anxieties and dependency, and depoliticizing social differences (Scutt 1990) have been questioned by those who salute new reproductive technologies as postmodern forms of deconstruction allowing for new ways of being (Farquhar 1996).

It is important to notice that rather than simply being blurred, the key analytical categories organizing our world and deriving from the division between technology and nature are being reconfigured and fought over. New technological domains are ambivalent spaces. The idea that new information technologies offer a world of masquerade in which we can represent our bodies with complete flexibility does not mean that the body is transcended altogether nor that the heterosexual ideology disappears (Slater 1998). The representation of technology is itself ambivalent. In contemporary science fiction dualistic thinking is articulated differently but it is not eluded (Holland 1995) while the popularization of genetics does not do without a rhetoric of nature and the (re)generation of value differences (Nelkin and Lindee 1995).

CONCLUDING REMARKS

Human bodies have been seen as clay, molded by political and economic constraints. With an emphasis on the power effects of classificatory systems, bodies have also been conceived as symbols speaking of the place their bearers occupy within the social order as well as of what counts as order and disorder. More recently bodies have been described as texts, emphasizing not so much their metaphoric quality, but rather readership and persuasion, the power to create reality through interpretation and representation. The immateriality discerned in textuality has been amended by a notion of the body as mimesis, whereby the body is practiced in every day life, shaped by dealing with the situations, rules, and classifications encountered. Despite their differences, Foucault, Bourdieu, and Butler seem to incline towards such notion. Furthermore, although each emphasizes different aspects of power – respectively bio-politics as part of governmentality, taste as related to political economy and symbolic power, the incorporation of binaries and classificatory power – they all try to widen the notion of power from its confinement to the political strictly conceived.

The map which I have been drawing is therefore both a topographic device and a trajectory for navigation. Within the social sciences, sociology in particular, there has been a general move away from considering the shaping of the body merely as a ghastly by-product of domination – like in Marx's analysis of the physical effects of factory work – and towards the designation of embodiment as a crucial aspect of social struggles and structure. What body politics teaches us is that the body is a battlefield, molded by conflicts between groups with different values and different political and economic interests. Furthermore, the body – its images, definitions, boundaries, etc. – is itself the focal point for conflicts over the shape of power, for the modern power to govern life can only crystallize a variety of identities which in turn become the basis for resistance against it. This seems to require a new conception of politics, one which considers, to restate Foucault, that we have become very peculiar animals, animals in whose politics our own life as living beings is put into question. This should help us consider the ambivalence of plasticity. Body politics is coterminous with the progressive consolidation of a notion of the body as plastic, both in its meanings and its materiality. To be sure, plasticity often takes the explicitly programmatic tone of a political project. Precisely because of this we cannot be satisfied with its location as the blind spot of our reflection on the body-power relation and should address the ways in which it is implicated in formations of both domination and freedom.

Further Reading

Brook, B. 1999: *Feminist Perspectives on the Body.* Harlow: Addison-Wesley-Longman.
Harvey, J. and Sparks, R. 1991: "The politics of the body in the context of modernity." *Quest* 43: 164–89.
Turner, B. S. 1987: "The rationalization of the body: Reflections on modernity and discipline." In S. Whimster and S. Lash (eds.) *Max Weber. Rationality and Modernity.* London: Allen & Unwin.

30

Citizenship
Citizenship and Gender

Ruth Lister

Feminist scholarship has revealed how citizenship has been male, in theory and practice. Central to this is the gendered public–private dichotomy, which has contributed to women's admission to citizenship on male terms and also to the way this has generally been ignored by theorists of citizenship. Citizenship is itself a contested concept, with roots in the very different traditions of liberalism and republicanism. What is needed is a critical synthesis of the rights and responsibilities of political participation. The three main feminist approaches to citizenship are "gender-neutrality," working with a model of women as equal with men; "gender-differentiation," working with a model of the sexes as different; and "gender-pluralism," in which both women and men are seen as members of multiple groups. Lister argues that the regendering of citizenship requires change in public and private spheres to enable both women and men to combine paid work and caring responsibilities.

"Is citizenship gendered?" The answer to this question, posed by Sylvia Walby (1994) has to be a resounding "yes." Citizenship has always been gendered in the sense that women and men have stood in a different relationship to it, to the disadvantage of women. Yet, for much of its history, a veil of gender-neutrality has obscured the nature of this differential relationship. Today, as feminist theorists have stripped away this veil, the challenge is to reconceptualize citizenship in gendered terms in the image of women as well as men. We are thus talking about citizenship and gender from two angles: as an historical relationship and as a normative or political and theoretical project.

This chapter will discuss each in turn. It will focus in particular on the key debates around what we might call the "regendering" of citizenship. These relate to the meaning of citizenship itself and, more centrally, to the nature of this "re-gendering": is the aim a genuinely "gender-neutral" or a "gender-differentiated" model? Or can we, as I shall argue, avoid getting stuck in this particular formulation of the traditional "equality" vs. "difference" dilemma through a synthesis of the two and through a pluralist "conception of citizenship which would accommodate all social cleavages simultaneously"? (Leca 1992: 30).

CITIZENSHIP AND GENDER: AN HISTORICAL RELATIONSHIP

Citizenship as both a theory and a practice operates simultaneously as a force for inclusion and exclusion, both within and at the borders of nation-states (see Soysal, chapter 31, in this volume). Women have been denied the full and effective title of citizen for much of history, ancient and modern. The twentieth-century mainstream theorization of citizenship has tended to ignore the ways in which women's gradual achievement of civil, political, and social rights often followed a different pattern from men's. Likewise, it has tended to dismiss women's earlier exclusion as a historical aberration, now more or less effectively remedied. Thus, for example, Adrian Oldfield asserts that it does not "require too much imagination... to extend the concept of 'citizen' to include women"; leaving aside Machiavelli and even allowing for the "citizen-soldier," there is, he claims, "nothing aggressively male" about the concept (1990: 59).

The excavations of feminist scholarship have, on the contrary, revealed how, in both theory and practice, despite its claims to universalism, citizenship has been quintessentially male. While the purpose of these excavations has generally been to spotlight women's exclusion from citizenship, critical studies in masculinities are beginning to problematize the other side of the gender equation: men's relationship to citizenship. Jeff Hearn (1997), for instance, underlines the need to interrogate "the silence that has persisted on the category of men [as gendered actors] in both theory and practice around citizenship," but in a way which both names and decenters men.

The exposure of the quintessential maleness of citizenship helps us to understand that women's exclusion (and the chequered nature of their inclusion) far from being an aberration has been integral to the theory and practice of citizenship. Nowhere was this more obvious than in classical Greece where the active participation of male citizens in the public sphere was predicated on women's labor in the "private" domestic sphere which rendered them as unfit for citizenship. The public–private dichotomy, and the male–female qualities associated with it, stands at the heart of the gendered citizenship relationship. On the "public" side stands the disembodied citizen *qua* man who displays the necessary qualities of impartiality, rationality, independence, and political agency. This is upheld by the "private" side to which embodied women are relegated and from whence they are deemed incapable of developing the "male" qualities of citizenship (Pateman 1989). The continued power of this deeply gendered dichotomy has meant that women's admission to citizenship has been on male terms. It has also meant that much mainstream theorizing about citizenship continues to discount the relevance of what happens in the private sphere to the practice of citizenship in the public sphere. Thus, for example, it ignores the ways in which the gendered division of labor in the private sphere shapes the access of both women and men to the public sphere and to the political, economic, and social rights of citizenship which derive from such access (Lister 1997).

WHY RE-GENDER CITIZENSHIP?

For some, the historically gendered nature of citizenship, together with its inherently exclusive tendencies at the boundaries of nation-states, renders it a concept of little value for contemporary feminism. This rejection of the very concept of citizenship is rarely articulated in print, although Gillian Pascall (1993) expresses deep ambivalence about a concept which is so problematic for women. Likewise, Anne Phillips has warned that "in a period in which feminism is exploring the problems in abstract universals, citizenship may seem a particularly unpromising avenue to pursue" (1993: 87). Nevertheless, it is an avenue which has become positively crowded by feminist scholars, in a wide range of countries, intent on re-gendering citizenship from the standpoints of women (for an overview, see Voet 1998).

This feminist preoccupation with citizenship in part reflects a wider desire to (re)claim concepts which have been hi-jacked in the interests of men. Citizenship is a pivotal contested concept in contemporary political and social theory. As such, feminists cannot afford to be absent from the contest. More positively, citizenship is seen by many as an analytical and political tool of considerable potential value (Walby 1994; Lister 1997; Yuval-Davis 1997; Bussemaker and Voet 1998; Voet 1998). It has also been deployed by a range of social movements, in which women are active, reminding us that women do not necessarily claim citizenship simply as women but as, for example, Black women, disabled women or lesbian women.

Given citizenship's status as a "contested concept," it is hardly surprising that the issue of how to re-gender it is not straightforward. The debates can be grouped around two questions concerning the nature of citizenship and the nature of its re-gendering.

THE NATURE OF CITIZENSHIP

One reason why citizenship is a contested concept is that it has its roots in two very different, and at times antagonistic, political traditions: liberalism and civic republicanism. The former casts citizenship as a *status* involving, primarily, rights accorded to individuals; the latter casts it as a *practice* involving responsibilities to the wider society (Heater 1990; Oldfield 1990). Whereas under classical liberalism, rights were confined to the civil and political spheres, the twentieth century saw their extension to the social sphere and more recently their embrace of new categories, such as reproductive rights, demanded by social movements. Within civic republicanism, the citizen is primarily a political actor, exercising "his" civic duty within the public sphere. In the late twentieth century, though, the more prominent duties discourse centers on work obligations as one element in what has been described as a communitarian strand to citizenship (Bussemaker and Voet 1998).

Rights

Until relatively recently, it is a rights discourse which has been more dominant. Women have struggled to achieve equal rights with men in the civil, political, and social spheres as crucial to their achievement of full citizenship. Although some contemporary feminists reject a legal rights discourse as individualistic and male-inspired, many others acknowledge "the dual nature of the law – as an agent of emancipation as well as oppression" and that, for all its shortcomings, it "has played a vital role in securing for women the prerequisites of citizenship" (Vogel 1988: 155).

Political Participation

From the perspective of re-gendering citizenship, there have been two main sources of challenge to a rights-based approach, centering on political participation and on promoting care as a citizenship obligation. In a recent text on feminism and citizenship, Rian Voet argues that "instead of seeing citizenship as the means to realize rights, we should see rights as one of the means to realize equal citizenship. This implies that feminism ought to be more than a movement for women's rights; it ought to be a movement for women's participation" (1998: 73). She goes on to argue that having acquired citizenship rights, it is the exercise of those rights, especially in the political sphere, which is crucial to the full development of women's citizenship as part of what she calls "an active and sex-equal citizenship" (1998: ch. 11).

The most forceful case for a feminist civic republican model of citizenship is that made by Mary Dietz. She advocates "a vision of citizenship" which is "expressly political" and, more exactly, "participatory and democratic." In this vision, politics involves "the collective and participatory engagement of citizens in the determination of the affairs of their community" and we conceive of ourselves as "'speakers of words and doers of deeds' mutually participating in the public realm." It is only, she contends, when active political participation is valued as an expression of citizenship in contrast to the "politically barren" construction of the "citizen as bearer of rights" alone, that feminists will "be able to claim a truly liberatory politics of their own" (1987: 13–15). Other feminists, sympathetic to Dietz's vision, such as Anne Phillips (1991, 1993) and Iris Young (1990), nevertheless caution against an uncritical reading of civic republicanism which, *inter alia*, defines the political in narrow terms and ignores the domestic constraints on many women's political participation.

Responsibilities

Central to these domestic constraints is the unpaid care work which many women still undertake in the home. Under present models of citizenship, such work does not tend to appear in the pantheon of citizenship responsibilities as does paid work, nor does it carry the same access to social rights. This has led some feminists, such as Pascall (1993), to be wary of claims to citizenship based on duties. In contrast, Diemut Bubeck has suggested that by focusing on citizenship obligations, feminists can turn conventional understandings of citizenship on their head through the introduction "of a revised conception of citizenship in which the performance of her or his share of care has become a general citizen's obligation" (1995: 29). Such a reconceptualization could be particularly significant in the context of debates about the work responsibilities of lone parents and I will return to it below (Lister 1999a).

A CRITICAL SYNTHESIS

Most would accept that citizenship involves a balance of rights and responsibilities; what is at issue is where that balance should lie and what should be the link, if any, between them. With regard to whether the re-gendering of citizenship is better pursued in terms of citizenship as a status or as a practice, my own position (echoing that of, for example, Chantal Mouffe 1992) is that we need a critical synthesis of the two. While the rights and participatory approaches to citizenship have developed along separate parallel tracks, they are not necessarily in conflict. On the contrary, they can be seen as mutually supportive, even if a tension remains between their primary concerns with the individual or the wider community. The development of women's position as citizens in the twentieth century can be understood as the outcome of the interplay between women's exercise of their political capacities and their emergent social rights.

The re-gendering of citizenship needs, first, to embrace both individual rights (and in particular social and reproductive rights) and political participation, broadly defined to include informal modes of politics, and, second, to analyze the relationship between the two (Sarvasy and Siim 1994). The notion of human agency helps us to knit the two together. Citizenship as participation can be understood as an expression of human agency in the political arena, broadly defined; citizenship as rights enables people to exercise their agency as citizens. As citizenship rights remain the object of political struggles to defend, reinterpret, and extend them, a dynamic is set in motion in which the rights and participatory elements of citizenship stand in a dialectical relationship with one another. Re-gendering citizenship in this way is particularly important in challenging the construction of women (and especially "minority group" women) as passive victims, while not losing sight of the structural and institutional constraints on their ability to act as citizens.

THE RE-GENDERING OF CITIZENSHIP

The different approaches to the re-gendering of citizenship can be summed up under the three headings of "gender-neutrality," "gender-differentiation," and "gender-pluralism." The first works with a model of women as equal with men; the second with a model of women as different from men, thereby reflecting the long-standing "equality vs. difference" debate within feminism. In the third model both women and men are members of multiple groups and/or holders of multiple identities. Individual theorists do not always fit neatly into any of the three categories, so that any views cited here should not necessarily be taken as definitive of the particular author's thinking. In my own work, I have attempted to develop a "woman-friendly" conceptualization of citizenship which draws on aspects of each of these models (Lister 1997).

The Gender-neutral Citizen

The model of the gender-neutral citizen is most commonly associated with liberal feminism, although it is not necessarily confined to it. The emphasis is on equal rights and equal obligations. The gender of the citizen should be irrelevant to the allocation and exercise of these rights and obligations. From the time of the French Revolution to the present day, some feminists have used the egalitarian and universalistic promise of citizenship in the cause of women's emancipation and autonomy (Bryson 1992; Voet 1998).

In the political sphere, this has meant an emphasis on women's full and equal participation in formal politics, first through the winning of the vote and then through formal political representation. Women's representation in parliament and government has been pressed as a matter of equality and justice rather than as a means of promoting a particular set of interests or a "different" way of doing politics (see Squires, chapter 34, in this volume).

In the social sphere, the priority has been to enable women to compete on equal terms with men in the labor market. This in turn opens up access to the social rights of citizenship linked to labor market status through social insurance schemes. In both cases, women are better able to achieve the economic independence seen as critical to full and effective citizenship. This approach prioritizes effective sex discrimination and equal pay legislation combined with "family-friendly" employment laws and practices which enable women to combine paid work with their caring responsibilities in the home. Its logic underlies the social security rules operative in many countries which require lone mothers and fathers claiming social security to be available for paid work (once their children reach a certain age, which in a number of US states is as young as 12 weeks) on the same basis as unemployed people.

While traditionally proponents of a gender-neutral citizenship have tended to focus on the changes in the public sphere necessary to achieve this ideal, today there tends to be a greater recognition of the changes which also need to be made in the private sphere, most notably in the gendered division of labor. A more equitable division of labor is, for example, central to Susan Moller Okin's vision of the "genderless" family and society which she sees as crucial to the transformation of women's position as citizens (1989: ch. 8). Likewise, Anne Phillips, one of the more prominent exponents of a gender-neutral citizenship places great emphasis on a more equitable domestic division of labor as providing the context in which "the notion of the citizen could begin to assume its full meaning, and people could participate as equals in deciding their common goals." Phillips' "vision is of a world in which gender should become less relevant and the abstractions of humanity more meaningful." However, she acknowledges that in the transition to such a world, an emphasis on sexual differentiation is necessary in order "to redress the imbalance that centuries of oppression have wrought" (1991: 7).

Phillips is thus well aware of the dangers of a gender-neutral model of citizenship in a gender-differentiated world and of lapsing into a false gender-neutrality which in practice privileges the male. Others see such dangers as inherent in a gender-neutral conception of citizenship. Ursula Vogel, for instance, dismisses as "futile" any attempt to insert women into "the ready-made, gender-neutral spaces of traditional conceptions of citizenship" which are a chimera (1994: 86). Kathleen B. Jones is critical of gender-neutral approaches which require women to mold themselves to fit a citizenship template which has developed in the interests of men and which ignore "the ways in which gender, as a socially constructed, historical reality, reflects different ways of being and knowing that fundamentally affect the practice and meaning of civic duties and responsibilities, and the enjoyment of civil and political rights" (1988: 20)

The Gender-differentiated Citizen

In an exploration of the possible meaning of citizenship in a "woman-friendly polity," Jones contends that:

> a polity that is friendly to women and the multiplicity of their interests must root its democracy in the experiences of women and transform the practice and concept of citizenship to fit thcsc varied experiences, rather than simply transform women to accommodate the practice of citizenship as it traditionally has been defined. (1990: 811)

Jones is primarily concerned with women's *political* citizenship. The dilemma she poses is "how to recognize the political relevance of sexual differences and how to include these differences within definitions of political action and civic virtue without constructing sexually segregated norms of citizenship?" (1988: 18). Historically, attempts to incorporate sexual "differences within definitions of political action" tended to be rooted in "maternalist" arguments for treating motherhood as the equivalent of a male civic republicanism grounded in active political participation and the ability to bear arms. Motherhood represented the embodiment of difference, for only women, *qua* mothers, could bear the next generation of citizcns (Pateman 1992). Another strand in maternalist thought made the case for women's full political participation with reference to the qualities and gifts which women could bring to politics as mothers.

Within contemporary feminism, this argument is echoed in Sarah Ruddick's exposition of "maternal thinking" which she defines as "the intellectual capacities [a mother] develops, the judgements she makes, the metaphysical attitudes she assumes, the values she affirms" (1989: 24). Although Ruddick does not herself write explicitly about citizenship, other "social feminists," such as Jean Bethke Elshtain, have made the connection for her. It is in Elshtain's work that the torch of political maternalism burns brightest among contemporary feminists. She celebrates mothering and the private familial sphere in contrast to a negative picture of "an ideal of citizenship and civic virtue that features a citizenry grimly going about their collective duty, or an elite band of citizens in their 'public space' cut off from a world that includes most of the rest of us" (1981: 351).

The maternalist approach has been attacked by those who see it as construct-ing the "sexually segregated norms of citizenship" which Jones warns against. As Carol Pateman (1992) has reminded us, it is just such sexually segregated norms which have served to subordinate and marginalize women as political citizens. Dietz rejects "maternal thinking" as the basis for citizenship on the grounds that it reinforces "a one-dimensional view of women as creatures of the family" and that it does not "necessarily promote the kind of democratic politics social feminism purports to foster." On the contrary, she argues that the exclusiveness and inequalities of power associated with the mother–child relationship make it a poor model for democratic citizenship (1985: 20; 1987).

In the face of the critique of a maternalist construction of citizenship, a number of feminists, sympathetic to some of the values promoted by maternal-ism, are arguing for a non-maternalistic conceptualization of difference in pol-itics around the broader notion of care and an ethic of care, which is not confined to women. This is underpinned by a commitment to human interde-pendence rather than a concern with (in)dependence, as in the gender-neutral model (Sevenhuijsen 1998). The case for care as a resource for political citizen-ship has been put by Bubeck (1995) on the grounds that the private concerns, values, skills, and understandings associated with the practice of caring can all enhance public practices of citizenship. One arena in which they can do so, in particular, is that of informal, often community-based, politics, which is often grounded in concerns which derive from women's responsibilities for care (Lister 1997). Part of Jones' case for a gender-differentiated citizenship is the need for "a new grammar and ethos of political action" which incorporates women's polit-ical activities rather than simply mirroring male definitions of what counts as politics (1988, 1990: 789).

The momentum for the incorporation of care into our thinking about citizen-ship is, though, stronger in relation to social citizenship. Again, historically maternalism has played a pivotal role in attempts to forge a gender-differentiated conceptualization of social citizenship. In the early twentieth century, in a number of countries, certain feminists drew on maternalist arguments to make the case for women's access to social rights. For instance, in both the US and Britain, the campaign for the endowment of motherhood drew on the imagery of motherhood as national service, the equivalent of men's military service, in the construction of their citizenship (Pederson 1990; Sarvasy 1992).

Today, a number of feminists are drawing on feminist theorizing around care to make the case for the incorporation of "care in the definition of citizenship, so the rights to time to care and to receive care are protected" as part of a more inclusive approach to citizenship (Knijn and Kremer 1997: 357). One policy implication often drawn is that those who stay at home to provide care should receive payment. Others, while agreeing with the need to place more value on care for citizenship, are worried lest such payments should undermine women's claims to citizenship through equal participation in the labor market.

Thus even if the care approach, by focusing on women's responsibilities rather than their supposed qualities, and by acknowledging that care is not gender-specific, is less vulnerable than maternalism to a biological essentialism that freezes the differences between women and men, it still shares certain risks with it. These are the risk of marginalization, mentioned earlier, and also the risk of ignoring the differences between women. Some disabled feminists, for instance, reject the very language of care as casting disabled people in the role of dependants and argue that the discourse of caring is incompatible with a commitment to disabled people's rights to be equal citizens (Morris 1993, 1996; see also Meekosha and Dowse 1997).

More broadly, Mouffe criticizes those who attempt to replace the false universalism of traditional conceptualizations of citizenship with "a sexually differentiated, 'bi-gendered' conception of the individual and to bring women's so-called specific tasks into the very definition of citizenship." Instead of "making sexual difference politically relevant to its definition" she argues for "a new conception of citizenship where sexual difference should become effectively nonpertinent" (1992b: 376).

The Gender-pluralist Citizen

This is not an argument for gender-neutrality but for what Mouffe terms "a radical democratic conception of citizenship" (1992b: 377). She interprets the feminist struggle for women's equality not "as a struggle for realizing the equality of a definable empirical group with a common essence and identity, women, but rather as a struggle against the multiple forms in which the category 'woman' is constructed in subordination." Thus she favors "an approach that permits us to understand how the subject is constructed through different discourses and subject positions" against one "that reduces our identity to one single position – be it class, race, or gender" (1992b: 382). Mouffe's concern is with citizenship as a political practice and as a "common political identity of persons who might be engaged in many different purposive enterprises and with differing conceptions of the good, but who are bound by their common identification" with pluralist democratic values (1992b: 378).

Mouffe explicitly distinguishes her own pluralist position from that of Iris Young who proposes a "group differentiated citizenship." In the name of a "heterogeneous public that acknowledges and affirms group differences," Young makes the case for a "politics of group assertion" which "takes as a basic principle that members of oppressed groups need separate organizations that exclude others, especially those from more privileged groups." To this end, "a democratic public should," she contends, "provide mechanisms for the effective recognition and representation of the distinct voices and perspectives of those of its constituent groups that are oppressed or disadvantaged" (1990: 10, 167, 184).

A key criticism which has been made of Young's proposal is that it runs the danger of freezing group identities, suppressing differences within groups and impeding wider solidarities (Mouffe 1992b; Phillips 1993). More fluid pluralist approaches, which are less prone to these dangers, have been articulated around the notions of a "politics of difference" (Yeatman 1993); a "transversal politics" (Yuval-Davis 1997) a "politics of solidarity in difference" (Lister 1997) and a "reflective solidarity" (Dean 1996).

Gender-pluralist approaches are best equipped to accommodate the range of social divisions, such as sexuality, class, "race," religion, and age, which intersect with gender to shape the citizenship of women and men. They help to diffuse the gender binary at the center of the equality vs. difference dichotomy. However, they do not offer guidance on one of the key questions for the re-gendering of citizenship which it raises: the respective value to be accorded to unpaid care work and paid work in the construction of citizenship responsibilities and rights. And a purely pluralist approach means that citizenship no longer offers a universal yardstick against which marginalized groups can stake their claim (Pascall 1993). A gender-pluralist approach, therefore, represents only one half of the re-gendering equation.

Toward a Woman-friendly Citizenship

Key to the other half of the equation is the reconstruction of citizenship's yardstick so that it no longer privileges the male through its false universalism. This means, in particular, the incorporation of care as an expression of citizenship, in line with the gender-differentiated model. However, this must not be at the expense of undermining progress toward gender equality and therefore the gender-neutral model cannot be totally discarded. What is needed is a synthesis of the two, within the framework of gender-pluralism, which, in the words of Pateman, enables "the substance of equality [to] differ according to the diverse circumstances and capacities of citizens, men and women" (1992: 29). Pivotal to the construction of the synthesis is the disruption of the public/private divide in recognition of the ways in which the interaction between public and private spheres sculpts the gendered contours of citizenship. From a policy perspective, this means, above all, measures to shift the gendered division of labor and to create the conditions in which both women and men can combine paid work and caring responsibilities (Lister1997, 1999b). Thus the re-gendering of citizenship will require change in both public and private spheres and in men's as well as women's relationship to citizenship.

Further Reading

Lister, R. 1997: *Citizenship: Feminist Perspectives*. Basingstoke: Macmillan.
Voet, R. 1998: *Feminism and Citizenship*. London: Sage.

31

Postnational Citizenship: Reconfiguring the Familiar Terrain

Yasemin Nuhoğlu Soysal

Predominant conceptions of citizenship treat it as national, denoting a territorially bounded population with a specific set of rights and duties. Immigration challenges the premises of this nation-state model. In the postwar era, individual rights have been increasingly legitimated as "human rights" at the transnational level. Furthermore, as in the case of the European Union for example, political authority is increasingly dispersed among local, national, and transnational political institutions. In terms of rights and identity, the development of postnational citizenship involves the extension of rights to noncitizen immigrants, which blurs the dichotomy between nationals and aliens. Mobilization around claims to collective rights generally involve particularistic identities, but they are connected to transnationally institutionalized discourses and agendas of human rights, sometimes invoking the rights of the individual to cultural difference. Furthermore, this mobilization is often organized and directed beyond the nation-state, toward transnational jurisdictions. However, Soysal argues that postnational citizenship does not imply the end of the nation-state, which remains important to the organization of rights and the safeguarding of national cultures; nor does it herald a global society. It is rather a paradoxical and contradictory process, but it does require that sociologists take transnational institutions and discourses more seriously than has previously been the case.

Citizenship is back with a vengeance. Since the 1990s it has made its way in noticeable strides into the discipline of Sociology. If one point of entry is the comparative and historical studies either reconceptualizing the Marshallian concept of citizenship as a more dynamic and relational one (Turner 1989; Sommers 1993; Wiener 1998) or renarrating the development of welfare and women's rights in the right historical order (Barbalet 1988; Fraser and Gordon 1992; Orloff 1993; Skocpol 1996), the other entry has been a growing literature on immigration and citizenship (Kymlicka and Norman 1994). Immigration provides a productive viewpoint to study citizenship since it challenges the very premises of the nation-state model that we political sociologists take for granted in our work.

Our theories are stubborn in assigning the nation-state a privileged position as a unit of analysis, even when conversing about global processes such as immigration. By doing so, they axiomatically embrace the dichotomy of citizen and alien, native and immigrant. This not only generates analytical quandaries as transnational institutions and discourses become increasingly salient, but also renders invisible changes in national citizenship and new formations of inclusion and exclusion.

The predominant conceptions of modern citizenship, as expressed in both scholarly and popular discourses, posit that populations are organized within nation-state boundaries by citizenship rules that acclaim "national belonging" as the legitimate basis of membership in modern states. As such, national citizenship is defined by two foundational principles: a congruence between territorial state and the national community; and, national belonging as the source of rights and duties of individuals as well as their collective identity. Hence, what national citizenship denotes is a territorially bounded population with a specific set of rights and duties, excluding others on the ground of nationality.

In the postwar era, a series of interlocking legal, institutional, and ideological changes affected the concept and organization of citizenship in the European state system. A significant development regards the intensification of the global discourse and instruments on individual rights. This emphasis on rights has been expressed through a codification of "human rights" as a world-level organizing principle in legal, scientific, and popular conventions. Individual rights that were once associated with belonging to a national community have become increasingly abstract and legitimated at the transnational level and within a larger framework of human rights.

As legitimized and celebrated by various international codes and laws, the discourse of human rights ascribes universal rights to the person. Even though they are frequently violated as a political practice, human rights increasingly constitute a world-level index of legitimate action and provide a hegemonic language for formulating claims to rights beyond national belonging. This elaboration of individual rights in the postwar era has laid the ground upon which more expansive claims and rights are advanced. The definition of individual rights as an abstract, universal category, as opposed to being attached to an absolute status of national citizenship, has licensed a variety of interests (environmentalists, regional movements, indigenous groups, as well as immigrants) to make further claims on the state.

A complementary development is the emergence of multilevel polities. The gradual unfolding of the European Union, for example, suggests that political authority is increasingly dispersed among local, national, and transnational political institutions. The diffusion and sharing of sovereignty, in turn, enables new actors, facilitates competition over resources, and makes possible new organizational strategies for practicing citizenship rights. The existence of multilevel polities creates new opportunities for mobilizing identities and advancing demands within and beyond national boundaries.

These developments have significant implications for the notions of identity and rights, on the one hand, and the organization and practice of citizenship, on the other. In Europe today, conventional conceptions of citizenship are no longer adequate to understand the dynamics of rights and membership. National citizenship or formal nationality is no longer a significant construction in terms of how it translates to rights and privileges; and, claims-making and participation are not axiomatically concomitant with the national order of things.

In the following sections, I will focus on two key aspects of the changing models of citizenship: the decoupling of rights and identity, and the expansion of collective claims-making and mobilization. Here I expand on what I called "postnational citizenship" elsewhere (Soysal 1994).

RIGHTS AND IDENTITY

The postwar elaboration of human rights as a global principle, in international agreements and institutions but also in scientific and popular discourses, legitimates the rights of persons beyond national collectivities. This authoritative discourse of individual rights has been influential in the formalization and expansion of many citizenship rights to those who were previously excluded or marginalized in society: women, children, gays and lesbians, religious and linguistic minorities, as well as immigrants. Particularly in the case of immigrants, the extension of various membership rights has significantly blurred the conventional dichotomy between national citizens and aliens.

The erosion of legal and institutional distinctions between nationals and aliens attests to a shift in models of citizenship across two phases of immigration in the twentieth century. The model of national citizenship, anchored in territorialized notions of cultural belonging, was dominant during the massive migrations at the turn of the century, when immigrants were either expected to be molded into national citizens (as in the case of European immigrants to the US) or categorically excluded from the polity (as in the case of the indentured Chinese laborers in the US). The postwar immigration experience reflects a time when national citizenship is losing ground to new forms of citizenship, which derive their legitimacy from deterritorialized notions of persons' rights, and thus are no longer unequivocally anchored in national collectivities. These postnational forms can be explicated in the membership of the long-term noncitizen immigrants in western countries, who hold various rights and privileges without a formal nationality status; in the increasing instances of dual citizenship, which breaches the traditional notions of political membership and loyalty in a single state; in European Union citizenship, which represents a multitiered form of membership; and in subnational citizenships in culturally or administratively autonomous regions of Europe (e.g. Basque country, Catalonia, and Scotland). The membership rights of noncitizen immigrants generally consist of full civil rights, social rights (education and many of the welfare benefits), and some political rights (including local voting rights in some countries). In the emerging European system, certain groups of individuals are more privileged than others – dual citizens and the nationals of European Union countries have more rights than (non-European) resident immigrants and political refugees; they in turn have more rights than temporary residents or those immigrants who do not hold a legal resident status. Thus, what is increasingly in place is a multiplicity of membership forms, which occasions exclusions and inclusions that no longer coincide with the bounds of the nation(al).

Paradoxically, as the source and legitimacy of rights increasingly shift to the transnational level, identities remain particularistic, and locally defined and organized. The same global rules and institutional frameworks which celebrate personhood and human rights, at the same time naturalize collective identities around national and ethno-religious particularisms, by legitimating the right to "one's own culture" and identity. Through massive decolonizations in the postwar period and the subsequent work of the international organizations such as the United Nations, UNESCO, and the Council of Europe, the universal right to "one's own culture" has gained increasing legitimacy, and collective identity has been redefined as a category of human rights. In the process, what we normally consider as unique characteristics of collectivities – culture, language, and standard ethnic traits – have become variants of the universal core of humanness or selfhood. Once institutionalized as a right, identities occupy a crucial place in individual and collective actor's narratives and strategies. In turn, identities proliferate and become more and more expressive, authorizing ethnic nationalisms and particularistic group claims of various sorts. Accordingly, even when previous nation-states are dissolving (for example, the Soviet Union and Yugoslavia), the "emerging" units aspire to become a territorial state with self-determination, and the world political community grants them this right. In national and world polities, identity emerges as a pervasive discourse of participation, and is enacted as a symbolic (and organizational) tool for creating new group solidarities and mobilizing claims.

Thus, while rights acquire a more universalistic form and are divorced from national belonging, at the same time identities become particularistic and expressive. This decoupling of rights and identity is one of the most elemental characteristics of postnational citizenship. Individuals attain rights and protection, and thus membership, within states that are not "their own." An immigrant in Germany, for instance, need not have a "primordial" attachment of cultural and historical kind to Germanness in order to attain social, economic, and political rights. Their rights derive from transnational discourses and structures celebrating human rights as a world-level organizing principle. The idea of nation, on the other hand, persists as an intense metaphor of identity, and at times an idiom of war. It is still the source of a pronounced distinctiveness, but divested from its hold on citizenship rights.

COLLECTIVE CLAIMS-MAKING AND MOBILIZATION: THE PRACTICE OF CITIZENSHIP

With the postwar reconfigurations in citizenship, along with dissociation of rights and identity, the old categories that attach individuals to national welfare systems and distributory mechanisms become blurred. The postwar reification of personhood and individual rights expands the boundaries of political community, by legitimating individuals' claims to rights beyond their membership status in a particular nation-state. This inevitably changes the nature and locus of struggles for social equality and rights. New forms of mobilizing and advancing claims emerge, beyond the frame of national citizenship.

Two features of these emerging forms are crucial:

First, while collective groups increasingly mobilize around claims for particularistic identities, they connect their claims to transnationally institutionalized discourses and agendas of human rights. Immigrant groups in Europe mobilize around claims for group-specific provisions and emphasize their group identities. Their claims, however, are not simply grounded in the particularities of religious or ethnic narratives. On the contrary, they appeal to the universalistic principles and dominant discourses of equality, emancipation, and individual rights.

When immigrant associations advocate the educational rights and needs of immigrant children in school, they employ a discourse that appropriates the rights of the individual as its central themes. They directly invoke the international instruments and conventions on human rights to frame their position. They forward demands about mother-tongue instruction, Islamic *foulard*, or *halal* food by asserting the "natural" rights of individuals to their own cultures, rather than drawing upon religious teachings and traditions. For instance, the issue of wearing the Islamic *foulard* in school, which erupted into a national crisis in France in early 1990s, was not only a topical contention over immigrant integration or French *laicism*, but entered into the public arena as a matter of rights of individuals (see Feldblum 1993; Kastoryano 1996; Kepel 1997). During the debates, the head of the Great Mosque of Paris (one of the highest authorities for the Muslim community) declared the rules preventing wearing scarves in school to be discriminatory on the grounds of individual rights. His emphasis was on personal rights, rather than religious traditions or duties: "If a girl asks to have her hair covered, I believe it is her most basic right" (*Washington Post*, October 23, 1989). As exemplified in this case, immigrants advance claims for difference which are affirmed by universalistic and homogenizing ideologies of human rights. And by doing so, they appropriate host country discourses, participate in the host country public spaces, and exercise civic projects as they amplify and practice difference.

The second feature of the new forms of claims-making is that the organizational strategies employed by collective groups increasingly acquire a transnational and subnational character. Their participation extends beyond the confines of a unitary national community, cover multiple localities, and transnationally connect public spheres. In the case of immigrant groups, for example, we find political parties, mosque organizations, and community associations which operate at local levels but also assume transnational forms, and develop organizational connections between places of origin and destination. They carry back and forth institutional forms, bridging a diverse set of public spaces. An example of this is the Alevite groups (a subsect of Islam), organized both in Turkey and Germany. Based on their experience in, and borrowing models from the German education system, they have raised demands for the recognition of denominational schools in Turkey, which do not have a legal standing in the current system. In a similar vein, during the last local elections in Berlin, Turkish immigrant groups pushed for their local voting rights, while at the same time put pressure on the Turkish government to facilitate their rights to vote in Turkish national elections. As such, they envision their participation in multiple civic spaces, both in Berlin and in Turkey. Similar claims are being made by the Mexican and Central American immigrant communities in the United States. They demand dual citizenship and dual voting rights in their countries of origin and residence. And, indeed, the governments of Mexico, Columbia, and the Dominican Republic recently passed legislation allowing dual nationality.

All of this implies that the public spheres within which immigrants act, mobilize, and advance claims, have broadened. In pursuing their claims, the mobilization of immigrant groups entails multiple states and political agencies, and they target trans-and subnational institutions, as much as the national ones. For example, the much debated Islamic *foulard* issue was not simply a matter confined to the discretion of a local school board, but has traversed the realms of local, national, and transnational jurisdictions – from local educational authorities to the European Court of Human Rights.

While the claims and mobilization of immigrant groups aim to further particularistic solidarities, paradoxically, they make appeals to universalistic principles of human rights and connect themselves to a diverse set of public spheres. As such, their mobilization is not simply a reinvention of cultural particularisms. Drawing upon universalistic repertoires of making claims, they participate in and contribute to the reification of host society and global discourses.

The experience of immigrant communities in Europe indicates a diversion from classical forms of claims-making and participation in the public sphere. Much of the decolonization and civil rights movements of the 1960s and the early women's movements were attempts to redefine individuals as part of the national collectivity. Similarly, labor movements were historically linked to the shaping of a national citizenry. It is no coincidence that the welfare state developed as part of the national project, attaching labor movements to nations (as in Bismarckian Germany). However, the emerging forms of collective participation and claims-making in Europe are less and less nationally defined citizenship projects. Individuals and collective groups set their agenda for realization of rights through particularistic identities, which are embedded in, and driven by, universalistic discourses of human rights. This shift in focus from national collectivity to particularistic claims does not necessarily imply disengagement from public spheres. Neither does it mean the disintegration of civic arenas. On the contrary, they are evidence for the emerging participatory forms, and multiple arenas and levels that individuals enact and practice their citizenship.

This new form of claims-making and participation, which discursively and organizationally goes beyond nationally demarcated parameters, highlights the other important aspect of postnational citizenship. Postnational citizenship is not simply a set of legal rights and privileges or a legal status attached to a person, as implied in Marshallian definitions of citizenship. It signifies a set of practices through which individuals and groups activate their membership within and without the nation-state. Individuals and collectivities interact with and partake in multiple public spheres – hence, altering the locus of participation and setting the stage for new mobilizations.

In concluding, I would like to clarify three major confusions that discussions of postnational citizenship seem to raise. In so doing, my intention is to differentiate postnational citizenship from other theoretical constructs (such as cosmopolitanism and globalization), which are also deployed to account for the shifts in the national order of things. I also intend to rearticulate its theoretical expanse in depicting the new topography of rights and membership and the contemporary dynamics of exclusion and inclusion.

First, postnational citizenship does not refer to an identity or a unitary legal status. It is a sociological category to narrate the changes in the very institutions of rights and identity, which locate citizenship and its practice in multilevel discourses and multiple public spheres (and national is only one of these multiple scripts and arenas). It does not mark the emergence of a legal status or identity at the global level, ascribed by a single, unified world society and political structure. If anything, postnational citizenship projects that identities remain constructed at local levels and get more and more attached to local spaces (see also Gupta and Ferguson 1992; Malkki 1995).

Thus, it is superfluous to associate postnational citizenship with ideologies of cosmopolitanism, which profess a moral, universalistic individual and identity. Likewise, it is unproductive to conflate postnational citizenship with theoretical formulations regarding "transnational communities," which presumptively accept the formation of tightly bounded communities and solidarities (on the basis of common cultural and ethnic references) between places of origin and arrival (see Basch, Schiller, and Blanc 1994; Cheah and Robbins 1998; Portes 1998). Postnational citizenship does not imply the necessary advent of transnational solidarities or communal bonds, or the existence of individuals devoid of (local) commitments, identities, and interests. Rather, it emphasizes the multiconnectedness of public spheres and the increasingly universalistic conceptions and discourses of rights, which are no longer limited by national constellations.

Second, postnational citizenship does not imply the "withering of the nation-state." The same transnational rules and institutions reify the nation-state's agency and sovereignty as much as they celebrate human rights and foster postnational citizenship. The normative and institutional domain of the transnational is not host to a harmonious and coherent rule system. It accommodates a multiplicity of principles often with contradictory outcomes and effects. Inasmuch as they are contradictory, the principles of human rights and nation-state sovereignty are equally part of the same transnational discourse and institutional terrain. Thus, as the source and legitimacy of rights increasingly move to the transnational level, rights and membership of individuals remain organized within nation-states. The nation-state remains a persistent depository of cultures of nationhood and still the most viable political organizational structure. This is what leads to the incongruity between the legitimation and location of postnational citizenship, which has paradoxical implications for the exercise of citizenship rights. Nation-states and their boundaries persist as reasserted by restrictive immigration practices and sovereignty narratives, while universalistic personhood rights transcend the same boundaries, giving rise to new models and understandings of membership.

Hence, postnational citizenship is not a sign of a linear procession from national to transnational. That is, we cannot (should not) postulate postnational citizenship as a stage within the much assumed dichotomy of national and transnational, and the expected transition between the two. There is much confusion around this issue and much time and energy is spent in arguing whether we are approaching a transnational stage or not. Postnational citizenship confirms that in postwar Europe the national no longer has primacy but it coexists with the transnational, mutually reinforcing and reconfiguring each other. Into the analytical realm of postnational citizenship, the national and transnational determinants figure in as mutual variables and as concurrent levels, within which the current practices of citizenship and participation should be understood.

Postnational citizenship is also mistakenly associated with globalization. This oversight arises from misconstruing globalization as the world becoming a homogeneous and/or disorderly entity. This extremely rudimentary notion is hardly entertained by any proponent of globalization. Even the most unyielding proponents describe a much more differentiated process (see Sassen 1996, 1998). A more useful definition of globalization refers to world-level structural changes, which shorten distances and connect local articulations to social events and relations seemingly located afar (see Giddens 1990; Robertson 1992; and Appadurai 1996). Although they signify correlated processes, postnational citizenship is not one and the same as globalization and does not singularly derive from it. The intensification of discourses and institutions of human rights at the global level, a novel development in the postwar era, indeed underline the development of postnational citizenship. But postnational citizenship itself does not assume or predict a uniform modality of citizenship in a converging world (citizenship institutions, although being transformed, still keep certain distinctiveness, based on their historical and institutional specificities at national level).

Lastly, postnational citizenship is not in itself a normative prescription, nor does it presume public spheres free of conflict or devoid of exclusions. That is to say, on the one hand, postnational citizenship reveals an ongoing process of definition and redefinition of rights and participation. On the other, it productively brings to the fore the fact that there are no longer absolute and clear-cut patterns of exclusion and inclusion which simply coincide with the bounds of the national. In today's Europe, access to a formal nationality status is not the main indicator of inclusion and exclusion. Rights, membership, and participation are increasingly matters beyond the vocabulary of national citizenship. Under the rubric of postnational citizenship, inclusions and exclusions shape simultaneously and at multiple levels – local, national, and European.

The increasingly expansive definition of rights may appear as a contradiction in the face of recent attempts to deregulate the welfare state and eliminate policy categories based on the collective (e.g., affirmative action and welfare provisions). However, the copresence of postnational citizenship and/with the breakdown of the welfare state is no coincidence. Both trends derive from the global dominance of the ideologies and institutions of liberal individualism. While these ideologies contribute to the dismantling of the welfare state project, at the same time, they enable various groups in advancing identity-based claims justified on the basis of individual rights. Thus, the same transnational processes that lead to new marginalizations and exclusions also create new grounds for and spaces of claims-making and mobilization, and facilitate the expansion of rights.

However, the new spaces of citizenship and claims-making are not necessarily free of conflict. By emphasizing the hegemony of discourses and strategies of human or personhood rights, which resolutely underlines postnational citizenship, one should not take a naive position and assume that individuals and groups effortlessly attain rights, or that they readily bond together and arrive at agreeable positions. Postnational rights are results of struggles, negotiations, and arbitrations by actors at local, national, and transnational levels, and are contingent upon issues of distribution and equity. And like any set of rights, they are subject to retraction and negation. Rather than denying the certitude of conflict and contestation for rights, postnational citizenship as a category and practice draws attention to the multilayered and diverse forms that they take and new arenas in which they are enacted.

Our dominant theories and conceptualizations have yet to catch up with the changes in the institutions of citizenship, rights, and identity. They have yet to respond to the challenge posed by emergent actors, border-crossings, and non-conventional mobilizations. Postnational citizenship is an attempt to capture and incorporate these changes by assigning transnational institutions and discourses a more predominant analytical role than it is usually granted in the prevailing studies. Otherwise, we will continue to have models that do not work, anomalies in existing paradigms, and incongruities between official rhetoric and institutional actualities.

Further Reading

Gupta, A. and Ferguson, J. 1992: "Beyond 'culture': Space, identity, and the politics of difference." *Cultural Anthropology* 7: 6–23.

Hobsbawm, E. 1990. *Nations and Nationalism since 1780: Programme, Myth, Reality.* Cambridge: Cambridge University Press.

Sassen, S. 1996: *Losing Control? Sovereignty in an Age of Globalization.* New York: Columbia University Press.

Soysal, Y. N. 1994: *Limits of Citizenship: Migrants and Postnational Membership in Europe.* Chicago: University of Chicago Press.

32

Governmentality and Citizenship

Giovanna Procacci

Citizenship is classically analyzed, by T. H. Marshall for example, as referring to the nation-state. However, it may also be analyzed from the Foucauldian perspective of governmentality. The judicial approach has been dominant, but Marshall's model also stresses the importance of the welfare state and the building of social consensus, which is not readily analyzed in terms of a given set of rights. Increasingly, with the crisis of the nation-state, it is evident that citizenship is less an expression of belonging to a national community and more the practice of such a belonging. Procacci argues that criticisms of the classical paradigm do not generally move beyond a traditional focus on the transcendent moral subject of citizenship. In contrast, the study of governmentality shifts attention away from state sovereignty and the opposition between subject and power to look at the specific field of actions it constitutes, including forms of political subjectivity. From this perspective, liberal techniques of power are new: they act through the state in the name of sovereignty while at the same time acting directly in a detailed way on individuals' lives and conduct. The social dimension of citizenship is exemplary of a different logic from that of civil and political rights: it is founded on the fact of being a living being rather than on liberty, and oriented toward society as a new subject of rights rather than toward the rights of other individuals.

In recent years, the concept of citizenship has known a remarkable renewal of interest within the field of political theory. It has not been just a fashionable promotion from the media; in a much more fundamental way, the concept itself has undergone a semantic extension, losing its predominantly bureaucratic meaning to cover a larger scope of experiences at the core of our political sensibility. At the same time, citizenship nowadays is at the core of conflicts marking current political transformations, above all the crisis of the nation-state: it has become a hot issue in terms of policy making and a target of a variety of criticisms.

This chapter will discuss the crisis of T. H. Marshall's paradigm of citizenship, in so far as it refers centrally to the nation-state. The theory of Marshall also points in another direction for analyzing citizenship phenomena, however, by treating them from a concrete perspective of government. Michel Foucault's work on government and governmentality offers a chance to further elaborate such a view of citizenship, interpreting the latter less as an institution than as strategies governing processes of social change by transforming citizens' attributes, expectations, and practices. The contingent character of citizenship strategies might prove helpful to appreciate the specificity of our present problems of citizenship, as well as current attacks against it; namely, the tendency to individualize and marketize social problems (as in the new social policies) or to reduce citizenship to cultural identity claims (as in multiculturalism). They express two sides of a "post-modern" revolt of particularities against "modern" universalism, which fits these times of welfare crisis and neo-liberal attempts to govern without social regulations (Rose 1996).

THE NATURE OF CITIZENSHIP

Citizenship emerged historically from the political struggle of western societies against medieval orders and the fragmentation of collective life due to communitarian particular rights, in the attempt to emancipate at the same time individuals and society. Modern societies have been characterized by a tendency to dissolve communitarian particularities into the general – society, the state, and so on – on the one hand, and into the individual on the other. Citizenship is the territory where such a search for both generality and individuality simultaneously is inscribed. Therefore its nature is inextricably collective *and* individual: the common quality of all members of society and the practices of each of them expressing their sense of belonging. Citizenship conceptualizes at the same time a status – the status of a citizen, the ties to social community – with their implications in terms of rights, loyalty, and identity; and the reasons legitimating the inclusion in, or exclusion from the community. The history of citizenship has been marked by inevitable tensions due to this complexity, and by the need to find institutional devices able to master them; this is why citizenship cannot be separated from the practices of government organizing it, and from the forms of subjectivity corresponding to them. Indeed, here lies the main theoretical interest of the concept of citizenship: it allows us to describe the political through the subjectivity constructed in relation to it, and to criticize the functioning of political institutions from the point of view of citizens' entitlements (Zolo 1994: 4).

Unquestionably, all this matters for the social sciences; and yet, the analysis of citizenship has for a long time been dominated by the juridical approach. As a consequence, citizenship has been identified with institutional processes sanctioning inclusion or exclusion within the political space of modern nations. From this vantage point, citizenship expresses essentially the ascription of a subject to a national state and the derived set of rights; citizenship is thus the basis of the political relationship to the state, embodied in the passport; yet it is reduced to, and becomes in fact interchangeable with nationality. The study of citizenship has thus been caught in the traditional emphasis of political studies on the legitimacy of the political body and institutions representing it – that is, on issues of sovereignty.

As a matter of fact, the juridical reflection on citizenship also offers a different perspective, concerned with individuals and their liberties (Costa 1999). Under this different light, citizenship expresses an attempt to ground a pre-political order founded on a consensual integration of members; it is less concerned with the legitimacy of the sovereign, than with its delimitation. Here citizenship is seen as participating in the gradual separation of the sphere of society from the sphere of sovereignty: in this way, the concrete order of social and political practices in which the former is organized is regained as a theoretical object for the social sciences.

THE SOCIOLOGICAL DISCOVERY OF CITIZENSHIP

We are used to dating the sociological discovery of citizenship from the path-breaking essay by T. H. Marshall (1950 and 1963), first given as lectures in 1949 under the impulsion of postwar reconstruction and the birth of the British welfare experience. Marshall proposed viewing citizenship as a multilevel phenomenon, with civil, political, and social dimensions equally crucial to it. They mark the different steps of a dynamic moving citizenship in conformity with the modern political imperative to reduce inequality in order to generalize the status of citizen. It is true that the political actor of such development is the state, up to the construction of welfare systems. However, from this point, citizenship can no longer be seen as just a given set of granted rights. It is rather to be understood as a process of government developing strategies of rights and driven by the need to enlarge social consensus. The social pact itself changes, and changes are to be analyzed from the concrete perspective of government. Both sides, the state's institutional action and changes in concrete strategies of government, are equally important to Marshall's narrative of citizenship.

Under the pressure of the civil rights movement during the 1960s, political sociology amplified the importance of Marshall's proposal. It seemed to open new perspectives for analyzing social differentiation according to a progressive, pluralist ideal of extended democracy, without attacking communitarian cultural identities. Such a progress was to take place within the nation-state, strengthened by its role in redistribution and welfare organization. For Reinhart Bendix (1964) or Talcott Parsons (1969), the definition of rights and duties of the citizen was a crucial moment of the making of the nation-state, in so far as it needs the active participation of all citizens. Thus, citizenship might play a crucial role in mobilizing human resources, countering inequalities exacerbated by capitalism, and favoring integration, particularly of the disadvantaged, under the firm control of the nation-state. In the end, sociology's reception of Marshall's narrative did not break the traditional association of citizenship with the state, and via the state, with the problematic of legitimacy and sovereignty.

Such a progressive ideal, and above all its promotion by the state, has proved frail before the crises of recent years – the crisis of the nation-state, of welfare, and of universalism; as a result, the very orientation of Marshall's paradigm is called into question. Nowadays the explosion of interest around citizenship goes together, most often, with an exclusively cultural definition of citizenship; it is as if, once the role of the state becomes less clear, citizenship loses its progressive political strength against inequality. There is no doubt that the crisis of the nation-state is not just an ideological effect of this historical moment: it calls seriously into question its ability to maintain a frame for citizenship. Massive migrations are generating communities of nonnationals who more and more claim rights reserved to citizens, undermining the coincidence of citizenship and nationality; citizenship itself is denounced as "the last privilege." At the same time, processes of globalization decompose the state politically, to the advantage of supranational political organizations and of new regionalisms (see Le Galès, chapter 37, in this volume). The link between citizenship and nationality breaks, provoking reactions which all tend to interpret the nation as synonymous with nationalism (Gellner 1983). To the extent that Marshall's theory of citizenship relies on the state, the crisis of the latter makes its paradigm problematic (see Soysal, chapter 31, in this volume).

In fact, nationality and citizenship have not worked politically in the same way. While the concept of nationality connects national identity and the political link to the state, citizenship has worked as a criterion to separate society from its political expression – organizing not only inclusion, but also internal exclusions among the nationals. This is why, for instance, social rights and social citizenship have worked in relative independence from nationality, rooted in collective aggregations different from the state (such as professions, generations, and the like). Citizenship has not been synonymous with belonging to a community, it rather expresses a practice of such belonging; it consists less in a way of being, than a way of acting. The political issue under citizenship is not communitarian identity, but public activity (Tassin 1994); this makes it possible to work to further dissociate citizenship from its nationalistic reference, as the condition of viewing the state as a site for public activity, rather than the institutional expression of a national identity.

THE CRISIS OF MARSHALL'S PARADIGM

There are many reasons to criticize Marshall's narrative of citizenship. Some authors point out the dominance of the Anglo-Saxon experience behind his theory although this is far from being the unique model of citizenship – it is, for instance, very different from French citizenship, with respect to the secularization of the public space (Birnbaum 1996: 65) as well as to conflicts between formal equality and positive inequality (Procacci 1993). Others show that even within the British experience, citizenship was not exclusively produced by the action of the nation-state; it was built on local public spaces as well (Somers 1993). Further criticisms address the evolutionist character of citizenship dynamics in Marshall's model; the "natural" evolution of expanding rights undermines political changes, namely those introduced by social rights with respect to civil and political rights (Procacci 2000).

However, criticisms of Marshall do not always move forward to overcome the limits of his theory; as Birnbaum remarks, the big typological descriptions of citizenship opened up by the crisis of his paradigm tend to revive more traditional questions about the *nature* of the citizen; they reactivate traditional oppositions such as passive/active, public/private, bourgeois/citizen, with the result that the transcendental moral subject of citizenship again becomes the focus. This becomes particularly true when the debate on citizenship enacts the opposition of liberals and communitarians, which currently dominates political debate, especially its US academic version. While the former have to face the crisis of the nation-state, affecting, as we have seen, the conception of citizenship attached to it, and look unable to counter a nationalistic turn, communitarians tend to see the weakening of the state more favorably. They attack citizenship as an abstract network of social ties built by advanced liberal societies: modern social developments have gradually weakened the original civic impulse inherent in the model of classic republican citizenship, molded on *active* participation in the public sphere, to the advantage of a *passive*, consumer-wise version of citizenship where rights, more than duties and commitment, are the bulk of citizens' expectations. Citizenship has become "a status, an entitlement, a right or a set of rights passively enjoyed" (Walzer 1989). Against this passivity, due to the abstract character of citizenship, we ought to valorize *difference and identity*, both based on community values. On these bases, theories of multiculturalism tend to present citizenship as synonymous with cultural identity claims (Kymlicka 1995), going together with a weak, mostly instrumental membership within a national space. David Burchell (1995) points out here the danger of a "politics of civic nostalgia," longing for the return of a classic citizen devoted to public affairs, badly replaced by a privatized citizen only caring for his/her rights.

Against a defense of the state at the risk of nationalism, and against the reduction of citizenship to particular cultural claims, it can be fruitful to try a different path, working out the other analytical indication offered by Marshall: citizenship as concrete practices of government, as specific requirements and expectations, rights and duties, involving public action and subjectivity. Freed from the burden of an evolutionist narrative, this perspective might help us to appreciate the specificity of our present problems of citizenship.

GOVERNMENTALITY: A STRATEGIC VIEW OF CITIZENSHIP

To this purpose, some crucial concepts shaped by Michel Foucault to analyze power might prove helpful. He suggested treating power as *strategic thought*, a rationally reflected "way of doing things." Political theory usually attends too much to institutions, too little to *practices* (Gordon 1991); it therefore tends to focus on the analysis of the state as it was prior to the set of practices it embodies. Institutions tend to present themselves as self-consistent, given once for all, unavoidable; whereas the meaning of practices is a highly contingent construction (Veyne 1978). After all, political practices share an important feature with scientific ones: "It is not *reason in general* that is implemented, but always a specific type of rationality" (Foucault 1982b: 242). As Paul Veyne put it, there are no *natural* objects in politics – universals such as the state, or its subjects; rather, there only exist specific historical figures. Problems might well be old, yet we experience only the momentary patterns they assume, and their specific ration-

ality. Against the illusion of self-evidence and the certitude of everlasting continuity, contingency only makes sense of the present, which is in the end nothing
but "a difference in history" (Foucault 1988b).

In his lectures to the Collège de France – still unpublished, with the exception
of the 1975 and 1976 Lectures – Foucault proposed the concepts of *government*
and governmentality to conceptualize political practices, distancing them from
issues of legitimacy and sovereignty. No doubt these do matter in analyzing
political power; yet, behind their persistence, people govern and are governed
in specific ways – as legal subjects, as economic resources, as living beings, as
citizens – and they do not mean the same thing. The concept of government, then,
shifts analytical attention from legitimate institutions embodying sovereignty
toward the specific practices through which political power is acted. From the
sixteenth century onwards, beside the theme of legitimacy, the study of power
thematized an art of government, treating its practices on a continuum with all
social relations. Power, Foucault (1976) had established, is no-one's property; it
can only be exercised: it consists of a system of actions and reactions. The point
becomes, then, to analyze the specific field of actions it constitutes. This requires
an analysis that does not reduce the political element to law, but studies also the
extrajuridical constraints hanging over individuals.

Brought down to practices, power appears intertwined with the subjectivity of
individuals on whom it is exercised; analytically, it is impossible to separate
them: forms of subjectivity become crucial to political relations. There is no
fundamental opposition of a subject to an object of power, as the theory of
sovereignty claims by sharply distinguishing between the sovereign and subjects.
To govern means "to structure the possible field of action of others" (Foucault
1982a: 221); it is an action over action, a conduct of others' conduct. This means
that the governed are active subjects; in the same moment that they obey, they are
free to act within a range of possible actions. In this way, government is the
source of a critical attitude (or counter-conducts); it always involves some
resistance against it, expressing the will not to be governed, or at least not in
such a way (Gordon, forthcoming). "The intransigence of freedom" establishes
an agonistic interaction, within which grows an autonomous subjectivity (Owen
1995). There is, Foucault says, a continuity between governing and governed
people, an "upward and downward" continuity (Foucault 1991: 91–2); even
more, government is the contact point where techniques of domination and
techniques of the self meet (1988b). The activity of the governed thus raises the
problem of subjectivity at the core of politics (Veyne 1987) that the concept of
government allows us to conceptualize, referring it to the specific actions
required or expected from them.

Now, this link between political practices and subjectivity is crucial to citizenship, as we have seen. From the point of view of governmental strategies, citizenship regimes describe the different ways in which people are governed – that is, at
the same time their identity as subjects and the actions of power to which they are
exposed. There is no such thing as *the citizen*; there exist only the specific figures
corresponding to different regimes of citizenship: the citizen is an historical
persona, a social creation; ways of governing people as citizens change, just as
citizens' subjectivity changes. The classical model of citizenship sharply separated

the political order of the *polis* and the domestic order – *oikos*. This is not *the* model, as civic humanism claims by positing the citizen as the condition for the emergence of the political. Already in Marshall there are several patterns of citizen corresponding to specific attributes required from him/her as a result of changes occurring in the political sphere. The notion of government allows us to conceptualize the emergence of new forms of subjectivity and conduct, and therefore of a different experience of citizenship – namely the growing import- ance of private and professional conducts. This destroys the myth that civic virtue can exhaust the field of politics (Burchell 1991).

From the vantage point of a genealogy of modern politics, its specific feature is neither violent imposition (warlike) nor the voluntary tie of a contract (juridical), but the existence of a repertoire of techniques involving the subjectivity of the governed which are not marked by the regime using them. Foucault saw govern- ment as a useful concept for thinking about liberalism. Liberalism had to face the complexity of political subjectivity, confronted social and economic expectations and reassembled, thus, the antinomy of classic citizenship. Looking at it as an activity ("the liberal way of doing"), rather than as a set of institutions, liberalism itself appears as a revolution: it is a critique of the state, of the need to govern, in the name of society, and a principle of limitation of sovereignty. Why govern? The state is no longer the natural subject and object of political knowledge; nor is civil society a natural object, always opposed to the state; rather it is a strategic goal, the effect of a liberal technique of government (Foucault 1997b).

Modern power consists in a new political configuration, where a political power acting in the name of sovereignty, expressing its unity through the state and legal forms of intervention, is combined with a more detailed governmental action concerned with individuals' lives and conducts. The state itself, in order to act, needs to know regularities and processes of an objective social reality, existing independently of law and state action, and for this purpose it needs to get closer to it. "Government is the right disposition of things arranged so as to lead to a convenient end" (Guillaume La Perrière quoted in Foucault 1991: 93). "Things" here are men, their relationships, customs, habits, and so on. Govern- ment is something like personal guidance. It marks the emergence of a bio-power, a power exerted over living beings, over their lives, instead of threatening them with violence and death (Foucault 1984c). At the source of modern power, the biological element enters into the sphere of politics, multiplying techniques investing the body and health. Such bio-power has two targets: the individual body (discipline) and the population (regulation).

A condition of possibility of government is, then, the political discovery of *population*: as the wealth and power of a state lie in its population, the latter appears as the subject of transformations, regularities, needs, and aspirations that have to be addressed in a specific way. Foucault named this emergence into the political arena of the problems raised by a population, *bio-politics*: life and death, health, longevity, and race become politically significant phenomena, which need to be governed so that individual lives can develop in "such a way that their development also fosters the strength of the state" (Foucault 1997b). This link between individual lives and the common lot gives modern power a fundamentally antinomic character that Foucault conceptualized through the formula *omnes et singulatim* – the title of his 1979 Tanner Lectures at the University of Stanford. By this he meant that the peculiar feature of the political rationality of the modern state is not centralization, nor the growth of bourgeois individualism; rather it is a combination of individualizing techniques of care for the souls and lives of each one, together with a rational totalizing principle of statehood governing the *polis* through juridical general measures. The former is referred to as a pastoral model of Christian origins that had penetrated into the secular political culture. Such a combination of the antinomic principles of the individual and the general is so typical of modern political rationality that Foucault concluded: "right from the start, the state is both individualizing and totalitarian. Opposing the individual and his interests to it is just as hazardous as opposing it with the community and its requirements" (Foucault 1988b: 84).

Here again we meet an essential character of citizenship as the territory of a twofold process of generalization and individuation, impossible to separate from each other. Its historical developments show that a political rationality tending to govern a population as citizens strategically combines the two kinds of techniques. What Marshall had presented as different dimensions within citizenship marking gradual steps corresponds, in fact, to the strategic complexity of governing citizens, using civil, political, and social rights according to multiple goals. However, this presents a difficulty for liberalism: it is suspicious of government in the name of society, and yet society demands government for sake of its own security and order, against the disorder provoked by excessive vulnerability and inequality. Problems of population are a constant challenge to liberalism, because they cannot be managed through purely legal means; they engage a bio-political rationality that follows a different logic with respect to individuals' rights and liberties. Once they become an object of government, a significant part of our identity and citizenship is produced through our relation to the state which is by no means a purely juridical relation. While the legal codification of citizenship reveals its limits, a claim for liberation – to be freed from the burden of need – is addressed to the state and spreads, despite its non-liberal character, throughout the political.

THE CASE FOR SOCIAL CITIZENSHIP

We can now replace Marshall's evolutionist narrative of citizenship with an interpretation that is able to account for strategic transformations within the field of citizenship. In particular, we can acknowledge the importance of citizenship's social dimension – the main contribution of Marshall's sociology to the theory of citizenship – other than as a continuation from civil and political citizenship. Through social citizenship Marshall conceptualized the experience of the British welfare state and the expansion of citizenship and rights due to social-democracy. Underneath this ideological feature, however, social citizenship points at a difficulty in governing citizens, due to the fact that civil and political rights are only potentially universal: in fact, they are unable to attack the structure of inequality, and so leave the space for it to prevent the generalization of citizenship status. A social dimension has always been crucial to citizenship and it has been the source of a socialization process of citizenship and rights according to a different logic from liberalism. Social rights mark a rupture, originating in the space opened up within the political rationality of liberal rights and law, a space they were unable to fill.

Changes are strategic; they have to be analyzed in relation to their targets. So it is for social citizenship and social rights; from this point of view, welfare appears as a goal rather than the condition for a natural expansion of citizenship. More generally, interpreted from the vantage point of governmental strategies, the whole process of socialization (of citizenship, of rights, of risk, etc.) looks like a response to difficulties in governing social transformations linked to problems of inequality in a society built on egalitarian premises. Social rights are exemplary of a different logic from that of liberal, civil, and political rights: here the subject of rights is less founded on liberty than on the pure fact of being a living being. Social rights express a right to life embodied in positive rights which are not related to others' rights so much as to a new subject of rights: *society*. Society grants or rejects positive claims that aim to reach some standards of well-being; social rights are more a matter of liberation than of liberties. They require that society is acknowledged as the subject of its own claims, needs, interests, and rights, irreducible to those of individuals or of the state; that it is acknowledged as the site of specific involuntary processes. As for social rights, "social" here means that society legitimates them – and not social actors. The political transformation of the relationship of citizens to the state originates neither at the level of the state nor at the level of individuals, but at the level of society, an independent field of practices and knowledge with respect to the juridical and the economic spheres. Not only does the market fail if inequality is so great as to exclude too many people; it is society as a whole that is threatened. The political need to reduce inequality by organizing the social has, thus, been a crucial moment of an intellectual movement at the heart of modernity, bringing back intermediate institutions that the rise of liberalism had exiled from the social space.

Finally, social citizenship expresses a political strategy aimed at producing the forms of subjectivity corresponding to this project of socialization. As such, it has become an important part of our present experience as citizens. Such a project, however, far from being realized "naturally" within a liberal society, only took place through deep tensions due to the antinomic principles of modern power, which are both emancipating and regulating at the same time. Foucault (1983) stressed that bio-politics lacks internal principles of limitation; it deals with needs which tend to expand indefinitely. This might account for some intolerance nowadays toward the burdens of the social. Yet, the idea that it is possible to govern only by *singulatim*, as suggested by a new celebration of particularities and individualism, overlooks the fact that the crisis we are living through is a crisis of public action and social regulation. Denouncing, as so often happens today, socialization (of citizenship, of rights, of risk) as the price in abstraction and bureaucratic control that individuals have suffered for their emancipation obscures the way in which it also generates liberation and conceals the limits of the liberal project with which modern society ought to come to terms.

Further Reading

Burchell, G., Gordon, C., and Miller, P. 1991: *The Foucault Effect. Studies on Governmentality*. London: Harvester.

Foucault, M. 1997, 1999, forthcoming: *The Essential Works of Michel Foucault 1954–1984*, 3 vols. Ed. P. Rabinow et al. London: Allen Lane.

Part IV

Political Transformations

33

Democratization
Transformation, Transition, Consolidation: Democratization in Latin America

Joe Foweraker

Democratic transition is usually understood as a critical moment in historical time created by the strategic decisions of elite actors. Although such moments may be the culmination of prolonged struggles in civil society that transform the political terrain, they do not automatically create the conditions for fully consolidated democracy. Democratic transformation, transition, and consolidation are three distinct but interrelated aspects of the more encompassing process of democratization. In Latin America democratic transformation was achieved by popular struggles for citizenship rights, with urban social movements playing a leading role, but it was elite actors and political parties that forged a new democratic consensus. But the failure to instil a secure regime of universal rights, and the continuing strength of clientelist politics, led to a constricted form of democracy that remains unconsolidated. Yet the formal institutions of democratic governance appear to work reasonably well in many countries, and there is hope that democratic performance will improve.

DEMOCRATIZATION DURING THE "THIRD WAVE"

Democracy may be defined in a minimal and procedural fashion, as a political system where multiple political parties compete for control of the government through relatively free and fair elections. By this definition, the number of democracies in the world has grown from just 35 in 1974, mainly rich and industrialized nations of the West, to some 120 today (Hun tington 1993: 3; Diamond 1997a: 22). With democratic states now comprising more than half of the total, it is suggested that democracy is now the typical form of government (Jaggers and Gurr 1995). It is also argued that liberal democracy, which includes an emphasis on individual freedoms and the rule of law, now serves as the almost universal legitimating principle of state authority (Fukuyama 1992: xi). Indeed this sea change, often characterized as the "third wave" of democratization, can be interpreted as a genuinely global democratic revolution.

Latin America has been at the heart of the "third wave" of democratization, with democratic governments gradually replacing the military dictatorships of the 1970s and 1980s. Indeed, 1989 "was the first time that all the Ibero-American nations, excepting Cuba, enjoyed the benefits of elected constitutional governments at the same time" (Valenzuela 1993: 3). This result was not as dramatic or visible as the collapse of the Communist dictatorships in Eastern and Central Europe, which began in the same year, but it did mark an historical watershed. Almost two centuries after their independence, the states of Latin America now comprised a new democratic universe.

In modern times, democracy is understood as the opposite of dictatorship, and democratization is the process of replacing dictatorial government with democracy. This process is mainly imagined as a critical moment in historical time, characterized as a democratic transition. This corresponds to the original usage of dictatorship as emergency powers vested temporarily in the executive (Bobbio 1989: 158–9), and to the way that Latin American military dictatorships often defended their rule. But, in reality, democratization usually involves "a prolonged and inconclusive political struggle" (Rustow 1970: 352) over at least one generation. It is therefore important to distinguish democratic transition from the period of democratic transformation that precedes it, and that "creates the political conditions in which the transition takes place" (Foweraker 1989: 2). Transformation refers to the changes in civil society that prepare the political ground for a transition to a new regime, and both are required for an understanding of democratic consolidation, often seen – in rather teleological fashion – as democratization's destination. I shall address democratic transition, transformation, and consolidation, in turn.

DEMOCRATIC TRANSITION

Most studies of democratic transition in Latin America focus exclusively on the "short-term maneuvring" of elite actors (Levine 1988: 385), and explanations of transition are often confined to the ex post modeling of elite decision-making. These decisions are either characterized as the choices of attitudinal groups such as "liberalizers" and "hardliners" (e.g. Przeworski 1986, 1991), or as the terms of elite pacts and settlements required to found a new regime (e.g. Hagopian 1990; Higley and Gunther 1992). But these moments of elite interaction are "not measurable according to a common scale" (O'Donnell and Schmitter 1986: 9), so that the typologies derived from them tend to have as many categories as cases. Consequently, comparative studies of democratic transition are usually organized as a series of case studies, bound by rather abstract generalizations (e.g. O'Donnell and Schmitter 1986; Diamond, Linz, and Lipset 1988–9).

Elite motives are a proper part of any explanation of democratic transition, and these studies demonstrate how military elites in particular came to find the business of government both exhausting and often damaging to the military as an institution (Stepan 1988). But they cannot explain the close historical coincidence of the Latin American transitions, which has invited inquiry into broader patterns of causation that are international. On the one hand, it is argued that

Latin America's growth rate was slower than the rest of the world in the 1980s, and that military dictatorships were especially vulnerable to economic downturn and crisis (Limongi and Przeworski 1994: 24). On the other, the clear shift of the United States' foreign policy toward a strong preference for democracy, and the conditionality clauses of the international funding agencies, provided both carrot and stick for a change of regime (Whitehead 1996). Many Latin American democrats believe Jimmy Carter to be the greatest of postwar US presidents. Yet, a balance between the international and the national must be struck, and it is possibly misleading to suggest that domestic conflicts were only important in "a limited number of South American cases" (Whitehead 1996: 23), where the transitions were "peculiarly national" (Schmitter 1996: 28).

The focus on elite decision-making explores the boundary conditions for procedural consensus among elite actors, and seeks to establish the institutional arrangements that will underpin elite pacts and settlements. Broadly speaking, this is the Lockean approach to the creation of the civic culture of democracy, which, in the contemporary context, is imagined as a process of "institutionalizing uncertainty" (Przeworski 1986: 58–9). Once the process of transition is underway, the main concerns are the institutional constraints and opportunities that bind competing elites to the political outcome. Both DiPalma (1990) and Sartori (1994) have investigated the choice and construction of institutions, and their consequences, intended or otherwise.

But the truism that "the process of establishing a democracy is a process of institutionalizing uncertainty" rings less true in Latin America where "little institutional innovation has occurred" (Mainwaring 1990: 171). Either the authoritarian legacy predominates, with no new constitution being written or agreed (as in Chile), or there is a strong influence of the "preauthoritarian institutional legacy on the choice of institutions" (Geddes 1996: 30). In sum, democratic transition takes place through "institutionally regulated institutional change" (Offe 1996: 209), and the choice of institutions is severely limited because they have to "make sense" to political actors, as well as being fit for the political tasks at hand. In particular, the presidential tradition determines presidential outcomes, for where there is a "presidential constitution... the transition to democracy takes place through the free election of a new president, presumably under the old constitution, for either a normal or a reduced mandate" (Linz 1994: 68). Hence, there is really very little "institutional uncertainty," and democratic transitions are characterized by "political gardening" rather than by institutional "designer activism" (Stark 1992).

Yet institutional constraints do not operate uniformly throughout the "political society" where control of public power is contested (Stepan 1989), since it includes not only constitutional and electoral rules, but also political party programs, party alliances and coalitions, and legislative procedure. The political parties themselves may appear to rise "phoenix-like from the ashes" and "have little to gain from making risky changes to the political rules" (Geddes 1996: 31) when acting as a "natural focal point for negotiated transition" (Cohen and Arato 1992: 53). But they do have to appeal to a mass public, and "organize" that public for participation in electoral politics; while some sectors of the public may have both organized and mobilized in the struggle against the dictatorship.

But the elite-centered view stops short at this point, and "ignores the many ties that bind leaders to mass publics, for example, through political parties, trade unions, and secondary associations of all kinds" (Levine 1988: 385). In particular, there are no bridges to the burgeoning literature on social movements, so "we are left with reified social forces moving at one level, and leaders interacting at another" (Levine 1988: 388). The focus on democratic transition must therefore be complemented with an account of popular agency in civil society.

DEMOCRATIC TRANSFORMATION

The first major comparative study of democratic transition in Latin America asserted that the fall of authoritarian regimes has the "crucial component" of large-scale mobilization, and that the liberalization of these regimes may elicit the "resurrection of civil society" required to push the transition forward (O'Donnell and Schmitter 1986: 18–26). Civil society remained undefined, but the widespread assumption – here and elsewhere in the literature – was that civil society was a uniquely popular possibility that was expressed in the rise of social movements. The state had often crushed trade unions, banned political parties, and invaded the universities. There was no freedom of assembly, speech, information, or even habeas corpus. Society had been demobilized. Hence, in Mexico the surge of social movement activity was described as "society getting organized," while in Brazil it was said that "if civil society did not exist it had to be invented." Social movements were not the same as civil society, but they were seen as participating in the process of constructing this society, or recovering it from the state.

Most mobilization in the 1970s and 1980s took the form of urban social movements that represented the popular response to state repression and economic austerity. Depending on time, place, and circumstances, they could include women's, teachers', student, and ethnic movements, and movements on behalf of the "disappeared" and exiled. None of this should imply that the labor and agrarian movements suddenly disappeared. On the contrary, the labor movement often took the lead in opposing the military and authoritarian regimes (Foweraker and Landman 1997), confirming its role as the major democratic actor of the past 100 years (Reuschmeyer, Stephens, and Stephens 1992). But rapid urban expansion did provide a fecund context for the emergence of new social actors and for the discovery of new forms of associational activity that appeared to (re)-create civil society.

The mobilization of civil society becomes political once social movements begin to state their demands in terms of rights. And mobilization for material and economic objectives will generate demands for civil and political rights when met by the political constraints or repression of dictatorial regimes (Foweraker and Craig 1990; Foweraker 1993). Hence, what all the movements came to have in common was the discovery and defense of rights (Cardoso 1983). Land rights, labor rights, educational rights, human rights. In the liberal polities of Western Europe and North America social movements are seen to claim or defend very particular rights because universal rights are already secure. In

Latin America, in contrast, where civil liberties were suppressed and political rights denied, the specific demands of social movements added up to a struggle for popular citizenship, once they were translated into the language of rights. (There is a radical difference between contexts where citizenship is enshrined and others where its elements are still inchoate.) This discovery and affirmation of citizenship rights is central to the process of democratic transformation.

The struggle for citizenship is also the platform for the projection of social movements into political society. By acting as "schools of democracy" (Foweraker 1993) in caucuses, assemblies, demonstrations, and occupations, and by protesting when rules were infringed or promises broken, they created the kind of civic and political associationalism that is essential to political education and contestation (Dahl 1971, 1989). In this way they sought to restore the public sphere and free it from authoritarian constraints and control. It was a fight for "new rights" (Mainwaring and Viola 1984: 33), for "equal rights" and social inclusion (Jelin 1990: 206), and for the positive rights of political participation (Cohen and Arato 1992: 446) that defined a "sphere of freedom" where political society could decide its own rules (Weffort 1989). During the dictatorships it was all too evident that political society required new legal and electoral rules to guarantee freedom of speech and association, as well as political representation through free and fair elections.

A sense of this democratic transformation can correct the Lockean bias of democratic transition by a more Humean emphasis on the delivery of tangible benefits, or the "wish to be rid of tangible evils" (Rustow 1970: 354). In other words, democracy is a matter of mass as well as elite, and the elite pacts which underpin democratic transition must be transmitted "to the citizenry at large" (Rustow 1970: 357) in order to win its support for the newly minted democratic arrangements. Otherwise, too little attention will be paid to non-elite adherence to basic democratic values, and too little made of equality before the law, the right to dissent, and government accountability (Moisés 1993). Since it is only rights and the rule of law that can eliminate arbitrary rule, it is only rights that can create diffuse support for the emerging democratic system (in contrast to the specific support for particular governments that varies with their performance in delivering social goods) (Easton 1975). It is the constitutional presence of civil liberties and political rights that guarantees the key democratic principle of "all power to nobody" (Sartori 1987: 72), and so delivers the substance of democracy to the individuals who compose the polity.

With the democratic transition, political parties (re)-emerge and begin to carry the struggle for citizenship rights into the political and constitutional sphere. Every modern state administration must institutionalize positive law and so create "subjects capable of political obligation, and later the rights of citizens" (Cohen and Arato 1992: 439); and a newly democratic regime will seek to build legitimacy by insisting on these rights. Citizenship becomes a universal identity that is defended by the regime in opposition to the specific identities and claims of social movements (Touraine 1988: 75). Insofar as the rights claimed during the period of democratic transformation are delivered with democratic transition, the movements' claims are met and they lose impetus. "Successful social movements inevitably lose their reason for being" (Jaquette 1989: 194).

The social movements do decline, but their contribution – and that of civil society overall – to democratization remains important. First, their piecemeal impact on state policies and institutional reforms can succeed in reshaping the broad contours of the legal-institutional terrain linking civil society to the state (Foweraker 1993, 1995). Second, they can secure a (temporary) place in political society, and their partial co-optation or "institutionalization" may be a proper price to pay for the emergence of agile political actors that can negotiate with incumbent regimes (Cohen and Arato 1992: 470). Third, although there is some consensus that "the governing bloc must decompose" (Garretón 1989: 262) before democratic transition can occur, it may be social mobilization in civil society that opens the breach (Mainwaring 1992), as well as influencing the strategic calculations of elite actors (Foweraker 1989). Finally, the perception of "decline" is linked to a sense of democratic transition as a singular historical event. Yet social movements have only recently begun to insist on the rights of citizenship, and democratic transitions themselves may still have some way to go.

DEMOCRATIC CONSOLIDATION

Democratic consolidation is said to occur when democracy "becomes routinized and deeply internalized in social, institutional and even psychological life, as well as in political calculations for achieving success" (Linz and Stepan 1997: 16). In the full version of this definition, it depends on the effective operation of ingrained expectations across the five key democratic arenas of civil society, political society, economic society, the state apparatus, and the rule of law (Linz and Stepan 1996: 14). Democracy has become the "only game in town" (Linz and Stepan 1997: 15) and "all major political actors take for granted the fact that democratic processes dictate government renewal" (Mainwaring 1992: 3). [This sense of consensus about the rules of the game is clearly linked to Przeworski's notion of "institutionalizing uncertainty" (Przeworski 1986: 58), since these "major actors" must be convinced of the institutional guarantees that minimize the threat to their longer-term interests. In the reiterative game of electoral democracy, today's losers must be able to think of themselves as tomorrow's winners.]

One of the problems with this definition is that it tends to mix normative and descriptive approaches to democracy (so ignoring the warnings of Sartori 1987), and takes as its "comparative yardstick, a generic and somewhat idealized view of the old polyarchies" (O'Donnell 1997: 44). Consequently the threshold of consolidation is set too high for the Latin American democracies that are not deemed consolidated because they are insufficiently "institutionalized." Expectations of "lawlessness and distrust" are reinforced by the "weakness of both state and the rule of law" (Diamond 1998: 55). This weakness is manifested – for example – in a lack of the kind of horizontal accountability that might curb politicized militaries, or hold them responsible for human rights abuses. The result is seen as "democracy by default" where "façade arrangements" disguise "traditional power relations" and "the persistence of undemocratic structures" (Whitehead 1992: 158).

The attitudinal and behavioral conditions of democracy as "the only game in town" are understood to constitute the "widespread legitimation of democracy" (Diamond 1997b: xix), with legitimacy serving as a salient criterion of democratic consolidation. The (possibly tautological) presumption here is that certain values that comprise a democratic culture "are closely linked with the persistence of stable democracy" (Inglehart and Carballo 1997: 40), so that the "greater the belief in the legitimacy of the institutions of polyarchy, the greater the chances of polyarchy" (Dahl 1989: 262). But it is not always clear "who must accept formal democratic rules, and how deep must this acceptance run" (O'Donnell 1997: 48), and, in particular, whether it is just the elites or the mass of the population that must support democracy. Although most survey data seeks out the general attitudes of the population, the Latin American historical record demonstrates that "democracies are overthrown by elite conspiracies, not popular revolt," with loss of popular support neither "a necessary nor sufficient condition for democratic breakdown" (Remmer 1995: 113).

Despite this caveat, it is just such survey data that are adduced as evidence of Latin America's precarious democratization, with average support for democracy not reaching "the two thirds level" that is a "minimum threshold" for a "consolidated regime" (Diamond 1998: 12–13). Sixty three percent show such support, compared with averages of 78 percent in southern Europe and 79 percent in Eastern Europe (Diamond 1998: 10). But this figure can be seen as encouraging in democracies that are "unconnected with the lived experience of the mass of the population" (Whitehead 1992: 154), where "a very partial form of democratic politics" leads to the "limited or non-participation" of the majority of this population (Held 1992: 20). Moreover, contrary to widely-held assumptions, it appears that "political factors – especially relating to how democratically the regime is performing or being seen to perform – are much more important than economic ones in shaping perceptions of legitimacy," especially those relating to "increased freedom, responsiveness and transparency" (Diamond 1998: 62).

Nevertheless, Latin American democracy continues to be judged as unconsolidated by the literature's main criterion of "a reasonably close fit between formal rules and actual behavior" (O'Donnell 1997: 47). No matter that established democracies like India, or even Japan and Italy, are called consolidated even though they plainly fail to qualify by this criterion. This suggests that there is no lack of institutionalization per se – whether in these cases or Latin America – but it is an institutionalization of informal rules – rather than formal ones – that in Latin America coalesce in clientelism, nepotism, and other particularistic practices. Together with patrimonialism, these informal rules breach and blur the division between public and private, so that particularism comes to "vigorously inhabit most formal political institutions" (O'Donnell 1997: 49). In some degree this is a consequence of "transition through transaction" (Share and Mainwaring 1986), and of the way authoritarian elites retain an influential presence in the state apparatus. But, more importantly, these are pervasive traits of the political culture since time immemorial. Insofar as the informal rules constitute corruption plain and simple, it is a corruption that has grown fat and bloated on the privatization of state assets and the narcotics trade. But both traditional clientelism and modern corruption now affect the core institutions of the state.

There is one major exception to the rule of informal rules (partial or complete, depending on the country in question) and this is the electoral-institutional arena, where "the incumbency of the top government posts is decided by a universalistic process of fairly counting each vote as one" (O'Donnell 1997: 49). This "ring-fencing" of elections is achieved through the measure of horizontal accountability implicit in political party competition, driven by the requirements of international legitimation and finance. And the result is that citizens of the Latin American democracies may enjoy the basic political freedoms implicit in (relatively) free and fair elections, with freedom of opinion, movement, and association, even while their civil rights of personal integrity and equality before the law are infringed or ignored. The division is overdrawn (free and fair elections require civil liberties), but it does help to explain the nature of the gap "between formal rights and actual rights, between commitments to treat citizens as free and equal and practices which do neither sufficiently" (Held

Figure 33.1   Political and civil rights in Latin America

Note: Figure drawn from database funded by Economic and Social Research Council project on Comparative Democratic Performance: Institutional Efficacy and Individual Rights. Variables selected are: executive accountability = Polity III Executive recruitment Competition (ordinal 0-3); civilian control = Binghamton Civilian Control over Military (ordinal 0-5); civil rights = Purdue Political Terror Scale (ordinal 1-5); minority rights = Minorities at Risk Political Discrimination against Minorities (ordinal 0-4)

1992: 20). My current research into democratic performance in Latin America demonstrates that electoral accountability advances rapidly with the transitions to democracy in Latin America, while the provision of civil rights remains static (as shown in figure 33.1):

DEMOCRATIC STABILITY AND DEMOCRATIC PERFORMANCE

The concern with consolidation arises because "it is one thing for a democratic transition to take place; but it is quite another matter for democracy to survive" (Leftwich 1997: 524). The concern is felt acutely in Latin America, where democracies have tended to come and go prior to the swell of the "third wave," but it is always present in processes of democratization. In 1919 the whole of Europe west of Russia and Turkey was systematically reorganized into democratic states, "yet how many democracies remained in Europe in 1939?" (Hobsbawm 1987: 111). Despite the concern, however, it proves difficult to specify exactly when a democracy becomes consolidated, or to define consolidation other than in the teleological sense of serving to sustain democracy. Conversely, "democracies are never completely consolidated" because it is impossible to know the limits where "contingent consent" breaks down (Schmitter 1995: 17). Consolidation then becomes a synonym for democratic stability, in the sense of regime survival and endurance. Yet the current Latin American democracies remain unconsolidated by the usual criteria, although they are surviving. Consequently, "all we can say at present is that, as long as elections are institutionalized, (these democracies) are likely to endure" (O'Donnell 1997: 45).

But the quality of Latin American democracy remains in question. It is argued that the combination of institutionalized elections with informal rules and clientelist politics leads to a "delegative" rather than representative style of political authority, with a "plebiscitarian executive" that acts to subvert the formal authority of congress and the judiciary (O'Donnell 1997: 50). Elite actors and powerful economic interests then tend to target the executive and capture "benefits that flow more as patronage and privileges than as universal rights," while "operating through parties and legislatures only to defend achieved privileges" (Malloy 1987: 252). It is also alleged that these tendencies are exaggerated by a common pattern of presidential government with proportional representation in the assembly. A frequent result is "a fractionalized multiparty system" (Mainwaring 1990: 168) that leaves it very unlikely that the presidential party will enjoy a majority or near majority in the assembly (Mainwaring 1993: 200); and this can create the kind of "gridlock" that stymies the legislative process. Although there is very real variation in the design of these presidential-PR systems (Shugart and Carey 1992: 77), their critics see all of them as beset by the same problems of governance, so that "the Latin American model remains a particularly unattractive option" (Lijphart 1993: 151).

This argument may be overstated on both counts. On the first count, it is true that executives initiate most legislation in Latin America, and tend to have total and line-item vetoes, as well as extensive decree and emergency powers, including that of the state-of-siege (Mainwaring 1993). The received wisdom is that these powers threaten democracy (Shugart and Carey 1992), and that undisciplined political parties in the assembly do little to protect it, with the oft-cited exceptions of Chile, Costa Rica, and Uruguay (Mainwaring 1990). But, on the record, the assemblies are neither weak nor subservient, and certainly do not willingly delegate their powers to the executive in order to overcome stalemate and immobilism (as alleged by Geddes 1996). On the contrary, the available evidence suggests that assemblies are powerful agents that retain a strong ability to check the executive (in countries as different as Brazil, Ecuador, Uruguay, and Venezuela) (Jones 1995). Indeed, the executive is often hard pressed to put through a legislative agenda, lacking effective means for levering recalcitrant assemblies, and it is this executive incapacity that may lead to the decretismo (government by decree) so characteristic of "delegative democracy" (O'Donnell 1992).

Gridlock is inherent to all presidential systems in some degree, since these systems embody two separate agents of the electorate, and lack of policy agreement between executive and assembly can always "cause stress in the regime" (Shugart and Carey 1992: 2). In these circumstances the assembly can always block executive initiatives, even if it cannot directly control the president, while the president remains constitutionally incapable of forcing a majority in the assembly through threat of dissolution (Mainwaring 1993: Valenzuela 1993). But the gridlock of Latin American government is not a fundamental problem, and party indiscipline and party system fragmentation are not so damaging as often alleged (Mainwaring and Shugart 1997: 52). Conversely, governability – understood as government stability, legislative capacity, and the avoidance of gridlock – is greatly enhanced by processes of (pre- and post-electoral) coalition-formation, that go a long way to creating governing majorities or near-majorities in many assemblies (Foweraker 1998). Naturally, this effect is not universal. Coalition-based majorities enabled the Bolivian government to implement a difficult stabilization package, and the Brazilian government to pass a constitutional reform allowing reelection of the president himself. But minority governments precipitated the closure of the congress in Peru, the impeachment of the president in Venezuela, and social protest and the forced resignation of the president in Ecuador.

Overall, the Latin American presidential model works better than the theory predicts. Institutionally, the governability of Latin American democratic systems varies according to party systems and electoral rules, and some institutional designs clearly work better than others in generating "working majorities" in the assembly (Foweraker 1998). Politically, governability is enhanced by processes of coalition-formation that are only possible in a pragmatic and "non-ideological" context; and although not all ideological divisions have disappeared, they do not drive the political process as they did in the 1960s and 1970s. In the main, democratic politics in Latin America are about governability, order, and "accommodation." And here the informal rules and particularism of the political culture may play a positive role. For the particularism does not simply contaminate pristine democratic institutions, so preventing government from delivering in practice the values to which it subscribes in principle. On the contrary, it is the stuff of democratic deliberation, negotiation, and "trade-offs."

So, current democratic government in Latin America is far from perfect, and is rarely as responsive, transparent, or accountable as popular sovereignty would require. It is not yet "good government" (Torres Rivas 1995: 55). But there is political learning, and at least some governments are finding new ways of doing democratic politics. There is, therefore, some hope that democratic performance will improve, and that the current "wave" of democratization in Latin America will endure.

Further Reading

Collier, Ruth Berins 1999: *Paths towards Democracy: the Working Class and Elites in Western Europe and South America*. Cambridge: Cambridge University Press.

Diamond, Larry 1999: *Developing Democracy: Toward Consolidation*. Baltimore and London: Johns Hopkins University Press.

34

Feminism and Democracy

Judith Squires

Second-wave feminists were initially concerned with exploring participatory forms of democracy, but recently attention has shifted to institutions of parliamentary democracy. Although women now have equal formal rights to vote and be elected, the percentage of women in national parliaments is consistently low (with significant variations between countries). However, the grounds for the claim that there should be increased numbers of women in decision-making structures are controversial. While some feminists advocate an interest-based approach, others see the inclusion of women as requiring a more radical challenge to existing political institutions. In her influential argument for a "politics of presence," Anne Phillips synthesizes interest-based and identity-based approaches. Iris Marion Young's theory of group representation stresses that identities must be understood in relational, not essentialist, terms. Her attempt to distinguish her position from interest-group pluralism leads her toward the ideals of deliberative democracy, which she has, on other occasions, criticized as over-universal. Chantal Mouffe's theory of radical democracy is against the instrumentalism of interest-group pluralism and anti-essentialist with regard to identity-based group recognition. She is also opposed to deliberative democracy as embodying an ideal of the common good that is morally incompatible with pluralism. Feminist reflections on the representation of women in the formal institutions of politics provoke reflection on the democratization of representative systems as such.

The two traditions of democracy and feminism share many common preoccupations, but have had a complex, and at times fraught, association. The democratic tradition long predates feminism: only in the nineteenth century did democrats begin to take seriously the issue of women's democratic rights. The feminist tradition on the other hand has always been concerned to be democratic and has frequently aimed to revitalize democratic theory and practice. Second-wave feminism emerged in western liberal democracies in the 1960s, simultaneous with a growing scepticism amongst political activists about formal representative democracy and an active exploration of more participatory forms of democracy. Both developments shifted attention away from the formal representative and decision-making mechanisms of government toward more diffuse and informal practices of participation. Carole Pateman's *Participation and Democratic Theory* (1970) was an early example of this enthusiasm for workplace democracy. The Women's Movement actively experimented with democratic practices, attempting to develop new forms of democratic inclusion for women. Such experiments influenced the practices of the Left, as documented by Hilary Wainwright, Sheila Rowbotham, and Lynne Segal in *Beyond the Fragments* (1979).

By the end of the 1980s the focus of democratic theorists' attention had turned back to the institutions of parliamentary democracy. The events in Eastern Europe focused attention on the importance of democratic elections and representative government. Meanwhile the social movements in the West had lost much of their energy and enthusiasm for active participation. Both the democratic and feminist traditions turned their attention to liberal democracy, with its focus on individual rights, periodic elections, and representative government. "The reinstatement of liberal democracy as something positive," comments Anne Phillips, "is one of the major theoretical phenomena of our time." (1991: 13). For many participatory democrats this turn to representative government is something of a capitulation to pragmatism. Yet, ironically, the more limited goals of equal representation within local and national government have proved far from accessible for women.

Since 1788 when women first gained the right to stand for election in the United States of America, women's right to vote and be elected has been slowly recognized throughout the sovereign states of the world. Only Kuwait and the United Arab Emirates continue to refuse women the right to vote and stand for election. Yet active participation in national parliaments by women is still notoriously low; the percentage of women in national parliaments globally rose from 3 percent in 1945 to only 11.6 percent in 1995. As of July 1999 the world average for the percentage of women in national parliaments was 12.7 percent. The rate of change in women's electoral success has not therefore been as great as many people had expected given that legal restrictions have largely been removed. Moreover, the comparative percentage of women in parliaments internationally is proving increasingly intriguing. On the one hand there is a notable degree of uniformity. Whilst the Nordic countries have achieved the high of 38.9 percent, women in their parliaments and the Arab States maintain their low of 3.4 percent, the overwhelming majority of states (including the Americas, Europe, Asia, the Pacific, and Sub-Saharan Africa) have very consistent proportions of women in their parliaments; ranging between 10.2 percent and 15.1 percent only (see http://www.ipu.org/wmn-e/world.htm for current information). On the other hand, the variation between countries (between Sweden, for example, on 42.7 percent and France on 10.9 percent) does not seem to be as clearly related to employment practices, social structures, or cultural values as many scholars had predicted. It is now widely accepted that one of the most significant factors explaining cross-cultural differences in the representation of women is the electoral system. Recent research indicates that electoral systems with a high number of seats in multi-member constituencies facilitate the entry of women (Norris 1993: 312).

In the context of this data, the rather conventional issue of the number of women in the national legislature has now become the subject of greater theoretical interest to feminists than it was throughout the 1960s and 1970s. Whereas the persistent under-representation of women was previously thought by many feminists to be an issue of limited interest (there being many more radical issues of structural importance to address), it is now recognized to be a significant and complex issue in its own right. As Phillips notes, "politics appears to be more of an independent variable than might have been expected and substantial political equalities look possible even in the absence of thorough-going social or economic reform" (Phillips 1991: 19).

THE REPRESENTATION OF WOMEN

Most forms of feminist activism during the 1990s have asserted an explicit claim for an increased presence of women in decision-making structures. These demands are often based on a presumption that women have interests that are best represented by women. Yet, as Lovenduski notes, "that understanding has been fiercely contested by feminists, their sympathizers and their opponents in a continuing and sometimes acrimonious debate" (Lovenduski and Norris 1996: 1). Given that women, even those claiming the title feminist, currently articulate such distinct political positions, it is hard to judge what might be an accurate representation of their interests.

Sapiro explores the claim that women share particular experiences and have common "representable interests" (Sapiro 1998: 164). To assess whether women are an "interest group" and, if so, what interests they have, Sapiro claims that one needs to consider both women's "objective situation" and their conscious-ness of their own interests. For saying "that women are in a different social position from that of men and therefore have interests to be represented is not the same as saying that women are conscious of these differences, that they define themselves as having special interests requiring representation, or that men and women as groups now disagree on policy issues on which women might have a special interest" (Sapiro 1998: 167).

This is politically significant because, contrary to the Burkean notion of paternalistic representation of the interests of others, political systems are – Sapiro notes – not likely to represent previously underrepresented groups "until those groups develop a sense of their own interests and place demands upon the system" (Sapiro 1998: 167). Moreover, if the interests in question are not clear and preformed, but are still in the process of being uncovered via processes of consciousness-raising, it will then be more difficult to distinguish between the represented and the representative. In these circumstances women would seem to be best placed to advocate the interests of women.

Other advocates of group representation reject this interest-based approach. Diamond and Hartsock argue against casting women as simply another interest group among many, and refute the idea that fairness requires that women promote their interests within the existing political system equally with all other such interest groups. This, they claim, underplays the distinctive and radical challenge posed by the recognition of women's experiences and political ambitions. It also overlooks the new political and methodological questions raised by their position: "if the inclusion of women into politics threatens the most basic structures of society, one cannot fit their concerns into the framework of interests" (Diamond and Hartsock 1998: 193). The very language of interests, they argue, emerges with and then perpetuates the division of labor that creates the ideal of rational economic men seeking to maximize their satisfactions. They propose that it be replaced by more encompassing categories of analysis, which more adequately capture the range of human emotions, such as needs.

Their basic resistance to Sapiro's focus on interests is that it implies that the issue of women's fair representation is an issue of inclusion: that women are seeking to catch up with men (Diamond and Hartsock 1998: 197). In direct contrast, they argue that women's demands cannot simply be integrated into the system; the inclusion of questions of reproduction and sexuality into the political process will transform the very concept of the political, eroding the public/private distinction and, presumably (though they do not state this directly), undermining the current system of representative democracy in favor of a more participatory one. Nonetheless, within the confines of the current representative system they are clear that "only women can 'act for' women in identifying 'invisible' problems affecting the lives of large numbers of women" (Diamond and Hartsock 1998: 198). In short, they too argue for group representation, but the group in question is conceived as an identity group not an interest group.

More recent work on feminism and democracy usually attempts to resolve this apparent opposition between those who seek the more effective representation of women's interests within interest-group pluralism, and those who seek the transformation of the representative system itself. In her influential work, Phillips adopts an integrative position, synthesizing the interest-based and identity-based approaches.

THE POLITICS OF PRESENCE

Phillips's "rather commonsensical" solution is to use both the terms "interests" and "needs" together (Phillips 1995: 73). Both positions, she claims, have their strengths and weaknesses: "Interests can sound rather grasping and competitive, but it does at least serve to remind us that there may be conflicts between different groups. Need has more obvious moral resonance, but it originates from a paternalist discourse which lends itself more readily to decisions by experts on behalf of the need group" (Phillips 1995: 73). The first may be overly individualistic but there are contrasting worries that the second may be overly assimilatory. In an attempt to synthesize the best of these approaches and provide a firmer normative basis from which to consider the arguments for the increased representation of women, Phillips proposes a "politics of presence."

A "politics of ideas" is Phillips' term for politics that focuses on policies and representation that focuses on people's beliefs and interests. Fair representation is, on this ideas-based model of politics, realized in the ongoing responsiveness of representatives to those they are representing. The accountability of representatives to their electorate is therefore paramount. As long as they are responsive, it matters little who the representatives are: "the messages will vary, but it hardly matters if the messengers are the same" (Phillips 1995: 6). A politics of presence, on the other hand, is Phillips' term for politics that focuses on the messengers as well, generating forms of representation that recognize both interests and identities. Fair representation, on this conception of politics, requires that the overly cerebral concentration on beliefs and interests be extended to recognize the political significance of the identity of the representatives. Fair representation, from the perspective of a politics of presence, regards the gender (and any other social identity deemed politically significant) of the representative to be "an important part of what makes them representative..." (Phillips 1995: 13). The descriptive similarity of the representatives in relation to their electorate is vital.

This endorsement of a politics of presence is controversial. Phillips lists three central objections. The first two originate from within the interest-based model of politics and the third from the participatory democracy model of politics (there being internal divisions within these camps as to whether group representation is the best way forward). First, there is the argument that such a politics poses a threat to national unity and leads to a "balkanisation" of the polity, in that it encourages intransigence rather than cohesion. Secondly, there is a concern that it undermines the basis for political accountability in that it is much harder to clearly define what a social group, as opposed to an interest group, really wants (what its interests are and whether they are being pursued). The third objection, made not by advocates of interest-based politics but by civic republicans and deliberative democrats, is that this is yet another capitulation to representative politics (albeit group-based rather than individualistic), which detracts from the pursuit of a truly inclusive and participatory politics of the common good (Phillips 1995: 21–4). We could also add a fourth objection, which arises from a more deconstructive concern that any institutionalization of group identity will work to reify and normalize identities in a way that might then be used to resubordinate the group in question.

It is the second concern about accountability that Phillips takes to be the most serious in relation to debates about the political representation of women. As accountability "is best understood in relation to the politics of ideas" it is essential that a politics of ideas is not jettisoned altogether in any move toward a politics of presence (Phillips 1995: 56). Accordingly, she argues that: "It is in the relationship between ideas and presence that we can best hope to find a fairer system of representation, not in a false opposition between one or the other" (Phillips 1995: 25). Phillips also takes the third concern seriously, acknowledging that arguments for group representation are at their strongest when placed in the context of wider arguments for participatory democracy (Phillips 1995: 145–65). Accordingly, she proposes "active intervention to include members of groups currently under-represented in politics..." (Phillips 1995: 167). Theorists grounded in a tradition of deliberative and participatory democracy are, Phillips feels, able to offer more than those within the overly narrow traditions of interest-group pluralism or identity-based politics. Notably, Phillips commends Young's particular vision of group representation in that: "it recognizes the potential diversity and disagreement within any social group; and it provides some basis for the accountability of representatives to those they might claim to represent" (Phillips 1995: 54).

GROUP REPRESENTATION

Like Phillips, Young claims that existing electoral and legislative processes are "unrepresentative" in the sense that they fail to reflect the diversity of the population, leading her to demand that a certain number of seats in the legislature be reserved for the members of marginalized groups. She suggests that groups which have suffered oppression need guaranteed representation in order that their distinct voice can be heard. For a just polity requires the participation and inclusion of all groups, which is only secured by differential treatment for oppressed groups.

This rejection of the assimilationist ideal is based in a belief that attachment to specific traditions, practices, language, and other culturally specific forms is a crucial aspect of social existence. A democratic public should therefore provide mechanisms for "the effective recognition and representation of the distinct voices and perspectives of those of its constituent groups that are oppressed or disadvantaged" (Young 1990: 184). These mechanisms will involve three distinct features. First, the provision of public resources, which will be used to support the self-organization of group members, "so that they achieve collective empowerment and a reflective understanding of their collective experiences and interests in the context of the society" (Young 1990: 184). Secondly, the provision of public resources to enable the group to analyze and generate policy proposals in institutionalized contexts, and the formal requirement that decision-makers show that they have taken these perspectives into account. Thirdly, the group veto power regarding specific policies that affect a group directly, "... such as reproductive rights for women" (Young 1990: 184).

Rather than transcending particularity Young proposes that "... attention to social group differentiation is an important resource for democratic communication" (Young 1997: 385). But social groups are not to be confused with interest groups. Young is keen to point out that these groups should be understood in relational, not essentialist, terms. The social groups she would positively recognize in her vision of differentiated citizenship are products of social relations and are therefore fluid and intersecting. Social groups are neither "any aggregate or association of persons who seek a particular goal, or desire the same policy..." nor "a collective of persons with shared political beliefs" (Young 1990: 186). Rather, "... the social positioning of group differentiation gives to individuals some shared *perspectives* on social life" (Young 1997: 385).

Despite this attempt to define social groups as clearly relational, some commentators have confused Young's position with identity politics (Elshtain 1995), and others feel that she moves too close to an interest-based politics. Mouffe, for example, claims that Young's vision is actually nothing more than a rearticulation of interest-group pluralism (Mouffe 1992: 369–85). But these are both charges that Young rejects. In response to Elshtain she insists that her "politics of difference" is not an identity politics; indeed it offers a basis from which to critique a politics of identity (Young 1997: 385–97). In response to Mouffe she claims that her vision of group representation is fundamentally different from interest-group pluralism in that it promotes public discussion and decision-making rather than the pursuit of predefined interests (Young 1990: 186–90). In other words, she avoids the problems of essentialism and unaccountability of an identity-group politics only to be charged with adopting a form of interest-group pluralism, which she also wants to reject.

Young's attempt to distinguish her position from interest-group pluralism propels her to invoke the norms of just deliberation that arise from a deliberative democracy framework, which she has, on other occasions, criticized as overly universalistic. Her argument is that interest groups simply promote their own interests in a political marketplace, with no reference to a conception of social justice or the common good. The social groups argued by Young to require special representation are, on the other hand, defined with reference to a specific vision of justice which generates criteria for assessing social oppression, and hence criteria for establishing which groups require such representative guarantees. This vision of justice offers guidance regarding which groups require special representation rights, and how they should act in the political realm. A distinction is made between demands stemming from self-interest and those stemming from justice: "the test of whether a claim upon the public is just or merely an expression of self-interest is best made when those making it must confront the opinion of others who have explicitly different, though not necessarily conflicting, experiences, priorities and needs" (Young 1990: 186). In other words, to engage in deliberation with other social groups marks a just political dialogue as opposed to a simple expression of instrumental interest.

Young's particular defense of group representation rests on a notion of social groups. This notion in turn invokes a tradition of deliberative democracy, which frequently makes appeal to a Habermassian notion of discourse ethics. Young argues that even though Habermas "seems unwilling to abandon a standpoint of universal normative reason that transcends particularist perspectives" he "has gone further than any other contemporary thinker in elaborating the project of a moral reason that recognized the plurality of subjects" (Young 1990: 106). Significantly, although Young criticizes deliberative democracy because of its appeal to the ideal of impartiality, her attempt to distance herself from the instrumentalism of interest-group pluralism actually propels her towards precisely this endorsement of impartiality and deliberation. Indeed, as Phillips notes (Phillips 1995: 147), whereas Young's initial formulation of her argument for group representation relied on heavily criticizing deliberative democracy, she now uses this framework, in a slightly modified form, which she labels communicative democracy, to defend her own vision of group representation (Young 1996: 120–36).

Significant modifications of the basic deliberative model are proposed however. Young recommends that the forms of communication considered significant in debates about justice be extended to include greeting, rhetoric, and storytelling. Greeting entails non-linguistic gestures, such as smiles and handshakes, which bring bodies into communication. Rhetoric entails humor, wordplay, images, and metaphors, which bring desire into communication.

Storytelling entails narratives that exhibit subjective experience and evoke sympathy, which brings experience into communication (Young 1996: 129–32). But whether this ideal of communicative ethics really stands in opposition to impartiality, or simply articulates a form of impartiality that attempts to be attentive to difference is, however, worth considering. Whilst advocates of deliberative democracy tend to view Young as an oppositional voice (Dryzek 1999; Miller 1999), critics of the deliberative model of democracy see her as located broadly within this camp (Mouffe 1993: 85–6).

RADICAL DEMOCRACY

Chantal Mouffe is sceptical about the deliberative model of democracy. She offers another attempt at a resolution of the rights-based and participatory approaches to democracy, stressing the centrality of the notion of rights complemented by a more active sense of political participation and belonging (Mouffe 1992a: 378). Whilst she endorses a participatory vision of democracy, Mouffe endorses the centrality of rights and warns of the dangers of a substantive notion of common good. She distances herself from republican models of democracy by clearly differentiating between social and political communities. Arguing that all other communities are partial and exclusionary, the only community that Mouffe allows as the basis for political action in a political community is a group "bound by their common identification with a given interpretation of a set of ethico-political values" (Mouffe 1992a: 378). The community of women is an identity-based community, which ought not to be a basis for political action.

The central problem with the liberal conception of citizenship, she argues, is that it has "reduced citizenship to a merely legal status, indicating the rights that the individual holds against the state" (Mouffe 1992a: 377). She notes, as generations of republican thinkers have noted, that notions of public-spiritedness, civic activity, and political participation have been excluded by this overly narrow rights-based approach. However, she also acknowledges, along with liberal theorists, that the communitarian insistence on a substantive notion of the common good and shared moral values is incompatible with pluralism (Mouffe 1992a: 378). A "modern pluralist democracy" would, in Mouffe's estimation, negotiate both of these potential dangers by casting citizenship as a political identity that consists in the identification with the assertion of liberty and equality for all. Whereas liberalism evacuates the idea of a common good and republicanism reifies it, a radical democratic approach views the common good as something that we constantly refer to but that can never be reached.

Her model of representative democracy is not simply instrumental – it is not about the articulation and representation of preformed interests. It is about the constitution and contingent negotiation of identities and interests within the political realm itself. This, she argues, will always be an antagonistic process: "To negate the ineradicable character of antagonism and aim at a universal rational consensus – this is the real threat to democracy" (Mouffe 1996: 247). And it is here that she is clearly at odds with the communicative democracy offered by Young. Despite Young's own scepticism about universality, Mouffe finds her too accepting of the deliberative vision of discourse ethics for comfort.

Mouffe also rejects Young's proposals for group representation, objecting to the idea that sexual difference should be a valid distinction in the domain of politics (Mouffe 1992a: 377). She dislikes the idea of group representation as a positive political strategy. She, like all feminist theorists situated firmly within the deconstructive frame, is determined to avoid both instrumental interest-group pluralism and essentializing identity-based group recognition. These theorists highlight the very real dangers of these two approaches.

But, unlike the more integrative and deliberative work of Phillips and Young, the nature of the specific proposals for mechanisms of political representation that emerge from this perspective are largely undeveloped. Critics argue that this is an inevitable consequence of the deconstructive approach, which lacks a normative account of citizenship; "it is only a method to be used," states Voet, "it is not a substantial political theory in itself" (Voet 1998: 131). Yet, even if this is accepted, an increasing number of theorists are appealing to its method in order to reappraise the potential of liberal democracy.

CONCLUSION

The debates within feminist theory outlined here may appear to be far removed from the daily practice of democracy and the pressing issue of the low levels of participation of women in formal politics, but there are important links. The emphasis of early second-wave feminism on informal grass-roots democratic practices has done much to draw attention, in both theory and practice, to the limitations of defining politics too narrowly and locating democratic practice within the formal institutions only. The democratization of everyday life has come to be seen as a central requirement for the realization of active democratic participation for all. The more recent turn within feminist theory toward consideration about the mechanisms for realizing full participation within the formal institutions of politics is now focusing attention on the equally significant issue of democratization of the representative systems itself. These two developments combined highlight the democratic significance of ensuring the active participation of all social groups in the various decision-making bodies of the polity. The current reflections on mechanisms of fair representation invigorate existing democratic theory and suggest new, more inclusive, forms of democratic practice.

Further Reading

Nash, Kate 1998: "Beyond liberalism? Feminist theories of democracy." In Vicky Randall and Georgina Waylen (eds.) *Gender, Politics and the State*. London: Routledge.
Phillips, A. 1991: *Engendering Democracy*. Cambridge: Polity Press.

35

Postmodernization, Fragmentation, Globalization
Postmodernization

Jan Pakulski

Political modernization is generally agreed to have involved differentiation
of politics from religion and morality, bureaucratization of the "body
politic" and increasing political participation; the "freezing" of sociopolitical divisions; and the centrality of the sovereign nation-state. There is also
a broad consensus on the corporatist contours of late modernity. "Postmodernization" and "postmodernity," on the other hand, are much more
contentious concepts. Nevertheless, there are a number of common trends
in postmodern analyses. The state is shrinking as its modern role in providing external defense, internal surveillance, and citizenship rights is undermined. Furthermore, states are increasingly interdependent in a way that
undermines sovereignty. "Transnational society" is a network of groups
and organizations that operate outside and (at least partly) independently
of the state. International and "post-international" politics generate a new
"multicentric world." There is a dedifferentiation of politics from private
concerns, as democratic principles are extended beyond the political
sphere, while politics becomes mass spectacle. Party-class dealignment
and the rise of new political identities, particularly those mobilized by
"new social movements," further undermine the autonomy of political
elites. Modern ideologies are eroded – especially socialism – and the left–
right continuum is questioned. Civic nationalism vies with ethno-nationalism in many advanced societies. These changes suggest a major historical
discontinuity, though it is still too early to make a definitive diagnosis of
postmodernity.

There seems to be broad agreement among social scientists on the main processes of political modernization or, in the Marxist lingo, political ascendancy of
bourgeois capitalism. These include differentiation of politics from religion and
morality; organization and bureaucratization of the "body politic," especially of
the state and political parties; and increasing political participation combined
with the emergence of social cleavage politics. The latter involves the emergence
and subsequent "freezing" of sociopolitical (mainly class, regional, and religious)
divisions in the process of industrial and national revolutions. The agreement
also extends to such key features as the centrality of territorial nation-states
operating according to an internationally recognized principle of sovereignty; of

cleavage-based political parties that organize and mobilize mass support; and of elaborate ideologies that underlie mass political contests. The late modernity, it has also been widely agreed, added to this general picture some details and clearer contours: the ascendancy of corporate elites; the growth of mass, catch-all political parties with highly bureaucratized party machines; corporatist "deals" between governments, big business, and central unions that helped to diffuse social, mainly class, conflicts; and progressive "mass-mediation" of politics. While Marxists, liberals, and conservatives differ in their interpretations of the sources and distribution of political power, evaluate differently the core political institutions, and chart differently the future, they share the broad consensus concerning the key ingredients and directions of political modernization which, for Marxists, has been synonymous with entrenchment of the bourgeois political order.

There is no such agreement about contemporary political processes and the notions of "postmodernization" and "postmodernity." These are contentious concepts unifying in opposition both Marxist and "mainstream" scholars. They signify a breach and discontinuity in sociopolitical developments, a contrast with, rather than continuation of, modern patterns and trends, regardless of whether conceptualized as "democratic class struggles" or "corporate-bureaucratic trends," as interpreted by "mainstream" liberal and conservative thinkers. "[T]o speak about postmodernity," according to Featherstone (1988: 198), "is to suggest an epochal shift or break from modernity involving the emergence of a new social totality with its own distinctive organizing principles." They also signify a different way of understanding and explaining contemporary change. Advocates of postmodern change not only highlight discontinuities, and often the reversals, of historical trends, but also emphasize the tentative nature of generalizations about them. The very prefix "post-" reflects uncertainty as to the nature of these new developments and scepticism about the "grand" or "meta-" narratives of modernization, including ideological constructs of socialism, liberalism, conservatism, and welfarism, and the accompanying beliefs in progress.

While these are the common elements of postmodern analyses, differences are equally important. Those like Zygmunt Bauman see the advanced societies as already "postmodern." By contrast, those like Stephen Crook et al. analyze "postmodernization" as an ongoing – and by no means even or complete – social process. Those like David Harvey and Mike Featherstone see it as a phase in capitalist development, while those like Malcolm Waters (1996) see an inversion of modern trends. Those who follow a neo-Marxist tradition in social analysis tend to see contemporary politics as either a "disorganized" or even chaotic face of contemporary capitalism (e.g. Lash 1990), or as "a new cultural logic of late capitalism" (e.g. Jameson 1991). Their analyses of the postmodern condition tend to be most critical and sombre – not unlike their neo-Marxist predecessors. The critical "culturalists," by contrast, focus on value change (e.g. Inglehart 1996), the decline of ideological meta-narratives and return to the local and vernacular (e.g. Lyotard 1984), the ascendancy of autonomous but empty symbols or simulacra (e.g. Baudrillard 1983), and the rise of plural and diverse "identity politics."

Let us ignore, for a moment, these differences and focus instead on the key post-modernizing trends seen as symptomatic of historical discontinuities. By doing that, we remain faithful to the core intuitions of postmodern analyses which are sceptical of sweeping generalizations and grand narratives.

THE SHRINKING STATE

The modern state has emerged as a centralized administrative machine involved in warfare and welfare – the former securing international position and the latter attenuating internal social conflicts. The corporatist settlements established under the aegis of this interventionist state in the early twentieth century began to show evidence of considerable dysfunction in the 1970s and 1980s, thus prompting the diagnoses of welfare, legitimacy, fiscal and governing "crises," and attempts to "roll the state back." More importantly, the three essential functions of the modern state – external defense, internal surveillance, and the maintenance of citizenship rights – have been undermined by new developments in military technology and public attitudes.

The defensive functions of the state in advanced societies have been under-mined by the combined force of nuclear proliferation, multilateral alliances and agreements (including NATO and the disarmament plus arms control treaties), the declining role of the military elites, and the spread of individualistic and libertarian orientations among the young and educated segments of the popula-tion. Nuclear weapons make military confrontations risky for both sides, regard-less of the overall balance of military might. The awareness of these risks has been increased by campaigns conducted by the pacifist movements. The world-wide coverage of hostilities by the mass movements and media has made the use of violence a politically risky option. Military ventures are routinely condemned by the public unwilling to tolerate the loss of life, as well as by influential political groups sceptical of political effectiveness and opposed to the high costs of warfare. Even when they occur, such ventures are difficult to sustain. This is due not only to organized public pressures, but also to the waning of relative powers of military elites. The ties of military establishments with the corporate elites, especially in Europe, have been weakened by a decentralization of economic decision-making, increasing difficulties in legitimizing vast military expenditure, and the impact of anti-militaristic peace movements.

The role of the state as provider and guardian of citizenship rights and political freedoms has been eroded by spiralling costs and publicity given to unintended side effects. Welfare provisions and entitlements, in particular, have been singled out as unsustainable in the light of climbing costs, declining capa-city to extract taxes, and publicity given to welfare dependencies. The alternative "workfare principle" found its supporters among the right-of-center liberals and left-of-center libertarians prompting calls for "rolling back" of the etatist welfare project. Restricting the welfare and other regulative functions of the state became something of the common wisdom of political elites, including the New Labor. Moreover, an increasing range of rights and freedoms have been depoliticized and thus defined as "human rights" and "individual freedoms" located above and beyond the control of the state, while state violations of these rights have been publicized thus undermining the core elements of state legitimacy as the principal guardian of citizenship rights.

This shrinking of the regulative functions reflects both the declining willingness and the waning capacities of the state elites to control economy and society. Increasing economic globalization and involvement in international agreements reduces the capacity of governments to affect economic performance, levels of unemployment, and allocation of rights and privileges. The net result of these declining capacities has been a leaner and more humble state.

Erosion of Sovereignty and the Politics of Trust

One may see these developments as a redistribution of state powers and responsibilities formerly concentrated in national governments. They are redistributed horizontally to autonomous corporate bodies; "downwards" to autonomous quangos, civic initiatives, and extra-state self-governing bodies; "sideways" through marketization and privatization of previously state-run enterprises; and "upwards" to suprastate bodies, including the UN, World Bank, and the WTO. The last of these redistributive shifts is particularly conspicuous in Western Europe. The European integration marks a decline in individual states' capacities to shape their policies, both internally and internationally, and in their sovereignty. This, in turn, attracts the ire of right-of-center nationalist groups, as well as the opposition from the traditional left concerned with the erosion of states' capacities to prevent unemployment, regulate labor conditions, and control immigration.

The role of the state in international relations has also been changing in an equally dramatic fashion. The modern states have always operated according to the principle of territorial sovereignty and power politics. This starts to change. The advanced societies of Western Europe, North America, and Australasia have been witnessing a "postmodern shift" toward mutual constraints and surveillance reflecting the recognition of mutual dependence and vulnerability, and resulting in open interference and monitoring (Cooper 1997). This shift encompasses economic, military, and social affairs. While the Treaty of Westphalia (1648) legitimized the modernist principle of sovereignty and power-politics, the Treaty of Rome (1972), arms control deals, and the multiple trade extension and tariffs reduction agreements in the second half of the twentieth century mark the birth of codependent and interfering "postmodern states." The security of such states and societies depends increasingly on international constraints, openness, and trust-building measures, which include mutual surveillance. Similarly, their economic affairs, as well as such "internal-domestic" matters as crime controls and treatment of minorities, are subject to multilateral monitoring and controls. This shift, it must be stressed again, affects the advanced (largely western) societies; most states in the developing world still follow the modern principles and paths of development.

TRANSNATIONAL SOCIETY AND MULTICENTRIC WORLD

Another aspect of this trend is the proliferation of multifarious groups and organizations operating outside and (at least partly) independently of states. According to Rosenau (1990), these bodies form an increasingly powerful network of "transnational society." The network includes, first of all, such transnational structures as global financial networks, networks of technology and knowledge production, and networks of transnational manufacturing, connected through nodes of transnational corporations. Secondly, it includes increasingly vocal trans-and international communities based on religion (e.g. Islamic communities), creeds and lifestyles (e.g. the greens), ideology (e.g. the New Right) or sexual preferences (e.g. gay communities). Transnational organizations constitute a third element of the multicentric transnational societies. They include the old ones, such as the Catholic Church, the newer, such as NATO and the UN, and the very new bodies, such as Greenpeace, World Bank, and the IMF. The proliferation of these new bodies, with increasing powers and interconnections, is further prompted by publicity given to transnational problems, i.e. problems beyond the control of any single state, such as pollution, illegal drug trade, the AIDS epidemic, and the banking crisis. Such publicity also generates "transnational events," such as green and pro-democratic mobilizations.

It must be stressed again that these transnational structures, organizations, and events symptomatic of what Rosenau calls "post-international politics," coexist and interact with state and national organizations, and with international, interstate politics. It is a combination of these two types of structures and politics – international and postinternational – that generate a new dynamic of the "multicentric world."

Another aspect of this transnational trend is the erosion of international boundaries and a rapid spread of ideas ("interdependence" according to Waters (1996); "time-space distantiation" according to Giddens (1990: 14); and "time–space compression" according to Harvey (1989: 240)). Floating ideas and institutional copies become widely available and are applied in diverse cultural settings thus producing hybridized institutional orders (institutional bricolage). Good examples of such floating ideas and institutions are "Thatcherism" and the "round table." The former included a set of political-ideological preferences combined with dry liberal strategies of economic management and administration, and it has been adopted in advanced, postcommunist, and developing societies in a way reminiscent of cultural trends and fashions. Similarly, the "round table" model of political negotiations pioneered successfully in Poland in 1988/9 was subsuquently adopted in other postcommunist societies, as well as South Africa, Cambodia, and the Philippines.

BLURRING BOUNDARIES, POLITICAL SPECTACLES, AND PLEBISCITARY PRESSURES

While democratic pressures prompt the spread of international politics of trust, they also result in a weakening of institutional separation. To reiterate, this institutional separation and differentiation, including the separation of politics from morality and public from private spheres, has been diagnosed as a core modern trend. Diffusion of democratic values and practices has resulted in dedifferentiation, in a blurring of these divisions. The politicization of private spheres (e.g. gender and domestic relations, sexual preferences, etc.) coincides with what may be described as privatization of politics. Its immediate symptoms include demands for extension of democratic principles well beyond what in the past constituted the "political sphere" and into familial, domestic, and gender relations. The slogan of feminist activists "the personal is political" has its numerous equivalents among the "moralist" right-of-center movements campaigning against abortion, pornography, and "declining moral standards." The rising political moralism, and the ascendancy of "politics of rights and convictions" herald a declining differentiation and separation of private and public spheres.

These pressures, it must also be noted, are reinforced by the electronic mass media, especially television. TV and the other electronic media (including the daily press) represent political events as a spectacle, often framed in a manner resembling popular culture dramas and commercials. Such "pop-formatted" coverage of electoral contests, crime, and atrocities committed by political groups and regimes, generates immediate and powerful audience reactions, as well as demands for morally rectifying action. These demands are increasingly difficult to resist by politicians whose power and autonomy are eroded by weakening party apparatuses and dealignment (discussed below). The first victim of such pressures is political consistency and long-term policy cohesion. The sober *Realpolitik* based on long-term calculus gives way to fickle populist politics propelled by media coverage and responding to momentary swings of public sentiments.

By making politics a mass spectacle, the media contribute to the weakening of institutional insulation of elites. Such insulation from immediate pressures allowed the elites for autonomous, responsible, and calculative decision-making. The weakening of the insulation results in mounting plebiscitary pressures, and in the widening adoption by elites of populist management techniques of image-cultivation. To critics, this amounts to the end of political leadership; to supporters of grassroots politics, this is a welcome symptom of increasing political responsiveness.

POLITICAL DEALIGNMENT AND DECLINING CLEAVAGE POLITICS

The autonomy of elite action is also eroded by party-class dealignment. Dealignment refers to four parallel processes: a decline in class voting; the fragmentation of the major "class parties"; the declining partisanship and consistency of voting; and a decline in class-specific appeals by political parties. The most popular measures of dealignment, the Alford Index and Thomsen Index of class voting, have declined since the 1960s in all advanced societies for which longitudinal data on voting behavior are available (e.g. Clark, Lipset, and Rempel 1993; Nieuwbeerta 1997). The decline varies in speed and intensity, but it appears to be a universal trend throughout the post Second World War period, particularly strong in societies with an initially high level of class voting. The dealignment has been accompanied by the rise of various "third" and "unallied" forces, including "single-issue parties," protest parties, and by the proliferation of "independents."

Another aspect of the dealignment process is declining trust in, and loyalty to, the old political parties (e.g. Blondel 1978; Franklin et al. 1992). This results in the collapse of the inter-generational transmission of party loyalties. Taken together, these trends mark the waning of stable political constituencies, ascendancy of temporary alignments, and the proliferation of fickle issue-voting.

Also weakening is the nexus between political attitudes and political activism. Studies of the relationship between images of attitudes and political activism show a wide disparity between them (e.g. Graetz 1983, 1992). This is linked with the ascendancy of new identities formed around such highly publicized and politically prominent issues as ethnicity, gender, and lifestyle. These identities seem to be displacing the old (especially class-based) identities as generators of political preference and action, at least among the young and educated urbanities.

It is hard to find a consistent explanation of these trends. As noted above, it has been linked with mass mediation of politics, mass democratization, and the spread of postmaterial value priorities. It has also been suggested that advanced societies undergo de-traditionalization resulting in a breakdown of political socialization and the widening generation gap; that high social and territorial mobility in metropolitan areas undermines class communities and creates marginal and floating electorates; and that the new issues displace the old class-specific repertoires of concerns. Whatever combination of factors is responsible, there is little doubt that the old pattern of social cleavage-based political behavior has been in decline (e.g. Dunleavy 1980; Pakulski and Waters 1996).

THE NEW BASES OF POLITICAL PREFERENCES

Many students of political behavior suggest that political preferences today detach themselves from social divisions (e.g. Rose and McAllister 1985; Franklin, Mackie, and Valen 1992; Kitschelt 1994). The shift seems to be from a stable structurally-based and ideologically oriented political behavior to a new configuration that is more contingent, volatile, and issue-specific. For example, Kitschelt (1994) has shown a progressive destructuring of votes throughout Western Europe, "though with a different pace and rhythm." Increasingly, voter preferences and party choices are based on such factors as market and organizational location, production sector, generation and lifecycle, gender, and consumption style. Support for the new political forces, especially the emergent "third" and Left-Libertarian parties, reflects the growing salience of these new divisions.

The contemporary "politics of difference," like the post-Fordist production, becomes a politics of highly specialized, issue-centered niches. It responds to specific demands of smaller segments of the population differentiated along the lines of localities, lifestyles, education and skills, gender, generation, cultural consumption, as well as type of production, and productive sector (internationally competitive vs. protected). These divisions do not form a stable cleavage pattern; they themselves vary from region to region, and reflect both social locations and social trajectories and are subject to significant conjectural variation. Some of them detach themselves from social locations to the extent that suggest the social decoupling of political orientations and preferences (Crook, Pakulski, and Waters 1992).

NEW POLITICS AND NEW SOCIAL MOVEMENTS

Analysts of postmodern change point to the growing salience in advanced societies of "new politics" propelled by new collective actors, new social movements. These new actors are transfunctional, and they attract diffuse social categories formed along locality, gender, ethnicity, and lifestyle lines. Their membership is transient and fluid, and their organizational structure is decentralized, informal, and polymorphous (e.g. Offe 1985; Scott 1990; Maheu and Urry 1994). The concepts of "new politics" and "new social movements" embrace a broad spectrum of social activities transcending the domain of conventional ("old") politics. Perhaps the most popular interpretation sees the new politics as a reflection of new social values (Inglehart 1991). These new post-materialist values are detached from economic interests and issues of national security. They involve concerns with the quality of life, self-actualization, and civil liberties. The new values cut across the old political loyalties and do not fit the established ideological cleavages. They mark the emergence of multipolar ideological-political space "beyond left and right" (Giddens 1996).

The "new social movements" mobilize diverse constituencies that form along new issue clusters (Dalton and Kuechler 1990), generational divisions (Abramson and Inglehart 1992), gender and status blocs (Turner 1988), "life politics" (Giddens 1991), and other dimensions of civil society (Cohen and Arato 1992). More recent analyses identify right-populist counter-movements that form in opposition to left-libertarian new social movements. Anti-green, anti-feminist, anti-minority and anti-gay movements further erode the old patterns of political alliances and supplement the rich gallery of new political actors (Betz 1994).

DECOMPOSING IDEOLOGICAL PACKAGES

Modern ideologies "proper" – liberalism, conservatism, and socialism – crystallized in the nineteenth century. Socialism, in particular, was an ideological child of the industrial class conflict. Modern liberalism and conservatism were reformulated in response to the socialist challenge. The formation of these ideological packages coincided with the organizational crystallization of "milieu parties" (*Volksparteien*) and the spread of electoral democracy. The "imagined communities" of nations and classes relied heavily on these ideological packages for cohesion and legitimacy.

The emergence of new movements, the rise of "life politics," the mobilization of the "ideologically mixed categories," such as the American New Fiscal Populists and the North European Progressivists, and the ascendancy of highly pragmatic and non-ideological (for critics ideologically incoherent) New Labor, may be seen as a symptom of decomposition of these old ideological packages. Similarly, the emergence of "lifestyle politics" and new political actors indicates the new "end of ideology." Despite desperate attempts at accommodation of new concerns within old ideological packages (viz. the "green socialists"), the new issues split and erode the old ideological polarities and weaken their hold over mass audiences and elites. Consequently, many contemporary political analysts question the validity of the old left-right continuum and replace it with a multi-dimensional ideological-political space (e.g. Inglehart 1991; Poguntke 1993; Kitschelt 1994). Even these complex ideological maps, however, are evaded by proliferating and increasingly diverse issue concerns.

THE WANING OF SOCIALISM AND THE RISE OF NEW LABOR

Socialism seems to be most strongly affected by the decline of ideological packages. The collapse of the state socialist project in Eastern Europe, combined with the implosion of the Soviet empire, marked a dramatic ideological and political shift from competing ideological camps to the triumphant – but also increasingly vague – liberalism, from bi-polar to multi-polar global power arrangements, and – among the west European societies – from politics based on the balance of power to politics of multilateral agreements.

The Soviet model of socialism was thoroughly modernist. At the center of this model lay the authoritarian interventionist state fused with the central party apparatus. The comprehensive socioeconomic planning, reflecting the ideological principles and goals, was organized and implemented through the apparatuses of a quasi-corporatist state that dominated the civil society. The goals and the logic of operation of the party-state were unmistakably modern: socialism was defined as synonymous with scientific outlook, progress, industrialization, rationalization, and secularization from above. The implosion of the Soviet bloc opened the way for autonomization and selective democratization of the formerly subordinated states. While the Czech Republic, Slovakia, Poland, and Hungary enter the path of western "postmodernization," vast areas of the bloc face economic uncertainty and political instability.

The collapse of the Soviet model coincided with the erosion of the socialist (Labor and SD) programs in the West. Though embracing the principles of democracy, these programs were thoroughly modernist in their ideological foundations. The old Labor embraced a scientistic vision of organized and controlled society, with the central plank of nationalization cum corporatist "partnership" with private enterprise. The New Labor disposes of this model and the underlying ideologically guided politics. It lacks a consistent ideological vision; the underlying social values are vague and there is no consistent strategic plan for their realization. In fact, the highly publicized "third way" resembles a constantly updated melange of fashionable slogans. For social democratic supporters, this is a virtue, rather than a vice; the new SD/Labor is depicted as liberated from ideological rigidities and doctrinal shackles. For the critics, this is a symptom of ideological and programmatic decomposition (e.g. Lipset 1991; Giddens 1996). One may add that a similar process of decomposition seems to affect the liberal and conservative ideologies. Triumphant liberalism turns into an increasingly vague and weak creed (Fukuyama 1992). The popularity of "fiscal conservatism" and communitarianism, in turn, mark a decomposition of the conservative ideological package.

From Ethnic to Civic Nationalism

Together with socialism, nationalism has been seen as the core ideological force of modernity. It underlined the formation of the modern state, formed the foundation of modern democracy, and reshaped the modern citizenship (Greenfeld 1992). While the post-Soviet societies experience the resurgence of ethno-nationalism – which played a central role in the process of autonomization in 1989–91 – in the most advanced societies ethno-nationalism seems to be in retreat. It survives in regional pockets, mainly among the less educated and the aged, especially in areas affected by economic decline. The anti-migrant and anti-refugee sentiments there are mobilized by the right-of-center new social movements. The mainstream form of collective sentiment, especially among the younger sections of the educated urban strata, is "civic nationalism" – an inclusive, universalistic, and open form of solidarity and collective fervor.

The weakening of nationalist (as well as class) ideological grand narratives, coincides with the rise of "little narratives" (*petits réctis*). They are small scale quasi-ideological constructs that are internal to local communities, including regional groups and ethnic minorities. Campaigns for minority and regional autonomy and the proliferation of subnational ethnic and regional identities (regionalism and multiculturalism) are more compatible with civic spirit than with the "classic" nationalism.

Many aspects of political conflicts in advanced societies reflect the confrontation between the ethno-nationalism and civic nationalism. While the latter spreads, together with rising levels of education and generational replacement, the ethno-nationalist groups, typically in regional pockets, become more radical and vociferous, and therefore highly visible due to sensational media coverage. This vocality and radicalization, however, are symptomatic of decline rather than ascendancy.

Do these trends amount to a major discontinuity, a postmodernization of politics? The answer, in our view, has to be cautiously affirmative. This caution is best reflected by a number of final qualifications and caveats.

First and foremost, it must be remembered that it is still very early in the day. If it is true that Minerva's owl spreads its wings at dusk, we can comprehend modernity, but are still not ready for a definitive diagnosis of what may follow. Indeed, the very fact that we can now define and circumscribe the features of modernity with a high degree of clarity and consensus may indicate that we are leaving the modern era behind. Second, the processes of postmodernization seem to be uneven. The elements of cultural postmodernization, for example, seem to be more advanced and widespread than postmodern politics. Moreover, the latter, as we stress throughout, are largely restricted to the advanced (and largely western) societies. Postmodern states and politics, to use Cooper's term, coexist with and confront the modern ones. Third, the rapid pace of change, combined with hybridization of institutional orders (itself, we claim, a distinctly postmodern feature), make diagnoses difficult. We are aiming at the moving target, and our aiming devices – the analytic and theoretical tools – are *in statu nascendi*.

Further Reading

Cooper, R. (1997): *The Postmodern State and the World Order*. London: Demos.
Crook, S., Pakulski, J., and Waters, M. (1992): *Postmodernization*. London: Sage.

36

Nationalism and Fragmentation Since 1989

John Schwarzmantel

Nationalism is both cause and consequence of the fragmentation of political units exemplified by the break-up of the Soviet Empire and the rise of regionalist and nationalist identities demanding recognition. Nationalism is fundamentally ambiguous. The creation of a civic nation is part of the process of democratization in Eastern and Central Europe, but nationalism can also destroy civic unity and polarize communities on ethnic lines. It is implied in accounts of the relation between nationalism and modernity that nationalism is redundant as a mobilizing force once nation-states are established. Fragmentation raises the question of whether the ideal unifying nation-state of modernity is possible or desirable. In the changed conditions of postmodernity, internal and external challenges to the nation-state reduce the progressive significance of nationalism, leaving it to assert exclusive ethnic identities that undermine democracy and common citizenship. Nevertheless, there has been a proliferation of nationalisms since 1989, especially in the post-Communist world, and nationalism remains powerful in established liberal–democratic systems. Its divisive tendencies can not be avoided by a straightforward rejection. A form of political nationalism can prevent fragmentation, while preserving the balance between abstract universalism and divisive particularism.

The Concept of Fragmentation

The concept of "fragmentation" is a key to understanding the contemporary world. The break-up of the Soviet Empire accompanying the collapse of communism, the rise of regionalist, nationalist, and separatist movements, and more broadly the emergence of a range of different identities and subcultures demanding recognition within nation-states, are all indications of the dissolution of what were formerly more unified fields of social action. Beyond that, analysis of globalization has raised the question whether this process erodes particular and local identities, or on the contrary stimulates a fragmenting localism as a protest against the onward march of globalization (Bahador 1999).

With regard to nationalism, the issue is whether the continued salience of nationalism and appeals to national identity is a cause or a consequence of the increased fragmentation of larger political units. Is it the case that nationalism itself is the cause of the splitting up of empires, as well as of civic nation-states, which become prey to divisive nationalisms offering a more appealing focus for political identity? Or is the causal relationship the other way around: has nationalism gained in importance because the collapse of more inclusive identities has left the field open for more exclusive and particular appeals, such as those of ethnically defined nationalism?

It is argued here that nationalism is both cause and consequence of the fragmentation of politics, and that the degree to which it contributes to this splitting up of wider units depends on the nature of the nationalist movement in question. The creation of a civic nation, "shaping a healthy national identity without xenophobia and national hatred" (Agh 1998: 77) is part of the process of democratization in the countries of Eastern and Central Europe. Such a process of nation-building can reconcile national and ethnic minorities to their membership of a recently established democratic nation-state. Yet, as the uses of nationalism in former Yugoslavia demonstrate all too clearly, nationalism remains one of the most fissiparous and divisive forces in modern politics, fragmenting civic unity and polarizing communities on ethnic lines. How to cope with this fundamental ambiguity in nationalism is the focus of debate in the social sciences, and raises basic questions of political practice.

It is necessary, first of all, to define what is meant by the term "fragmentation." In its most general sense it clearly refers to the break-up of overarching identities and institutions. Fragmentation suggests a process of dissolution, which can be applied in a number of ways. In the context of post-Communist systems, it should be remembered that the process of democratization can give rise to a "worrying accompaniment" of "nationalist mobilization and the emphasis on national identity" (Harris-Grossbergerova 1998: 380). The removal of the Communist one-party system and the transition to political pluralism allowed the expression of nationalist demands and minority grievances. Because the "new meaning of democracy" in the countries of post-Communism is bound up with "the activation of all kinds of minorities, including ethnic-national minorities" (Agh 1998: 80), fragmentation is one consequence of the transition to democracy in these countries. The "triple transition" (Agh 1998) of political democratization, economic change, and a different social structure opens up a range of possibilities, leading to a much more diverse range of identities and loyalties.

What is involved in the discussion of these problems is the nature and significance of nationalism in contemporary politics. More specifically, the issues at stake can be explained as follows:

- First is the question of whether nationalism has a future, in a world which is increasingly global in its structure, where the nation-state is faced with severe challenges internally and externally. In such a globalizing world, is nationalism destined to lose its mobilizing power, and is the nation-state fated to become an anachronism?

- The second issue is the question of nationalism and identity. Can the nation-state still offer a framework of identity and community which commands the loyalty of its citizens? Alternatively, is the nation-state a unit which cannot rival the stronger appeals of ethnic movements, sometimes of a separatist kind, which involve more particular identities which fragment the unity of the nation-state?
- Thirdly, there is the problem of the nature of nationalism in the contemporary world order: is nationalism taking on more ethnic forms, which are potentially more fragmentary and disruptive, or is there still a future for an inclusive and tolerant concept of the nation which can provide symbols of political identity and a unifying framework for political action?

These are all issues which are central to a wide range of discussion in the social sciences. Nationalism has become the center of attention of a vast amount of work from historians, political scientists, sociologists, and normative political philosophers. The purpose of what follows is to draw out from some of the contemporary discussion lines of argument which help to answer the questions concerning the future of nationalism, the idea of the nation, and the nature of the nation-state.

Nationalism and Modernity

The death or demise of nationalism has been often predicted, yet obituaries of nationalism seem somewhat premature. Classical modernist analysts of nationalism such as Hobsbawm and Gellner suggest that nationalism has come to be a force of declining significance. For Hobsbawm, it is doubtful whether nationalism can continue to be a program of politics in the twenty-first century (Hobsbawm 1990: 182). In somewhat similar vein, Gellner's analysis of nationalism indicates the diminishing significance of nationalism in contemporary politics. For Gellner, nationalism was functional, indeed fundamental, to the transition from agrarian to industrial society (see Gellner 1983; Hall 1998). The corollary of this is that once societies have made the transition to industrial society, then the need for nationalism is less intense. After industrial society has been achieved throughout the globe, national identities come to be less salient, losing their mobilizing ability in a postindustrial society.

While there seems to be general endorsement of this modernist interpretation of nationalism, to the extent that nationalism is generally accepted to be part and parcel of modernity, there is less agreement on the prognosis of the declining power of nationalism in contemporary politics. The break-up of the Soviet Union has witnessed the resurgence of a range of nationalist movements and parties in the countries which constituted that supranational empire. Indeed, for some commentators the collapse of the USSR was the final proof of the "return of the repressed," signifying the perennial power of nationalism and the futility of attempts to suppress it. On this analysis, the attempt by the communists to create a supranational state appealing to values of socialist internationalism and aspiring to the ultimate fusion of nations, was doomed to fail, and nationalism was the cause of the fragmentation of the multinational state.

More nuanced observers (Suny 1993) have pointed out that the Soviet Union, for all its rhetoric of socialist internationalism, was a system which in many ways built up its constituent nations. Throughout the history of the Soviet Union, nation-building was very much on the agenda: every member of the Soviet Union had their national identity inscribed in their passport, and national languages and cultures were fostered, even in the Stalinist period.

The resurgence of nationalism and the appeal to national identity as powerful features of post-Communist politics built on this legacy of the Communist system. Post-Communist elites were able to turn to nationalism as a potent means of mass mobilization. Nowhere was this truer, and with more disastrous effect, than in Yugoslavia, and in particular in Bosnia, where ethnic and religious divisions led to war. In Serbia, Milosevic is the prime example of ex-Communist turned nationalist mobilizer, using the appeals of nationalism to replace those of defunct Communism, and using a discourse of national identity to build up his following. This points to the continuing force of nationalism in the countries of ex-Communism, and the potency of symbols of national identity, such as the use made of the 1389 battle of Kosovo (see Malcolm 1998).

The thrust of nationalism in the period of modernity was to function as a unifying force. Nation-building or nation-defending (for those nations who already had achieved nation-statehood) meant the creation of large internally-unified nations. Their size and effectiveness would provide their citizens with the triple goal of political cohesion, economic unity, and cultural uniformity. Socialist perspectives on the nation shared this view, seeing large nations as functional and progressive for economic development and hence, in the long run, for socialist transformation. Advocates of the leading philosophies of modernity, liberalism and socialism, agreed that while ultimately the nation would be transcended, the large nation-state represented a progressive and necessary stage for economic development and shared political rights (Smith 1995; Schwarzmantel 1998: ch. 6).

The issue for contemporary social science is whether the tendencies toward fragmentation, noted above, have changed the nature and significance of nationalism so that the nation assumes a different function from that which it assumed in the period of modernity. Nationalism has been seen from a host of competing perspectives, including those views which see it as a form of politics aiming at capture and control of the modern state (Breuilly 1993). Nationalism is a particularly effective mobilizing device, as it involves emotions, myths, feelings of shared ancestry and common culture, which bring the members of the nation together in sentiments of solidarity and community. Hence the power of the nation as a focus of identity, giving people a sense of who they are in the modern world. The nation has been the chief source of identity in the conditions of modern politics, demarcating the citizens of one nation from those of another, furnishing individuals with a sense of bonding and cohesion. In that way it can be said that the nation was the bedrock of community in modern politics, the "imagined community" which provided individuals with an identity broader than that of their immediate families and kin, yet narrower than cosmopolitan affiliations with "the human race" in general.

It is true that such forms of identity have taken pathological forms, mobilizing the members of a nation in total unity against some "Other," against an outsider group seen as threatening to the culture and identity of the "in-group." Nationalism and the concept of the nation acquired what Greenfeld calls "ethnic baggage," which elevated ideas of national identity and national particularity to an exaggerated extent (Greenfeld 1992). Obviously the chief example here is the use made of nationalism by movements of fascism and national-socialism. These redefined the idea of the nation, and made it a closed and narrowly defined national community. However, the point remains that the force of nationalism in the period of modernity was to overcome fragmentation, to create large and cohesive units within which citizens would find their economic security, political rights, and their cultural community. The program of nationalism has been one of the great success stories of modern times in successfully transcending localism and in bringing citizens together in the unit of the nation-state. However, as critics of nationalism have never tired of pointing out, the dangers remain that this unity of the nation is purchased at the expense of denying wider affiliations which cross national boundaries. The cost of national unity is often hostility to the outsider and non-national.

Challenges to the Nation-State

If the aim, and to some extent the achievement, of nationalism in the period of modernity was the overcoming of fragmentation through the creation of a world of nation-states, current controversies in the social sciences focus on the challenges to the nation-state and nationalism in the changed conditions of postmodernity. These challenges can be defined as internal and external. Internal challenges relate to problems of migration and plural loyalties or multiple affiliations within the nation. External challenges are those of supranational institutions and international loyalties which rival those of the nation-state (see Le Galès, chapter 37, in this volume).

Taking each of these in turn, the internal problems call into question the picture of a nation-state peopled almost entirely by those who are its citizens with shared political rights. There is a growing gap between the rights of citizens, who benefit from a cluster of political rights, and the denial of rights to those, like immigrant workers in Germany, for example, who may be living and working in the particular country but are deprived of any political rights, including that basic right of citizenship, the right to vote (cf. Soysal, chapter 31, in this volume). The internal challenges also involve the idea that the nation can no longer offer a central focus of loyalty which creates a sense of unified citizenship in all those who live within its borders. In a nation of multicultural citizenship (Kymlicka 1995) a variety of groups and cultures attract the loyalty of citizens and act as diverse sources of identity, so that unifying ideas of civic nationalism become less viable.

To these internal challenges to the nation can be added the external ones, which provide rival sources for identity and power in the changing world of contemporary politics. Ideas of "postnational identity" suggest that the force of nationalism and the framework of the nation no longer have anything to offer in a transformed society, in which supranational loyalties are more prominent. The democratic framework of the nation-state and its representative institutions are powerless and relatively ineffectual compared with international centers of economic power which are not constrained by structures of democratic account-ability and control. Following this line of argument, the main source of frag-mentation of the nation-state and the decline of nationalism would stem from the globalized and international structure of the world, where culture, power, and identities are formed through a flow of supranational forces which render the nation-state and the appeal of nationalism obsolete. Some writers (Held 1995a) suggest that democracy needs to be reconceptualized on a "cosmopoli-tan" level and argue that the nation-state is no longer an adequate framework for understanding democracy and realizing it. Democracy and the struggle to extend democratic rights can only be understood in terms of a cosmopolitan structure of institutions. Taken together, these arguments suggest that there is indeed a process of fragmentation in contemporary society which renders nationalism and the nation-state much less significant than in the era of modernity and of "nation-building." The process of fragmentation in a postmodern world reduces the significance of nationalism, leaving it as a belated and futile attempt to assert identity in a world of growing homogeneity, taking increasingly exclusive ethnic forms which undermine democracy and challenge ideas of common citizenship and civic nationalism.

The ideal of civic nationalism takes as its central theme the definition of the nation as an association of citizens, bound together by shared political rights and allegiance to democratic procedures. The concept of the nation is a political one, and is distinguished from ethnic nationalism which sees the nation as a commun-ity of descent and birth. Such a deterministic criterion for a nation is distinct from the "voluntaristic" bonding which characterizes the civic concept of the nation. Classically, this civic concept of the nation is exemplified in Renan's famous lecture of 1882, *Qu'est-ce qu'une nation?* which saw the nation as a "daily plebiscite" dependent on the will of its members to continue living together (see extracts in Hutchinson and Smith 1994).

In a more contemporary vein, the idea of "civic nationalism" is akin to what Habermas calls "constitutional patriotism," seeing the nation as the totality of "*Staatsbürger.*" In his words "citizens are supposed to constitute themselves as an association for free and equal persons by choice" (Habermas 1996: 287). This view of the nation is contrasted by Habermas with a concept of the nation as formed by "*Volksgenossen,*" which he defines as "nationals (who) *find* them-selves formed by an inherited form of life and the fateful experience of a shared history." This antithesis represents the contrast between a universalist concept, "the universalism of an egalitarian legal community" and, on the other hand, "the particularism of a cultural community bound together by origin and fate." Indeed, one could suggest that this goes to the heart of the problem of nation-alism and fragmentation: the idea of nationalism involves a universalist message (everyone should be part of a nation which has its own right to self-determina-tion) along with the assertion of cultural particularity (this particular nation is special and valuable) which provides a focus of identity in times of rapid transition. The problem is of reconciling the universal with the particular, of seeing whether civic nationalism can preserve its inclusive and integrative character.

Some writers (see Spencer and Wollman 1998) criticize the binary division between "civic" and "ethnic" nationalism as too simplistic and value-laden, inviting a crude division between "good" and "bad" nationalism. The value of the distinction is itself a focus of discussion in contemporary writing on nationalism. However much it is questioned, it is argued here that it remains a useful device for distinguishing between different definitions and concepts of the nation, which each have contrasting political implications. While it is true that civic nationalism can often have a hidden ethnic basis, and can rest on certain unquestioned assumptions which make it less inclusive than it claims, the distinction points to the different ways in which the concept of "the nation," an essentially malleable idea, can be constructed. From the point of view of the problem of fragmentation, the central question remains whether civic nationalism can resist the fissiparous or fragmentary tendencies of different cultural groups in civil society to assert their own identity and make it prominent. If such tendencies become too strong, the power of the nation weakens as a framework for democratic action. The rallying appeal of the symbols of civic nationalism become less powerful and less able to provide a common focus of citizen identity. The nation would become less of a politically inclusive framework for common citizenship, and would find its integrative power challenged by other more particularistic and more exclusive identities. However, in opposition to such a view, it is argued here that a more nuanced view needs to be taken, which sees nationalism in contemporary politics as both cause and consequence of the fragmentation which is an undoubted feature of the world situation. Furthermore, nationalism needs to be understood as a protean and fluid force which can take a variety of forms; it appeals to ideas of community and identity, which is why it possesses such resilience. The way different nationalisms incorporate these ideas have important consequences for understanding the politics of our time. There are thus three concluding themes in what follows.

SURVIVAL AND RESURGENCE OF NATIONALISM

First, it is true that the world since 1989 has witnessed a proliferation of nationalisms, especially in but not restricted to the post-Communist world. It is also true that these nationalisms have been fissiparous, they have been separatist and divisive, for the most part involving the wish to form independent nation-states, on the part of areas that were formerly part of larger units. The phenomenon is most marked in the post-Soviet area, though Scotland is an example from Western Europe. Two points can be made about this continued salience of nationalism and its separatist implications. The first is that in a world which is becoming more global, more supra-national, nationalism remains important as a source of identity. The more the world moves towards a global culture, the more the nation is valued as a means of affirming a particular culture, history, and is seen as a repository of a special identity and tradition. Hence we reach the paradoxical conclusion that globalization and nationalism can go hand in hand, with the former stimulating the affirmation of national identity and the values of a shared community. This can indeed take exclusive and dangerous forms if national identity is couched in terms of ethnicity and common descent.

Second, much recent discussion in the political sociology of nationalism has made it clear that what Suny calls the "sleeping beauty" theory of nationalism is an inadequate guide to explaining the persistence of nationalism and its contribution to a world of greater fragmentation. The "sleeping beauty" theory asserted that nationalism was always present, presumably everywhere, but certainly in the countries of the former Soviet Union. It slumbered during the years of the Soviet repression of nationalism, but the "Prince" of communist collapse awoke the sleeping beauty of nationalism from its slumbers and led it to its triumph in the conditions of post-Communist transition. While this is, of course, a caricature, the critique of such theories is correct in asserting that national identities were nurtured during the period of Communism, and that the Soviet system was responsible for an ambitious programme of "nation-building." This suggests that nationalism is not a natural force, or an inherent identity which people automatically have, but is at least in part the product of conscious creation. Hence, the assertion of national identities in the period following the collapse of Communism was paradoxically prepared by the Communist regime itself. The Communist system sought to control the force of nationalism by fostering national identities and national culture, by giving some of the nationalities of the former Soviet Union their "own" republics, of which groups like Ukrainians and Armenians were the "owners." Of course the aim was that these national affiliations would be held in check and transcended, both by the supranational ideology of Communism, and by the supranational force of the Communist Party of the Soviet Union (CPSU). The hope was also that economic development and intermarriage would lead to the growing together of nationalities and to the ultimate triumph of "Soviet man" as the model citizen. Hence, the salience of nationalism in post-Communism, with its fissiparous implications, was the product, if an unintended one, of the Soviet regime itself. That system prepared the institutional framework for the resurgence of nationalism and appeal to national identity, which marked the period after the collapse of Communism.

This analysis owes much to the framework put forward by the American sociologist Rogers Brubaker, who sees nationalism as the product of a "field" of three forces (Brubaker 1996). These elements he calls "nationalizing states," "national minorities," and "external homelands." The merit of his analysis is that he sees nationalism not as some inherent quality, but as the result of a series of actions and political processes. In the period after Communism, political elites tried to make their states "nationalizing states," they sought to make the state the state of their particular ethnic or national group, they wished to make their ethnic group the "owners" of that particular state. In the conditions of Eastern and Central Europe, where different ethnic and national groups inhabit the same geographical area, this attempt to make a state the vehicle for one dominant ethnic group, to create a nationalizing state, inevitably risks the victimization of those living on the same territory who are not members of the dominant group.

Hence arises a conflict between such "nationalizing states" and "national minorities." Where the national minorities can look to a state of their co-nationals, such as members of the Hungarian minority in Slovakia who can look to the Hungarian state, then the presence of such an "external homeland" can often exacerbate national tensions and nationalist rivalries. The result of this "field of tension" between nationalizing states, national minorities and external homelands can be a process which heightens nationalist discourse, and leads the participants to feel that their particular culture and national identity are imperilled. Hence the resurfacing of nationalism, its refusal to go away in a world of ethnic tension and transition from Communism to democracy.

Third, nationalism remains highly powerful both in the post-Communist world since 1989 as well as in established liberal–democratic systems. Social science and political sociology have sought explanations for this continuing prominence of nationalism, and the implications for the future shape of politics and social movements. Nationalism has contributed to a sense of fragmentation in contemporary politics. In a world of increased globalization, it has highlighted particularistic affiliation to one national group. This is both the strength of nationalism and its potential danger for any transition to democracy. Nationalist movements draw their strength from their validation of one particular culture; the force of nationalism lies in its appeal to a particular community and feeling of identity. Yet this appeal has its dangers, especially when the nation is conceptualized as an ethnic group or community of descent. Nationalism, or appeals to national identity, if successful, create a more fragmented and divided world, in which national cohesion is often purchased at the expense of the "other," the non-national, the outsider. Yet nationalism was also the product of a more fragmented and divided world, in which the collapse of the Communist system left the way open for these more divisive identities based on nationalism and ethnicity.

The conclusion defended here is that the anti-democratic and divisive tendencies of nationalism cannot be avoided by a straightforward rejection of nationalism *tout court*. A civic nationalism which links nationalism and national identity to democratic procedures and institutions can provide a sense of identity, particular yet open to all who are citizens, which can aid the transition to or the maintenance of democratic society. Such a civic nationalism itself is challenged by more fragmentary and intense identities, yet it may provide one means of averting the rise and domination of narrower, more exclusive nationalisms. Finally, such a civic nationalism would be a source of identity, but only one among others, asserting a national identity as one identity, compatible with regional or subnational identities as well as with more global ones, such as a European identity. The evils of nationalism in the past stem from its attempt to make the nation exclusively defined, the one and only source of identity. This is doomed to failure in an ever more pluralistic world. A form of political nationalism can prevent the process of ever more fragmentation and division, while preserving a balance between a totally abstract universalism and a narrow divisive particularism. Political sociology has recently given renewed attention to the phenomenon of nationalism and its contemporary significance. Some might think that this is a sign that nationalism has passed its peak, and therefore a more adequate analysis is possible now that it is a force of diminishing significance. The analysis presented here suggests that the controversies in contemporary social science mirror the ongoing power, for good or ill, of nationalism and national identity as forces that retain the capacity to crucially affect the stability and security of the world today.

Further Reading

Brubaker, R. 1996: *Nationalism Reframed. Nationhood and the National Question in the New Europe*. Cambridge: Cambridge University Press.

Caplan, R. and Feffer, J. (eds.) 1996: *Europe's New Nationalism. States and Minorities in Conflict*. Oxford: Oxford University Press.

Hall, J. (ed.) 1998: *The State of the Nation. Ernest Gellner and the Theory of Nationalism*. Cambridge: Cambridge University Press.

37

A New Phase of the State Story in Europe

Patrick Le Galès

European states have faced serious disjunctures that make classical definitions of the state redundant. There is a dynamic combination of changes,
including: the retreat of national legal systems; pressure on taxation
policies from the European Union and business; the fragmentation of
centralized bureaucracy; the growing interdependence of national military-industrial complexes and policing; postnational citizenship rights;
the permeability of frontiers; the globalization of the economy. Nation-
states in Europe are being restructured to accommodate the European
Union. However, they also have a good deal of control over its construction. There is a dynamic of institution-building at work which is more than
just adapting to markets. At the same time national societies are also
undergoing change. Organized around a modern industrial economy, a
national class structure, institutions, rules, values, organized interests,
and concrete infrastructures, the national society is now subject to processes of individualization, fragmentation, pluralization, and de-traditionalization. The European Union apparently has relatively little impact so
far on national societies, though a European society, articulated on diversity, may be emerging. Much more significant are challenges from the local
and regional level. Le Galès concludes that the end of the state is not in
sight, but there is an end to the meta-narrative of the nation-state.

Ideas concerning the demise of the nation-state are not new. The coming age of
"Le dépérissement de l'Etat" (the decaying state) was announced even before the
nation-state was fully in place. There have been no shortage of prophets announ-
cing its death over the past 150 years. Globalizing processes (however diverse
they might be), dynamics of internal differentiation and the fashioning of large
regional areas (the European Union), have produced new work which yet again
ranges powerful arguments against the nation-state. Such work suggests the
coming age of "the dismantling state," the "virtual state," "the retreating
state," "the hollowing out of the state," "l'Etat en miettes" (the state in pieces).
The state "obsolete or obstinate?" asks John Hoffman (1995). However, as the
nation-state in Europe has so far proved remarkably resilient, anybody
concerned with its changing forms should be inclined towards caution (Mann
1997).

There are three main strands of analysis that try to explain the changing form of the state. Wright and Cassese (1996) points to the dynamic combination of the following factors: economic recession, a paradigm shift in favor of the market, changing forms of politics, globalization, europeanization, liberalization, technological progress, decentralization and fragmentation, reforms of the public sector, and a new political agenda. In contrast, neo-Marxist writers explain the restructuring of the state with reference to the changing forms and scale of capitalism (Jessop 1997). Postmodernization theory offers yet a third interpretation (see Pakulski, chapter 34, in this volume).

This chapter examines the concrete form of the state and its transformations. I argue that European states have faced serious disjunctures which render classic definitions inappropriate. But strong states also adapt and react to new sets of conditions and processes of change. What we are now witnessing may therefore mark a new phase, rather than the end, of the state story.

DISJUNCTURES AND WEAKENING OF THE STATE

Weber's famous definition of the state (see Poggi, chapter 9, in this volume) may no longer be appropriate in Europe due to the loss of monopoly of violence over a bounded territory, decreasing potential for domination, and less centrality; in other words a less "hard" politics. Building upon Poggi's presentation, several changes are briefly reviewed, thus underlining the dynamic combination of changes.

1 *National legal systems are in retreat*: In the classic understanding of state sovereignty, there is no legal power superior to the state. However, first, for EU states, a significant proportion of new legislation originates at the European level. Conflicts between national courts of justice, or councils of state and the commission, bear witness to the importance of these changes and to the sometimes painful acknowledgment of a superior source of law accompanying European legal integration (Dehousse 1996). Second, international agreements (e.g. trade agreements, human rights, environmental questions, etc.) are an increasing source of law and rules with varying degrees of binding capacity. Third, it is increasingly difficult to differentiate private and public laws at the international level. Accounting and consulting firms, multinationals, private organizations (e.g. International Chambers of Commerce) are themselves sources of norms and rules, creating a new *lex mercatoria*, or a private system of transnational governance which has direct impact on national systems and which reconfigures the public and private spheres (Cutler 1997; Dezalay and Garth 1998). Countries with strong traditions of national public laws such as Germany, Italy, or France are finding the latter particularly destabilizing.

2 *Taxation*: The European Union marks a transfer of state sovereignty. The introduction of the Euro and the creation of the European Central Bank constitute major symbolic and real changes for nation-states used to old currencies. The nation-state is constrained by pressures from below and from Europe, as well as from financial markets. In practice it has lost part of its taxing and

spending powers. Though not without conflict, the rise of meso level government in Europe has a financial element that renders the state's monopoly problematic. Furthermore, the European Union has pushed forward a degree of harmonization, in particular in the field of VAT, which constrains diversity of taxation between member states. Taxation comparisons in Europe – stressed in particular by business organizations and the media – are creating pressure for harmonization, and European norms may be in the making. Pressure on taxation policy is also developing far beyond the European union in international organizations, for instance the OECD. Trends toward globalization, in their neo-liberal variation, are usually associated with demands for less regulation and less tax for firms. What is at stake here is, of course, more than just taxation. Questions are raised about what belongs and what does not belong in the public sphere; what the state should or should not be doing (including public investment in utilities and the organization of public services and the welfare state). Business pressure toward the private financing and organization of the public sector (but also national insurance, some social services, and pensions) in other words, a new round of commodification, goes hand to hand with the contested issue of the role of the state, the general interest and the "appropriate" level of taxation.

3   *From hierarchy to mosaic*: Centralized differentiated bureaucracy is apparently being replaced by the fragmented "organizational state." Literature in the sociology of organization (Crozier and Friedberg 1976; Mayntz 1993), governance (Kooiman 1993), public policy (Dente 1990; Heclo and Wildavsky 1994) and on policy networks (see John, chapter 13, in this volume) has questioned the unity of the state. The state is seen as fragmented (made up of multiple agencies, networks, individuals, and different political arenas); public policies do not work in terms of commands and hierarchies but by negotiation, flexibility, and *ad hoc* arrangements. This suggests a dissolution of the state. Fragmentation is also emphasized not only because the frontiers between public and private actors are blurring, but because policy domains are becoming increasingly difficult to identify. The making of a European polity has increased the centrifugal trends within individual nation-states, opening new avenues at different levels for different groups and organizations (so-called multilevel governance – Marks, Hooghe, and Kermit 1996). European governance building can be seen as a massive redistribution of authority in which no one single center is able to dominate the system (cf. Lange and Schimank, chapter 6, in this volume). This confusion of power does not *necessarily* lead to fragmentation. In some domains hierarchies still prevail or may be reconfigured. In the European governance in the making most empirical research points to new institutionalization processes (Stone and Sandholz 1998). Reforms of the civil service epitomize these changes (see Palumbo, chapter 12, this volume).

4   *Monopoly of violence: the rise of postmilitarism?* One may argue, as Shaw does (1997), that nation-states in Europe lost their military independence after the Second World War, particularly through the role of NATO. But many European states have kept some autonomy, if not the independence claimed by France and Britain. International Relations scholars also often point to the dismantling of the national military–industrial complex. For reasons of techno-

logical and economic interdependence, globalization and the European market, national champions of national military independence are on their way out. In other words, as Mann suggests (1997) conflict-ridden Western Europe has weakened the pressure for what he calls "hard politics." European states are slowly coming to play a role in that field only on close collaboration with nation-states (see Scott, chapter 17, in this volume).

Similarly, with respect to policing, a steady movement toward europeaniza-tion is on the cards (Bigo 1996). But here nation-states remain cautious. These changes are more pronounced within armies themselves as they have to face radical pressures for change: different goals, pressure for coordination with others, new technologies, introduction of market mechanisms, the end of con-scription in several countries (Boesne and Dandekker 1998). It remains to be seen whether the making of Europe will lead to some form of accumulation of constraint at that level, probably remaining closely articulated to existing national forces, or if Europe will remain part of and dominated by NATO. In the last instance, no single European state is able to protect its citizens from various threats or to engage in a war with another European state. The whole idea of sovereignty and the link between state and violence (Giddens 1990) is therefore in jeopardy, imperfect and incomplete as it may have been (there were sometimes competing centers of authority and alternate purveyors of violence, see Caporaso 1996; Badie 1999).

5   *Citizenship*: elements of European citizenship now exist (EU passports, rights to vote at local elections) in particular within the Schengen zone. Seven articles in the Maastricht Treaty introduce a citizenship of the Union in articula-tion with national ones (Shore and Black 1996) but the whole issue of creating a postnational citizenship is a crucial debate in Europe (Garcia 1993). The question of social rights (pensions and social security) is high on the agenda of the European Union. There are also increasing elements of citizenship at the infra-national level. In cities or regions, for instance, the decentrali-zation of social policy is leading toward specific social and political rights (Garcia 1996). Differentiated patterns of political participation (elections, procedural democracy, associations) may also be leading to more diverse forms of local or regional citizenship, obvious in the case of federal or quasi-federal states.

6   *Frontiers*: sociologists of globalization have underlined the dynamics of flux: telecommunications, pollution, capital, norms, tourists, immigrants, cultures, technologies, terrorism, social movements, ideas, knowledge. They permeate frontiers and are clearly "points of disjuncture" (Held and McGrew 1993; Castells 1996) marking the end of the classic view of the national territory (Badie 1995). The European Union plays an essential role in this process and has pursued an agenda of reducing barriers and frontiers (first for trade but also for citizen) within its political limits. Within the Schengen zone, there is now a free circulation of individuals. The Commission also actively promotes exchanges (students) and finances programs to develop cooperation between regions close to borders. Frontiers have not disappeared, and they take different forms and meanings (Linklater 1998), but clearly, incomplete or recent as it may have been, the monopoly of control over a bounded territory is nowadays

largely irrelevant in theory and in practice in most European nation-states. The end of the Westphalian era – the organization of the world into territorially exclusive, sovereign nation-states – is signalled by competing territorial logics and decentralized systems of political authority (Rosenau 1990; Badie 1995).

7   *State and the economy*: national states have kept a strong capacity to play a role in the economy but there is also a huge literature to suggest that it is a domain where they have lost a lot of power. The globalization of the economy (and most importantly financial markets (see Soysal, chapter 31 in this volume) and multinational firms), and its dematerialization, are leading to the disembeddedness of the economy (Strange 1996). There are limits and many paradoxes to this argument (Boyer and Drache 1997; Scott 1997; Storper 1997). However, the increase in economic flux and the ever-increasing accumulation of wealth (and therefore power) within global organizations questions the capacity of nation-states to guide firms' strategies, to impose regulations and taxes to extract wealth to redistribute to other social and political priorities. Large movements of deregulation and privatization (again not without paradoxes and limits) have benefitted major firms rather than reinforcing state power over the economy. Moreover, the European Union now plays an important regulatory role which severely limits the room to maneuvre of nation-states (trade negotiation, competition policy limiting state aid, social and environmental regulations). National champions, although they seem to remain rooted within their national environments, are nevertheless more and more taken by their global strategies and the large movements of restructuring and mergers. They are therefore becoming more sensitive to pressures from non-national actors, to financial markets rather than national trade unions for instance. Over the past 30 years, the idea of national regulation of the economy (whatever its limits), which was so powerful during the time of national regimes of regulation or the national Keynesian welfare state (Jessop 1994; Crouch and Streeck 1996), has clearly been severely undermined.

Something profound has therefore changed for European nations. Postmodern authors such as Ruggie (1993) suggest the need to change our conception of the state in order to take into account the detachment of the state from a given territory, its fragmentation, the dismantling of the general interest and stabilized organized social and political forces. That view of a postmodern state is also emphasized by legal scholars breaking away from the positivist view of legal systems. But the loss of centrality of nation-states also allows for the restructuring of the nation state.

State Restructuring and the European Union

The redistribution of authority that goes with the making of the European political space is also taking place *within* the state apparatus. A more complex political space allows for some groups of powerful actors within states to distance themselves from established interest groups and to gain more latitude in choosing their priorities; for instance, to send social and political pressure upwards or downwards. Decentralizing the implementation of welfare rationalization or using the EU as a device to impose domestic reforms have become very common features in Europe. States' administrative and political elites can no longer pretend to fully protect their citizens, but they can use the pressures and the risks of the new economic and political environment to justify an expansion of intervention in some domains and retreat from others. Majone (1996) has shown how the European Union tends to behave as a regulatory state, dealing with market failures, rather than voluntarist public interventions or redistribution. This trend is also at work in European countries, as shown for instance by the proliferation of the regulatory agency model (Wright and Cassese 1996). Cerny interprets these changes as the making of the "competitive state" (1990), mainly preoccupied with economic competition and entrepreneurship, a view also expressed in Jessop's conceptualization of the postnational Schumpeterian workfare state (1994). Most of the changes can be interpreted in terms of the denationalization of the state or "destatization" (Jessop 1997), or as economic reorganization under the guidance of the state in accordance with market logics and requirements.

Marxist writers interpret this as the retreat of the state in favor of a European governance adapted to market demands; disembedded from political pressures and the organized interests of disadvantaged groups. An alternative interpretation suggests that the rise of market logics and institutions in the European Union was indeed used to promote internal changes but that nation-states and the European Union will then regain control to impose their political priorities in cooperation or in conflict with economic actors. Last but not least, if the EU is a political space in the making, it may be the case that gradually social actors will reorganize accordingly. Already, both major economic interests and some groups (anti-poverty, environment, and those organized for women's interests) are influential and the EU is increasingly a site for political activity. The increasing influence of the European Parliament and the organization of social forces may take some time but Europe may become a more classic, though complex, form of state even without taking the road of federalism.

However, at the same time, most nation-states in Europe have not gone very far in cutting welfare. Most comparative analysis points to "frozen welfare states in Europe" (Esping-Andersen 1996) rather than their full-scale dismantling. Most nation-states are also very active in revitalizing national systems of education. Pressures exist and coalitions are active to push forward a radical liberal agenda for European states in accordance with the more ideological conception of globalization, but political elites are entrenched in social structures and ideologies which are far from inclined to just adapt to market demands. Political and ideological conflict over the restructuring of the state is now principally fought at the European level.

The impact of European integration marks a real change for nation-states but states are not simply retreating in the face of this. Milward has demonstrated how states have used the construction of Europe to reorganize and modernize their economy (Milward 1993). In a similar vein, Moravscik (1999) suggests that the making of the European Union is very much under the control of the nation-states. Political and administrative elites use it to promote economic reforms, change political priorities, and initiate the restructuring of the state apparatus itself.

A significant factor is the division of labor which will take place between local and regional, national and European levels. Even if most agree that there is the making of a structure of governance (Amstrong and Bulmer 1998), Europe still does not have the attribute of a state (Schmitter 1996). Caporaso (1996) suggests that we should consider the EU as a form of state, but not a Westphalian state (although it involves some processes similar to state building), and not just a regulatory state either (which would leave social and redistribution issues at the national level). The EU has now developed a large set of public policies (Meny, Muller, and Quermonne 1997), and it is taking over some social issues. There is a dynamic of institution-building at play which involves more than just adapting to markets. Neo-institutionalist authors underline the temporal aspect of building institutions and the gradual europeanization of norms and rules (Stone and Sandholz 1998), or even the *de facto* constitutionalization of Treaties (Weiler 1994).

As the result of this process, existing nation-states may retreat, become organized as part of European federation, or still call the tune in renovated form at the European level. If earlier phases of construction of the European Union, undertaken by national state elites, have clearly both given strong impetus to market forces *and* left nation-states in control, there is no reason why future political conflicts will not lead to different forms of institutionalization of the market and different kinds of state structure.

ARE NATIONAL SOCIETIES EVADING THE NATION-STATE?

Neo-institutionalist authors (usually within the Weberian tradition) and neo-Marxists alike have emphasized the embeddedness of the state in national societies (Skocpol 1979; Jessop 1990). Changing scales of social structures therefore place nation-states in difficulty. Two points are emphasized here: first, the increased individualization and fragmentation of societies; second, the changing scales and tensions associated both with the pressures from localities and regions and pressures related to transnational networks and flows.

For sociologists, the nation-state is usually defined in the terms set out by Weber and Gellner (i.e. a bounded monopoly of legitimate violence, administration, and culture) and the national society includes the coherence of a modern industrial economy, a national class structure, a set of national institutions, rules, values, organized interests (political parties, churches, welfare states, economic interests) and concrete infrastructures (Touraine 1990). All this was more or less in place by the end of the nineteenth century. The post-1945 decades marked the completion of national, modern, industrialized, European societies although many characteristics were to be found elsewhere. Thanks to TV, national cultures became fully dominant and national languages triumphed nearly everywhere. Regional differences were on the way out thanks to massive redistribution, national labor markets, and the strength of national institutions as an integrating factor, not to mention mass consumption. Society meant national society. Of course, nuances should be noted, because the near completion of the political project of the national society is fairly recent in most European countries. Mann (1997) argues that the "caging" of society was never complete; non-national forces always played a role in the structuring of national societies. But if our time horizon is the contrast with the postwar period, the coherence of national European societies was rather the dominant picture since 1945.

In most areas of social life – work, family, consumption, education, leisure, politics, religion – social science research tends to stress the following points: individualization (but also the rearticulation of groups), differentiation, pluralization, de-traditionalization, and deinstitutionalization. These processes are often proposed under the heading of the fragmentation of societies (Mingione 1991; Lash and Urry 1993; Dubet and Martucelli 1998) and the apparently ever increasing autonomy of individuals *vis-à-vis* national institutions. Hence, political parties, national economic interests, national churches, national armies (the military-industrial complex), but also welfare states and school systems, are facing increased pressure in most European countries from below and from above (Therborn 1995; Mendras 1997). That does not mean they are disappearing. But national institutions which used to structure societies, to organize interactions, provide social links, representations, norms and social practices, are less and less able to impose their logic. They are less able to work as hierarchies or structures of control and domination. Individuals and groups, or some of them, have more autonomy to negotiate their exit. In polarized societies (Netherlands–Belgium) or national societies organized around the dynamics of two conflicting forces (Catholicism and communism in Italy for instance), national sets of institutions bringing together schools, parties, trade unions, and various organizations are less able to integrate individuals, to structure and define boundaries. Immigration is an important feature which reinforces the processes of differentiation and pluralization of national societies, although far less so in Europe than in the USA. This is a contested process in many cases (Rex 1997; Jopke 1998).

Beyond national societies, sociologists of globalization suggest that ever-stronger cross-national flows of people, money, information and images, make nations less important in people's lives. On the one hand, there is an increasing role for transnational practices and networks from above and below. Changing national societies are increasingly analyzed in terms of growing interdependence, transnational practices, and the ever growing dynamism and expansion of social networks (Hannerz 1996). This raises the question of what is left of national societies when there is growing pluralization of the population (immigrants from different backgrounds, illegal workers, and high flyers) together with cross-border flux. Transnationalism (Appaduraï 1996) from above (for instance related to the transnationalization of firms) is matched by transnationalism from below. If the development of flux and networks leads to interdependent national societies, what is left of national society?

On the other hand, Sklair (1995) and Robertson (1992) have put forward a different argument; namely, that there is a global system of social processes. Evidence can be found for instance in the organization of interests on a European or global scale, including the development of a new repertoire for social movements, but also new procedures and new tools to organize and influence the EU to combat international organizations. In this case, the global social system in the making is no longer related to the state. The forces (transnational corporations) at the forefront of these processes are escaping national rules and constraints. They have profound destabilizing effects on nation-states and national societies because these are no longer the only focus structuring conflicts between social classes. Sklair (1995) suggests, for instance, the making of a new hegemonic global capitalist class in relation to a new phase of global capitalism; the national economy and national bourgeoisie are undermined, for instance, as they can avoid the constraints of national societies. Immigrants also create transnational social spaces which have a dynamic of their own (Faist 1999). Appaduraï, from a cultural point of view, announces the rise of the "postnational global cultural economy" (Appaduraï 1990). Uncertainties about what a national society is further undermine the embeddedness of the state. But social changes of that scale do not happen over night and existing national social structures are only slowly being eroded, a point emphasized in social mobility research (Breen and Rottman 1998), or value surveys.

And what of Europe? Is the making of the European Union having an impact on national societies, or even, should it have an impact? Recent overviews of social changes in contemporary Europe (e.g. Crouch 1999) have clearly underlined the fact that there is no such thing as a European society. Most key elements of national societies (labor market, family structure, values, social classes, conflicts) tend to remain quite different within Europe or even within countries, or to be comparable with other industrial or postindustrial societies. Such studies stress the role of technologies, the baby boom, and the role of women in the labor market, rather than the making of the European Union. The diversity between and within countries remains very strong and relatively stable.

However, the making of the European union is also a political project which aims, to a lesser extent than the project of nation building, to promote a European model of society (including welfare, universal services, and a contrast with the USA on social cohesion). The development of European indicators (social indicators, values, tax, inequality) goes hand in hand with elements of rationalization and normalization around European standards (for instance in higher education). European public policies strengthen some groups, are associated with representations of society, and become the central focus for interest groups. Increased mobility (students, tourists, immigrants, business) within Europe enhances interdependencies. Groups involved in Brussels learn about other countries and enter discussions about European norms and policies (a competitive game), which may eventually become binding rules. The slow emergence of a fragmentary European society, articulated upon increasing diversity, is led by discourses, images, rules, and interest groups. It is pushed in particular by the middle classes who have the skills to take advantage of all ranges of opportunities, but increasingly other groups and social actors are involved.

Last but not least, the question of the level of social organization has been raised at the infra-national level. At the time of the triumphant modern nation-state in the 1960s, new counterforces started to appear which used localities and regions to contest national homogenizing tendencies: new social movements and regionalist movements. While regions and localities were seen as less constraining for individuals, thanks to social and geographic mobility, they became increasingly significant for the formation of social groups and the invention or reinvention of identities and solidarities within or against the nation-state. While national symbols started to lose their significance in the face of the uncertainties and variability of economic relations and the state became less central, local and regional cultures became valorizing codes for the satisfaction of needs for self-expression and identity.

In Europe, the dynamic of infra-national territories was first led by cultural minorities which resisted the homogenizing forces of nation-states and/or which were economically losing ground within the national economy. As previously noted, few states were homogeneous to start with and national integration was never complete because cultures, identities, and traditions were not eliminated (Keating and Loughlin 1997). However, if the renaissance of regionalism and localism has often been interpreted in cultural terms, the most important question is not whether the rediscovery of local cultures stems from the need to express identity, since this may be the case without it having much effect on social organization. As Bagnasco suggests, drawing on the celebrated Italian case, economies are less and less able to consider themselves in isolation: a cultural and a political idiosyncrasy can endure only by being associated with an economy that can withstand the free market (Balme 1997).

To explain the general rise of meso-government in Europe, Anderson (1994) emphasized the fact that the end of wars in Europe relaxed the constraints of state mobilization and made possible differentiated political scenes. Gradually, the top-down logic of service management and political mobilization reinforced the bottom-up demands for autonomy, thus leading to a more complex political national space. In different ways, localities and (some) regions gained resources, expertise, autonomy, and legitimacy. In some cases, federal or quasi-federal states have now clearly become competitors of the nation-state and the breakdown of some states is not unthinkable; for example in Belgium or Spain or even the UK.

The revival of identity-seeking claims is perhaps less important in Western Europe for explaining regional and local mobilization than the (offensive and defensive) reaction to globalization processes. The reinforcement of subnational, territorial, and political mobilization is pushed by the need to face the destructuring of local and regional societies, keeping in mind globalization processes on the one hand, and rivalries among subnational territories on the other. Faced with logics of fragmentation, social groups, organized interests, and political elites mobilize for collective projects, reinvent local identities and organize in governance regimes either to resist politically, culturally, and economically or to adapt to globalization processes. But pressures on nation-states also apply to regions or localities and fragmentation often prevails.

Pressures on national societies and the restructuring of the state itself within the European Union marks the end of one cycle of the state story. In Europe, some political sociologists are looking forward to the postnation-state period and the making of a more tolerant, pluralist (postmodern?) society within some form of constitutionalized state (Habermas 1996). On the other hand, Touraine (1996) and others stress the crisis of European nation-states. He suggests a need to distinguish between the national state – defined as the political and institutional "expression" of a national (cultural) reality where politics is determined by some more general social reality such as the nation or race – and the nation-state – where politics (in particular the state) plays a role in the organization and structuration of society. Touraine stresses the risks associated on the one hand with the rise of the national state in Europe and on the other reorganized states which are more and more separated from national societies and nations. The European Union is an interesting case in that regard, but it is not the only one.

Rather than the end of the state, the chapter suggests "la fin du grand récit de l'Etat nation"; the end of the idealized articulation of a state and a national society brought together in a modernist narrative.

Further Reading

On social and political change in Europe, see Colin Crouch *Social Change in Western Europe*. (Oxford University Press 1999). The special edition of *Review of International Political Economy*, edited by Andrew Chitty (vol. 4., no. 3, 1997), contains a number of important essays (e.g. those by Mann, Jessop, and Shaw). On the political (and other) aspects of globalization, see David Held, Anthony McGrew, David Goldblatt, and Jonathan Perraton's *Global Transformations* (Polity Press 1999).

38

The "Singapore Model": Democracy, Communication, and Globalization

Danilo Zolo

Translated by Laura Serratrice

Singapore is an antipolis in which unquestionable political consensus is maintained by authoritarian means. It is the actuality of the possible development of western democracies. The postwar consensus in the West depended on the production of economic resources for social welfare, the safeguarding of national identity and the protection of fundamental rights. Today the balance between these three variables is problematic. Globalization threatens the stability of democratic countries, undermining the cohesion of national states with the weakening of political identities and the continuing crisis of welfare provision. The bureaucratization and "self-referentiality" of political decision-making, the deficit of "constructive power" and the proliferation of "invisible powers" affecting politics threaten democratic pluralism. The mass media has reduced the public to "political consumers," and strategies are being developed to manipulate us at a more "subliminal" level. As the entitlements to citizenship rights have grown, their effectiveness and enforceability have diminished. These tendencies do not point precisely toward the realization of the disciplinary authoritarianism of Singapore, but they do indicate "evolutionary risks" of a similar outcome in the West in terms of the erosion of personal and political freedoms.

A NEGATIVE UTOPIA

In a book I wrote a few years ago I referred to the "Singapore Model" as the theoretical nightmare of western democratic thought – the genuine portrait of a "distopian" archetype *à la* Orwell or Huxley (Zolo 1992: 184). Singapore, it is a well-known fact, is one of the most aggressive "Asian tigers" of the Pacific. Its political regime is a striking example of a contemporary *antipolis*. For the last thirty years this modern city-state has been governed by a sort of platonic king-philosopher, Lee Kuan Yew, who decided to turn the country into "a highly disciplined society, determined, educated and willing to work hard."

Without drawing inspiration from any political ideology or eastern religious tradition, Lee Kuan Yew has meticulously planned and prescribed the rhythms of life and the collective and individual goals of his three million fellow citizens, mostly Chinese and Malayan, including the prohibition of spitting in public and smoking outside designated areas which are closely monitored. The less serious violations are dealt with corporal punishments (violent lashes on the buttocks with a bamboo cane), the more serious ones with capital punishment, which in Singapore is probably looked upon even more favorably than it is in the United States.

Thanks to the very high technological efficiency and the vast use of information and telecommunication systems, wealth is widespread and constantly growing. Public services are excellent, schools and hospitals in particular, the traffic is free flowing and quiet, air pollution is moderate, unemployment is virtually non-existent, almost everyone is a home owner, and the education level is very high. To all that we only have to add, or perhaps subtract, the total absence of political opinions and public discussion. Singapore is a "City of the Sun" in which the prudential motto *de rege paucum, de Deo nihil* is a custom that it is not necessary to enforce by means of administrative pressure. Political consensus is, in all senses of the term, unquestionable.

The image of Singapore generates unease in western countries (but also interest and at times even enthusiasm) because its authoritarian model seems to have a potential that goes beyond its current realizations in South-East Asia. Singapore seems to be the actuality of the possible evolution (or involution) of the western democratic regimes. The success of the "Singapore Model" in the West could lead to the demise of democracy without causing any traumas, since it would be compatible with both market economy and economic liberty.

Free Market Economy and Political Legitimization

Ralf Dahrendorf has said that in the postwar years the western countries managed to "square the circle." They kept under control, and in a mutual and dynamic balance, the production of economic resources needed for social welfare, the safeguard of the sense of national identity, and the protection of fundamental rights (Dahrendorf 1995: 15). Today, the balance between these variables has become problematic, especially because of the push toward globalization. Globalization is jeopardizing the stability of democratic countries because it introduces forms of relentless competition, makes many types of jobs precarious, denies the protection of fundamental rights to foreigners, and creates privileged areas for the indigenous majorities (as is the case of highly civilized Switzerland).

I shall use the three variables proposed by Dahrendorf to assess the democratic quality of a modern, complex, and differentiated society and compare the experience of western democracies to the "Asian authoritarianism" of the Singapore model.

Concerning the first variable, it has now become apparent that the market economy (I stick to this generic, but in my opinion useful, expression regardless of the variety of its forms in contemporary capitalism) has no rivals as an effective system of production. The market economy is by now rooted in every corner of the world and it is taking on a global dimension which seems irreversible. Nowadays, after the inglorious decline of "really existing socialism," any attempt to plan or even conceive alternative "forms of production" to the market would be unthinkable both on a theoretical and a political level.

Obviously, the rhetoric about the beneficial effects of globalization, in particular of economic globalization, is pervasive. There is also excessive optimism concerning the ability of these phenomena of functional interdependence to pave the way to tackling crucial international issues. Just as optimistic is the expectancy that the global opening of the markets – it is a classic thesis re-proposed by contemporary neo-liberalism – could help overcome the disparity that exists today between the restricted number of industrial powers and the great majority of less developed or underdeveloped countries.

However, there is no doubt that in western countries the market economy, with its powerful globalizing drive, acts not only as an effective form of production and distribution of material goods, but also as a stimulating factor with regard to scientific research and technological development, especially in the areas of new materials, electronics, telecommunications, and artificial intelligence. In western countries the market and the information and technological development take on the role of important factors of political legitimization, reaching beyond their specific economic and productive functions. They are, despite their anonymous and abstract nature, one of the elements of popular consensus and an essential condition for the citizens' loyalty toward political institutions.

The increase in production and consumption in the industrialized countries, from Japan to Europe to North America, is today the pattern that not only inspires the strategies of the political *elite* in power, but that also dominates collective consciousness: it is a deep and generalized conformity that homogenizes rhythms of life, patterns of consumption, and political inclinations. Italy, for example, seems to be less and less identifiable on the basis of traditional values such as religion, customs, language, culture, or the concept of family. The "motherland" has lost a large part of its romantic aura and nationalistic intensity, even in the language and culture of the right-wing parties (cf. Rusconi 1993). Much more important is the collective expectation – and the relevant political guarantee – of an economic development in terms of Gross National Product in order to enable Italy to keep on being an internationally respected country by virtue of its economic strength and its technological progress, on a par with the major European countries. The drive toward secessionism (or half- secessionism) of the Padania region seems to confirm this commercial and economic logic as well as the low level of consensus that it can guarantee. The spur of this separatist claim does not stem from ethno-cultural identity or shared history or some myth of foundation. It is more of an uprising, justified or not, against the fiscal burdens imposed by the Italian government on small and medium businesses in Northern Italy to support other less flourishing regions of the country. It is therefore a rebellion that, more or less consciously, reflects that particular logic of economic globalization that, for Kenichi Ohmae (1995), tends to undermine the cohesion of the national states.

Something similar could be argued about the European Union, at least judging by its most recent developments, after the treaties of Schengen and Maastricht and their prevailing "Euro-technocratic" interpretations. It is the economic and financial dimension (not to mention the monetary and banking dimension) that seems to hold the power of uniting, or possibly dividing, Europe rather than the compliance with shared political values or a sense of belonging to a "European civil society," and therefore to a common history, culture, and destiny.

In fact, it is the logic of commercial and financial globalization that suggests the creation of extended economic areas, where either the strongest factors of production and the most sophisticated commodities (such as financial capitals and high-tech products) can compete and flourish. This does not constitute, however, an obstacle to the development of new protective policies against labor-intensive industries and unskilled-labor manufactures (Gilpin 1987: 204–9; Greenaway, Hine, and O'Brien 1991). In other words, these are processes of economic integration which are also favored because of their effects of exclusion with regard to weaker economies, which in the case of the European Union is in regard to the whole of the non-EEC Mediterranean countries. The ideal of a *civitas maxima* of a liberalized world economy where all the factors of production are free to circulate, is part of the propaganda of the economic powers, but is an ideal which fails to have an effect on their industrial and commercial policies. In fact, as Robert Gilpin has shown, the industrial powers – and Europe is by no means an exception – implement complex strategies which combine commercial competition between states, economic regionalism, and sector-based protectionism (1987: 394–408).

THE DECLINE OF THE WELFARE STATE

Economic globalization does not only cause a weakening of the political identity of the national states, European democracies included, as well as a consequent fading of the collective identity of citizens. It also detracts from the ability of the national states to manage their economies in an autonomous way and to protect their less well-off citizens from the negative consequences of world competition. This is one of the main reasons why, after the collapse of the Soviet Union, the end of the cold war and the world victory of the market economy, European countries have started to restructure the Welfare State. This phenomenon, too, bears consequences where matters of political loyalty and collective identity of the citizens are concerned (namely, the "second variable" suggested by Dahrendorf).

Representative democracy, with the mass parties at its core, has survived in western countries over the last 40 years thanks to its welfarist metamorphosis. The social cohesion and the political loyalty of the working classes have been secured through a contamination of the mechanisms of market economy and the representative procedures with the balancing logic of the Welfare State.

Nowadays, this political exchange is more difficult to realize, and the balance that it had generated is put under constant pressure. In all western countries the Welfare State is in crisis and no political party defends it any longer without substantial reserves, even among left-wing parties. It is obviously undeniable that, despite the large investment of public resources and the bureaucratic pressure on individual freedom, the Welfare State did not manage to assure a fair distribution of wealth. In all industrialized countries, welfarist principles have generated new forms of social layering. Next to a large middle class, whose essential needs are solidly guaranteed, the distributive policies of the Welfare State have produced on the one hand an affluent minority – looked after by both the market and the state – and on the other hand an underclass: a layer of citizens and foreigners marginalized not only in terms of economic status and private consumption, but also in ethnic and cultural terms. As matter of fact, the latter have been excluded from any entitlement to fundamental rights, including the "social rights" to work and education (Roche 1992: 57–62).

Among the marginalized subjects are the non-EEC immigrants coming from countries with economies still lagging behind and with high demographic rates. By pushing their way into the meanders of western populations, they face an up hill battle for equality. The request of this growing number of non-autochthonous individuals to become *pleno iure* citizens challenges the very structure of citizenship underlying the countries where they have moved to live and work. This is a radical challenge because the dialectical relation between "citizen" and "foreigner" is altered by the magnitude of the migratory phenomenon and by its uncontrollability and irreversibility. It is also a powerful challenge because it tends to undermine the "pre-political" basis of citizenship, the sociological processes which account for collective identity and, finally, the institutions of the rule of law. For the latter are requested to acknowledge the multiethnic nature not only of the individual rights of immigrated citizens, but also of the ethnic identities of minorities who experience a remarkable cultural gap with the host countries.

In his recent book entitled *Was ist Globalisierung?*, Ulrich Beck states that the Welfare State is doomed (1997). Globalization makes it possible for big business to avoid the burdens imposed by national legislations – tax revenue in particular. At the same time the development of electronic technology – automation, information systems, telecommunications – increases the productivity of big corporations that, in turn, tend to lay-off work force which is not highly specialized. A global capitalism is taking shape that can afford to avoid the fiscal costs of labor and, potentially, even labor itself. So, while the profits of the big corporations are growing, the western countries are running out of those financial resources that were traditionally set aside for pensions, social services, and care for the elderly. It is therefore not only work that is starting to become increasingly scarce – public resources are also starting to wither away.

The upshot is the rejection of welfarist heterodoxies, that tried to replace the allocation of resources imposed by an unbounded market with its welfarist logic, and the return to the "pure liberal state'(Luhmann 1981, see chapter 6 in this volume) – or "private law society." As Marshall wrote, the Welfare State attempted to introduce an egalitarian logic of citizenship rights into the possessive logic of contractual relations, since it subordinated, at least partially, free market rules to political allocative principles (Marshall 1950). Globalization reacts against this attempt by exposing the weaknesses and distortions of the welfarist logic. Everywhere in Europe the reaction against the waste and the corruption brought about by the "mixed economy" has made fashionable a host of stock phrases like privatization, subordination of workers, both in the public and private sectors, to the rules of the market, cutting of public funds that are not motivated by absolute necessity, dropping full employment policies and the alleged right to work, lowering of the safety net for the elderly and the young. The upshot is a further fragmentation of the social fabric, especially in terms of lack of civil commitment, fading of the sense of belonging, violence and self-destructive reaction to the conditions of marginality.

THE COLLAPSE OF DEMOCRATIC PLURALISM

I have pointed out that a distinctive feature of the "Singapore model" is the absence of differentiated political programs and therefore the lack of public debates and confrontations about viable political alternatives. In Singapore, political representation is more than ever a procedural pretence since the power is irreversibly held by the bureaucratic and administrative apparatus. And it is the tip of this governmental iceberg that regulates the rest of society and that defines the duties of the individual citizens. Some features are missing which are considered the fundamental requirements for a political regime to be called democratic, and this is regardless of whether we choose a "classic defini-tion" or more recent ones suggested by authors like Schumpeter, Sartori, Dahl, and Bobbio. Such requirements are: a plurality of elites in competition against one another to assert their leadership; an informed public opinion able to assess political alternatives; free elections which give the citizens real power to deter-mine the outcome of the political competition.

I therefore maintain that, if we consider these three elements – pluralism, alternative programs, free elections – as the minimal requirements to distinguish between a democratic regime and a nondemocratic one, the Singapore model represents a potential "evolutionary regression," so to speak, on the western democratic experience.

To defend this thesis it is mandatory to refer to the transformations that have affected the western political systems over the last decades. I mean to refer to what I have called the "evolutionary risks" of democracy in complex societies (Bobbio 1987; Zolo 1992: 121–70). That is, phenomena such as the bureau-cratization of political decision-making and of political parties in particular, the deficit of "constructive power" *vis-à-vis* the increase of vetoing powers (powers which annihilate the planning ability of the institutions formally entitled to decision-making), the weakening of the political consensus and, finally, the proliferation of the "invisible powers" – *arcana imperii* and *arcana seditionis* – which operates in a sort of unfathomable underground of democratic pluralism with the aim of undermining its institutions and objectives.

One key case is the "self-referentiality" of the party system; that is the tendency of political parties to operate in a circular fashion as the source of both their legitimization and their reproduction. In fact, my thesis is that the political parties today do not fulfil their traditional task of gathering the demands coming from society and of placing them in competition with one another in the public arena. They are, therefore, by no means tools of political representation. Their function is, on the contrary, that of systematically reinvesting their power to reconstitute the bases of that same power within informal, and often obscure circuits, through which they distribute resources, advantages, and privileges in order to fuel the flow of solidarity and mutual interest on which they are based.

The most striking consequence of the logic of self-referentiality is the progressive fading of what the theorists of democratic pluralism consider as the very foundation of democracy: the competition for leadership on the basis of alternative programs and therefore the existence of a genuine "political opposition" (Dahrendorf 1988: 77–100). This is not a merely procedural requirement: it calls for differentiated political proposals upon which the electorate can express its will and decide the outcome of the political process, making one party win and another one lose. In other words, this is a requirement that gives meaning to the concept of the "political sovereignty" of the electorate and that makes electoral procedures effective means of decision-making rather than folk rituals.

This is a crucial point: the self-referentiality of the party system tends to hollow out democratic pluralism, because it establishes such strong ties between the parties that it ends up neutralizing any programmatic differentiation. As for the economic competition between businesses, the aim of the race between self-referring parties is the gaining of larger portions of the electoral market, rather than changing the rules of the market. However, in the case of the political market the rules are by no means neutral when compared to the interests at stake: things like the definition of the form of government, the constitutional structure of the state, and the fundamental rights to which people are entitled.

Consequently, if the competition between the parties is too superficial, the "positive" political freedom of the electorate – their actual and autonomous ability to choose between alternative political purposes – is largely lost. What is left is a bare formalistic, "negative" freedom to vote, meaning that the individual is free to take part – or not as the case may be – in the electoral process and to express a political preference without being forced to do it. But obviously – and here the analogy with Singapore becomes even more meaningful – it is not the electorate that decides on fundamental political issues: somebody else before it, and instead of it, has tacitly agreed on what needs to be voted for and what must be left to the self-referencing negotiation between political parties. In other words, the restricted elite at the top of the party system has decided beforehand what the agenda of the electorate is going to be, counteracting in advance any risk of destabilization.

MASS MEDIA AND POLITICAL COMMUNICATION

It could be argued that the new political agents are no longer the "parties" but rather an elite of electoral entrepreneurs that, in an advertising competition with one another, address the citizens-consumers directly, offering them their own symbolic products through the television and according precise marketing strategies.

"Public debate" itself – totally absent in Singapore – is the monopoly of TV stations that organize political discussions in the spectacular and personalized form of the direct confrontation between a restricted number of telegenic leaders who sit permanently in TV studios. They sit there to show off their dialectic abilities in a sort of advertising competition that aims at the public of "political consumers" which, in turn, is systematically "surveyed" for a feedback on the persuasive effects of such communication.

The aim of "opinion polls" is not to offer choices to political consumers, start a debate for the public, record their development, and reach in the end more rational and "democratic" decisions. The public is not informed of certain issues, it is not engaged in discussing them "rationally" and taking care of them. It is rather bombarded with elementary incentives and contextually monitored for its immediate reactions. The public opinion thus "forged" and "verified" is typically extremely pliable and at the same time, it can be presented as the authoritative opinion of the majority of the citizens, at any stage of the communication, and ultimately as the truth to abide by (Martin 1984; Creeps 1989; Mann and Orren 1992; Brahma 1993).

Naturally, I am not arguing here that television and information systems are not central phenomena of contemporary society, both in its public and in its domestic and professional dimensions. On the contrary, it is a process that seems destined to generate a real anthropological mutation since it affects the cognitive parameters, the emotional dispositions, the collective consciousness, and the meaning, rhythms, and contents of daily life. And it is easy to foresee that over the next few decades this process will have an even bigger impact upon the functioning of political institutions. Communication is going to increase quantitatively while, at the same time, there will also be an increase in the differentiation of both the technical instruments of communication and of the social and economic structures within which it will be organized. The future seems to belong to forms of communication that, like pay-TV for instance, are resilient to the demand of a progressively more fragmented market and that specialize in providing different solutions to a differentiated public of consumers.

One of the positive consequences, we are assured, will be the increase in political information and knowledge and, in particular, the beginning of new forms of participation. Thanks to the sophisticated electronic appliances, citizens will finally be able to engage in a daily "political patchwork." The electronic *agorà* will cease to be a myth and it will take the form of an instant referendum democracy. The Clinton administration, for instance, has already launched the new catchphrase – civic networking.

In my opinion, this optimism is ungrounded. The asymmetrical, selective and noninteractive character of mass communication will not be altered by any means. The power the users have to control the procedures of selection of the communication will not grow, nor will their critical ability concerning the contents of communication. On the contrary, their cognitive autonomy will probably be exposed to higher risks. The excessive symbolic pressure under which we will find ourselves will make it difficult for all of us to rationally select the contents of communication.

Furthermore, it seems that our voluntary attention span and our long-term concentration span tend to shrink more and more rather than expanding in an effort to keep up with the social complexity. It shrinks exactly because of the increase in the variety of the quality and the intensity of the stimulation that bombards us and that, if only for a moment, succeeds in catching our attention. We find ourselves stuck in some sort of evolutionary bottleneck from which, for the time being, it is not easy to forecast the outcome or the development.

It is probably for these reasons that nowadays the strategies of multimedia communication – first and foremost commercial advertising, opinion polls, and political campaigning – seem to aim more and more overtly at forms of "subliminal" persuasion (Benjamin 1982; Qualter 1985; Kaid, Nimmo, and Sanders 1986; Baker 1994; Poster 1995). Instead of addressing our conscious attention of citizens and consumers, such communication techniques tend to target it indirectly, relying on cognitive and emotional stimulation secretly associated with the contents or the means of the message that is being communicated. This situation raises delicate issues related to personal identity, individual autonomy, manipulation of public opinion and, ultimately, of the functioning of the decision-making mechanisms of a democratic state. Deep down the very nature of politics is changing: it is becoming subliminal politics.

DEMOCRATIC CITIZENSHIP AND INDIVIDUAL RIGHTS

Let's now take into consideration the "third variable" that, according to Dahrendorf, a democratic regime must be able to keep in synergical balance with the production of material resources and with political loyalty: the protection of individual rights. On this point the gap between the regime of Singapore and that of a western democratic state may look abyssal. On the one hand, the emphasis is on authority, discipline, and collective duties; on the other hand, the stress is on the limitation of power dictated by the constitution, political freedom, and individual rights. Undoubtedly, this is a crucial point.

And yet the debate cannot end here. The *thema decidendum* is not whether there is an objective difference between the two political models – the difference is certainly there and it is remarkable – but whether the "protection of rights" is nowadays, in the countries considered as democratic, a variable in equilibrium with other variables and not subordinated to variables considered as independent – which could lead to a tendency to restrict or not sufficiently protect the set of liberties. My hypothesis is that this tendency does exist and that it is the consequence of the all-important role taken on by technological development, production, and consumption.

In *Citizenship and Social Class* Thomas Marshall linked the development of the modern concept of citizenship – liberal–democratic and social–democratic – to the acknowledgment of individual rights. According to Marshall, while the premodern forms of political belonging were elitist and exclusive, modern citizenship is open and in steady expansion, in the sense that it consistently includes new rights and new individuals. Marshall foresaw that in the Welfare State society there would have been, ultimately, a simple inequality of income and private consumption, and not any longer an inequality of status, which affects the accessibility of fundamental rights (Marshall 1950: 127).

Even though I do not agree with the evolutionary optimism of Marshall's view, and I am taking here the opposite ideological position, I believe it can offer a useful approach to the issue of the relationship between the development of market economy, the evolution of modern citizenship, and the institution of individual rights. It could be possible to argue the following thesis: as the "container" of citizenship has gone from the acknowledgment of civil rights to that of political rights and finally social rights, the protection of rights has become increasingly selective, juridically defective, and politically reversible. It would be possible to talk of some sort of "law of marginal decreasing value" of the acknowledgment of individual rights. And the reason for this lies, most likely, in the different relationship that has taken shape between the acknowledgment of rights and the claims of market economy.

Paradoxically, in the long history of democratic constitutions, the greater the entitlement to new categories of rights the lower the endowment for the citizens. And the main consequence of this thesis is that while civil rights belong, so to speak, to the physiological functionality of liberal and democratic governments, only a permanent "struggle for the law" can ensure the effectiveness of political rights, social rights and, even more importantly, those that we can call "new rights": women rights, the rights of foreigners, environmental rights, and the right to biological integrity, the right to cognitive autonomy.

If by effectiveness of political rights we mean the opportunity that the electorate has of putting forward its independent will through the formal procedure of parliamentary representation, such opportunity is strongly threatened, as has been said earlier, by the self-referencing system of political parties and by the excessive power of mass media communication.

However, the effectiveness of social rights is even more uncertain than that of political rights because they are directly exposed to the contingencies of the market. Due to their direct influence on the mechanisms of wealth accumulation and the fiscal burdens, social rights have a far more uncertain nature compared to the procedures that are supposed to safeguard civil rights. It is true that under exceptional circumstances even civil and political rights can be limited or even withdrawn; but if ineffectiveness of the right to work, for instance, is a normal situation – a physiological one, I might add – within the rule of law, Welfare State included, the same cannot be said for the denial of the inviolability of privacy, or of the guarantees of private property or of freedom of contract.

It is important to add that nowadays, following the crisis of the Welfare State, the very normative structure of social rights is going through a change, in the sense that they are losing their universality and juridical enforceability. Rather than real rights that, ultimately, citizens can put forward in a courtroom – it is the case, in particular, of the rights to health and education – "social rights" are now mere charitable services. Even when they are not withdrawn, they are available at the discretion of the institutions that provide them, mainly because of the necessity to keep public order and because of an "opportunistic" management of critical situations. And therefore Jacques Barbalet has rightly claimed today that rather than "social rights" we should talk of "social services" (Barbalet 1988).

CONCLUSION

Do we then have to conclude that the "Singapore model" is the political form into which the western democracies are rapidly turning? Do we have reason to fear that Asian authoritarianism is the only possible outcome of the current crisis of the western democracies and of the Welfare State?

Such a conclusion would undoubtedly be over simplistic. What can be argued on the basis of the analysis that I have suggested is something much more complex, even though not less worrying. What can be realistically affirmed is that the three variables indicated by Dahrendorf – the production of resources, the political cohesion, and the protection of individual rights – are not in equilibrium in western countries today. Political cohesion is based much more on conformism brought about by private consumption rather than by a sense of identity rooted in a vigorous civil society. The traditional forms of democratic life – the party system above all – seem to have lost all potential of participation and have been reduced to mere rituals of designation of political authority on the basis of an increasingly weak consensus. On the other hand market economy is not only a successful "production method" – it tends to become, also thanks to the globalizing drive, a dominating factor in both public and private life.

If the overall scenario that emerges from this discussion is not the disciplinary authoritarianism of Singapore, it is something that comes close to it in a "dis-topical" way. The *open society* idealized by authors like Friedrich Hayek and Karl Popper, tends to become closed and stiff through a political and cultural process that threatens individual freedom at its deeper level because it affects the way in which personal identity, and both intellectual and political preferences, are formed. Paradoxically, social integration is achieved through the break-up of the public sector and the privatization-dispersion of the political agents, rather than, as in the case of Singapore, on the basis of a discipline imposed by the top levels of the administration.

If this is the case, then the reference to the "Singapore model" is not a futile theoretical and political provocation, but a plausible argument because it invites us to reflect upon, and keep a close eye on, the "evolutionary risks" of western democracy. It also emphasizes the need for a "struggle for rights" that, without denying the traditional political liberties, reaches far beyond the "physiological" protection of civil rights and negative freedom.

Further Reading

Bobbio, N. 1987: *The Future of Democracy*. Cambridge: Polity Press.
Gilpin, R. 1987: *The Political Economy of International Relations*. Princeton: Princeton University Press.
Qualter, T. H. 1985: *Opinion Control in the Democracies*. London: Macmillan.

Bibliography

Abercrombie, N. and Turner, B. S. 1978: "The dominant ideology thesis." *British Journal of Sociology* 29: 149–70.

Abramson, P. and Inglehart, R. 1992: "Generational replacement and value change in eight West European societies." *British Journal of Political Science* 22(2): 183–228.

Adorno, T. and Horkheimer, M. 1972 [1944]: *The Dialectic of Enlightenment*. London: Verso.

Adorno, T. W. 1991: *The Culture Industry: Selected Essays on Mass Culture*. London: Routledge.

Agh, A. 1998: *The Politics of Central Europe*. London: Sage.

Aglietta, M. 1979: *A Theory of Capitalist Regulation*. London: Verso.

Ahmed, S. 1997: "'It's a sun-tan, isn't it?' Autobiography as an identificatory practice." In H. S. Mirza (ed.) *Black British Feminism. A Reader*. London: Routledge.

Ahrne, G. 1996: "Civil society and civil organizations." *Organization* 3(1): 109–210.

Alcoff, L. M. 1999a: "Philosophy and racial identity." In M. Bulmer and J. Solomos (eds.) *Ethnic and Racial Studies Today*. London: Routledge.

Alcoff, L. M. 1999b: "Towards a phenomenology of racial embodiment." *Radical Philosophy* 95: 15–26.

Aldrich, J. 1995: *Why Parties?* Chicago: Chicago University Press.

Almond, A. and Verba, S. 1963: *The Civic Culture: Political Attitudes and Democracy in Five Nations*. Princeton: Princeton University Press.

Altman, D. 1996: "Rupture or continuity?: The internationalization of gay identities." *Social Text* 48: 77–94.

Ames, B. 1995: "Electoral strategy under open-list proportional representation." *American Journal of Political Science* 39(2): 406–33.

Amstrong, K. and Bulmer, S. 1998: *Governance of the Single European Market*. Manchester: Manchester University Press.

Anderson, B. 1991: *Imagined Communities*, second edition. London: Verso.

Anderson, P. 1974a: *Lineages of the Absolutist State*. London: New Left Books.

Anderson, P. 1974b: *Passages from Antiquity to Feudalism*. London: New Left Books.

Anderson, P. 1994: *The Invention of Regions*. Florence: EUI Working papers, no. 2.

Andreski, S. 1971: *Military Organization and Society*. Berkeley, CA: University of California Press.

Ang, L. 1996: *Living Room Wars: Re-Thinking Media Audiences for a Postmodern World*. London: Routledge.

Appaduraï, A. 1990 : "Disjuncture and difference in the global cultural economy." In M. Featherstone (ed.) *Global Culture: Nationalism, Globalization and Modernity*. London: Sage.

Appaduraï, A. 1996a: *Modernity at Large: Cultural Dimensions of Globalization*. University of Minnesota Press.

Appaduraï, A. 1996b: *The Social Life of Things : Commodities in Cultural Perspective*. Cambridge: Cambridge University Press.

Arato, A. 1981: "Civil society against the state: Poland 1980–81." *Telos*, Spring 47: 23–47.

Archibugi, D. and Held, D. (eds.) 1995: *Cosmopolitan Democracy: An Agenda for a New World Order*. Cambridge: Polity Press.

Arendt, H. 1951: *The Origins of Totalitarianism*. Orlando, Florida: Harcourt Brace and Co.

Aries, P. 1978: *The Hour of our Death*. Harmondsworth: Penguin.

Aristotle. 1988: *The Politics*. Cambridge: Cambridge University Press.

Arrighi, G. 1994: *The Long Twentieth Century: Money, Power and the Origins of Our Times*. London: Verso.

Arrow, K. J. 1951: *Social Choice and Individual Values*. New York: John Wiley and Sons.

Ashenden, S. 1996: "Reflexive governance of child sexual abuse." *Economy and Society* 25(1): 64–88.

Ashenden, S. and Owen, D. (eds.) 1999: *Foucault contra Habermas: Recasting the Dialogue between Genealogy and Critical Theory*. London: Sage.

Atkinson, M. and Coleman, W. 1989: "Strong states and weak states: sectoral policy networks in advanced capitalist economies." *British Journal of Political Science* 19(1): 47–67.

Aya, R. 1994: "Explaining revolutionary violence: A refutation." *Theory and Society* 23(6): 771–6.

Bachrach, P. 1969: *The Theory of Democratic Elitism: A Critique*. London: University of London Press.

Bachrach, P. and Baratz, M. S. 1962: "The two faces of power." *American Political Science Review* 56(4): 947–52.

Bachrach, P. and Baratz, M. S. 1963: "Decisions and nondecisions: an analytical framework." In *American Political Science Review* 57(3): 632–42. Reprinted in Scott (ed.), *Power*, 1994.

Bachrach, P. and Baratz, M. S. 1975: "Power and its two faces revisited: reply to Geoffrey Debnam." *American Political Science Review* 69(3): 900–4.

Badie, B. 1995: *La Fin des Territoires*. Paris: Fayard.

Badie, B, 1999: *Un Monde sans Souveraineté*. Paris: Fayard.

Badie, B. and Birnbaum, P. 1994: "Sociologie de l'Etat revisitée." In *Revue Internationale de Sciences Sociales*, no. 140, June.

Bagdikian, B. H. 2000: *The Media Monopoly*, sixth edition. Boston: Beacon.

Bahador, B. 1999: "Fragmentation in an era of globalization." *Bulletin of the Association for the Study of Ethnicity and Nationalism* 16: 9–16.

Baker, C. E. 1994: *Advertising and a Democratic Press*. Princeton: Princeton University Press.

Balibar, E. 1991: "The nation form: History and ideology." In E. Balibar and I. Wallerstein (eds.) *Race, Nation, Class. Ambiguous Identities*. London: Verso.

Balibar, E. 1995: *The Philosophy of Marx*. London: Verso.

Balme, R. 1996: "Pourquoi le gouvernement change-t-il d'échelle ?" In R. Balme (ed.) *Les politiques du néo-régionalisme*. Paris: Economica.

Banfield, E. 1958: *The Moral Basis of A Backward Society*. Glencoe, IL: The Free Press.

Barbalet, J. M. 1988: *Citizenship. Rights, Struggle and Class Inequality*. Milton Keynes: Open University Press; University of Minnesota Press.

Barrow, C. W. 1993: *Critical Theories of the State: Marxist, neo-Marxist, post-Marxist*. Madison: University of Wisconsin Press.

Barry, A., Osborne, T., and Rose, N. (eds.) 1996: *Foucault and Political Reason: Liberalism, neo-Liberalism and Rationalities of Government*. Chicago: University of Chicago Press.

Barry, B. 1970: *Sociologists, Economists and Democracy*. London: Macmillan.

Barry, B. 1975: "Political accommodation and consociational democracy." *British Journal of Political Science* 5: 477–505.

Barry, B. 1991: "Is it better to be powerful or lucky?" In B. Barry (ed.) *Democracy and Power*. Oxford: Clarendon Press.

Bartelson, J. 1995: *A Genealogy of Sovereignty*. Cambridge: Cambridge University Press.

Barth, F. 1969: *Ethnic Groups and Boundaries. The Social Organization of Culture and Difference*. Oslo: Universitetsforlaget.

Bartolini, S. and Mair, P. 1990: *Identity, Competition, and Electoral Availability*. Cambridge: Cambridge University Press.

Basch, L., Schiller, N. G., and Blanc, C. S. 1994: *Nations Unbound: Trans-national Projects, Postcolonial Predicaments, and Deterritorialized Nation-States*. Langhorne, PA: Gordon and Breach.

Bataille, G. 1985: *Visions of Excess*. Manchester: Manchester University Press.

Baudrillard, J. 1983a: *In the Shadow of the Silent Majority*. New York: Semiotext(e).

Baudrillard, J. 1983b: *Simulations*. New York: Semiotext(e).

Baudrillard, J. 1995: *The Gulf War Did Not Take Place*. Sydney: Power Publications.

Baudrillard, J. 1998: *The Consumer Society*. London: Sage.

Bauman, Z. 1989: *Modernity and the Holocaust*. Cambridge: Polity Press.

Bauman, Z. 1992: *Intimations of Postmodernity*. London and New York: Routledge.

Baumann, G. 1992: "Ritual implicates 'Others': Rereading Durkheim in a plural society." In D. de Coppet (ed.) *Understanding Rituals*. London: Routledge.

Beck, U. 1992: *Risk Society: Towards a New Modernity*. London: Sage.

Beck, U. 1994: "The debate on the 'individualization theory' in today's sociology in Germany." *Soziologie* 3: 191–200.

Beck, U. 1997: *Was ist Globalisierung?* Frankfurt am Main: Suhrkamp Verlag.

Becker, G. 1964: *Human Capital*. New York: National Bureau of Economic Research, Columbia University Press.

Becker, G. S. 1981: *A Treatise on the Family*. Cambridge, MA: Harvard University Press.

Beetham, D. 1991: *The Legitimation of Power*. Basingstoke: Macmillan.

Beetham, D. 1993: "Four theorems about the market and democracy." *European Journal of Political Research* 23: 187–201.

Beetham, D. 1996: *Bureaucracy*, second edition. Buckingham: Open University Press.

Beetham, D. and Lord, C. J. 1998: *Legitimacy and the European Union*. Harlow: Addison-Wesley-Longman.

Behrenbeck, S. 1998: "Gefallenengedenken in der Weimarer Republik und im 'Dritten Reich'." In S. Arnold et al. (eds.) *Politische Inszenierung im 20. Jahrhundert. Zur Sinnlichkeit der Macht*. Wien: Böhlau.

Bell, D. 1987: "The world and the US in 2013." *Deadlus* 116(3): 1–32.

Bell, R. 1985: *Holy Anorexia*. Chicago: University of Chicago Press.

Bellah, R. S. 1968: "Civil religion in America." In W. G. McLoughlin and R. S. Bellah (eds.) *Religion in America*. Boston: Houghton Mifflin.

Bellamy, R. P. 1987: *Modern Italian Social Theory: Ideology and Politics from Pareto to the Present*. Cambridge: Polity Press.

Bellamy, R. P. 1992: *Liberalism and Modern Society: An Historical Argument*. Cambridge: Polity Press.

Bellamy, R. P. 1999: *Liberalism and Pluralism: Towards a Politics of Compromise*. London and New York: Routledge.

Bendix, R. 1964: *Nation-Building and Citizenship*. Berkeley: University of California Press.

Benhabib, S. (ed.) 1996: *Democracy and Difference: Contesting the Boundaries of the Political*. Princeton: Princeton University Press.

Benjamin, G. (ed.) 1982: *The Communication Revolution in Politics*. New York: Academy of Political Science.

Bennett, R. and Krebs, G. 1993: "Local economic development partnerships: an analysis of policy networks in EC-LEDA local employment development strategies." *Regional Studies* 28(2): 119–40.

Bensel, R. F. 1990: *Yankee Leviathan: The Origins of Central State Authority in America, 1859–1877*. Cambridge: Cambridge University Press.

Bentley, A. F. 1908: *The Process of Government*. Chicago: University of Chicago Press.

Berger, P. L. and Luckmann, T. 1972 [1966]: *The Social Construction of Reality. A Treatise in the Sociology of Knowledge*. Harmondsworth: Penguin.

Berle, A. A. and Means, G. C. 1932: *The Modern Corporation and Private Property*. London: Macmillan.

Berman, H. J. 1983: *Law and Revolution: The Formation of the Western Legal Tradition*. Cambridge, MA: Harvard University Press.

Bernard, M. 1996: "Civil society after the first transition." *Communist and Post-Communist Studies* 29(3): 309–33.

Betz, H-G. 1994: *Radical Right-Wing Populism in Western Europe*. London: Macmillan.

Bhabha, H. K. (ed.) 1990: *Nation and Narration*. London: Routledge.

Bhabha, H. K. 1994a: "Frontlines/borderposts." In A. Bammer (ed.) *Displacements. Cultural Identities in Question*. Bloomington: Indiana University Press.

Bhabha, H. K. 1994b: *The Location of Culture*. London: Routledge.

Bigo, D. 1996: *Polices en réseaux, l'exemple Européen*. Paris: Presses de Sciences Politiques.

Billig, M. 1995: *Banal Nationalism*. London: Sage.

Birch, A. H. 1959: *Small Town Politics*. Oxford: Oxford University Press.

Birnbaum, P. 1996: "Sur la citoyenneté." *L'Année Sociologique* 46(1): 57–85.

Blackburn, R. (ed.) 1991: *After the Fall: The Failure of Communism and the Future of Europe*. London: Verso.

Blair, T. 1998: *The Third Way: New Politics for the New Century*. London: The Fabian Society.

Block, F. 1987: *Revising State Theory: Essays in Politics and Postindustrialism*. Philadelphia: Temple University Press.

Blondel, J. 1978: *Political Parties: A Genuine Case for Discontent?* Aldershot: Wildwood.

Bloom, A. 1987: *The Closing of the American Mind*. New York: Simon & Schuster.

Blumer, J. G. et al. 1971: "Attitudes to the monarchy: Their structure and development during ceremonial occasion." *Political Studies* 19: 149–71.

Bobbio, N. 1987: *The Future of Democracy*. Cambridge: Polity Press.

Bobbio, N. 1989: *Democracy and Dictatorship: The Nature and Limits of State Power*. Cambridge: Polity Press.

Boesne, B. and Dandekker, C. (eds.) 1998: *Les armées en Europe*. Paris: La Découverte.

Boissevain, J. (ed.) 1991: *Revitalizing European Rituals*. London: Routledge.

Bomberg, E. 1998: "Issue networks and the environment: Explaining European Union environmental policy." In D. Marsh (ed.) *Comparing Policy Networks*. Buckingham: Open University Press.

Bordo. S. 1993: *Unbearable Weight. Feminism, Western Culture and the Body*. Berkeley: University of California Press.

Borzel, T. 1998: "Organizing Babylon – on the different conceptions of policy networks." *Public Administration* 76: 253–73.

Bottomore, T. B. 1964: *Elites and Society*. London: C. A. Watts.

Boudon, R. 1982: *The Unintended Consequences of Social Action*. London: Macmillan.

Bourdieu, P. 1977a: "Remarques provisoires sur la perception sociale du corps." *Actes de la Recherche en Sciences Sociales* 14: 51–4.

Bourdieu. P. 1977b: *Outline of a Theory of Practice*. Cambridge: Cambridge University Press.

Bourdieu, P. 1980: "Le capital social. Notes provisoires." *Actes de la Recherche en Sciences Sociales* 3: 2–3.

Bourdieu, P. 1982: *Ce que parle veut dire. L'economie des echanges linguistiques*. Paris: Fayard.

Bourdieu, P. 1984a: *Distinction*. Cambridge, MA: Harvard University Press.

Bourdieu, P. 1984b: "La delegation et le fetichisme politique." *Actes de la Recherche en Sciences Sociales* 52(5): 49–55.

Bourdieu, P. 1998: *La Domination Masculine*. Paris: Seuil.

Boyer, R. 2000: "The unanticipated fallout of European monetary union: an essay on the political and institutional deficits of the euro." In C. Crouch (ed.) *After the Euro: Shaping Institutions for Governance in the Wake of European Monetary Union*. Oxford: Oxford University Press.

Boyer, R. and Drache, D. (eds.) 1997: *States Against, Markets*. London: Routledge.

Boyer, R. and Durand, J-P. 1997: *After Fordism*. Trans. S. H. Mair. Basingstoke: Macmillan.

Brahma, J. 1993: *The Phantom Respondents. Opinion Surveys and Political Representation*. Ann Arbor: The University of Michigan Press.

Brandes, U., Kenis, P., Raab, J., Schneider, V., and Wagner, D. 1998: "Explorations into the visualisation of policy networks." *Konstanzer Schriften in Mathematik und Informatik* no. 60, April.

Breen, R. and Rottman, B. 1998: "Is the national state the appropriate geographical unit for class analysis?" *Sociology* 32(1): 1–22

Breines, W. 1982: *Community and Organization in the New Left, 1962–1968: The Great Refusal*. New York: Praeger.

Breuilly, J. 1982: *Nationalism and the State*. Manchester: Manchester University Press.

Breuilly, J. 1993: *Nationalism and the State*, second edition. Manchester: Manchester University Press.

Breuilly, J. 1996: "Approaches to Nationalism." In G. Balakrishnan and B. Anderson (eds.) *Mapping the Nation*. London: Verso.

Browne, W. P. 1995: *Cultivating Congress*. Kansas: Lawrence.

Brubaker, R. 1992: *Citizenship and Nationhood in France and Germany*. Harvard: Harvard University Press.

Brubaker, R. 1996: *Nationalism Reframed. Nationhood and the National Question in the New Europe*. Cambridge: Cambridge University Press.

Brunsson, N. 1989: *The Organization of Hypocrisy. Talk, Decisions, and Actions in Organizations*. Chichester: John Wiley.

Bryant, C. G. A. 1995: "Civic nation, civil society, civil religion." In J. A. Hall (ed.) *Civil Society: Theory, History, Comparison*. Cambridge: Polity Press.

Bryson, V. 1992: *Feminist Political Theory*. Basingstoke: Macmillan.

Bubeck, D. 1995: *A Feminist Approach to Citizenship*. Florence: European University Institute.

Buchanan, J. 1984: "Politics without romance: A sketch of positive public choice theory and its normative implications." In J. M. Buchanan and R. D. Tollison (eds.) *The Theory of Public Choice – II*. Ann Arbor: University of Michigan Press.

Buchanan, J. and Tullock, G. 1962: *The Calculus of Consent*. Ann Arbor: University of Michigan Press.

Budge, I. and Farlie, D. 1983: *Explaining and Predicting Elections. Issue Effects and Party Strategies in Twenty-Three Democracies*. London: Allen & Unwin.

Bulbeck, C. 1992: *Australian Women in Papua New Guinea: Colonial Passages 1920–1960*. Cambridge: Cambridge University Press.

Bulbeck, C. 1998: *Re-orienting Western Feminisms: Women's Diversity in a Postcolonial World*. Cambridge: Cambridge University Press.

Bulmer, M. (ed.) 1974: *Working-Class Images of Society*. London: Routledge and Kegan Paul.

Burchell, D. 1995: "The attributes of citizens: Virtue, manners and the activity of citizenship." *Economy and Society* 24(4): 540–58.

Burchell, G. 1991: "Peculiar interests: Civil society and governing the system of natural liberty." In G. Burchell, C. Gordon, and P. Miller (eds.) *The Foucault Effect. Studies on Governmentality*. London: Harvester.

Burchell, G., Gordon, C., and Miller, P. (eds.) 1991: *The Foucault Effect. Studies in Governmentality*. Chicago: University of Chicago Press; Hemel Hempstead: Simon and Schuster.

Burke, P. 1992: *The Fabrication of Louis XIV*. New Haven, CT, and London: Yale University Press.

Burleigh, M. and Wipperman, W. 1991: *The Racial State, 1933–1945*. Cambridge: Cambridge University Press.

Burnham, J. 1941: *The Managerial Revolution*. New York: John Day.

Bussemaker, J. and Voet, R. 1998: "Citizenship and gender: Theoretical approaches and historical legacies." *Critical Social Policy* 18(3): 277–307.

Butler, J. 1990: *Gender Trouble. Feminism and the Subversion of Identity*. London: Routledge.

Butler, J. 1993: *Bodies that Matter: The Discursive Limits of Sex*. London: Routledge.

Butler, J. 1997: *Excitable Speech. A Politics of the Performative*. London: Routledge.

Cairns, D. and Richards, S. 1988: *Writing Ireland: Colonialism, Nationalism and Culture*. Manchester. Manchester University Press.

Calvert, P. 1996: *Revolution and International Politics*, second edition. London: Pinter.

Campbell, D. 1998: *Writing Security*, revised second edition. Manchester: Manchester University Press.

Caporaso, J. 1996: "The European Union and forms of state : Westphalian, regulatory or post-modern." *Journal of Common Market Studies* 34(1).

Cardoso, R. C. L. 1983: "Movimentos sociais urbanos: balanço critico." In B. Sorj and M. H. Tavares de Almeida (eds.) *Sociedade y Política no Brasil Pos-1964*. São Paulo: Editora Brasiliense.

Carey, J. W. 1998: "Political ritual on television: Episodes in the history of shame, degradation and excommunication." In T. Liebes and J. Curran (eds.) *Media, Ritual and Identity*. London: Routledge.

Carey, J. M. and Shugart, M. S. 1995: "Incentives to cultivate a personal vote: a rank ordering of electoral formulas." *Electoral Studies* 14(4): 417–39.

Carpenter, D., Esterling, K., and Lazer, D. 1998: "The strength of weak ties in lobbying networks." *Journal of Theoretical Politics* 10(4): 417–44.

Carter, E., Donald, J., and Squires, J. (eds.) 1993: *Space and Place: Theories of Identity and Location*. London: Lawrence & Wishart.

Cassirer, E. 1955: *The Philosophy of Symbolic Forms*. New Haven, CT: Yale University Press.

Castells, M. 1996: *The Rise of the Network Society*, vol. I of *The Information Age: Economy, Society and Culture*. Oxford: Blackwell.

Castells, M. 1997: *The Power of Identity*, vol. II of *The Information Age: Economy, Society and Culture*. Oxford: Blackwell.

Castoriadis, C. 1987: *The Imaginary Institution of Society*. Oxford: Oxford University Press.

Cater, D. 1964: *Power in Washington*. New York: Random House.

Caygill, H. 1993: "Violence, Civility and the prediconent of Philosophy." In D. Campbell and M. Dillan (eds.) *The Political Subject of Violence*. Manchester: Manchester University Press.

CCCS 1982: *The Empire Strikes Back: Race and Racism in 70s Britain*. London: Hutchinson in association with the Center for Contemporary Cultural.

Cerny, P. 1990: *The Changing Architecture of Politics*. London: Sage.

Chaney, D. 1993: *Fictions of Collective Life. Public Drama in Late Modern Culture*. London: Routledge.

Cheah, P. and Robbins, B. (eds.) 1998: *Cosmopolitics: Thinking and Feeling Beyond the Nation*. Minneapolis: University of Minnesota Press.

Cheal, D. 1988: "The postmodern origin of ritual." *Journal for the Theory of Social Behavior* 18(3): 269–90.

Clark, J. C. D. 1990: "National identity. State formation and patriotism: The role of history in the public mind." *History Workshop Journal* 29: 95–102.

Clark, T. N. and Goetz, E. 1994: "The antigrowth machine: Can city governments control, limit or manage growth?" In T. N. Clark (ed.) *Urban Innovation: Creative Strategies for Turbulent Times*. London: Sage.

Clark, T., Lipset, S., and Rempel, M. 1993: "The declining political significance of social class." *International Sociology* 8(3): 279–93.

Clarke, S. (ed.) 1990: *The State Debate*. Basingstoke: Macmillan.

Cloonan, M. 1998: "Massive Attack." *Index on Censorship* 6: 184–7.

Coase, R. 1937: "The nature of the firm." *Economica* 4: 386–405.

Cohen, A. 1985: *The Symbolic Construction of Community*. London: Routledge.

Cohen, A. 1993: *Masquerade Politics. Explorations in the Structure of Urban Cultural Movements*. Oxford: Berg.

Cohen, J. and Arato, A. 1994 [1992]: *Civil Society and Political Theory*. Cambridge, MA: MITP.

Cohen, J. and Rogers, J. 1995: *Associations and Democracy*. London: Verso.

Cole, G. D. H. 1920: *Guild Socialism Re-Stated*. London: Leonard Parsons.

Coleman, J. S. 1988: "Social capital in the creation of human capital." *American Journal of Sociology* 94: 95–120.

Coleman, J. S. 1990: *Foundations of Social Theory*. Cambridge, MA: The Belknap Press of Harvard University Press.

Coleman, J. S. 1994: "A rational choice perspective on economic sociology." In N. J. Smelser and R. Swedberg (eds.) *The Handbook of Economic Sociology*. Princeton: Princeton University Press.

Coleman, J. S. and Fararo, T. J. (eds.) 1992: *Rational Choice Theory: Advocacy and Critique*. Newbury Park: Sage.

Collier, Ruth Berins and Collier, David. 1991: *Shaping the Political Arena*. Princeton: Princeton University Press.

Collins, R. 1975: *Conflict Sociology: Toward an Explanatory Science*. New York: Academic Press.

Colomy, P. 1990: "Revisions and progress in differentiation theory." In Jeffrey C. Alexander and Paul Colomy (eds.) *Differentiation Theory and Social Change. Comparative and Historical Perspectives*. New York: Columbia University Press, 465–97.

Condorcet, M. J. A. 1976 [1794]: "Sketch for the historical picture of the progress of the human mind." In *Selected Writings*, ed. K. M. Baker. Indianapolis: Bobbs-Merrill.

Connell, R. W. 1987: *Gender and Power: Society, the Person and Sexual Politics*. Cambridge: Polity Press.

Connell, R. W. 1990: "The state, gender and sexual politics: Theory and appraisal." *Theory and Society* 19: 507–44.

Connell, R. W. 1995: *Masculinities*. Cambridge: Polity Press.

Connolly, W. E. 1991: *Identity\Difference*. Ithaca: Cornell University Press.

Connolly, W. E. 1995: *The Ethos of Pluralization*. Minneapolis: University of Minnesota Press.

Connor, W. 1978: "A nation is a nation, is a state, is an ethnic group, is a . . . ." *Ethnic and Racial Studies* 4: 377–400.

Connor, W. 1994: *Ethnonationalism: The Quest for Understanding*. Princeton: Princeton University Press.

Cooper, R. 1997: *The Postmodern State and the World Order*. London: Demos.

Corner, J. 1995: *Television Form and Public Address*. London: Edward Arnold.

Costa, P. 1999: *Storia della cittadinanza in Europa*, vol. 1. Bari: Laterza.

Costain, A. N. 1992: *Inviting Women's Rebellion*. Baltimore: Johns Hopkins University.

Cox, G. 1997: *Making Votes Count. Strategic Coordination in the World's Electoral Systems*. New York: Cambridge University Press.

Crawford, B. (ed.) 1995: *Markets, States and Democracy: The Political Economy of Post-Communist Transition*. Boulder, CO: Westview Press.

Creeps, I. 1989: *Public Opinion, Polls and Democracy*. Boulder, CO: Westview Press.

Crenshaw, M. 1981: "The causes of terrorism." *Comparative Politics* 13: 379–99.

Crenshaw, Martha (ed.) 1995: *Terrorism in Context*. Philadelphia: Penn State University Press.

Crewe, I. 1974: "Introduction: Studying elites in Britain." In I. Crewe (ed.) *British Political Sociology Yearbook, Volume 1: Elites in Western Democracies*. London: Croom Helm.

Crook, S., Pakulski, J., and Waters. M. 1992: *Postmodernization*. London: Sage.

Crossley. N. 1996: "Body-subject/Body-power: Agency. Inscription and control in Foucault and Merleau-Ponty." *Body and Society* 2(2): 99–116.

Crouch, C. 1999: *Social Change in Western Europe*. Oxford: Oxford University Press.

Crouch, C. and Streeck, W. (eds.) 1996: *The Diversity of Capitalism*. London: Sage.

Crowley. T, (ed.) 1991: *Proper English?: Readings in Language. History and Cultural Identity*. London: Routledge.

Crozier, M. and Friedberg, E. 1976: *L'acteur et le Système*. Paris: le Seuil.

Cruikshank, B. 1999: *The Will to Empower: Democratic Citizens and Other Subjects*. Ithaca: Cornell University Press.

Cutler, A. 1997: "Artifice, ideology and paradox : the public/private distinction in international law." *Review of International Political Economy* 4(2): 261–85.

Dahl, R. 1956: *A Preface to Democratic Theory*. Chicago: University of Chicago Press.

Dahl, R. 1957: "The concept of power." *Behavioral Science*, vol. 2. Reprinted in Scott (ed.) *Power*, 1994.

Dahl, R. 1961: *Who Governs?* New Haven: Yale University Press.

Dahl, R. 1971: *Polyarchy: Participation and Opposition.* New Haven and London: Yale University Press.

Dahl, R. 1985: *A Preface to Economic Democracy.* Cambridge: Polity Press.

Dahl, R. 1989: *Democracy and its Critics.* New Haven, CT and London: Yale University Press.

Dahrendorf, R. 1988: "Declino delle opposizioni e minoranze morali." *Micromega* 3(2): 77–100.

Dahrendorf, R. 1995: *Quadrare il cerchio.* Roma–Bari: Laterza.

Dalton, R. and Kuechler, M. (eds.) 1990: *Challenging the Political Order: New Social and Political Movements in Western Democracies.* Cambridge: Polity Press.

Dalton, R. J., Flanagan, S. C., and Beck, P. A. (eds.) 1984: *Electoral Change in Advanced Industrial Societies: Realignment or Dealignment?* Princeton: Princeton University Press.

Davies, C. A. 1998: "'A ves heddwch?' Contesting meanings and identities in the Welsh National Eisteddfod." In Felicia Hughes-Freeland (ed.) *Ritual, Performance, Media.* London: Routledge.

Davies, J. C. 1969: "The J-curve of rising and declining satisfaction as a cause of some great revolution and a contained rebellion." In H. D. Graham and T. R. Gurr (eds.) *Violence in America: Historical and Comparative Perspective.* Beverly Hills: Sage.

Davis, A. B. et al. 1941: *Deep South.* Chicago: Chicago University Press.

Davis, K. 1995: *Reshaping the Female Body: The Dilemma of Cosmetic Surgery.* London: Routledge.

Dayan, D. and Katz, E. 1992: *Media Events: The Live Broadcasting of History.* Cambridge, MA: Harvard University Press.

Dean, J. 1996: *Solidarity of Strangers.* Berkeley: University of California Press.

Dean, M. 1994: *Critical and Effective Histories.* London: Routledge.

Dean, M. 1997: "Sociology after society." In D. Owen (ed.) *Sociology after Postmodernism.* London: Sage.

Dean, M. 1999: *Governmentality: Power and Rule in Modern Society.* London: Sage.

Dean, M. and Hindess, B. (eds.) 1998: *Governing Australia: Studies in Contemporary Rationalities of Government.* Melbourne: Cambridge University Press.

Dearing, J. W. and Rogers, E. M. 1996: *Agenda-Setting.* Thousand Oaks, CA and London: Sage.

Defert, D. 1991: "'Popular life' and insurance technology." In G. Burchell, C. Gordon, and P. Miller (eds.) *The Foucault Effect*, 1991.

Dehousse, R. 1996: "Les Etats et l'Union Européenne, les effets de l'intégration." In V. Wright and S. Cassese (eds.) *Le recomposition de l'Etat en Europe*, 1996.

Deleuze, G. 1988: *Foucault.* Minneapolis: Minneapolis University Press.

della Porta, D. 1990: *Il Terrorismo di Sinistra in Italia.* Bologna: Il Mulino.

della Porta, D. (ed.) 1992: *Social Movement and Violence: Participation in Underground Organizations.* Greenwich, CT: Jai Press.

della Porta, D. 1995. *Social Movements, Political Violence and the State.* New York: Cambridge University Press.

della Porta, D. and Diani, M. 1999: *Social Movements: An Introduction.* Oxford: Blackwell.

della Porta, D. and Reiter, H. (eds.) 1998: *Policing Protest: The Control of Mass Demonstrations in Western Democracies.* Minneapolis: The University of Minnesota Press.

della Porta, D. and Tarrow, S. 1987: "Unwanted children. Political violence and the cycle of protest in Italy. 1966–1973." *European Journal of Political Research* 14: 607–32.

Dente, B. 1990: "Metropolitan governance reconsidered or how to avoid errors of the third type." *Governance* 3 (1).

Deutsch, K. 1966: *Nationalism and Social Communication*. Cambridge, MA: MIT Press.

Dezalay, Y. and Garth, B. 1998: *Dealing in Virtue*. Chicago: University of Chicago Press.

Diamond, I. and Hartsock, N. 1998: "Beyond interests in politics: A comment on Virginia Sapiro's 'When are Women's Interests Interesting?'" In A. Phillips (ed.) *Feminism and Politics*, 1998.

Diamond, L. 1997a: *The End of the Third Wave and the Global Future of Democracy*. Reihe Polikwissenschaft/Political Science Series no. 45. Vienna: Institute for Advanced Studies.

Diamond, L. 1997b: "Introduction: In search of consolidation." In L. Diamond, F. Marc, M. F. Plattner, Y-h. Chu, and H-m. Tien (eds.) *Consolidating the Third Wave Democracies: Themes and Perspectives*. Baltimore and London: Johns Hopkins University Press.

Diamond, L. 1998: *Political Culture and Democratic Consolidation*. Working Paper 118. Madrid: Juan March Institute.

Diamond, L., Linz J. J., and Lipset, S. M. (eds.) 1988–9: *Democracy in Developing Countries*. Boulder, CO: Lynne Rienner and London: Adamantine Press.

Dietz, M. 1985: "Citizenship with a feminist face: the problem with maternal thinking." *Political Theory* 13: 119–37.

Dietz, M. 1987: "Context is all: Feminism and theories of citizenship." *Daedalus* 116(4): 1–24.

DiPalma, G. 1990: *To Craft Democracies: An Essay on Democratic Transitions*. Berkeley: University of California Press.

Dix, R. 1989: "Cleavage structures and party systems in Latin America." *Comparative Politics* 22(1): 23–37.

Dobash, R. E. and Dobash, R. P. 1992: *Women, Violence and Social Change*. London: Routledge.

Domhoff, G. W. 1967: *Who Rules America?* Englewood Cliffs: Prentice Hall.

Domhoff, G. W. 1971: *The Higher Circles: The Governing Class in America*. New York: Vintage Books.

Domhoff, G. W. 1979: *The Powers That Be: Processes of Ruling Class Domination in America*. New York: Vintage.

Domhoff, G. W. 1998: *Who Rules America? Power and Politics in the Year 2000*. Mountain View: Mayfield Publishing.

Dörner, A. 1996: *Politischer Mythos und Symbolische Politik. Der Herrmannmythos: zur Entstehung des Nationalbewuatseins der Deutschen*. Opladen: Westdeutscher Verlag.

Douglas, M. 1966: *Purity and Danger. An Analysis of Concepts of Pollution and Taboo*. London: Routledge.

Douglas, M. 1992: "The normative debate and the origins of culture." In M. Douglas (ed.) *Risk and Blame. Essays in Cultural Theory*. London: Routledge.

Dowding, K. 1991: *Rational Choice and Political Power*. Aldershot: Edward Elgar.

Dowding, K. 1995a: "Model or metaphor? A critical review of the policy network approach." *Political Studies* 43: 136–58.

Dowding, K. 1995b: *The Civil Service*. London: Routledge.

Dowding, K. 1996: *Power*. Buckingham: Open University Press.

Dowding, K. and King, D. (eds.) 1995: *Preferences, Institutions and Rational Choice*. Oxford: Clarendon Press.

Downing, B. M. 1992: *The Military Revolution and Political Change: Origins of Democracy and Autocracy in Early Modern Europe*. Princeton: Princeton University Press.

Downs, A. 1957: *An Economic Theory of Democracy*. New York: Harper and Row.

Downs, A. 1967: *Inside Bureaucracy*. Boston: Little Brown.

Downs, A. 1972: "Up and down with ecology: The issue attention cycle." *Public Interest* 28: 38–50.

Downs, A. 1998: *Political Theory and Public Choice*. Cheltenham: Elgar.

Drago, M. E. 1998: *The Institutional Bases of Chile's Economic "Miracle."* Unpublished Ph.D. thesis. Florence: European University Institute.

Drake, M. 1999: "They made a desert and called it peace." *Sociological Research Online* 4(2) at *http://www.socresonline.org.uk/socresonline/4/2/drake.html*.

Dryzek, J. 1999: "Reassessing deliberative democracy." Unpublished paper.

Dubet, F. and Martucelli, D. 1998: *Dans Quelle Société Vivons-Nous?* Paris: Seuil.

Dunleavy, P. 1980: "The urban basis of political alignment." *British Journal of Political Science* 9: 409–44.

Dunleavy, P. 1991: *Democracy, Bureaucracy and Public Choice: Economic Explanations in Political Science*. New York and Hemel Hempstead: Harvester Wheatsheaf.

Durkheim, E. 1915: *The Elementary Forms of Religious Life: A Study in Religious Sociology*. Translation of the French edition of 1912 by J. W. Swain. London: Allen & Unwin; New York: Macmillan.

Durkheim, E. 1957: *Professional Ethics and Civic Morals*. London: Routledge.

Durkheim, E. 1969: "Individualism and the intellectuals." *Political Studies* 17: 14–30.

Durkheim. E. 1987: *Selected Writings*, edited by Anthony Giddens. Cambridge: Cambridge University Press.

Durkheim, E. 1993: *The Division of Labor*. New York: Free Press.

Duverger, Maurice 1954: *Political Parties*. London: Methuen.

Eade, J. 1996: "Ethnicity and the politics of cultural difference: an agenda for the 1990s?" In T. Ranger, Y. Samad, and O. Stuart (eds.) *Culture, Identity and Politics. Ethnic Minorities in Britain*. Aldershot: Avebury.

Easton, D. 1975: "A reassessment of the concept of political support." *British Journal of Political Science* 5(4): 435–58.

Eckstein, H. 1980: "Theoretical approaches to explaining collective political violence." In T. R. Gurr (ed.) *Handbook of Political Conflict*. New York: Free Press.

Edelman, M. 1971: *Politics as Symbolic Action*. Chicago: Markham.

Edelman, M. 1985: *The Symbolic Uses of Politics*, second edition. Urbana/Chicago: University of Illinois Press.

Edelman, M. 1988: *Constructing the Political Spectacle*. Chicago: University of Chicago Press.

Eder, K. 1993: *The New Politics of Class: Social Movements and Cultural Dynamics in Advanced Societies*. London: Sage.

Eisenstein, H. 1991: *Gender Shock: Practising Feminism on Two Continents*. Sydney: Allen & Unwin.

Elias, N. 1987: *The Loneliness of the Dying*. Oxford: Blackwell.

Elias, N. 1988: "Violence and civilization." In J. Keane (ed.) *Civil Society and the State*. London: Verso.

Elias, N. 1991 [1939]: *The Civilizing Process: The History of Manners and State Formation*. Oxford: Blackwell.

Elias, N. 1994 [1939]: *Civilizing Process*. Oxford: Blackwell.

Elias, N. and Dunning, E. 1986: *Quest for Excitement: Sport and Leisure in the Civilizing Process*. Oxford: Blackwell.

Elliott, J. H. 1985: "Power and propaganda in the Spain of Philip IV." In S. Wilentz (ed.) *Rites of Power: Symbolism, Ritual, and Politics since the Middle Ages*. Philadelphia: University of Pennsylvania Press.

Elshtain, J. B. 1981: *Public Man, Private Woman*. Oxford: Martin Robertson.

Elshtain, J. B. 1995: *Democracy on Trial*. New York: Basic Books.

Elster, J. (ed.) 1986: *Rational Choice*. Oxford: Blackwell.

Ely, J. 1992: "The politics of 'Civil Society'." *Telos* 93: 173–91.

Enelow, J. and Hinich, M. J. 1984: *The Spatial Theory of Voting. An Introduction*. New York: Cambridge University Press.

Enelow, J. M. and Hinich, M. J. (eds.) 1990: *Advances in the Spatial Theory of Voting*. Cambridge: Cambridge University Press.

Enloe, C. 1990: *Bananas, Beaches and Bases: Making Feminist Sense of International Politics*. Berkeley: University of California Press.

Epstein, J. and Straub, K. (eds.) 1991: *Body Guards: The Cultural Politics of Gender Ambiguity*. New York and London: Routledge.

Eriksen, T. H. 1993: *Ethnicity and Nationalism. Anthropological Perspectives*. London: Pluto.

Ertman, T. 1997: *Birth of the Leviathan: Building States and Regimes in Medieval and Early Modern Europe*. Cambridge: Cambridge University Press.

Esping-Andersen, G. 1990: *The Three Worlds of Capitalism*. Cambridge: Cambridge University Press.

Esping-Andersen, G. 1996: *Welfare States in Transition*. London: Sage.

Etzioni, A. 1995: *The Spirit of Community – Rights, Responsibilities and the Communitarian Agenda*. London: Fontana Press.

Evans, G. and Whitefield, S. 1993: "Identifying the bases of party competition in eastern Europe." *British Journal of Political Science* 23(4): 521–48.

Evans, P. B., Rueschemeyer, D., and Skocpol, T. (eds.) 1985: *Bringing the State Back In*. Cambridge: Cambridge University Press.

Ewald, F. 1991: "Insurance and Risk." In G. Burchell, C. Gordon, P. Miller (eds.) *The Foucault Effect*.

Eyerman, R. and Jamison, A. 1998: *Music and Social Movements: Mobilizing Traditions in the Twentieth Century*. Cambridge: Cambridge University Press.

Fainstein, S. S. and Hirst, C. 1995: "Urban social movements." In D. Judge, G. Stoker, and H. Wolman (eds.) *Theories of Urban Politics*. London: Sage.

Faist, T. 1999: "Transnational social spaces out of international migration: Evolution, significance and future prospects." *European Archives of Sociology* 1.

Fantasia, R. 1988: *Cultures of Solidarity*. Berkeley: University of California.

Farhi, F. 1994: "Comments on Jeff Goodwin's 'Toward a new sociology of revolutions'." *Theory and Society* 23(6): 785–8.

Farquhar, D. 1996: *The Other Machine. Discourse and Reproductive Technologies*. London: Routledge.

Favazza, A. 1996: *Bodies Under Siege: Self-Mutilation and Body Modification in Culture and Psychiatry*. Baltimore: Johns Hopkins University Press.

Fay, R. G. 1997: *Making the Public Employment Service More Effective through the Introduction of Market Signals*. Paris: OECD.

Featherstone, M. 1988: "Towards the sociology of postmodern culture." In H. Haferkamp (ed.) *Culture and Social Structure*. Berlin and New York: de Gruyter.

Featherstone, M. (ed.) 1990: *Global Culture*. London: Sage.

Featherstone, M., Hepworth, M., and Turner, B. S. (eds.) 1991: *The Body. Social Processes and Cultural Theory*. London: Sage.

Fehér, F. and Heller, A. 1986: *Eastern Left – Western Left*. Cambridge: Polity Press.

Feher, M., Daddaff, R., and Tazi, N. (eds.) 1989: *Fragments for a History of the Human Body*, 3 vols. New York: Zone.

Feldblum, M. 1993: "Paradoxes of ethnic politics: The case of Franco-Maghrebis in France." *Ethnic and Racial Studies* 16: 52–74.

Felsenthal, D. S. and Machover, M. 1998: *The Measurement of Voting Power*. Cheltenham: Edward Elgar.

Ferguson, A. 1966 [1767]: *An Essay on the History of Civil Society*. Edinburgh: Edinburgh University Press.

Ferrajoli, L. 1993: "Cittadinanzae diritti fondamentali." *Teoria Politica* ix(3): 63-76.

Figgis, J. N. 1913: *Churches in the Modern State*. London: Longman, Green & Co.

Finlayson, A. 1998a: "The discourse of nation and the discourse of sexuality." In T. Carver and V. Mottier (eds.) *The Politics of Sexuality*. London: Routledege.

Finlayson, A. 1998b: "Ideology discourse and nationalism." *Journal of Political Ideologies* 31: 99–118.

Fish, S. 1995: "The advent of multipartism in Russia, 1993–95." *Post-Soviet Affairs* 11: 340–83.

Flap, H. D and De Graaf, N. D. 1986: "Social capital and the attained occupational status." *The Netherlands' Journal of Sociology* 22: 145–61.

Foley, M. and Edwards, B. 1996: "The paradox of civil society." *Journal of Democracy* 7(3): 38–52.

Foster, H. 1983: *Postmodern Culture*. London: Pluto Press.

Foucault, M. 1976: *The Birth of the Clinic*. London: Tavistock.

Foucault, M. 1977: *Discipline and Punish*. Harmondsworth: Penguin.

Foucault, M. 1978: *The History of Sexuality: An Introduction*. Harmondsworth: Penguin.

Foucault, M. 1980a: "Two lectures." In C. Gordon (ed.) *Power/Knowledge: Selected Interviews and Other Writings 1972–1977*. Hemel Hempstead: Harvester Press.

Foucault. M. 1980b: *Herculin Barbin: Being the Recently Discovered Memoirs of a Nineteenth Century Hermaphrodite*. New York: Pantheon.

Foucault, M. 1981: "Omnes et Singulatim: Towards a Criticism of 'Political Reason'." In S. McMurrin (ed.) *The Tanner Lectures on Human Values, II*. Salt Lake City: University of Utah Press.

Foucault, M. 1982a: "The Subject and Power." In H. Dreyfus and P. Rabinow (eds.) *Michel Foucault: Beyond Structuralism and Hermeneutics*. London: Harvester Wheatsheaf.

Foucault, M. 1982b: "Le sujet et le pouvoir." *Dits et Écrit* 4: 222–43.

Foucault, M. 1983: "Un système fini face à une demande infinie." *Dits et Écrits* 6: 376–83.

Foucault, M. 1984a: "What is Enlightenment?" In P. Rabinow (ed.) *The Foucault Reader*. London: Penguin.

Foucault, M. 1984b: *The Foucault Reader*, edited by P. Rabinow. Harmondsworth, Penguin.

Foucault, M. 1984c: *History of Sexuality*, vol. 1. Harmondsworth: Penguin.

Foucault, M. 1985: *The Use of Pleasure*. Harmondsworth: Penguin.

Foucault, M. 1986: "La gouvernementalité." *Actes* 54: 6–15.

Foucault. M. 1988a: "Social security." In L. D. Kritzman (ed.) *Michel Foucault: Politics, Philosophy and Culture: Interviews and Other Writings, 1977–1984*. London: Routledge.

Foucault, M. 1988b: "Politics and reason." In L. D. Kritzman (ed.) *Michel Foucault: Politics, Philosophy, Culture: Interviews and Other Writings, 1977–1984*. London: Routledge.

Foucault, M. 1988c: "The ethic of care for the self as a practice of freedom." In J. Bernauer and D. Rasmussen (eds.) *The Final Foucault*. Boston, MA: MIT Press.

Foucault, M. 1988d: "Iran: The spirit of a world without spirit." In L. D. Kritzman (ed.) *Politics, Philosophy and Culture: Interviews and Other Writings, 1977–84*. London: Routledge.

Foucault, M. 1988e: "Kant on enlightenment and revolution." *Economy and Society* 15(1): 88–96.

Foucault, M. 1991: "Governmentality." In G. Burchell, C. Gordon, and P. Miller (eds.) *The Foucault Effect*. Chicago: University of Chicago Press.

Foucault, M. 1994: "Foucault, Michel, 1926– ." In G. Gutting (ed.) *The Cambridge Companion to Foucault*. Cambridge: Cambridge University Press.

Foucault, M. 1997a [1975]: *Discipline and Punish: The Birth of the Prison*. Harmondsworth: Penguin.

Foucault, M. 1997b: "The birth of biopolitics." In P. Rabinow (ed.) *Ethics, Subjectivity and Truth*. London: Allen Lane.

Foucault, M. 1997c: "Society must be defended." In P. Rabinow (ed.) *Ethics, Subjectivity and Truth*. London: Allen Lane.

Foweraker, J. 1989: *Making Democracy in Spain: Grass-Roots Struggle in the South, 1955–1975*. Cambridge: Cambridge University Press.

Foweraker, J. 1993: *Popular Mobilization in Mexico: The Teacher's Movement, 1977–1987*. Cambridge: Cambridge University Press.

Foweraker, J. 1995: *Theorizing Social Movements*. London: Pluto Press.

Foweraker, J. 1998: "Institutional design, party systems and governability – differentiating the presidential regimes of Latin America." *British Journal of Political Science* 28: 651–76.

Foweraker, J. and Craig, A. 1990: *Popular Movements and Political Change in Mexico*. Boulder, CO: Lynne Rienner.

Foweraker, J. and Landman, T. 1997: *Citizenship Rights and Social Movements: A Comparative and Statistical Analysis*. New York: Oxford University Press.

Franklin, M., Mackie, T., and Valen, H. 1992: *Electoral Change: Responses to Evolving Social and Attitudinal Structures in Western Countries*. Cambridge: CUP.

Franzway, S., Court, D., and Connell, R. W. 1989: *Staking a Claim: Feminism, Bureaucracy and the State*. Sydney: Allen & Unwin.

Fraser, N. 1989: "Foucault on modern power: Empirical insights and normative confucions." In N. Fraser (ed.) *Unruly Practices: Power, Discourse and Gender in Contemporary Social Theory*. Cambridge: Polity Press.

Fraser, N. and Gordon, L. 1992: "Contract versus charity: Why is there no social citizenship in the United States?" *Socialist Review* 22(3): 45–67.

Freeman, J. L. 1955: *The Political Process: Executive Bureau – Legislative Committee Relations*. Garden City, New York: Doubleday.

Ferejohn, J. 1974: *Pork Barrel Politics*. Stanford: Stanford University Press.

Freud, S. 1976 [1930]: *Civilization and its Discontents*. London: Hogarth Press.

Friedman, D. and McAdam, D. 1992: "Collective identity and activism: Network, choices, and life of a social movement." In A. Morris and C. McClurg Mueller (eds.) *Frontiers in Social Movement Theory*. New Haven and London: Yale University Press.

Friedman, J. (ed.) 1996: *The Rational Choice Controversy: Economic Models of Politics Reconsidered*. New Haven: Yale University Press.

Friedman, M. 1962: *Capitalism and Freedom*. Chicago: University of Chicago Press.

Friedman, M. and Friedman, R. 1990: *Free to Choose: A Personal Statement*. San Diego: Harcourt Brace Jovanovich.

Frith, S. 1996: *Performing Rites: On the Value of Popular Music.* Oxford: Oxford University Press.

Frost, M. 1998: "Migrants, civil society and sovereign states: Investigating an ethical hierarchy." *Political Studies* 46(5): 871–85.

Fukuyama, F. 1992: *The End of History and the Last Man.* London: Hamish Hamilton.

Fukuyama, F. 1995: *Trust: The Social Virtues and the Creation of Prosperity.* New York: The Free Press.

Gais, T., Peterson, M., and Walker, J. 1984: "Interest groups, iron triangles, and representative institutions in American National Government." *British Journal of Political Science* 14: 161–85.

Galbraith, J. K. 1992: *The Culture of Contentment.* London: Sinclair-Stevenson.

Gamble, A. 1994: *The Free Economy and the Strong State: The Politics of Thatcherism,* second edition. London: Macmillan.

Gamson, W. A. and Meyer, D. S. 1996: "Framing political opportunity." In D. McAdam, J. D. McCarthy, and M. N. Zald (eds.) *Comparative Perspectives on Social Movements: Opportunities, Mobilizing Structures, and Cultural Framings.* Cambridge: Cambridge University.

Garcia, S. 1996: "Cities and citizenship: Special issue." *International Journal of Urban and Regional Research* 20(1).

Garfinkel H. 1967: "Passing and the managed achievement of sex status in an 'intersexed' person." In H. Garfinkel, *Studies in Ethnomethodology.* Englewood Cliffs: Prentice Hall.

Garret, G. and Tsebelis, G. 1999: "Why resist the temptation to apply power indices to the EU?" *Journal of Theoretical Politics* 11: 291–307.

Garretón, M. A. 1989: *The Chilean Political Process.* London: Unwin Hyman.

Geddes, B. 1996: "Initiation of new democratic institutions in eastern Europe and Latin America." In A. Lijphart and C. H. Waisman (eds.) *Institutional Design in New Democracies.* Boulder, CO: Westview Press.

Geertz, C. 1973: *The Interpretation of Cultures: Selected Essays.* New York: Basic Books.

Gellner, E. 1983: *Nations and Nationalism.* Oxford: Blackwell.

Gellner, E. 1992: *Postmodernism, Reason and Religion.* London: Routledge.

Gellner, E. 1994: *Conditions of Liberty, Civil Society and its Rivals.* Harmondsworth: Penguin.

Gellner, E. 1995: "The importance of being modular." In J. Hall (ed.) *Civil Society: Theory, History, Comparison.* Cambridge: Polity Press.

Gerth, H. H. and Mills, C. Wright (eds.) 1948: *From Max Weber: Essays in Sociology.* London: Routledge Kegan Paul.

Giddens, A. 1973: "Elites in the British class structure." *Sociological Review.* Reprinted in J. Scott (ed.) *Power,* 1990.

Giddens, A. 1984: *The Constitution of Society.* Cambridge: Polity Press.

Giddens, A. 1985: *The Nation-State and Violence,* vol. 2 of *A Contemporary Critique of Historical Materialism.* Cambridge: Polity Press.

Giddens, A. 1990: *The Consequences of Modernity.* Cambridge: Polity Press.

Giddens, A. 1991: *Modernity and Self-Identity.* Cambridge: Polity Press.

Giddens, A. 1994: *Beyond Left and Right: The Future of Radical Politics.* Cambridge: Polity Press.

Giddens, A. 1998: *The Third Way: The Renewal of Social Democracy.* Cambridge: Polity Press.

Gillespie, R. 1982: *Soldiers of Peron: Argentina's Montoneros.* New York: Oxford University Press.

Gilpin, R. 1987: *The Political Economy of International Relations*. Princeton: Princeton University Press.

Gilroy, P. 1987: *Ain't No Black in the Union Jack*. London: Hutchinson.

Gitlin, T. 1978: "Media sociology: The dominant paradigm." *Theory and Society* 6: 205–53.

Gitlin, T. 1997: "The anti-political populism of cultural studies." *Dissent*, Spring: 77–82.

Glasman, M. 1994: "The great deformation: Polanyi, Poland and the terrors of planned spontaneity." *New Left Review* 204: 59–86.

Glazer, N. and Moynihan, D. P. (eds.) 1975: *Ethnicity. Theory and Experience*. London: Harvard University Press.

Goffman, E. 1963: *Behavior in Public Places. Notes on the Social Organization of Gatherings*. New York: The Free Press.

Goffman, E. 1963b: *Stigma. Notes on the Management of Spoiled Identities*. Englewood Cliffs: Prentice Hall.

Goffman, E. 1967: *Interaction Rituals. Essays on Face-to-Face Behavior*. New York: Pantheon Books.

Golberg, E. 1996: "Thinking about how democracy works." *Politics and Society* 24: 7–18.

Goodwin, J. 1994: "Toward a new sociology of revolutions." *Theory and Society* 23(6): 731–66.

Gordon, C. 1991: "Governmental rationality: An introduction." In G. Burchell, C. Gordon, and P. Miller, (eds.) *The Foucault Effect*, 1991.

Gordon, C. forthcoming: "Introduction" to M. Foucault. *The Essential Works of Michel Foucault, 1954–1984*, vol.3. London: Allenhane.

Graetz, B. 1983: "Images of class in modern society." *Sociology* 17(1): 79–96.

Graetz, B. 1992: "Inequality and political activism in Australia." *Research in Inequality and Social Conflict* 2: 157–77.

Graham, H. and Gurr, T. R. 1969: *Violence in America: Historical and Comparative Perspective*. New York: Praeger.

Gramsci, A. 1971: *Selections from the Prison Notebooks*. London: Lawrence and Wishart.

Granovetter, M. 1973: "The strength of weak ties." *American Journal of Sociology* 78: 1360–80.

Granovetter, M. 1985: "Economic action, social structure, and embeddedness." *American Journal of Sociology* 83: 1420–43.

Grant, J. and Tancred, P. 1992: "A feminist perspective on state bureaucracy." In A. J. Mills and P. Tancred (eds.) *Gendering Organizational Analysis*. Newbury Park: Sage.

Gray, C. 1994: *Government Beyond the Center*. Basingstoke: Macmillan.

Greenaway, D., Hine, R. C., and O'Brien, A. P. (eds.) 1991: *Global Protectionism*. London: Macmillan.

Greenberg, D. F. 1988: *The Construction of Homosexuality*. Chicago: University of Chicago Press.

Greenfeld, L. 1992: *Nationalism, Five Roads to Modernity*. Cambridge, MA and London: Harvard University Press.

Griffith, E. S. 1939: *The Impasse of Democracy*. New York: Harrison-Hilton.

Gupta, A. and Ferguson, J. 1992: "Beyond 'culture': Space, identity, and the politics of difference." *Cultural Anthropology* 7: 6–23.

Gurr, T. R. 1970: *Why Men Rebel*. Princeton: Princeton University Press.

Gurr, T. R. 1988: "Empirical research on political terrorism: The state of the art and how it might be improved." In R. O. Slater and M. Stohl (eds.) *Current Perspectives on International Terrorism*. London: Macmillan.

Gurvitch, G. 1941: "Mass, community, communion." *Journal of Philosophy* 2(28): 485–96.

Guttsman, W. L. 1963: *The British Political Elite*. London: MacGibbon and Kee.

Haas, P. 1992: "Introduction: Epistemic communities and international policy co-ordination." *International Organization* 46: 1–35.

Habermas, J. 1976: *Legitimation Crisis*. Cambridge: Polity Press.

Habermas, J. 1984 and 1987: *The Theory of Communicative Action, Reason and the Rationalization of Society*, vol.1. Boston: Beacon Press.

Habermas, J. 1989a: *The Theory of Communicative Action, Lifeworld and System: A Critique of Functionalist Reason*, vol. 2. Cambridge: Polity Press.

Habermas, J. 1989b [1962]: *The Structural Transformation of the Public Sphere: An Inquiry into a Category of Bourgeois Society*. Cambridge: Polity Press.

Habermas, J. 1991: "What does socialism mean today? The revolutions of recuperation and the need for new thinking." In R. Blackburn (ed.) *After the Fall: The Failure of Communism and the Future of Socialism*. London: Verso.

Habermas, J. 1992: "Citizenship and national identity: Some reflections on the future of Europe." *Praxis International* 12 (1): 1–19.

Habermas, J. 1996 [1992]. *Between Facts and Norms. Contributions to a Discourse Theory of Law and Democracy*. Cambridge, MA: MIT Press.

Habermas, J. 1996: "The European nation-state – its achievements and its limits. On the past and future of sovereignty and citizenship." In G. Balakrishnan (ed.) *Mapping the Nation*. London: Verso.

Habermas, J. 1999: "Bestialität und Humanität: ein krieg an der Grenze zwischen Recht und Moral." *Die Zeit*, 18, 29th April: 1, 6–7.

Hagopian, F. 1990: "Democracy by undemocratic means? Elites, political pacts and regime transition in Brazil." *Comparative Political Studies* 23(2): 147–70.

Hajer, M. 1993: "Discourse coalitions and the institutionalisation of practice: The case of acid rain in Britain." In F. Fischer and J. Forester (eds.) *The Argumentative Turn in Policy Analysis and Planning*. London: UCL Press.

Hajer, M. 1997: *The Politics of Environmental Discourse: Ecological Modernization and the Policy Process*. Oxford: Oxford University Press.

Hall, J. (ed.) 1995: *Civil Society – Theory, History, Comparison*. Cambridge: Polity Press.

Hall, J. (ed.) 1998: *The State of the Nation. Ernest Gellner and the Theory of Nationalism*. Cambridge: Cambridge University Press.

Hall, S. 1978: *Policing the Crisis: Mugging, the State, and Law and Order*. London: Macmillan.

Hall, S. 1981: "Notes on deconstructing 'the popular'." In R. Samuel (ed.) *People's History and Socialist Theory*. London: Routledge.

Hall, S. 1988a: "New ethnicities." In K. Mercer (ed.) *Black Film, British Cinema*. London: Institute of Contemporary Arts.

Hall, S. 1988b: "Popular democratic vs authoritarian populism: Two ways of taking democracy seriously." In S. Hall (ed.) *The Hard Road to Renewal: Thatcherism and the Crisis Of the Left*. London: Verso.

Hall, S. 1988c: "Authoritarian populism: A reply to Jessop et al." In S. Hall (ed.) *The Hard Road to Renewal: Thatcherism and the Crisis Of the Left*. London: Verso.

Hall, S. 1992a: "The new ethnicities." In J. Donald and A. Rattansi (eds.) *Race, Culture and Difference*. London: Sage.

Hall, S. 1992b: "The question of cultural identity." In S. Hall, D. Held, and T. Mcgrew (eds.) *Modernity and its Futures*. Cambridge: Polity Press.

Hall, S. 1996: "Politics of identity." In T. Ranger, Y. Samad, and O. Stuart (eds.) *Culture, Identity and Politics. Ethnic Minorities in Britain*. Aldershot: Avebury.

Hall, S. and Gieben, B. (eds.) 1992: *Formations of Modernity*. Cambridge: Polity Press in association with the Open University.

Hall, S. and Jefferson, T. 1993: *Resistance through Rituals. Youth Subcultures in Postwar Britain*. London: Routledge.

Hamel, P. 1993: "Contrôle ou changement social à l'heure du partenariat." *Sociologie et Sociétés* 25(1): 173–88.

Hamel, P., Lustiger-Thaler, H., and Maheu, L. 1999: "Is there a role for social movements?" In J. Abu-Lugoh (ed.) *Continuities and Cutting Edges: Sociology for the Twenty-First Century*. Chicago: University of Chicago Press.

Handelman, D. 1990: *Models and Mirrors: Towards an Anthropology of Public Events*. Cambridge: Cambridge University Press.

Hann, C. M. 1995: "'Philosophers' Models on the Carpathian Lowands." In J. Hall (ed.) *Civil Society*, 1995.

Hannerz, U. (ed.) 1996: *Transnational Connections, Culture, People, Places*. London: Routledge.

Haraway, D. J. 1991: *Simians, Cyborg and Women. The Reinvention of Nature*. London: Free Association.

Harmel, R. and Janda, K. 1982: *Parties and Their Environment*. London: Longman.

Harris-Grossbergerova, E. 1998: "The Slovak question at the end of the twentieth century: National identity, political culture and democratization." In A. Cindric (ed.) *A Festschrift for Ludvik Carnic. Studies in Humanities and Social Sciences*. Ljubljana: Faculty of Arts in Ljubljana, Department of Sociology.

Harrop, M. 1986: "The press and post-war elections." In I. Crewe and M. Harrop (eds.) *Political Communications: The General Election Campaign of 1983*. Cambridge: Cambridge University Press.

Harvey, D. 1989: *The Condition of Postmodernity*. Oxford: Blackwell.

Haslam, M. (ed.) 1986: *Psycho-legal Aspects of Sexual Problems*. Burgess Hill: Sussex Shering.

Havel, V. 1985: "The power of the powerless." In Havel et al. (eds.) *The Power of the Powerless*. Armonk, NY: M.E. Sharpe.

Havel, V. 1988: "Anti-political politics." In J. Keane (ed.) *Civil Society*.

Hay, C. 1996: *Re-stating Social and Political Change*. Buckingham: Open University Press.

Hayek, F. A. 1948: *Individualism and Economic Order*. London: Routledge & Kegan Paul.

Hayek, F. A. 1960: *The Constitution of Liberty*. London: Routledge.

Hayek, F. A. 1978: *The Mirage of Social Justice*. London: Routledge & Kegan Paul.

Hearn, J. 1992: *Men in the Public Eye: The Construction and Deconstruction of Public Men and Public Patriarchies*. London: Routledge.

Hearn, J. 1997: "Men and power: Citizenship, welfare, nation and global relations," paper given at European Sociological Association Conference, University of Essex, August.

Heater, D. 1990: *Citizenship*. London: Longman.

Hebdige, D. 1979: *Subculture: The Meaning of Style*. London: Methuen.

Hechter, M. 1986: "Rational choice theory and the study of race and ethnic relations." In J. Rex and D. Mason (eds.) *Theories of Race and Ethnic Relations*. Cambridge: Cambridge University Press.

Heclo, H. 1978: "Issue networks and the executive establishment." In A. King (ed.) *The New American Political System*. Washington, DC: Enterprise Institute for Public Policy Research.

Heclo, H. and Wildavsky, A. 1974: *The Private Government of Public Money*. London: Macmillan.

Hegel, G. 1967 [1821]: *Philosophy of Right*. Oxford: Oxford University Press.

Heinz, J., Laumann, E., Nelson, R., and Salisbury, R. 1993: *The Hollow Core: Private Interests in National Policy-Making*. Cambridge: Harvard University Press.

Held, D. 1980: *Introduction to Critical Theory*. London: Hutchinson.

Held, D. 1992: "Democracy: From city-states to a cosmopolitan order?" *Political Studies* 40, special edition on "Prospects for Democracy," ed. D. Held.

Held, D. 1995a: *Democracy and the Global Order. From the Modern State to Cosmopolitan Governance*. Cambridge: Polity Press.

Held, D. 1995b: *The Problem of Autonomy and the Global Order*. Cambridge: Polity Press.

Held, D. and McGrew, A. 1993: "Globalization and the liberal democratic state." *Government and Opposition* 28(2): 261–88.

Helgerson, R. 1992: *Forms of Nationhood: The Elizabethan Writing of England*. Chicago: University of Chicago Press.

Heller, A. 1982: "Phases of legitimation in Soviet-type societies." In T. H. Rigby and F. Feher (eds.) *Political Legitimation in Communist States*. London: Macmillan.

Hendin, H. 1997: *Seduced by Death. Doctors, Patients and the Dutch Cure*. New York: Norton.

Henley, N. M. 1977: *Body Politics: Power, Sex and Non Verbal Communication*. Englewood Cliffs: Prentice Hall.

Hérault, B. and Lapeyronnie, D. 1998: "Le statut de l'identité: Les conflits sociaux et la protestation collective." Paper presented at the International Sociological Association World Congress, Montreal, August.

Heritier, A. and Knill, C. 1996: *Ringing the Changes in Europe: Regulatory Competition and the Transformation of the State, Britain, France, Germany*. Berlin: Walter de Geuyter.

Herman, E. S. and McChesney, R. W. 1997: *The Global Media: The New Missionaries of Corporate Capitalism*. London: Cassell.

Hesmondhalgh, D. 1997: "Post-Punk's attempt to democratize the music industry: the success and failure of Rough Trade." *Popular Music* 16(3): 255–74.

Hewitt, C. 1974: "Policy-making in post-war Britain: A national level test of elitist and pluralist hypotheses." *British Journal of Political Science* 4(2): 187–216. Reprinted in Scott (ed.) *Power*, 1994.

Hewitt, M. 1991: "Bio-politics and Social Policy: Foucault's account of welfare." In M. Featherstone, M. Hepworth and B. S. Turner (eds.) *The Body*.

Higley, J. and Gunther, R. 1992: *Elites and Democratic Consolidation in Latin America and Southern Europe*. Cambridge: Cambridge University Press.

Higson, A. 1995: *Waving the Flag: Constructing a National Cinema in Britain*. Oxford: Clarendon Press.

Hindess, B. 1996: *Discourses of Power: From Hobbes to Foucault*. Oxford: Blackwell.

Hindess, B. 1998: "Divide and rule: The international character of modern citizenship." *European Journal of Social Theory* 1(1): 57–70.

Hindmoor, A. 1998: "The importance of being trusted: Transaction costs and policy network theory." *Public Administration* 76(1): 25–43.

Hinich, M. J. and Munger, M. C. 1996: *Ideology and the Theory of Political Choice*. Ann Arbor: University of Michigan Press.

Hintze, O. 1970: "Staatsverfassungs und Heeresverfassung." In O. Hintze (ed.) *Staat und Verfassung*. Goettingen: Vandenhoeck und Ruprecht, 52–83.

Hirst, P. Q. 1997: *From Statism to Pluralism*. London: UCL Press.

Hirst, P. Q. (ed.) 1989: *The Pluralist Theory of The State: Selected Writings of G. D. H. Cole, J. N. Figgis, and H. J. Laski*. London: Routledge.

Hirst, P. Q. 1994: *Associative Democracy: New Forms of Economic and Social Governance*. Cambridge: Polity Press.

Hix, S. 1999: *European Union: Institutions and Policies*. London: Macmillan.

Hobbes, T. 1994 [1660]: *Leviathan*. London: Everyman.

Hobsbawm, E. 1987: *The Age of Empire 1875–1914*. London: Weidenfield and Nicolson.

Hobsbawm, E. J. 1990: *Nations and Nationalism Since 1780. Programme, Myth, Reality*. Cambridge: Cambridge University Press.

Hobsbawm, E. and Ranger, T. (eds.) 1983: *The Invention of Tradition*. Cambridge: Cambridge University Press.

Hoffer, E. 1951: *The True Believer: Thoughts on the Nature of Mass Movement*. New York: Harper and Brothers.

Hoffman, J. 1995: *Beyond the State*. Oxford: Blackwell.

Holland, S. 1995: "Descartes goes to Hollywood: Mind, body and gender in contemporary cyborg cinema." *Body and Society* 1(3/4): 157–74.

Holloway, J. and Piciotto, S. (eds.) 1978: *State and Capital: A Marxist Debate*. London: Arnold.

Hollway, W. 1994: "Separation, integration and difference: Contradictions in a gender regime." In H. L. Radtke and H. Stam (eds.) *Power/Gender: Social Relations in Theory and Practice*. London: Sage.

hooks, b. 1992: *Black Looks. Race and Representation*. Toronto: Between the Lines.

Horkheimer, M. and Adorno, T. W. 1972: *Dialectic of Enlightenment*. New York: Seabury.

Horowitz, D. 1985: *Ethnic Groups in Conflict*. Berkeley: University of California Press.

Hume, David. 1987 [1742]: *Essays: Moral, Political and Literary*. Indianapolis: Liberty Fund.

Humphrey, C. and Laidlaw, J. 1994: *The Archetypal Actions of Ritual. A Theory of Ritual Illustrated by the Jain Rite of Worship*. Oxford: Clarendon Press.

Hunter, D. and Wistow 1987: "The paradox of policy diversity in a unitary state: Community care in Britain." *Public Administration* 65: 3–24.

Hunter, F. 1953: *Community Power Structure*. Chapel Hill: University of North Carolina Press.

Huntington, S. 1993: "Democracy's third wave." In L. Diamond and M. Plattner (eds.) *The Global Resurgence of Democracy*. Baltimore: Johns Hopkins University Press.

Hutchinson, J. 1987: *The Dynamics of Cultural Nationalism: The Gaelic Revival and the Creation of the Irish Nation-State*. London: Allen & Unwin.

Hutchinson, J. and Smith, A. D. (eds.) 1994: *Nationalism*. Oxford: Oxford University Press.

Hutchinson, J. and Smith, A. D. 1996: "Introduction." In J. Hutchinson and A. D. Smith (eds.) *Ethnicity*. Oxford Readers, Oxford: Oxford University Press.

Ibarra, P. 1989: *La Evolucion Estrategica de Eta*. Donostia: Kriselu.

Index on Censorship 1998: *Smashed Hits: The Book of Banned Music*.

Inglehart, R. 1990: "Values, ideology and cognitive mobilization in new social movements." In R. Dalton and M. Kuechler (eds.) *Challenging the Political Order*. Cambridge: Polity Press, 43–66.

Inglehart, R. 1991: *Culture Shift in Advanced Industrial Society*. Princeton: Princeton University Press.

Inglehart, R. and Carballo, M. 1997: "Does Latin America exist? And is there a Confucian culture?: A global analysis of cross-cultural differences." *PS: Political Science and Politics* 30(1): 34–46.

Inglehart, R. 1996. *Postmodernization*. Princeton: Princeton University Press.

Inman, R. P. 1987: "Markets, governments, and the 'new' political economy." In A. J. Auerbach and M. Feldstein (eds.) *Handbook of Public Economics*, vol. 2. North-Holland: Elsevier Science Publishers.

Innis, H. A. 1950: *Empire and Communications*. Oxford: Oxford University Press.

Ion, J. 1994: "L'évolution des formes de l'engagement public." In P. Perrineau (ed.) *L'Engagement Politique, Déclin ou Mutation?* Paris: Presses de la Fondation nationale de science politique.

Isaac, J. C. 1987: *Power and Marxist Theory: A Realist Approach*. Ithaca: Cornell University Press.

Iversen, T. 1994: "Political leadership and representation in west European democracies. A test of three models of voting." *American Journal of Political Science* 38(1): 45–74.

Jacobs, J. 1961: *The Death and Life of Great American Cities*. New York: Vintage Books.

Jaggers, K. and Gurr, T. R. 1995: "Tracking democracy's third wave with the polity III data." *Journal of Peace Research* 32(4): 469–82.

Jameson, F. 1991: "The cultural logic of late capitalism." In F. Jameson *Postmodernism or the Cultural Logic of Late Capitalism*. London: Verso.

Jamieson, K. H. 1984: *Packaging the Presidency: A History and Criticism of Presidential Advertizing*. New York: Oxford University Press.

Jamieson, K. H. 1988: *Eloquence in an Electronic Age: The Transformation of Political Speechmaking*. New York: Oxford University Press.

Janda, K. and King, D. S. 1985: "Formalizing and testing Duverger's theories on political parties." *Comparative Political Studies* 18(2): 139–69.

Janowitz, M. 1960: *The Professional Soldier: A Social and Political Portrait*. New York: Free Press.

Jaquette, J. (ed.) 1989: *The Women's Movement in Latin America: Feminism and the Transition to Democracy*. Winchester, MA: Unwin Hyman.

Jáuregui Bereciartu, G. 1981: *Ideología y Estrategia Política de Eta (1959–1968)*. Madrid: Siglo XXI.

Jeffery, C. (ed.) 1997: *The Regional Dimension of the European Union*. London: Frank Cass.

Jelin, E. 1990: *Women and Social Change in Latin America*. London: UNRISD/Zed Books.

Jenkins, R. 1997: *Rethinking Ethnicity. Arguments and Explorations*. London: Sage.

Jenkins-Smith, H., St Clair, G., and Woods, B. 1991: "Explaining change in policy subsystems: Analysis of coalition stability and defection over time." *American Journal of Political Science* 35: 851–80.

Jessop, B. 1982: *The Capitalist State: Marxist Theories and Methods*. Oxford: Martin Robertson.

Jessop, B. 1990: *State Theory: Putting Capitalist States in their Place*. Cambridge: Polity Press.

Jessop, B. 1994: "Post-fordism and the state." In A. Amin (ed.) *Post-fordism*. Oxford: Blackwell.

Jessop, B. 1997 : "Capitalism and its future: Remarks on regulation, government, and governance." *Review of International Political Economy* 4 (3): 561–81.

Jessop, B. 1999: "Globalization and the national state." Draft, published by the Department of Sociology, Lancaster University at: *http: //www.lancaster.ac.uk/sociology/soc012rj.html* .

Jessop, B., Bonnet, K., Bromley, S., and Ling, T. 1988: *Thatcherism: A Tale of Two Nations*. Cambridge: Polity Press.

Jessop, B., Bonnet, K., and Bromley, S. 1990: "Farewell to Thatcherism? Neo-liberalism and 'new times'." *New Left Review* 179: 81–102.

Joas, H. 1991: "Between Power Politics and Pacifist Utopia: Peace and war in socio-logical theory." *Current Sociology* 39(1): 47–66.

Jobert, B. and Muller, P. 1987: *L'Etat en Action: politiques, publiques et corporatismes.* Paris: PUF.

John, P. and Cole, A. 2000: "When do institutions, policy sectors and cities matter? Comparing networks of local policy-makers in Britain and France." *Comparative Political Studies* 33(2): 248–68.

Johnston, R. J. 1995: "The conflict over qualified majority voting in the European council of ministers: An analysis of the UK negotiating stance using power indices." *British Journal of Political Science* 25: 245–54.

Jones, K. B. 1988: "Towards the revision of politics." In K. B. Jones and A. G. Jónasdóttir (eds.) *The Political Interests of Gender.* London: Sage.

Jones, K. B. 1990: "Citizenship in a woman-friendly polity." *Signs* 15(4): 781–812.

Jones, M. P. 1995: *Electoral Laws and the Survival of Presidential Democracy.* Notre Dame: University of Notre Dame Press.

Jopke, C. (ed.) 1998: *Challenges to the Nation-State.* Oxford: Oxford University Press.

Jordan, G. 1990: "Sub-governments, policy communities and networks." *Journal of Theoretical Politics* 2(3): 319–38.

Jordan, G., Maloney, W., and McLaughlin, A. 1994: "Characterising agricultural policy-making." *Public Administration* 72: 505–26.

Jordan, T. 1995: "Collective bodies: Raving and the politics of Gilles Deleuze and Felix Guattari." *Body and Society* 1(1): 125–44.

Jouvenel, B. de 1962: *On Power: Its Nature and the History of its Growth.* Boston: Beacon Press.

Juteau, D. 1996: "Theorising ethnicity and ethnic communalisms at the margins: From Quebec to the world system." *Nations and Nationalism* 2(1): 45–66.

Kaid, L. L., Nimmo, D., and Sanders, K. (eds.) 1986: *New Perspectives in Political Advertising.* Carbondale: South Illinois University Press.

Kaldor, M. 1993: "Yugoslavia and the new nationalism." *New Left Review* 197: 96–112.

Kaldor, M. 1999: *New and Old Wars: Organized Violence in a Global Era.* Cambridge: Polity Press.

Kassim, H. 1994: "Policy networks, networks and European Union policy making: A sceptical view." *West European Politics* 17(4): 15–27.

Kastoryano, R. 1996: *Négocier l'Identité: La France, l'Allemagne et leurs Immigrés.* Paris: Armand Colin.

Katz, E. and Lazarsfeld, P. F. 1955: *Personal Influence: The Part Played by People in the Flow of Mass Communications.* Glencoe, IL: The Free Press.

Katz, R. 1980: *A Theory of Parties and Electoral Systems.* Baltimore: Johns Hopkins University Press.

Katz, R. and Mair, P. (eds.) 1994: *Party Organizations. A Data Handbook.* London: Sage.

Keane, J. (ed) 1988: *Civil Society and the State: New European Perspectives.* London: Verso.

Keating, M. and Loughlin, J. (eds.) 1997: *The Political Economy of Regionalism.* London: Frank Cass.

Kelley, R. 1998: *Yo' Mama's Disfunktional! Fighting the Culture Wars in Urban America.* Boston: Beacon Press.

Kellner, D. 1995: *Media Culture.* London: Routledge.

Kenis, P. and Schneider, V. 1991: "Policy networks and policy analysis: Scrutinizing the new analytical toolbox." In B. Marin and R. Mayntz (eds.) *Policy Networks: Empirical Evidence and Theoretical Considerations*. Frankfurt: Campus.

Kenniston, K. 1968: *Young Radicals*. New York: Harcourt, Brace, and World.

Kepel, G. 1997: *Allah in the West: Islamic Movements in America and Europe*. Stanford: Stanford University Press.

Kertzer, D. 1988: *Ritual, Politics and Power*. New Haven, CT and London: Yale University Press.

Kimball, R. 1990: *Tenured Radicals*. New York: Harper Row.

Kimmel, M. 1990: *Revolution: A Sociological Interpretation*. Cambridge: Polity Press.

Kirchheimer, O. 1965: "The transformation of the western European party systems." In J. Lapalombar and M. Weiner (eds.) *Political Parties and Political Development*. Princeton: Princeton University Press.

Kishwar, M. and Vanita, R. 1984: *In Search of Answers: Indian Women's Voices from Manushi*. London: Zed Books.

Kitschelt, H. 1989: *The Logics of Party Formation*. Ithaca, NY: Cornell University Press.

Kitschelt, H. 1992: "The formation of party systems in East Central Europe." *Politics and Society* 20(1): 7–50.

Kitschelt, H. 1994: *The Transformation of European Social Democracy*. Cambridge: Cambridge University Press.

Kitschelt, H. (in collaboration with Anthony J. McGann) 1995: *The Radical Right in Western Europe. A Comparative Analysis*. Ann Arbor: Michigan University Press.

Kitschelt, H. 2000: "Citizens, politicians, and party cartellization. Political representation and state failure in post-industrial democracies." To appear in *European Journal of Political Research*.

Kitschelt, H., Mansfeldova, Z., Markowski, R., and Toka, G. 1999: *Post-Communist Party Systems. Competition, Representation, and Inter-Party Cooperation*. Cambridge: Cambridge University Press.

Klapper, J. T. 1960: *The Effects of Mass Communication*. Glencoe, IL: The Free Press.

Knijn, T. and Kremer, M. 1997: "Gender and the caring dimension of welfare states: Toward inclusive citizenship." *Social Politics* 4(3): 328–61.

Knoke, D. 1994: *Political Networks*. Cambridge: Cambridge University Press.

Knoke, D., Pappi, F., Broadbent, J., and Tsujinaka, Y. 1996: *Comparing Policy Networks*. Cambridge: Cambridge University Press.

Knutsen, O. and Scarbrough, E. 1995: "Cleavage politics and value conflict." In Jan van Deth and Elinor Scarbrough (eds.) *The Impact of Values*. Oxford: Oxford University Press.

Konig, T. 1997: "Macro stability and micro change. German policy networks before and after unification." Paper to annual meeting of the American Political Science Association, Washington.

Konig, T. and Brauninger, T. 1998: "The formation of policy networks." *Journal of Theoretical Politics* 10(4): 445–71.

Konrad, G. 1984: *Antipolitics*. London: Harcourt Brace Jovanovich.

Kooiman, J. (ed.) 1993: *Modern Governance*. London: Sage.

Kornhauser, W. 1959: *The Politics of Mass Society*. Glencoe, IL: The Free Press.

Kreps, D. 1990: *A Course in Microeconomic Theory*. Brighton: Harvester Wheatsheaf.

Kuechler, M. and Dalton, R. J. 1990: "New social movements and the political order: Inducing change for long-term stability?" In R. J. Dalton and M. Kuechler (eds.) *Challenging the Political Order: New Social and Political Movements in Western Democracies*. Cambridge: Polity Press.

Kumar, K. 1971: *Revolution: The Theory and Practice of a European Idea*. London: Weidenfeld and Nicolson.

Kumar, K. 1993: "Civil Society: An inquiry into the usefulness of an historical term." *British Journal of Sociology* 44(3): 375–95.

Kumar, K. 1996: "The revolutions of 1989 in East-central Europe and the idea of revolution." In R. Kilminster and I. Varcoe (eds.) *Culture, Modernity and Revolution: Essays in Honor of Zygmunt Bauman*. London: Routledge.

Kymlicka, W. 1995: *Multicultural Citizenship. A Liberal Theory of Minority Rights*. Oxford: Clarendon Press.

Kymlicka, W. and Norman, W. 1994: "Return of the citizen: A survey of recent work on citizenship theory." *Ethics* (January): 352–81.

Laborde, C. 2000: *Pluralist Thought and the State in British and French Political Thought 1900–1925*. London: Macmillan/St Anthony's.

Laitin, D. D. 1995: "The civic culture at thirty." *American Political Science Review* 89: 168–73.

Lane, J.-E. (ed.) 1987: *Bureaucracy and Public Choice*. London: Sage.

Laqueur, T. 1990: *Making Sex. Body and Gender from the Greeks to Freud*. Harvard: Harvard University Press.

Lasch, C. 1979: *The Culture of Narcissism*. New York: Norton.

Lash, S. 1990: *The Sociology of Postmodernity*. London: Routledge.

Lash, S. and Urry, J. 1987: *The End of Organized Capitalism*. Cambridge: Polity Press.

Lash, S. and Urry, J. 1993: *Economies of Signs and Space*. London: Sage.

Laski, H. J. 1921: *The Foundations of Sovereignty and Other Essays*. London: Allen & Unwin.

Laumann, E. and Knoke, D. 1987: *The Organizational State: A Perspective on National Energy and Health Domains*. Madison: University of Wisconsin Press.

Laumann, E., Marsden, P., and Prensky, D. 1992: "The boundary specification problem in network analysis." In L. Freeman, D. White, and A. Romney (eds.) *Research Methods in Network Analysis*. New Brunswick: Transaction.

Laver, M. and Schofield, N. 1990: *Multi-Party Government*. Oxford: Oxford University Press.

Laver, M. and Shepsle, K. 1996: *Making and Breaking Governments. Cabinets and Legislatures in Parliamentary Democracies*. New York: Cambridge University Press.

Lazarsfeld, P. F., Berelson, B., and Gaudet, H. 1948: *The People's Choice*. New York: Columbia University Press.

Le Galès, P. and Thatcher, M. 1995: *Les Réseaux de Politique Publique, Débats Autour des Policy Networks*. Paris: LHarmattan.

LeBon, G. 1896: *The Crowd: A Study of the Popular Mind*. London: Ernest Benn.

Leca, J. 1992: "Questions on citizenship." In C. Mouffe (ed.) *Dimensions of a Radical Democracy*. London: Verso.

Lefort, C. 1986: *The Political Forms of Modern Society: Bureaucracy. Democracy. Totalitarianism*. Cambridge: Polity Press.

Leftwich, A. 1997: "From democratization to democratic consolidation." In D. Potter, D. Goldblatt, M. Kiloh, and P. Lewis (eds.) *Democratization*. Cambridge: Polity Press.

Lentin, R. 1999: "The rape of the nation: Women narrativising genocide." *Sociological Research Online* 4(2) at *http://www.socresonline.org.uk/socresonline/4/2/lentin.html*.

Levine, D. 1988: "Paradigm lost: Dependency to democracy." *World Politics* 40(3): 377–94.

Lewin, L. and Vedung, E. (eds.) 1980: *Politics as Rational Action: Essays in Public Choice and Policy Analysis*. Dordrecht: Reidel.

Lijphart, A. 1968: *The Politics of Accommodation: Pluralism and Democracy in the Netherlands*. Berkeley: University of California Press.

Lijphart, A. 1977: *Democracy in Plural Societies. A Comparative Exploration*. New Haven, CT: Yale University Press.

Lijphart, A. 1984: *Democracies*. New Haven, CT: Yale University Press.

Lijphart, A. 1993: "Constitutional choices for new democracies." In L. Diamond and M. F. Plattner (eds.) *The Global Resurgence of Democracy*. Baltimore and London: Johns Hopkins University Press.

Limongi, F. and Przeworski, A. 1994: *Democracy and Development in South America, 1946–1988*. Madrid: Juan March Institute.

Lindblom, C. E. 1959: "The science of 'muddling through'." In Amitai Etzioni (ed.) *Readings on Modern Organizations*, second print. Englewood Cliffs: Prentice Hall, 154–73.

Lindblom, C. E. 1977: *Politics and Markets*. New York: Basic Books.

Linklater, A. 1998: *The Transformation of Political Community: Ethical Foundations of the Post-Westphalian Era*. Chapel Hill: University of South Carolina Press.

Linz, J. J. 1994: "Presidential or parliamentary democracy: Does it make a difference?" In J. J. Linz, and A. Valenzuela *The Failure of Presidential Democracy*. Baltimore and London: Johns Hopkins University Press.

Linz, J. J. and Stepan, A. 1996: *Problems of Democratic Transition and Consolidation: Southern Europe, South America, and Post-Communist Europe*. Baltimore and London: Johns Hopkins University Press.

Linz, J. J. and Stepan, A. 1997: "Toward consolidated democracies." In L. Diamond, M. F. Plattner, Y-h. Chu, and H-m. Tien (eds.) *Consolidating the Third Wave Democracies: Themes and Perspectives*. Baltimore and London: Johns Hopkins University Press.

Linz, J. J. and Valenzuela, A. (eds.) 1994: *The Failure of Presidential Democracy. Comparative Perspectives*. Baltimore: Johns Hopkins University Press.

Lipietz, A. 1987: *Mirages and Miracles: The Crisis in Global Fordism*. Trans. D. Macey. London: Verso.

Lipset, S. M. 1960/1981: *Political Man*, first/second edition. New York/Baltimore: Doubleday/Johns Hopkins University Press.

Lipset, S. M. 1991: "No third way: A comparative perspective on the left." In D. Chirot (ed.) *The Crisis of Leninism and the Decline of the Left*. London: Washington University Press.

Lipset, S. M. and Rokkan, S. 1967: "Cleavage structures, party systems, and voter alignments. An introduction." In S. M. Lipset and S. Rokkan (eds.) *Party Systems and Voter Alignments. Cross-National Perspectives*. New York: Free Press.

Lipsitz, G. 1990: *Time Passages: Collective Memory and American Popular Culture*. Minneapolis: University of Minnesota Press.

Lipsky, M. 1968: "Protest as a political resource." *American Political Science Review* 62: 1144–58.

Lister, R. 1997: *Citizenship: Feminist Perspectives*. Basingstoke: Macmillan.

Lister, R. 1999a: "Reforming welfare around the work ethic: New gendered and ethical perspectives on work and care." *Policy and Politics* 27(2): 233–46.

Lister, R. 1999b: "What welfare provisions do women need to become full citizens?" In S. Walby (ed.) *New Agendas for Women*. Basingstoke: Macmillan.

Locke, J. 1980 [1681–83]: *Second Treatise on Civil Government*. Ed. C. B. Macpherson. Indianapolis, IN: Hackett.

Lockwood, D. 1966: "Sources of variation in working-class images of society." *Sociological Review* 14(3): 244–67.

Lomax, B. 1997: "The strange death of civil society in Hungary." *Journal of Communist Studies and Transition Studies* 13(1): 41–63.

Lorber, J. 1994: *Paradoxes of Gender.* New Haven: Yale University Press.

Loury, G. 1977: "A dynamic theory of racial income differences." In P. A.Wallace and A. Le Mund (eds.) *Women Minorities and Employment Discrimination.* Lexington, MA: Lexington Books.

Loury, G. 1987: "Why should we care about group inequality?" *Social Philosophy and Policy* 5: 249–71.

Lovenduski, J. and Norris, P. (eds.) 1996: *Women in Politics.* Oxford: Oxford University Press.

Luhmann, N. 1970 [1967]: "Soziologie als Theorie sozialer Systeme." In Niklas Luhmann *Soziologische Aufklärung 1. Aufsätze zur Theorie Sozialer Systeme.* Opladen: Westdeutscher Verlag, 113–36.

Luhmann, N. 1970 [1968]: "Soziologie des politischen Systems." In Niklas Luhmann *Soziologische Aufklärung 1. Aufsätze zur Theorie Sozialer Systeme.* Opladen: Westdeutscher Verlag, 154–77.

Luhmann, N. 1974: "Der politische Code. 'Konservativ' und 'progressiv' in systemtheoretischer Sicht." In *Zeitschrift für Politik* 21: 253–71.

Luhmann, N. 1981: *Politische Theorie im Wohlfahrtsstaat.* München Wien: Olzog.

Luhmann, N. 1982: *The Differentiation of Society.* New York: Colombia University Press.

Luhmann, N. 1983: "Anspruchsinflation im Krankheitssystem. Eine Stellungnahme aus gesellschaftstheoretischer Sicht." In Phillip Herder-Dorneich and Alexander Schuller (Hrsg.) *Die Anspruchsspirale. Schicksal oder Systemdefekt?* Stuttgart: Kohlhammer, 28–49.

Luhmann, N. 1984: *Soziale Systeme. Grundriß einer Allgemeinen Theorie.* Frankfurt am Main: Suhrkamp.

Luhmann, N. 1989: "Politische Steuerung: Ein Diskussionsbeitrag." *Politische Vierteljahresschrift* 30: 4–9.

Luhmann, N. 1990a [1986]: *Ökologische Kommunikation. Kann die moderne Gesellschaft sich auf ökologische Gefährdungen einstellen?* 3 Aufl. Opladen: Westdeutscher Verlag.

Luhmann, N. 1990b: "The paradox of system differentiation and the evolution of society." In Jeffrey C. Alexander and Paul Colomy (eds.) *Differentiation Theory and Social Change. Comparative and Historical Perspectives.* New York: Columbia University Press, 409–40.

Luhmann, N. 1991: "Steuerung durch Recht? Einige klarstellende Bemerkungen." In *Zeitschrift für Rechtssoziologie* 12: 142–6.

Luhmann, N. 1992: *Beobachtungen der Moderne.* Opladen: Westdeutscher Verlag.

Luhmann, N. 1993a [1969]: *Legitimation durch Verfahren.* 3 Aufl. Frankfurt am Main: Suhrkamp.

Luhmann, N. 1993b [1984]: *Soziale Systeme. Grundriß einer allgemeinen Theorie.* 4 Aufl. Frankfurt am Main: Suhrkamp.

Luhmann, N. 1993c: "Politische Steuerungsfähigkeit eines Gemeinwesens." In Reinhard Göhner (Hrsg.) *Die Gesellschaft für Morgen.* München and Zürich: Piper, 50–65.

Luhmann, N. 1994: "Die Gesellschaft und ihre Organisationen." In Hans-Ulrich Derlien, Uta Gerhardt, and Fritz W. Scharpf (Hrsg.) *Systemrationalität und Partialinteresse. Festschrift für Renate Mayntz.* Baden-Baden: Nomos, 189–201.

Luhmann, N. 1995: "Probleme mit operativer Schließung." In Niklas Luhmann (ed.) *Soziologische Aufklärung 6. Die Soziologie und der Mensch.* Opladen: Westdeutscher Verlag, 12–24.

Luhmann, N. 1997: *Die Gesellschaft der Gesellschaft*, 2 Bde. Frankfurt am Main: Suhrkamp.

Lukes, S. 1974: *Power: A Radical View.* London: Macmillan.

Lukes, S. 1975: "Political ritual and social integration." *Sociology* 9: 289–308.

Lyotard, J. 1984: *The Postmodern Condition.* Manchester: Manchester University Press.

Maarek, P. J. 1993: *Political Marketing and Communication.* Luton: Luton University Press.

Maas, A. 1951: *Muddy Waters.* Cambridge: Harvard University Press.

Mach, Z. 1992: "Continuity and change in political ritual: May Day in Poland." In Jeremy Boissevain (ed.) *Revitalizing European Rituals.* London: Routledge, 43–61.

MacKinnon, C. A. 1989: *Toward a Feminist Theory of the State.* Cambridge, MA: Harvard University Press.

Maheu, L. 1995: "Introduction." In L. Maheu (ed.) *Social Movements and Social Classes: The Future of Collective Action.* London: Sage.

Maheu, L. 1996: "A modernist look at post-industrialization and the ambivalence of social movements." In J. Clark and M. Diani (eds.) *Alain Touraine.* London: The Falmer Press.

Mainwaring, S. 1990: "Presidentialism in Latin America." *Latin American Research Review* 25(1): 157–79.

Mainwaring, S. 1992: "Transitions to democracy and democratic consolidation: Theoretical and comparative issues." In S. Mainwaring, G. O'Donnell, and J. S. Valenzuela (eds.) *Issues in Democratic Consolidation: The New South American Democracies in Comparative Perspective.* South Bend, IN: University of Notre Dame Press.

Mainwaring, S. 1993: "Presidentialism, multipartism, and democracy: The difficult combination." *Comparative Political Studies* 26(2): 198–228.

Mainwaring, S. and Shugart, M. S. (eds.) 1997: *Presidentialism and Democracy in Latin America.* Cambridge: Cambridge University Press.

Mainwaring, S. and Viola, E. 1984: "New social movements, political culture and democracy: Brazil and Argentina in the 1980s." *Telos* 61: 17–52.

Mair, P. 1997: *Party System Change. Approaches and Interpretations.* Oxford: Oxford University Press.

Majone, G. 1994: *Independence versus Accountability?: Non-Majoritarian Institutions and Democratic Government in Europe.* Florence: European University Institute.

Majone, G. (ed.) 1996: *Regulating Europe.* London: Routledge.

Majone, G. 1997: *From the Positive to the Regulatory State: Causes and Consequences of Changes in the Mode of Governance.* Madrid: Instituto Juan March de estudios e investigaciones.

Malcolm, N. 1998: *Kosovo, A Short History.* London and Basingstoke: Macmillan.

Malkki, I. H. 1995: *Purity and Exile: Violence, Memory, and National Cosmology among Hutu Refugees in Tanzania.* Chicago: University of Chicago Press.

Malloy, J. 1987: "The politics of transition in Latin America." In J. M. Malloy and M. A. Seligson (eds.) *Authoritarians and Democrats: Regime Transition in Latin America.* Pittsburgh: University of Pittsburgh Press.

Maltese, J. A. 1994: *Spin Control: The White House Office of Communications and the Management of Presidential News*, second edition. Chapel Hill, NC: University of North Carolina Press.

Mann, M. 1988: *States, War and Capitalism.* Oxford: Blackwell.

Mann, M. 1997: "Has globalisation ended the rise and rise of the nation-state?" *Review International of Political Economy* 4(3): 472–96.

Mann, T. E. and Orren, G. R. (eds.) 1992: *Media Polls in American Politics.* Washington, DC: The Brooking Institution.

Manning, F. E. 1983: "Cosmos and chaos: Celebrating the modern world." In F. E. Manning (ed.) *The Celebration of Society: Perspectives on Contemporary Cultural Performances.* Bowling Green, Ohio: Bowling Green University Press.

Marcuse, H. 1969: *Eros and Civilization.* New York: Sphere Books.

Marks, G., Hooghe, L., and Kermit, K. 1996: "European integration from the 1980's: State-centric versus multi-level governance." *Journal of Common Market Studies* 34 (3): 341–78.

Marsh, D. (ed.) 1998: *Comparing Policy Networks.* Buckingham: Open University Press.

Marsh, D. 1998: *Comparing Policy Networks.* Buckingham: Open University Press.

Marsh, D. and Rhodes, R. (eds.) 1992: *Policy Networks in British Government.* Oxford: Oxford University Press.

Marshall, T. H. 1950: *Citizenship and Social Class and other Essays.* Cambridge: Cambridge University Press.

Marshall, T. H. 1963: *Class, Citizenship and Social Development.* Westport: Greenwood Press.

Martin, L. J. (ed.) 1984: *Polling and the Democratic Consensus.* Beverly Hills, CA: Sage Publications.

Marwick, A. 1977: *War and Social Change in the Twentieth Century.* London: Macmillan.

Marx, K. 1975: "Theses on Feuerbach." In *Early Writings of Karl Marx.* Harmondsworth: Penguin Books.

Marx, K. 1978 [1847]: *The Poverty of Philosophy.* Peking: Foreign Languages Press.

Marx, K. and Engels, F. 1976a [1845–46]: *The German Ideology.* In *Marx-Engels Collected Works*, vol. 5. London: Lawrence & Wishart.

Marx, K. and Engels, F. 1976b [1848]: *The Manifesto of the Communist Party.* In *Marx-Engels Collected Works*, vol. 6. London: Lawrence & Wishart.

Marx, K. 1977 [1887]: *Capital*, vol. 1. London: Lawrence & Wishart.

Marx, K. 1981 [1844]: *Economic and Philosophic Manuscripts.* London: Lawrence & Wishart.

Mason, D. 1999: "The continuing significance of race? Teaching ethnic and racial studies in sociology." In M. Bulmer and J. Solomos (eds.) *Ethnic and Racial Studies Today.* London: Routledge.

Masson, D. 1998: *With and Despite the State: Doing Women's Movement Politics in Local Service Groups in the 1980s in Québec*, Ph.D. Thesis, Department of Sociology and Anthropology, Ottawa, Carleton University.

Mattern, M. 1998: *Acting in Concert: Music, Community and Political Action.* New Brunswick: Rutgers University Press.

Matthews, T. D. 1994: *Censored.* London: Chatto & Windus.

Mauss, M. 1973 [1936] "Techniques of the body." *Economy and Society* 2: 70–87.

May, J. D. 1973: "Opinion structure of political parties: The special law of curvilinear disparity." *Political Studies* 21(2): 135–51.

Mayntz, R. 1988: "Funktionelle Teilsysteme in der Theorie sozialer Differenzierung." In Renate Mayntz, Bernd Rosewitz, Uwe Schimank, and Rudolf Stichweh (eds.) *Differenzierung und Verselbständigung. Zur Entwicklung gesellschaftlicher Teilsysteme.* Frankfurt am Main and New York: Campus, 11–44.

Mayntz, R. 1993: "Governing failures and the problem of governability." In Kooiman (ed.) *Modern Governance*, 1993.

McAdam, D. 1988: *Freedom Summer.* New York: Oxford University Press.

McAdam, D., Tarrow, S., and Tilly, C. 1996: "To map contentious politics." *Mobilization* 1(1): 17–34.

McCarthy, J. D. and Zald, M. N. 1977: "Resource mobilization and social movements: A partial theory." *American Sociological Review* 82: 1212–41.

McCarthy, T. 1992: "The critique of impure reason: Foucault and the Frankfurt school." In T. E. Wartenberg (ed.) *Rethinking Power*. Albany: State University of New York Press.

McClurg Mueller, C. 1992: "Building social movement theory." In A. D. Morris and C. McClurg Mueller (eds.) *Frontiers in Social Movement Theory*. New Haven, CT: Yale University Press.

McCombs, M. E. and Shaw, D. L. 1972: "The agenda-setting function of mass media." *Public Opinion Quarterly* 36: 176–87.

McConnell, G. 1970: *Private Power and American Democracy*. New York: Knopf.

McGarry, R. H. and O'Leary, B. (eds.) 1993: *The Politics of Ethnic Conflict Regulation*. London: Routledge.

McGinniss, J. 1970: *The Selling of the President, 1968*. London: André Deutsch.

McKay, G. 1996: *Senseless Acts of Beauty*. London: Verso.

McLean, I. 1987: *Public Choice: An Introduction*. Oxford: Blackwell.

McRobbie, A. 1991: *Feminism and Youth Culture*. Basingstoke: Macmillan.

Mead, L. M. 1986: *Beyond Entitlement: The Social Obligations of Citizenship*. New York: Free Press.

Mead, L. M. 1997: *From Welfare to Work: Lessons from America*. A. Deacon (ed.). London: IEA Health and Welfare Unit.

Meekosha, H. and Dowse, L. 1997: "Enabling citizenship: Gender, disability and citizenship in Australia." *Feminist Review* 57: 49–72.

Melbeck, C. 1998: "Comparing local policy networks." *Journal of Theoretical Politics* 10(4): 531–52.

Melucci, A. 1989: *Nomads of the Present: Social Movements and Individual Needs in Contemporary Society*. London: Hutchinson Radius.

Melucci, A. 1996: *Challenging Codes: Collective Action in the Information Age*. Cambridge: Cambridge University Press.

Mendras, H. 1997: *L'Europe des européens*. Paris: Gallimard.

Mennell, S. 1995: "Civilisation and decivilisation, civil society and violence." *Irish Journal of Sociology* 5: 1–21.

Mény, Y., Muller, P., and Quermonne, J. L. (eds.) 1997: *Public Policies in Europe*. London: Routledge.

Messerschmidt, J. W. 1993: *Masculinities and Crime: Critique and Reconceptualization of Theory*. Lanham: Rowman & Littlefield.

Meyer, D. S. 1990: *A Winter of Discontent: The Nuclear Freeze and American Politics*. New York: Praeger.

Meyer, D. S. 2000: "Social movements: Creating communities of change." In M. A. Tetreault and R. L. Teske (eds.) *Feminist Approaches to Social Movements, Community, and Power*. Columbia, SC: University of South Carolina Press.

Meyer, D. S. and Marullo, S. 1992: "Grassroots mobilization and international politics: Peace protest and the end of the Cold War." *Research in Social Movements, Conflict, and Change* 14: 99–140.

Meyer, D. S. and Staggenborg, S. 1996: "Movements, countermovements, and the structure of political opportunity." *American Journal of Sociology* 101: 1628–60.

Meyer, D. S. and Tarrow, S. (eds.) 1998: *The Social Movement Society*. Lanham, MD: Rowman & Littlefield.

Meyer, D. S. and Whittier, N. 1994: "Social movement spillover." *Social Problems* 41(2): 277–98.

Michels, R. 1958: *Political Parties*. Glencoe, IL: Free Press.

Mies, M. 1986: *Patriarchy and Accumulation on a World Scale: Women in the International Division of Labor*. London: Zed Books.

Miliband, R. 1969: *The State in Capitalist Society*. London: Weidenfeld and Nicolson.

Mill, J. S. 1967: *Essays on Government, Jurisprudence, Liberty of the Press and Law of Nations*. New York: Kelly.

Mill, J. S. 1972: *Utilitarianism, On Liberty and Considerations on Representative Government*. London: Dent.

Mill, J. S. 1977 [1865]: "Considerations on representative government." In J. M. Robson (ed.) *Collected Works of John Stuart Mill*. Toronto: University of Toronto Press.

Miller, D. 1993: "Deliberative democracy and social choice." In D. Held (ed.) *Prospects for Democracy*. Cambridge: Polity Press.

Miller, D. 1999: "Does deliberative democracy deny difference?" Unpublished paper.

Miller, P. and Rose, N. 1990: "Governing economic life." *Economy and Society* 19(1): 1–31.

Miller, T. 1993: *The Well-Tempered Self: Citizenship, Culture, and the Post-Modern Subject*. London: Johns Hopkins University Press.

Miller, W. L. 1991: *Media and Voters: The Audience, Content, and Influence of Press and Television at the 1987 General Election*. Oxford: Oxford University Press.

Mills, C. Wright 1956: *The Power Elite*. New York: Oxford University Press.

Milward, A. 1993: *The European Rescue of the Nation-State*. Berkeley: University of California Press.

Mingione, E., 1991: *Fragmented Societies*. Oxford: Blackwell.

Mintrom, M. and Vergari, S. 1998: "Policy networks and innovation diffusion: The case of state education reforms." *The Journal of Politics* 60(1): 126–48.

Mintz, B. and Schwartz, M. 1985: *The Power Structure of American Business*. Chicago: Chicago University Press.

Mises (von), L. 1944: *Bureaucracy*. New Haven, CT: Yale University Press.

Misztal, B. 1996: *Trust in Modern Societies: The Search for the Bases of Social Order*. Cambridge: Polity Press.

Mitchell, W. C. and Simmons R. T. 1994: *Beyond Politics. Markets, Welfare, and the Failure of Bureaucracy*. Boulder, CO: Westview Press.

Mizruchi, M. S. 1982: *The American Corporate Network, 1900-1974*. London: Sage.

Modood, T. 1994: "Political blackness and British Asians." *Sociology* 28: 859–76.

Moe, T. M. 1997: "The positive theory of bureaucracy." In D. Mueller (ed.) *Perspectives on Public Choice*. Cambridge: Cambridge University Press.

Moisés, J. A. 1993: *Democratization, Mass Political Culture and Political Legitimacy in Brazil*. Madrid: Juan March Institute.

Montesquieu, C. de S. 1949 [1748]: *The Spirit of the Laws*. London: Collier-Macmillan.

Moodie, T. D. and Ndatshe, V. 1994: *Going for Gold: Men, Mines, and Migration*. Johannesburg: Witwatersrand University Press.

Moore, B. jr. 1969: *Social Origins of Dictatorship and Democracy: Lord and Peasant in the Making of the Modern World*. Harmondsworth: Penguin.

Moore, S. W. 1957: *The Critique of Capitalist Democracy*. New York: Paine-Whitman.

Moravscik, A. 1999: *The Choice of Europe*. London: Routledge.

Morris, J. 1993: *Independent Lives*. Basingstoke: Macmillan.

Morris, J. (ed.) 1996: *Encounters with Strangers. Feminism and Disability*. London: Women's Press.

Morriss, P. 1987: *Power: A Philosophical Analysis*. Manchester: Manchester University Press.

Mosca, G. 1939: *The Ruling Class*. New York: McGraw Hill.

Mouffe, C. (ed.) 1992a: *Dimensions of Radical Democracy: Pluralism, Citizenship, Community*. Verso: London.

Mouffe, C. 1992b: "Feminism, citizenship and radical democratic politics." In J. Butler and J. W. Scott (eds.) *Feminists Theorize the Political*. New York and London: Routledge.

Mouffe, C. 1993: *The Return of the Political*. Verso: London.

Mouffe, C. 1996: *Democracy, Power and the "Political."* In Benhabib (ed.) *Democracy and Difference*, 1996.

Moyano, M. J. 1995: *Argentina's Lost Patrol: Armed Struggle, 1969–1979*. New Haven, CT: Yale University Press.

Moyser, G. and Wagstaffe, M. (eds.) 1987a: *Research Methods in Elite Studies*. London: Allen and Unwin.

Moyser, G. and Wagstaffe, M. 1987b: "Studying elites: Theoretical and methodological issues." In G. Moyser and M. Wagstaffe (eds.) *Research Methods in Elite Studies*. London: Allen & Unwin.

Mueller, D. 1989: *Public Choice II*. Cambridge: Cambridge University Press.

Negus, K. 1998: "Cultural production and the corporation: Musical genres and the strategic management of creativity in the US recording industry." *Media, Culture and Society* 20(3): 359–79.

Neidhardt, F. 1981: "Über Zufall, Eigendynamik und Institutionalisierbarkeit absurder Prozesse. Notizen am Beispiel der Entstehung und Einrichtung einer terroristischen Gruppe." In H. von Alemann and H. P. Thurn (eds.) *Soziologie in weltbürgerlicher Absicht*. Opladen: Westdeutscher.

Nieuwbeerta, P. 1997: *The Democratic Class Struggle in Twenty Countries, 1945–1990*. Den Haag: CIP-Data KB.

Nelkin, D. and Lindec, M. S. 1995: "The mediated gene." In J. Terry and J. Urla (eds.) *Deviant Bodies*.

Nisbet, R. 1966: *The Sociological Tradition*. New York: Basic Books.

Niskanen, W. A. 1971: *Bureaucracy and Representative Government*. Chicago: Aldine Press [reprinted in 1994].

Niskanen, W. A. 1973: *Bureaucracy: Servant or Master?* London: Institute of Economic Affairs.

Niskanen, W. A. 1975: "Bureaucrats and politicians." *Journal of Law and Economics* 18: 617–44 [reprinted in 1994: 243–67].

Niskanen, W. A. 1993: "A Reassessment" [reprinted in 1994: 269–83].

Nixon, S. 1996: *Hard Looks. Masculinity, Spectatorship and Contemporary Consumption*. London: UCL Press.

Norris, P. 1993: "Comparing legislative recruitment." In Joni Lovenduski and Pippa Norris (eds.) *Gender and Party Politics*. London: Sage.

North, D. C. 1990: *Institutions, Institutional Change and Economic Performance*. Cambridge: Cambridge University Press.

Norval, A. J. 1993: "Minoritarian politics and the pluralisation of democracy." *Acta Philosophica* 14(2): 21–40.

Norval, A. J. 1996: *Deconstructing Apartheid Discourse*. London: Verso.

Norval, A. J. 1999: "Hybridization: the im/purity of the political." In J. Edkins, N. Persram, and V. Pin-Fat (eds.) *Sovereignty and Subjectivity*. London: Lynne Rienner.

O'Donnell, G. 1992: *Delegative Democracy?* Working Paper, 172, Helen Kellogg Institute, South Bend, IN: University of Notre Dame.

O'Donnell, G. 1997: "Illusions about consolidation." In L. Diamond, M. F. Plattner, Y-h. Chu, and H-m. Tien (eds.) *Consolidating the Third Wave Democracies: Themes and Perspectives*. Baltimore and London: Johns Hopkins University Press.

O'Donnell, G. and Schmitter, P. C. 1986: *Transitions from Authoritarian Rule: Tentative Conclusions about Uncertain Democracies*. Baltimore: Johns Hopkins University Press.

O'Shaughnessy, N. J. 1990: *The Phenomenon of Political Marketing*. Basingstoke: Macmillan.

O' Neill. J. 1985: *Five Bodies: The Human Shape of Modern Society*. Ithaca: Cornell University Press.

Offe, C. 1972: *Strukturprobleme des kapitalistischen Staates*. Frankfurt am Main: Suhrkamp Verlag.

Offe, C. 1984: *Contradictions of the Welfare State*. London: Hutchinson.

Offe, C. 1985: "New social movements: Challenging the boundaries of institutional politics." *Social Research* 52(4): 817–68.

Offe, C. 1996: "Designing institutions in east European transitions." In R. E. Goodin (ed.) *The Theory of Institutional Design*. Cambridge: Cambridge University Press.

Offe, C. 1997: "Les nouveaux mouveaux sociaux: Un défi aux limites de la politique institutionnelle." In C. Offe (ed.) *Les démocraties modernes à l'épreuve*, 98–132. Papers presented by Y. Sintomer and D. La Saout. Paris: L'Harmattan.

Offe, C. and Preuss, U. 1991: "Democratic institutions and moral resources." In D. Held (ed.) *Political Theory Today*. Cambridge: Polity Press.

Ohmae, K. 1995: *The End of the Nation-State. The Rise of Regional Economies*. New York: The Free Press.

Okin, S. M. 1989: *Justice, Gender and the Family*. New York: Basic Books.

Okin, S. M. 1991: "Gender, the public and the private." In D. Held (ed.) *Political Theory Today*. Cambridge: Polity Press.

Oldfield, A. 1990: *Citizenship and Community, Civic Republicanism and the Modern World*. London: Routledge.

Olson, M. 1965: *The Logic of Collective Action*. Cambridge, MA: Harvard University Press.

Omi, M. and Winant, H. 1986: *Racial Formations in the United States: From the 1960s to the 1980s*. New York: Routledge.

Ordeshook, P. C. 1997: "The spatial analysis of elections and committees: Four decades of research." In D. C. Mueller (ed.) *Perspectives on Public Choice. A Handbook*. Cambridge: Cambridge University Press.

Orloff, A. S. 1993: "Gender and the social rights of citizenship: The comparative analysis of gender relations and welfare states." *American Sociological Review* 58: 303–28.

Osborne, D. and Gaebler, T. 1992: *Reinventing Government: How the Entrepreneurial Spirit is Transforming the Public Sector*. Reading, MA: Addison-Wesley-Longman.

Osborne, T. 1998: *Aspects of Enlightenment*. London: UCL Press.

Ostrom, E. 1994: "Constituting social capital and collective action." *Journal of Theoretical Politics* 6(4): 527–62.

Owen, D. 1995: "Genealogy as exemplary critique: Reflections on Foucault and the imagination of the political." *Economy and Society* 24(4): 489–506.

Pakulski, J. and Waters, M. 1996: *The Death of Class*. London: Sage.

Palmer, D. S. 1995: "The revolutionary terrorism of Peru's Shining Path." In Martha Crenshaw (ed.) *Terrorism in Context*. Philadelphia: Penn State Press, 249–307.

Palumbo, A. 1996: "Closing down central government? An inquiry into the civil service managerial reform." University of East Anglia: Center for Social and Public Choice. Discussion Paper, no. 27.

Panebianco, A. 1988. *Political Parties. Organization and Power*. Cambridge: Cambridge University Press.

Papastergiadis, N. 1997: "Tracing hybridity in theory." In P. Werbner and T. Modood (eds.) *Debating Cultural Hybridity: Multi-Cultural Identities and the Politics of Anti-Racism*. London: Zed Books.

Pareto, V. 1935: *The Mind and Society*. New York: Harcourt Brace.

Parker, A. et al. (eds.) 1992: *Nationalisms and Sexualities*. London: Routledge.

Parker, N. 1999: *Revolutions and History: An Essay in Interpretation*. Cambridge: Polity Press.

Parry, G. 1969: *Political Elites*. London: Allen & Unwin.

Parsons, T. 1969: "Full citizenship for the negro Americans?" In T. Parsons (ed.) *Politics and Social Structures*. New York: Free Press.

Parsons, T. and Smelser, N. 1956: *Economy and Society*. London: Routledge & Kegan Paul.

Pascall, G. 1993: "Citizenship – a feminist analysis." In G. Drover and P. Kerans (eds.) *New Approaches to Welfare Theory*. Aldershot: Edward Elgar.

Pateman, C. 1970: *Participation and Democratic Theory*. Cambridge: Cambridge University Press.

Pateman, C. 1988: *The Sexual Contract*. Cambridge: Polity Press.

Pateman, C. 1989: *The Disorder of Women*. Cambridge: Polity Press.

Pateman, C. 1992: "Equality, difference and subordination: The politics of motherhood and women's citizenship." In G. Bock and S. James (eds.) *Beyond Equality and Difference*. London and New York: Routledge.

Patomáki H. and Pursianen, C. 1999: "Western models and the Russian idea: Beyond 'inside/outside' in discourses on civil society." *Millennium* 28(1): 53–77.

Pederson, S. 1990: "Gender, welfare and citizenship in Britain during the Great War." *The American Historical Review* 95(4): 983–1006.

Pelczynski, Z. A. 1988: "Solidarity and the rebirth of civil society in Poland 1976–81." In J. Keane (ed.) *Civil Society and the State: New European Perspectives*. London: Verso.

Peterson, J. 1989: "Hormones, heifers and high politics: Biotechnology and the Common Agricultural Policy." *Public Administration* 67(4): 451–71.

Peterson, J. 1995: "Decision-making in the European Union: A framework for analysis." *Journal of European Public Policy* 2(1): 69–93.

Peterson, V. S. (ed.) 1992: *Gendered States: Feminist (Re)Visions of International Relations Theory*. Boulder, CO: Lynne Rienner.

Phillips, A. 1991: *Engendering Democracy*. Cambridge: Polity Press.

Phillips, A. 1993: *Democracy and Difference*. Cambridge: Polity Press.

Phillips, A. 1995: *The Politics of Presence*. Oxford: Clarendon Press.

Phillips A. (ed.) 1998: *Feminism and Politics*. Oxford: Oxford University Press.

Pickvance, C. 1985: "The rise and fall of urban movements and the role of comparative analysis." *Environment and Planning D: Society and Space* 3: 31–53.

Piven, F. F. and Cloward, R. A. 1971: *Regulating the Poor*. New York: Pantheon.

Poguntke, T. 1993: *Alternative Politics: The German Green Party*. Edinburgh: Edinburgh University Press.

Polsby, N. 1980: *Community Power and Political Theory*, second edition. New Haven, CT: Yale University Press.

Popper, K. R. 1979 [1961]: *The Poverty of Historicism*, second revised edition. London: Routledge & Kegan Paul.

Porter, R. 1991: "History of the body." In P. Burke (ed.) *Perspectives on Historical Writing*. Cambridge: Polity Press.

Portes, A. 1998a: "Divergent destinies: Immigration, the second generation, and the rise of transnational communities." In P. H. Schuck and R. Muenz (eds.) *Paths to Inclusion: The Integration of Migrants in the United States and Germany*. New York: Berghahn Books.

Portes, A. 1998b: "Social capital: Its origins and applications in modern sociology." *Annual Review of Sociology* 24: 1–24

Poster, M. 1995: *The Second Media Age*. Cambridge: Polity Press.

Poulantzas, N. 1978: *State, Power, Socialism*. London: Verso.

Procacci, G. 1993: *Gouverner la misère*. Paris: Seuil.

Procacci, G. 2000: "Poor citizens: Social citizenship versus individualization of welfare." In K. Eder, C. Crouch, and D. Tambini (eds.) *States, Markets and Citizenship*. Oxford: Oxford University Press.

Przeworski, A. 1985: *Capitalism and Social Democracy*. Cambridge: Cambridge University Press.

Przeworski, A. 1986: "Some problems in the study of the transition to democracy." In G. O'Donnell, P. C. Schmitter, and L. Whitehead (eds.) *Transitions from Authoritarian Rule: Comparative Perspectives*. Baltimore: Johns Hopkins University Press.

Przeworski, A. 1991: *Democracy and the Market: Political and Economic Reforms in Eastern Europe and Latin America*. Cambridge: Cambridge University Press.

Putnam, R. D. 1973: *The Beliefs of Politicians: Ideology, Conflict and Democracy in Britain and Italy*. New Haven, CT: Yale University Press.

Putnam, R. D. 1993: *Making Democracy Work: Civic Traditions in Modern Italy*. Princeton: Princeton University Press.

Putnam, R. D. 1995: "Bowling alone: America's declining social capital." *Journal of Democracy* 6: 65–78.

Putnam, R. D. 1996: "The strange disappearance of civic America." *American Prospect* 24: 34–48.

Qualter, T. H. 1985: *Opinion Control in the Democracies*. London: Macmillan.

Raab, C. 1992: "Taking networks seriously: Education policy in Britain." *European Journal of Political Research* 21: 69–90.

Rabinowitz, G. and McDonald, S. E. 1989: "A directional theory of issue voting." *American Political Science Review* 83(1): 93–121.

Rae, D. and Taylor, M. 1970: *The Analysis of Political Cleavages*. New Haven, CT: Yale University Press.

Ray, L. J. 1993: *Rethinking Critical Theory – Emancipation in an Age of Global Social Movements*. London: Sage.

Ray, L. J. 1996: *Social Theory and the Crisis of State Socialism*. Cheltenham: Edward Elgar.

Ray, L. I. 1999: "Memory, trauma and genocidal nationalism." *Sociological Research Online* 4(2) at *http://www.socresonline.org.uk/4/2/ray.html*.

Reilly, P. R. 1991: *The Surgical Solution*. Baltimore: Johns Hopkins University Press.

Remmer, K. L. 1995: "New theoretical perspectives on democratization." Review article, *Comparative Politics* 28 October: 103–22.

Renan, E. 1990: "What is a Nation?" In H. Bhabha (ed.) *Nation and Narration*. London: Routledge.

Rueschemeyer, D., Stephens, E. H., and Stephens, J. D. 1992: *Capitalist Development and Democracy*. Cambridge: Polity Press.

Rex, J. 1997: "Immigrants in Europe." In R. Axtmann (ed.) *Globalisation and Europe*. New York: Brookings.

Rhodes, R. 1986: *The National World of Local Government*. London: Allen & Unwin.

Rhodes, R. A. W. 1988: *Beyond Westminster and Whitehall*. London: Unwin Hyman.

Rhodes, R. A. W. 1990: "Policy networks: A British perspective." *Journal of Theoretical Politics* 2: 293–317.

Rhodes, R. A. W. and Marsh, D. 1992: "New directions in the study of policy networks." *European Journal of Political Research* 21:181–205.

Rhodes, R. A. W. and Marsh, D. 1994: "Policy networks: Defensive comments, modest claims, and plausible research strategies." Paper to PSA annual conference, University of Swansea, 29–31 March.

Richardson, J. J. and Jordan, G. 1979: *Governing Under Pressure: The Policy Process in a Post-Parliamentary Democracy*. Oxford: Martin Robertson.

Richardson, J., Maloney, W., and Rudig, W. 1992: "The dynamics of policy change: Lobbying and water privatisation." *Public Administration* 70: 157–75.

Riker, W. 1982: *Liberalism versus Populism*. San Francisco: Freeman.

Ritter, G. 1979: *The Corrupting Influence of Power*. Westport, CT: Hyperion Press.

Robertson, R. 1992: *Globalization: Social Theory and Global Culture*. London: Sage Publications.

Roche, M. 1992: *Rethinking Citizenship*. Cambridge: Polity Press.

Rödel, U., Frankenberg, G., and Dubiel, H. 1989: *Die Demokratisch Frage*. Frankfurt am Main: Suhrkamp Verlag.

Rorty, R. 1980: *Philosophy and the Mirror of Nature*. Oxford: Blackwell.

Rosas, A. 1995: "State sovereignty and human rights: Towards a global constitutional project." In D. Beetham (ed.) *Politics and Human Rights*. Oxford: Blackwell.

Rose, A. M. 1967: *The Power Structure: Political Process in American Society*. New York: Oxford University Press.

Rose, N. 1996: "The Death of the social? Re-figuring the territory of government." *Economy and Society* 25(3): 327–56.

Rose, N. 1999: *Powers of Freedom: Reframing Political Thought*. Cambridge: Cambridge University Press.

Rose, R. and McAllister, I. 1985: *Voters Begin to Choose*. London: Sage.

Rosenau, J. N. 1990: *Turbulence in World Politics: A Theory of Change and Continuity*. Princeton: Princeton University Press.

Roth, A. E. (ed.) 1988: *The Shapley Value: Essays in Honor of Lloyd S. Shapley*. Cambridge: Cambridge University Press.

Rousseau, J-J. 1963 [1762]: *The Social Contract and Discourses*. London: Dent.

Rowbotham, S., Segal, L., and Wainwright, H. 1979: *Beyond the Fragments: Feminism and the Making of Socialism*. Merlin Press: London.

Rowley, C. K. (ed.) 1987: *Democracy and Public Choice: Essays In Honor of Gordon Tullock*. Oxford: Blackwell.

Rowley, C. K. 1993: *Liberty and the State*. Aldershot: Edward Elgar.

Rowley, C. K. (ed.) 1997: *Constitutional Political Economy in a Public Choice Perspective*. Dordrecht: Kluwer Academic.

Ruddick, S. 1989: *Maternal Thinking. Towards a Politics of Peace*. London: Women's Press.

Rueschemeyer, D., Huber Stephens, E., and Stephens, J. D. 1992: *Capitalist Development and Democracy*. Cambridge: Polity Press.

Ruggie, J. 1993: "Territoriality and beyond: Problematizing modernity in international relations." *International Organisation* 47(1): 139–74.

Rusconi, G. E. 1993: *Se cessiamo di essere una nazione. Tra etnodemocrazie e cittadinanza europea*. Bologna: Il Mulino.

Russell, C. S. (ed.) 1979: *Collective Decision Making: Applications from Public Choice Theory*. Baltimore: Johns Hopkins University Press.

Rustow, D. A. 1970: "Transitions to democracy: Toward a dynamic model." *Comparative Politics* 2: 337–63.

Rutten, P. 1991: "Local popular music in the national and international markets." *Cultural Studies* 5(3): 294–305.

Sabatier, Paul A. and Jenkins-Smith, Hank C. 1993: *Policy Change and Learning: An Advocacy Coalition Approach*. Boulder, CO: Westview Press.

Salecl, R. 1993: "National identity and socialist moral majority." In E. Carter et al. (eds.) *Space and Place*. London: Lawrence & Wishart.

Sandefur, R. L. and Laumann, E. O. 1998: "A paradigm for social capital." *Rationality and Society* 10(4): 481–501.

Sani, G. and Sartori, G. 1983: "Polarization, fragmentation and competition in western democracies." In Hans Daalder and Peter Mair (eds.) *Western European Party Systems. Continuity and Change*. Beverley Hills: Sage.

Sapiro, V. 1998: "When are interests interesting?" In A. Phillips (ed.) *Feminism and Politics*, 1998.

Sartori, G. 1976. *Parties and Party Systems*. Cambridge: Cambridge University Press.

Sartori, G. 1987: *The Theory of Democracy Revisted*. Chatham, NJ: Chatham House Publishers.

Sartori, G. 1994: *Comparative Constitutional Engineering: An Inquiry into Structures, Incentives and Outcomes*. Basingstoke and London: Macmillan.

Sarvasy, W. 1992: "Beyond the difference versus equality policy debate: Postsuffrage feminism, citizenship and the quest for a feminist welfare state." *Signs* 17(2): 329–62.

Sarvasy, W. and Siim, B. 1994: "Gender, transitions to democracy and citizenship." *Social Politics* 1(3): 249–55.

Sassen, S. 1996: *Losing Control? Sovereignty in an Age of Globalization*. New York: Columbia University Press.

Sassen, S. 1998: *Globalization and Its Discontents*. New York: The New Press.

Sayer, D. 1991: *Capitalism and Modernity:An excursus on Marx and Weber*. London: Routledge.

Scammell, M. 1995: *Designer Politics: How Elections are Won*. Basingstoke: Macmillan.

Schiff, M. 1992: "Social capital, labor mobility and welfare." *Rationality and Society* 4: 157–75.

Scharpf, F. W. 1989: "Politische Steuerung und politische Institutionen." *Politische Vierteljahresschrift* 30: 10–22.

Schimank, U. 1992: "Determinanten sozialer Steuerung – akteurtheoretisch betrachtet. Ein Themenkatalog." In Heinrich Buahoff (ed.) *Politische Steuerung. Steuerbarkeit und Steuerungsfähigkeit. Beiträge zur Grundlagendiskussion*. Baden-Baden: Nomos, 165–92.

Schlesinger, J. A. 1984: "On the theory of party organization." *Journal of Politics* 46(2): 369–400.

Schmitter, P. C. 1995: "Transitology: The science or the art of democratization?" In J. S. Tulchin and B. Romero (eds.) *The Consolidation of Democracy in Latin America*. Boulder and London: Lynne Rienner.

Schmitter, P. C. 1996a: "The influence of international context on the choice of national institutions and policies in neo-democracies." In L. Whitehead (ed.) *The International Dimensions of Democratization: Europe and the Americas*. Oxford: Oxford University Press.

Schmitter, P. C. 1996b: "Examining the present Euro-polity with the help of past theories." In Marks, G. et al., *Journal of Common Market Studies*, 1996.

Schneider, M. 1996: "Sacredness, status and bodily violation." *Body and Society* 2(4): 75–92.

Schofield, N. 1993: "Political competition and multi-party coalition governments." *European Journal of Political Research* 23(1): 1–33.

Schofield, N. 1997: "Multiparty electoral politics." In D. C. Mueller (ed.) *Perspectives on Public Choice. A Handbook*. Cambridge: Cambridge University Press.

Schubert, K. and Jordan, G. (eds.) 1992: *European Journal of Political Research: Special Issue on Policy Networks* 21: 1–2.

Schumpeter, J. 1956: *Capitalism, Socialism and Democracy*. New York: Harper.

Schwarzmantel, J. 1998: *The Age of Ideology. Political Ideologies from the American Revolution to Post-Modern Times*. Basingstoke: Macmillan

Scott, A. 1990: *Ideology and the New Social Movements*. London: Unwin Hyman/ Routledge.

Scott, A. (ed.) 1997: *The Limits of Globalisation*. London: Routledge.

Scott, A. 1999: "War and the public intellectual: Cosmopolitanism and anticosmopolitanism in the Kosovo debate in Germany." *Sociological Research Online* 4(2) *http:// www.socresonline.org.uk/4/2/scott.html*.

Scott, J. (ed.) 1990a: *The Sociology of Elites, Three Volumes*. Cheltenham: Edward Elgar Publishing.

Scott, J. 1990b: *A Matter of Record: Documentary Sources in Social Research*. Cambridge: Polity Press.

Scott, J. 1991a: "Networks of corporate power: A comparative assessment." *Annual Review of Sociology* 17: 181–203.

Scott, J. 1991b: *Social Network Analysis*. London: Sage.

Scott, J. 1991c: *Who Rules Britain?* Cambridge: Polity Press.

Scott, J. (ed.) 1994: *Power*. London: Routledge.

Scott, J. 1997: *Corporate Business and Capitalist Classes*. Oxford: Oxford University Press.

Scott, J. and Griff, C. 1984: *Directors of Industry*. Cambridge: Polity Press.

Scott, J. C. 1990: *Domination and the Arts of Resistance*. New Haven, CT: Yale University Press.

Scott, S. and Morgan, D. (eds.) 1993: *Body Matters. Essays on the Sociology of the Body*. London: The Falmer Press.

Scutt, J. A. (ed.) 1990: *The Baby Machine*. London: Green Print.

Séguin, M. 1998: *L'émergence des mouvements sociaux de l'environnement dans l'enjeu des déchets solides à Montréal*, Ph.D. Thesis, Department of Sociology, Montréal, Université de Montréal.

Seligman, A. 1993: "The fragile ethical vision of civil society." In B. S. Turner (ed.) *Citizenship and Social Theory*. London: Sage.

Seligman, A. 1995: "Animadversions upon civil society and civic virtue in the last decade of the twentieth century." In J. Hall (ed.) *Civil Society*, 1995.

Sevenhuijsen, S. 1998: *Citizenship and the Ethics of Care*. London and New York: Routledge.

Shapley, L. S. 1953: "A value for *n*-person games." In H. W. Kuhn and A. W. Tucker (eds.) *Contributions to the Theory of Games*, vol. 2. Princeton: Princeton University Press. Reprinted in Roth (ed.) *The Shapley Valve*, 1988.

Shapley, L. S. and Shubik, M. 1954: "A method for evaluating the distribution of power in a committee system." *American Political Science Review* 48: 787–92. Reprinted in Roth (ed.) *The Shapely Valve*, 1988.

Share, D. and Mainwaring, S. 1986: "Transitions through transaction: Democratization in Brazil and Spain." In W. Selcher (ed.) *Political Liberalization in Brazil*. Boulder, CO: Westview.

Shaver, S. 1989: "Gender, class and the welfare state: The case of income security in Australia." *Feminist Review* 32: 90–110.

Shaw, M. 1991: *Post-Military Society*. Cambridge: Polity Press.

Shaw, M. 1997: "The state of globalization: Towards a theory of state transformation." *Review of International Political Economy* 4(3): 497–514.

Shaw, M. 1999: "The Kosovan War, 1998–99: Transformations of state, war and genocide in the global revolution." *Sociological Research Online* (2) at *http://www.socresonline.org.uk/socresonline/4/2/shaw.html*.

Shefter, M. 1978: "Party and patronage: Germany, England, and Italy." *Politics and Society* 7(4): 403–51.

Shilling, C. 1993: *The Body and Social Theory*. London: Sage.

Shils, E. 1957: "Primordial, personal, sacred and civil ties." *British Journal of Sociology* 7: 130–45.

Shils, E. and Young, M. 1953: "The meaning of the coronation." *Sociological Review* 1: 63–81.

Shonfield, A. 1965: *Modern Capitalism*. Oxford: Oxford University Press.

Shore, C. and Black, A. 1996: "Citizens Europe and the construction of European identity." In V. Goddard et al. (eds.) *The Anthropology of Europe*. London: Berg.

Shrum, W. M. 1996: *Fringe and Fortune: The Role of Critics in High and Popular Art*. Princeton: Princeton University Press.

Shugart, M. S. and Carey, J. M. 1992: *Presidents and Assemblies: Constitutional Design and Electoral Dynamics*. Cambridge: Cambridge University Press.

Simmel, G. 1997 [1908]: "Sociology of senses." In D. Frisby and M. Featherstone (eds.) *Simmel on Culture*. London: Routledge.

Simons, J. 1995: *Foucault and the Political*. London: Routledge.

Sitkoff, H. 1981: *The Struggle for Black Equality, 1954–1980*. New York: Hill and Wang.

Sivan, E. 1989: "The Islamic resurgence: Civil society strikes back." *Journal of Contemporary History* 25(2/3): 353–62.

Skinner, Q. 1998: *Liberty before Liberalism*. Cambridge: Cambridge University Press.

Sklair, L. 1995: *Sociology of the Global System*. Baltimore: Johns Hopkins University Press.

Skocpol, T. 1979: *States and Social Revolution: A Comparative Analysis of France, Russia and China*. Cambridge: Cambridge University Press.

Skocpol, T. 1996: *Protecting Mothers and Soldiers*. Cambridge, MA: Harvard University Press.

Slater, D. 1998: "Trading sexpics on IRC: Embodiment and authenticity on the internet." *Body and Society* 4(4): 90–118.

Slobin, M. (ed.) 1996: *Retuning Culture: Musical Changes in Central and Eastern Europe*. London: Duke University Press.

Smith, A. 1976 [1776]: *An Inquiry into the Nature and Causes of the Wealth of Nations*. Ed. R. H. Campbell and A. S. Skinner. Oxford: Clarendon Press.

Smith, A. D. 1981: *The Ethnic Revival in the Modern World*. Cambridge: Cambridge University Press.

Smith, A. D. 1986: *The Ethnic Origins of Nations*. Oxford: Basil Blackwell.

Smith, A. D. 1991: *National Identity*. London: Penguin.

Smith, A. D. 1995: *Nations and Nationalism in a Global Era*. Cambridge: Polity Press.

Smith, A-M. 1995: "A symptomology of an authoritarian discourse." In Carter et al. (eds.) *Cultural Remix*. London: Lawrence & Wishart.

Smith, J. 1998: "Global civil society? Transnational social movement organizations and social capital." *American Behavioral Scientist* 42(1): 93–107.

Smith, M. 1990: *The Politics of Agricultural Support in Britain*. Aldershot: Dartmouth.

Smith, M. 1991: "From policy community to issue network: Salmonella in eggs and the new politics of food." *Public Administration* 69, Summer: 235–55.

Soeffner, H-G. 1992: "Zur Soziologie des Symbols und des Rituals." In J. Oelkers (ed.) *Das Symbol – Brücke des Verstehens*. Stuttgart: Kohlammer.

Sofsky, W. 1993: *Ordnung des Terrors: Das Konzentrationslager*. Frankfurt am Main: Fischer Verlag. Trans. W. Templar as *Order of Terror: The Concentration Camp*. Princeton: Princeton University Press, 1996.

Sofsky, W. 1999: "Kreig und Illusion." *Die Zeit* 21, 20th May: 56.

Soguk, N. 1999: *States and Strangers*. Minneapolis: University of Minnesota Press.

Somers, M. R. 1993: "Citizenship and the place of the public sphere: Law, community, and political culture in the transition to democracy." *American Sociological Review* 58: 587–620.

Sontag, S. 1988: *AIDS and its Metaphors*. New York: Ferrar, Straus, and Giroux.

Soysal, Y. N. 1994: *Limits of Citizenship: Migrants and Postnational Membership in Europe*. Chicago: University of Chicago Press.

Spencer, P. and Wollman, H. 1998: "Good and bad nationalisms: A critique of dualism." *Journal of Political Ideologies* 3(3): 255–74.

Stacey, J. 1983: *Patriarchy and Socialist Revolution in China*. Berkeley: University of California Press.

Stark, D. 1992: "Path dependence and privatization strategies in east central Europe." *East European Politics and Societies* 6(1): 17–54.

Starr, F. 1983: *Red and Hot: The Fate of Jazz in the Soviet Union*. Oxford: Oxford University Press.

Stehr, N. 1994: *Knowledge Societies*. London: Sage.

Stein, R. M. and Bickers, K. 1995: *Perpetuating the Pork Barrel: Policy Subsystems and American Democracy*. Cambridge: Cambridge University Press.

Steinhoff, P. 1991: "Death by defeatism and other fables: The social dynamics of the Rengo Sekigun Purge." In T. S. Lebra (ed.) *Japanese Social Orgnization*. Honolulu: University of Hawaii Press.

Steneunberg, B., Schmidtchen, D., and Koboldt, C. 1999: "Strategic power in the European Union: Evaluating the distribution of power in policy games." *Journal of Theoretical Politics* 11: 343–70.

Stepan, A. 1988: *Rethinking Military Politics: Brazil and the Southern Cone*. Princeton: Princeton University Press.

Stepan, A. 1989: *Democratizing Brazil: Problems of Transition and Consolidation*. New York: Oxford University Press.

Stokman, F. and Berveling, J. 1998: "Dynamic modelling of policy networks in Amsterdam." *Journal of Theoretical Politics* 10(4): 577–601.

Stokman, F. and Zeggelink, E. 1996: "Is politics power or policy orientated? A comparative analysis of dynamic access models in policy networks." *Journal of Mathematical Sociology* 21(1/2): 77–111.

Stokman, F., Ziegler, R., and Scott, J. (eds.) 1985: *Networks of Corporate Power*. Cambridge: Polity Press.

Stoler, A. L. 1995: *Race and the Education of Desire: Foucault's History of Sexuality and the Colonial Order of Things*. Durham: Duke University Press.

Stone, A. and Sandholz, W. (eds.) 1998: *European Integration and Supranational Governance*. Oxford: Oxford University Press.

Storey, H. 1995: "Human rights and the new Europe." In D. Beetham (ed.) *Politics and Human Rights*. Oxford: Blackwell.

Storper, M. 1997: *The Regional World*. New York: Guilford.

Strange, S. 1996: *The Retreat of the State, the Diffusion of Power in the World Economy*. Cambridge: Cambridge University Press.

Straw, W. 1993: "The English Canadian recording industry since 1970." In T. Bennett, S. Frith, L. Grossberg, J. Shepherd, and G. Turner (eds.) *Rock and Popular Music: Politics, Policies, Institutions*. London: Routledge.

Strayer, J. R. 1970: *On the Medieval Origins of the Modern State*. Princeton: Princeton University Press.

Street, J. 1997: *Politics and Popular Culture*. Cambridge: Polity Press.

Strom, K. 1990a: "A behavioral theory of competitive political parties." *American Journal of Political Science* 34(2): 565–98.

Strom, K. 1990b: *Minority Government and Majority Rule.* Cambridge: Cambridge University Press.

Stromquist, N. P. 1995: "State policies and gender equity: Comparative perspectives." Paper presented to second annual Missouri Symposium on Research and Educational Policy, University of Missouri-Columbia.

Suny, R. G. 1993: *The Revenge of the Past. Nationalism, Revolution, and the Collapse of the Soviet Union.* Stanford: Stanford University Press.

Sztompka, P. 1993: *The Sociology of Social Change.* Oxford: Blackwell.

Tamás, G. M. 1994: "A disquisition on civil society." *Social Research* 61(2): 205–22.

Targ, H. R. 1979: "Societal structure and revolutionary terrorism: A preliminary investigation." In Michael Stohl (ed.) *The Politics of Terrorism.* New York: Dekkar, 119–43.

Tarrow, S. 1994: *Power in Movement: Social Movements, Collective Action and Politics.* Cambridge: Cambridge University Press.

Tarrow, S. 1996: "Making social science work across space and time. A critical reflection on Robert Putnam's *Making Democracy Work.*" *American Political Science Review* 90: 389–97.

Tarrow, S. 1998. *Power in Movement,* second edition. Cambridge: Cambridge University Press.

Tassin, E. 1994: "Identités nationales et citoyenneté politique". *Esprit.*

Taylor, C. 1994: "The politics of recognition." In A. Gutmann (ed.) *Multiculturalism and the Politics of Recognition.* Princeton: Princeton University Press.

Taylor, M. (ed.) 1988: *Rationality and Revolution.* Cambridge: Cambridge University Press.

Taylor, R. 1999: "Political science encounters 'race' and 'ethnicity'." In M. Bulmer and J. Solomos (eds.) *Ethnic and Racial Studies Today.* London: Routledge, 115–23.

Terry, J. and Urla, J. (eds.) 1995: *Deviant Bodies.* Bloomington: Indiana University Press.

Teubner, G. and Willke, H. 1984: *Kontext und Autonomie. Gesellschaftliche Selbststeuerung durch reflexives Recht, EUI-Working-Paper 93,* Florence: European University Institute.

Thatcher, M. 1998: "The development of policy network analyses." *Journal of Theoretical Politics* 10(4): 389–416.

Therborn, G. 1995: *European Modernity and Beyond. The Trajectory of European Societies.* London: Sage.

Thompson, E. P. 1982: "Exterminism: The last stage of civilization." In E. P. Thompson (ed.) *Exterminism and Cold War.* London: Verso.

Thompson, J. B. 1995: *The Media and Modernity: A Social Theory of the Media.* Cambridge: Polity Press.

Thompson, J. B. 1997: "Scandal and social theory." In J. Lull and S. Hinerman (eds.) *Media Scandals: Morality and Desire in the Popular Culture Marketplace.* Cambridge: Polity Press.

Thompson, J. B. 2000: *Political Scandal.* Cambridge: Polity Press.

Thornton, S. 1995: *Club Cultures.* Cambridge: Polity Press.

Tilly, C. 1978: *From Mobilization to Revolution.* Reading, MA: Addison-Wesley-Longman.

Tilly, C. 1992: *Coercion, Capital, and European States: A.D. 990–1990.* Oxford: Blackwell.

Tilly, C. 1993: *European Revolutions, 1492–1992.* Oxford: Blackwell.

Tilly, C. 1994: "In search of revolution." *Theory and Society* 23(6): 799–804.

Tilly, C. 1995: "To explain political processes." *American Journal of Sociology* 100(6): 1594–610.

Tismaneanu, V. 1989: "Nascent civil society in the German Democratic Republic." *Problems of Communism* 38: 91–111.

Tocqueville, A. 1946 [1835]: *Democracy in America*. London: Oxford University Press.

Tohidi, N. 1991: "Gender and Islamic Fundamentalism: Feminist politics in Iran." In C. T. Mohanty, A. Russo, and L. Torres (eds.) *Third World Women and the Politics of Feminism*. Bloomington: Indiana University Press.

Tönnies, F. 1974 [1887]: *Community and Association*. London: Routledge & Kegan Paul.

Torres Rivas, E. 1995: "Democracy and the metaphor of good government." In J. S. Tulchin and B. Romero (eds.) *The Consolidation of Democracy in Latin America*. Boulder and London: Lynne Rienner.

Touraine, A. 1988: *The Return of the Actor: Social Theory in Post-Industrial Society*. Minneapolis: University of Minnesota Press.

Touraine, A. 1990: "Existe-t-il encore une société française." *Tocqueville Review* 11.

Touraine, A. 1996: "Le nationalisme contre la nation." *L'Année sociologique* 46(1): 15–41.

Touraine, A. 1997: *Pourrons-nous vivre ensemble?* Paris: Fayard.

Trigilia, C. 1998: *Sociologia economica. Stato, mercato e società nel capitalismo moderno*. Bologna: Il Mulino.

Truman, D. 1951: *The Governmental Process*. New York: Alfred A. Knopf.

Tsebelis, G. 1994: "The power of the European Parliament as a conditional agenda setter." *American Political Science Review* 88: 128–42.

Tullock, G. 1965: *The Politics of Bureaucracy*. Washington, DC: Public Affairs Press.

Tullock, G. 1976: *The Vote Motive. An Essay in the Economics of Politics, with Applications to the British Economy*. London: Institute of Economic Affairs.

Tully, J. 1995: *Strange Multiplicity: Constitutionalism in an Age of Diversity*. Cambridge: Cambridge University Press.

Tully, J. 1999: "To think and act differently." In S. Ashenden and D. Owen (eds.) *Foucault contra Habermas*. London: Sage.

Turner, B. S. 1984: *The Body and Society*. Oxford: Blackwell.

Turner, B. S. 1988: *Status*. Milton Keynes: Open University Press.

Turner, B. S. 1989: "Outline of a theory of citizenship." *Sociology* 24:189–217.

Turner, V. 1969: *The Ritual Process. Structure and Anti-Structure*. London: Routledge.

Udehn, L. 1996: *The Limits of Public Choice: A Sociological Critique of the Economic Theory of Politics*. London: Routledge.

Ullmann-Margalit, E. 1978: "Invisible-hand explanations." *Synthese* 39: 263–91.

Vajda, M. 1988: "East-Central European perspectives." In J. Keane (ed.) *Civil Society and the State*, 1988.

Valenzuela, A. 1993: "Latin America: Presidentialism in crisis." *Journal of Democracy* 4(4): 3–16.

Valverde, M. 1996: "'Despotism' and ethical liberal governance." *Economy and Society* 25(3): 357–72.

Valverde, M. 1998: *Diseases of the Will: Alcohol and the Dilemmas of Freedom*. Cambridge: Cambridge University Press.

Van den Berghe, P. L. 1986: "Ethnicity and the sociobiology debate." In J. Rex and D. Mason (eds.) *Theories of Race and Ethnic Relations*. Cambridge: Cambridge University Press.

Van Waarden, F. 1992: "Dimensions and types of policy networks." *European Journal of Political Research* 21: 29–52.

Velody, I. 1989: "Socialism as a sociological problem." In P. Lassman (ed.) *Politics and Social Theory*. London: Routledge.

Verba, S. 1965: "The Kennedy assassination and the nature of political commitment." In B. S. Greenberg and E. B. Parker (eds.) *The Kennedy Assassination and the American Public: Social Communication in Crisis*. Stanford: Stanford University Press.

Verdier, D. 1995: "The politics of public aid to private industry." *Comparative Political Studies* 28(1): 3–42.

Veyne, P. 1978: "Foucault révolutionne l'histoire." In P. Veyne *Comment on écrit l'histoire*. Paris: Seuil.

Veyne, P. 1987: "L'individu atteint au coeur de la puissance publique." In P. Veyne, *Sur l'Individu*. Paris: Seuil.

Vickers, J. 1994: "Notes toward a political theory of sex and power." In H. L. Radtke and H. J. Stam (eds.) *Power/Gender: Social Relations in Theory and Practice*. London: Sage.

Vidich, A. J. and Bensman, J. 1968: *Small Town in Mass Society*. Princeton: Princeton University Press.

Vigarello, G. 1988: *The Concept of Cleanliness*. Cambridge: Cambridge University Press.

Virilio, P. 1994: *Bunker Architecture*. Princeton: Princeton University Press.

Voet, R. 1998: *Feminism and Citizenship*. London: Sage.

Vogel, U. 1988: "Under permanent guardianship: Women's condition under modern civil law." In K. B. Jones and A. G. Jónasdóttir (eds.) *The Political Interests of Gender*. London: Sage.

Vogel, U. 1994: "Marriage and the boundaries of citizenship." In B. van Steenbergen (ed.) *The Condition of Citizenship*. London: Sage.

von Neumann, J. and Morgenstern, O. 1944: *The Theory of Games and Economic Behavior*. New York: Wiley.

Wacquant, L. J. D. 1995: "Why men desire muscles." *Body and Society* 1(1): 163–79.

Walby, S. 1994: "Is citizenship gendered?" *Sociology* 28(2): 379–95.

Waldman, P. (ed.) 1993: *Beruf: Terrorist. Lebensläufe im Untergrund*. Monaco: Beck Verlag.

Walker, R. 1994: "Social movements/world politics." *Millennium* 23(3): 669–700.

Wallman, S. 1978: "The boundaries of race: Processes of ethnicity in England." *Man* 13: 200–17.

Walton, J. 1966: "Substance and artifact: The current status of research on community power structure." *American Journal of Sociology* 71(4): 430–8.

Walzer, M. 1989: "Citizenship." In T. Ball, J. Farr, and R. L. Hanson (eds.) *Political Innovation and Conceptual Change*. Cambridge: Cambridge University Press.

Warner, L. W. 1959: *The Living and the Dead: A Study of the Symbolic Life of Americans*. New Haven, CT: Yale University Press.

Warner, L. W. 1962: *American Life: Dream and Reality*. Chicago: Chicago University Press.

Warner, L. W. 1936: "American class and caste." *American Journal of Sociology* 42: 234–7.

Warner, W. L. 1949: *Social Class in America*. New York: Harper and Row.

Wasserman, S. and Faust, K. 1994: *Social Network Analysis: Methods and Applications*. New York: Cambridge University Press.

Wasserman, S. and Galaskiewicz, J. (eds.) 1994: *Advances in Social Network Analysis: Research in the Social and Behavioral Sciences*. Thousand Oaks, CA: Sage.

Waters, M. 1996: *Globalization*. London: Routledge.

Waters, M. 1997: "Sociology after class." In D. Owen (ed.) *Sociology after Postmodernism*. London: Sage.

Watson, S. (ed.) 1990: *Playing the State: Australian Feminist Interventions.* Sydney: Allen & Unwin.

Weber, M. 1922: *Wirtschaft und Gesellschaft.* Tübingen: J. C. B. Mohr (Paul Siebeck).

Weber, M. 1949: *The Methodology of the Social Sciences.* New York: The Free Press.

Weber, M. 1958 [1919]: "Politics as a vocation." In H. H. Gerth and C. W. Mills (eds.) *From Max Weber. Essays in Sociology.* New York: Oxford University Press.

Weber, M. 1967 [1919]: *Wissenschaft als Beruf,* 5 Aufl., Berlin: Duncker & Humblot.

Weber, M. 1976 [1905] *The Protestant Ethic and the Spirit of Capitalism.* London: Allen & Unwin.

Weber, M. 1978 [1922]: *Economy and Society. An Outline of Interpretative Sociology.* Ed. G. Roth and C. Wittich, trans. E. Fischoff et al., 2 vols. Berkeley: University of California Press.

Weber, M. ca. 1991 [1921]: "Bureaucracy." In H. H. Gerth and C. Wright Mills (eds.) *From Max Weber: Essays in Sociology.* London: Routledge.

Weber, M. 1994a: *Political Writings.* Ed. P. Lassman and R. Spiers. Cambridge: Cambridge University Press.

Weber, M. 1994b [1919]: "The profession and vocation of politics." In Peter Lassman and Ronald Spiers (eds.) *Max Weber: Political Writings.* Cambridge: Cambridge University Press.

Weffort, F. 1989: "Why democracy?" In A. Stepan (ed.) *Democratizing Brazil.* New York: Oxford University Press.

Weiler, J. 1994: "A quiet revolution. The European Court of Justice and its interlocutors." *Comparative Political Studies* 26: 510–34.

Weitz, R. (ed.) 1998: *The Politics of Women's Bodies. Sexuality, Appearance and Behavior.* Oxford: Oxford University Press.

Wellmer, A. 1981: "Terrorism and social criticism." *Telos* 48: 66–78.

Westholm, A. 1997: "Distance versus direction: The illusory defeat of the proximity theory of electoral choice." *American Political Science Review* 91(4): 865–84.

White, R. W. 1993: *Provisional Irish Republicans: An Oral and Interpretative History.* Westport, CT: Greenwood Press.

White, S., Gill, G., and Slider, D. 1993: *The Politics of Transition: Shaping a Post-Soviet Future.* Cambridge: Cambridge University Press.

Whitehead, L. 1992: "The alternatives to liberal democracy: A Latin American perspective." *Political Studies* 40. Special Edition on "Prospects for democracy" ed. D. Held: 146–59.

Whitehead, L. 1996: "Three international dimensions of democratization." In L. Whitehead (ed.) *The International Dimensions of Democratization: Europe and the Americas.* Oxford: Oxford University Press.

Whittier, N. 1995: *Feminist Generations: The Persistence of the Radical Women's Movement.* Philadelphia: Temple University Press.

Whyte, J. 1990: *Interpreting Northern Ireland.* Oxford: Clarendon.

Wiener, A. 1998: *"European" Citizenship Practice: Building Institutions of a Non-State.* Boulder, CO: Westview Press.

Wieviorka, M. 1988: *Société et terrorisme.* Paris. Fayard.

Wildavsky, A. 1964: *Leadership in a Small Town.* Totowa, New Jersey: Bedminster Press.

Wilkinson, P. 1979: "Social scientific theory and civil violence." In Yona Alexander, David Carlton, and Paul Wilkinson (eds.) *Terrorism: Theory and Practice.* Boulder CO: Westview Press, 45–72.

Wilkinson, P. 1986: *Terrorism and the Liberal State,* second edition. London: Macmillan.

Wilks, S. and Wright, M. (eds.) 1987: *Comparative Government–Industry Relations.* Oxford: Oxford University Press.

Williams, W. L. 1986: *The Spirit and the Flesh: Sexual Diversity in American Indian Culture*. Boston: Beacon Press.

Willke, H. 1992: *Ironie des Staates. Grundlinien einer Staatstheorie polyzentrischer Gesellschaften*. Frankfurt am Main: Suhrkamp Verlag.

Wintrobe, R. 1997: "Modern bureaucratic theory." In D. Mueller (ed.) *Perspectives on Public Choice*. Cambridge: Cambridge University Press.

Wolf, E. 1988: "Inventing society." *American Ethnologist* 15(4): 752–61.

Wolf, N. 1991: *The Beauty Myth. How Images of Beauty are used Against Women*. London: Vintage.

Wolpe, H. 1988: *Race, Class and the Apartheid State*. London: James Curry.

Wouters, C. 1986: "Formalization and informalization: Changing tension balances in civilizing process." *Theory, Culture and Society* 3(2): 1–18.

Wright, P. 1985: *On Living in an Old Country*. London: Verso.

Wright, V. (ed.) 1993: *Les privatisations en Europe*. Arles: Actes Sud.

Wright, V. and Cassese, S. (eds.) 1996: *La recomposition de l'Etat en Europe*. Paris: La Découverte.

Yeatman, A. 1990: *Bureaucrats, Technocrats, Femocrats: Essays on the Contemporary Australian State*. Sydney: Allen & Unwin.

Yeatman, A. 1993: *Post-Modern Revisionings of the Political*. London: Routledge.

Young, I. M. 1990: *Justice and the Politics of Difference*. Princeton: Princeton University Press.

Young, I. M. 1996: "Communication and the other: Beyond deliberative democracy." In Benhabib (ed.) *Democracy and Difference*, 1996.

Young, I. M. 1997. "Difference as a resource for democratic communication." In J. Bohman and W. Rehg (eds.) *Deliberative Democracy: Essays on Reason and Politics*. Cambridge, MA: MIT Press.

Yuval-Davis, N. 1997: *Gender and Nation*. London: Sage.

Zald, M. N. 1992: "Looking backward to look forward: Reflections on the past and future of the resource mobilization research program." In A. Morris and C. McClurg Mueller (eds.) *Frontiers in Social Movement Theory*. New Haven and London: Yale University Press.

Zizek, S. 1989: *The Sublime Object Of Ideology*. London: Verso.

Zolo, D. 1992: *Democracy and Complexity. A Realist Approach*. Cambridge: Polity Press.

Zolo, D. (ed.) 1994: *La cittadinanza*. Bari: Laterza.

Zolo, D. 1997: *Cosmopolis: The Prospects for World Government*. Cambridge: Polity Press.

Zwerman, G. 1992: "Conservative and feminist images of women associated with armed, clandestine organizations in the United States." In D. della Porta (ed.) *Social Movements and Violence: Participation in Underground Organizations*. Greenwich, CO: JAI Press.

Index

Page numbers in bold type indicate main or detailed references